JUDICIAL TYRANNY

by

Carrol D. Kilgore

**An Inquiry into the Integrity of the Federal Judiciary
published at the beginning of the
Third Century of American Independence**

THOMAS NELSON INC., PUBLISHERS
Nashville / New York

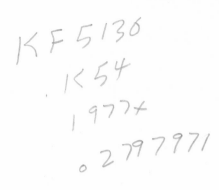
To Hilda,
who urged me to return to this book's abandoned beginnings,
and to the children—
Laura, Roger, Shirley and Jennifer,
who waited patiently during the
long week-ends of the writer's solitude,
this book is dedicated.

Library of Congress Cataloging in Publication Data
Kilgore, Carrol D
  Judicial tyranny.
  "Published at the beginning of the third century of American independence."
  Includes bibliographical references.
  1. Judicial power—United States. 2. Judges—United States. I. Title.
KF5130.K54   347'.73'1   77-2174
ISBN 0-8407-4060-3

TABLE OF CONTENTS

Part I

THE PLACE OF JUDGES
IN
CONSTITUTIONAL GOVERNMENT

I.

ON JUDGING JUDGES

IN THE FOURTEENTH CENTURY, the English Parliament enacted a law which commanded that "the judges shall not cease to do right . . ." [1]

This law expresses an inborn love for just treatment, shared by all men. But even apart from man's inability to achieve perfection in any endeavor, the desire to achieve perfect justice never has been realized and never will be realized for as Emerson said, *one man's justice is another's injustice.* Each man, in his affairs, sees the just result from his own biased viewpoint. When perfect justice is attained for one disputant, the same decision tramples justice underfoot in the view of his adversary.

You may build your house on a towering hill, and I may build mine in the valley below. When you start to build a massive dam to impound the waters of a little stream, and I have you brought before a magistrate, the decision cannot fail to be unjust in the selfish view of one of us.

If you are prevented from building the dam, you will seethe with frustration for a long time, because you spent many hours dreaming of the view of a lovely little lake beside your house, built with materials you had accumulated at great expense, *your* materials, bought with *your* money, to build *your* dam on *your* land to collect *your* water. And if you had been permitted to achieve this dream so long dreamt, it would have harmed me not the least, because your water would have filled your dam in a few months, and then the water would have cascaded down the spillway you planned and into the same old stream-bed where it would once again meander past my little house in the valley.

And if you win, then I will seethe over the injustice of it, over the fact that during the very best part of an entire year, when I always take my rest beside the flowing stream in the late afternoons, my stream is taken from me, all because my wealthy neighbor stole my water with the help of some judge, who must have been affected by some reason which does not meet the eye. I not only lose my stream for a year, but when the water again begins to flow it will not be pleasant to sit beside because it will look so muddy. If others claim they can see no mud in it, *my* eyes will be able to perceive that it no longer has the clear sparkle that once made it so pleasant. Even if I can dismiss this from my mind, I know that I still cannot enjoy my little stream because of the infernal noise from that waterfall, whose sound can be heard in every part of my home. Its loudness is aggravated by the fact that it will never cease until the day when that home-made dam shall burst and let the water come running down to destroy my home and drown its occupants, a threat that occurs to my fearful mind every time I go to bed at night.

As men can never achieve perfect justice, men will never cease to dispute their rights. In the most primitive and least-organized type of society, there will arise a chieftan or ruler who must settle these disputes. As the civilization be-

---

1. I Blackstone, *Commentaries,* p. 142.

comes more complex, the people inevitably provide judges to settle this unending stream of disputes.

But there are few Solomons, and when disputes are left to be settled by the innate wisdom of those set over the people as judges, it always becomes obvious that judges cannot be expected to be free of bias and prejudices, because they are human. It is soon perceived by all that the justice enforced by the wisdom of individual judges falls with a heavy hand upon some and rests very lightly upon others, as the differing philosophies of different or succeeding judges lead them to decisions viewed as unjust by increasing numbers of people.

Always, there comes a time when the unguided whim or sense of justice of the individual judge is replaced by a body of law having some certainty in its content—law enabling men to know in advance how they should act in order to avoid the future wrath of judgment. The body of law substituted for the whim of the individual judge is always both God-like and merciless. It is always based upon ideas and the rationalization of fundamental concepts of justice. It claims for itself a perfect rightness, wisdom of concept, and strict accord with abstract principles of justice accepted by all. But once the rules are made, they fall without mercy upon those subjected to the governing authority of law. This continues until the merciless quality gives rise to new specific laws based on different abstract principles of justice, born of experience.

This yearning for just law to govern conduct and a governmental machinery dedicated to following that just law in the settlement of individual disputes gives rise to codes of laws, such as the Code of Hammurabi, later the Justinian Code, still later the French Code Napoleon, and many others.

Because of historical accidents,[2] the desire for certainty in law led to a unique system of law in England. Not to a code of laws, but to a body of law enunciated in judicial opinions in the decisions of many controversies, and this body of law was known as the Common Law. It grew slowly by an evolutionary process, accommodating itself in subtle ways to the gradual changes and the abrupt changes that occurred through the course of centuries.

This magnificent body of law sometimes moved in unjust directions, but there was then a corrective device—a legislative body known as the Commons of Great Britain in Parliament assembled, which enacted new laws to change unjust parts of the common law. Some parliamentary enactments, like some parts of the Common Law, were imperfect and proved unjust in their application.

The greatest fundamental procedural device of the Common Law was trial by jury, not always a welcome device. Some people felt that trial by jury subjected them to judgment by the rabble, when they should be able to receive the benefit of the studied wisdom of a learned judge.[3] The system came to be revered when experience showed the jury's capacity to stand between the individual and governmental demands for unjust punishment.

Although jurors could be biased and prejudiced just as individual judges might be, this English institution of trial by jury had great advantages. The large

---

2. See below, pp. 15, 95, 124.
3. In those days when many crimes were punishable by death, it was theorized that the individual would choose the jurors to try him, and nothing could be more fair. Actually, the sheriff chose the jurors, but the defendant could excuse jurors whom he did not trust. But he reached the outer limit when he excused 36 jurors. At this point, he had done more than fail to find jurors he could trust. He had rejected one entire jury of his peers, then another entire jury of twelve good men and true. When he

number of jurors required unanimously to agree in order to reach a verdict increased the probability that some jurors, if unable to overcome the prejudices of others, might refuse any decision, causing the case to be tried again before a different jury, making a just decision more likely.

Two other major advantages were not so immediately obvious. One, if an individual judge were influenced by undetected prejudices, his mind might warp the law to an almost imperceptible degree, and then warp the facts shown by the evidence sufficiently to meet this distorted view of the law. Thus, his prejudice, rather than the law, dictated his decision. But the jury system required the jury to decide all facts in the case, and the judge to instruct the jury as to the content of the law. This led to another benefit of the jury system—freeing the judges to concern themselves solely with law without bothering with the factual disputes as to what the people had actually done. The judge's instructions, when studiously considered, must be a correct statement of the applicable law so that the judges above him would find it to have been correct. When every imaginable variation of factual disputes came before judges, this naturally led them into a studious consideration of the law and a vigorous endeavor to be absolutely correct in their statements of the law, permitting the law itself to develop along rational lines with full consideration given to every recognized concept of justice.

This Common Law system was and is most excellent.[4]

When the ships crossed the Atlantic, bringing settlers to the forested continents of the Western Hemisphere, those settlers brought with them the law they knew and had lived under. The French brought to Louisiana and the Spanish to Florida and New Mexico their national adaptations of the Roman Code. And the English ships which landed in Massachusetts and Virginia, and then in all the coastal area north of Florida, brought with them the great system of the English Common Law.

Wherever they settled, the people soon required the designation of judges to interpret and apply the law to individual disputes. As law came to be more pervasive, judges were called upon to interpret and apply these details of the ever-growing body of law that governs the people, protecting them or burdening them. With today's proliferation of law, the quality of life and of civilization itself, in the last analysis, rests to a great degree upon the quality of judgment of the judges of the land.

As today's pervasive effect of judicial actions reaches into every level of society and every aspect of life, as times become troublesome, as governmental burdens become heavy, as governmental protections approach the vanishing point, the concerned citizen eventually is driven to examine the conduct of

---

rejected the third panel, he demonstrated that he would not consent to be tried by any jury. He refused, in the quaint old words, to put himself upon the country—to subject himself to the power and authority of the law. He was then tied to the ground and stones were piled upon him until he was crushed to death without any determination that he was guilty. This penalty of death without judgment had its attractive aspect: It avoided an additional consequence of a judgment of guilt—forfeiture of the defendant's property, leaving his wife and children homeless and destitute.

4. The finest book on the superiority of the common law system over the system of statutory law was written by one trained under the Roman rather than the common law, Italian jurist Bruno Leoni, *Freedom and the Law.*

the judiciary. Only by such studious examination, can one hope to find solutions for the burdens of mis-government.

During most of our history, the judiciary has been surrounded by an aura of purity and respectability like that which usually has surrounded the clergy. Indeed, one could describe the American judiciary as the priesthood of the American civilization.

From the earliest civilizations, a priesthood has often stood between the supreme power—God—and the people's human rulers. In the American civilization, a handful of robed judges boldly speak in the name of the supreme power— the Constitution—to impose rules upon the rule-making legislative bodies of the nation, to stay the hands of executives in the execution of "laws," and to nullify the acts of the electorate in the exercise of democratic self-governing powers they supposed themselves to possess.

This robed priesthood of the American civilization has led the people in the nation's greatest movement of moral repentence, the rise of the Negro citizen in his place in society. With the concurrent transformation of America into a predominently urban society, the Federal judiciary acted to remove "the shackles of rural domination" from state legislatures, with the effect of state laws gradually changing to reflect the mores of the dominant urban majority.

Great racial tensions have been *caused* by the decisions of this modern priesthood: From them, the downtrodden Negro has received hope and encouragement, without which the downtrodden cannot conceive the inspiration to revolt or to demand better treatment.[5] Those unrepentent white citizens bent upon preserving their prerogatives regard such judicial changes and the resulting legislated changes as injuries to their interests, which is accurate. By such changes, those white citizens have been deprived of their power to utilize local law and many elements of the economic and social structure to keep succeeding generations of Negro citizens in a position of legal and social inferiority, both essential to the maintenance of their position of economic inferiority.

Other tensions between yesterday's and tomorrow's American societies have been abetted by the judicial priesthood. The revolt of the excitable college populace, speeded by the permissive attitude of educational administrators, has been legitimized by judicial protection in the form of the extension to students on campus of procedural rights formerly reserved to citizens being subjected to the power of government acting as government as distinguished from government acting as the proprietor of an educational institution. Students given the right to speak freely, came to view this guarantee as imposing upon *someone* an obligation to listen, while the older generations obstinately viewed students as inmates in the educational institutions, inmates who owned obligations of respectful attention and obedience in exchange for the gift of education as the passport to an intellectually and economically rewarding life.

The scism between the older and younger generations—far greater than before due to the acceleration of technological advances and scientific discoveries—has been broadened by a new sexual morality. The eventual demise of the puritanical outlook was bound to follow the older generation's contraceptive inventiveness, but it is unlikely that such total rejection could have occurred with such rapidity but for the freedom from restraint enjoyed by *Playboy* and those who imitated it in the publishing field, the entertainment industries, and finally in popular dress. The freedom from restraint which made the popular distribution of those

---

5. According to the theory of Eric Hoffer, *The True Believer.*

provocative publications possible was accomplished by Federal judicial decisions that terminated strict governmental censorship previously exercised by local, state, and Federal governments alike.

An older generation remembered the patriotic fervor of Americans in World Wars I and II, and sometimes viewed youth's anti-war stance with bewilderment or as a loss of patriotism brought about by cowardice, aided by judicial decisions that greatly broadened the conscientious objection immunity from combat service. While one segment of the populace engaged in or approved violence and rioting, another segment hoped for prompt and forcible suppression of disorder by the police, who said that the proper performance of their duties had been rendered almost impossible by the judicial decisions of the 1960s.

These vast social changes, wrought or considerably aided by judicial decisions, have been accomplished by judgments unaided by legislated changes in law. Until the Civil Rights Act of 1964, the legislated law remained virtually unchanged in its language and provisions, and by judicial decisions the law was changed in its practical application.

Historically, the courts, and particularly the Supreme Court of the United States, have been deeply respected by most citizens. Citizens have recognized their obligation to conduct their affairs in accordance with law. They have accepted as correct the final judicial determinations of law made by the United States Supreme Court and the various state supreme courts. Public respect for the impartiality of the judiciary has been so strong that when President Franklin D. Roosevelt found some of his New Deal reforms frustrated by judicial decisions and sought to "pack" the Supreme Court by increasing its membership, Congress rejected his attempt to use his power of judicial appointment to influence the Court's decisions. Congress was popularly supported despite Roosevelt's immense popularity, because of the veneration of the Constitution and the Supreme Court as its protector.

In the popular view, the sanctity of the Supreme Court and the protection of the courts from political pressure were far more important even than the realization of *popular* government programs.

Protecting judges from political pressures, the people expect judges to be non-political in their decisions. This may appear to be an unrealistic expectation, because the prime consideration in the appointment of every Federal judge is almost always the one factor which is never a valid consideration: *Politics.* Thus it will remain, and in spite of it, in the alchemy of transforming a political lawyer into a federal judge, judges will continue in their decisions to be non-political in the usual sense.

Within the past twenty years, these judges, so insulated from any need to be affected by political pressures, have engaged in a course of aggressive decision-making so extensive that its effects have touched all citizens, and have aroused many to anger. Though former Chief Justice Earl Warren had only one vote, and though his voice carried no more weight in decision-making than did the voices of each of the other eight justices of the Supreme Court, the Court then came to be known as the Warren Court. "Impeach Earl Warren" was the ineffective war cry of a small minority.

The integrity of the federal judicial processes came under real or feigned suspicion. Where once they were respected, decisions were met with sullen resistance, open condemnation from many official governmental sources, and anonymous acts of violence. The National Guard was called out in one state to enforce and in another state to oppose final judicial decisions. The mayor of one southern city charged that the federal bench was "infested with a new breed of sociologists" and that educators were "diverted from their mission of education to the changing whims of a perverted federal judicial system . . ."

Such criticisms and responses to judicial decisions have had their effect upon the public esteem for the Supreme Court and have also had their effect in Congress. The House of Representatives moved steadily toward achieving a threat to impeach Justice Fortas, and Fortas resigned; two judges were nominated by President Nixon for elevation to the Supreme Court and were rejected by the Senate after tremendous battles, interpreted by many politically-oriented writers as purely political.

None can dispute the fact that the Supreme Court has suffered a great loss of the public respect it once enjoyed. Much of the written criticism of federal courts appearing in the public press has been directed at disapproval of the results of decisions and most of the praise has been an expression of approval of those results: Anger over the compelled association between races versus applause for the final accord of legal equality to the Negro; frustration over the relative loss of voice in state government by the rural electorate versus urban relief at being freed from outmoded laws formerly perpetuated by a provincial minority; vague unrest over the increase in crime which the police are crippled by judicial restraints in their efforts to combat versus unrestrained joy in the right to be dirty, hairy, naked and noisy.

But none of these is a legitimate reason either to praise or to condemn the courts. Each of these could have been accomplished by the exercise of legislative power to change the laws. Any or all of these changes can be nullified by the people's elected representatives by passing new laws or by amending the Constitution if either be required. If such considerations be—as they appear to be—the only basis for criticism of the Supreme Court, then the criticism is undeserved.

There is but one valid basis for criticising a judge. That is that he has incorrectly decided cases because of his intellectual dishonesty, intellectual laziness, or intellectual inferiority. Seldom are there men of low mentality on the United States Supreme Court. The Court is not subject to legitimate criticism unless its justices have decided cases incorrectly by not doing the considerable work necessary to discover the state of law, and thereby been intellectually lazy, or unless they have substituted their desire for what the law should be for their endeavor to determine what the law is, and thereby been intellectually dishonest.

Tyranny cannot come to America except by a failure of the judiciary to consistently be intellectually honest and a failure of the people to keep a close and understanding watch on their own government, realizing that government and the incumbents in its offices are not proper subjects of worship or adulation. If the judiciary has been true to its obligations of office, it should be supported and defended, however any individual may respond to the *effects* of its decisions. If the judiciary has not been true to its obligations of office, this becomes an occasion for action: Americans have complete power over their government, and if there is a defect in any part of it, they have the power to remedy the defect if they perceive it and if enough of them want it remedied.

With the United States Supreme Court having departed from so many past precedents in the last two decades, the purpose of this book is to help the individual citizen pass judgment upon the Supreme Court, by seeking an answer to the question of whether the Court has substituted its will as to what the law shall be for its *judgment* as to what the law is.

II.

JUDICIAL POWER

JUDICIAL POWER IS fundamentally the power to decide lawsuits: Shall this man be sent to jail? Shall this woman be granted a divorce? Who owns this land? Such questions are decided by a trial court in accordance with evidence presented to the court and in accordance with law. Assuming no jury, the trial judge decides what the facts are from the evidence and decides what the law is from his study of law. As he combines those two elements, we have legal responsibility imposed upon us according to our own acts—the facts—and according to the law which was in effect *when we acted*. In this manner, it is hoped that arbitrary rulings will be avoided, and we will not be compelled to make amends for acts that were right and lawful when we did them: That we will not be ruled by arbitrary whim.

Above the trial court sits an appellate court structure in which the United States Supreme Court is the highest court. In these appellate courts, the same people appear through their attorneys, but the nature of the case has changed. It has become, in effect, a lawsuit by the losing party against the trial judge, in which the losing party argues that the judge made a legal error, requiring the reversal of his decision, and in which the winning party defends the trial judge's decision favorable to him.

Thus, in both the trial and appellate courts, the search to discover the law is not a search performed for the purpose of informing the people what is to be required of them in the future. Instead, it is merely one step in determining what are the legal results of acts *already committed*, looking backward to what the law *was* at that time, instead of looking forward to determine what the law *should* be. Such labor is an academic inquiry, never to be affected by any speculation as to what popular desire might dictate that the law should be. Such popular desires bring their pressures to bear upon the legislative bodies, which respond to public pressures in deciding what the law will be henceforth.

This is the tradition of American law: The English Common Law, evolved over centuries by judges who felt a strong obligation to decide in accordance with the law. Judges in this system did not feel that they were making law. Instead, they were discovering, from past decisions, the present state of the law. While today there might be uncertainty as to what the rule of law is on a particular point until after it shall have been decided, when the case is decided and the law established or discovered, it is later seen to fit perfectly into the mosaic of law.

This common law system has an advantage over the code or civil law system of handing down written rules of law, because when the growth of the law occurs slowly, and judges are faced with conflicting rules of law, the natural desire to render just decisions will result in the blending of conflicting rules to arrive at just results and just law.

By this method, the English Common Law had built up a body of intricate law by the time of American Independence, such as the body of criminal law, the law of contracts, the law of trusts, with relatively little formal legislative influence.

15

We are still largely governed by this common law in most of our activities, and it is administered for the most part by the various state courts. For example, until the quite recent past, all important statutory law in the law of contracts could easily be copied onto a single sheet of paper. The principal contract law statutes were known as statutes of frauds, requiring certain types of contracts to be in writing to be enforced, and the statutes of limitations, establishing time limits for filing suits to enforce different types of contracts.

When the English Parliament enacted a statute, the statute would be "absorbed" into the Common Law, and sometimes would give rise to a new body of common law. In this manner, the law of trusts originated and had become a firmly established, complex body of law before the time of American Independence. This body of law, used so profitably by the trust departments of thousands of banks and used by estate planners in diminishing the burden of federal estate taxation, is the offshoot of two ancient statutes enacted by the English Parliament, the Statute Mortmain, and the Statute of Uses.

The Statute Mortmain was enacted to combat the ever-increasing church ownership of property, with more and more of England's limited real estate falling into the church's "dead hand," and the church's dead hand would never deed the property back to living people so that ownership could change hands from generation to generation. The Statute Mortmain simply decreed that churches should be incompetent to own property. Today, partly from tradition, most American church property is still owned by individuals constituting a board of aldermen, board of deacons, or the like.

After the Statute Mortmain was enacted, many devout individuals evaded the prohibition by transferring property to another person for the use of the church. This high moral obligation of the new "owner" to respect the church's exclusive right to use the property soon came to find judicial enforcement by the chancery courts, whose judges were men of ecclesiastical training. As time passed, more and more property came to be "owned" by people who had no right to enjoy the fruits of ownership, whose enjoyment was reserved to the beneficiary of the "use." Legal ownership and beneficial ownership of real property were separated.

To conform the law to popular practice so that legal ownership would be vested in the actual beneficial owners of the property, the Parliament enacted the Statute of Uses. This statute converted the "use" into legal ownership. But by this time, people had perceived advantages to being able to separate legal ownership from beneficial ownership, so they sought to preserve those advantages. Some unknown lawyer devised a method which came to be known as a "use on a use." He drafted a transfer of property to an individual for the use of a second individual, who was directed to hold the property under tightly limited discretion for the use of a third individual. The "use on a use" did work, and has long been known as the trust.

The trustee might have total legal ownership, total power to decide how to use trust property and invest trust money, but the benefit or income goes to the trust beneficiary. The trust derived its life from the former enforcement given to uses for religious purposes. Still today, the standard of conduct imposed upon trustees is the strictest known to the law—more strict than that imposed upon Congressmen, Senators, judges.

So the Common Law continually evolved in the course of the decision of individual cases between individual people, and the judges and the people were dedicated to the principle that cases should be decided according to law rather than by the whims of different judges. The judge was trusted with as little power as

possible. He was restricted to determining the law, and the decision of the facts—
the real point of dispute in most cases—was left to a jury of laymen, who did not
sit long enough to form habits in the decision of cases. If the jury were moved by
passion, the judge might be persuaded to set aside their verdict and grant a
second trial before a new jury. The next decision hopefully would be a product
of evidence and reason rather than passion.

If the decision of facts were entrusted to a judge and he were moved by the
same passion instead of reason, this error could be corrected by taking it before a
higher judge, for whom the printed page of transcript can seldom recreate the
passion of the courtroom. That judges can dangerously succumb to human passions is demonstrated by a federal judge's instructions given to a jury in frontier
days. A Mr. Starr was on trial for murdering a marshal, and the Supreme Court
quoted the judge's instructions to the jury in *Starr v. United States:*

> "How unjust, how cruel, what a mockery, what a sham, what a bloody crime it
> would be upon the part of this government to send a man out . . . and to say . . . I
> am unable as chief executive of this government to assure you that you have any pro-
> tection whatever. . . . What was this posse [marshal] to do? What was he commanded
> to do? To go into the Indian country and hunt up Mr. Starr, and say to him that
> on a certain day the judge of the Federal court at Fort Smith will want your
> attendance at a little trial down there wherein you are charged with horse stealing,
> and you will be kind enough, sir, to put in your attendance on that day; and the
> judge sends his compliments to you, Mr. Starr. . . . Without these officers what is
> the use of this court? It takes men who are brave to uphold the law here. I say,
> because of this, and because there is no protection unless the law is upheld by
> men of this kind, if it be true that you are satisfied of the fact beyond a reasonable
> doubt that Floyd Wilson was a man of this kind, that he was properly in the exe-
> cution of the high duty devolving upon him, and while so properly executing it by
> the light of these principles of law I have given you, his life was taken by this
> defendant, your solemn duty would be to say that he is guilty of the crime of
> murder, because the law has been violated it is to be vindicated; you are to stand
> by the nation; you are to say to all the people that no man can trample upon the
> law wickedly, violently, and ruthlessly; that it must be upheld if it has been
> violated."

Under our traditions, whether in deciding appellate cases or in charging a jury,
the judge's proper domain has always been to decide questions of law in accordance with the law already established—to look backward to discover the past
content of law, not to command the state of the law henceforth. In endeavoring
to approach the ideal of government of laws rather than government according
to the varying wills of individual men, this system of Common Law we fortunate-
ly inherited from the English had as its bedrock the doctrine of *stare decisis:*
That on questions of law, every court is bound to follow the law, as evidenced by
its own prior decisions and the prior decisions of its superior courts.

Thus, yesterday's decisions represent yesterday's law, and unless that law has
been changed, these decisions are today's law. On a particular point, we study
together an 1808 decision, an 1870 decision, and a 1935 decision to discover the
state of the law on that point in 1970. If the past decision was directly on the
identical legal point under consideration, that decision is very likely conclusive
unless the Legislature has changed the law on that point.

To illustrate the working of *stare decisis,* consider the law of slander. This is
the law that imposes monetary liability upon a person for speaking false statements about another person. In a particular state, there may have been many

decisions on many elements of the law of slander—the effect of innuendo, whether one may be held liable for slander committed while he was testifying on the witness stand in a trial, or while speaking on the floor of the Legislature, and rulings on evidence that have been made in slander trials.

Finally, a suit for slander is brought where one man made false statements about another to his face, with no witnesses present. The Defense: The right to receive damages for slander is based upon injury to the slandered man's reputation, and I have not injured his reputation when I have made the false statement to none but him; a man's reputation lies wholly in the opinions of third persons, and I have not injured his reputation unless I have made the false statement to some of those third persons.

To discover what the law is, the court considers its past rulings—perhaps that where slander has been committed, the amount of damages should be determined by the extent that reputation is injured, whether the slander was innately absurd and unbelievable so that it would not greatly damage the reputation, and the fact that in a prosecution for assault and battery, prior decisions have established that it is no defense that the "victim" provoked the assault by making insulting statements to his assailant. The court may also study the rulings of the courts of other states or of England or Canada for whatever insight they may contain that is consistent with local law; and the court may finally be persuaded that it is the law of this state that there is no right to receive damages for slanderous statements made to no one but the person slandered. And all this is done to determine whether John Jones owes money to Bill Smith for falsely calling him a thief to his face. Now the state of the established law has been discovered from past decisions after considerable study and deliberation, and has been announced in the decision of a lawsuit. This is the exercise of judicial power. It is *stare decisis.*

Ten years pass, without any new laws being passed on the subject. Then such a situation may occur again, but under far more aggravated circumstances, so aggravated that the judges' sympathies are excited to the point that they feel it almost immoral not to allow the victim of the slander to recover monetary damages for the tremendous mental strain wrongly imposed upon him. They may question whether the right to utter private insults is so precious that it should, in effect, be licensed by the courts. But in their proper adherence to the doctrine of *stare decisis,* the judges follow their past decision, and rule against the victim of the "slander." In so doing, they may express dissatisfaction with the law, and may recommend that the Legislature consider changing it, though the Legislature did not make the law in the first place. This is the proper exercise of judicial power and a proper application of *stare decisis.*

But in the exercise of purely judicial power, judges sometimes do overrule their prior decisions, denounce as incorrect their past declarations of the law, and judges do this in full accord with the command of *stare decisis.* How can this be if judges are bound by their prior decisions?

Sometimes this occurs because of the simple failure to locate a past decision. The court then may re-decide the same question and may decide it differently. Later, presented with the two directly conflicting decisions, both of which cannot correctly represent the law, the judges must reconsider and decide which correctly represents the law, which fits more perfectly into the overall legal scheme. One decision, as a result, must be overruled, because it can be seen that it was a decision contrary to law.

On other occasions, what appears to be an overruling of past cases does not actually overrule the holdings. Under *stare decisis,* the only actual holdings on the law are those legal rulings which are necessary to the decision of the case. In deciding cases, judges sometimes write extensively on comparable legal rules to illustrate the correctness of their actual decision. These supportive ramblings, and even the solution of actual questions of law which, in the manner in which the case is actually disposed of, do not actually contribute to the decision of whether to affirm or reverse the trial court, are not holdings but are *obiter dicta*— "other words." *Stare decisis* does not require that the court and its inferior courts follow such other words not necessary to the real decision but only that they follow the actual holdings. This limitation on *stare decisis* recognizes the true nature of judicial power—that it is limited to the decision of controversies between people and does not include the power to enunciate broad rules of law for the future government of the people. This is the legislative or imperial power to enunciate future law, not the judicial *function* of discovering past law.

Sometimes a subsidiary rule of law becomes so outmoded by changing times that it comes into conflict with the principal rule of law from which it was derived, and it must be overruled not because it was incorrect when decided, but because changing facts have made it incorrect.[1] Under this excellent Common Law system, law grows by a slow evolutionary process, and has the flexibility to meet changing conditions without radical departures or even noticible departures from existing law.

The English Common Law became the American Common Law. It governed men in their affairs during all the years before the American Colonies declared themselves a separate and independent nation. In each state, that state's common law determined property rights, the rights and duties involved in the relations of husband and wife, parent and child, debtor and creditor—it provided for the resolution of all important disputes that arose between men in society.

Property ownership and marital relationships were not dissolved when the Declaration of Independence was signed, nor were debts forgiven, though it was only by law that the duties involved in these relations were enforcd. The Common Law continued in effect and continues today in the separate states. It still has as its bedrock the doctrine of *stare decisis*—that past judicial decisions evidence the past state of the law, and the law is still the same unless it has been changed.

Even when statutes are enacted by a legislature, the courts, to decide cases in accordance with law, must still decide: What is the law? This means that the courts must construe statutes and declare their meaning, and the meaning of a statute is not always obvious. Lawyers are customarily reluctant positively to assert the meaning of a new statute until a court has construed it in the process

---

1. In the law of negligence, the fundamental rule of conduct has always been that every man must conduct himself as a reasonably prudent man would under the same or similar circumstances. Juries are instructed to compare individual conduct with this rule. In the early days of the automobile, there developed a subsidiary rule that in driving at night, the driver must drive slowly enough so he could stop his car within the range of his headlights; if he did not, he was demonstrating a reckless disregard for the safety of wagons, horses and pedestrians, who might so suddenly loom into sight before his dim headlights that he could not stop in time due to his high speed. In time, the horses and wagons departed, and everyone began driving much faster. The man who drove slowly within the stopping range of his lights was in fact not acting prudently under the changed circumstances, but was a traffic hazard. Courts began overruling the "range of headlights" rule and did so in full accord with the requirement that they follow past law as found in earlier decisions.

of deciding a case, and has authoritatively demonstrated its meaning. This careful judicial demonstration of the meaning of a statute sometimes leads the legislature to re-study the matter and decide that it actually enacted more or less than it had intended to enact.[2]

The amendatory power of legislative authority suggests a slight chink in the wall of solidarity of *stare decisis,* the present validity of past judicial decisions. When the Supreme Court expounds the meaning of a stature, it does not proclaim future law. Future law was previously proclaimed by Congress in enacting law, and the Supreme Court merely explained the meaning of that past proclamation. Then when Congress amends or repeals the law, Congress immediately renders the old Supreme Court decision an inaccurate statement of today's law.

Obviously, an old decision explaining the meaning of a repealed law is not only no longer binding upon inferior courts: It is no longer even persuasive. Inferior courts, in enforcing laws enacted by Congress, can thus become *obligated to disregard Supreme Court authority*. So when reading judicial opinions that are based upon statutes, one must regard them with suspicion until he has carefully checked to be sure that the legislative authority has not changed the stature in the meantime. The sanctity of judicial decisions under *stare decisis* must yield to the superior law-changing authority of the legislative body.

A consideration of judicial power in relation to statutes leads to one of the strangest decisions ever rendered by the United States Supreme Court, and thence to the subject of the place of dissenting opinions in the proper exercise of judicial power. The decision is *James* v. *United States*. It presents opinions, dissenting opinions, and opinions partly concurring and partly dissenting. The case was decided under the definition of "income" in the income tax laws, and is generally accepted as establishing a principal of law, but from a legal viewpoint, all it established was that Mr. James did not have to go to prison.

The case involved Mr. James' embezzlement of a large sum of money. The statutory definition of income was designed to include all gains and income, whether legal or illegal, with some exceptions such as true gifts, which are not taxable under the income tax laws. The Supreme Court had earlier considered the question of the taxability of embezzled money, and other federal courts had considered many other types of illegal gains. There was some similarity between embezzled money and money won by gambling, although the gambler-loser's wife might be able to sue and get back the lost money. There was some similarity to money obtained by fraud, as by the sale of a fake money-making machine for a large sum of money. There was some similarity to money obtained by extortion, as the kidnapper's ransom. But in all these cases of illegal gains, the ownership was transferred by the original owner, and the gambler, extortionist, or con artist was enriched by the amount of the illegal gain. This was taxable as income.

But money stolen or embezzled was different. Though the thief might spend it, he was not spending his own money, but someone else's. In a sense, it was similar

---

2. An example of the corrective change of law can be seen in the original wording of the secondary boycott provisions of the Taft-Hartley Act. These provisions made it illegal under given circumstances to cause a concerted refusal by employees to work. A case came before the Supreme Court in which a union had caused a single truck driver to refuse to deliver his cargo. The Supreme Court held this not to be illegal because there can be no "concerted" refusal to work by a single employee. Congress amended that Taft-Hartley provision to make it apply to causing a single employee to quit work under the illegal circumstances.

to borrowed money, which does not enrich the borrower because he still owes the full amount that he borrowed. But if he borrows $10,000 one year and becomes insolvent and settles his debt for $6,000 the next year for a discharge from any obligation to pay the full $10,000, he has had a $4,000 gain, or income the year he settled his liability. The Supreme Court has earlier held that embezzled money should receive the same treatment as borrowed money—not taxable at all in the year it was stolen, but taxable in a later year to the extent of any "saving" realized by the thief if he settled his liability by making partial repayment.

This holding fitted well into general property law concepts, or at least into those particular property concepts that the Court mentioned in its opinion. But the holding was not conducive to successful tax collection. It immunized the embezzler from tax liability during the year when the embezzler had all the stolen money in his hands and could easily have paid the tax, and it imposed liability for tax upon him in the year when he had most strained his financial resources to repay all of the stolen money he could—when he was least able to raise money to pay additional income tax. The decision was not popular with the Internal Revenue Service.

So the Government had Mr. James indicted for tax evasion for the year during which he embezzled the money, and James was convicted. The Supreme Court reversed the conviction and dismissed the case, with six of the nine justices voting for the reversal and dismissal.

Of the six justices whose votes joined to free Mr. James, three followed the earlier holding, saying that he had no income from the embezzlement in the year he stole the money, therefore couldn't be guilty of attempted tax evasion that year. The other three justices who voted to free Mr. James completely disagreed. They thought the money was income to Mr. James the year he stole it, but they said that until we this moment decided that money became income when it was stolen, Mr. James could not have known he had taxable income, therefore could not be guilty of *wilfully* attempting to evade payment of his tax, wilfulness having to be proven to prove commission of the crime.

Three other justices could not agree that the record entitled Mr. James to a judgment of acquittal. Two justices thought that the record did not establish whether Mr. James was innocent or guilty: They agreed that the embezzler has income when he steals but said the case should be sent back for another trial on the added issue of whether Mr. James actually knew of the earlier Supreme Court decision that embezzled money is not income, *i.e.*, whether he acted wilfully in failing to report it on his tax return. The final justice agreed that embezzled money is income, but thought Mr. James was guilty and his conviction should be upheld because there wasn't any evidence that he actually had known of the earlier Supreme Court decision and felt protected by it in not reporting this money as income.

Thus the Court's actual decision that Mr. James was innocent as a matter of law could have been expressed by a brief *per curiam* opinion (an unsigned opinion "by the Court") that the Court held Mr. James innocent but that no majority of its members could agree upon the reasons for such holding; or more properly, the Court could have ordered the case re-argued.

The Government and its Internal Revenue Service, as one of the disputing litigants in the *James* decision, seized upon the decision as establishing that money embezzled, stolen, or extorted is taxable as income the year of its illicit receipt. This view can be accepted by combining the votes of those justices who held that Mr. James was innocent as a matter of law with the vote of justices who held that he was guilty as a matter of law or that he might be innocent or guilty, as could not be determined without another trial. The Government's happy view of the *James* case is based upon a vision of the Supreme Court not as a body empowered to decide the outcome of lawsuits, but as a council empowered by majority vote to determine the future state of the law.

It is the judicial function to judge the past acts of people and to weigh them against past law, as corrected if the past decision can be demonstrated to be incorrect—whether those acts consist of the failure to render true accounts to the Government for income taxation, trespass upon another's land under a claim of some right to use the land, or a state's discriminatory exclusion of a Negro child from a white school on account of his race—and to impose judicial remedies in the form of orders for imprisonment, award of monetary damages, or an injunctive order requiring the State to admit the child to the school.

The question before the Supreme Court in *United States v. James* was whether the trial court's judgment of Mr. James' guilt of tax evasion should stand, and as a step to such decision, the Supreme Court had to consider the question of whether embezzled money was actually taxable income. It would appear unthinkable that Mr. James should be imprisoned for doing what the Supreme Court had already held that he should do in his income tax reporting. If the Supreme Court had set out not to exercise judicial power but to seize upon the *James* case as an opportunity to announce a change in substantive law, this would have led to a course of opinions no different from those actually handed down.

A people who will consent to having their laws handed down to them, made and changed by nine men enthroned for life, differ only in degree from a people who will tolerate government by a single man enthroned for life. Lawmakers should be subject to expulsion by the people when they make unacceptable laws. Judges should be immunized from the effects of such unpopularity because their task is to make academic search to learn the content of existing law, and if that law is unpopular, it is not the fault of the judges, but of the lawmakers.

United States v. James can be considered to establish the law as to the taxability of embezzled money only by joining concurring opinions with dissenting opinions, totally contrary to the legal effect previously given dissenting opinions everywhere except in the *James* case. In all American courts, state and federal, it has been considered that dissenting opinions are not law, are properly totally disregarded in determining what is the law, and are no part of the judicial decision.

Under the Common Law tradition, the court's actual decision of a case, and so much of its opinion as is necessary to its decision of the case, are evidence of the law. The rest merely complicates the task of determining the content of the law. The dissenter refuses to join the rest of the judges on the court in determining what the outcome of the case will be, and he writes a dissenting opinion to express why he cannot join in the decision of the case. It is *always* impossible for the dissenting opinion to be a part of the reasoning by which the decision of the case is rendered. The acceptance of the *James* case as establishing the taxability of embezzled money thus rests upon an extremely poor quality of legal scholarship in its unquestioning acceptance of dissenting opinions as evidence of the law.

More dangerously, the lower courts' acceptance of *James* as authoritative implies an acceptance of the premise that the Supreme Court somewhere, somehow obtained the power to sit around and vote on the future content of the law, as distinguished from the obligation to discover the past content of law to the extent needed to decide a case of controversy between people.

But though dissenting opinions, as such, are in no way authoritative, individual dissenting opinions legitimately have tremendous effect at times. The value of dissenting opinions inheres in the distinction between judicial and legislative powers.

When legislative authority enacts a statute to control future conduct, the statute becomes law solely because the legislature had the power to make law and it exercised that power. The resulting law might be good or bad, well or ill-designed to remedy the defects it was enacted to cure, but these considerations are of no effect. The statute is law by virtue of the power of government to impose its will upon those subject to its power.

But when a court declares the meaning of a statute or constitutional provision, the court's opinion is secondary, the statute or constitution itself is the primary declaration of the law, and the judicial explanation of its meaning may or may not be correct. If at any time, the judges perceive their past explanations of the meaning of a statute to be wrong, they are obligated to correct their past errors. The judgments and opinions of courts are themselves subject to judgment, and the standard against which they are judged is truth.

Dissenting opinions can have great value in judging the validity of judicial decisions, in determining whether those decisions are true to the law. The value of dissenting opinions depends entirely upon their intrinsic value because truth is where one finds it, not enhanced in the slightest by the fact that the writer of the opinion was a justice of the United States Supreme Court. The value of the dissent arises from the indestructability of truth and of ideas which embody truths. Such criticisms later *force* their way into the law by their own power. Similarly, ideas propounded by legal writers and professors of law have at times had such intrinsic force that they simply could not be kept out of judicial decisions, because they embodied truth.

Many of the dissenting opinions of Justice Oliver Wendell Holmes, Jr., as to the meaning of various parts of the Constitution have withstood the test of time and have come to be accepted as more accurate and truthful expositions of the Constitution than the opinions from which he dissented. More recent times have seen other magnificent dissenting opinions on occasion, particularly by Justices Hugo L. Black and John M. Harlan.

These dissenting opinions often evince strong feelings of the impropriety of Supreme Court decisions. Witness language by Justice Black in his dissent from a decision holding a particular type of union conduct immune from the anti-trust laws in *American Federation of Musicians v. Carroll:*

"I am sure that the Clayton and Norris-LaGuardia Acts never intended to give unions this kind of stranglehold on any industry. It may be that the Court views this industry as having special problems of supply and demand requiring special treatment under the antitrust laws. If this is the case, the Court should frankly say so and seek to confine the misguided rules of law it announces. More appropriately, *the Court should leave to Congress* the task of making special provisions in the antitrust laws for the special circumstances of the music industry.[3]

3. Witness, also, the outcry of judicial conscience in Justice Harlan's dissent to one of the leading legislative reapportionment decisions, *Reynolds v. Sims.* After asserting the Constitution does not permit the federal judiciary to compel the redrawing of legislative district lines within a state, he said:

When dissenting opinions proceed from such strong convictions as to lead justices openly to charge that their fellow justices have exercised power not given to
them, such dissents eventually are bound to have effect on future judgments as
to the correctness of the decision, and as to the fidelity of those justices who
rendered it.

Dissenting opinions thus attack the correctness of the court's decision, and seek
to pinpoint reasons why the dissenter believes the court is departing from law in
its decision. If the contentions of the dissenter are adequately answered in the
court's opinion, then the dissent is a futile protest. But if the court's opinion *makes
no attempt* to answer the dissent, here is ground for suspicion that the court *could
not answer* it. From this, and from the fact that the court itself necessarily knew
of the dissent by one of its members, there arises a justifiable suspicion that the
court has *consciously* failed to seek to discover and obey the commands of law,
and has instead wilfully usurped the legislative power to make rules for the future
government of the people. This is dishonesty in judicial office.

The doctrine of *stare decisis* requires the courts to follow their past decisions to
the extent that those decisions have actually decided the legal questions they claim
to have decided. But when a court construes a statute, the doctrine of *stare decisis*
is much less effective as a restraint on the court's future decisions, because the
actual law is the statute rather than the court's explanation of the statute, and if the
court later discovers that its prior decision was incorrect or untrue to the statute's
meaning, the court is *obligated* to overrule its prior decision.

America complicated the subject of judicial power and its exercise by adopting
a written constitution that actually restrains governmental power. Sweden furnished the world an example of a government of combined city-states which had
an adjudicative system to settle disputes between the city-states; each city-state
obligated itself to obey such judgments, and all of them agreed to force the loser to
obey the judgment if it failed to do so voluntarily. So those city-state governments
were subjected to law, but the law was *externally applied* by the force of arms of
their fellow-governments.

In some bygone civilizations, of which the ancient Jewish is the best-known example, there was the restraining influence of a priesthood communicating to the
government the external restraints of the commands of God.[4] But these commands

---

"Finally, these decisions give support to a current mistaken view of the
Constitution and the constitutional function of this Court. This view, in a
nutshell, is that every major social ill in this country can find its cure in some
constitutional 'principle,' and that this Court should 'take the lead' in promoting
reform when other branches of government fail to act. The Constitution is not
a panacea for every blot upon the public welfare, nor should this Court,
ordained as a judicial body, be thought of as a general haven for reform
movements. The Constitution is an instrument of government, fundamental to
which is the premise that in a diffusion of governmental authority lies the
greatest promise that this Nation will realize liberty for all its citizens. This
Court, limited in function in accordance with that premise, does not serve
its high purpose *when it exceeds its authority,* even to satisfy justified impatience
with the slow workings of the political process. For when, in the name of
constitutional interpretation, the Court *adds something to the Constitution that
was deliberately excluded from it,* the Court in reality substitutes its view of
what should be so for the amending process." [Emphasis by Justice Harlan].
4. See above, p. 12.

were never effective as a restraint upon governmental power except to the extent that the king heeded the prophetic influence, and sometimes kings were more influenced by Jezabels than by Jehovah.

The American colonies were charted by the English king and were subject to the external restraints of the king's government. Many of these regal restraints upon the colonies' exercise of governmental powers came to be misused, and their misuses were catalogued in the Declaration of Independence:

> "He has refused his Assent to Laws, the most wholesome and necessary for the public good.—He has forbidden his Governors to pass Laws of immediate and pressing importance, unless suspended in their operation till his Assent should be obtained; and when so suspended, he has utterly neglected to attend to them.—He has refused to pass other Laws for the accommodation of large districts of people, unless those people would relinquish the right of Representation in the Legislature, a right inestimable to them and formidable to tyrants only. . . .—He has dissolved Representative Houses repeatedly, for opposing with manly firmness his invasions on the rights of the people. . . .—He has made Judges dependent upon his Will alone, for the tenure of their offices, and the amount and payment of their salaries.—He has erected a multitude of New Offices, and sent hither swarms of Officers to harass our people, and eat out their substance. . . ."

Thus the colonial American governments were themselves governed by the superior and external authority of the English king sitting in council.[5]

With the abolition of the English king's authority, the governments of the American states became ungoverned except to the extent that the people in each state might restrain their own government, and some of these state governments occasionally exhibited an unneighborly attitude toward their fellow governments.

The Constitution of the United States was designed to establish a government, but was also designed as a set of mandatory rules to govern the government itself, without *any external force* to enforce those rules! What a dream: A charter, a set of limitations, to govern what all history had proven to be ungovernable! Thoreau,[6] only seventy years after its creation, was to describe the government so established:

> "This American government,—what is it but a tradition, though a recent one, endeavoring to transmit itself unimpaired to posterity, *but each instant losing some of its integrity?* It has not the vitality and force of a single living man; for a single man can bend it to his will. . . . It is excellent, we must all allow; yet this government never of itself furthered any enterprise, but by the alacrity with which it got out of its way. *It* does not keep the country free. *It* does not settle the West. *It* does not educate. The character inherent in the American people has done all that has been accomplished; and it would have done somewhat more, if the government had not sometimes got in its way. . . . Trade and commerce, if they were not made of India rubber, would never manage to

---

5. Though regal unfairness was charged in both the *Declaration of Independence* and Thomas Payne's popular writings, most English governmental power had passed from the king to the parliament, and as a matter of historical accuracy, most American mistreatment came at the hands of the parliament. This was recognized in the debates in the Federal Constitutional Convention. See *Documents Illustrative of the Formation of the Union*, p. 846.

6. Henry David Thoreau, *Civil Disobedience.*

bounce over the obstancles which legislators are continually putting in their way; and, if one were to Judge these men wholly by the effects of their actions, and not partly by their intentions, they would deserve to be classed and punished with those mischievous persons who put obstructions on the railroads.*

To impose the rule of law upon ungovernable government not restrained by any superior external force, the draftsmen of the Constitution looked to what they considered the weakest department of government, the judiciary. Hamilton, urging his fellow New Yorkers to adopt the Constitution, wrote in *The Federalist:*

> The judiciary, from the nature of its functions, will always be the least dangerous to the political rights of the Constitution; because it will be the least in a capacity to annoy or injure them. The Executive not only dispenses the honors, but holds the sword of the community. The legislature not only commands the purse, but prescribes the rules by which the duties and rights of every citizen are to be regulated. The judiciary, on the contrary, has no influence over either the sword or the purse; no direction either of the strength or of the wealth of society; and can take no active resolution whatever. It may be truly said to have neither FORCE nor WILL, but merely judgment; and must ultimately depend upon the aid of the executive arm even for the efficacy of its judgments."

And the accuracy of this last forecast was demonstrated in recent times by President Eisenhower's use of his executive authority to command troops to Little Rock essentially to enforce federal court orders.

To this weakest of all the branches of government, it is assumed that the writers of the Constitution left the task of upholding the Constitution—the rule for the government of government itself. But the Constitution did not actually leave to judges alone the obligation of subservience to the Constitution.

To assure that there would be no doubt but that the Constitution was forever meant—subject to its continued acceptance by the people—to govern the government itself, the document provides: "This Constitution, and the Laws of the United States which shall be made in Pursuance thereof; and all Treaties made, or which shall be made, under the authority of the United States, shall be the supreme Law of the Land . . ." Thus its supremacy was declared by the people in adopting the Constitution, and the supremacy was shared by laws made pursuant to the Constitution. Laws enacted by Congress outside the scope permitted by the Constitution were not made a part of the supreme law; nor were state laws, or even state constitutions, a part of the supreme law of the land. To assure that even state constitutions and laws would be nullified if they conflicted with the supreme law, the Constitution provided that all state and federal judges, legislators, and executives, would be bound by the Constitution, "any Thing in the Constitution or Laws of any State to the Contrary notwithstanding."

But ink on paper fades, and written laws have no force except as they are enforced or voluntarily obeyed. What assurance was there that the supremacy of every provision of the Constitution would be kept alive in the future? There was none. None, except the honor of public officials, and especially judges, impelling

---

*In this book, where quotations are marked with an asterisk, some or all of the italics are by the original writer. Where not so marked, all italics are by this author.

them to abide by their oaths of office, and the omnipresence of an entire populace with the good sense to insist that public officials live up to their oaths of office, and with the intelligence and awareness to perceive when those officials should dishonor their obligations.

But as the past recedes, people who have not experienced tyranny come to public office, and the urgency of constitutional safeguards tends to weigh less heavily than the demands of living, voting people, who are here today, will be gone tomorrow, and expect their stay to be made as painless and pleasant as possible. So as a final device to perpetuate constitutional safeguards for the benefit of future generations, judges were surrounded by powerful protections to insulate them, as much as possible, from all political demands. Being born and trained to the great Common Law tradition which would instill in them a reverence for law, for the precedent of past decisions, and for the intellectual challenge of discovering the law, it was anticipated that judges would devote themselves to the continual study which would lead them to increasing understanding of the protections afforded by the Constitution.

People accept the role of the Supreme Court as the protector of the Constitution and its power to declare upon the constitutionality of the acts of state governments and the enactments of Congress, but where did the Supreme Court get this power? There is no provision in the Constitution giving courts supremacy over the Congress. Judges are required to swear to support the Constitution, but the identical requirement is imposed upon Congressmen, and by the very same sentence of the Constitution. Is the actual supremacy of the courts in declaring upon questions of constitutionality a power acquired by usurpation condoned by Congressional inaction?

The Supreme Court has repeatedly shown itself aware that the only power it can exercise is judicial power, and that it has no authority over either the president or the Congress. In the Supreme Court's decision of *Massachusetts v. Mellon,* the Court said: "We have no power *per se* to review and annul acts of Congress on the ground that they are unconstitutional. . . . [The] power exercised is that of ascertaining and declaring the law applicable to the controversy. It amounts to little more than the negative power to disregard an unconstitutional enactment, which otherwise would stand in the way of the enforcement of a legal right."

There is *only one reason* for the supremacy of the Supreme Court's opinions on questions of constitutionality: It has the 'last word. Laws without enforcement accomplish nothing. Congress may vote to impose a tax, but the Congressmen cannot go armed to compel citizens to pay it, and except for the imposition of martial law and the abandonment of all pretense of constitutional government, the tax payment can be enforced only by court actions, requiring judges to determine whether the tax statute violates the Constitution. This is what the Supreme Court referred to as the negative power to disregard an unconstitutional enactment.

We have seen that in the Common Law adjudicative system, judges must search past decisions to learn the content of the law, they must consult and interpret statutes to see whether the legislative authority has changed the Common Law, and then having discovered the content of the law, they must apply it to the facts of the case to arrive at their judgment. The written constitution adds an additional complexity: The judges must now compare the law as they find it with the Constitution—the rule for the government of government—to determine whether the government has the power to enforce that law as the court has found it to exist or whether the Constitution denies government the power to make or enforce such a law.

This power of judges to declare laws unconstitutional is accepted without question, but it was not always so. In helping to "sell" the new constitution to the people of New York, Hamilton insisted that judges would have to rule upon constitutionality, but others held different opinions. They considered that the president had sworn to uphold the Constitution, and so had the congressmen and senators, that each would have to answer to his own conscience, and that each would have to decide for himself whether an action he was called upon to take was within his power under the Constitution. And clearly, some constitutional questions could never be ruled upon by a judge. For example, the Constitution prohibits any state from engaging in war, but if Neveda should make war against Utah, no court orders could stop it; this would call for more serious response. The president, as commander-in-chief of the army, would have to exercise his judgment as to what action his oath of office required.

From its position as the speaker of the last word in the actual imposition of law upon individuals, it was inevitable that the Supreme Court would become the preeminent guide on questions of constitutionality. The Court's province—and *every* judge's duty—to rule upon constitutionality was effectively established by the persuasiviness of a single judicial opinion, that of Chief Justice John Marshall in *Marbury v. Madison*. The masterful opinion is worth reading in its entirety. It concludes:

"This original and supreme will organizes the government, and assigns to different departments their respective powers. It may either stop here, or establish certain limits not to be transcended by those departments.

"The government of the United States is of the latter description. The powers of the legislature are defined and limited; and that those limits may not be mistaken, or forgotten, the Constitution is written. To what purpose is that limitation committed to writing, if these limits may, at any time, be passed by those intended to be restrained? The distinction between a government with limited and unlimited powers is abolished, if those limits do not confine the persons on whom they are imposed, and if acts prohibited and acts allowed are of equal obligation. It is a proposition too plain to be contested, that the constitution controls any legislative Act repugnant to it; or, that the legislature may alter the constitution by an ordinary Act.

"Between these alternatives there is no middle ground. The constitution is either a superior paramount law, unchangeable by ordinary means, or it is on a level with ordinary legislative acts, and, like other acts, is alterable when the legislature shall please to alter it.

"If the former part of the alternative be true, then a legislative act contrary to the constitution is not law; if the latter part be true, then written constitutions are absurd attempts, on the part of the people, to limit a power in its own nature illimitable.

"Certainly all those who have framed written constitutions contemplate them as forming the fundamental and paramount law of the nation, and, consequently, the theory of every such government must be, that an act of the legislature, repugnant to the constitution, is void.

* * * *

"If an act of the legislature, repugnant to the constitution, is void, does it, not withstanding its invalidity, bind the courts, and oblige them to give it effect? Or, in other words, though it be not law, does it constitute a rule as operative as it was a law? This would be to overthrow in fact what was established in theory; and would seem, at first view, an absurdity too gross to be insisted on. It shall, however, receive a more attentive consideration.

"It is emphatically the province and duty of the judicial department to say what the law is. Those who apply the rule to particular cases, must of necessity expound and interpret that rule. If two laws conflict with each other, the courts must decide on the operation of each.

"So if a law be in opposition to the constitution; if both the law and the constitution apply to a particular case, so that the court must either decide that case conformably to the law, disregarding the constitution; or conformably to the constitution, disregarding the law; the court must determine which of these conflicting rules governs the case. This is of the very essence of judicial duty.

"If, then, the courts are to regard the constitution, and the constitution is superior to any ordinary act of the legislature, the constitution, and not such ordinary act, must govern the case to which they both apply.

"Those, then, who controvert the principle that the constitution is to be considered, in court, as a paramount law, are reduced to the necessity of maintaining that courts must close their eyes on the constitution, and see only the law.

"This doctrine would subvert the very foundation of all written constitutions. It would declare that an act which, according to the principles and theory of our government, is entirely void, is yet, in practice, completely obligatory. It would declare that if the legislature shall do what is expressly forbidden, such act, notwithstanding the express prohibition, is in reality effectual. It would be giving to the legislature a practical and real omnipotence, with the same breath which professes to restrict their powers within narrow limits. It is prescribing limits, and declaring that those limits may be passed at pleasure.

* * * *

"There are many parts of the constitution which serve to illustrate this subject.

It is declared that "no tax or duty shall be laid on articles exported from any state." Suppose a duty on the export of cotton, of tobacco, or of flour; and a suit instituted to recover it. Ought judgment to be rendered in such a case. Ought the judges to close their eyes on the constitution, and only see the law?

The constitution declares "that no bill of attainder or ex post facto law shall be passed."

"If, however, such a bill should be passed, and a person should be prosecuted under it; must the court condemn to death those victims whom the constitution endeavors to preserve? [7]

* * * *

"From these, and many other selections which might be made, it is apparent that the framers of the constitution contemplated that instrument as a rule for the government of courts, as well as of the legislature.

"Why otherwise does it direct the judges to take an oath to support it? This oath certainly applies in an especial manner to their conduct in their official character. How immoral to impose it on them, if they were to be used as the instruments, and the knowing instruments, for violating what they swear to support!

* * * *

---

7. The bill of attainder was a parliamentary death sentence that pretended to be an ordinary enactment. In its most tyrannical use, Parliament would enact a law requiring a named person, upon penalty of death, appear before the bar of Parliament before a certain date, but would require that the enactment be kept secret until the date had passed. When arrested for violating this "law," it only had to be proven that the arrested person was the individual named in it and that he had failed to appear.

"Why does a judge swear to discharge his duties agreeably to the constitution of the United States, if that constitution forms no rule for his government—if it is closed upon him, and cannot be inspected by him?

"If such be the real state of things, this is worse than a solemn mockery. To prescribe, or to take this oath, becomes equally a crime."

Marshall's great intellect proved beyond dispute that simple honesty and the avoidance of criminal misconduct in the performance of judicial duties require every judge to uphold the supremacy of the Constitution over all inferior law, whether that law be contained in Congressional enactments, state constitutions, or state legislation. He demonstrated that studious determination of the way different laws apply to facts—to people's past actions—is the essence of the performance of judicial duty. The judge is obligated to know this short document, the Constitution,[8] and to recognize that some provision of it may apply to the facts of a particular dispute.

Under Marshall's plain and rational exposition of the Constitution, if Congress should pass a law authorizing the President to issue an edict forbidding all the people to charge prices or to pay wages above such levels as the President might deem wise, if the President should issue his edict and a citizen should be prosecuted for violating it, simple honesty requires the judge to compare the presidential edict with the Constitution. If the judge sees that the Constitution gives the President the Government's law-enforcing powers, but gives its law-making powers only to the Congress, Marshall's view maintains that simple honesty requires the judge to question whether Congress can *enact* that the law-making powers may be exercised by the President; or whether this conflicts with the Constitution's grant of all law-making power to Congress, then to be exercised only by following a particular procedure required to make an enactment become a law.

Going further, Marshall's rationale demonstrates that if the Constitution says Congress can change this precise and detailed law-making procedure, giving the President the power to rule by edict instead of merely *enforcing laws,* that Congress may do this by enacting the details of the new law-making procedure and by submitting the enactment to all fifty states; and that when thirty-eight of those states' legislatures should consent to federal law being made in the manner provided by the new enactment, federal law could then be made by following the new procedure: Then there is a clear conflict between the Constitution's provisions as to how the law-making system may be changed and the Congressional attempt to change the law-making system by a simple enactment not approved by thirty-eight state legislatures. Marshall demonstrated that honesty requires the judge to determine whether the presidential edict is law to be enforced by him when Congress did not follow the procedure provided by the Constitution for empowering the President to rule by edict.

If Congress enacts a definition of murder and makes it a felony punishable by imprisonment for anyone to commit murder in a passenger boat traveling any navigable river within the United States, the method of Marshall's masterful rationale demonstrates that honesty requires the judge to question whether Congress can make such a law, when the Constitution gives Congress the power to "define and punish piracies and felonies committed on the high seas," but nowhere gives Congress the power to define felonies committed on inland rivers; and that

---

8. A copy of the Constitution appears for convenient reference as an appendix to this book.

this obligation of honesty requires the judge always to uphold the Constitution instead of the inferior Congressional enactment if Congress is given no power to make the enactment.

In this magnificent opinion, rightly honored as America's finest judicial decision, Marshall made no pretense that he was claiming some power for judges. Instead, he demonstrated that honor and the oath of office impose upon the judge an unavoidable *duty* to discern the meanings of both the statute and the pertinent constitutional provision when both appear to control the decision to be rendered.

Chief Justice Marshall's compelling logic in *Marbury v. Madison* has often been forgotten, but it has never been refuted. Measured against the standard of truth in the declaration of principles, it has withstood the test of time for over a hundred and sixty years. It has demonstrated that it is an accurate and fundamental statement of constitutional law: That the Constitution is a law for the government of courts as well as the other branches of government, that if judges fail to adhere to it, they violate the obligation of their oaths of office, and that they must, when they find law to be in conflict with the Constitution, declare the law void, refuse to follow it, and instead follow the supreme law.

Marbury v. Madison was not a proclamation made by the Supreme Court for the guidance of all the courts of the nation; courts have no power to issue and send out proclamations. *Marbury v. Madison* was the decision of a lawsuit, and to give judgment, the Supreme Court had to rule on whether it was obligated to obey the Constitution or a conflicting statute.[9] It was and is accepted as correctly determining that all courts not only are permitted but are required to rule upon the constitutionality of laws they are called upon to enforce.

We have seen that judicial determinations of constitutionality, as a practical matter, are the most authoritative determinations solely because the courts have the last word, because laws have no effect except as they are enforced, and because it is only through the instrumentality of the courts that the power of government can be brought to bear upon people to enforce the law. In this practical world, it is impractical to risk too much upon the validity of a new law of questionable constitutionality, until the courts have decided whether the law is valid.

Forgetting mere theory, in fact we see that Congress enacts laws initiating great changes—such as a 1970 enactment reducing the voting age to eighteen—and the people await the Supreme Court's determination of whether the enactment is law. In fact, lower federal courts emit sweeping orders compelling great changes in local governmental practices, basing their decision upon their understanding of past Supreme Court opinions, and the people, the President, and the Congress await decision by the Supreme Court as to whether the law actually requires the changes in local governmental practices that have been ordered by lower federal courts.

Then in practice, theory aside, have the Supreme Court and its inferior federal courts become the most powerful branch of government? Is the Supreme Court superior to Congress, and has Congress become inferior to the Court? Has this weakest of the three branches of government, envisioned in *The Federalist* as being the least in capacity to annoy or injure the "political rights of the Constitution" become the most powerful of the branches of government?

Government clearly cannot concede to each person the right (without risking

---

9. The statute in question was one by which Congress attempted to give additional power to the Supreme Court itself, and the Court's holding was that the Constitution does not permit it to exercise the power Congress sought to give it.

the penalty) to determine for himself the content of the law applicable to him, for this would produce instant anarchy. Some agency must be given the power to determine constitutionality when law is brought to bear upon the individual citizen, and the Constitution leaves this function to the courts, as Marshall demonstrated. How can the courts have this power without their being superior to the President and to the Congress? Is *Marbury v. Madison* merely a footnote to history, a governmental act by which the judicial duty to rule upon constitutionality was established? Was its logical exposition of the supremacy of the Constitution merely a game of words, divorced from reality, and the means by which the supremacy of the judiciary rather than the Constitution was established?

To pass judgment upon whether judges have truly endeavored to decide cases according to law, or whether their decisions have been infected by intellectual inferiority, intellectual laziness, or intellectual dishonesty, we must in this connection examine more closely the nature of judicial power; the nature of power often determines its limitations. A concession to the church of the "power" to interpret the Ten Commandments concedes no power to expound a state's criminal laws.

Accepting the power of the courts to pass upon questions of constitutionality, Americans—including judges and lawyers—generally accept the reasoning that an enactment of Congress must be constitutional if it is to be law, the Supreme Court has declared the enactment to be constitutional, and the enactment is therefore law. This may be accepted as approximately correct IF we accept the additional unspoken premise in the logical chain: That the decisions of the Supreme Court are *always* correct. No thinking person can accept this unspoken proposition claiming the infallibility of any court.

Every appellate court owes its existence to the recognition of the fact that occasional errors by trial courts are inevitable. Errors by the United States Supreme Court are inevitable, and if one lacks the understanding to perceive this, it is demonstrated by the number of times the Supreme Court has reversed its own past declarations on the meaning of constitutional provisions. In dealing with complex questions, erroneous decisions and personal honesty are compatible.

The Supreme Court ruled in *Plessy v. Ferguson* that the constitutional guaranty of equal protection of the laws was not violated by state laws requiring separation according to race, so long as each race was equally denied the right to associate with the other. More than fifty years later, the Court acknowledged that the separation of races by state law was in itself a denial of equal protection of the laws in public education. *Plessy v. Ferguson* may now be forgotten and, as we shall see,[10] was never legitimately a part of the law.

But as recent literature on the past mode of life of Negro citizens has demonstrated, millions of them endured great suffering from the leadership and legitimation furnished by the Court's decision of that case. The decision may theoretically be regarded as not a part of the law and never a part of the law, but the tragedy of it was that nobody knew it was not law. The courts of the land acted as if it were law. In a very real and practical sense, when the Supreme Court reverses one of its prior decisions, it has changed the law in the practical affairs of life, though changing the law is a legislative act and the Constitution gives the legislative power to Congress, not to the courts.

The Supreme Court has on occasion struggled with the doctrine of *stare decisis.* Justice Brandeis wrote [11] in 1924 that the Court could hold a new Congressional enactment valid without being required to overrule a rule of past decisions:

10. See below, Chapter IV.
11. In *Washington v. W. C. Dawson & Co.*

"[This] would require merely that we should limit the application of the rule therein announced, and that we should declare our disapproval of certain expressions used in the opinions. Such limitation of principles previously announced, and such express disapproval of dicta, are often necessary. It is an unavoidable incident of the search by courts of last resort[12] for the true rule. . . . The doctrine of *stare decisis* should not deter us from overruling that case and those which follow it. . . . *Stare decisis* is ordinarily a wise rule of action. But it is not a universal, inexorable command. The instances in which this court has disregarded its admonition are many."

In 1936, Justice Harlan F. Stone wrote in his concurring opinion in *St. Joseph Stock Yards Co. v. United States:* "The doctrine of *stare decisis,* however appropriate and even necessary at times, has only a limited application in the field of constitutional law."

Stare decisis is the rule that past decisions of law are binding upon the court and its inferior courts in the decision of future cases, and the rule under which federal and state courts viewed as law past Supreme Court decisions expounding the Constitution; yet Justice Stone, with the concurrence of Justice Benjamin N. Cardozo, said it had only limited application. *Stare decisis* is the rule under which lower courts have struggled with the meaning of particular Supreme Court phraseology in constitutional law cases, such as "with all deliberate speed" and "unitary school system" in racial cases, the "totality of circumstances" in some criminal cases, "without redeeming social importance" in obscenity cases, and "invidious discrimination" in decisions under the Equal Protection Clause of the Fourteenth Amendment; yet *stare decisis* was said to have but limited application, though to American judges schooled in the Common Law, its application is almost second nature.

More careful analysis demonstrates that Justices Brandeis, Stone, and Cardozo were incorrect in their assertion of the limited application of *stare decisis* in constitutional law. When one considers the nature of judicial power given the courts by the Constitution against the central theme of the Constitution itself—that it is the supreme law for the government of Government, instead of considering it against the central theme of the common law—that prior judicial decisions establish the law by which the courts are bound, one is driven to quite a different conclusion: In constitutional law, the rule of *stare decisis* has *no legitimate application at all!* In constitutional law, there is no reason why any court should consider itself bound by past Supreme Court decisions merely because those cases were decided by the highest court. There is every reason to view Supreme Court determinations of questions of constitutional law as not being binding on lower courts in their future decisions, even to the slightest extent.

Dissenting Justice George Sutherland once wrote [13] of the individual judge's duty:

"And in passing upon the validity of a statute, [a judge] discharges a duty imposed upon him, which cannot be consummated justly by an automatic acceptance of the views of others which have neither convinced, nor created

---

12. The court of last resort is the highest court to which an appeal can be taken, sometimes the United States Supreme Court, sometimes a lower court. In limited classes of cases, the United States Supreme Court is both the trial court and the court of last resort, there being no appeal at all.

13. In *West Coast Hotel Co. v. Parrish.*

a reasonable doubt in, his mind. If upon a question so important he thus surrender his deliberate judgment, he *stands forsworn*. He cannot subordinate his convictions to that extent and keep faith with his oath or retain his judicial and moral independence. . . . The judicial function is that of interpretation; it does not include the power of amendment under the guise of interpretation. To miss the point of difference between the two is to miss all that the phrase 'supreme law of the land' stands for and to convert what was intended as inescapable and enduring mandates into mere moral reflections.*

The Senate has shown a conscientious determination to keep the Supreme Court from being peopled by men of mediocre intellect, and the Court has traditionally included men of high intelligence and insight. The cases coming before it are often important cases, and the lawyers on both sides customarily do a far more thorough job of legal research and write their briefs with much greater care than in lower appellate courts. The Supreme Court has every opportunity to be correct in its decisions. It is nevertheless not always right.

Material and persuasive arguments that might lead to a different conclusion are sometimes simply not conceived, either by the justices or by any of the participating lawyers. In one recent case of immense public importance, a dissenting opinion covered in lengthy detail a different but related constitutional provision than the one being relied upon and stated that none of his fellow justices and none of the lawyers presenting the issues had even noticed *the existence* of these constitutional provisions in their briefs or arguments! And the lawyers involved in such presentation included the Solicitor-General of the United States, a number of state attorneys-general, and many private attorneys of highest professional qualifications and reputations.

Are Supreme Court opinions as to the meaning of the Constitution to be regarded as binding law by inferior judges? There is nothing in Chief Justice Marshall's exposition of the supremacy of the Constitution in *Marbury v. Madison* that does not apply just as much to the "law" established by Supreme Court opinions as it does to statutes established by Congress.

The Constitution is the rule of government that applies to every court, not just to the Supreme Court. Inferior judges must either grant supremacy to the "law" declared by the Supreme Court, or they must grant supremacy to the Constitution, which they have sworn to do. Any judge, state or federal, who honestly views any Supreme Court decision as to the meaning of a constitutional provision as being incorrect not only has the right, but the duty, to refuse to follow the precedent of Supreme Court decisions. If he does not perform that duty, then he is giving his loyalty to Supreme Court rulings, and denying his loyalty to the Constitution as the Supreme Law of the Land.

It would be inexcusable for judges to blind themselves to the Constitution and see only the law enacted by Congress, refusing to rule upon its constitutionality, but such a judge would at least have this to be said for his morality: That the enactment, though in substance repugnant to some provision of the Constitution, was at least made pursuant to the Constitution in the sense that it was voted by Senators and Congressmen chosen in the manner provided by the Constitution, who were sworn to support the Constitution, and who followed the procedures provided by the Constitution for converting a bill before Congress into an enactment of Congress.

But a judge who considers himself bound to follow past Supreme Court decisions in his future actions, though he considers such decisions to be incorrect expositions of the Constitution, has not even this much to be said for him. No provision of the Constitution makes Supreme Court opinions a part of the supreme law of the land. The supreme law of the land consists solely of the Constitution, laws enacted pursuant to it, and treaties made under the authority of the United States. Nothing else.

To the extent that Supreme Court opinions may be considered law, as cogent evidence of the meaning of the Constitution, they are secondary law, and judges who find a conflict are bound by honor to follow their own understanding of the Constitution instead of following the higher court's decision. Whenever a judge cannot accept a Supreme Court decision as correct, then human intelligence and the English language should be adequate to enable him to write a respectful opinion demonstrating why he believes the Supreme Court decision to be an incorrect interpretation of the law.

The greatest failing of the American judicial brotherhood is the pretense that Supreme Court decisions are law for no other reason than that they are decisions handed down by the Supreme Court instead of some other court.

It being obvious that Supreme Court decisions are not binding law upon lower courts in their future decisions of constitutional questions, one might ask, in what manner, then, is the Supreme Court supreme? Or is it supreme?

The Supreme Court is supreme in the exercise of the only power given to it by the Constitution, the exercise of judicial power in the decision of cases and controversies: Who owns this land? Can the Government send this man to prison? Can the Government sell this man's land for taxes claimed to be due under a particular taxing act, or is that act void? Must this citizen submit to compulsory induction into the armed forces under the Selective Service Act? In the exercise of this power, the Supreme Court is supreme.

As an example, suppose there is a city in which the poor areas are greatly under-represented and the more prosperous areas greatly over-represented in the city council as a result of historic councilmanic district patterns, worsened by changes caused by highway locations and urban renewal projects which cause further population shifts among the poor.

A suit is then filed in the federal district court to compel the councilmen to re-district the city on the theory that the Equal Protection Clause of the Fourteenth Amendment requires it; this theory is based upon the then-recent Supreme Court decision that the Clause requires each state to draw district lines so that all legislative districts will be approximately equally populated.

The district judge views the Supreme Court's legislative apportionment ruling as incorrect, but he also believes that even if the Supreme Court's view of the constitutional provision is correct when applied to the apportionment of voters to elect a state legislature, this view could not be correct when applied to a mere city council election. So as he should, the judge refuses to order reapportionment and dismisses the case, as required by his view of the Constitution and his oath to support it.

On appeal, the Supreme Court rules that the Equal Protection Clause requires apportionment into equally-populated districts for the election of city councilmen as well as for the election of state legislators, and the Court remands the case with directions that the reapportionment be ordered. Upon receipt of the Supreme Court's mandate, the district judge may be entirely unpersuaded by the Supreme Court's opinion; he may be convinced, from his study of both the Equal Protection Clause and other parts of the Constitution, that the Constitution does not require voting district reapportionment; he will then regard the Supreme Court's decision as an act of usurpation, an unauthorized intervention by the federal judiciary into the purely local and internal affairs of state government.

What, then, is the district judge's duty? He is obligated to totally disregard his beliefs as to the meaning of the Constitution and to fully enforce the decision of the Supreme Court without reluctance, without evasiveness, without hesitation. He is a judicial officer, exercising the judicial power of the United States. The supreme judicial power was exercised, and it finally determined the law governing this particular lawsuit: That these defendants who are city councilmen owe to these plaintiffs who are residents of the city the duty to redraw the council district lines according to population. The trial judge no longer has any power to exercise his own judgment, he only has the duty to effectuate the judgment already exercised by a court superior to his.

This is the manner, and the only manner, in which the Supreme Court is legitimately supreme, in the exercise of judicial power to determine the outcome of particular lawsuits, one at the time. The decision is binding on the parties to the lawsuit, even if the decision is wrong, even if the decision itself violates the Constitution.

The next week, if another city council reapportionment case involving another city in the same judicial district is brought before the same judge, it then becomes his obligation to again follow his own understanding of the meaning of the Constitution, not the Supreme Court's understanding, and to write an opinion explaining why he believes the Supreme Court's past decision was wrong.

If he does not follow his own convictions as to the meaning of the Constitution, then he substitutes the Supreme Court's interpretations for the Constitution itself as the supreme law of the land. He yields to the Supreme Court the power to be not only the supreme adjudicator of cases and controversies, but also the Supreme Law-Giver. This power the Supreme Court does not have under the Constitution and cannot obtain except by constitutional amendment or by usurpation—usurpation condoned by Senators, Representatives, by the President, and by the entire body of state and federal judges, each of whom has bound himself to support the Constitution as the leading component of the supreme law of the land.

III.

THE CONSTITUTION OF THE UNITED STATES

IF A CITIZEN would judge how well the courts have discharged their steward-ship as interpreters of the Constitution, he must know something about the Con-stitution. Except by taking this approach, one's judgment of the courts is reduced to an opinion as to the desirability or undesirability of the decisions or the con-servatism or liberality of particular judges.

Such approaches are inane *unless* we concede to judges the power to govern instead of merely the function of discovering, interpreting, and applying pre-determined law to individual controversies. But if we do consent to government by judges, to the unquestioning acceptance of their interpretations instead of the Constitution as our supreme law, then our *prime considerations* should be the quality of the judge's liberality, conservatism, sense of justice, and political acu-men in discerning the will of the body politic and in sensing the limits of rules that can be imposed upon the people and be accepted by them in the spirit of good citizenship.

By 1967, most of the recent Supreme Court decisions departing from past precedent had been handed down. Long before 1967, the Supreme Court had come to be generally regarded as *the* authoritative enunciator of the meaning of the Constitution. Long before 1967, the President had become firmly established as the national leader who should give Congress guidance in making enactments to support the presidential policy, he being the only officer of the Federal Govern-ment, except for his running mate, elected by the people of the entire nation. Long before 1967, there had been a mounting acceleration of the tendency toward ineffectiveness of the state governments as instrumentalities for achieving popular demands or demands thought to be popular; state governments had been thought conservatively unresponsive to new national movements and the federal govern-ment had expanded its powers to fill the vacuum of unresponsiveness; and in turn, the expansion of federal law, carried out by a vast bureaucracy and necessarily supported by a great increase in the burden of federal taxation contributed further to the ever-increasing impotence of state governments as effective instrumentali-ties to respond wisely and rapidly to the popular aims of changing times.

Long before 1967, America had fought a war "to make the world safe for democracy," and it had come to be popularly accepted that any change that tends to make government more democratic is a desirable change.

In 1967, the Constitutional Convention which wrote our Constitution stood at mid-point in American history. Yet we had come to view that equal period of time between the first settlement at Jamestown and the time of the adoption of our Constitution and the foundation of our government as an introduction to American history, consisting of the first Thanksgiving Day, George Washington and the cherry tree, the Revolutionary War, Paul Revere's ride, Patrick Henry's speeches, and little else.

Yet this long period before the formation of our government contributed greatly to the spirit of 1776 and to the years immediately following. It was a period of great personal independence, and contemporaneously, Edmund Burke spoke in Parliament in favor of loosening the controls over the American Colonists, extolling the American accomplishments, vigor and spirit.[1] As America's civilizations began to develop in the separate colonies, if any man found the light restraints of government too restrictive, he had but to move deeper into the wilderness to regain total freedom. And in the industriousness born of freedom and necessity, they had converted that wilderness into a highly civilized society by the time of the American Revolution. They had learned to be free and to love their freedom.

But before the American Revolution, the king and parliament had imposed ever-increasing restrictions upon the liberties they had known and considered to be their birthright. Heavy taxation by a government said to contribute nothing to their well-being was but one aspect of the growing range of tyrannical government. Others, including the stationing of soldiers in their homes without their consent, were listed briefly in the Declaration of Independence. The burden of tyrannical, arbitrary and repressive government so bore down upon the leaders of the thirteen English colonies, bred to a tradition of generations of liberty, that they joined hands to publicly and openly commit treason against their king and their government. The fact of victory, of success, of actual achievement of separation, and that alone, converted their treasonous insurrection into the American Revolution.

Eleven years after the Declaration of Independence was signed, a handful of those who had led the Revolution assembled with others in convention and wrote the Constitution of the United States. We are today under no obligation to follow the thinking of those men but are completely free to follow our own ideas. But we should show considerable deference to their reasons, because they enjoyed freedom greater than we enjoy, they lived under tyranny more burdensome than we—if only because it came upon them more suddenly, instead of by gradual stages, and they had the good sense to recognize it for what it was and to nip it in the bud. Then they attempted, after much study, to design a government they hoped would be able to withstand government's natural tendency to tyranny. So they deserve to be heard, not for their sake, but for ours.

The freed Americans attempted to form a central government not once, but twice. The first attempt was under the Articles of Confederation. The states were in fact thirteen separate nations, and the interests of mighty Virginia differed considerably from those of the tiny state of Rhode Island and Providence Plantations. But all realized the desirability of having a central government, if for no other purpose than to make war and to assure the freedom of citizens—"paupers, vagabonds, and fugitives from justice excepted" [2]—to move freely and to enjoy the rights of free men in every state.

But they had suffered before because of the existence of another government

---

1. Of the American whaling industry: "We know that whilst some of them draw the line and strike the harpoon on the coast of Africa, others run the longitude and pursue their gigantic game along the coast of Brazil. No sea but what is vexed by their fisheries; no climate that is not witness to their toils. Neither the perserverance of Holland, nor the activity of France, nor the dexterous and firm sagacity of English enterprise ever carried this most perilous mode of hard industry to the extent to which it has been pushed by this recent people; a people who are still, as it were, but in the gristle; and not yet hardened into the bone of manhood." I *Works of the Right Honourable Edmund Burke,* 462.
2. Article IV, Articles of Confederation.

having authority over their local governments and people, and they feared abuse of power by the new central government being established by the Articles of Confederation and Perpetual Union. To guard against any abuse of power by the new central government under the Articles of Confederation, they adopted a very simple device—they didn't give the new government any power. In truth, the Articles of Confederation did not establish a government. The document was not actually a constitution, but was a treaty between thirteen separate nations.[3] The Confederation provided no single executive to carry out laws, and no courts to enforce law upon individual citizens.

Each state had one vote in Congress, but within limits could choose the number of delegates it would send, could recall them and appoint substitutes at will, and could choose them however it wished. This loose arrangement, under which the Congressmen were actually ambassadors, might be thought to make it difficult for Congress to exercise its law-making powers, but it did not, because Congress was given no law-making powers over the people within the states.

The Congress under the Articles of Confederation could declare war, but could not levy taxes, and the only way it could either raise troops or obtain money was to request a quota by ratio formula from each state, and each state was free to refuse to contribute either money or troops.

When this Congress provided for a convention to propose amendments to the Articles of Confederation, the convention met in Philadelphia. There, mutually sworn to secrecy, they wrote the Constitution in sessions held behind closed doors from which the public and the press were excluded.

The Articles of Confederation provided that it could be amended by amendments submitted by the Congress and accepted by the legislatures of every state. The Constitution transmitted by George Washington to the Congress departed from this governing law by providing for its approval not by the state legislatures, but by the people through constitutional conventions to be held in each state. In writing the Constitution, the Philadelphia convention had commenced with the words: "We, the People of the United States, . . . do ordain and establish this CONSTITUTION for the United States of America."

While Americans today generally know little about the content of our Constitution, the general populace of that day, who had painfully experienced both the tyranny of too much government and the disorder of too little government, read and understood every word of the proposed constitution.[4] Words spoken in those state conventions speak eloquently of both the practical necessity which compelled the people to give increased power to a central government and the fears

---

3. The entire government can best be understood by reading the central and basic agreement set out in the treaty known as the Articles of Confederation: "The said States hereby severally enter into a firm league of friendship with each other, for their common defence, the security of their liberties, and their mutual and general welfare, binding themselves to assist each other against all force offered to, or attacks made upon them, or any of them, on account of religion, sovereignty, trade, or any other pretence whatever." [Article III, Articles of Confederation.]

4. In the Massachusetts convention, as quoted by Carl Van Doren in *The Great Rehearsal,* farmer-delegate Jonathan Smith spoke of the anarchy of a recent armed rebellion that so distressed the people that they would have flocked to a monarch if he had appeared to offer protection, even if the monarch had proven a tyrant, "so that you see that anarchy leads to tyranny, the better to have one tyrant than so many at once." Smith continued:

which led those who wrote it in Philadelphia to attempt to restrict those powers given to the central government as much as practicality would allow.

But though practicality dictated the formation of a central government having the power to govern, the fear of the concentration of power beyond control of the local body politic was a very great fear. The Constitution provided for the District of Columbia by stating that there should be a ten-mile square area set aside as the seat of government, and this provision was publicly envisioned as carrying the threat that it could become a fortress from which armed troops could be sent out to suppress the populace.[5]

Patrick Henry found ground for criticism. Acknowledging respect for the writers of the new constitution, he questioned, "but, Sir, give me leave to demand, what right had they to say, *We the people?* My political curiosity, exclusive of my anxious solicitude for the public welfare leads me to ask, who authorized them to speak the language of *We the people,* instead of *We, the states?"*

Compelled by practicality to give power to the central government, the founding fathers so greatly feared the concentration of power that a central theme permeates the entire Constitution. *Government* is not to be trusted. Hardly less obvious is the secondary theme: *The people* are not to be trusted, either.

Democracy was not viewed by the founding fathers as an end to be sought after, but as an evil to be avoided. They recognized pure democracy as being the most tyrannical of all forms of government, government by the whim of the majority instead of the whim of a single dictator. When a single ruler becomes tyrannical, he can be murdered, but when a majority of the people become tyrannical, their numbers are such that the tyranny cannot be overcome except by foreign conquest.

So for America, the republican form of government was chosen: The people were to choose those who would exercise the power of government, but the power was to be exercised by the people's chosen representatives, not by the people themselves. But elected representatives must be responsive to popular will, and it

---

"Now, Mr. President, when I saw this constitution, I found that it was a cure for these disorders. It was just such a thing as we wanted. I got a copy of it and read it over and over. I had been a member of the convention to form our own state constitution, and had learnt something of the checks and balances of power, and I found them all here. I did not go to any lawyer, to ask his opinion—we have no lawyer in our town, and we do well enough without. I formed my own opinion, and was pleased with this constitution. My honorable old daddy there wont think that I expect to be a congress-man and swallow up the liberties of the people. I never had any post, nor do I want one. But I don't think worse of the constitution because lawyers and men of learning, and monied men are fond of it. . . .—these lawyers, these monied men, these men of learning, are all embarked in the same cause with us, and we must all swim or sink together; and shall we throw the constitution overboard, because it does not please all alike? . . . Some gentlemen say, dont be in a hurry, take time to consider, and don't take a leap in the dark. I say, take things in time—gather fruit when it is ripe. There is a time to sew and a time to reap; we sewed our seed when we sent men to the federal convention, now is the harvest, now is the time to reap the fruit of our labor, and if we wont do it now, I am afraid we never shall have another opportunity."
[Quoted, Carl Van Doren, *The Great Rehearsal,* 198–200].

5. Van Doren, *The Great Rehearsal,* 179.

was noticed that in past experience, republics deteriorated into democracies. Attempting to avoid dictatorial government, the framers of the Constitution sought to create a unique government organization designed to block *all the roads to tyranny*.

The Confederation charter was not junked. Many provisions of the Constitution came directly from the Articles of Confederation, often in verbatim language. But its power structure, which depended entirely upon the continuing authorization by the states for its effectiveness, was replaced by an effective power structure empowered to govern *people*.

In the structure of the government, the fundamental safeguard was to split governmental power between different groups, so that each would protect its power from intrusions by the other. The entire governmental power, as in every government, consisted of the power of government to impose its will upon individual citizens by force. In non-tyrannical governments, this power to govern consists of making rules for the people to obey, sending our agents to enforce the rules, and then deciding, before finally improsing the legal penalty for violating the rules, whether the individual has in fact violated such rule.

So these different types of power were divided: *All* the legislative power was given to Congress and none to the President or the courts, except that the President could veto new laws, subject to Congress' power to override his veto if the law were popular enough to gain the necessary two-thirds majority in both houses of Congress. *All* the executive powers to enforce laws and to appoint public officials was given to the President, subject to the power of the Congress to authorize the courts to appoint some officials and to provide other methods for the appointment of inferior officers. *All* of the judicial power of the United States was vested in the Supreme Court and such inferior courts as Congress might create, with the judicial power of the United States extending to all cases and controversies arising under the Constitution, laws, and treaties of the United States, and to certain other limited catagories, such as suits between citizens of different states, suits between states themselves, and a few other instances where it appeared wiser for the cases to be decided by national courts instead of state courts.[6]

To protect against abuses of power by the executive or the judicial branches, Congress was given the power to impeach and remove from office any officer of government. And Congress had the additional power to control the extent of the President's power by simply enacting or repealing laws, thereby increasing or decreasing the laws he was empowered to enforce, hence enlarging or diminishing his power.

The power of Congress—and thereby the power of the entire Federal Government—was restricted by denying it the general power to govern, giving it the power to enact laws only on particular subjects, and leaving all other law-making powers to the states. Thus, a tension was created between the national government and state governments which, through their senators, were expected to resist Congressional attempts to exceed the scope of Federal law-making powers. The Congress was organized in a manner thought adequate to help enable the states resist encroachments by the Federal Government.

Congress was divided into the Senate and the House of Representatives. The Senate was composed of representatives of the *government* of each state and the

---

6. This separation of governmental powers is described in greater detail below, Chapter VIII.

House was composed of representatives of the *people* of each state. The Congressman in the House were the ONLY officers of the Federal Government to be elected by the people, and the House was to be the "People's House" of the Congress. Its members had to stand for election every two years, and they alone could originate bills to levy taxes.

The Senators were to be a more restraining, conservative influence; they were to be elected by the state legislatures, not by the people, and for six-year terms. The states surrendered their sovereignty in foreign affairs. Their representatives, the Senators, were given the power to affirm or disaffirm treaties, and the House had no part in foreign agreements. While the House, responsive to popular feelings, was given the power to impeach officers of the government, the Senate had the sole power to try such impeachments and decide whether the accused officer should forfeit his office and his right to hold office in the future. And to guard further against encroachments on state powers, the state legislatures, not the people, were given the power to approve or disapprove amendments to the Constitution proposed by the federal Congress.

This system was devised to retain to the people the power to effectively influence government to make change—indeed, it invited them to compel change—and it still so organized the government as to permit officeholders to resist pressure to make unwise changes under the compulsion of sudden popular aims that lacked the substance to persist and grow stronger.

Representatives were subjected to the full fury of the election processes and the unrestrained demands of voters, representing comparatively small districts and being elected directly by the voters, constitutionally defined as the same "electors" permitted to vote for the members of the largest house of the state legislature. But the Congressmen could make no laws without the concurrence of the Senate, and the Senators were elected by the state legislature—both houses, whose members were better qualified than ordinary voters to understand the demands of governmental responsibility because state legislators had felt the weight of such responsibility.

But the Senators were also subject to public pressure *if* the pressure were sufficiently persistent. Citizens had much more convenient access to their state legislators, living in the same county, than to their Congressmen, and the legislators were in a position to both screen irresponsible demands and transmit legitimate demands and arguments to Senators far more forcefully than could the ordinary citizen. A single vote of a legislator might be decisive in the Senator's re-election, but an individual vote in a public election is almost never decisive, and the importance of a single voter's opinion depends upon his ability to influence other voters to agree with him.

This portion of the constitutional scheme to protect the republic against the mob spirit that sometimes seizes democracy disappeared in 1913 with the adoption of the Seventeenth Amendment providing for the popular election of Senators by those qualified to vote for election of members of the lower house of the state legislature. Then came the voting amendments.[7]

---

7. The reader may wish to read those amendments concerning voting rights, bearing in mind that all the ends achieved by these Twentieth Century voting right amendments could have been achieved without amending the Constitution, and after reading the latter part of the book, consider which was the wiser way to expand voting rights, the mode provided by the Constitution or the use of constitutional amendments.

The preservation of the state governments was not viewed as an unavoidable evil compelled by the circumstance that they were there and could not be destroyed. The protection of these governments under the constitutional scheme was regarded as an integral and essential part of sound government. It was intended to preserve for local determination those matters whose nature did not require national uniformity, leaving to each body of people in a fairly small geographical area the freedom to develop and control their own societies and give political form to their own peculiar traditions. A unique example of the way local traditions lead to different governmental devices can be seen in the independent-minded people of Arizona: Arizona's new laws do not become effective for ninety days, and during that time, a popular petition procedure may prevent a new law from ever becoming effective until the people have approved it by popular referendum.

The preservation of local state governments also served to partially insulate the federal Congress from the sometimes irresponsible demands of democracy because it was in local matters of everyday life that the public was apt to be most insistent, and such local concerns were to be only within the authority of the local state government to deal with. Local state governments were also to provide a place where developing politicians could give evidence of their ability and integrity before being entrusted with the broader and less controllable powers of the national government. That this purpose has been fulfilled so far is demonstrated by the number of local politicians who have enjoyed immense popularity in their own states but had little influence in the rest of the nation.

The executive power of the United States was concentrated in a single person, the president, to whom the executive department heads were to be responsible. The presidency was designed to be a powerful office, in some ways paralleling the power of a king, but with limited tenure of office, and without either the regal power to make law or the regal power to suspend law. The president was given the power to make treaties, subject to the senate's "advice and consent," and the power to appoint officers of government. He was given a position of influence over the content of laws by being required to make a report to Congress each year on the state of the union and by being empowered to veto new laws enacted by Congress, subject to the congressional power to override his veto. He was given the power to enforce laws, but had no power to determine their content, except in enactments of such limited popularity that his veto could not be overridden, nor was he given power to finally determine in individual cases—the point of application of all laws—whether the full imposition of governmental power should be granted or withheld.

The need for a powerful executive had been proven by the delegates' experience of the weakness of government under the Articles of Confederation and the efficiency of government under the Governors-General in pre-Revolutionary days, but the method of choice of such an officer was a difficult problem. It was solved by giving to each state the number of electors equal to the total of its senators and congressmen, and by leaving to each state's legislature the method of selection of such electors. Each legislature was free to choose whatever method it desired, and if the votes of all the electors did not result in a majority of the electoral votes being cast for any candidate, then the president should be elected by the federal House of Representatives.

With the inevitable development of political parties to control the new center of power, the electoral candidates soon ceased exercising their own judgment and became committed in advance to candidates of a particular party; and they were usually so committed by state law. The electoral system, with some changes by amendments, remains in effect, and has resulted in no constitutional crises: The president has always been chosen in the precise manner required by the Constitution. The system has its advantages and disadvantages, and though it is not as democratic as direct popular elections, it has almost always arrived at the same result, and on those few occasions when a minority candidate has been chosen, the popular vote has been so close that the less popular candidate has commanded enough popular support to induce opponents to recognize his right to the office. In the usual election, it gives the majority winner an appearance of a larger majority than he actually commanded and aids in the bi-partisan acceptance of a new president despite the immense minority that rejected his candidacy.

There were other provisions designed to more carefully delineate the state-federal powers to minimize conflicts between the two governments and to govern relations between state governments. These provisions expressly limited the power of state governments or imposed express duties upon state governments or officials.

Under Article I of the Constitution, concerned with the legislative or general governing power of the government, there were provisions forbidding states to impose taxes on imports or exports, to keep troops or ships of war in peace time or to engage in war "unless actually invaded, or in such imminent danger as will not admit of delay."

While Article I contained limitations upon the powers of states, a separate article, Article IV, contains the other provisions of the Constitution applicable to state governments as governments and to the Federal government,[8] and Article V provides for constitutional amendments.[9]

This, except for a consideration of the precise subjects as to which Congress was given the supreme power to govern, summarizes the complex governmental structure established by the Constitution, designed to make a national government as powerful as it had to be and yet to render the total governing power—federal and state—as harmless as possible.

People today are aware of the pervasive powers claimed and exercised by the Federal Government, but the central idea of the founding fathers for protecting the people in local areas from interference by a central government was that Congress was not to be empowered to govern generally, but only to make laws to govern the people on particular subjects. In view of this fundamental scheme for limiting federal governmental power, the writers of *The Federalist* urged that no Bill of Rights was necessary—that the limitation on governmental powers itself made the Federal Government incapable of infringing the rights already protected by local law.

As to this lack of any Federal power over purely local affairs, consider: When a law-abiding farmer living in the center of a state wants to shoot wild ducks on the shore of a lake on his farm, he waits until the duck-hunting season opens, he obtains the required hunting license, and he shoots no more ducks than the limited number set by law. The law he is obeying is Federal law. There is no

---

8. These include the guarantee to citizens of each state the privileges and immunities of citizenship in each of the other states, the provision for extraditing fugitives from one state to another, and the command that the United States guarantee each state a republican form of government.

9. By Congressional proposal of Amendments or such proposal by a convention, followed by ratification by three-fourths of the state legislatures. Congress is required to call a convention when two-thirds of the state legislatures request it.

word in the Constitution from which there can be implied any grant of power to Congress to prohibit the hunting of wild game or birds within the borders of a state. We are aware of the pervasive powers of Congress to tax and to regulate interstate commerce, and although wild birds fly across state lines, there is no slight commercial aspect to a wild bird flying through the air. There is nothing either interstate or commercial about a farmer shooting a bird on his own land for his wife to cook and serve to their family. Yet in *Missouri* v. *Holland,* the United States Supreme Court held the federal hunting season law to be valid.

This basic law came into being by the second method provided by the Constitution for making a rule a part of the supreme law of the land. Great Britain, as governing authority of the Dominion of Canada, signed a migratory bird treaty with the President of the United States, the agreement was approved by two-thirds of the members of the United States Senate, and it thus became a treaty "made under the authority of the United States," hence a part of the supreme law, invalidating all conflicting laws of the state of Missouri and of every other state.

The greatest deterrent to law-making by the President through his treaty power is the ability of thirty-four of the one hundred senators to vote against a treaty already signed, and to thereby prevent it from ever becoming a treaty. The President cannot make a treaty which violates some specific prohibition in the Constitution.

Though treaties are a part of the supreme law of the land, they are in no way superior to Acts of Congress. The law embodied in a treaty may be nullified by a simple Act of Congress, and the treaty, to the extent Congress has changed the law, ceases to be a part of the supreme law of the land. When Congress does this, the United States may have violated its treaty unless, under the generally-accepted rules of international law, disregard of the treaty is viewed as rightful. But nations do at times violate the most solemn treaties, and the offended nation has its remedies—severance of diplomatic relations, embargo of ports, seizure of foreign industrial interests within its borders, war, and any other remedy within the power of its armies to enforce. So treaties are not unchangeable law, but in the United States, treaties, so long as they remain effective, are as much a part of our law as is legislated law, no matter how "local" their subject may be.

But as distinguished from treaty making, more than adherence to the Constitution's law-making *procedures* is necessary for an Act of Congress to become law. For such an enactment to be valid, Congress must have enacted it in the exercise of some specific power given to Congress by the Constitution and the enactment must not violate any of the prohibitions imposed upon Congress by the Constitution.

Congress can do things like making war and authorizing the purchase of property, but these things could be done by the United States in Congress Assembled under the Articles of Confederation. This is different from legislating in the usual sense, which consists of making rules that people must obey under the compulsion of the power of government: Pay your income taxes, and if you wilfully seek to evade payment, you will be imprisoned; do not ship guns in interstate commerce, or you will be imprisoned; perform your contracts, or you will be held liable for damages and your home may be sold or your bank account seized to enforce payment.

The Congress under the Articles of Confederation had no real law-making power because it lacked the element of governmental compulsion, and it had no organized structure vested with executive and judicial powers over individuals. Theoretically, it was given some law-making power, but that power extended to only one subject: Rules governing commerce with the Indian tribes. Nothing else. Even if the confederacy government had been designed with a governmental structure, it would have been a government of little consequence, because it was given virtually nothing to regulate.

This was cured in the Constitution. But the Confederacy's central theme of distrust of a national government except to the extent necessary was retained by the Constitution. No general law-making power was given to Congress, but only the power to govern specific subjects or specific geographical areas. The distrust of a national government far from home was a part of the distrust of *any government* as a threat to the individual's liberty. But the list of congressional powers was lengthened in the Constitution. The states had learned, by living with the mistaken but valuable experience of the Articles of Confederation, that they must have uniform national rule on more subjects than trade with the Indians.

The Convention delegates increased the list by adding those subjects on which they believed *uniformity of law* was necessary, and by adding none other. As time passed, the people have felt a need for uniformity in other areas, and constitutional amendments have added a few other subjects to Congress' legislative powers.

Financial security became the first and most pressing need of the new government, and taxation the method of financing government. Taxes were divided into direct taxes levied directly on the people, their property and wealth, and indirect taxes, such as those on imports, manufacturing, and selling which would be reflected in increased sales prices and thereby indirectly paid by the people, so that the eventual source of these tax payments would be within the various states in which the people made their purchases. The Constitution requires apportionment of the direct taxes among the states according to population, but requires the indirect taxes to be uniform. No apportionment is required for income tax, a direct tax, because of a constitutional amendment permitting income taxation without apportionment.

The careful wording of the grant of taxing powers by the Constitution illustrates the care legislators must take in their choice of words. After the substance of the new constitution was generally agreed by the Convention, it was referred to a Committee on Detail to write out all details in orderly form, and the committee reported a simple clause granting the taxing power: "The Legislature of the United States shall have the power to lay and collect taxes, duties, imposts and excises;"—followed by a list of other powers.

The entire Convention, seeing this proposed unlimited power to tax, reverted to the Articles of Confederation, which had required the states to contribute only for those expenditures incurred and approved by Congress for the purpose within the jurisdiction of the general government, "for the common defense or general welfare." And so, as it emerged in the Constitution actually adopted by the people, the Congress was given power "To lay and collect Taxes, Duties, Imposts and Excises, to pay the debts and provide for the common Defense and general Welfare of the United States; but all Duties, Imposts and Excises shall be uniform throughout the United States; . . ."

Other constitutional provisions limit state and federal taxing powers,[10] and the second power given Congress was the power to borrow money.

The third power is the power to regulate foreign and interstate commerce,

---

10. Congress may not tax exports, and states may not tax either exports or imports, but the states may charge inspection fees, with all inspection fee profits going into the federal treasury.

which is the basis of most of the expansion of Federal powers under the original provisions of the Constitution. A few of the laws Congress declared to be based upon its commerce power are most federal labor legislation, most of the Civil Rights Act of 1964, the anti-trust laws, the criminal kidnapping and stolen car laws.

The Commerce Clause empowers Congress "To regulate Commerce with foreign Nations, and among the several States, and with the Indian Tribes;" the final phrase coming from the Articles of Confederation. But under the Confederation, the regulation of commerce with the Indians was severely limited by a provision that "provided that the legislative right of any state within its own limits shall not be infringed or violated [by the Confederacy Government]." Such a limitation under the new Constitution would have rendered any control of interstate commerce quite impossible, because the commercial activity occurs entirely within one state or another except for the moment of movement of the shipment across the state line.

Next came grants of powers to establish uniform naturalization and bankruptcy laws, to coin and regulate the value of money and to provide for the punishment of counterfeiting; to fix the standards of weights and measures, establish post offices and provide for patents and copyrights; and to constitute the inferior federal courts.

Then the Constitution turns to matters beyond the nation's borders, empowering Congress "To define and punish Piracies and Felonies committed on the high Seas, and Offenses against the Law of Nations." Next is the power to declare war, to grant letters of marque and reprisal and other war-connected powers. Congress was given the power to provide armies and a Navy, and to provide for the organizing of a militia (National Guard), with the power reserved to each state to appoint the officers of the militia and to train the militia, but according to "the discipline prescribed by Congress."

Congress was given the power to provide for (as, by empowering the President if it saw fit) calling the militia into National services for only three purposes: to execute the laws of the nation, to suppress insurrections, and to repel invasions. There is no mention of any power to call the militia out to either fight an offensive war or to act defensively beyond the Nation's borders. For either the suppression of insurrection against the United States or for the enforcement of Federal law, Congress alone has the power to prescribe all the rules under which the President may be empowered to call out the state militia.

Two other provisions give Congress the total power of government, not limited to specific types of legislation: The government of the armed forces and the government of areas that have come to be known as "Federal Enclaves." These include the District of Columbia and other areas purchased within states with the consent of the state legislatures, for the construction of buildings and other listed types of installations. There are many such areas in the United States, which have been purchased with state legislative consent and are occupied by forts, military bases, post offices and other office buildings owned by the Government. These areas (though there are also areas owned by the Government but acquired by other means and not within Congress' geographical governing authority) are no longer within state authority, but are governed wholly by federal law.

One unique example of property owned by the Government but not within its exclusive governing authority is Yosemite National Park, which was owned by the Government when California was admitted to statehood, and the Supreme Court held, as required by the Constitution, that the United States did not retain power of government over Yosemite, but only owned it, with the area governed by the laws of California.[11] Except for the District of Columbia, Congress governs most such federal enclaves, such as post offices, by occasionally enacting an "assimilation law," under which Congress adopts for each enclave the civil and criminal laws of the surrounding state. The principal practical effect is that if a citizen commits a crime in such a building within an enclave purchased with the consent of the state legislature, he is prosecuted by the Federal government in a Federal court for violation of a statute, such as a murder law, enacted by a state legislature.

The final power is a very expansive provision known as the Necessary and Proper Clause, empowering Congress "To make all Laws which shall be necessary and proper for carrying into Execution the foregoing Powers, and all other Powers vested by this Constitution in the Government of the United States, or in any Department or officer thereof." These, except for a few other powers such as the power to make regulations for the conduct of the Federal courts and the power to appropriate money, are the powers granted to Congress by the Constitution.

Following the grant of powers by Section 8 of the Legislative Article, Section 9 contains the express restrictions upon Congressional powers. In addition to those already discussed, there are prohibitions against the suspension of the writ of *habeas corpus* except when required by rebellion or invasion, and against the enactment of bills of attainder and *ex post facto* laws. Congress is also forbidden to make any commerce or revenue regulation giving preference to ports of one state over ports of another, and is forbidden to grant any title of nobility. The provision also prohibits any officer of the Federal Government from accepting any title, gift, or office from any foreign state. It is noteworthy that in the entire Constitution, there is not one single command addressed to the private individual or to the people generally. The Constitution is the instrument for the government of government, while government engages in its business of governing the people.

Similar prohibitions, plus others arising from the necessary inferiority of the state governments in relation to the federal, are imposed upon all state governments, with one addition: The states are forbidden to make any law impairing the obligations of contracts.

This was the Constitution as it stood before any amendments. It was designed to splinter powers and place them in tension against each other so that the people could be protected from the likely tyrannical power if the entire power of government were concentrated in one man or in one group of men. Between the different groups, wise government could be attained and governmental power would be subject to the political pressure of popular will whenever the popular will should become strong enough. It was made to change without revolution, yet to be strong enough to withstand mere majority desires which might be viewed as grossly unfair by sizeable minorities. By limiting the Congressional legislating power to particular subjects and by placing the three types of powers held by the Federal government—legislative, executive, and judicial—in opposition to each other, it was hoped that absolute federal supremacy would be achieved in national defense and in a few matters where uniformity was believed essential, but that outside those areas, each state government would remain supreme in the government of its people.

Though the Constitution contained some provisions for the protection of individual rights,[12] it was the view of many, as we have noted,[13] that the Consti-

---

11. *Collins v. Yosemite Park & Curry Co.*

12. The Privileges and Immunities Clause, the prohibition against federal suspension of the writ of *habeas corpus*, and the prohibition against state legislation impairing the obligation of contracts.

tution itself was a bill of rights, because it gave the Government no powers which could be used to infringe the rights already existing under state laws. But the idea of a Bill of Rights was popular in the conventions held in each state to consider ratification of the Constitution. In the Massachusetts convention, Convention President John Hancock [14] suggested that the Constitution should have a provision that "all powers not expressly delegated to Congress are reserved to the several states, to be by them exercised."

Responding to this suggestion, Delegate John Adams commented:

> "This appears, to my mind to be a summary of a bill of rights, which gentlemen are anxious to obtain. It removes a doubt which many have entertained respecting the matter, and gives assurance that, if any law made by the federal government shall be extended beyond the power granted by the proposed Constitution, and inconsistent with the constitution of this state, it will be an error, and adjudged by the courts of law to be void.[15]

And this provision, with some important and beneficial changes, ended up where the great mind of Adams said it belonged, as the Tenth Amendment, the capstone of the Bill of Rights.

Parts of some of the constitutional amendments are discussed below in some detail, and all are reprinted in the Appendix [16] where they may be read. But we might here note some generalities. The Amendments form patterns. The first ten are the Bill of Rights, designed for the sole purpose of protecting people in America from the use of power by our own government, done either by guaranteeing rights, directly limiting the power of the Government, or, as in the case of the Tenth Amendment, by giving instructions to judges. The next two amendments were adopted quite early, the Eleventh to further limit the powers of the Federal Government, and the Twelfth to change the original unwise procedure for vice-presidential selection. The Thirteenth, Fourteenth, and Fifteenth Amendments were occasioned by the Civil War and the changes it wrought, and were rapidly adopted after its end.

All the remaining amendments were adopted in the Twentieth Century. Of these, one authorized the income tax, whose unlimited authorization is considered unwise by many, and another amendment authorized the prohibition of alcoholic beverages, declared a mistake by a third amendment repealing it. All other Twentieth Century amendments are concerned with voting rights [17] and with procedures for filling political offices.

One other aspect of the amendments, and indeed of the entire Constitution, that may be noticed is that there are no provisions having changing meanings with the single exception of the Eighth Amendment, which prohibits "excessive" fines or bail bonds and cruel *and* unusual punishments.[18] Such comparative and value judgmental terms always vary from generation to generation.

Another general quality of the entire Constitution and its amendments is that many words are used that appear to have common meanings, but which, contrary to appearances, have behind them a history of legal usage, oftentimes growing from historical events which gave rise to such protective provisions. An ex-

---

13. See above, p. 44.

14. A signer of the Declaration of Independence, Hancock was not a member of the Federal Convention in Philadelphia.

15. *II Elliot, Debates,* 131.

16. See below, pp. 364-369.

17. See below, pp. 367-369.

18. A sentence for "horse stealing," not considered cruel when it was rendered

ample of such language which cannot be judged by today's everyday usage is the plain language of the Second Amendment's prohibition against governmental infringement of "the right of the people to keep and bear arms."[19]

Notes kept by various delegates to the secret convention that wrote the Constitution make exciting reading as one can see prejudice pitted against prejudice, resolved into reason pitted against reason to reach the wisest answer, with outbursts of anger approaching rudeness. But the anger served to bring home to all delegates the sure knowledge that there would be no Constitution unless they could reach compromises adequate to protect the essential interests of all. There can be no doubt that the achievement of the same constitutional provisions would have been impossible had the meetings not been conducted in total secrecy.

Benjamin Franklin, as governor (President of the Respublica of Pennsylvania), was host to the convention, and was then quite aged and world revered. After the convention, a lady asked him whether the people were to have a monarchy or a republic, and he replied, "A republic if you can keep it." Urging the delegates to unanimously support the recommended constitution, the weakened old man prepared comments read to the convention by another delegate. In them, he appraised their work:

> "I doubt whether any other Convention we can obtain may be able to make a better Constitution. For when you assemble a number of men to have their advantage of their joint wisdom, you inevitably assemble with these men, all their prejudices, their passions, their errors of opinion, their local interests and their selfish views. From such an Assembly, can a perfect product be expected? It therefore astonishes me, Sir, to find this system approaching so near to perfection as it does; and I think it will astonish our enemies, who are waiting with confidence to hear that our councils are confounded like those of the Builders of Babel; and that our States are on the point of separation, only to meet hereafter for the purpose of cutting one another's throats. Thus I consent, Sir, to this Constitution because I expect no better, and because I am not sure, that it is not the best.[20]

And this has been history's acclaim of the Constitution they produced: The most perfect instrument ever designed to govern a government without outside force to compel obedience. Its genius is not merely in written rules and limitations, but in its device of dividing total governing powers between four separate groups—the state governments and the supreme federal legislature, executive and judiciary, and in the methods it provided for choosing the officers of government, so that the officers would be sufficiently remote to help prevent their domination by mob spirit, but sufficiently dependent on the people that they could not withstand a long-sustained mass demand for change.

---

about the time of the Constitution would be rejected today:
> "That the said _____ shall stand in the pillory one hour, and shall be publicly whipped on his bare back with thirty-nine lashes well laid on, and at the same time shall have both his ears nailed to the pillory and cut off, and shall be branded on the right cheek with the letter H of the length of three quarters of an inch and on the left cheek with the letter T of the same dimensions as the letter H in a plain and visible manner."

19. This guaranty was originally achieved in England after a period during which the law-abiding majority was disarmed by law, while a favored and oppressing minority enjoyed the right to bear arms.

20. From Madison's notes, *Documents Illustrative of the Formation of the Union*, p. 739.

Part II

LESSONS FROM JUDICIAL ERRORS

IV.

FROM *PLESSY* TO *SHELLEY*

THE CAUSE OF Negro equality was doomed in October, 1896, when the Supreme Court decided *Plessy v. Ferguson.* Cause for hope came in May, 1948, when the Court decided *Shelley v. Kraemer.*

All have some familiarity with the "separate but equal" ruling in *Plessy v. Ferguson,* which upheld the power of state governments to enact laws requiring racial segregation. But the fame of *Shelley v. Kraemer* has been overshadowed by the Supreme Court's first school desegregation decision, *Brown v. Board of Education. Shelley v. Kraemer* held state courts could not enforce racial real property covenants by barring black people from buying property in white neighborhoods. The case has been rendered of little practical value because of subsequent legislation and judicial decisions. Both cases remain landmarks in the history of the fight for racial equality, but in that continuing battle, the cases have no interest other than as historical events.

However, our subject is not race relations. Our subject is the discovery of legitimate standards by which citizens may pass judgment upon the judges who judge them; to consider the quality of the stewardship of judges as interpreters of the Constitution. From these decisions, much can be learned.

Let us examine the battles of J. D. Shelley and his wife, Ethel Lee Shelley, with the Missouri law of real property, which led them eventually into the Supreme Court of the United States. The Supreme Court of Missouri had held that this black couple, who had bought, paid for, and moved into their home, were barred from owning or occupying it. In arriving at this result, the Missouri court did nothing but grant enforcement to a racially restrictive covenant, a private contract, which had been entered into in 1911.

The Common Law had long since erected an extremely complex body of law to govern real property, and the central theme of this property law was to grant the greatest possible freedom to owners of property. Real property was viewed as being eternal in nature, while personal property could be burned, thrown into the sea, or otherwise destroyed, and then all ownership of that property would cease. But where real property was concerned, the property would always last longer than its owner. The total ownership of real property was regarded as being eternal ownership, with the ownership always held by the present owner or those who "hold under" the original owner, who derived his ownership from the state or formerly, from the King.

The acquisition of eternal ownership was more than a mere theoretical contrivance, because formerly, when the owner died, the ownership of the land immediately went back to the King. In achieving eternal ownership, the landowners in England took from the King his prime or eternal ownership and acquired the right to pass their land on to their children. Now having eternal ownership, they began selling less than the eternal ownership—selling land only for lesser periods, such as one year, ninety-nine years, or for the lifetime of the buyer. Then when the one or ninety-nine years passed, or the life tenant died, the interest of that tenant terminated, and the one who held eternal ownership, or his heirs, still owned the land and again had the right to take possession of their property.

The owner of property could qualify his transfer of ownership in almost any way. He could sell it to a buyer for a limited time, such as "so long as used for the operation of a school, and no longer." Then if the owner of the school should find school operations unprofitable, and should close the school and install manufacturing equipment in the building to operate a factory, the ownership of the property would immediately revert to the original owner. Many of the donated parks in America occupy land that was deeded to the government body only for so long as used for that purpose, and if the government abandons its use as a park, the land immediately reverts to the heirs of the original owner.

A system of restrictive covenants has also long been used in real estate transactions. These covenants are customarily used in real estate developments, where an owner will sell a large tract of land for subdivision, and the deed will contain covenants restricting the use of the land. The covenants customarily contain such restrictions as set-back building lines, minimum square footage, types of construction and other provisions to promote uniform property values. The restrictions help persuade purchasers to buy, secure in the knowledge that the neighborhood will develop into the type of neighborhood they want to live in.

It was only one small step from these buyer-seller covenants to covenants between neighbors, containing any kind of restrictions the owners might desire. These agreements or covenants might cover any type of restrictions the owners might jointly desire to impose upon the use of their property, the law had to meet this exercise of the owners' freedom by either enforcing the covenants or denying enforcement, and there was no reason to deny enforcement.

None of this had anything to do with racial discrimination, and all of it was well-formulated and in full force in the American colonies long before the Revolution. It came to be used by white owners to assure that none of the property in their neighborhood would be occupied by Negro people.

The racially-restrictive covenants which interfered with Mr. and Mrs. Shelley's ownership of their land were executed by thirty of the thirty-nine property owners on Labadie Avenue in St. Louis in 1911; the covenants were duly recorded so that any buyer would see the private restrictions on ownership that were effective on each lot. The Constitution of the United States, in its provisions restricting each state's legislative powers provides that no state shall pass any "law impairing the obligation of contracts," and Missouri did not do this. Missouri simply enforced ancient property law, enforcing superior property rights in the land that the Shelleys purchased after those rights had come into existence.

Only the people involved were impelled by any racially-discriminatory motivations, but it is clear that nothing in the Constitution interferes with any citizen's right to hate or hold prejudices. The right of each citizen to follow his own likes and dislikes, attractions and prejudices, is the essence of individual liberty.

There had been cases earlier in which local governments had acted on purely prejudicial grounds, though possibly to protect property values, by passing laws designed to stop black expansion into hitherto white neighborhoods. Those state laws and local ordinances were designed to separate neighborhoods according to race. They often prohibited the sale of property to a person of a different race from the race of the majority of the property-owners on the block, unless the majority of the owners of the other race should give their written consent. These state laws denied the citizen the right to purchase property from a buyer who was willing to sell to him, and the decisive factor in the denial *by* the state of the citizen's right to own property was that citizen's race. This constituted state action denying the right to own property because of race, and the Supreme Court had held in 1917 that such laws were a denial of equal protection of the laws to Negro citizens in violation of the Fourteenth Amendment.

But this was purely state action, in which the state had made the determination that race would be the deciding factor in determining whether a certain citizen could acquire ownership of a certain house. In *Shelley v. Kraemer,* however, the State of Missouri formulated no racial policy. It merely enforced restrictive property rights that Mr. and Mrs. Kraemer owned in the land purchased by the Shelleys, the right not to have the land owned or occupied by black people. The law itself was a body of real property law having no connection with racial considerations. The only possible racial motivation was that of private citizens, not of Missouri.

Courts enforce citizens' property rights as a matter of course, regardless of the individual property-owners' motivations; many property disputes are motivated by pure spite, but this makes no difference.

So racially-discriminatory motivations were present in the *Shelley* case, and as the Supreme Court stated in its decision, ". . . the principle has become firmly embedded in our constitutional law that the action inhibited by the first section of the Fourteenth Amendment is only such action as may fairly be said to be that of the States. That Amendment erects no shield against merely private conduct, however discriminatory or wrongful."

The Court concluded that racial agreements between private citizens do not violate the Equal Protection Clause, and that the private agreement to exclude Negro citizens from property ownership in the Kraemer's neighborhood was not rendered void by the Constitution, even as the action of an individual murder is not action by a state.

However, the Court did not stop here. It said: "But here was more. These are cases in which the purposes of the agreements were secured only by judicial enforcement by state courts of the restrictive terms of the agreements."

The Court went on to hold that the action of the Missouri Supreme Court was action by the State of Missouri on the basis of race, that even though the private discriminatory agreement did not violate the Fourteenth Amendment, the enforcement of that agreement by the State did deny the Shelleys equal protection of the laws of Missouri.

The Supreme Court said:

> "It is clear that but for the active intervention of the state courts, supported by the full panoply of state power, petitioners would have been free to occupy the properties in question without restraint. . . . Now State action, as that phrase is understood for the purposes of the Fourteenth Amendment, refers to exertions of state power in all forms. . . . We hold that in granting judicial enforcement of the restrictive agreements in these cases, the States have denied petitioners the equal protection of the laws and that, therefore, the action of the state courts cannot stand."

The Supreme Court quite properly looked through ancient real property law to the final decisive fact on whose basis the Missouri courts denied the Shelleys the right to own the property they had bought and paid for: The Shelleys were black. If they had been white, the Missouri courts would not have denied them the right to own the property that they purchased. The prime fact which led to the Missouri decision, the decisive fact upon which the State acted, was an inherent individual trait, and the plain language of the Equal Protection Clause forbade state denial of equal protection of the laws to any *person.*

Shelley v. Kraemer, though primarily of historical interest in relation to the history of racial conflicts, remains an impressive decision for another reason. In it, the Supreme Court carried Chief Justice Marshall's logic and decision in *Marbury v. Madison* to their next inevitable step.

Marbury v. Madison demonstrated that the Constitution is a law for the government of the Federal Government and in some respects, the state governments; that obedience to the Constitution is required of those in every branch of each of those governments; and that in the decision of cases, courts must measure the laws of Congress against the Constitution, and if they find that the Constitution did not empower Congress to enact the law involved in the case, the courts must disregard the law because of the supremacy of the Constitution.

Shelley v. Kraemer shifted emphasis from the usual view of courts as guardians and interpreters of the Constitution, whose incorrect interpretations of the Constitution in relation to both procedural law and the law governing citizens were subject to reversal by the Supreme Court: Now, attention was concentrated upon state courts as instrumentalities of state government. When the judgment of the Supreme Court of Missouri conflicted with the Equal Protection Clause, and the two were irreconcilable, the Supreme Court of Missouri had violated the Fourteenth Amendment to the Constitution. It was an arm and a part of the government of Missouri, no less than those exercising the legislative and executive powers of Missouri, and when the state court's violation of the Constitution occurred, the State of Missouri, through its courts, had itself violated the Constitution. The state court was a wrongdoer.

This natural corollary to *Marbury v. Madison,* recognizing that an act of a court in violation of the Supreme Law is no less a violation of law than a violation by a legislature or by an individual policeman wielding a portion of the government's executive power, was essential to the Supreme Court's reversal of the Missouri court's decision, because the Constitution only condemned action *by the state* denying people equal protection of its laws.

This salutary principle expounded in *Shelley v. Kraemer* necessarily places both judicial acts and "law" enunciated in judicial interpretations in their proper place of inferiority to the Constitution. It obviously follows that a decision by a federal court in violation of the Constitution may constitute a judicial violation of the Constitution, and may then be a violation of the Constitution by the Government of the United States.[1]

---

1. Such a judicial violation of the Constitution occurred early in the history of the United States. Congress enacted a law that when people sued in federal court on the ground that they were citizens of different states, the federal court should decide according to state law, usually the common law, the law which governed the conduct of the people in the happening of the incident that gave rise to the lawsuit. The Court never paused to ask itself whether even Congress could authorize it to disregard the governing law in the decision of lawsuits, but held in this decision of *Swift v. Tyson* that Federal courts only had to follow state statutes, and should use their own judgment as to what the common law is or should be. This condition under which the federal judiciary decided cases without regard to the governing law continued for a hundred years. Finally, the Supreme Court recognized and corrected its mistake in *Erie Railroad Co. v. Tompkins,* saying:

When police officers exercising governmental power have violated the supreme law, by torturing prisoners or by other less uncivilized but no less illegal conduct, such as by unreasonably searching a citizen's home without a search warrant, the Supreme Court has quite properly branded such official misconduct as governmental lawlessness. The best-known example of such deserved criticism appears in a criminal case, *Elkins v. United States:*

> "Our Government is a potent, omni-present teacher. For good or ill, it teaches the whole people by its example. Crime is contagious. If the Government becomes a law-breaker, it breeds contempt for law; it invites every man to become a law unto himself; it invites anarchy. To declare that in the administration of the criminal law the end justifies the means—to declare that Government may commit crimes in order to secure the conviction of a private criminal—would bring terrible retribution. Against that pernicious doctrine this Court should resolutely turn its face."

The principal distinction between a violation of the Constitution by a single police officer and a violation by an appellate court is that the police officer may be acting under pressure to solve crimes, out of dedication to the work of seeing that criminals will be penalized for the crimes they have committed, and in ignorance of the nice legal distinctions often made by lawyers and judges; while appellate judges are never required to act in haste, but are obligated to do the necessary studying to assure that they will not violate the Constitution nor exceed the powers it has given them. The distinction between a violation of the Constitution by a policeman and by a judge reduces itself to the difference between simple wrongdoing by one who does not pretend to be learned in the law and that of one who is *obligated* to be learned in the law—wrongdoing heightened by hypocrisy.

The Missouri restrictive covenant case of *Shelley v. Kraemer* heralded the end of the era of *Plessy v. Ferguson*. In *Brown v. Board of Education*, the Supreme Court, declaring state-imposed segregation of children by race in the public schools to be a violation of the Constitution, abandoned the rule of its 1896 decision, *Plessy v. Ferguson*. *Plessy v. Ferguson* stands discredited. As the best-known example of judicial wrong-doing, it is a good place to start in discovering the ways courts can incorrectly construe the Constitution and thereby fail to enforce its supremacy over conflicting laws.

Plessy v. Ferguson legitimatized the "separate but equal" doctrine under which segregated public schooling was maintained for over a half-century and under which in many areas black children were required to attend public schools far from their homes and denied the right to attend nearby public schools; pursuant to that doctrine, theaters, restaurants, and many other businesses were required by some states to maintain separate facilities for the two races or else serve only one race; and laws prohibited the marriage of persons of different races.

Plessy v. Ferguson did not err by going contrary to the prevailing legal opinions of the day to throw up a new barricade against the advance of black citizens to an equal place in society. It was in full accord with the recognized legal opinions of the day, including opinions by the Supreme Courts of Ohio, California, New

---

"Thus the doctrine of *Swift* v. *Tyson* is, as Mr. Justice Holmes said, 'an unconstitutional assumption of powers by the Courts of the United States . . .'" This confession of judicial wrong-doing is still accepted as a case correctly determining the law in accordance with the Constitution.

York, and Indiana. It was in full accord with Congressional opinion, as evidenced by acts of Congress requiring school segregation by race in the District of Columbia, but this should have carried no weight because Congress exercised total governmental power over the District of Columbia, and there was no constitutional provision requiring that the United States accord equal protection of the laws to all people within its jurisdiction.

In the matter of showing respect for any past judicial decisions that merit careful consideration, *Plessy v. Ferguson* was far more respectable than the decision that effectively destroyed it, *Brown v. Board of Education*. Though the phrase "Equal Protection of the Laws" had not before appeared in the Constitution of the United States, the legislators who wrote the phrase did not originate it. The idea came from phraseology in the Constitution of Massachusetts, and the Supreme Court of Massachusetts had carefully considered and expounded the meaning of equal protection of the laws for many years. It might well have been argued then that those who wrote the Fourteenth Amendment and the state legislatures which accepted it as a part of the Constitution did so partly on the basis of the general understanding of the meaning of equal protection, derived partly from the decisions of the Massachusetts courts. For this reason, Massachusetts decisions predating the adoption of the Fourteenth Amendment might legitimately be regarded as the most persuasive evidence of the meaning of the Equal Protection Clause.

Before the adoption of the Fourteenth Amendment, Massachusetts courts had ruled that the state's equal protection clause did not prohibit laws requiring separate schools for black and white children. In *Plessy v. Ferguson,* the Supreme Court quoted a portion of an earlier Massachusetts opinion:

> "[By] the Constitution and laws of Massachusetts, all persons without distinction of age or sex, birth or color, origin or condition, are equal before the law. . . . But when this great principle comes to be applied to the actual and various conditions of persons in society, it will not warrant the assertion that men and women are legally clothed with the same civil and political powers, and that children and adults are legally to have the same functions and be subject to the same treatment; but only that the rights of all, as they are settled and regulated by law, are equally entitled to the paternal considerations and protection of the law for their maintenance and security."

So *Plessy v. Ferguson* cannot be criticised on the ground that it was out of step with the accepted and settled legal authority of the day, though each comment about *Brown v. Board of Education* would be accurate.

Plessy was a Louisiana citizen "of mixed descent, in the proportion of seven eights Caucasian and one eighth African blood" and he had the appearance of a white man. Ferguson was the Louisiana judge before whom Plessy was brought to be tried in New Orleans for the criminal offense of refusing to go from the railroad car reserved for white passengers to the car reserved for "colored" passengers. The prosecution was under a state law that required railroad companies to maintain separate or partitioned cars for the two races, and the law prohibited any member of one race from occupying a car reserved for passengers of the other race. The law was written in totally impartial terms—its prohibitions were addressed equally to each race, and there was but one exception to the total segregation on railroad cars: Servants caring for children of a different race could go with the children to their assigned railroad car to care for them.

Mr. Plessy contended before Judge Ferguson that he could not be tried at all, arguing that the state law violated the Equal Protection Clause of the federal Constitution. Judge Ferguson disagreed.

So the case of *Plessy v. Ferguson* was filed by Mr. Plessy in the Supreme Court of Louisiana, seeking a special order known as a writ of prohibition [2] to prohibit Judge Ferguson from even trying the case of *State v. Plessy*. The Supreme Court of Louisiana refused to prohibit the trial, and followed the generally accepted view that while the law must treat citizens equally, it cannot blind itself to natural differences. These natural differences permit the law to require the adult to feed, clothe, educate and care for the small child, while it simultaneously says to the adult: Work or starve.

The United States Supreme Court followed this view on its review of the case. Here are some of its comments:

"We consider the underlying fallacy of the plaintiff's argument to consist in the assumption that the enforced separation of the two races stamps the colored race with a badge of inferiority. If this be so, it is not by reason of anything found in the act, *but solely because the colored race chooses to put that construction upon it.* The argument necessarily assumes that if, as has been more than once the case, and is not unlikely to be so again, the colored race should become the dominant power in the state legislature,[3] and should enact a law in precisely similar terms, it would thereby relegate the white race to an inferior position. *We imagine the white race, at best, would not acquiesce in this assumption.* The argument also assumes that social prejudices may be overcome by legislation, and that equal rights cannot be secured to the negro except by an enforced commingling of the two races. We cannot accept this proposition. If the two races are to meet on terms of social equality, it must be the result of natural affinities, a mutual appreciation of each other's merits and a voluntary consent of individuals. . . . Legislation is powerless to eradicate racial instincts or to abolish distinctions based upon physical differences, and the attempt to do so can only result in accentuating the difficulties of the present situation. If the civil and political rights of both races be equal, one cannot be inferior to the other civilly or politically. If one race be inferior to the other socially, the Constitution of the United States cannot put them upon the same plane."

There is considerable truth in some of the Court's comments. People cannot be made to love. Change of moral standards cannot be enforced by law; indeed, all governments are utterly powerless in the face of strong popular moral sentiments. Regardless of the extent of political and social equality, many people will hate different groups of people, including those who hate none but bigots.

Precisely what is wrong with *Plessy v. Ferguson?* It was more in accordance with established lines of legal decisions than was *Brown v. Board of Education.* It was in agreement with the prevailing thinking of the day that Equal Protection, or equality before the law, did not command social equality, just as *Brown v. Board of Education* was more in accord with the prevailing theoretical thinking of the 1950's that the maintenance of racially segregated schools by state governments had done immense social harm to black children, and apparent black inferiority

---

2. Described at pp. 226, 244, this is an order prohibiting a government official from doing something the law does not authorize him to do.

3. This assumption is untrue. At no time in American history have black legislators constituted the majority of both legislative houses of any state.

was segregation's result rather than its justification.[4] If this is the only difference, then neither decision is better than the other, but they only reflect changes in the prevailing public opinion. Public opinion is none of the business of courts. Making response to changes in public opinion is the legislative obligation.

Some might say that a difference between the two decisions is that *Brown* gave effect to the Equal Protection Clause as a part of the Supreme Law of the Land and that *Plessy* refused to do so. But to say this merely declares that the currently-accepted decision is the correct one.

Plessy v. Ferguson deserves more attention than that. It is a handbook in a method of deciding cases incorrectly and a stark portrait of judges so blinded by bias that they were incapable of seeing the truth.

By crediting the Massachusetts decisions and decisions by other state courts, the Supreme Court credited decisions which themselves had proceeded from pre-Civil War thinking, when half the nation held the ownership of human slaves to be morally right, and when the Constitution itself recognized and protected both the right to own human slaves and the right of the slaveowner to go to another state and recapture his escaped slaves, the Constitution requiring the sanctuary state to deliver the escaped slave to his master.

This traditional thinking about race as a factor that the state could legitimately notice as a basis of according different—but equal—treatment had also led to the pre-Civil War Supreme Court decision of *Dred Scott v. Sanford,* that free black people were not and could not become American citizens.[5] But the Fourteenth Amendment did more than to prohibit states from denying equal protection of the laws. It rejected the *Dred Scott* decision and granted American and state citizenship to all persons born in America.

The pre-Civil War Massachusetts thinking treated women and children as persons whom the law could treat differently because they were viewed as weak and in need of protection, while the segregation of the Negro and the white was based upon commonly-accepted beliefs in black inferiority, which in fact and in theory denied equal citizenship to the Negro on account of race. The Fourteenth Amendment's accord of citizenship to the Negro at the same time undermined the validity of the Massachusetts decisions as to the meaning of equal protection.

The principal error of the Supreme Court in *Plessy v. Ferguson* was that it disregarded the language of the Equal Protection Clause and based its thinking upon prevailing thinking instead of upon carefully-chosen constitutional language. The Clause does not speak of masses of white and black people, but it speaks only of the *individual,* the person, in commanding that no state shall deny any person

---

4. The leading exposition of this theory is Myrdal, *An American Dilemma.*

5. In that decision, Chief Justice Taney had described the historic American view of the Negro—"[They] had for more than a century before [the Revolution] been regarded as beings of an inferior race, and altogether unfit to associate with the white race, either in social or political relations, and so far inferior that they had no rights which the white man was bound to respect, and that the Negro might justly and lawfully be reduced to slavery for [the white man's] benefit, . . . bought and sold and treated as an ordinary article of merchandise and traffic, whenever a profit could be made by it. . . . [This view] was regarded as an axiom in morals as well as in politics, which no one thought of disputing, or supposed to be open to dispute; and men in every grade and position in society daily and habitually acted upon it in their private pursuits, as well as in matters of public concern, without for a moment doubting the correctness of this opinion."

equal protection of the laws. When all white men who might seek admission would have been admitted to the "white" railroad car, and Mr. Plessy, because of his inherent attributes as a person—not because of anything he did or failed to do—was denied admission to the "white" car, Louisiana was denying that person equal protection of its laws. Persons as persons were treated unequally. It could make no difference that Louisiana was also ready to violate the Constitution by denying a white man admission to the "colored" car: A violation of a white person's constitional rights to equal treatment could not justify a violation of a black person's constitutional rights.

But even assuming that the Equal Protection Clause concerned itself with masses of people instead of the individual, as it says, the Supreme Court's decision showed infidelity to truth because it disregarded important facts. Though some of the generally-known facts were discussed in parts of *Plessy v. Ferguson* not quoted above, none were discussed to ascertain the purpose and necessary effect of the Louisiana segregation statute.

First, there were historical facts that all citizens knew. Southern economy and society had been built upon slavery since before the Revolutionary War. The Constitution contained pro-slavery compromises already mentioned, plus a provision forbidding Congress to place any restrictions upon the importation of persons the states desired to import until after 1808. After that twenty-year lapse, Congress would have the power under the Commerce Clause to abolish the slave trade.

This tension between those intent on preserving their wealth in slaves and those morally offended by human slavery continued in other compromises after the Federal Government was formed. But where slavery existed, Negro slaves were property, to be bought and sold, willed and inherited, to be kept isolated from any considerable absorption of knowledge, and to be given the care that humane people give to those incapable of caring for themselves.

"Give me liberty or give me death!" demanded Patrick Henry with the fervor of a true believer. He demanded this in a slave state, addressing his slave-owning peers in Virginia's House of Burgesses, and did so in the presence of another slave-owner, Thomas Jefferson, who wrote in the Declaration of Independence: "All men are created equal . . ." A society believing in human liberty and equality could not maintain virtually all black people in a state of slavery and in the category of owned property except upon a rationalization that the slaves were less than equal people, a race that had never maintained a great empire, a race that would still be squatting around forest campfires had the superior race not possessed and civilized them.

The slave-holding society had formed its separate nation and warred mightily to protect its property and its way of life, but it was defeated, and the victor imposed the Thirteenth Amendment's declaration that neither slavery nor involuntary servitude should exist in the United States.

Their property no longer belonged to them, the law was the law, but the property—now a huge body of freed paupers lacking even the rudimentary training to enable them to handle money and plan their futures—still were not really citizens. They were still unfit to associate as equals with their former owners or with any members of the white race. These views prevailed among the white people: the people who owned the land, had the knowledge, and were a part of the web of society which elected their legislators from among their numbers. The Legislatures passed their laws, and the laws were not designed to improve the *status quo* of the freed property.

So to prevent the use of state government powers to keep the Negro from earning and taking his equal place in society, the Fourteenth and Fifteenth Amendments were adopted. The Fourteenth Amendment defined citizenship to assure that the former slaves would be citizens of both the Nation and their own states, and entitled to the rights of citizenship. These amendments were adopted in part to assure that the white majority, in the battle to maintain vast social superiority and economic superiority over the black minority, would never be able to use the tremendous power of state government to block or hinder the minority's labors to rise from slavery except by laws that applied equally to white men.

Even disregarding their own memories and their own knowledge of the state of affairs, these historical facts were known to all the justices who decided *Plessy v. Ferguson* from nothing more than the records of Congress and the published opinions of the Supreme Court's own past cases. The Fourteenth Amendment was adopted partly to remedy this evil, and the very least that its Equal Protection Clause could possibly mean is that the Negro and the White must always receive equal treatment by the laws of the state, with no differentiation on account of race, and with not the slightest use of state law to aid one against the other.[6]

By what means did the Supreme Court make it appear in this case that it was granting supremacy to the Equal Protection Clause? It simply turned the clause upside down. The Court took something the Equal Protection Clause *did not do*— directly command social equality—and converted it into something the clause *could not do*. By this means, the Court prevented the clause from accomplishing what it was intended to accomplish.

The purpose and command of the Thirteenth Amendment, freeing the slaves, was to convert these people from property into free people so they could live to the limits of their abilities like other people.[7] The Fourteenth Amendment's purpose was to allow the Negro to attain such position as he could, without having to fight the state, as well as his fellow men, for the attainment. But all realized that friendship and social acceptance could never be compelled, so the Fourteenth Amendment contained no restrictions applicable to the people, but only restrained the power of the state governments.[8]

So although the gradual attainment of social acceptance of the Negro was among the motivations for the Fourteenth Amendment, it was not among the commands of the Fourteenth Amendment.

Plessy v. Ferguson stands beside *Marbury v. Madison* as a decision deserving

---

6. This amendatory clause was written as a permanent and impartial statement of principle, differs in tone and phraseology from the reconstruction legislation Congress enacted to govern the conquered southern territory. Much of that legislation was written expressly for the protection of the freedmen and no others, and could not have rationally been applied to women, children, or any other group accorded different treatment. The meaning of the Equal Protection Clause is explored in greater detail below, pp. 256, 331.

7. "The law in its majestic equality, forbids the rich as well as the poor to sleep under bridges, to beg in the streets, and to steal bread."—Anatole France.

8. It is impossible rationally to construe the Equal Protection Clause, a command expressly addressed to states as states, as either restraining individual discriminatory conduct or authorizing Congress to restrain such conduct. This was thoroughly demonstrated in an 1883 Supreme Court opinion reported under the title, *Civil Rights Cases*. Most modern civil rights legislation has been enacted under the Congressional power to regulate interstate commerce, government contracts, appropriation, and other such subjects.

thorough and thoughtful study by every judge in the nation. *Marbury v. Madison* demonstrated that courts have the duty to declare laws unconstitutional, but only to the extent necessary when a particular law is involved in the decision of a lawsuit. *Plessy v. Ferguson* stands as an example of the abuse of judicial power to be assiduously avoided by all judges who take to heart their solemn oaths of office.

By that decision of the Supreme Court, the United States Government permitted the state governments to support and even require social racial discrimination. By this act of the United States Government, and under its leadership, sixty years of racial repression were imposed on citizens of the Negro race. Surely at some time during those decades, there must have been some judge somewhere in the country (and racial legislation existed in even such progressive states as California) with the perception to realize that separate-but-equal legislation denied equal protection of the laws to both white and Negro people, by denying each access to the place assigned exclusively to the other. Surely some judge would have written an opinion refuting the segregation laws' claim to legitimacy and pointing out the errors in *Plessy v. Ferguson* had it not been for the unquestioning acceptance by the entire judicial body of the nation of the false premise that a Supreme Court interpretation of a constitutional provision "settles" the meaning of that provision.

Plessy v. Ferguson inspires one to wonder what would have been the history of the Negro race in America and of race relations if all judges had realized and understood that mere Supreme Court interpretations of the Constitution cannot displace the Constitution itself as the supreme law? If all judges had accepted the proposition that, except in the case being decided by the Supreme Court, its opinions on constitutionality have no legitimate weight with inferior courts beyond the persuasiveness and scholarship contained in each opinion? If each judge had insisted that he could not be true to his oath to support the Constitution by adhering to the Supreme Court's interpretation of that document, when his own interpretation and study led to a different opinion?

If judges had recognized their prime allegiance was to the Constitution instead of other judges' interpretations of the Constitution, they would not have even had to do extensive labor to demonstrate the incorrectness of *Plessy v. Ferguson:* the work was done for them. One of the members of the Supreme Court, Justice John M. Harlan, grandfather of the justice of that same name who so recently sat, dissented. His dissent effectively demonstrated the incorrectness of the Court's decision.[9] Though his dissent refuted the opinion of the Court, the Court made no effort to demonstrate any error in the dissenting opinion. When a dissenting judge asserts in any case, as did Justice Harlan, that the Court's decision exceeds the bounds of judicial propriety, the dissenting opinion may be incorrect in its con-

---

9. Among his comments: "Everyone knows that the statute in question had its origin in the purpose, not so much to exclude white persons from railroad cars occupied by blacks, as to exclude colored people from coaches occupied by or assigned to white persons. . . . Our Constitution is color-blind, and neither knows nor tolerates classes among citizens. In respect of civil rights, all citizens are equal before the law. . . . We boast of the freedom enjoyed by our people above all other peoples. But it is difficult to reconcile that boast with a state of the law which, practically puts the brand of servitude and degradation upon a large class of our fellow citizens, our equals before the law. The thin disguise of 'equal' accommodations for passengers in railroad coaches will not mislead anyone, or atone for the wrong this day done."

tentions. But if it is incorrect, the majority should have the professional capacity to discern and demonstrate in writing the error of the dissenter's views. Any time an appellate court fails to notice and endeavor to refute such a strong dissenting opinion, the failure casts grave doubt upon the correctness of the Court's opinion, and the doubt cannot be dispelled by the passage of time, unless the dissent is patently incorrect on its face.

The majority of the votes on any appellate court determines the disposition of the case, that is, it exercises the judicial power, but in the quest for truth, votes can never establish truth. Truth is beyond the power of government to destroy, and falsehood beyond the power of government to legitimize. When government pretends that one is the other, government neither destroys truth nor legitimizes falsehood, it only demonstrates its own inability to discern truth or its own willingness to admit truth. Such practices tend toward tyranny.

V.

IMPROPER JUDICIAL TACTICS

WE WOULD LIKE to think that every man can take his case to the Supreme Court, but the court of last resort is usually an appellate court inferior to the Supreme Court. The Supreme Court cannot review every decision of every appellate court in the country, and of those who ask, few are permitted to present their arguments to the Court.

Thus, though the Supreme Court is given no power but judicial power, and though its interpretations of the meaning of the Constitution cannot legitimately displace the Constitution as the Supreme Law of the Land, the prime consideration in the determination of whether the Supreme Court will decide a case must be the importance of the legal questions involved. The screening process to determine which cases are important enough to be re-decided by the Supreme Court is performed by the Court itself. With very few exceptions, the Supreme Court hears no cases except those it decides to hear. The decision to hear a case is "announced" by the issuance of an order to the lower court, known as a writ of *certiorari*. The writ deprives the lower court of any further jurisdiction and transfers the case to the Supreme Court.[1]

Sometimes the Court grants *certiorari* in a few cases involving the same subject, and takes no action for the time being on many other similar cases in which petitions have been filed. Then when the Court decides the argued cases, it will simultaneously grant the writ of *certiorari* in the other pending cases, nullify ("vacate") the lower appellate court judgment, and remand the cases with an order that the judges reconsider them in the light of the Court's new decision.[2] This power of the Supreme Court to vacate the decisions of lower appellate courts and to require those courts to reconsider their decisions in light of particular Supreme Court opinions furnishes control over lower appellate court decisions. It assures that there would be no chaos if lower judges considered themselves bound by the Constitution they have sworn to support instead of being bound by Supreme Court interpretations.

In cases in which the Supreme Court, on petitions to review, has not ordered a lower appellate court to reconsider in light of some named decision, a broad acceptance of the obvious truth that Supreme Court interpretations of the Constitution cannot be substituted for the Constitution itself would leave the Court very

---

1. The issuance of certiorari is based on a petition filed by the loser in the lower court. It presents the loser's reasons why he thinks the lower court's decision was wrong and why he things the case important enough to be reviewed by the Supreme Court. The case is reviewed if as many as four of the Court's nine justices vote to issue the writ; if less vote to review, the writ is denied and the lower court's decision allowed to become final.

2. The remand is in the exercise of the Supreme Court's supreme judicial power—power in the decision of individual cases, so that the judges on remand are not free to totally disregard the authority of the Court's new decision.

much in control in the exercise of its *certiorari* powers. At the same time, if in federal-question cases, the lower appellate judges would dedicate themselves to obeying the Constitution instead of to an attempt to decipher the often obscure language of Supreme Court opinions (*e.g.,* obscenity as that which lacks any redeeming social value, whatever that might mean), this would make communication a two-way street. It would inevitably lead the Supreme Court to an earlier acceptance, on occasion, of the error of its own past decisions.

During the sixty years that followed *Plessy v. Ferguson,* the Supreme Court did not grant *certiorari* in a single public school racial segregation case. With the state courts hiding behind the Supreme Court's improper refusal to correct its past errors as to the meaning of the Equal Protection Clause, the Court's systematic denial of *certiorari* contributed to the tragic continued violation of the Amendment.

The refusal by any judicial system to hear serious arguments before imposing judgment is an inexcusable failure to properly perform the judicial function—to hear and consider before inflicting the will of government upon individuals. This refusal to hear and consider may be accomplished by the *systematic refusal* over an extended period of time to grant *certiorari* on cases in a particular field of law or to a particular class of litigants. The refusal to hear before deciding can be accomplished by writing an opinion which fails to mention a serious legal or constitutional argument raised, and so pretends that the question was not raised at all. The refusal to hear and consider may be accomplished by re-stating a party's legal contentions in such different language that the court does not answer the questions and arguments advanced by the citizen, but answers entirely different arguments that the citizen would not have made at all. The refusal to consider before rendering judgment may be accomplished by responding with a snide comment, which neither answers nor gives any hint as to possible errors in the constitutional argument.[3]

When a court makes an incorrect decision as to the meaning of a constitutional provision, it abandons that provision as a part of the supreme law binding upon the court. There remains nothing to guide the judges in their future decisions but their own imaginations, poor substitutes for constitutional provisions governing the powers of courts—provisions reduced to writing in order that they may not be forgotten. The assumption that incorrect interpretations of the Constitution are law that must be followed is false. Lawyers who, out of "respect" for high courts, refuse to urge upon those courts the obligation to undo their own errors actually exhibit disrespect for the high judges in the implication that the judges lack the one judicial trait prized above all others—intellectual integrity. At the very least, the bench and bar should rise to the level of clear vision and plain language of Hans Christian Anderson's little boy, who declared against all adult pretense the truth

---

3. For example, my friends and I think about dogs and decide that a dog has four legs, a head and a tail, and conversely, we postulate that an animal with those attributes is a dog. As the animal before us has four legs, a head and a tail, we conclude it is a dog. You rudely point out that anyone can tell by looking that the animal is a horse. We forcefully demolish your argument: "We are talking about dogs, your comments about horses are not relevant and we are not impressed by them." You attacked our basic assumption that *every* animal with four legs, a head and a tail is a dog, and we refused to attempt to answer your unanswerable attack: Instead of trying to answer you, we overwhelmed you by the power of our numbers. The horse, of course, remained a horse.

that everyone knew—that the king in his new suit was as naked as the day that he was born.

To better judge the illegitimate judicial tendencies we have noticed, we will consider some decisions of the United States Supreme Court that illustrate these improper tactics.

The Selective Service Cases:

The major American wars were fought to be won, were supported by a strong current of patriotism among the people, to the extent that in World War II, virtually the entire portion of the population not in uniform referred to itself as the "home front." The Korean War was a new experience—war fought for a purpose other than victory. If victory could be achieved only by causing loss of face to another great nuclear power and thereby risking nuclear holocaust, it was honorable to forego victory to avoid contaminating the entire world.

By the time of the Vietnam War, young people had come to accept an American war as an engagement that did not have to end in victory. Without victory as the aim, much of the excitement disappeared from war. There can be a moral commitment to crushing evil, but it is difficult to be committed to the thought of losing one's life for the purpose of establishing a stalemate line in the middle of an obscure little country to stop a Communist advance. Those asked to risk death might question why that advance could not be stopped along the outer borders of the little country without loss of American lives.

Many people developed strong moral feelings opposed to the Vietnam War, war in general, the cruelty of war, the unreasonableness of compelling young men to fight in a war to which they were morally opposed. And the opposition was truly moral. But perhaps a moral belief differs from a philosophical belief mainly because it is often more a result of intuition supported by rationalization rather than being derived by ratiocination from demonstrated principles.

Moral and philosophical beliefs differ in nature from religious beliefs. Religious beliefs proceed from belief in the existence of a deity having power superior to that of any government or other human force. Mere moral beliefs admit that they are based upon the human intellect, but religious beliefs insist they are commanded by Almighty God and may not even be intelligible to man.

Two men may hold beliefs of equal intensity, each so strongly opposed to killing that he will die rather than to kill another; the only difference between their beliefs is that for one, the beliefs are acknowledged to proceed from his own intellect and for the other, they are believed, even *known,* to be commanded by divine power. To one who reveres individual freedom, it is unreasonable to respect the beliefs of one of these men and trample upon the beliefs of another. But in the enforcement of federal statutes and constitutional provisions, judges are not empowered to be guided by their personal philosophies, personal senses of morality, or sympathies for the philosophies or moral codes of others.

Under Federal law, there is one essential difference between one compelled by religious beliefs and one compelled by moral or ethical beliefs. The First Amendment prohibits the enactment of any law abridging the freedom of religion. If religion positively commands a believer not to do an act, and Congress positively commands him to do that very act, Congress has infringed his freedom of religion in violation of the First Amendment. But no provision of the Constitution exempts mere moral or ethical beliefs from the compulsion of laws made by Congress pursuant to the Constitution.[4]

Congress has customarily enacted its compulsory draft laws to attempt to spread the military service obligation evenly, but it has stopped at the door of the church in recognition of its lack of power to infringe the freedom of religion. Congress cannot be accused of discriminating simply because it *excludes* from the compulsion of the draft laws the only group the Constitution denies it the power to include.

An early compulsory draft law exempted conscientious objectors affiliated with a well-recognized religious organization with an existing creed forbidding participation in war.[5] Congress later broadened this statutory conscientious objector exemption to exclude from required military service anyone who "by reason of religious training and belief, is conscientiously opposed to participation in war in any form." This change eliminated any need for a connection with an established religious organization, but posed the question of what is "religious training and belief?" One of the federal courts of appeals held that strong *moral beliefs* were religious beliefs, though the individual seeking to be excused from military service in that case did not believe in the existence of God. Another court of appeals ruled that religious belief essential to entitle the believer to the conscientious objector immunity encompassed only beliefs based upon the belief in God, in an "authority higher and beyond any worldly one."

So the issue was joined as to the meaning of this law enacted by Congress. Times had changed, the march of science had defeated the belief in God in the minds of many people, and the growth of substitutes for religion was in progress—astrology, dedication to political and humane causes, to drugs, and to science itself as the search for truth.[6] With the change in times, perhaps Congress used "religious training and belief" in a more contemporaneous sense than the phrase "freedom of religion" means in the First Amendment.[7]

So Congress settled the dispute between the two federal appellate courts as to who should be excluded from compulsory military service. It changed the law to make the meaning clear and to make the scope of the conscientious objection ex-

---

4. Men have always been morally opposed to rules made by government. Law itself is but a set of rules which the individual is compelled to obey by force: Prison, fine, the electric chair. The Whiskey Rebellion soon after the formation of our government arose from moral belief in free man's right to grow his own corn on his own land and convert it into whiskey to drink or sell without having to seek any government's permission. If the United States Government should decide to yield to strong moral beliefs—an inconvenience to government with so many moral beliefs abounding—then the power to decide to yield rests in Congress alone.

5. It is doubtful if this definition of those immune from military obligations was constitutionally valid. Jesus' beliefs were religious, yet He would not come within this definition.

6. One scientist has suggested that a new religion should be created, the existence of a living God should be discarded as a rejected premise, and truth as revealed by science should become the object of worship. Ralph W. Burhoe, "Salvation in the Twentieth Century," *Science Ponders Religion.*

7. There was no doubt about the meaning of religion in those days. It meant the Christian religion, the competing religions of those who worshipped God but were mistaken about His name, or at the very least, the existence of a divine system of rewards and punishments, possibly here but most probably in an afterworld.

emption very precise. In 1948, Congress amended the exemption statute to define the statute's use of the term "religious training and belief": "an individual's belief in relation to a Supreme Being involving duties superior to those arising from any human relation, but does not include essentially political, sociological, or philosophical views or a merely personal moral code."

Assuming the validity of the compulsory military service laws, Congress had thereby made the decision within its power—that a refusal to obey the governmental command to enter military service would not be tolerated by the Government if based only upon moral grounds, philosophical, political, or sociological views, but would be permitted if it was the conscientious objector's belief that he must act under a command from God superior to and conflicting with the command of law made by human government.

In 1970, the Supreme Court came to the rescue of large numbers of people who objected to service in the Vietnam War. In *Welsh v. United States,* the Supreme Court held the statutory *religious* conscientious objector exemption to be extended to those who objected on *moral* grounds so firmly held that the men's moral or philosophical beliefs "would give them no rest or peace if they allowed themselves to become a part of an instrument of war."

The decision may be applauded for the recognition it gave to the demands of many deeply-concerned people; it may thus be applauded for doing what Congress could have done had the popular pressure been strong enough to move Congress to amend the Selective Service Act. If Congress had exercised its *legislative power* to change the law, this would be a change in law achieved in the sole manner provided by the Constitution to change law, by legislation. But the Supreme Court is given no legislative power. Its obligation is to accord supremacy to the Constitution and to enactments of Congress made pursuant to it, even when it thinks it can improve upon the Congressional enactments. The Court pretended Congress had not outlawed the excusing of men who objected to serving only on moral or philosophical grounds.

The Supreme Court was not ignorant of the legislative changes, because Justice Harlan described those legislative developments in his concurring opinion [8] in *Welsh v. United States.* It was impossible to intelligently interpret the Selective Service Act as extending the draft law immunity to people who objected only on moral grounds, however strong, while admitting they did not believe in the existence of God. In so interpreting it, the Supreme Court openly and knowingly misinterpreted the plain language of the statute and refused to grant enforcement to the Act of Congress. By its fiat, it allowed mere moral and philosophical beliefs to overcome law which, if otherwise valid, was part of the Supreme Law. The Court's stated reason was compassion.

The difficulty with permitting moral objections to immunize citizens from the duty to obey the law is that, if courts be legitimately empowered to grant immunity from the commands of law on such basis,[9] the courts will be enforcing

---

8. Justice Harlan concurred on a different basis. He considered the 1948 amendment illegal because it discriminated between those who object on religious grounds and those who object on moral grounds; his opinion involved the rationale the Supreme Court has assigned to the Equal Protection Clause, but that Clause by its plain language is addressed only to state governments, not to the Federal Government. His opinion in this case is patently unsound.

9. A systematic and persuasive exposition of the proper scope of law, which would condemn most of the law presently in existence in America, was brilliantly developed by Bastiat, *The Law.*

morality rather than the law they are sworn to enforce. One's receipt of this judicially-granted immunity from the duty to obey the law's commands must depend upon how much the courts are attracted to one's moral beliefs. How about the Ku Klux Klan? The Black Panthers? Communists? WASPs? [10] The power to respond to popular moral convictions by changing federal law is vested in the legislative authority, not the judicial authority, and when judicial authority claims this power—or exercises it while pretending not to claim it, the judiciary dishonors its obligation of office.

But what of the power of the United States to compel men to submit to military service against their will? Can Congress constitutionally interrupt a man's private life, deprive him of all his liberty, and compel him to take arms against his will? Can this Congressional power to impose military service obligations upon objecting citizens exist under a Constitution that prohibits the *existence* of involuntary servitude?

We may regard the question as completely settled, because the Supreme Court held compulsory draft laws to be valid in 1918 during the patriotic excitement of World War I. That settles it *if we concede* to the Supreme Court or to the Government the right to substitute judicial interpretations of the Constitution for the Constitution itself as the supreme law. If we are unwilling to yield this power of substitution, then the 1918 decision of *Arver v. United States* cannot be viewed as settling the question unless the opinion contains reasoning adequate to persuade the unbiased reader of its correctness.

Joseph F. Arver strenuously objected to being compelled to enter the Army in World War I. His case and those of five other men were joined by the Supreme Court in a single opinion under the heading of *Selective Draft Law Cases.* Among the men, they contended upon almost every conceivable ground that Congress could not compel their military service. Among these was the objection that the law offended the involuntary servitude prohibition of the Fourteenth Amendment.

The Court thoroughly and competently demonstrated that prior to the adoption of the Thirteenth Amendment, the United States had the power to adopt and enforce a compulsory draft law.[11] But this demonstration did not touch upon the change brought into the Constitution by the adoption of the Thirteenth Amendment right after the Civil War. At any time before then, Congress could have passed a commerce law providing for licensing people and ships to engage in the slave trade, and could have authorized people to bring newly-captured black slaves from Africa to sell in America, but when the Thirteenth Amendment was adopted, Congress no longer had that power.

The Thirteenth Amendment prohibits involuntary servitude, and in the Supreme Court's twenty-five-page opinion in the *Arver* case, the Court wrote only one paragraph about this objection, the most serious and difficult objection to the continued existence of Congressional power to compel military service. This is *all* the Court wrote on the subject:

---

10. A popular abbreviation, from the 1960's for White Anglo-Saxon Prostestants.

11. Most of the Court's opinion was taken up with an excellent demonstration that under the original Constitution, before the Thirteenth Amendment, the Government had the power to compel military service. The Court demonstrated that every government in history had used the power to compel citizens to fight, both offensively and defensively. Congress is empowered to raise armies, and to pass laws necessary and proper to carry out that power, American history proved the use of compulsory draft laws was necessary and the history of the entire world showed it to be the proper means of raising armies, so it was quite clear that the Federal Government *originally* had this power.

"Finally, as we are unable to conceive upon what theory the exaction by government from the citizen of the performance of his supreme and noble duty of contributing to the defense of the right and honor of the nation as the result of a war declared by the great representative body of the people can be said to be the imposition of involuntary servitude, in violation of the prohibitions of the 13th Amendment, we are constrained to the conclusion that the contention to that effect is refuted by its mere statement."

The Supreme Court, admitting that it could not even understand the contention, made no attempt to refute it, but instead rhetorically re-stated the contention in an insulting manner and in accordance with the then-popular political or patriotic view. In truth, selective service is entirely involuntary. That is what *Arver v. United States* was all about. It is servitude to the extent that every minute of the soldier's life is ordered; he is told when to rise and when to go to bed, what to wear, when he may be at liberty, the exact day and hour that his personal liberty will terminate, and he can be imprisoned for returning late; he is totally deprived of the right to follow his own will, he is obligated to perform personal services as well as military services upon the direction of his commander, and it is all based upon governmental compulsion rather than voluntary consent. Compulsory military service has all the attributes of involuntary servitude. "Involuntary servitude" is not simply another word for "slavery," because the Thirteenth Amendment expressly prohibits slavery and also expressly prohibits involuntary servitude as something different from slavery, lacking slavery's ownership of the slave's body.

The Thirteenth Amendment was both proposed by Congress and approved by the state legislatures in 1865, shortly after Congress had exercised its power to compel military service in the Civil War. It was within the memory of Congress that large numbers of people in New York City had conscientiously protested those draft laws, and had carried their protest against them to the point of rioting for four straight days! Congress had shown itself aware of the need for involuntary service in the military organization by itself enacting the draft laws. Yet this was the language of the Thirteenth Amendment as originated in Congress at the end of the Civil War: "Neither slavery nor involuntary servitude, *except as a punishment for crime whereof the party shall have been duly convicted,* shall exist within the United States, or any place subject to their jurisdiction."

The expression of one exception to a rule implies that there are no other exceptions. The involuntary servitude expressly excepted from the prohibition of the Thirteenth Amendment was a servitude imposed by *governments,* and this was made lawful only if it were for the commission of a crime for which the citizen had already been convicted! The exception proves that the Amendment prohibits all American governments to impose involuntary servitude for any other reason or under any other circumstances.

To exclude compulsory military service from the Amendment's prohibition against involuntary servitude, it would have been quite simple for Congress to have added another exception in writing the amendment, such as "and except for compulsory military service during war or imminent threat of war." But Congress adopted no language to exclude this type of involuntary servitude that had so recently been required by it and that had driven citizens to violent protest.

The Amendment, as worded and adopted, by its plain words terminated Congress' once unquestionable power to impose compulsory military service. Any judicial opinion seeking to demonstrate Congress' continuing power to impose involuntary military servitude would have to incorporate some knowledge not readily apparent and evidently not readily apparent to the Supreme Court in 1918. If it had been, the Court would have written an intelligent opinion utilizing reason instead of merely insulting the serious question it faced and could not answer. The Court here blinded itself to the Thirteenth Amendment in favor of the patriotism of the day, as it later blinded itself to statutory commands in *Welsh v. United States* [12] in favor of changing morals and the popular revulsion to the Vietnam War.

Any time judges permit their clear vision and accurate interpretation of the Constitution and statutes to be warped, whether by reason of feelings or racial superiority, sympathy for the plight of litigants, strong patriotism, or any other emotion, so that they fail to correctly construe and obey Constitutional commands, the Constitution as a set of absolute rules to govern the government is eroded. Continued erosion will necessarily eventuate in a reduction of the Constitution to nothing more than whatever the current membership of the courts may be pleased to say it means. Strengthened by the false pretense that past Supreme Court decisions are binding, though contrary to reason and to the Constitution, this will inevitably lead to the destruction of all remnants of a wisely-drawn Constitution, and the enthronement of a body of judge-made law, often invidiously discriminatory in its application, but continuing to claim to speak as the institutional protector of the "Constitution."

Under judges less dedicated to human freedom and dignity than most who have sat as justices of the United States Supreme Court, this use of judicial power can deteriorate into an awful form of tyranny. It does no good to write words down so that Constitutional limitations on governmental powers may be remembered, when judges claim the power to change the meaning of written words. The absolute preservation of constitutional supremacy is essential to the protection of the liberties of people now living and those yet to come.

Of Death and Taxation:

We in America enjoy every form of taxation. This is not surprising, because it is generally accepted that there are only three types of taxes: Taxes on people, taxes on property, and taxes on acts people do. The last category is today generally called an excise in legal circles. There are many sub-categories. The taxes on imports and exports are sometimes called imposts and exposts, and are universally based upon value, cost, or quantity of the thing imported or exported. One might consider these duties to be taxes on property being imported or exported, or taxes on the act of importing or exporting. In America, it makes no difference which we may choose to call them, because the Constitution is quite specific about imposts and exposts. All states are denied the power to impose either of them,[13] the Federal Government is denied the power to impose exposts, but has unlimited power to impose duties on goods imported into the country.

Speaking of governments generally, the tax imposed upon particular acts is immensely important to the taxing authority, usually legislatures. There is nothing much that can be done with taxes on people and on property but to continue or

---

12. See above, p. 68.

13. The Constitution permits states to inspect products coming across state lines, and to charge inspection fees, but requires profits from inspection fees to be paid by the States into the Federal treasury.

abolish the tax or change the tax rates or exemption levels. But the concept of taxing people's acts offers great range to legislative ingenuity. If the people tire of one type of tax, the tax can be abolished, and the range of human activity is so broad that another small "excise" can be applied to some entirely different type of activity.

Legislative salesmanship can choose subjects of taxation least likely to provoke mass anger. Taxes on whiskey are wonderful. They reward the good by exempting them from the tax and those intent upon drinking derive enough satisfaction from the goods purchased that they will not allow high tax rates to stand in their way. During World War II, a new tax on the act of selling—a sales tax—was imposed by the Federal Government on the sale of certain products, including luggage, jewelry, theater admissions. Called a "luxury tax," it both raised money and aided the wartime spirit of sacrifice at home to match the sacrifices of the men overseas,[14] with those who insisted upon enjoying luxuries having to pay the twenty per cent tax for the privilege.

Nations have at times had taxes to suppress sumptuous living, known as sumptuary taxes. The sumptuary tax could tax either acts or property, such as the act of eating a third meal in a single day, or a tax on each individual's second pair of shoes, increased geometrically with each additional pair.

Why all the names? What good do they do? Why not just call all of them taxes? They are traditional and had become traditional long ago, just as the offspring of horses and lions were known as colts and cubs. But in America, words describing types of taxes have real importance because different words relating to taxation are used in the Constitution to define the taxing power of the United States Government.

It is quite important to determine—and be guided by—the meaning of the words "taxes, duties, imposts and excises" and of "direct taxes" as they are the words that measure the Government's taxing power.[15] Clearly, the power of the government to tax cannot be expanded by the simple expedient of declaring the words to mean something other than what they meant when they were written into the Constitution. This would be but a refusal to honor the constitutional limitations upon governmental taxing power.

One of the great sources of Federal internal revenue is the estate and gift tax structure. It is designed to discriminate against the rich by taking large percentages of their wealth and by leaving poorer people totally immune from the tax; there is a minimum of $60,000 that passes tax-free. The tax is carefully designed to take a substantial portion of the entire accumulation of wealth achieved by an individual (or a married couple) during the entire lifetime. The citizen may choose during his lifetime to give much of his money to his children, but this

---

14. In some places outside shelling range, the overseas sacrifices were not too great. Whiskey, free of taxation, could be purchased for one dollar a fifth and cigarettes for five cents a pack.

15. The most valuable federal tax source is the income tax, the greatest means of taking money from people in all the states and using it not only for general national purposes, but also to build hospitals, provide school lunches, and do many other good deeds locally beneficial to people in each separate state. This tax was authorized by the Sixteenth Amendment, empowering Congress to tax incomes "from whatever source derived, without apportionment among the several states, and without regard to any census or enumeration." Aside from this direct tax authorization, the rest of the Federal taxing power, if governed by the Constitution, remains precisely what it was when the Constitution was adopted.

would defeat the passage of that wealth to his children upon his death and would diminish the amount of the estate tax, so there is a gift tax imposed, at a lesser rate. When the citizen dies, if the government views the lifetime gifts as having been made in contemplation of death, the gifts are added as a part of the estate and taxed at higher rates, with credits given for the earlier payments of gift taxes.

The tax is immensely profitable not only to the Government but also to banks, to tax lawyers engaged in estate-planning, and to insurance companies.[16] Those most expert in the technicalities of the tax and most competent to advise people with tax problems have a huge, vested interest in perpetuating the tax, which thus enjoys a practical immunity from attack by them.[17] But is the Federal estate tax constitutional?

The Constitution requires that all direct taxes be apportioned among the states on the basis of population, which requires variable tax rates for the different states. The estate tax is uniform throughout the country, and if it were considered a direct tax, it would have to be apportioned among the states: If a direct tax, the total amount collected from California each year during the 1970's would have to be exactly 9.82% of the national total and that collected from Nevada estates would have to be 0.24% of the national total. Thus, the rate imposed on individual estates would not only vary from state to state, but would vary from year to year, according to the number of extremely wealthy people who might die during different years. If the tax were viewed as a direct tax, Federal estate taxation would be very difficult to achieve as a practical matter.

How can this tax uniformly levied upon the accumulated wealth—homes, insurance benefits, savings accounts, stocks and bonds—exist, when it takes a share of accumulated wealth directly from the people without apportionment among the states?

It exists because the courts have long since satisfied themselves—incorrectly— that it is actually an excise, and the Constitution requires excises to be uniformly assessed throughout the nation instead of being apportioned by population. Therefore, the theory goes, an excise is not a direct tax, and can and must be uniformly assessed. The death taxes are declared to be assessed against particular acts by which ownership is transferred.[18] All property owned by the citizen must be transmitted upon his death to someone living or to some government or organization.

---

16. To diminish the amount of this burdensome tax, banks have trust departments to serve the wealthy, complex trusts are created to hold part of the wealth for the third generation, so that it will not be taxed twice, once when grandfather dies and again when father dies. Insurance companies sell large insurance policies not to provide money for distribution to heirs, but to pay the estate tax on both the citizen's wealth and the insurance he has purchased to pay the tax. Citizens who fail to show this foresight are often unsuccessful in transmitting their property to their children.

17. Small taxpayers, whose tax liability is comparatively insignificant, are effectively barred from legally contesting taxation because they must first follow the bureaucratic procedures within the IRS. These procedures are claimed to be for the benefit of the taxpayer by furnishing him hearings, but when the defensive objections to the tax are complex, the expense of employing a lawyer to follow these inane procedures conducted by adversaries rather than impartial judges, followed by the expense of litigation in the federal courts, is so great that it either exceeds the tax saving to be gained or is too great an expense to be risked against the possibility of an anti-government decision.

18. The Federal Government declares that it taxes the act of transmitting property by reason of death, and most state governments declare they tax the act

Both death and the transmission of property by reason of death are inevitable unless the individual dies without property. This may be a tax upon an "act" or it may be a tax upon each citizen's accumulated wealth, with death being the event that fixes the time for assessment and payment of the tax. Constitutionally, it makes no difference which it is.

The Constitution prohibits the levying of capitations (such as poll taxes) and other *direct taxes* by Congress except upon an apportioned basis. What if Congress should levy a tax annually on the act of growing hair, uniformly imposed upon all hair-growers throughout the country? This would obviously be a head tax and because of population shifts, births, deaths, and diseases that destroy hair, would never be accurately apportioned by the last census. The courts have uniformly and consistently held that any federal taxes on persons and on real property must be apportioned, and the apportionment is so impractical Congress does not even attempt to exercise this taxing power. But what if Congress, declaring itself to be levying an excise, should impose an annual tax upon the act of heating or cooling a dwelling house by means of natural gas, artificial gas, fossil fuels, wood or electricity? Would not this tax, measured at the rate of one per cent the value of the house being heated or cooled, actually be a tax on realty?

These suppositions merely assume that these taxes are actually taxes upon property and persons, acknowledged to be beyond the Government's power to levy without apportionment. If an excise actually meant a tax on doing an act when the Constitution was written, then the taxes would actually be excises upon growing hair or heating houses; they would be required to be uniform although they are identical to the forbidden capitation and tax on real property. The only way we can discover the meaning of Congress' power to impose excises is to return to the time of the Constitution.

Under the Articles of Confederation, there was no taxing power, but contributions were requested from each state on the basis of the total value of land and houses in the state. In the Constitutional Convention, it was determined that the basis of apportionment should be shifted to a population formula as a measure of relative wealth; this cumbersome formula would give the Federal Government the power to levy taxes directly against the people when the need for money was sufficiently crucial to impel Congress to set up a workable direct tax structure, but as a practical matter, it would restrict the Federal Government to indirect taxation as a source of revenue.

So in the Convention's early resolutions, referred to the Committee on Detail, it was provided that there should be a periodic census, "And that the Legislature of the United States shall proportion the direct Taxation accordingly." It was implied in this resolution that indirect taxes did not have to be apportioned, but there was no mention of duties, excises, imposts or exposts. The Committee on Detail added the language "to lay and collect taxes, duties, imposts, and excises" and among the limitations on Congressional power, it placed the apportionment formula for direct taxes and capitations.[19]

The Committee added no provision for the uniformity of duties, imposts

---

of inheriting property by reason of someone else's death. The definitions are fictitious.

19. The Committee added another faint restraint upon Federal taxing powers, by providing that the taxing power could be used only "to pay the debts and provide for the common defence & general welfare, of the U.S." Notes of James Madison, *Documents Illustrative of the Formation of the Union*, p. 660.

and excises. This provision was added by the Convention itself to assure non-discrimination among the states. It is clear that these men, so dedicated to the apportionment principle, would have instantly recognized the uniformity-of-excises requirement as totally destructive of the scheme for apportioning direct taxes *if "excises" actually meant taxes imposed upon acts rather than property and persons.* They would have perceived that so many acts are done in relation to property that any one of these could be seized upon as a pretense to tax property itself in evasion of the apportionment principle. In fact, "excise" did not have the meaning now assigned to it—a tax on acts done by people. It meant a tax on products to be marketed, so that the actual tax burden would be indirectly paid by the purchaser as part of the purchase price.

The words of American law came from England, and these men's leading easy-reading source for discussion of English law and its development was a set of books published twenty years earlier, Blackstone's *Commentaries.* The Revolutionary cry against "Taxation without Representation" echoed a principle gained from the king in *Magna Carta,* but the catchy phraseology was straight from Blackstone.

We have seen that in America, Congress has the power, and the states lack the power, to tax imports. It makes no difference whether one considers an impost to be a tax on the property imported or on the act of importing property because these would simply be an arbitrary naming of the same thing, and Congress has the power to tax imports no matter what you may call the tax. So neither Congress nor the courts have concerned themselves about whether property or the act of importing is being taxed when an import duty is added to the cost of a Volkswagen from Europe or a television set from Japan.

The same attitude applied to English taxation at the time of the American Revolution and earlier on June 23, 1753, when Oxford University announced: "In Michaelmus Term next will begin a Course of Lectures on the Laws of England by Dr. Blackstone, of All-Souls College." It made no difference whether a tax be called an impost, expost, duty or excise—Parliament imposed all of them, the power to impose them was vested in "the Commons of Great Britain in Parliament assembled," and the only limitation on Parliament's taxing power was the degree of taxation the people would endure. Whether taxation was direct or indirect and whether a tax was an excise or a duty had not the slightest legal significance.

The King's revenues, says Blackstone,[20] were divided by historical tradition into the king's ordinary revenues and his extradorinary revenues, and examination reveals that this distinction had no connection with the difference between direct and indirect taxation. The King's ordinary revenues [21] belonged to him by tradition and his extraordinary revenues were those he had been compelled by

---

20. I Blackstone, *Commentaries*, Ch. 8.

21. The King's ordinary revenues were simply those heriditary revenues he had not been compelled to surrender to the House of Commons. Many of these rights to receive money had been sold to noblemen or passed to inferior government units, and no longer formed a part of England's tax structure. They included, for example, the right to wrecks washed ashore and those remaining at sea, distinguished "by the barbarous and uncouth appelations of *jetsam, flotsam* and *ligan*" and these heriditary revenues also included the forfeited property of those whom the king had to care for, such as the lunatic, who has "lucid intervals, sometimes enjoying his senses, and sometimes not, and that frequently depending upon the change of the moon."

force to surrender to Parliament, those which could not be levied except by the House of Commons. The principal English division of taxes was based not upon restraints on taxing power but upon habit, the way Parliament customarily imposed taxes: Annual taxes fixed each year and perpetual taxes enacted once and remaining in effect until repealed. This distinction has no relation to the direct/indirect taxation dichotomy.

Blackstone's list of perpetual taxes included a list of real property taxes and even a type of capitation, expressly defined by our Constitution as a direct tax. Yet the name with which Parliament chose to dub them was "duties," [22] a general name for taxes which our Constitution includes in its list of indirect taxes. The perpetual taxes also included a license privilege tax on the operation of hackney-coaches, which American courts have concluded to be an excise because it is imposed upon the act, or privilege of performing the act, of driving a taxi. Blackstone called it a "duty" rather than an excise.[23]

But elsewhere in Blackstone's discussion of taxation, in this most common and popular legal handbook [24] at the time our Constitution was written, we do find a discussion of direct and indirect taxation. It was in no sense a discussion of terms having *legal* significance in the law of England, but a discussion of the *economic* theory of taxation and the problem of how to get the most tax with the least chance of rebellion.[25] After discussing the details of the English customs tariffs, which included duties on both imports and exports, Blackstone discussed this economic theory. From his comments:

> Directly opposite [to the customs tariff] is the *excise duty;* which is an inland imposition paid sometimes upon the consumption of the commodity or frequently upon the retail sale, which is the last stage before consumption."

---

22. At various times, there were duties imposed upon every house except cottages, there was a head tax on each servant employed, called a duty on servants, and there were taxes on all the chimneys, "vulgarly called smoke farthings," on all the hearths, and on all the windows in each house above an exempt number, usually six or nine. All were named "duties" by Parliament, but the occasional naming in this manner was only a habit without legal significance. The Parliament did not use it, as did those who wrote our Constitution, as a part of the category of indirect taxes.

23. With the collection of this tax being in the hands of designated commissioners, they not only raised money but also adopted regulations, so that the hackney drivers, "a very refractory race of men, may be kept in some tolerable order."

24. Far more authoritative was Coke's *Institutes*, which, while known to the best-educated American lawyers, was even then almost impossible to understand, and was not as well known as Blackstone. The difficulty of understanding Coke is accurately portrayed in Chapter X of Catherine Drinker Bowen's excellent biography of one of our founding fathers, *John Adams and the American Revolution.*

25. At times, when direct taxes imposed upon the people as people and their property became too heavy, the people had killed the king's tax collectors for coming on their property. For the direct taxes fell directly upon the people, they had to pay the taxes from their own property or wealth, and they were quite conscious of the extent of the tax. If they fail to pay such a tax voluntarily, the tax cannot be collected except by jailing the citizen or seizing his property. The efficacy of the direct tax depends upon the people's acceptance of both the tax and its rates.

Blackstone continued briefly his discussion of the economic theory and placed the excise duty in the same category with the customs tariff—the tax imposed at some point along the route that led to consumer purchase, by which the burden of taxation would be laid upon the consumer as a part of the purchase price. He discussed a list of excises, some in the form of taxes on property to be sold (e.g., starch and hair powder in the hands of the manufacturer, gold and silver wire taxable at the wiredrawer's, silver plate taxable by an annual license tax on the retail seller). He followed his discussion of the new system of excise taxation [26] with a discussion of the older perpetual taxes. The first of these was the ancient salt tax, described by Blackstone as an excise levied upon each bushel of salt.[27]

It is thus clear beyond dispute that when the Constitution was written, Parliament could and did label taxes with whatever name it chose, and the name made no difference—Parliament could and did label both direct and indirect taxes as "duties." Further, excises were understood to mean taxation indirectly imposed at some point in the process leading to consumer purchase, and "excise" *did not mean* a tax on doing an act as distinguished from taxes on people and things.

The Federalist demonstrates that this was the best understanding of the difference between the mutually exclusive direct tax and "duties, imposts and excises." Its every example of excises is an example of taxation on the route leading to consumer purchase. In No. 36, Hamilton discussed the difference between direct and indirect taxes, describing the latter as "duties and excises on articles of consumption." [28]

It was the constitutional purpose to require that Federal taxes be apportioned according to the census, considering population an indicator of wealth. The tax burden imposed directly upon the wealth of the people was required to be apportioned. There is obviously no tax more direct than death taxes based upon an entire lifetime's accumulation in property and other forms of wealth. Uniformity in the rates of indirect taxation—duties, imposts and excises—was required, so that although *tax receipts* would be highest from the importing and manufacturing states, the *tax burden* would fall upon each state in accordance with its population and wealth, for these determine how much the people in each state would spend for consumer goods, and therefore the amount of indirect tax burden borne by each state.

26. This system of excises upon many products, Blackstone told the American lawyers who were among his readers, was first introduced into England in the 1640's in imitation of the Dutch taxing system. The year before it was first proposed, rumors of the impending system of taxation spread to the point that the Journal of the House of Commons stated that "aspersions were cast by malignant persons upon the house of commons, that they intended to introduce excises, the house for its vindication therein did declare, that these rumors were false and scandalous; and that their authors should be apprehended and brought to condign punishment."
27. "This is not generally called an excise, because under the management of different commissioners, but the commissioners of the salt duties have by statute the same powers, and must oberve the same regulations, as those of other excises."
28. Hamilton also noted that the total income from excises on particular articles is subject to the consent of the purchasers, because if an excise were made unreasonably high, the price increase would reduce consumption of the taxed product, and reduce the receipts from taxation of that product, this aspect of excise taxes being "a natural limitation of the power of imposing them." *The Federalist*, No. 21.

Even the derivation of the word excise, from the Latin *ad*, or toward the *census* tax, through the old French *accens* to *acceis,* supports the then common understanding of the excise as taxation on the people, added indirectly to the taxes imposed directly upon them, by being included and usually hidden in the cost of consumer goods. It was the Constitutional intent to apportion all taxes among the states according to population, to be achieved by commanding the opposed systems of apportionment of direct taxes and uniformity of indirect taxes.

Yet by judicially changing the meaning of excise from a consumer goods tax to a tax on doing an act—any kind of act—the Federal Government has been able to impose tremendous and almost confiscatory taxation upon the accumulations of each citizen during his lifetime on the assumption that the thing being taxed is the act of willing, the act of inheriting, or the process of succession of heirs to inherited property, and that the tax is therefore an excise and *cannot be apportioned.* Thus does learning obscure knowledge when study is restricted to the uncritical amplification of past errors. By the simple expedient of changing the meaning of words in constitutional provisions, there is no constitutional protection that cannot be abolished under the pretense that it is being preserved.

When we demonstrate the illegality of Federal estate taxation achieved by converting the power to tax products on their way to market into the power to tax human acts of any nature, we do not concern ourselves with protecting the interests of the weathy [29] but with the need to protect the Constitution from the erosion of time, when new generations of judges forget the meaning of constitutional provisions, do not bother to educate themselves as to the meaning of those provisions when they were adopted, and by perpetuating the past unwarranted substitution of suppositions for the clear meanings of constitutional safeguards, rob the safeguards of all value.[30]

---

29. This is not to imply that the right of the wealthy to retain their honestly-gained or inherited wealth is in any way morally inferior to the right of the poor to retain the property they have honestly earned. While naked envy alone is adequate motivation to attack wealth and the wealthy, Abraham Lincoln maintained that the presence of some wealthy people serves as an inspiration and example to others to strive toward that end, and theoretically, it has been quite convincingly demonstrated that in a free society, wealth and its preservation in honorable business endeavors are absolutely essential to the improvement of the lot of every financial level of society. See, e.g., Ludwig von Mises, *Human Action.*

30. There is no constitutional right or safeguard that cannot be completely destroyed by this pernicious type of official forgetfulness. Even the right to trial by jury may be warped by successive slight changes with each generation of judges comparing it with what it was a decade ago rather than comparing it with the inherited ideal of trial by jury. This has already happened to the grand jury, which is today mostly a rubber-stamp of governmental desires for prosecutions, though at the height of its effectiveness as a device for the protection of human rights, the grand jurors were free of undue governmental influence. The attorney for the Crown, or prosecuting attorney, could not even go into the presence of the grand jury, so he could not influence them; there was no unfairness about a defendant not being able to have his attorney appear and argue before the grand jury, because neither side could appear there, and if the grand jurors needed advice, they went before the judge to seek it. In Michigan, as described in the Supreme Court opinion in *Re William Oliver*, this ancient and valuable institution was reduced to a farce labelled the "One-Man Grand Jury," Single judges were by statute empowered to act as grand juries, to conduct secret interrogations: "And those secret interrogations

The destruction of the meaning of "excise" and its rebirth with a new meaning adequate to greatly expand governmental power began in a 1796 Supreme Court decision, *Hylton v. United States*. John Marshall had not yet been appointed to the Court, and his *Marbury v. Madison* had not yet fully answered all arguments as to the Court's obligation to rule upon constitutionality.

Congress had enacted a new tax, which it called a carriage duty, levied uniformly upon all carriages "for the conveyance of persons." Daniel Hylton, of Virginia, had 125 carriages and refused to pay the tax. In the lawsuit over his tax liability, he and the Government stipulated that Hylton owned the 125 carriages for the conveyance of persons, but that he kept them for his own separate use, did not rent them out, and did not furnish carriage service to people for hire.[31] He objected that the duty was a direct tax on his carriage, not apportioned as required by the Constitution, and so void.

Each justice delivered his opinion separately and orally from the bench, as was then the custom. All agreed that "duties, imposts, and excises" referred to indirect taxes required to be uniform instead of being apportioned.

None of the justices made any reference to any theoretical distinction between direct and indirect taxes, nor to the practical reason for such distinction, nor did any refer to Blackstone or *The Federalist*.

Each justice assumed, from the many duties levied in England, that the United States must have the power to tax carriages, though the American taxing power was limited and the English unlimited. Each who discussed the matter at any length undertook to demonstrate the difficulty of apportioning a tax on carriages on the basis of population. One justice built factual inequality into a mathematical assumption and did a computation to demonstrate that it would result in a tax inequality. He assumed that the number of carriages in the United States was equal to the number of congressmen, 105, and that the total tax was to be $1,050. He then proceeded, by computation, to demonstrate the gross inequality of the tax as applied to Virginia and Connecticut by assuming that, though Virginia's population was less than three times that of Connecticut, Virginia would have twenty-five times as many carriages, and by assuming that, though the two states had in combination less than one-fourth the nation's population, they would own almost seventy percent of the nation's carriages! He thus proved to a mathematical certainty that if you start out with a false assumption, you will reach a false conclusion every time. Not one of the justices noticed that Congress had the unquestionable power to tax carriages being rented or used in a carriage service or carriages being imported, manufactured, or sold, where the tax burden could ultimately be passed to the consumer![32]

---

can be carried on day or night, in a public place or a 'hideout,' a court-house, an office building, a hotel room, a home, or a place of business; so well is this ambulatory power understood in Michigan that the one-man grand jury is also popularly referred to as the 'portable grand jury.' " One such portable grand jury compelled William Oliver to testify before him, decided Oliver's testimony did not "jell," and so "the judge-grand jury immediately charged him with contempt, immediately convicted him, and immediately sentenced him to sixty days in jail."

31. What possible use one man could have for 125 carriages did not appear, and for all that the Supreme Court could tell, he may have used the carriages to operate a slave trade business, so that a tax on the carriages would have been an indirect tax he could have passed on to the slave-buyers.

32. One justice, concluding that a tax imposed directly upon an owner's carriages

Here are the errors of judicial technique in the decision: (1) the judges assumed the conclusion they were required to reach, i.e., they assumed that the United States *had to have the power to tax carriages,* because a carriage "duty" was imposed in England, whose legislative body was subject to no constitutional taxing restraints; (2) they were utterly confused as to the subject they were deciding, which was understandable, because the word "duty" appearing in the Constitution was absolutely meaningless in relation to the direct-indirect taxation dichotomy, except in its colloquial application to excises and tariffs; and (3) they showed no evidence of having attempted to educate and thereby qualify themselves to decide the matter by studying either the leading popular legal authority of the day or the leading popular writing of the day as to the meaning of the entire Constitution.

For the next ninety-nine years, whenever Congress found urgent need to impose taxes directly on the people and their wealth, and failed to take time to apportion the taxes, the Supreme Court found ways to uphold these illegal direct taxes. When Congress imposed an illegal tax on incomes (before this was legalized by Constitutional amendment), the Court opined that if a carriage tax is an indirect tax, then a tax on incomes is bound to be indirect,[33] and then when Congress imposed a direct death tax on decedents' estates, the Court said that it had already held income taxes to be indirect, and they could not be distinguished in principle from death taxes,[34] which indeed they cannot.

In the income tax case, as in the carriage tax case before it and the estate tax case after it, the Supreme Court substituted its judgment of fairness for the Constitutional mandate as to the only way Congress was empowered to exercise its direct taxing power; and the unfairness was assumed on the basis of far-fetched factual assumptions whose truth or falsity were totally unknown to the Court.

But finally, in 1895, the Supreme Court actually gave mature consideration to the distinction between direct and indirect taxation by centering its attention upon the Constitution instead of upon temporary governmental objectives, and it found what those terms meant when the Constitution was written.

---

is not a direct tax, quoted from the basic 1776 work on economic theory, Adam Smith's *Wealth of Nations.* However, the quotation from Smith did not concern itself with the general taxing power, but with direct and indirect methods of taxing income. As expenditures are usually made from income, Smith postulated that government could indirectly tax income by taxing expenditures, taxing things rapidly consumed while they are still in the hands of the dealer, and taxing things kept a long time, such as silver plate and carriages, after the consumer purchases them. This has nothing to do with the division of the entire governmental taxing power into direct and indirect taxes.

33. This was asserted by the Supreme Court in *Pacific Insurance Company v. Soule,* in upholding an unapportioned income tax enacted by Congress under the impetus of Civil War financial needs. The Court quoted a single sentence from page 318 of I Blackstone, *Commentaries,* but disregarded the fact that everything preceeding and everything following that isolated sentence on page 318 was concerned with indirect taxation by excise duties on commodities, where the actual burden is passed to the purchaser who pays the tax as a portion of the purchase price.

34. *Scholey v. Rew,* sustaining an unapportioned Civil War Tax on the succession to ownership of property upon death. The Court mentioned *The Federalist's* statement that duties and excises must be uniform instead of being apportioned, but made no mention of the statement in the same article of *The Federalist,* No. 36, that excises are taxes on products which would be passed indirectly to the consumer as a part of his purchase price.

The case was *Pollock v. Farmers' Loan & Trust Co.* In it the Supreme Court declared unconstitutional a newly-enacted Federal income tax. The Court did not pretend that opposing opinions did not exist—it met and destroyed them by demonstrating their incorrectness. It engaged in no attempts at mathematical computations based upon assumed and false figures, but yielded to the supremacy of the Constitution.

The Court noted that the tax and decision on Hylton's carriages came when the United States feared war and was in special need of additional revenue. The Court stated what direct taxation actually consisted of—"direct taxation on accumulated property," and reviewed the thinking of the Constitutional Convention, that this direct taxing power, substituted for the apportioned contributions under the Articles of Confederation, was expected to be used by the Federal Government only when necessary, and then by following the apportionment command. The Court quoted from both the writings of Blackstone and *The Federalist* as to the clear distinction between direct and indirect taxation.

The Court discussed what had been one of the strongest reasons to assume the *Hylton* decision correct, that Alexander Hamilton, as Secretary of the Treasury needing to raise money, had argued the case for the Government. Hamilton's superiority in advocacy was obvious and was acknowledged.[35] Most of Hamilton's arguments, which were not available in writing until many years after the *Hylton* decision, concentrated upon examples of things it had pleased the English Parliament to label "excises" at various times, and his argument mostly avoided the subject of the meaning of direct taxation. What he said in arguing for his right to receive carriage tax money into the treasury was contrary (and far inferior) to what he had written so well in *The Federalist.*

Hamilton had argued that direct taxes included poll taxes, real property taxes, and taxes against the total of the citizen's wealth, real and personal; he made no effort to advance any theory as to how a tax imposed by the government upon all of a man's personal property could be "direct" and a tax on only half of his property "indirect." In *Pollock v. Farmers' Loan & Trust Co.*, Chief Justice Fuller properly assessed Hamilton's carriage argument: "Any loose expressions in definition of the word 'direct,' so far as conflicting with his well considered views in *The Federalist*, must be regarded as the liberty which the advocate usually thinks himself entitled to take with his subject."

The Court insisted that neither claimed injustices from tax apportionment,[36] nor the claimed great need for the tax [37] could justify the judiciary's disregard of

---

35. Chief Justice Spencer, of New York, said: "Alexander Hamilton was the greatest man this country has ever produced. I knew him well. . . . He argued cases before me while I sat as judge on the bench. Webster has done the same. In power of reasoning Hamilton was the equal of Webster, and more than this can be said of no man. . . . I can truly say that hundreds of politicians and statesmen of the day got both the web and woof of their thought from Hamilton's brains. He, more than any other man, did the thinking of the time." Veeder, *Legal Masterpieces.*

36. "If, in the changes of wealth and population in particular states, apportionment produced inequality, it was inequality stipulated for, just as the equal representation of the states, however small, in the Senate, was stipulated for. . . . If it be true that the Constitution should have been so framed that a tax of this kind could not be laid, the instrument defines the way for its amendment."

37. "We are not here concerned with the question of whether an income tax be or be not desirable, nor whether such a tax would enable the government to diminish taxes on consumption and duties on imports, and to enter upon what

Constitutional limitations upon governmental taxing power. In short, the Court insisted that its only function was the judicial function—not to shape the law, but to discover and enforce it, having no responsibility for the content of either the Constitution or the acts of Congress. Under this great decision, the finest ever written on the Federal taxing power, but more importantly under the Constitution itself, the Federal estate tax levied now is an obvious violation of the Constitution.

How, then, do we happen to have such an unconstitutional tax? One reason is that *Pollock v. Farmers' Loan & Trust Co.* involved income tax. Such tax without apportionment has now been legalized by constitutional amendment, so the teaching of the decision is never read. Another reason we have federal estate taxation is *Knowlton v. Moore.*

In 1898, three years after the Supreme Court demonstrated the unconstitutionality of the income tax, Congress enacted a "War Revenue Act" which included an estate tax. Congress had done this before, and such a tax had been held valid in *Scholey v. Rew* [38] on the rationale that if carriages are taxable, so is income, and if income is, so are estates.

Knowlton died leaving an estate valued at over two and a half million dollars. His executors paid the estate tax under protest, and *Knowlton v. Moore* was their suit for refund of the tax money. The Supreme Court held the unapportioned estate tax not to be a direct tax, in an opinion written by Justice Edward D. White, who had written a dissenting opinion in the *Pollock* case. Justice White did not approach it from the premise of the Constitution, but instead discussed the historical and present nature of "death duties" both here and in other nations. [39] The Court thoroughly established that most countries had found death taxes useful, which clearly cannot affect the meaning of any provision of the Constitution.

Finally, the Court came to the question of whether the tax directly on Mr. Knowlton's entire accumulated wealth was a direct tax. The Court began this attempt by noting that it had long ago been held in *Scholey v. Rew* that an estate tax is an indirect tax because the Court held it to be an excise. The Court then attempted to demonstrate that the recent income tax decision of *Pollock v. Farmers' Loan & Trust Co.* did not overrule the old estate tax decision. This was quite true in the sense that Chief Justice Fuller did not expressly declare the old case overruled—he merely demonstrated the falsity of the assumptions on which all the *past decisions* upholding unapportioned direct taxes had been based.

---

may be believed to be a reform of its fiscal and commercial system. Questions of that character belong to the controversies of political parties, and cannot be settled by judicial decision."

38. Discussed above, n. 34.

39. The Court showed that ancient Rome, France, Germany and England all had death taxes considered to be taxes upon the transmission of ownership at the time of death, which is correct but has nothing to do whether these taxes are direct or indirect. The Court quoted a definition enacted by the French legislative authority: "Direct taxes bear immediately upon persons, upon the possession and enjoyment of rights; indirect taxes are levied upon the happening of an event or exchange." The Court did not assert those foreign governments were subject to the taxing restraints found in the Constitution of the United States, nor did the Court enunciate any rationale as to how French legal theories, totally foreign to the Anglo-American common law, might be related to the meaning of any phrase in our Constitution.

The Court then asserted there was nothing in the *Pollock* decision to imply that inheritance taxes "which had from all time been considered as being imposed, not on property, . . . but . . . on the transmission or receipt of property . . ." were direct taxes.[40] The Court merely *asserted* the recent decision's lack of any implication that inheritance taxes were direct taxes, making no effort to demonstrate the correctness of this assertion; this is understandable, because the assertion was false. At one point in working his way to the conclusion that the estate tax was lawful and while discussing a particular aspect of this new wartime tax, Justice White even inadvertently but accurately referred to it as a tax on property!

The Court then proceeded to discuss whether "a tax is a direct tax on property which has at all times been considered as the antithesis of such a tax; that is, has ever been treated as a duty or excise, because of the particular occasion which gives rise to its levy." The Court stated the Knowlton executors' contention that any tax is a direct tax unless the tax burden can be shifted to another person in paying a purchase price, and that such was the holding of the recent *Pollock* income tax decision. The Court answered this by saying: "The fallacy is in the premise. It is true that in the income tax cases the theory of certain economists by which direct and indirect taxes are classified with reference to the ability to shift the same was averted to. The constitutional meaning of the word direct was the matter decided." The Court thus blinded itself to the fact that in the income tax decision, the chief justice had carefully and thoroughly proven that this "economic theory" of direct/indirect taxation was written into the Constitution.

Thus, by a series of decisions, did the Supreme Court refuse to enforce the direct taxation provisions of the Constitution, every such decision involving a tax levied for war purposes. The Court destroyed the clear meaning of "excise" and substituted a new and artificial meaning, equating it to a tax on the doing of an act, though its meaning when the words were written had not the slightest implication that it was based upon a differentiation between acts and things.[42]

Running through these decisions are the very worst examples of the malperformance of the judicial function: The utilization of supposed facts that are false, because although presented as suppositions, they are impossible suppositions; and the utilization of contrived facts and arguments to demonstrate the injustice or impracticality of constitutional provisions, when any provisions that may be unjust or impractical are subject to change by using the procedure for constitutional amendment. When judges usurp this fundamental amendatory power, they dishonor their oaths of office.

Of Crime and Punishment:

Mapp, Miranda, Stovall, Katz, Desist, Escobido, Chimel are the names of some of those who were accused of criminal offenses and whose cases were considered by the Supreme Court during the past decade. To the police officer, the most

---

40. N. 34 above.

41. Actually, the tax involved in *Nichol v. Ames* was an excise, a stamp tax upon documents executed in the sales of commodities in the exchanges, in that case the Chicago Board of Trade, and the taxpayers there in fact did attempt to avoid payment of the excise on abstruse economic theories.

42. As we have seen, "duty" was merely a word Parliament had applied to anything it chose, including such direct taxes as head taxes and taxes on real and personal property, and "excise" was applied to taxes on the license, or right, to engage in particular businesses, but primarily to property itself, such as silver wire in the hands of the wiremaker and plate in the hands of the retail seller.

famous of these is *Miranda v. Arizona,* which involved warnings a police officer should give to an arrested suspect. Ernesto Miranda's name has since been immortalized, both in judicial opinions and police lingo, as the name of the "Miranda Warning." Most good police officers carry cards on which the "Miranda Warning" is printed, so they can read the exact language to suspects.

It is not our purpose to discover the content of criminal law, which is the lawyer's usual reason for reading judicial decisions. Our purpose is to discover guidelines for judging the quality of judicial fidelity to the Constitution and to the law in the decision of lawsuits. For this purpose, we seek cases that have been incorrectly decided, not to learn from their wisdom, but to examine them as samples of the wrong way to perform the judicial function.

The criminal decisions of the 1960's are invaluable for this purpose because there are so many of them in a narrow field, decided on the basis of the Constitution, declaring past constitutional decisions to be incorrect. Each such overruling decision presents an unavoidable question: Was the Supreme Court's old decision wrong, or is the Court wrong now in holding the old decision wrong? Or are both of them wrong? The only valid measure of judicial integrity is the standard of truth, and by this standard the fact that one decision was decided today and one a hundred years ago is immaterial. Either decision may be but the result of the day's madness.

One of the more recent (June 23, 1969) beneficiaries of the overruling process was Ted Steven Chimel, a man who, according to the facts stated in the Supreme Court's opinion, took pride in his work. He had shown a neighbor in Santa Ana, California, a stack of typewriters in his home and had told the neighbor they were "hotter than a $3 bill." Afterward, he told the neighbor he couldn't go bike riding with him that night because he was planning to "knock over" a coin shop. He later told the neighbor he started to break into a coin shop that night but had not gone through with it. The next day, the neighbor read a newspaper account of a coin shop burglary the night before, became suspicious, called the police, and Chimel was subsequently tried and his conviction upheld by the Supreme Court of California.

In *Chimel v. California,* the United States Supreme Court reversed the conviction on the ground that some of the evidence—the stolen coins—used to convict Chimel had been obtained by an illegal search in violation of the Constitution. California was free to try Chimel again, but it could not introduce in evidence the stolen coins, nor prove by police officers' testimony that the stolen coins were found in Chimel's home.

As an example of judicial technique in overruling earlier decisions, *Chimel v. California* is a good decision. The right protected by this decision is set out in most precise language in the Fourth Amendment:

> "The right of the people to be secure in their persons, houses, papers, and effects, against unreasonable searches and seizures, shall not be violated, and no Warrants shall issue, but upon probable cause, supported by Oath or affirmation, and particularly describing the place to be searched, and the persons or things to be seized."

This amendment brought into the Constitution the English insistence that every man's home is his castle, into which Government cannot intrude except by meeting the most stringent conditions required by necessity. The policeman is pitted against the individual citizen suspected of having committed a crime, and if the policeman is permitted to judge for himself whether he has reasonable grounds to search a citizen's home, he can usually persuade himself that he has ample reason for suspicion. Hence the requirements for search and arrest warrants are spelled out: If the policeman has reason to believe a citizen has burglarized a store and is hiding stolen merchandise in his home, the policeman and his witnesses can go before a magistrate, execute affidavits stating the facts that have made them suspicious. If the magistrate finds from the affidavits that it is probable that the citizen committed the crime or is concealing the stolen goods, the magistrate will issue arrest or search warrants, not merely authorizing, but *commanding* the officer to arrest the citizen, search his home, and seize the described property.

But sometimes it is quite reasonable for the officer to arrest a man without a warrant, and the Amendment only prohibits unreasonable searches and seizures. The most obvious example is when a policeman sees a man running from the scene of a robbery, where the victim stands shouting, "Stop thief!" It is quite reasonable for the officer to chase and capture the thief, and would be foolish for him to waste his time going to the courthouse to get an arrest warrant for one whose name he does not even know.[43] Having arrested the thief, if the officer does not search him, the thief may produce a concealed pistol and kill the officer, or he may be able to destroy the stolen money. This search of the prisoner's person at the time of arrest has long been known as a search incident to a lawful arrest, recognized as a lawful search permitted by the Constitution because of its reasonableness, born of necessity.

The search incident to arrest was the subject of the *Chimel* coin burglary case. The officers there clearly had enough facts to go to a magistrate and obtain an arrest warrant and a warrant to search Chimel's house; but they only sought and obtained an arrest warrant. They arrested Chimel in his home and searched not only his person, but his entire house, including drawers in his furniture, claiming this to be a search incident to the arrest. The Supreme Court rejected this argument, ruling illegal the meticulous search of the entire house when there had been ample time to seek a search warrant from a magistrate.

In so doing, the Court overruled a long series of earlier decisions which had expanded the search demanded by necessity to the extent that law enforcement officers were not only justified in violating the search warrant requirements of the Constitution, but were even enticed into violating those provisions. The decision exemplifies the proper manner of overruling past decisions, because the Court did not simply announce the overruling as if it were exercising some supposed power to change law, but it reviewed the past decisions and demonstrated why they were wrong, why they were not legitimately law at all.

The Court went back to an excellent and famous 1914 decision, *Weeks v. United States,* to discover the starting point in the improper expansion of the search incident to the arrest far beyond the demands of necessity. In the *Weeks* case, the Supreme Court had sought to pinpoint the issue before the Court by pointing out similar problems which were not involved:

---

43. The policeman's ignorance of the suspect's identity, though the suspicion of guilt is very strong, would likely result in his being unable to locate the thief after obtaining a warrant. This is a reasonable arrest because of the strong probability of guilt *and* because it is impossible to both make the arrest and seek a warrant.

"It is not an assertion of the right on the part of the Government, always recognized under English and American law, to search *the person* of the accused when legally arrested to discover and seize *the fruits or evidences of crime.*"

This little quotation about what the court was not deciding grew and grew. In the *Chimel* case, the Court said that it had "embellished" the *Weeks* quotation in *Carroll v. United States* by another statement not necessary to, and therefore not a holding, in that decision:

"When a man is legally arrested for an offense, whatever is found upon his person or *in his control* which it is unlawful for him to have and which may be used to prove the offense may be seized and used as evidence in the prosecution.*

Thus the emergency right to search the person, primarily for self-protection, grew into a right to seize things not on his person but merely under his control, without any reason given for this unwarranted expansion of governmental power.

The Court then discussed its subsequent decision of *Agnello v. United States,* in which the Court had announced in passing that the right to search "the *place where the arrest is made . . .* is not to be doubted." So by simple declaration, without reference to any historical or other justification, did the Supreme Court expand the right to search the person, dictated by necessity, into a right to search a place as well; a room, automobile, office, or home in which the suspect is arrested.

This method of violating the Constitution's search warrant requirements came into full bloom in *Harris v. United States,* in which the F.B.I. obtained only a warrant to arrest Harris, arrested him in the living-room of his apartment, then conducted a four-hour search of his apartment and all its contents, until they found a sealed envelope marked "George Harris Personal Papers." They ripped it open and found documents which sent Harris to prison for a crime totally different from the one for which he was arrested under the arrest warrant. The Supreme Court condoned this violation of the magistrate requirements of the Constitution by holding the ransacking search to be a search incident to a lawful arrest.

In overruling this series of decisions, described as starting with a hint, loosely converting it into dictum and finally elevating it into an actual holding, the Supreme Court in *Chimel v. California* quoted an earlier case:

"We are not dealing with formalities. The presence of a search warrant serves a high function. Absent some grave emergency, the Fourth Amendment has interposed a magistrate between the citizen and the police. This was done not to shield criminals nor to make the home a safe haven for illegal activities. It was done so that an objective mind might weigh the need to invade that privacy in order to enforce the law. The right of privacy was deemed too precious to entrust to the discretion of those whose job is the detection of crime and the arrest of criminals. . . . And so the Constitution requires a magistrate to pass on the desires of the police before they violate the privacy of the home. We cannot be true to that constitutional requirement and excuse the absence of a search warrant without a showing by those who seek exemption from the constitutional mandate that the exigencies of the situation made that course imperative."

The Court demonstrated in the *Chimel* case that this entire cancerous growth of improper decisions proceeded from statements made which were unnecessary, expanded in subsequent decisions in which the Court was not discharging the judicial obligation to decide the particular point on which it speculated, and finally arriving at a holding on no basis but unsupported decisions, all without first analyzing the language of the Fourth Amendment itself and approaching the problem from obvious inferences based upon the language of the Constitution.

These decisions enticed law enforcers to disregard the search warrant requirements of the Constitution. The constitutional search warrant requirements were strict. They required that the warrant specifically describe the place to be searched and the things to be seized. Once an officer found the thing he was ordered to seize, it was his obligation to stop searching and to terminate his invasion of the citizen's home. If in searching, he saw something else that would be an excellent piece of evidence, such as a hand-written note, a bloody garment, a sealed envelope, he could not seize them because the search warrant did not order him to seize those things.

But the Supreme Court decisions on search incident to an arrest repeatedly said that in conducting a search incident to a lawful arrest, the officer could seize not only the fruits of the crime and the instrumentalities used in committing the crime (a gun, burglary tools, a note passed by a bank robber to a teller commanding her to hand over her currency), but could also seize any *evidence* for use in the prosecution. It would take a dense law-enforcement officer not to realize that if he should happen to "catch up" with the suspect when the suspect was sitting in a house the officer wanted to search, it would be far better if the officer did not even have a restrictive search warrant, but only had an arrest warrant.

From almost the first, it was uniformly accepted that the Fourth Amendment and the rest of the Bill of Rights did not govern state governments to any extent: As far as the Federal Constitution was concerned, states were free to abolish trial by jury, to permit arbitrary searches of private homes, to abolish the freedom of the press, to maintain official state religions. It was not until the adoption of the Fourteenth Amendment with its clauses prohibiting particular actions by state governments,[44] that there arose any recognized constitutional basis for imposing the restrictions of the Federal Bill of Rights on any state.[45]

For the most part, the Federal Government did not even have any law of arrest until the enactment of the National Prohibition Act. Before that, the power of a federal officer to make an arrest was governed by the law of the state where he made the arrest. It is not surprising, therefore, that it was not until the Twentieth Century that the Supreme Court had occasion tò give much attention to the effect of violations of the Fourth Amendment prohibitions concerning arrest, search, and seizure of property. By then, the state courts had thoroughly adjudicated these common-law and state constitutional questions without reference to the Constitution of the United States.

---

44. The Supreme Court still has not held that the entire Federal Bill of Rights is effective to prohibit violation of those rights by the states.

45. For more than a hundred years after the Constitution was adopted, Congress enacted few criminal laws, and these within narrow fields; extensive Federal criminal prosecutions did not begin until the Prohibition fiasco, and broad criminal policing by the Federal Government did not begin until the 1930's. During this period, most criminal law enforcement was handled by the states, and it was in state courts that most of the law as to the rights of criminal defendants was developed or restated from the common law.

The first Fourth Amendment decision [46] as to the effect of an illegal search and seizure of property came in the 1914 decision of *Weeks v. United States*. A U.S. Marshal went into Weeks' home, searched it, and seized some papers. Weeks was criminally prosecuted and asked the Federal Court to order the marshal to return his papers, but the court refused to do this; and the court permitted the jury to receive and consider Weeks' papers stolen by the marshal. The Supreme Court held these papers could not be received in evidence, but must be returned to Weeks, the Court saying:

> "The effect of the Fourth Amendment is to put the *courts of the United States and federal officers*, in the exercise of their power and authority, under limitations and restraints as to the exercise of such power and authority, and to forever secure the people, their persons, houses, papers, and effects, against all unreasonable searches and seizures under the guise of law. . . . The case in the aspect in which we are dealing with it involves the *right* of the court in a criminal prosecution to retain for the purposes of evidence the letters and correspondence of the accused, seized in his house in his absence and without his authority, by a United States marshal holding no warrant for his arrest and none for the search of his premises. . . . If letters and private documents can thus be seized and held and used in evidence against a citizen accused of an offense, the protection of the Fourth Amendment, declaring his right to be secure against such searches and seizures, is of no value, and, so far as those thus placed are concerned, might as well be stricken from the Constitution. The efforts of *the courts and their officials* to bring the guilty to punishment, praiseworthy as they are, are not to be aided by the sacrifice of those great principles established by years of endeavor and suffering which have resulted in their embodiment in the fundamental law of the land. . . ."

This constitutional rule commanding exclusion of evidence—not really a rule so much as an act of judicial obedience to the Constitution—was met with criticism. The strongest criticism was that the rule of exclusion was an illogical rule of evidence, that it excluded evidence which would aid the jury in determining the truth, the establishment of truth being the purpose of the courts' existence.[47]

Such arguments overlooked the fact that the constitutionally required ruling did not create a rule of evidence. It obliterated evidence which should never have come into the Government's possession. Equally important, the arguments over-

---

46. An earlier landmark case, *Boyd v. United States*, arose under the Fifth Amendment, rather than the Fourth Amendment. The case was criminal in practical effect, the government tried to subpoena Boyd's papers to be used against him, and the Supreme Court held this couldn't be done because of the Fifth Amendment's prohibition against compelling a person to be a witness against himself in a criminal prosecution. The result was that the desired evidence was excluded from a trial, a result *expressly commanded* by the Fifth Amendment.

47. The argument was most forcefully made by the nation's most respected authority on the law of evidence, Professor John Henry Wigmore. It was urged that the truth-finding functions of the courts (this being the central idea of the law of evidence, the reliability of evidence to prove that which it is offered to prove) should be protected, and that law-enforcement officers' violations of the Constitution should be punished by criminal prosecutions for violating the Constitution, or by allowing the wronged citizen to sue the officer for violating his Fourth Amendment rights, as in the common law suits for false arrest and malicious prosecution.

looked the fact that both the courts and the law of evidence are inferior to the Constitution. In short, the criticism itself was irrational. It was based upon a false premise, a premise which converted obedience to a constitutional command into a supposed rule of evidence.

But the criticism on the basis of theories of the law of evidence persisted. In time, the Supreme Court enunciated other theoretical bases for holding that illegal evidence could not be introduced. One was that the Supreme Court, in the exercise of its supervisory authority over federal officers, could enforce rules designed to discourage violations of the Constitution by those officers. From a constitutional viewpoint, this rationale did not rise above the critics' rationale: There is not one word in the Constitution granting judges any supervisory power over federal policemen. All federal investigative agencies are parts of different departments which in turn are a part of the executive branch of the government; all such officers, in the performance of their duties, are subject to the supervisory power of the President. Indeed the Constitution imposes named duties [48] upon the President, including: "he shall take Care that the Laws be faithfully executed and shall Commission all the Officers of the United States."

In 1949, after the critical arguments that the *Weeks'* decision excluding illegally-seized evidence from trials was not good evidence law, the Supreme Court decided *Wolf v. Colorado*. The Court decided in that case, for the first time in all the years since the Fourteenth Amendment was adopted in 1868, that the Amendment's prohibition against states depriving people of their lives, liberty or property but by due process of law extended to the people the Fourth Amendment's protection against unreasonable searches and seizures, and gave the people this immunity from action by their own state governments as well as by the Federal Government. As we shall see, the determination that the restrictions of the Fourth Amendment limit the powers of state governments is correct.[49]

But then the Court went on to characterize the *Weeks* decision as a choice of a means of "enforcing" the Fourth Amendment search and seizure prohibitions, an inaccurate characterization.[50] The Court held Colorado was forbidden by the Fourteenth Amendment to conduct unreasonable searches and seizures, but Colorado was not required to observe the rule binding upon Federal Courts to refuse to receive in evidence that which had been obtained by illegal searches. How "to enforce" the prohibition against unreasonable searches was left to Colorado, now empowered to devise "other methods which, if consistently enforced, would be equally effective."

With *Wolf v. Colorado's* decision that the Federal Constitution's Fourth Amendment was now binding upon the states, but that each state could decide for itself what it wanted to do about the matter, and with the Supreme Court's supposed "supervisory power" over Federal agents working under the President, but with the Court claiming no supervisory powers over state investigators working under the authority of governors, county sheriffs, and city chiefs of police,

---

48. Though the Constitution gives the President certain executive powers, it imposes no *duties* upon him but these: To appoint the officers of the government, report to Congress on the State of the Union, recommend legislation, receive Ambassadors, and enforce the laws.
49. But on a rationale entirely different from that improvised by the Supreme Court. See below, Chapter VII.
50. See *Weeks* decision, p. 88.

they being parts of different governments, one might expect from this mélange some bizarre results.

An immediate result was the "Silver Platter Doctrine," announced by the Supreme Court in *Lustig v. United States* the same day the Court decided the *Wolf* case. It held the obvious in view of the Supreme Court's *Wolf* analysis: If a state officer searched a home in violation of the Constitution of the United States, the problem of what to do about the officer's illegal conduct was a problem the state could handle, but if the offense involved were also a Federal offense and the state officer should present the illegal evidence on a silver platter to a Federal officer, it could be used in a Federal prosecution as evidence which would help the trial court in its endeavor to discover the truth.

Was it proper for the Supreme Court to delegate to the states the power to devise rules to enforce the search and seizure immunity held incorporated into the Fourteenth Amendment by its Due Process Clause? It would be more correct to inquire whether the Supreme Court itself actually has any power to devise rules to "enforce" any provision of the Constitution. It clearly had not only the power but the duty to compare laws and acts of officers of government with the Constitution when required in its decision of lawsuits. But the power to "enforce?" Enforcement is a more active thing than the negative disregard of unconstitutional laws or the negative refusal to help government officials benefit from their violations of the Constitution.

The Constitution contemplates that it shall be obeyed,[51] not enforced. That each legislative, executive and judicial officer shall bind himself by oath to support the Constitution, which sets each branch of the Government apart from and opposition to the other two branches, in the hope that the jealousy of each for its own powers will preserve the supremacy of the Constitution and the right of the people to be protected from the prime source of tyranny—one's own government.

It is true that the Constitution gives Congress the power to make necessary and proper laws to carry into execution any *power* given by the Constitution to any department or officer of government, but this law-making power was given to Congress, not to the courts. And the Fourth Amendment provides that our immunity from "unreasonable searches and seizures, shall not be violated, . . ." This is not a grant of power to be enforced by laws. It is a denial of power to be respected by every executive and judicial officer in the performance of the duties of his office.

But a change was wrought by the Fourteenth Amendment. It was through the Due Process Clause of the Fourteenth Amendment that the Supreme Court held that every citizen's immunity from unreasonable searches and seizures by the Federal Government was broadened to protect the citizen from the state governments as well. The Fourteenth Amendment does provide for its enforcement against the state governments subjected to its commands: "The Congress shall have power to enforce, by appropriate legislation, the provisions of this article." This is where the United States Government's rule-making power lies—in our congressmen and senators, whom we can influence by our votes, not in the judiciary.

The Supreme Court's great *Wolf v. Colorado* experiment of delegating to the states the Congressional power to decide how to "enforce" against those same

---

51. Laws may be enforced against individual citizens commanded to obey, but the Constitution directs no command to any private citizen, with the single exception of the prohibition against the existence of slavery and involuntary servitude.

states the prohibitions of the Fourteenth Amendment came to an end in the Court's June 19, 1961, decision of *Mapp v. Ohio*. In *Mapp v. Ohio*, the Court ruled that in state criminal trials, the "imperative of judicial integrity" required the exclusion of evidence illegally seized by state officers, and that if the acts of state officers in violating the Constitution instead of proceeding properly upon written search warrants should result in the guilty escaping punishment, "it is the law that sets him free."

If one restricted his reading to these short quotations and some of the other rhetorical writing in *Mapp v. Ohio*, one might conclude that the Court had now reasserted its prior allegience to the view that it and every other court is inferior to the Constitution, each obligated to assure that its judgments will not violate the Constitution.

Not so. In *Mapp v. Ohio*, the Court only treated the symptoms of its past mistakes, and did so by reaffirming its incorrect view of its own position in relation to the Constitution, which had led it into its past errors: The supposition that the Constitution permitted the Court *any* choice as to whether illegal evidence could be used in criminal trials; the supposition that the Court had some power from some source to design rules of greater or lesser severity for the enforcement of the Fourteenth Amendment.

Having thus completed its actual holding, the Court then wrote at approximately twice the length [52] to demonstrate the *wisdom* of overruling the delegation aspect of *Wolf v. Colorado*, prefacing this with a statement recognizing it was not necessary to the decision.

Instead of roundly condemning *Wolf v. Colorado* as a decision both incorrect and violative of the Constitution, the Court actually sought to demonstrate its own nobility as an experimenter in the improvement of Federal-State relations, whose experiment had to be overruled because the few incorrigible states had failed to improvise adequate alternative methods of enforcing the Fourteenth Amendment. The states were given a chance; they failed to perform adequately, so the grace period extended to them by the magnanimity of *Wolf v. Colorado* was withdrawn by *Mapp v. Ohio*.

The next development of *Mapp v. Ohio* is a leader of many decisions that followed it, and as a leader, it deserves special attention. Though subsequent cases have carried much further the reasoning in the Supreme Court's 1965 decision of *Linkletter v. Walker*, history must surely accord to *Linkletter v. Walker* the recognition it so richly deserves: One of the sorriest decisions ever rendered by the Supreme Court.

Linkletter v. Walker was the next "logical" step following *Mapp v. Ohio*. Notice the name of the case. Though its subject was the imposition of criminal punishment by using evidence obtained by an illegal search of Linkletter's home, its title does not have the name of a state in it, nor the name of the United States. It was a *habeas corpus* case, Linkletter was a convicted prisoner, and Walker was the warden of the Louisiana State Prison.

---

52. The Court pointed out that while formerly, the majority of the state courts did not exclude illegally-seized evidence, the pendulum had now swung so that exclusion of such evidence had become the popularly-supported rule among state courts; that it had earlier refused to rule that state courts must exclude such evidence, because *Wolf v. Colorado* was so recent that state courts had lacked time to come up with alternative enforcement methods. Hence the Court was impelled, as the Court put it, to close the last courthouse door to such evidence.

In *Mapp v. Ohio,* the Supreme Court's opinion was the final opinion in a series of appeals that directly followed Miss Mapp's conviction (for possessing obscene publications). The process of deciding guilt or innocence was not yet brought to its final conclusion, and the Supreme Court's reversal merely sent the case back to the Ohio trial court where the case could be re-tried without the illegal evidence. But when the entire adjudicative procedure has been completed, as in *Linkletter v. Walker,* even if the case has been decided incorrectly, the defendant sooner or later has no courts left to which he can appeal, and service of his penitentiary sentence begins. The only remaining judicial remedy by which he can escape imprisonment is *habeas corpus,* in which he claims that he is being illegally imprisoned, though he has been found guilty by a jury, sentenced by a judge, though his conviction has been affirmed by the state supreme court and in some cases by the Supreme Court of the United States.

Many people go to prison partly by virtue of their own free decisions that they *refuse to receive* the constitutional rights guaranteed to them.[53] Usually, whether from guilty plea or from trial, the prisoner's imprisonment is lawful and *habeas corpus* does not help him because he has been properly adjudged guilty and properly imprisoned. But sometimes, the judgment ordering imprisonment violates the Constitution so that it is void and does not justify imprisonment. Imprisonment becomes state imposition of involuntary servitude other than "as punishment for crime whereof the party shall have been *duly* convicted," and the imprisonment itself is prohibited by this language of the Thirteenth Amendment. This may occur when a man is tortured into falsely confessing or when a prosecuting attorney coerces a man into falsely pleading guilty. Thus, though the court record beautifully reflects a perfectly ordinary guilty plea, that beautiful court record was built upon state coercion which deprived the defendant of *all* the constitutional rights created to assure fair trials, usually without the trial judge having the slightest inkling of it.

Such constitutional defects may bring the judgment of the court ordering imprisonment into conflict with the Constitution's supremacy, and render the court order void as justification for continuing to hold the man in prison. *Habeas corpus* can then free the citizen, leaving the state free to try him again. The only alternative is to disregard the supremacy of the Constitution and to nullify the Bill of Rights and the Fourteenth Amendment.

Linkletter v. Walker presented such a constitutionally defective prosecution, based upon an illegal search of Linkletter's home. The search was illegal even under the Supreme Court's old expansion of the search incident to lawful arrest (then still "in effect," if one illogically considers the Supreme Court's decisions as part of the supreme law rather than as mere interpretations of that law), because Linkletter was not in the place being searched—his home—but was in jail when the officers searched his home. Police officers took his keys from him, used them to break into and search his home without first presenting their proof to a magistrate and seeking a warrant. The Supreme Court ruled on the *Linkletter* case in 1965, four years after it had held in *Mapp v. Ohio* that the Constitution prohibited states from using in criminal prosecutions evidence seized in violation

---

53. The most common example of the surrender of constitutional rights is that of the defendant who pleads guilty, often because he knows the evidence against him is overwhelming. By his free choice, he surrendered constitutional rights: Representation by counsel, trial by jury, the right to be confronted with the witnesses against him, the right to remain free unless proven guilty beyond a reasonable doubt.

of the Fourteenth Amendment and that the imperative of judicial integrity prevented the Court from condoning this violation of the Constitution.

Linkletter was not one who stood silently under some secret threat and never openly claimed that his constitutional rights had been violated. He screamed all the way to the Supreme Court of Louisiana that his constitutional rights had been violated. The Louisiana Supreme Court held that the search of Linkletter's home was lawful, as an incident to his arrest, and that his conviction should be affirmed. But this holding by the Louisiana court came the year *before* the Supreme Court decided in *Mapp v. Ohio* that state courts could not use such illegal evidence in criminal trials.

The Supreme Court in the *Linkletter* case ruled that the writ of *habeas corpus* could not be used to free citizens whose rights to be immune from illegal searches had been violated, though the violation had formed the basis of the criminal prosecution, unless the prosecution was still "open" either in the course of trial or awaiting review by an appellate court, at the time the Supreme Court decided *Mapp v. Ohio*. Remember, all these cases stated they were decided under the Fourteenth Amendment's Due Process Clause, that clause prohibiting the states from taking any person's *liberty* without due process of law. If a court's judgment ordering imprisonment deprives a person of his liberty without due process of law, the citizen continues to be deprived of his liberty without due process of law until the moment he is released from prison. The time the individual spends in a cage or dungeon does not improve the quality of the state's past illegal conduct.

The manner in which the Supreme Court reached its *Linkletter* decision is amazing. The Supreme Court discovered in *Linkletter v. Walker,* for the first time in the more than 170-year history of its sitting, a new principle never before discerned: That when it determines, in the decision of a lawsuit, that certain government action violates a fundamental right long protected by the Constitution against violation by any government action, then the Court can fix the precise date on which the people shall become entitled to claim the full legal protection of the constitutional right. This accorded with the Supreme Court's determination, to its satisfaction, that *it* had the power to make rules for the enforcement of the Fourteenth Amendment and the power to grant or withhold from the states this rule-making power, given only to the Congress by the Constitution.

The Supreme Court's discovery in *Linkletter v. Walker* of its power to fix the exact future date on which the people would become entitled to the legal protection of particular constitutional rights was of obvious benefit. In the exercise of its claimed power to enforce the Fourteenth Amendment by devising rules to be obeyed by all the courts in the land, the Court could minimize the possible disruptive effects by providing an effective date that would not inconvenience the nation's governments too much. This power could be used, as it was in *Linkletter v. Walker,* to protect the states' power to continue holding in involuntary servitude those whom they had convicted and imprisoned in violation of the Constitution.

One of the quotations from the *Linkletter* decision to be favored in later cases came at the point when the Court concluded that it did have the power to deny Mr. Linkletter the benefit of the constitutional supremacy it had earlier held to shield Miss Mapp from state imprisonment. The Court's conclusion in the *Linkletter* case:

"While the cases discussed above deal with the invalidity of statutes or the effect of a decision overturning long-established common-law rules, there seems to be no impediment—constitutional or philosophical—to the use of the same rule in the constitutional area where the exigencies of the situation require such an application."

The rationale that it doesn't seem like the Constitution forbids us to make our decisions applicable only in the future is hardly a careful probing of the extent and nature of the Court's own power. In its conclusion, the Court took no note of obvious objections to the existence of this power never before claimed by the Court: Whether the fixing of dates for the enforcement of rules can ever be other than the exercise of legislative power the Court was forbidden to exercise; whether any branch of the government has the power to declare constitutional mandates unenforceable before a certain date fixed by that branch or any other branch of government; whether the suspension of "enforcement" of constitutional "rules" in favor of governmental convenience or "the exigencies of the situation" could be other than a denial of the supremacy of the Constitution.

In commencing its discussion of whether it had the power to give only future effect to its decisions—though the decisions themselves were claimed to be required by the Constitution—the Court came straight to the point that this was completely contrary to historical views as to the proper mode of exercising judicial power. The Court said:

> "At common law there *was no authority for the proposition that judicial decisions made law only for the future.* Blackstone stated the rule that the duty of the court was not to 'pronounce a new law, but to maintain and expound the old one.' I Blackstone, *Commentaries,* 69 (15th Ed., 1809). This Court followed that rule in *Norton v. Shelby County,* . . . holding that unconstitutional action 'confers no rights; it imposes no duties; it affords no protection; it creates no office; it is, in legal contemplation, as inoperative as though it had never been passed.' . . . The judge rather than being the creator of the law was but its discoverer. Gray, *Nature and Sources of Law* 222 (1st Ed., 1909). In the case of the overruled decision, *Wolf v. Colorado,* supra, it was thought to be only a failure at true discovery and was consequently never the law; while the overruling one, *Mapp,* was not 'new law but an application of what is, and therefore had been, the true law.' Shulman, Retroactive Legislation, 13 *Encyclopedia of the Social Sciences* 335, 336 (1934).
>
> "On the other hand, Austin maintained that judges do in fact do something more than discover law; they make it interstitially by filling in with judicial interpretation the vague, indefinite, or generic statutory or common-law terms that alone are but the empty crevices of the law.[54] Implicit in such an approach is the admission when a case is overruled that the earlier decision was wrongly decided. However, rather than being erased by the later overruling decision it is considered as an existing juridical fact until overruled, and intermediate cases finally decided under it are not to be disturbed."

So the Court started with two opposing views as to the nature of judicial work, but the Court did not follow this with any reasoning as to why the views differ.

One cannot intelligently judge between apparently conflicting theories without questioning what difference it makes.[55] What of the deeply conflicting Blackstonian view that judges discover law for the decision of cases by intellectual en-

---

54. As to the source of this amplified Austinian view, see below, p. 192.

55. In medieval times, it is said that theologians disputed the size of angels, and how many could dance on the head of a pin, but in practical matters it made no

deavor and the Austinian view that judges actually make law? Each is right in a sense. The Common Law viewpoint was a view of the correct attitude that should guide judges in the performance of their duties, the view in which all the people who wrote the Constitution and the Bill of Rights were schooled, the view that permeates the writings about judicial power in *The Federalist*. One lawyer [56] wrote in a brief of the origin of this view:

> "When William, the bastard son of Duke Robert the Devil of Normandy, grabbed the crown of England by force of arms, he was most anxious to have Englishmen accept him as the legitimate King of England. The price was that he and his successors pledge to observe the 'Laws of Edward the Confessor,' and they so pledged.
> "The wonder is not that they made the pledge nor how often they broke it (which was often); the wonder is how far they went to honor it in all matters not affecting their immediate safety on the throne.
> "William caused a great deal of time and talent of the few literate men available to be spent trying to find out what this vague body of law was. See 2 *Holdsworth, History of English Law*, pp. 150-54.
> "By the time of King John, long after Henry II had set the new national common law on its way with a system of royal justice that competed for business with the old local courts, the pledge to be extracted was no longer observance of 'the laws of Edward the Confessor' but 'the law of the land.' See *Magna Carta*, ch. 39."

The Austinian view has accuracy, not as a guideline for the proper performance of judicial duties but as a look backward over history to assess the product of judicial labor. All lawyers perceive that the common law was developed in judicial opinions. The law as to murder, burglary, contracts, the complex law of real property, were all written in judicial decisions. But this law was written by an evolutionary process, with the judge always seeking to discover the commands of existing law. The Austinian argument is a valid intellectual exercise containing much truth, but as a guideline for judicial conduct, it is demonstrably false.

In choosing between the two "conflicting" views in its *Linkletter* decision, the Supreme Court's clincher was to quote a statement by the respected Justice Holmes that the "life of the law has not been logic; it has been experience." Justice Holmes was speaking of the common law, not constitutional law, and the common law utilized logic enlightened by experience and a sense of justice, and did so in the decision of one lawsuit at a time in the proper exercise of judicial power.

The argument, in a backward look at the development of the Common Law, that judges consciously "made" law is simply untrue. It misstates experience when one views the past as a guideline for present judicial conduct. The common-law judges did not consciously make a rule and then consciously sit and ponder what would be the next development of the rule. They decided a lawsuit, and the legal

---

difference: The pin still pinned, there was no way you could either get rid of the angels or entice more angels into camping on your pinhead, so it was a harmless dispute. Each of the conflicting disputants was right as far as it made any difference and as far as it could be judged by anyone other than one already biased in favor of the view of one of the disputants.

56. Philip M. Carden, Attorney for *Tennessee Appellate Bulletin, Inc., Amicus Curiae* in *Bohanan v. State*, unreported.

decision became evidence of the law. A year later or fifty years later, people got into a slightly different dispute involving the same point of law. They brought it before a judge, the judge had to decide it, and he looked to past decisions in this evolutionary process for guidance as to how he was *required* to decide it. It is still done the same way.

In the experience of the Common Law, judges were ministers of the law, not its masters. Blackstone summarized some of the parliamentary acts requiring judges to ever be loyal to the law:

"[It] is enacted that no commands shall be sent under the great seal, . . . in disturbance of the law; . . . and, though such commandments should come, the judges shall not cease to do right; . . . that the pretended power of suspending, or dispensing with laws, or the execution of laws, by regal authority without the consent of parliament, is illegal."

To deliberately adopt the backward-looking view that judges make law, capsulizing decades and centuries of experience, in preference to the view that judges merely discover law, was to choose the alternative of government by the whim of judges over the alternative of government of laws.

The Supreme Court's summary of the Austinian view included reference to the fact that when common-law judges decided a case wrong, and the judgment became final, and the judges later found that the rule of law stated in the incorrect decision conflicted with other rules of law, so that old decision had to be declared incorrect, the incorrect decision remained a past accomplished fact which could not be remedied. The case could not be re-decided. One hanged pursuant to an incorrect criminal decision could not be resurrected. A divorce incorrectly granted under a misunderstanding of a point of divorce law could not be nullified years later when one of the parties had re-married. If a court incorrectly decided property ownership under a mistaken view of the law, the ownership of property could not be changed years later, particularly if it had been sold to new and innocent owners. But the recognition that occasional injustices existed and could not be corrected could never honestly be taken as a guide for judicial conduct, as a declaration that judges *should* decide incorrectly, to satisfy their own personal whims, on the theory that after sufficient time passed, no one would be empowered to correct their wrongdoing. A recognition of the inevitability of human error in judicial decisions could not justify the adoption of rules designed to perpetuate injustice.

In the field of constitutional law, the theory that past judicial errors must always stand beyond any power of correction is totally illogical. When a man has been placed in prison by means which violate the Constitution, and the court has his case before it, either the violation of the Constitution will be perpetuated by keeping the man in prison, or constitutional supremacy will be maintained by requiring the state to release him from prison until it has proven him guilty in a manner permitted by the Constitution. Any other viewpoint subordinates the Constitution's declared supremacy to government's temporary convenience, and abandons in practice that which theory and rationality establish as inescapable.

In the *Linkletter* case, the Supreme Court deliberately chose the alternative of perpetuating what it held to be—and what in fact was—a violation of the Constitution. The supreme considerations were whether state officers had relied on past Supreme Court decisions [57] in proceeding to violate citizens' constitutional rights, and how much it would inconvenience the states to discontinue their perpetuation of the effects of their past violations of the Constitution. Faced with a choice between convenience and the supremacy of the Constitution, the Court chose convenience.

Turning its back upon the experience of the Common Law as to the manner in which judges should perform their limited functions and choosing instead the backward look at the patterns of judicial decisions as justification for intentional judicial law-making, the Court then looked to some past decisions to legitimate its choice of government by edict over government of laws. As an attempt to demonstrate that the prior decisions justified, or even permitted, the exercise of this new power which the Supreme Court openly arrogated to itself, *Linkletter v. Walker* was a miserable failure.

In discussing the necessary retroactivity or non-retroactivity of constitutional law enunciated in judicial decisions, the Court described an old decision by Chief Justice Marshall, *United States v. Schooner Peggy*. The case did not involve some supposed power to interpret the Constitution as requiring a particular result and then suspending the right of the people to demand that result until a stated date. Instead, it recognized the judicial obligation to decide a case in accordance with law.

The *Schooner Peggy* was a French ship captured by Americans in time of war, and the case was a suit to "condemn" the ship so that the capturers could share the prize money; a Federal court ordered the ship condemned and the prize money awarded on September 23, 1800, but seven days later, before the trial court's judgment became final, the American and French Plenipotentiaries signed a treaty in Paris which provided in part:

"Property captured, and not yet definitely condemned, or which may be captured before the exchange of ratifications . . . shall be mutually restored."

The judgment definitely condemning The Peggy had not yet become final, an appeal to the Supreme Court kept it from ever becoming final, and before that Court ruled on the case, the Senate ratified the treaty and made it a part of the Supreme Law of the Land, a command to the Supreme Court to decree the return of the ship to France. Among Chief Justice Marshall's statements quoted by the Court in the *Linkletter* case was the statement that "the court must decide according to existing laws, and if it be necessary to set aside a judgment . . . which cannot be affirmed but in violation of law, that judgment must be set aside." This was a submission to the supremacy of law, not an attempted suspension of supreme law. It involved the exercise of law-making power—by the President and the Senate in the case of law made by treaty, as contrasted with the exercise of judicial power.

---

57. And at that, such past decisions did not declare the illegal state conduct to be other than a violation of the Constitution; without a showing that the states had decided to do anything about such illegal searches—not even making it a crime for an officer to commit such a violation, any claim that states have relied upon Supreme Court rulings is far-fetched, except that it may be said that state officers assumed they were free to violate constitutional prohibitions with perfect impugnity. This hardly seems a valid reason to suspend constitutional supremacy in favor of expediency.

One of the strongest quotations appearing in the *Linkletter* case which might be thought to indicate that the Supreme Court has some power to make its *own decisions* inapplicable except to future cases was from the Court's 1863 decision of *Gelpcke v. Dubuque:* "However we may regard the late [overruling] case in Iowa as affecting the future, it can have no effect upon the past."

This seems to imply that courts can make their constitutional decisions applicable only to disputes occurring in the future, but the *Gelpcke* decision contains no such implication. The Iowa constitution imposed a low debt limit on the state government, and when the state legislature in the past had authorized various Iowa cities to issue bonds above the permissible state bond limit, the Iowa Supreme Court had held that the cities could issue the bonds. After the legislature authorized Dubuque to issue the bonds in question and Dubuque issued them, but later failed to redeem them, suit was brought by Gelpcke to collect on the bonds he had purchased. The Supreme Court of Iowa held that the legislature exceeded its power, Dubuque had no authority to issue the bonds in question, and the bonds were void. The Supreme Court of the United States reversed this decision, held that Iowa courts could not, by new legal decisions, deny Gelpcke the enforcement of bonds. Why not? The bonds were contractual obligations, entered into on faith of past Iowa decisions that cities could be authorized to issue bonds regardless of whether they exceeded the state debt limit. Article I of the Constitution of the United States denies to every state the power to make laws "impairing the obligation of contracts . . ." This is what Iowa sought to do through its supreme court.

In denying Iowa the power denied to it by the Constitution, the power to impair the obligation of contracts, the Supreme Court quite appropriately made it clear that it was not attempting to interfere with Iowa's power in the future to prohibit the issuance of bonds so long as it did not attempt to impair the obligation of such bonds already issued. By new legislation, by injunctions against the issuance of new bonds which had not yet become contracts, Iowa could enforce its new interpretation contained in *Gelpcke v. Dubuque,* so long as this was not used in an attempt to invalidate past contracts. The case did not even approach a suggestion that the Supreme Court might decide what the law requires and then suspend the requirements of law.

The strongest language the Supreme Court found in support of the unprecedented action it decided to take in keeping Mr. Linkletter in prison though his imprisonment violated the Court's own interpretation of the requirements of the Due Process Clause of the Fourteenth Amendment was found in a 1932 Supreme Court decision, *Great Northern Railway Co. v. Sunburst Oil & Refining Co.* During the course of the decision, Justice Cardozo engaged in a philosophical legal discussion of the difference between judicial decisions affecting only future events, in the legislative manner, or affecting events which had already occurred, the subject with which judicial decisions are concerned.

The case was quite similar to the Iowa *Gelpcke* case except that the contracts involved were freight rate contracts rather than bonds. These rates were fixed by a Montana rate-fixing agency, and the Supreme Court of Montana had earlier held that these rates were only tentative, that a shipper could pay them and then contest their correctness by suing for a refund. In the *Sunburst* case, the Montana Supreme Court held it had been incorrect in its past decision, that the state-fixed rates were not tentative after all, but were final, so that once a shipper paid them, he could not sue for a refund. But the Montana court recognized that past holdings as to the tentative nature of the rates was incorporated in the contract between Great Northern and Sunburst Oil, that it could not impair the validity of that contract, and so Sunburst Oil could sue for a refund. The railroad brought this decision to the Supreme Court, claiming Montana had to give it the benefit of the correct view of Montana law that the rates as fixed are final and that the shipper cannot sue for a partial refund.

The opinion of the United States Supreme Court made it clear that the Montana Court's earlier explanation of the meaning of Montana statutes—that the railroad rates were tentative and not incontestable—was written into and formed a part of the freight contract between Great Northern and Sunburst, so that the Montana court merely enforced the contract as written, whose obligation it was constitutionally denied the power to impair.

In holding that Montana's action did not violate the Federal Constitution, the Supreme Court equated the action through Montana's judicial system to action that might have been taken by Montana's legislature—that the state could have changed the freight rate determination system for the future, without impairing the obligation of past contracts, and that this would not violate the Federal Constitution. This reasoning, of what the state can do through its legislature it can do through its courts, as far as the Federal Constitution's Obligation of Contracts Clause is concerned, obviously has no application to the structure of the Federal Government, nor actually even to state governmental structure.

In its *Linkletter* decision, the Supreme Court patched together and emphasized a number of past decisions, applying to past facts rules of law—statutes, constitutional amendments, state court decisions enunciating state law— which were unknown or non-existent during the trial of the cases being reviewed by the Supreme Court.

The law-making or state law decision, in each case, came from a source outside the federal judicial system.

So in the *Linkletter* case, the Supreme Court assumed the power to make rules to "enforce" the Fourteenth Amendment or to decide that the Constitution itself directly required the exclusion of evidence, and then to suspend the protection of the Constitution. The case, recognized that the search of Linkletter's home was illegal, was a miscarriage of justice in that it kept Linkletter in prison, while the earlier decision whose "effective date" was fixed by the *Linkletter* case, freed Miss Mapp, though the illegal search of her home occurred after the illegal search of Linkletter's.

More tragic than the personal injustice is the thinking evidenced by these decisions, placing the Supreme Court in a position of superiority to the Constitution itself, not driven by the commands of law to its decisions, but deriving from some source a monumental discretion: To seize upon any requirement of the Constitution and to exercise the judicial will by.making rules to actively enforce the Constitution, or to withhold the making of rules; to grant to the states this rule-making power, or to withdraw it from the states; and all the while never noticing that in the entire Constitution, there is no word giving the Supreme Court authority to exercise any type of power other than judicial power, with but one exception: *Congress* is empowered to authorize the courts to appoint such governmental officials as Congress may choose. This strongly implies that no other non-judicial power may be given to the courts.[58]

---

58. Congressional inability to give the Supreme Court powers not given to it by the Constitution was the substance of Marshall's decision in *Marbury v. Madison.*

The Supreme Court's 1965 discovery, in its *Linkletter* decision, of its power to suspend the effectiveness of rules required by the Constitution, laid the ground-work for its ever-expanding use of the legislative rule-making power during the following years.[59] The first important exercise of the Court's claimed power to make rules to enforce the Constitution and then suspend those rules until their

---

59. One of the strangest adventures in the development of rules for the suspension of rights declared to be required by the Constitution was the adventure of a Mr. Shott, who gave his name to a *habeas corpus* case, *Tehan v. Shott*. The right involved is the federal constitutional right of a defendant in a criminal case not to be compelled to be a witness against himself, paralled by a similar right against self-incrimination secured by constitutional or statutory provisions in many of the states. Federal courts had long held that the federal constitutional right against self-incrimination included the right to have the prosecutor and the judge refrain from making any comment about the fact that the defendant did not take the witness stand and testify in his own behalf. Many states which had provisions forbidding compulsory self-incrimination did not follow the "no comment" rule; they held that if the defendant were innocent, he should testify as to his innocence, and his failure to testify was an indication that he knew his testimony would prove his own guilt, and that the prosecutor, the judge, or both could comment upon the jury upon the defendant's silence as evidence of his guilt. It was not until 1964 that the Supreme Court held, in the *habeas corpus* case of *Malloy v. Hogan*, that states could not violate the right against self-incrimination as guaranteed by the Federal Bill of Rights, and not until 1965, in the direct criminal appeal of *Griffin v. California*, that the Court held the Constitution prohibits state prosecutors and judges from commenting upon a defendant's silence. Before either of these major criminal decisions was rendered, Mr. Shott was convicted in an Ohio state court, partly upon the basis of prosecutorial comments upon his failure to testify as evidence of his guilt. He appealed to the Ohio Supreme Court, which held such comments proper. He asked the United States to review this conviction as one obtained by violation of his federal constitutional rights, but the Supreme Court refused to grant *certiorari*. The only reason he was denied federal review of his conviction while his criminal case was still "open" or non-final was that the Supreme Court refused to hear him. So he started the *habeas corpus* route, sueing Sheriff Tehan, who had him in custody. He failed to gain his liberty, because it was then the Federal rule, as recognized by all Federal courts, that the Federal Bill of Rights does not apply to state governments in regard to the right against self-incrimination. He appealed to the Federal Court of Appeals in Ohio, and shortly before that court decided his appeal, the Supreme Court held in its Malloy *habeas corpus* decision that the Federal right against self-incrimination protects defendants in state cases. So the Court of Appeals, following the Supreme Court's *habeas corpus* case, ruled in its own *habeas corpus* case that the prosecutorial comment on Mr. Shott's failure to comment nullified his conviction. Then the Supreme Court held in its *Griffin* decision the same thing the Court of Appeals had held in its *Shott* decision, that such prosecutorial comment was constitutionally forbidden. Then came the Court's *Linkletter* decision, followed shortly by *Tehan v. Shott*, Sheriff Tehan having been granted review of the decision against him. In its decision, the Supreme Court held its constitutional no-comment ruling did not have to be observed by state courts except in cases still in the trial-appellate stage of the actual criminal prosecution when the Court rendered its 1965 *Griffin* decision on the point. The Supreme Court did not hold that the intermediate appellate court had to send Mr. Shott on to prison despite the violation of his constitutional rights, but sent the *habeas corpus* case back to the Court of Appeals for it to decide what to do about the matter, an issue that court had already decided in holding Mr. Shott entitled to his liberty because of the violation of his constitutional rights by Ohio. The Supreme Court

enforcement should be less inconvenient, were combined so skillfully as to deserve the admiration of any legislative body.

The occasion was actually two decisions, *Miranda v. Arizona* and *Johnson v. New Jersey.* Both cases were under consideration at the same time, having been argued one after the other before the Court. The *Miranda* decision was released on June 13, 1966, containing its promulgation of new rules to be followed by the states and the Federal Government as well, and the *Johnson* decision was released exactly one week later, declaring the effective date of the *Miranda* rules and also of the ruling in a previous decision, *Escobido v. Illinois.*[60]

The cases involved oral admissions or written confessions made by suspects while in the custody of police officers, and subsequently introduced against the confessors in their criminal trials. Confessions have always been most persuasive evidence of guilt, and have always been utilized by all police agencies, including those which are the very personification of official respect for the rights of the suspect, the F. B. I., the Secret Service, and the Special Agents of the Internal Revenue Service. Often many facts, whether indicating innocence or guilt, can be learned only by questioning the suspect. To restrict the police exercise of their question-asking functions necessarily makes more difficult the imposition of penalties for violation of the law.

The cases involved no police brutality, no beating, no torture of a suspect to sign a confession that might be either true or false. In *Escobido v. Illinois,* Danny Escobido was being questioned in the police station, and was demanding that he be allowed to see a lawyer; his lawyer, employed by relatives, was outside, demanding access to Escobido. During the two-hour interview with Escobido while his lawyer was seeking access to him, Escobido confessed and signed a written confession.

In the later *Miranda* case, Ernesto Miranda was held two hours by the Phoenix

---

stated it had "never considered" the merits of Shott's claim of right to be freed on *habeas corpus.* Also not considered, and not even mentioned by the Supreme Court, was this issue: In view of the express Federal Constitutional prohibition against suspension of the writ of *habeas corpus* except in the event of rebellion or invasion, whether the Supreme Court or any other court has the power to suspend the writ of *habeas corpus* by denying its benefits to one who has been convicted and imprisoned by methods that are forbidden by the Constitution of the United States.

60. The other convictions were New York and California state prosecutions and a federal prosecution. In the New York case, Vignera was held in custody for eight hours, then questioned by and confessed to an assistant district attorney; during the trial which led to a sentence of 60 years in prison, the trial judge told the jury: "The law doesn't say that the confession is void or invalidated because the police officer didn't advise the defendant as to his rights. Did you hear what I said? I am telling you what the law of the State of New York is." In the California conviction, Stewart was arrested in his home on an arrest warrant, his home was searched and items taken from robbery victims were found there. Stewart, his wife, and three visitors were locked in a California jail for five days, at the end of which Stewart confessed he murdered a robbery victim; the police then released his wife and friends, against whom they admitted they had no evidence of guilt. In the Federal case, Westover was arrested, booked and held in custody overnight by the Kansas City police, then questioned by the police throughout the morning of the next day; he was then turned over to three F. B. I. agents, to whom he confessed Federal crimes after three additional hours of questioning by those agents in another room of the Kansas City Police Station.

police and, after being identified by his victim, he confessed, signed a written confession, and was later convicted of kidnaping and rape. Several other cases were considered in the same opinion with the case of Ernesto Miranda. In its *Escobido* and *Miranda* decisions, the Supreme Court reversed all these convictions and sent them back for new trials without the use of confessions. The Court did this on the basis of the fact that the men did not have access to the benefit of representation by attorneys during their station-house interrogations.

The *Escobido* case was decided earlier in the usual manner of deciding lawsuits, except that it carried the constitutional protection of right to counsel to a point never before required by the Supreme Court, to the point of interrogation by the police before the person was officially accused and before any official trial proceedings had begun. The Court had earlier held, in a case cited in one of the dissenting opinions, that a citizen *was not guaranteed* by the Constitution the right to be represented by counsel while being interrogated; and the Sixth Amendment, covering the rights of accused persons in criminal trials, provides for the right "to have the Assistance of Counsel for his defence."

In *Escobido v. Illinois,* the Supreme Court held that to compel a man to give a statement during investigation in effect compelled him to be a witness against himself when the statement was used during the trial, and the Court held that to take a man's confession when he is a suspect, without first advising him of his right to be silent, and to do so by denying him the right to talk to his lawyer *upon his demand,* denies him the right to effective representation by counsel.[61] Within the framework of the facts of the case—all that the Court even pretended to decide—the decision was probably a decision required by the Sixth Amendment, assuming those fair trial requirements are a part of the Fourteenth Amendment's right not to be deprived of liberty without due process of law in state criminal prosecutions. In the case, the Court did not endeavor to exercise any rule-making power; it simply decided the lawsuit in the normal and proper exercise of judicial power.

But two years later in *Miranda v. Arizona,* on June 13, 1966, the Court did exercise its claimed power to make rules to enforce the Fourteenth Amendment, looked back to the *Escobido* decision, and declared formal rules to enforce the new right to be represented by counsel during police questioning, and then in the following week's decision of *Johnson v. New Jersey,* the Court expressly declared the dates on which citizens would be privileged to use legal procedures to enforce these constitutional rights.

And in looking about in the manner of a legislature—whose enactments are law solely because it has the power to make law and has exercised that power by voting that a proposed law shall become law—the Court abandoned its habit of the recent past of merely holding that the newly-discovered constitutional rights could not be enforced in Federal *habeas corpus* cases with the feared result of emptying the prisons. Instead, the Court chose more convenient or "reasonable" dates for citizens to be granted the privilege of these new constitutional rights based upon words written the first year of George Washington's presidency.

---

61. Speaking generally, interrogation may lead the police to conclude that a suspect is guilty or that he is innocent, so that this interrogation is no part of the trial; it, like a lawful or illegal search of a person's home, may produce evidence that will be used on the trial, but the interrogation itself is no more a trial than is the search a trial. The Supreme Court did not equate police interrogation with the constitutional phrase "criminal prosecution" in its *Escobido* decision.

The date it chose was the date the citizen's trial began. If the citizen's trial began on or after June 14, 1966, the day after the *Miranda* decision, and if his confession had not met all the guidelines announced in *Miranda v. Arizona*, then he had a constitutional right to require the state or federal judge not to admit his confession in evidence against him, if his trial began earlier, he had no right to have his confession excluded from the evidence submitted to the jury. The Court went even further, reached back to the ordinary judicial decision of the *Escobido* case, and announced the date when courts should become obligated to enforce its ruling. In short, the Court treated the cases as if they were enactments of statutes rather than the rendition of judicial decisions in obedience to law.

None of the convictions reversed in the *Miranda* decision came within the scope of the limited holding in the *Escobido* case, because in none did the suspect make demand to see his waiting lawyer, as did Escobido. The *Miranda* proclamation broadened this into a right to have a lawyer, whether the suspect asked for one or not. This time, the Supreme Court did not repeat its *Wolf v. Colorado* act of delegating to the states the power the Fourteenth Amendment gave to Congress to make laws to enforce the Amendment and then waiting for years to see what the states would do about it. The Court promulgated the rules itself, and immediately gave limited enforcement to the rules by reversing four convictions on the ground that each of them violated the rules proclaimed in 1966 to protect a constitutional right never recognized to exist in any Supreme Court decision in the nation's history until 1964, though all four of the confessions were given in 1960 or in 1963! All other citizens of the United States, who may have been persuaded to confess in violation of these then undeclared rules, would be denied the benefit of the supremacy of the Constitution unless their trials began after June 13, 1966, the date of the decision.

Miranda v. Arizona did not even pretend to be concerned primarily with the decision of the lawsuits. For the first 52 pages, it concerned itself with the promulgation, explanation and attempted justification of its new rules, in the course of which it did not so much as quote any provision of the *Constitution.*

But in its proclamation, the Supreme Court granted that Congress itself had some law-making power in this area—enforcement of the newly-discovered scope of the Fourteenth Amendment right: "Congress and the States are free to develop their own safeguards for the privilege, *so long as they are fully as effective as those described above. . . ."* The Court did not pause to inquire where Congress got this power, nor where the Court obtained its supposed power to give Congress advance notice of just how extensively Congress might exercise this power. Had the Court considered the Constitution instead of its own philosophy, the Court would have found that the Amendment does not impose any duty upon Congress to make rules to enforce it but does give Congress the power to make such rules; that the Amendment leaves to Congress the judgment as to whether it will make rules at all, rules less effective than the Supreme Court might think wise, or rules so sweeping as to affect the law-enforcing customs in every state. The Court also would have seen, if it had consulted the Amendment it claimed to construe, that the power to make rules to enforce it was given to no assembly on earth but the Congress.

The Court proclaimed its rules, with a paragraph or so following each rule, explaining the benefits to be derived from it. The Rules:

(1) At the outset, if a person in custody is to be subjected to interrogation, he must first be informed in clear and unequivocal terms that he has the right to remain silent.

(2) The warning of the right to remain silent must be accompanied by the explanation that anything said can and will be used against the individual in court. (3) . . . an individual held for interrogation must be clearly informed that he has the right to consult with a lawyer and to have the lawyer with him during interrogation under the system for protecting the privilege we deliniate today. (4) In order fully to apprise a person interrogated of the extent of his rights under this system then, it is necessary to warn him not only that he has the right to consult with an attorney, but also that if he is indigent a lawyer will be appointed to represent him.—A command not only to the police but also to all state legislatures and to the Congress to provide funds and procedures for the appointment of lawyers. (5) If the individual agrees to answer questions without a lawyer present: (a) If the individual indicates in any manner, at any time prior to or during questioning, that he wishes to remain silent, the interrogation must cease. (b) If the individual states that he wants an attorney, the interrogation must cease until an attorney is present.

So we see that this proclamation of new rules is a set of precise "Laws" sent out to govern the conduct of Federal investigators under the supervisory power of the President, state investigators under the supervisory authority of fifty governors, deputy sheriffs under the supervision of thousands of sheriffs, and city policemen under the supervision of many thousands of mayors, police commissioners and chiefs of police. As such, it is an exercise by a judicial body of power it could acquire only by usurpation.

The earlier portions of the opinion were designed to demonstrate the need for the proclamation of rules that followed. The Court referred to a number of earlier decisions in which brutality and torture had been used to extract involuntary confessions.

Toward combatting this evil, the Court took careful note of rules obligatory in modern England, Scotland, India, Ceylon, and under our own Uniform Code of Military Justice, without claiming any of this is supposed to be related to the meaning of any provision of the Constitution of the United States. To demonstrate the practicality of its new rules, the Court pointed to the F. B. I., which "can readily be emulated" by the states, as an agency which manages to solve crimes, though the F. B. I. warns suspects of their rights before they talk within the closed confines of the F. B. I. offices; to show the F. B. I. practices, the Court received in evidence a letter containing a report prepared for the Court by the FBI Director, which in fact failed to demonstrate that the F. B. I. actually met the more strict standards now proclaimed by the Court.[62]

What would have happened if the Court had put aside all suppositions that it was empowered to emit rules, all its humane aims, all consultation of police and psychiatriac manuals, all interest in the procedures of the FBI, India, Scotland, Ceylon and modern England, and had viewed the cases as lawsuits to be decided under the Constitution?

The Court's regulations were based upon the suspect's right to an attorney. Now available, what was the attorney to do for the suspect? The Court suggested that the lawyer's presence during interrogation would deter police from mistreating the prisoner—true, but only if officers who decide to beat a prisoner will be sure that they first comply with the Supreme Court's rules.[63] The Court also

---

62. Nor did the Court comment upon the propriety of its own conduct in receiving such evidence, the receipt of evidence being a trial court function, when the Supreme Court is not constitutionally permitted to function as a trial court in such cases.

63. After the prisoner has been beaten into truthfully confessing guilt and has

suggested that the lawyer's presence would help assure the accuracy of the resulting written statement, a benefit that can be better accomplished with a cheap tape recorder. And the Court also suggested that the lawyer could advise with the client as to whether to make a statement.

Here is the value of the lawyer. He will insist that the client say nothing to the police, answer not the most innocuous question, give no response even to statements made by detectives, except possibly, "On advice of counsel, I make no statement."

Then what does the lawyer do for the client when first summoned to represent him at the time of interrogation? If he can, he first tries to gain access to the client, instruct him forcefully not to open his mouth, perhaps leave an associate lawyer with the client (if permitted) to assure that the client will say nothing. In other words, the lawyer does what the Supreme Court's first regulation required the police to do, advise the client of his right to remain silent, but the lawyer does this much better than the police can ever do it, *because the police are not trying to keep the suspect from talking.* This is obvious to anyone whose thinking is centered upon the protection of constitutional rights instead of the enhancement of governmental powers.

If the lawyer cannot negotiate his client's freedom, he asks a court for a writ of *habeas corpus.* This commands the police to "have the body" of the prisoner before the court at a stated time, and then be prepared to prove the authority by which they claim the power to keep the citizen a prisoner.[64] When the police bring the prisoner before the court in obedience to the *habeas corpus* obtained by the lawyer, the police must produce a warrant or they must produce evidence of guilt on the basis of which the judge will at that time issue a warrant commanding the officer to arrest the suspect and *bring him before the judge*—the warrant does not command the officer to hold the prisoner incommunicado. In either event, the judge fixes bond and allows the suspect to go free when he posts the bond. Or if the police cannot prove legal justification for holding the citizen prisoner, the judge orders them to set him free. *Now.*

So what valuable service does this lawyer perform—the lawyer made available pursuant to the man's right "to have the Assistance of Counsel for his defence?" First, he helps the prisoner remain silent, and protects the prisoner's right not to "be compelled in any Criminal Case to be a witness against himself"—a right the prisoner has regardless of whether he has a lawyer to sit and hold his hand. This does not, in the psychologically-compelled confession situation, aid the man in his defense so much as it hinders the police in their investigation. And the principal service the lawyer performs in this emergency is not to aid the suspect in his defense, but to obtain for the suspect his freedom, his right to go where he wants to go and to be where he wants to be.

---

had time for healing and relaxation, a tenderly-delivered Miranda warning of the right to remain silent will not erase from the prisoner's mind the knowledge that the police know the full truth from his own mouth, and an occasional tortured confession may well result, clothed with all the trappings of *Miranda* legality.

64. If a grandmother refuses to release her grandchildren to their parents, it is by *habeas corpus* that she is commanded to bring the children into court and prove by what right she claims custody of them. If a hospital refuses to "release" a patient until his bill is paid, it is *habeas corpus* that commands the hospital administrators to bring the patient into court and prove what right it has to keep the patient prisoner, and the hospital loses, because there is legally no such thing in America as an owned, mortgaged, or pawned human being.

What was the common understanding about these problems—keeping prisoners incommunicado, coercing them into confessing, etc.—at the time the Bill of Rights was written? The most common, convenient and popular American source to the Common Law at that time was Blackstone's *Commentaries,* and the Common Law was still the law governing all thirteen of the states except for very limited legislated changes. Here is part of what Blackstone had to say to the men who wrote our Bill of Rights in 1789:

> ". . . And by [statute], commonly called the *habeas corpus* act, the methods of obtaining this writ are so plainly pointed out and enforced, that, so long as this statute remains unimpeached no subject of England can be long detained in prison, except in those cases in which the law requires and justifies such a detainer. And, *lest this act should be evaded by demanding unreasonable bail,* or sureties for the prisoner's appearance, it is declared by . . . (Bill of Rights, 1689), that excessive bail ought not to be required. . . . The confinement of a person, in any wise, is an imprisonment. So that keeping a man against his will in a private house, putting him in the stocks, arresting or forcibly detaining him in the street, is an imprisonment. . . . To make imprisonment lawful, it must either be by process from the courts of judicature, or by warrant from some legal officer having authority to commit to prison, which warrant must be in writing, under the hand and seal of the magistrate, and express the causes of the commitment, in order to be examined into (if necessary) upon a *habeas corpus.*"

These were the words most conveniently to be read by the men who wrote our Bill of Rights, and they had behind them many judicial decisions if more thorough study were desired. What do those amendments, and the original Constitution, have to say about these practical rules to protect citizens from deprivation of their freedom, the tool used, as the Supreme Court demonstrated in *Miranda v. Arizona,* to psychologically compel confessions?

In our Constitution: "The Privilege of the Writ of *Habeas Corpus shall not be* suspended, . . ." "The right of the people to be secure in their persons, . . . against unreasonable . . . seizures, shall not be violated, and no Warrants shall issue, but upon probable cause, . . . particularly describing . . . the persons . . . to be seized." "Excessive bail shall not be required. . . ."

Remember that most American law as to the power of police officers to arrest and hold people in custody was developed by states before the Fourteenth Amendment was viewed as protecting people against arrests and searches by their state governments. What of the police practice of holding citizens in custody for thirty minutes, two hours, five days, without any warrant? This is a denial of bail, either excessive or reasonable, in violation of the bail requirements of the Eighth Amendment. Such imprisonment, without any trial, conviction, or warrant, which totally subjects one man to the power of another, even in such fundamental needs as food, sleep, the bath-room, is this not involuntary servitude? Is this not clearly prohibited by the provisions of the Thirteenth Amendment outlawing all involuntary servitude "except as a punishment for a crime whereof the party *shall have been* duly convicted . . . ?"

If these constitutional provisions are violated by questioning when the police do not even have any right to be keeping the individual in their custody, the confession obtained by such violation is properly no more admissible in evidence than burglar tools obtained by an illegal search of the burglar's home. If police do not have enough evidence to go before a magistrate and obtain a search warrant, they may not then lawfully break in, search without a warrant, and still use the evidence against the man in court. When the Constitution does not permit the state to compel a man to get on a witness stand and answer whatever questions may be asked him touching upon his guilt, the state may not then lock him up, deny him bail, subject him to involuntary servitude, so pressurize him into confessing, and so gain by violating the Constitution what they are denied the power to gain openly.

Even if any of these constitutional provisions did not absolutely bar incommunicado questioning, with or without the presence of a lawyer—as they do, the Supreme Court still has no power to issue rules and declare them to be rules of conduct binding every law-enforcement officer in the country, because this power belongs exclusively to Congress. To recognize that any court has even a little of what has always been considered legislative power is apt to encourage that court to substitute its own personal ideas of justice for the more certain terms of the Constitution, particularly if the judges are inclined to impose their own ideas of justice on the nation anyway. It is most unwise to entrust judicial officials with such power, while allowing the people to believe they have a fixed and certain constitution.

What the Supreme Court actually did in the *Miranda* case was to *destroy* constitutional rights and to substitute for them a procedure for police interrogation of a suspect where the Constitution itself permits no such procedure even to exist. The Supreme Court nullified constitutional rights, under the claim that it was protecting them. Where the Constitution does not permit compulsory in-custody interrogation, by its requirements for admission to bail and its prohibition of involuntary servitude, the Supreme Court created a procedure, detailed and devoid of value, for systematically violating those constitutional rights, and did so by exercising usurped legislative power, which it may not lawfully do even to carry out constitutional commands.

Having satisfied itself that it had this legislative power to formulate rules and fix the effective dates of such rules, the Supreme Court continued through the 1960's to find new constitutional "protections." The decade's rule-making and effective date-fixing judicial inventiveness saw their finest hour when the Court came to grapple with the problems of electronic eavesdropping and recording. The new constitutional right was discovered by the Court in 1967 in *Katz v. United States* and the precise date when all other citizens should become entitled to share with Mr. Katz the benefit of this new rule was established and ordained the following year in *Desist v. United States*.

Even aside from wire-tapping, the Internal Revenue Service and the F. B. I. have on many occasions found valuable evidence in the use of the telephone. In an illegal bet-taking operation, when telephone company records show that the home of a reputed gambler has six telephone lines (possibly for taking local bets) and when the company's long-distance records show a pattern of calls at the right times every day to places that are known to furnish betting odds and to places where bets can be placed over the telephone, this furnishes evidence sufficient to convince the magistrate that a search warrant is justified. And when gamblers have become wary of this and begun using telephone booths, then an agent's personal observation recording the exact times that the suspect enters and leaves the booth, coupled with telephone company records of the times and points to which long-distance calls were made from each booth, have proven to be convincing evidence on trials.

Men have always sought privacy to do secret things. With the insecurity of telephone lines, people try to avoid them and speak face-to-face in most secret matters. The hotel room offers privacy but more opportunity for the eavesdropper, so that the greater privacy of the home is preferred. In criminal enterprises, the criminal has only his best judgment as to the dependability of his co-conspirators, who may later become witnesses against him. His protection can only be in his judgment of his cohort's reliability and his hope that, if he has judged wrong, he can speak to the jury as convincingly as the next man. But with the advent of the small recorder which actually proves which man is telling the truth, the security of the ability to lie convincingly disappeared; the wide open spaces became a good place for conspirators to talk in shirt sleeves, so it could be seen that no fairly bulky recording device was being worn.

Particularly where the work of undercover agents is involved, in the sale and purchase of whiskey, narcotics, counterfeit money, and other such contraband, criminals have always felt they were unfairly treated when they were brought into court and convicted by means of a tape recording in which the jury could hear the very words spoken by them in planning or committing a crime.

In the last analysis, the feeling of unfairness arises from the realization that the criminal cannot lie out of it: In the conflict between the testimony of the seller and buyer of heroin, or the law-violator and the undercover agent, who sometimes may himself have to violate criminal laws in order to maintain the confidence of his "co-conspirators," there is always a fighting chance that the testimony of the law-violator may be believed by the jury. But the recording of the actual voice of the law-violator leaves no doubt about who is telling the truth. The law-violator is then helplessly trapped during the trial, and there is little that can be said on his behalf to the jury in argument.

Criminals have sought to claim that this act of recording their voices and re-creating the crime in the courtroom violates their right against self-incrimination; but the courts usually have been able to discern the difference between the real immunity from being compelled to be a witness against oneself and the claimed right to privacy while one plots to overthrow the Government by force, plans to kidnap a child, or engages in the commission of some other crime. It is the distinction between the right of one who is in the clutches of government, subjected to criminal prosecution, and entitled to the protection of the Constitution's supremacy on the one hand, and the non-existent right, on the other hand, to commit crime in privacy.

The citizen has no right to commit crime. Crime is an act the law forbids a citizen to commit. But every citizen, innocent or guilty, has the right to the benefit of constitutional procedures when he is being criminally prosecuted. The use of modern electronic and laser eavesdropping and recording devices, as well as modern photographic equipment and films, comes under the heading of good detective work, detective work which *may* or *may not* violate some provision of the Constitution.

The Supreme Court earlier had occasion to examine these claims of unfairness. In *Goldman v. United States*, the Court held that the Constitution did not prohibit the use of testimony of Federal agents who had used a primitive eavesdropping device, the "dectaphone," to listen to the conversation of Goldman and his associates in an adjoining room in a public building. By talking in such a place which offered so little real privacy, Goldman took the chance that some curious little old lady in the adjoining room might be eavesdropping with an empty water glass held between her ear and the wall; the agents used a better device. The agents had as much right to use their room as had Goldman to use his, Goldman was not being forced to testify against himself but was engaging in a criminal conspiracy, and the agents did not enter and search his room, or his person.

The Supreme Court had also considered wire-tapping, and held that when a citizen uses the telephone, and sends his voice over telephone wires which may be tapped, his right to be immune from unreasonable search of his home, person, or effects has not been violated. Wire-tapped evidence, the Court held in *Olmstead v. United States,* could be used in criminal prosecutions in Federal courts. But Congress considered this too great an invasion of the individual's privacy, so it enacted a provision of the Federal Communications Act making it illegal to "intercept" and divulge the contents of intercepted telephone conversations; after this, because that law, as a part of the Supreme Law of the Land, prohibited everyone, including Federal courts, from divulging the contents of intercepted telephone conversations, the Court held that such wire-tapped evidence could not be used in Federal prosecutions.

Other cases were considered in which officers broke into homes or offices and concealed eavesdropping devices, and where eavesdropping was accomplished by physically inserting a listening device's pick-up into the external wall of a building. In the first of these, there was at least a "search" in that the intruder searched for the best place to hide the listening device; in the latter, there was no search at all, but only an intrusion upon private property. In both, the Supreme Court had held the searches to violate the unreasonable search and seizure prohibitions of the Fourth Amendment.

In construing constitutional provisions designed to protect the rights of individual citizens, it is easy to be misled from the starting point of the content of the Constitution, and to view the problem instead from the viewpoint of the citizen whose rights the Constitution was designed to protect. And from the viewpoint of the individual criminal, it is just as unreasonable to eavesdrop by nailing a listening device into his wall as it is to accomplish the same purpose by hiding a microphone under his desk, even if there is no search involved.

All these considerations came again before the Court in *Katz v. United States,* a prosecution under recent organized crime legislation forbidding the use of the telephone to transmit wagering information across state lines. The FBI proved Katz's guilt by attaching a radio transmitting device to the outside of a public telephone booth. They did not search the telephone booth. They watched, and began listening when a suspect entered the phone booth, and recordings made by them led to the conviction of Katz. This did not violate the Federal Communications Act, because there was no "interception" of the conversation at any point between the speaker in Los Angeles and the listener in Boston. There was only an eavesdropping upon one end of the conversation, accomplished by the use of modern miniturized electronic device, which did better than a directional microphone atop a nearby building.

But the Supreme Court held in the *Katz* case that the eavesdropping violated the Fourth Amendment. The Court held it to be an unreasonable "search" and "seizure." But if eavesdropping and searching are the same, does not this require application of the search warrant requirements of the Fourth Amendment? Indeed, yes. And it was on this ground—the lack of a search warrant, that the

Court ruled the electronically eavesdropped half conversation could not be introduced in evidence against Mr. Katz.

Lest the reader doubt that responsible men in high office could so far depart from the meaning of words they are called upon to construe, let him read the Court's own words:

"One who occupies [the telephone booth], shuts the door behind him, and pays the toll that permits him to place a call is surely entitled to assume that the words he utters into the mouthpiece will not be broadcast to the world. To read the Constitution more narrowly is to ignore the vital role that the public telephone has come to play in private communication. . . . The Government's activities in electronically listening to and recording the petitioner's words violated the privacy upon which he justifiably relied while using the telephone booth and thus constituted a 'search and seizure' within the meaning of the Fourth Amendment. . . . The agents confined their surveillance to the brief periods during which [Katz] used the telephone booth, and they took great care to overhear only the conversation of the petitioner himself. . . . The Government urges that, because its agents relied upon the decisions in *Olmstead* and *Goldman,* and because they did so more here than they might properly have done with prior judicial sanction, we should retroactively validate their conduct. *That we cannot do.* It is apparent that the agents in this case acted with restraint. Yet the inescapable fact is that this restraint was imposed by the agents themselves, not by a judicial officer. They were not required, before commencing the search, to present their estimate of probable cause for detached scrutiny by a neutral magistrate. They were not compelled, during the conduct of the search itself, to observe precise limits established in advance by a specific court order. Nor were they directed, after the search had been completed, to notify the authorizing magistrate in detail of all that had been seized."

Then the Court expressly held that the obtaining of a search warrant was a *"constitutional prerequisite"* to "the kind of electronic surveillance involved in this case."

Then having satisfied itself that the Constitution prohibited the electronic intrusion *anywhere* upon the individual's desired degree of privacy, and that it lacked the power (*"we cannot"*) to retroactively validate the "seizure" of private conversations without a search warrant, the Court proceeded to do that very thing fifteen months later in *Desist v. United States.* This was a case in which it, in the manner of a legislature, followed the recent course it had adopted of deciding when citizens should be permitted legal enforcement of their newly-discovered constitutional rights. Except that in this case, the Court went further.

If Congress were enacting a law to control the conduct of Federal investigators in the use of overly "snoopy" investigative techniques, Congress would provide an exact date as the date the investigators would have to change their practices. The decisive question would not be when the trial of some lawsuit begins, but whether the officer's investigation occurred before or after the effective date of the new law. This was the course adopted by the Supreme Court in the *Desist* case. The Court declared that unless the police illegally "seized" the conversation by recording it without a search warrant *after* the Court decided in the *Katz* case on December 18, 1967, that the freedom from such "seizures" was a constitutional right, the illegally seized conversation could be used to convict and imprison. Thus, under the Court's decision, the constitutional right to be free from electronic eavesdropping, though claimed to be commanded by the Fourth

Amendment, did not come into existence and could not be violated by police officers (in the *Desist* case, narcotics investigators) until the moment the Court declared the right to exist.

Such reasoning is a blatant substitution of the will and philosophy of the current membership of the Court for the Constitution as the supreme law of the land.

In its endeavor to make the Constitution conform to modern times and to the changes in the way people live, the Court lost touch with reality. If the FBI officer in the *Katz* case or the Narcotics Bureau officers in the *Desist* case had gone before a U. S. Magistrate to seek a warrant to eavesdrop, the Magistrate would probably have advised their superiors that the men were in need of psychiatric care. Or the Magistrate may have asked the agent: In order to get a search warrant to search the air in the telephone booth and seize the speaker's half of the telephone conversation, can you give me a particular description, as required by law, of the conversation to be seized?—If you will not know the telephone he is calling, and whether it is local or long-distance until you can later get access to the telephone company's automatic recordings of the time of the call and the number of the telephone called, and if you do not know who he will be talking to, how can you particularly describe the call not yet made?—Do you propose to listen to these calls as they are being made to be sure you will not "seize" any personal calls?—and if you listen as well as record by means of the eavesdropping equipment, and should actually "seize" Katz's half of a long-distance call regarding wagering, are you prepared to then go to Mr. Katz and deliever to him a written and signed "inventory" as required by law, describing the conversation you have seized?—Armed with the search warrant, and if you find Mr. Katz present, are you prepared to present the warrant to him and notify him in advance that you are about to begin making a search, as the law requires?—If this would interfere with your investigation, would you then ask the United States Attorney to provide me a copy of some new law enacted by Congress, authorizing me to issue a warrant to eavesdrop and providing some new and different procedure for you to follow when you have obeyed the warrant's command?—Where did I get any power to *order* you to eavesdrop?

Let us see how the Court arrived at the creation of this strange new constitutional right in the *Katz* decision, a right which legislative authority *could have created* in response to strong public pressure. Imitating language which the Court itself and its inferior courts had used in past decisions, the first question in the case framed by Katz's attorney was: "Whether a public telephone booth is a constitutionally protected area so that evidence obtained by attaching an electronic listening recording device to the top of such a booth is obtained in violation of the right of privacy of the user of the booth." The Court then characterized the statements of this and other issues as "the misleading way the issues have been formulated."

And of course the language used was misleading in a sense. It substituted general and different language, possibly with different shading of meanings, for the precise and specific language of the Constitution.[65]

---

65. The misleading effect can better be appreciated if we think of the Ten Commandments. There are commands that you shall not steal, kill or commit adultery. This may be transmuted into a statement that every man has the right (changing emphasis from *thy conduct to thy victim's rights*) to exclusive control

From this point, the Supreme Court went into its own paraphraseology of the plain language of the Fourth Amendment. The Court said that what the individual "seeks to preserve as private, even in an area accessible to the public, may be constitutionally protected." The Court did not endeavor to say why this was supposed to be true outside the individual's person and his effects, as the Fourth Amendment provides. To the objection that Katz knew he could be seen through the glass windows of the public telephone booth which was not Katz's house:

> "But what he *sought* to *exclude* when he entered the booth was not the intruding eye—it was the uninvited ear. He did not shed his right to do so simply because he made his calls from a place where he might be seen."

Thus the Court itself, as the starting point of its effort to "construe" the Fourth Amendment, substituted a three-part test—a generalized right to privacy, the citizen's desire for privacy, and the reasonableness of his expectation that he would attain privacy—for the specific constitutional protection of the sanctity of the individual's security against an unreasonable search of his house or his person and seizure of his property and effects.[66] Never once did the Supreme Court return to any inquiry as to the meaning of those words when they were written, nor note that "eavesdropping" and "peeping Tom" were words having well-known common or legal meanings when the Constitution was written, so that the writers of the Constitution and Bill of Rights could have written them to forbid this type of detective activity had they desired to do so.

In presuming to create the new constitutional right to privacy, the Supreme Court not only disregarded both the common-sense and historical meaning of the Fourth Amendment's search and seizure provisions, it also disregarded the posi-

---

of his life, his property, and his wife's sexual companionship. But, we realize, the enjoyment of sex is not the exclusive pleasure of the husband; the wife enjoys it, too. She is not property owned by her husband, but an individual in her own right, and if she finds her husband inadequate, and not only consents but joyfully initiates sexual relations with another man, is she not exercising *her right* to enjoy sexual relations? Does not her husband's exclusive right to her sexual companionship impose upon him the obligation to adequately fulfill his duties? Has the stranger's willing and happy cooperation really violated the husband's exclusive rights, or has the husband abandoned his exclusive rights by failing to keep his wife entranced? Surely, the stranger who only failed to resist the irresistible did not violate the Commandment when it was all the fault of the husband whose exclusive right the Commandment was designed to protect. Obviously not. There remains no room for doubt. . . . Thus, the technique of paraphrasing the precise language of the commandments can lead to violation of the command under the pretense that it is being obeyed. And in the violation, this rationalization disregards the fact that if this present happy view correctly states the meaning of the commandment, then the intellect that first framed its language could and would have said: Thou shall not seduce or rape another's wife.

66. This is quite similar to the Supreme Court's illegal expansion of the police authority to make a search incident to a lawful arrest, as condemned and proven improper by the Court's opinion in *Chimel v. California*, discussed above, pp. 84-87. A distinction is that the warping of constitutional meanings occurred in a single decision here, while it occurred in a series of expanding decisions in the developmnt of the rationale condemned by *Chimel v California*. Other interesting contrasts may be found by anyone who cares to compare the two opinions.

tion of Congress. After the Court had ruled in the *Olmstead* case that the wire-tapping interception of telephone conversations did not violate the Constitution, the people and their Congress nevertheless regarded wire-tapping as too much of an invasion of the privacy of the individual, and Congress enacted law to make wire-tapping illegal. The Supreme Court was not the sole agency provided by government to respond to popular desires for the protection of privacy in light of the sense of fairness and the need to catch criminals.

The *Goldman* decision on the use of the detectaphone was handed down [67] in 1942, and the refinement of electronic devices has continued since then. At all times, should popular feelings become strong enough, Congress and the state legislatures have been amenable to public pressure demanding the enactment of laws to create and give explicit protection to the right of privacy. Law-making is the function of Congress and the legislatures, never of the courts. The Supreme Court can *never* exercise legislative power except by usurpation, which dishonors the judicial oath of office.

A clear and present danger is that, if the nation concedes to nine men the power to make rules they think wise to enforce any provision of the Constitution and to actively discourage the violation of any Constitutional provision, then the business of making rules to govern state and federal officials and even the people themselves might become so entrancing as to lead to the abandonment of the adequate and arduous performance of the function of deciding lawsuits. The correct and proper performance of this function is essential to the protection of law and liberty.

By freeing itself from the shackles of deciding only as commanded by law instead of being the law-giver, the Supreme Court became free to promulgate specific and detailed rules without any great possibility of overly arousing public inquiry as to the propriety of its rule-making, and so the *Linkletter* decision fathered the sweeping changes we have noticed.

After the Supreme Court decided in its *Wade* and *Gilbert* decisions [68] that identifications based upon police line-ups at which the defendant was not represented by an attorney could not be used in evidence, it then declined to make the rule effective in its "later" decision, decided the same day, June 12, 1967, unless the line-up identification should occur after June 12 ,1967.[69] In deciding the "later" decision of June 12th, *Stovall v. Denno,* the Supreme Court said at the beginning and near the end of its opinion:

"This case therefore provides a vehicle for deciding the extent to which the rules announced in *Wade* and *Gilbert*—requiring the exclusion of identification evidence which is tainted by exhibiting the accused to identifying witnesses before

---

67. Described above, p. 108.

68. These decisions, *United States v. Wade* and *Gilbert v. California,* apply respectively to federal and state police line-ups, and are subject to the same criticisms as is *Miranda v. Arizona.*

69. In these cases, the Supreme Court simultaneously announced its decisions creating the new constitutional right and then denying enjoyment of that right to all Americans except Messrs. Wade and Gilbert until after the suspension period should pass. This differed from the Court's conduct in creating its Miranda rules, in which the Court waited a full week before announcing the suspension period in *Johnson v. New Jersey,* argued immediately after argument of the four cases whose decisions were announced under the leading title of *Miranda v. Arizona.*

trial in the absence of his counsel—are to be applied retroactively. . . . We recognize that Wade and Gilbert are, therefore, the only victims of pretrial confrontations in the absence of their counsel to have the benefit of the rules established in their cases. *That they must be given the benefit* is, however, an unavoidable consequence of the necessity that constitutional adjudications not stand as mere dictum. Inequity arguably results from according the benefit of a new rule to the parties in the case in which it is announced but not to other litigants similarly situated in the trial or appellate process who have raised the same issue. *But we regard the fact that the parties involved are chance beneficiaries as an insignificant cost for adherence to sound principles of decision-making.*"

But it is not judicial decision-making at all to use a lawsuit as a "vehicle" to announce a new rule, and almost reluctantly to give those particular people, to the exclusion of all other citizens of the United States until the suspension period shall have passed, the benefit of the new rule.

The *only basis* ever given for any assertion that the Supreme Court can declare upon constitutionality is that the determination of a lawsuit depends upon a statute or an act of a governmental official which conflicts with the Constitution, and the Court must give supremacy to either the Constitution or the inferior law or governmental act. In performing its duty to decide cases, the Court could not avoid the *obligation* to declare upon constitutionality—not a power to be weilded, but a duty to be performed. In the Seventh Decade of the Twentieth Century, this was perverted into a new attitude that in the exercise of its claimed power to make rules, the Court could not avoid the obligation to surround the rule with an existing lawsuit by reluctantly giving one or two individuals the benefit of the rule even though the supposed constitutional commands were suspended for the rest of the nation.

Such arrogant judicial exercise of the law-making powers of Congress was the inevitable result of the national pretense that the Constitution means whatever the Supreme Court may say it means, substituting mere interpretations for the Constitution. This is the cause, and if the people tolerate its continuance, then the people will deserve the even more unpleasant consequences that will inevitably follow.

Too much concern over keeping criminals in prison while imposing new and reformed rules on all the nation's law-enforcement officers? An exercise of law-making powers and a suspension of laws that could never touch the honest, law-abiding citizen?

Cipriano v. City of Houma, June 16. 1969:
"Therefore, we will apply our decision in this case prospectively. That is, we will apply it only where, under state law, the time for challenging the election result has not expired, or in cases brought within the time specified by state law for challenging the election and which are not yet final.

This is the path to tyranny.

Part III

THE JUDICIAL IMPERATIVE
IN
ERAS OF CHANGE

VI.

THE IMPERATIVE OF JUDICIAL INTEGRITY

IT MUST INTEREST the wealthy to consider whether Congress has lawful power to impose confiscatory estate taxes which make it impossible for people to transmit their accumulated wealth to their children. It must interest the police and criminal alike to consider judicial restraints upon police methods of combatting crime. This must also concern the individual law-abiding citizen, fearful that protection of his life, his property, his freedom may be found less important than the actual or claimed constitutional protections accorded the criminal.

For our purposes, we have neither examined nor criticized the Supreme Court's premise as to the meaning of the Due Process Clause of the Fourteenth Amendment, that it includes such fundamental protections as the right to trial by jury, the right against compulsory self-incrimination, the right to be immune from unreasonable searches and seizures by state governments; indeed, in discussing the Miranda Warning rules, we implicitly accepted a variant of the Court's premise by suggesting that the same benefits might better have been reached by reference to other provisions of the Bill of Rights and of the original Constitution before any amendments were added.[1]

In granting to each of us some of the protections of the Bill of Rights against encroachments by our own state governments,[2] the Court has done nothing more than it could have done if each of its members had given up on the task of discovering the meaning of Due Process of Law, had voted "Let's give them their right to trial by jury," and had written opinions to demonstrate how basic the particular right is to fundamental American traditions. There is a temptation simply to be happy that the Court has finally granted to Americans the protection of parts of the Bill of Rights, finally effective against the state governments. But before responding emotionally, we should place a counter-weight on the emotional scale: An inquiry as to whether, in claiming to protect human rights, the Supreme Court may not have damaged those rights far more than it protected them.

---

1. See above, pp. 105-107.
2. Not all rights secured by the Bill of Rights have received the Supreme Court's probing examination and enforcement against violations by state governments. The Eighth Amendment prohibits excessive bail, yet courts often appear to set bail in a high amount for the purpose of assuring suspects would not be released from jail and could not commit more crimes while awaiting trial; this could be better accomplished, and the bail requirement obeyed by statutes requiring that sentences for crimes committed while on bail be served consecutively rather than concurrently, or simply by laws making it a crime for a person on bail not to appear in court when required. While the search warrant requirements of the Fourth Amendment are generally respected, and warrants are based upon factual affidavits demonstrating the reasons for suspecting contraband is being kept in the place to be searched, arrest warrant affidavits seldom detail evidence from which it is assumed that the suspect is probably guilty. They customarily simply state that the suspect probably committed the named crime, with no summary of evidence, under oath, from which a magistrate could determine, by examining the affidavit upon a *habeas corpus,* that there was in fact probable cause to believe the suspect committed the crime.

Our inquiry hopefully is far more fundamental than questioning whether the results of particular decisions are gratifying to the wealthy, the criminal, the police, the young desirous of avoiding compulsory military service, the civil libertarian. Our inquiry is into the quality of judicial fidelity to law, the quality of judicial integrity, upon which all rights of all citizens must depend.

It must be obvious that at some point in its history, the Supreme Court has been grossly incorrect in its conception of the meaning of Due Process of Law. Either in its concept that the Fourteenth Amendment's Due Process Clause *did not* impose upon states the obligation to accord citizens specific protections found in the Federal Constitution's Bill of Rights, or in its new decisions that the states must conform to parts of the Bill of Rights, the Supreme Court erred.

One of these views must be true and one false. The difference between the two must be something greater than mere honest difference in viewpoints as to the meaning of due process of law. If this is the only difference between yesterday's Supreme Court view and today's Supreme Court view of due process of law, then the written guarantee of due process of law was not worth the writing: It guarantees us nothing more than the benefits and burdens of the current judges' philosophical viewpoints of justice, which as a permanent guarantee is no guarantee at all.

In our search through some of the past Supreme Court decisions, we took no note of the meaning of due process of law because this was not the purpose of our examination of those decisions. Instead, our examination was for the purpose of learning characteristics of the improper use of judicial power. This inquiry is essential to determine whether the Supreme Court is subject to criticism on the only basis for legitimate criticism of any appellate court—the incorrect decision of lawsuits caused by intellectual inferiority, intellectual laziness or intellectual dishonesty.

These three defects in the exercise of judicial power may accurately be combined into a lack of judicial integrity. It is impossible, and actually of no benefit, to determine in any case whether the loss of judicial integrity was caused by intellectual inferiority, intellectual laziness, or intellectual dishonesty—the result is the same, and one can determine which of the three contributed most strongly to the loss of judicial integrity only by following an individual judge's mental processes in the decision of the individual case.

To illustrate, we return to the most fundamental device for the protection of liberty, the right to trial by jury. We have noticed that the citizen's right to trial by jury, growing from *Magna Carta's* "judgment of his peers," was designed to insulate the citizen from governmental power by placing a body of his fellow citizens between him and the wrath of government. At least, trial by jury came to be revered because it had the capacity to operate in that manner. If Congress should provide for the creation of a corps of jurors, for civil service examinations to select them, for extensive training in the business of judging whether conflicting testimony was caused by untruthfulness, forgetfulness, or differences in the opportunity to see what each witness claimed to have seen; if Congress should provide for training in the complex business of drawing conclusions from proven facts; and if Congress should provide for the corps of jurors to be headquartered in different parts of the country, and sent out for limited times by an executive secretary to decide lawsuits, so that they would be less subject to bribery, less apt to defer to the interests of the rich or the powerful—this concentration upon the *functions* of jurors in the trial of lawsuits would violate the *right* to trial by jury, because it would totally defeat the primary *purpose* of the guaranty of jury trial, the purpose of using independent individuals to insulate the individual litigant from the awesome power of government.[3]

If Congress should enact such a system to be applied to ordinary federal jury trials in civil and criminal cases, no court could allow itself to use such jurors except by rationalization concentrated upon the fact-finding function of juries, in total disregard of the utility of "trial by jury" which led to its incorporation into the Constitution. This disregard of the meaning of "trial by jury" when the Constitution was written could result from any of the three deficiencies in judicial integrity we have noticed.

A judge could lack the intelligence to realize that by exalting the function of the jury, the congressional act has destroyed the jury as an institution designed to carry out the purpose of protecting the individual from the power of the government. If the judge realizes that the new jury scheme actually destroys the right to trial by jury, but he nevertheless holds the law constitutional and utilizes the government's professional jurors, then his decision can be branded as nothing but intellectual dishonesty.[4] If the judge is intelligent and honest, and considers the new "jury" system to be both "reasonable" and an improvement in the administration of the business of the courts, and thereby holds the new jury law to be constitutional, without ever realizing that it destroys the entire purpose of trial by jury, then his decision results from intellectual laziness, from his failure to do the work necessary to learn what "trail by jury" meant when it came to be revered.

Assuming intellectual honesty, intelligence, and dedication to labor, it is clear that intellectual integrity can be lessened by factors that interfere with the impartial exercise of judgment—strong compassion for those subjected to government's laws, patriotic feelings arising from war threatening the existence of government, natural sympathy for aims temporarily popular. Given judges who are not intellectually dishonest, inferior, or lazy, they are nevertheless obligated to constantly be on guard to assure that compassion, patriotism, sympathy, prejudices, and other such personal attitudes will not warp their judgment in deciding constitutional questions.

Given these ideal conditions, some erroneous decisions are still inevitable because the attainment of perfection is beyond our capacity. The most the people can expect from their judicial system is the labor of intelligent, honest, and hardworking judges dedicated to the avoidance of bias and prejudice in the performance of their duties. This is also the least the people should demand.

The Supreme Court has expressly and repeatedly reiterated that the imperative of judicial integrity requires judicial obedience to the Constitution.[5] And we have postulated that which cannot be denied, that the imperative of judicial integrity is violated when, under pretense that the Constitution's supremacy is being re-

---

3. Do not assume that this example is so far-fetched that it could never occur, because there already exist more than one such corps of fact-finders created by Congress in areas where it is supposed that the constitutional right to trial by jury does not exist.

4. This may possibly be self-justified under the pressure of fear of reversal, a rationalization as to the "reasonableness" of the new system, or a subconscious unwillingness to risk the security of position or the possibility of future promotion to higher judicial posts by opposing popular demands for better-trained jurors as an aid to better law enforcement.

5. Such statements include the explicit statement that this imperative does not permit the courts to disregard constitutional commands. See above, p. 91.

spected, it in fact is being denied when judges "change" the meanings of words in the Constitution.

This is not to say that the adoption of our Constitution petrified English law and imposed it on our new nation without regard to changing circumstances. A careful study of the meaning of Constitutional provisions when they were written into the Constitution will often reveal that changed circumstances permit the enactment of law which actually does not do violence to the Constitution, though such a law might have been thought to be beyond the power of government in more primitive circumstances of life.

But to begin with the meaning of constitutional language when it was written and to proceed to an inquiry of whether changed and modern circumstances keep from conflicting with the Constitution a law that might have been in conflict with the Constitution if the statute had been written in 1795 [6] is one thing; to totally disregard the meaning of the constitutional provision when it was written, and to make up a different meaning for it instead, is an entirely different thing.

The one recognizes the supremacy of the Constitution in compliance with the judicial oath of office, and labors to discover whether new laws conflict with the Constitution, while the other disregards the supremacy of the Constitution and substitutes newly written words for constitutional provisions as the supreme law of the land. The action of a judge who fails to make any endeavor to discover the meaning of constitutional provisions when they were written is incompatible with the imperative of judicial integrity.

In construing some such phrase as "cruel and unusual punishment," judges may take note of the fact that what is cruelty is always related to accepted views of what is humane and inhumane; that these views differ in cruel and gentle ages— *i.e.,* judges may demonstrate from study that a phrase such as this *always,* by its nature, relates to current mores.[7]

But this is entirely different from intentionally changing the meaning of constitutional phrases which had well-accepted and universally recognized meanings when they were written. It differs from the conscious abandonment of established meanings of constitutional provisions and the conscious substitution of new and different meanings. One approach endeavors to determine the meaning of constitutional provisions when they were adopted, and the other approach abandons the meaning and by so doing, denies the supremacy of the constitutional provision which, if it has become outdated, can be changed by constitutional amendment.[8]

The people's entitlement to constitutional government, our entitlement to a government of laws headed by a supreme law containing safeguards against tyranny, instead of government by the whim of current rulers, entitles us to the dedicated labor of judges in an endeavor to educate themselves as to the meaning of the Constitution when it was written and each amendment when it was adopted.

---

6. Compare the common-law "range of headlights" rule, which was invalidated by changing circumstances. Chapter II, n. 1.

7. But this type of thinking could not properly be carried to the point of outlawing punishment on humane theories based upon empathy. To the person punished, all punishment is cruel, yet the Eighth Amendment does not forbid the imposition of punishment. Punishment is supposed to be painful.

8. If a wise proposed constitutional amendment cannot command sufficient popular support to be adopted, then those who view the present provisions as being outdated, whether they be judges or litigants, simply hold a minority view that is not entitled to become a part of the supreme law of the land.

By accepting a federal judicial post, a man holds himself out as being learned in the meaning of the Constitution and intelligent enough to correctly interpret it.

We have viewed some of the evidences of disobedience to the imperative of judicial integrity: The substitution of different phrases for phrases written into the Constitution; the "change" of meaning of constitutional provisions into new and different meanings; the judicial failure to adequately guard against the effects of personal attitudes [9] in construing constitutional provisions or laws enacted by Congress; the assumption that mere judicial interpretations may legitimately be substituted for the provisions judges interpret as part of the supreme law of the land; the judicial claim of right to exercise executive or legislative powers; the failure of the judiciary to recognize and keep in its proper place of inferiority to the Constitution; and the assumption that the act of declaring unconstitutionality is a *power* judges may exercise rather than a *duty* they are *unavoidably compelled* to perform as a part of the proper discharge of the duty to decide lawsuits.

Now is the time to apply these tests to some of the great lines of decisions by the United States Supreme Court. This should lead us to a determination of whether constitutional supremacy is actually important enough to impel thinking people to insist that the imperative of judicial integrity be obeyed.

---

9. Including not only bias and prejudice, but sympathy, outrage, patriotism, yesterday's popular economic theories, today's popular humanistic and egalitarian theories, newly enunciated scientific theories now thought to be beyond possibility of refutation by anyone now living or yet to come, an urgent need to right the wrongs of the past, and current popular opinions.

VII.

DUE PROCESS AND THE BILL OF RIGHTS

THE 1968 SUPREME Court religious freedom decision of *Epperson v. Arkansas* was one of the Court's more trivial decisions—trivial in the sense that the point of law decided could have no application anywhere except in Arkansas and Mississippi, and trivial in the sense that the opinion does not leave the impression that anyone on either side was vitally concerned as to how the case should be decided. Arkansas and Mississippi were the only states in the nation that had not repealed their "monkey" or anti-evolution teaching laws, and Miss Epperson sued to establish her right to teach evolution.

Public school teachers, like all other public employees, have the same freedom of speech and of the press as do other citizens. But when the Supreme Court hires a bailiff to open Court each morning, the man is employed to say precisely what his superiors instruct him to say: "God save the United States and this Honorable Court." He is paid and accepts a salary from the Government to forego exercising his freedom of speech during certain hours of the day. School teachers are also paid to teach in accordance with the instructions given them.

Throughout the nation, when the people of a community tax themselves to build their schools and hire teachers to teach their children, they like to have their children taught in accordance with their own traditions, be they cosmopolitan or Calvinistic. This would appear to be strictly *their* business, unless there is something in the law to prohibit it.

The Supreme Court announced in the *Epperson* case that it found a prohibition against Arkansas' "anti-evolution" teaching law in the First Amendment's freedom of religion provisions. The Court discussed the fact the statute originated from the "fundamentalist" fervor which viewed Darwin's theory as an attack upon the creation account in the Bible; but the Court failed to consider whether this law may have maintained state neutrality toward religion by withdrawing religious disputes from the public classrooms. The Supreme Court held that, because the people of Arkansas were motivated by their religious beliefs, the Constitution of the United States rendered void their attempt to make a law forbidding the teaching of a secular scientific concept. The phrase "the people of Arkansas" is used correctly, because this law was enacted by the voters themselves, not by their chosen legislators.

Aside from obvious doubts as to whether this Arkansas law actually involved religion except to the extent that it kept religious disputes out of the classroom, if the Constitution actually commands that every state be barred from enacting legislation motivated by religious beliefs, then the decision in *Epperson v. Arkansas* was simply a proper exercise of judicial power, even though Arkansas' legislative power was exercised by the people rather than by their legislators.

On the other hand, if the Constitution did not command the result reached by the Supreme Court, then the decision has most dangerous aspects. By it, the Supreme Court deprived the *people* of one state, albeit a small and comparatively

121

poor state, of the power to make a law they wanted, a law that fitted in with their culture, in the exercise of their *self-governing* powers. If the Constitution did not command the decision, then the Supreme Court, by depriving the people of Arkansas of their self-governing powers, itself violated the Tenth Amendment:

> "The powers not delegated to the United States by the Constitution or prohibited by it to the States, are reserved to the States respectively, *or to the people.*"

In the course of its opinion in *Epperson v. Arkansas,* the Supreme Court said: "There is and can be no doubt that the First Amendment does not permit the State to require that teaching and learning must be tailored to the principles or prohibitions of any religious sect or dogma." Here is the exact language of the First Amendment:

> "*Congress* shall make no law respecting an establishment of religion, or prohibiting the free exercise thereof; or abridging the freedom of speech, or of the press; or the right of the people peaceably to assmble, and to petition the government for a redress of grievances."

By what alchemy was the express denial to the Congress of any power to make laws on particular subjects converted into a denial of power to make such laws *to the people themselves?* The alchemy did not occur in *Epperson v. Arkansas,* but it occurred over a period of many years before that decision through a large number of decisions as to the extent to which the various states' self-governing powers were restricted by the new command included in the Fourteenth Amendment: ". . . nor shall any State deprive any person of life, liberty or property without due process of law."

The freedoms of speech, religion, and the press are a part of liberty, which state governments cannot take from persons without "due process of law," as is the freedom to walk the streets, to lie in the parks, to choose one's mate for marriage, to choose one's friends, to choose to remain aloof from the close ties of friendship, to choose one's life work, to choose idleness if one can find some lawful means to stave off starvation. None of these liberties can be taken from people by a state government but by due process of law.

"Due process of law" is one of our most ancient and cherished legal concepts for the protection of the individual from the tyranny of government. The phrase was ancient and its meaning well-understood when it was first written into our Bill of Rights in 1791. It derives from the older phrase "the law of the land," which was committed to writing for the protection of the people of England in the *Magna Carta* in 1215. With such an ancient phrase, one would expect that all the judges in the nation would be in unanimous agreement as to the historically correct meaning of due process of law.

However, at no time within the past fifty years, and longer, have the justices of the Supreme Court been in unanimous agreement as to the fundamental meaning of due process of law. In its long series of post-Civil War decisions on the freedoms of speech, religion, and the press, the Court has not once given a searching examination of the meaning of "due process of law" when it was first written into our Constitution.

To the contrary, in its decisions on these great freedoms we so deeply and rightly value, the Court has engaged in all the practices we have identified as evidences of a breach of the "imperative of judicial integrity." The Court has engaged in the wholesale creation of new phraseology, without preceeding this with a studious examination of the meaning of "due process of law" in 1791, and it has then treated such phrases as if they had somehow become a part of the supreme law of the land, though no constitutional amendment has enacted those phrases into law.

In *Snyder v. Massachusetts,* the Supreme Court held that the Fourteenth Amendment's due process clause forbids state action that "offends some principle of justice so rooted in the traditions and conscience of our people as to be ranked as fundamental." In *Palko v. Connecticut,* the Court equated due process of law to a "scheme of ordered liberty." Mr. Justice Holmes created the phrase "clear and present danger," which is now judicially treated as if it were a part of the Constitution. Other recent decisions we will notice have utilized the phrase "without redeeming social value" as supposedly having some connection with the Constitution's protection of the freedom of the press. The *Snyder* and *Palko* ideas, claiming for judges the power to decide which rights are so fundamental and essential as to entitle them to constitutional protection, have been used to *deny* citizens the benefit of rights expressly stated in the Bill of Rights. The phrase "clear and present danger" has been used to *permit* Congress to pass laws restricting the freedom of the press and the freedom of speech, though the First Amendment does not say that Congress shall not make laws restricting freedom of the press unless urgency demands the law: The Amendment says that Congress shall make *no* law respecting that subject. None of this Supreme Court phraseology was even conceived when the phrase "due process of law" was first written into the Constitution, and none of it is mere translation of the precise meaning of due process of law into more modern language.

As "due process of law" comes more and more to be equated with ideas of "fundamental traditions," procedures essential to a "scheme of ordered liberty," and even to ideas of reasonableness and fairness of governmental action, such views are considered to empower judges to sit in judgment upon the reasonableness of all laws, though such reasonableness is judged by Congress and by the legislatures when they enact the laws. With the increase of such tendencies, judges inevitably come more and more to pass upon the *wisdom* of all legislative action, under the guise of constitutional interpretation, though this is no business of the judges of this nation. When judges add to the Constitution, they violate it no less than when they violate express prohibitions, because the power to amend it is given to Congress and the States, not to mere judges.

The right to pass upon the wisdom or reasonableness of government action or inaction, whether legislative or executive, is *our right*—the right of the people, through the weight of our numbers, to determine whether we want to be governed little or much, wisely or foolishly, reasonably or unreasonably. When judges presume to invade this common right of the people, they trespass into an area which will not be tolerated by any free people sufficiently alert to deserve to retain their freedom.

This is not to assert that the Fourteenth Amendment should be so read as to give the people of each state less protection against the actions of their own state governments; to the contrary, it insists that we are entitled to greater protection: But to the protection of law, rather than the protection of the overseeing benevolent guardianship of judges. This view also insists that the great protections of the Bill of Rights and the Fourteenth Amendment, not just its Due Process Clause, are so fundamental that they deserve to be perpetuated. This view insists that these fundamental rights and liberties are not protected when their original meanings are forgotten by substituting for them the varying ideas of justice held from time to time by different judges.

Due Process of Law:

Through the Due Process Clause of the Fourteenth Amendment the Supreme Court has held that some of the provisions of the Federal Bill of Rights protect people against actions by state governments. What did due process of law mean when it was written into our Constitution? It must be remembered that the Due Process Clause is written into our Constitution twice, once in the Fifth Amendment, long accepted as a restriction only upon the powers of the Federal Government, and again in the Fourteenth Amendment where it is expressly repeated as a restriction on the power of each state government. Its meaning did not change during the fifty-seven intervening years. The discernment of its meaning is not so much a matter of opinion as it is a matter of reading old books to find out what it meant in 1791.

The initial determination, before the Fourteenth Amendment, that the Bill of Rights in no way restrained actions by state governments, came in Chief Justice Marshall's 1833 decision of *Barron v. Baltimore*. In this case, the City of Baltimore had blocked off a wharf owned by Barron so that ships could not get to it, rendering the property worthless for use as a wharf, and Barron sued, claiming that the city had taken his property "for public use without just compensation," in violation of that clause of the Fifth Amendment.

Chief Justice Marshall's opinion was based upon both the assumption that powers of the state governments should not be limited unless the Constitution expressly required it, and on language of a number of provisions of the original Constitution which expressly stated that the states should not exercise certain powers; his decision was not based upon a thorough analysis of the Bill of Rights, drawn after the Constitutional Convention did its work, and drawn by a different group of men. Most of those amendments are written in language designed to perpetually secure human rights, rather than to limit governmental powers. However, it appears that some provisions of the original Constitution could require state action, though they do not specifically state that states shall do or refrain from doing things.

In Article IV of the Constitution, the provision for the return of escaped slaves or indentured servants says that each such person "shall be delivered up on the claim of the party to whom the service or labor may be due." If the slave-owner should file *habeas corpus* against an individual offering the slave sanctuary, surely the state court would have been required to order the slave delivered up on the hearing of the case, a duty imposed upon the state government without the Constitution saying "the State shall." And the provision in the same article that the "citizens of each State shall be entitled to all privileges and immunities of citizens in the several states" was written in terms of rights given to citizens, not of obligations imposed upon states; yet state judges would surely be bound to recognize the supremacy of this law to a law enacted by their own state's legislature requiring discrimination against citizens temporarily there from other states.

Likewise, the Second Amendment's guaranty of "the right of the people to keep and bear arms" would be just as totally destroyed if the laws of all states made the possession of firearms illegal as if federal law attempted to make such possession illegal.[1] When particular provisions of the Bill of Rights say that they guarantee the rights of individuals, an interpretation truer to the Bill of Rights would have been one which treated the guarantee of rights as a guarantee of rights rather than a limitation upon governmental powers, which is a different mode of attempting to protect rights.[2]

But Marshall's interpretation had become traditional by the time the Fourteenth Amendment was adopted, with its Due Process Clause and its many other provisions. In its post-Civil War experimentation with the meaning of Due Process of Law, the Supreme Court has failed to do that which is demanded by the imperative of judicial integrity: To go back to the time the Constitution was written and determine exactly what "due process of law" meant at that time, to determine whether some slight change of meaning was effected when it was placed in the Fifth Amendment as a part of the supreme law of the land, to determine whether some other change in meaning was effected when it was placed in the Fourteenth Amendment as a restriction on the powers of state governments, and to enunciate a coherent historical meaning of due process of law applicable to all types of cases, without regard to how well particular constitutional rights in the Bill of Rights might be received in the philosophies of particular judges.

Instead of doing this, the Court's approach is as if its members were agreed that they should assign some great, fundamental and beneficial meaning to "due process of law," but could not agree on what that meaning should be.

The meaning of due process of law when it was written into the Constitution was neither complicated nor imprecise. It was actually quite simple, and did not include "ordered concept of liberty" or any of the other paraphraseology the Supreme Court has substituted for it in the past seventy years.

All concede that the phrase "due process of law" evolved from the phrase "law of the land" as written into *Magna Carta*. The *Magna Carta,* like other such charters, was a compact between the powerful king of England and his subjects, in which he conceded restraints upon his powers and limits to his prerogatives.[3] As Hamilton related in *The Federalist, Magna Carta* was reconfirmed by the Petition of Right, assented to by King Charles I, and by the "Dec-

---

1. And though worded in terms of a guarantee of rights, it is clear that the Second Amendment would be violated by any Federal legislation attempting to declare it a crime for a citizen to possess firearms in his own home.

2. In regard to trial by jury, Cheif Justice Marshall rationale in holding state governments free to disregard the Bill of Rights is quite unimpressive. Before the Bill of Rights, the Judicial Article of the Constitution said: "The Trial of all Crimes, except in Cases of Impeachment, shall be by Jury; and such Trial shall be held in the State where the said Crimes shall have been committed . . ." Then Congress and the legislatures adopted the Sixth Amendment, including: "In all criminal prosecutions, the accused shall enjoy the right to a speedy and public trial, by an impartial jury of the State and district wherein the crime shall have been committed, . . ." With the right to jury trial in Federal cases having already been assured by commands to the judiciary, it could be cogently urged that the Sixth Amendment prohibited infringement of this right by any American government, state or Federal.

3. Cooley, a leading Nineteenth Century authority on constitutional law, wrote in his *Constitutional Limitations* of the *Magna Carta:* "The grant of Magna Carta did not make the English a constitutional monarchy; it was only after repeated violations and confirmations of the instrument, and when a further disregard of its provisions had become dangerous to the Crown, that fundamental rights could be said to have constitutional guaranties, and the government to be constitutional."

laration of Right assented to by the Prince of Orange in 1688 and afterwards thrown into the form of an act of Parliament, called the Bill of Rights."

Magna Carta was not written in meaningless generalities. It concerned itself with specific areas in which the king was wont to attempt to extend his prerogatives. "No community or individual shall be compelled to make bridges at riverbanks, except those who from old were legally bound to do so." Of the governmental taking of private property: "Neither we nor our bailiffs shall take, for our castles or for any other work of ours, wood which is not ours, against the will of the owner of the wood.[4] Many other specific rights were guaranteed in plain language.[5]

The Due Process guarantee appeared as the thirty-ninth Chapter of *Magna Carta:*

> "No freeman shall be arrested, or detained in prison, or deprived of his freehold [lands], or outlawed, or banished, or in any way molested; and we will not set forth against him, nor send against him, unless by the lawful judgment of his peers or by *the law of the land.*"

This had a very simple and clear meaning. No man could be deprived of his life (outlawry), liberty, or property except by the lawful judgment of a jury of his peers, in accordance with the law of the land, whether that law be fair or unfair, reasonable or unreasonable. When we speak today of our cherished aim of "government of laws," we are speaking of due process of law. It was arbitrary action, action not required by the existing law of the land, that was barred as a means of the deprivation of the citizen's life, liberty or property. And the content of that land differed depending upon ancient customs, meaning one thing in the City of London and having different variations in other cities, boroughs, towns, and ports.

Magna Carta's concept of Law of the Land had nothing to do with what judges might consider to be "concepts of ordered liberty," or the law's justice, reasonableness, or appropriateness. The concept of Law of the Land insisted that there was LAW in existence, and that it was only in accordance with that existing law that a man could suffer governmental deprivation of his life, liberty, or property.

Just as in later years, the *Habeas Corpus* Act was a specific device contrived by the English to protect their personal rights from governmental usurpation, *Magna Carta* had its practical devices designed to secure its observance. The king was compelled to promise that "we will banish from the Kingdom all foreignborn knights, cross-bowmen, serjeants, and mercinary soldiers, who have come with horses and arms to the kingdom's hurt." This cause of complaint was to recur in

---

4. Here was no guarantee that property could not be taken without just compensation, as promised by the Fifth Amendment—this greater guarantee denied the executive the right to take private property at all, but left the freedom only to purchase it by private bargaining.

5. Of the right to free and speedy justice: "To no one will we sell, to no one will we refuse or delay, right and justice." Of the necessity of proof: "No bailiff for the future shall put any man to his 'law' upon his own mere word of mouth, without credible witnesses brought for this purpose." Of particular ancient rights enjoyed in different places: "And the citizens of London shall have all their ancient liberties and free customs, as well by land as by water; furthermore, we decree and grant that all other cities, boroughs, towns, and ports shall have all their liberties and free customs."

the English battle against royal tyranny that led to the language of the English Bill of Rights in 1688:

> ". . . King James the Second, by the assistance of divers evil counsellors, judges, and ministers employed by him, did endeavor to subvert . . . the laws and liberties . . . By raising and keeping a standing army within this kingdom in time of peace, . . ."

In the repetitious manner of the history of tyranny, this theme was to recur in 1776 when Jefferson wrote of the king's misdeeds in our Declaration of Independence—"He has combined with others to subject us to a Jurisdiction foreign to our Constitution, and unacknowledged by our Laws; giving his Assent to their Acts of pretended Legislation: For quartering large Bodies of Armed Troops among us . . ."

In addition to depriving the King of his foreignborn troops, *Magna Carta's* device for the enforcement of the rights and immunities it granted was the creation of a council of twenty-five barons, chosen by all the barons of England. If the charter should be violated, they were directed to engage in armed insurrection,[6] leading all the people, with the king's advance written commitment to recognize the insurrection as lawful, a thing we have attempted to achieve by periodic elections.

By the time of the American Revolution, the phrases Law of the Land and Due Process of Law had come to be used almost interchangably, though perhaps due process of law referred more to the procedural aspects of law, such as the right not to be tried without indictment by a grand jury.

By this time, Blackstone had written his *Commentaries,* his writings had been widely distributed among the lawyers of America, and he had written of the concept of due process of law:

> "It were endless to enumerate all the *affirmative* acts of parliament, wherein justice is directed to be done according to the law of the land; and what the law is, every subject knows, or may know, if he pleases; for it depends not upon the arbitrary will [7] of any judge; but is permanent, fixed and unchangeable, unless *by authority of parliament. . . .* Not only the substantial part, or judicial decisions, of the law, but also the formal part, or method of proceeding cannot be altered *but by parliament . . .* "

The existence of law with some degree of certainty was essential, for without this there was but arbitrary government, but the security of due process of law,

---

6. The Charter charged that the assembly of barons should "be bound with all their might, to observe and hold, and cause to be observed, the peace and liberties we have granted and confirmed to them by this our present Charter . . ." It said if four barons should unsuccessfully petition the king to remedy any violation of the Charter, "those five-and-twenty barons shall, together with the community of the whole land, distrain and distress us in all possible ways, namely, by seizing our castles, lands, possessions, and in any other way they can, until redress has been obtained as *they deem fit,* saving harmless our own person, and the persons of our queen and children; and when redress has been obtained, they shall resume their old relations toward us."

7. The judicial claim of power to say whether certain rights are based upon "fundamental principles of liberty and justice" or are essential to a "scheme of ordered liberty" is simply a claim that the unguided will of judges is the sole measure of whether rights will be protected as necessary ingredients of "due process of law."

at the time of American Independence, meant that the citizen was entitled to the benefit of whatever was provided by the law of the land when government moved against him to take his life, his liberty, or his property.

What happened to this concept of Due Process of Law with the American Revolution? What happened to it fifteen years later, with the writing of the Constitution of the United States and the Bill of Rights to that Constitution? And more than seventy years after that, when it was placed in the Fourteenth Amendment?

With the American Revolution, the massive body of common law rights remained, but the king no longer existed for America, and the underlying compacts between king and people no longer existed. Due Process of Law still existed as a concept, but the *Magna Carta* was not actually a written part of American law; and Due Process of Law in England had guaranteed to English citizens the protection not only of the royal charters, but of the vast body of common law and Acts of Parliament, all to be followed by the government when it moved to deprive an English citizen of life, liberty, or property.

It so happened that this body of law included the right to trial by jury, indictment by grand jury, and the immunity from warrantless searches and seizures of person or property. But the protective devices of law were not restricted to those few rights. Whatever right happened to be most valuable to a particular person at a particular moment was the right whose violation might cost him his life or his liberty.

A rule of evidence, the hearsay rule, was and is of inestimable value in assuring that rights would be determined on the basis of true facts rather than generally-accepted rumor, and this rule was many times one of the most valuable parts of the law included in the concept of due process of law, included not because it was *fundamental* but because it was *law*.

When the Due Process Clause was adopted as a part of the Constitution in the Fifth Amendment, it entitled the American, at least when the Federal Government should move to take his life, liberty, or property, to obtain the judgment of a court as to whether such interests could be forfeited, and it entitled him to the full protection of the laws of the land, whatever the scope of that protection. But just as clearly, the American Congress was not forever shackled with the existing state of 1790 common law procedures,[8] and if Congress should change the law of the land by enacting new laws, then the citizen would be entitled to the benefit of whatever that law provided when government moved to take his life, liberty, or property.[9] And though the compacts with the king were gone, and the law of the land might be varied by Congress, the rest of the Bill of Rights carefully guaranteed some of the common-law parts of the law of the land as being beyond the power of even Congress to change.

---

8. Indeed, common law procedures as such were no part of federal law, except to the extent that they were made law by congressional acts or constitutional provisions.

9. Thus when Congress enacted the provision of the Federal Communications Act making it illegal for anyone to intercept a telephone message and divulge its contents, this, to the extent of its validity, became a part of the law of the land, and if evidence obtained by wire tapping were used to imprison a citizen or to fine him, then the government would be endeavoring to take his liberty or property without due process of law, without giving him the benefit of the law of the land. All the "suppression of illegal evidence" cases discussed in Chapter V involved the application—and often the violation—of the Due Process Clauses of the Fifth and Fourteenth Amendments.

Due process of law, before it was written into our Constitution, had not to do with the fairness of law, or whether particular laws were sufficiently fundamental to be cherished and obeyed, but with the *existence* and *certainty* of law, with the requirement that every citizen have the benefit of the judgment of the courts as to whether government could forfeit his life, liberty or property, and that the courts, in giving their judgments, themselves be governed by existing and pre-determined law.

What happened to this Due Process of Law clause when it was rewritten into the Fourteenth Amendment as a limitation on the power of the states to deprive people of their lives, liberty, or property?

It is that if New York desires to deprive a person of his liberty, New York must do so in accordance with *its laws,* and must give the person the benefit of all the laws of New York which bear upon his case. New York must move under pre-established law, its courts must be open to the person for determination of whether New York can take his liberty, and those courts must decide according to the fixed law of the State of New York as it existed the moment of the happening of the events which gave rise to the case.

The most natural meaning of the Due Process Clause of the Fourteenth Amendment, the *only meaning* dictated by scholarship, is that the Federal Constitution now requires each state to give the full due processes of its laws to any person in depriving him of his life, liberty, or property.

This was the construction given to the Fourteenth Amendment's Due Process Clause in 1890, in Chief Justice Fuller's opinion in *Ex Parte Kemmler.* Kemmler had been convicted of murdering his wife and sentenced to death under a new New York statute that provided for electrocutions; Kemmler claimed this to be cruel and unusual punishment, and evidence was introduced in the New York state courts proving it more humane than taking life by hanging. New York's constitution had the same prohibition against cruel and unusual punishment as did the Constitution of the United States, both copied from the English Declaration of Rights enacted by Parliament in 1688.

In refusing to review the New York sentence of death by electrocution, the Supreme Court said: "This Declaration of Rights had reference to the acts of the executive and judicial departments of the government of England; but the language in question as used in the Constitution of the State of New York was intended particularly to operate upon the Legislature of the State, to whose control the punishment of crime was almost wholly confided. So that, if the punishment prescribed for an offense against the laws of the State were manifestly cruel and unusual, as burning at the stake, crucifixion, breaking on the wheel or the like, it would be the duty of the courts to adjudge such penalties to be within the constitutional prohibition. . . . As due process of law in the Fifth Amendment referred to that law of the land which derives its authority from the legislative powers conferred on Congress by the Constitution of the United States, . . . so, in the Fourteenth Amendment, the same words refer to that law of the land in each State, which derives its authority from the inherent and reserved powers of the State, exerted within the limits of those fundamental principles of liberty and justice which lie at the base of all our civil and political institutions."

That final clause, indicating that the concept of the law of the land had something to do with "fundamental principles of liberty and justice" was Chief Justice Fuller's only departure from the meaning of Due Process of Law when it was first written into the Federal Constitution, and it overlooked the facts that the people in America have not trusted to the unguided judgment of judges the protection of their rights, but have written into their Federal and State constitutions such rules as they have deemed "fundamental principles of liberty and justice." If the people want to add more fundamental principles of justice as beyond the legislative power to alter, it is *their* business to add them, not the business of judges.

Eighteen years later, the Supreme Court considered *Twining v. New Jersey,* a state prosecution of a bank officer who had falsified bank records to make it appear that the bank's board had authorized an expenditure of money which in fact had not been authorized. The trial judge commented to the jury that in determining whether Twining had done acts, they could consider his failure to take the stand and give his version of the facts in testimony. In reviewing the case, the Supreme Court held that the comments on Twining's refusal to testify, and his resulting conviction, did not take his liberty without due process of law, New Jersey then being one of only two American states whose constitutions did not contain the customary prohibition that no person shall "be compelled in a criminal case to be a witness against himself."

Having determined that Twining received the full benefit of the law of the land in New Jersey, and having noted the existence of confusion as to the meaning of Due Process of Law, the Court then proceeded to add to the confusion, with citations to earlier decisions, that the requirements of due process of law would have to be determined by the settled law and usages of England before the emigration to America, not to "be fastened upon the American jurisprudence like a straight jacket, only to be unloosed by constitutional amendment," but to be "ascertained from time to time by judicial action, . . ."

Thus the Court declared to the judiciary the power to determine from time to time what rights are included in "due process of law," when in fact these are discoverable by judicial scholarship, not by the exercise of judicial will.

Thus, *Twining v. New Jersey* and its predecessors made of the Fourteenth Amendment's Due Process Clause an empty vessel to receive whatever fundamental rights the judges might place within it, contrary to the basic purpose of both the due process clause and the written constitution: To reduce to writing the rules for the government of government, so that those limitations may not be forgotten. It was inevitable that many of the privileges and immunities secured to the people by the Federal Bill of Rights would eventually drift into the realm of fundamental rights, but that they would be accomodated to government convenience, and some of them might be but insubstantial shadows of their original strength. But it was also inevitable that other ideas of right and justice, held from time to time by different judges, would be voted into and out of the empty vessel of due process of law, depriving the people of each state of the freedom to design the rules they might want to govern their state governments.[10] Does this mean that the Federal Bill of Rights does not legitimately afford the citizen any protection against state governments, as where the state, like New Jersey, has no constitutional prohibition against self-incrimination?

The Bill of Rights and State Governments:

The Supreme Court, in its repeated holdings as to the extensive rights enforceable against states under the Fourteenth Amendment's Due Process Clause

10. Such power seizure obviously may impose a requirement to honor rights or follow procedures which the majority of the people would reject in voting on a proposed constitutional amendment.

in criminal proceedings, has, without admitting it, constantly moved closer to the views of one of its former members that the clause imposes upon each state the exact protective obligations afforded by the first eight amendments in the Bill of Rights. The argument's best statement from the Supreme Court came in Mr. Justice Black's dissenting opinion in *Adamson v. California.* This 1946 case involved the conviction of Adamson for murder and the imposition of the death penalty, based partly upon his failure to take the stand and testify in his defense, which was made the subject of impressive argument by the prosecuting attorney. The Supreme Court held in the *Adamson* case that the right against self-incrimination, secured to the people against violation by the Federal Government by the Fifth Amendment, was not secured against violation by state governments by the Fourteenth Amendment. As we have seen, the Court recently changed its mind.[11]

In his dissent, Justice Black made a fairly thorough exploration of the legislative history of the Fourteenth Amendment. The historical information furnished by Justice Black included a statement made by Congressman Bingham in 1871, five years after the proposed Fourteenth Amendment had first been debated in Congress in its present form. Among the Congressman's comments:

". . . I had the honor to frame the amendment as reported in February, 1866, as it now stands, letter for letter, and syllable for syllable, in the fourteenth article of the amendments to the Constitution of the United States, . . .

"These eight articles [the first eight amendments] I have shown never were limitations upon the power of the States, until made so by the fourteenth amendment. The words of that amendment, 'no State shall make or enforce any law which shall abridge the privileges or immunities of citizens of the United States,' are an express prohibition upon every State of the Union, which may be enforced under existing laws of Congress, and such other laws for their better enforcement as Congress may make."

But the strange thing is that in claiming that the Fourteenth Amendment made the first eight amendments applicable to the state governments, the Congressman was not even talking about the Due Process Clause of the Fourteenth Amendment, under which the Supreme Court has now decided these criminal cases. He was talking about the amendment's Privileges and Immunities Clause.

The trouble with taking the meaning of a statute from the words of the legislators who wrote the statute, is that Congressman Bingham and those who worked with him did not have the power to ordain the amendment all by themselves. It had to be passed by both houses of Congress and be approved by the president in order to become a proposed amendment, then it had to be accepted by the legislatures of three-fourths of the states in order to become an amendment to the Constitution.

If legislators *intend* to make a law, the way they carry out their intent is to write it into language so that it will be understood, and if Congressman Bingham had written "the restraints upon the Federal Government's powers in the first eight amendments to this Constitution apply equally to the government of each state," then his meaning would have been clear, but whether the language would have passed both houses of Congress and the legislatures of three-fourths of the states is by no means certain.

To make their meaning clear, legislators often choose words that already have

---

11. In *Griffin v. California,* described above, p. 100, n. 59.

well-established legal meanings from their use in the common law or in older statutes; and for the same purpose, they sometimes *avoid* the use of words having legally established meanings, and use other words to spell out the statute's broader or more narrow application.[12]

Congressman Bingham's first version of his Fourteenth Amendment did not even remotely approach accomplishment of the aims he claimed for the revised language. In revising the amendment into its present language, Congressman Bingham chose words surrounded by an aura of legal understanding, which was of value in getting both Congress and the state legislatures to adopt the proposed amendment.

Congressman Bingham chose three phrases, and these were written into the Fourteenth Amendment to protect people against their state governments. One was the Due Process Clause, which had behind it hundreds of years of legal understanding and which was itself written into the Fifth Amendment, where it had served as a limitation upon the powers of the Federal Government. Another clause assured from each state government "the equal protection of the laws," based upon a clause in the Massachusetts constitution and then understood, as we have seen, *not to prohibit* state-required racial segregation.[13] Congressman Bingham's hope—and the entire Congress' intent—for making the Federal Bill of Rights applicable to state governments was the Privileges and Immunities Clause of his amendment.

Far more impressive than Bingham's statements five years after the Privileges and Immunities Clause were written into the Constitution were his statements on the floor of the House of Representatives as he persuaded Congress to adopt the language of the Clause. Congressman Bingham had a unique idea as to the effect of the Federal Bill of Rights on state governments. This idea was never noticed by Chief Justice Marshall—and apparently by no court since Congressman Bingham spoke—when Marshall ruled in *Barron v. Baltimore* that the Bill of Rights was applicable only to the Federal Government, not the state governments. Bingham reasoned that the Bill of Rights was a part of the Constitution, which it is, and that all state judges have taken solemn oaths to support the Constitution, which they have. Large parts of the Bill of Rights guarantee rights to individuals, such as the right not to be compelled to testify against oneself in criminal cases and the right not to be tried twice for the same offense, and Bingham reasoned that state judges, having sworn to support that Bill of Rights, no matter what state law might say, were bound to honor that obligation in the conduct of trials in state courts, as by refusing to try a man a second time or refusing to compel a man to be a witness against himself. This appears to be valid reasoning.

But Congressman Bingham further noticed—and spoke of it on the floor of the House of Representatives—that the law-making power of the Congress did

---

12. For example, when Congress passed the Dyer Act, making it illegal to transport stolen automobiles in interstate commerce, Congress utilized a word "stolen," and gave it the established legal meaning from the phrase "intent to steal" in the common-law definition of larceny. This referred to more than a mere unauthorized borrowing, but required an intent to permanently deprive the owner of the automobile. Under this law, a young man could violate a state "joy-riding" statute making it a crime to use another's automobile without permission, and still be innocent of the federal crime, even if he drove the automobile across the state line and there wrecked it.

13. As to the probable incorrectness of this meaning when the Clause was placed in a different environment in the Fourteenth Amendment, see above, Chapter IV.

not extend to the protection of *any constitutional rights*. He noticed that the Necessary and Proper Clause in the Legislative Article of the Constitution gives Congress the power to enact laws necessary and proper to carry out *powers* granted the Federal Government by the Constitution, but that there was no provision authorizing Congress to pass laws to protect the *rights* secured to citizens by the Constitution. Congressman Bingham proposed to remedy this, which he did by the final section of the Fourteenth Amendment. The First Section of the Fourteenth denies to each state the power to infringe the privileges and immunities of citizens of the United States, which Congressman Bingham and everybody else in Congress viewed as including principally the individual constitutional rights secured by the Federal Bill of Rights, and the final section of the Amendment authorizes Congress to enforce the entire amendment by appropriate legislation.

When Congressman Bingham began his battle to secure to citizens the protection of the Federal Bill of Rights against their state governments, he was challenged in his assertion that these rights were not already secured by the language of the Bill of Rights. Responding to the challenge on February 28, 1866, Congressman Bingham read to the House an excerpt from *Barron v. Baltimore*. He then made a lengthy speech,[14] in which he said:

"Why, sir, what an anomaly is presented today to the world! We have the power to vindicate the personal liberty and all the personal rights of the citizen on the remotest sea, under the frowning batteries of the remotest tyranny on this earth, while we have not the power in time of peace to enforce the citizens' rights to life, liberty, and property within the limits of South Carolina after her State government shall be recognized and her constitutional relations restored.

"As the whole Constitution was to be the supreme law in every State, it therefore results that the citizens of each State, being citizens of the United States, should be entitled to all the privileges and immunities of citizens of the United States in every State, and all persons, now that slavery has forever perished, should be entitled to equal protection in the rights of life, liberty and property."

This new Privileges and Immunities Clause forbade each state to "make or enforce any laws which shall abridge the privileges or immunities of citizens of the United States." This used a clause from a provision in the original Constitution: "The citizens of each State shall be entitled to all privileges and immunities of citizens in the several states."

"Several" in legal usage means "separate," and in the original constitutional provision, that Privileges and Immunities Clause, by its plain words, said that when a citizen of New Jersey went to New York, even for a day, he should have the same privileges and immunities as a citizen of New York, but no more. If New York let its citizens enter the state from surrounding states, then a New Jersey citizen had the rights to enter. If New York permitted each of its citizens to sell apples on street corners without licenses, then a citizen of New Jersey should enjoy the same right without any discrimination. If New York did not give its citizens the right to vote until they had resided in New York 5 years and attained the age of 21 years, then a forty-year-old New Jersey citizen moving to New York could not attain the right to vote until he, like New York citizens, had resided there for five years.[15]

---

14. Dated quotations from congressional proceedings during this period are from *The Congressional Globe* issue of the particular date.

15. This expounds the literal language of the clause and is not presented as a summary of judicial decisions.

But the slight language change when the clause was carried over into the Fourteenth Amendment raised an obvious question: "What are the privileges and immunities of American citizenship?"

Pre-Civil War decisions had held that the Bill of Rights only protected the citizen against the Federal Government, and an 1875 Ku Klux Klan case, *United States v. Chuikshank,* correctly made it clear that the protection of the Fourteenth Amendment's Privileges and Immunities Clause was not so broad as to protect individual citizens from injury by their fellow citizens, as distinguished from injury by the states. The rights to protection of one's life, person, and property from injury by other people are all governed by state laws, and always have been, so that the right to sue when a neighbor burns your home is not a privilege of American citizenship, controlled by laws made by Congress, but it is purely a matter of local state law.

In 1899, the new Privileges and Immunities Clause in the Fourteenth Amendment was effectively destroyed by the Supreme Court decision of *Maxwell v. Dow.* This was a *habeas corpus* case in which Maxwell had been convicted of armed robbery in Utah. The conviction was based upon a charge made by the prosecuting attorney instead of a grand jury indictment, and the trial and conviction were before an eight-man jury instead of the common-law jury of twelve. In these two respects, Maxwell's prosecution and conviction failed to conform to the Fifth and Sixth Amendments in the Federal Bill of Rights, and Maxwell claimed that these rights were among the privileges and immunities of American citizenship, secured against state violation by the Fourteenth Amendment. But the Supreme Court held that the protections afforded by the Federal Bill of Rights were not among the privileges and immunities of Amrican citizenship, saying of the first ten Amendments' provisions:

> "In none are they privileges or immunities granted and belonging to the individual as a *citizen* of the United States, but they are secured to *all persons* as against the Federal government, entirely irrespective of such citizenship."

So the Supreme Court construed "privileges and immunities" of citizens of the United States as consisting of none but those which were granted solely to American citizens on the basis of American citizenship. This included the right to become a citizen of any state in the nation by simply moving to that state and becoming a resident of it; the right to use any of the seaports of the nation; the right to move freely between states; the right to assemble and petition the Federal (but not a state) government for the redress of grievances. This places narrow limitations upon the privileges and immunities of American citizenship. Indeed, this list contains only privileges and no immunities at all.

Actually, all these rights of American citizenship were derived by judicial construction of constitutional provisions,[16] and dubious construction at that, except

---

16. Judicial reluctance to deal with the sweeping and powerful Privileges and Immunities Clauses follows the initial endeavor to expound the original clause, that by Mr. Justice Washington in *Corfield v. Coryell,* decided in his capacity as a circuit judge. He said, "We feel no hesitation in confining these expressions to those privileges and immunities which are, in their nature fundamental . . ." From this flowed the judicial habit of refusing to expound the meaning of the original Privileges and Immunities Clause, but holding that it must be determined in each case whether a particular privilege or a particular immunity were within the protection of the clause. The idea

the right to become a citizen of a state by simply residing there. This particular right was created by the very first sentence of the Fourteenth Amendment; it seems rather pointless to immediately re-create it in the very next sentence by the Privileges and Immunities Clause. Actually, the Constitution nowhere declares in so many words a specific list of privileges and immunities to be granted to citizens and denied to non-citizens.

Chief Justice Marshall's 1833 decision of *Barron v. Baltimore* was followed in word and spirit in *Maxwell v. Dow's* restrictive holding that the Privileges and Immunities Clause does not secure citizens from violation by the states of the specific rights protected by the Bill of Rights. Even assuming Marshall's decision entirely correct, it by no means follows that the human rights secured by the Bill of Rights are not privileges and immunities of American citizenship.[17]

The Constitution begins with the words, "We, the People," and the Second and Fourth Amendments are written in terms of rights guaranteed to the people: "the right of the people to keep and bear arms" and the "right of the people to be secure . . . against unreasonable searches and seizures . . ." Do these provisions not grant rights to the people, or citizens, of the United States: Surely, no one would insist that aliens temporarily living in the country are guaranteed by the Second Amendment the right to keep and bear arms! And the Fifth and Sixth Amendments' extensive guarantees of rights to "persons" and to "the accused" in criminal prosecutions are no less privileges of American citizenship because the Constitution secures them to aliens as well as citizens. In some cases, under treaties, these rights even follow citizens into foreign countries.

The rights of aliens to own property in foreign countries are generally treated by international law and by treaties, and the United States has many times seized the property of enemy aliens in time of war, with the final outcome settled by treaty, despite the Fifth Amendment's provision, "nor shall private property be taken for public use without just compensation." And in the matter of other protections furnished by the Bill of Rights, the Supreme Court's decision in *Fong Yue Ting v. United States,* as in other cases before and after it, accorded to the alien rights far less extensive than those accorded to citizens of the United States—such treatment including a denial of the right to trial by jury and a requirement that the individual Chinaman prove his innocence rather than requiring the Government to prove his guilt.

There is actually more reason to agree than to disagree with Congressman Bingham's claim of the meaning of the Privileges and Immunities Clause of the Fourteenth Amendment—that those rights guaranteed as rights by the Bill of Rights are privileges and immunities of American citizenship, even if some may be shared also by non-citizens and are protected against state action: That when the Fourteenth Amendment commands that "No state shall make or enforce any law which shall abridge the privileges or immunities of citizens of the United

---

that only fundamental privileges recognized by all the states was expressed by Justice Washington in this manner: He first wondered at the definition of "privileges and immunities of citizens *in* the several states . . ." and in the next sentence shifted to consideration of the rights of "citizens *of* the several states". His entire treatment was unsound. "Several" meant individual, separate, as contrasted with the conglomerated mass. The entire clause had a much broader meaning than indicated by Justice Washington.

17. The Bill of Rights contains both language guaranteeing rights and language limiting government powers.

States," it means that no state can take a citizen's private property for public use without just compensation any more than can the Federal Government, and that no state, in its own public or judicial proceedings, can deny to people any of the express rights guaranteed by the Federal Bill of Rights.

But not all of the Federal Bill of Rights is worded as a guarantee of rights; in parts, it is a limitation upon powers. The Seventh Amendment says the right of trial by jury shall be preserved in civil cases where the value in controversy exceeds twenty dollars, but it goes on to say that no fact determined by a jury "shall be otherwise reexamined in any court of the United States than according to the rules of the common law," a clear regulation of the manner of exercise of judicial power by the Federal court system, having nothing to do with a guarantee of rights nor with state courts. Also the Tenth Amendment, which we have discussed briefly,[18] can have no possible application to any government but the Federal Government.

But of primary importance is the First Amendment, which does not pretend to guarantee *any rights,* but instead totally forbids Congress, and Congress alone, to make any law regarding the freedoms of speech, the press, religion, and the freedom to assemble and petition the Government.

The Supreme Court has clung to the decisions of *Maxwell v. Dow* and similar cases,[19] holding that the rights guaranteed by the Bill of Rights are not among the privileges and immunities of citizens of the United States, and has instead held, often by claiming to exercise some rule-making power it declares itself to possess, that many of these rights are "protected by" the Due Process Clause of the Fourteenth Amendment.

The Supreme Court's superficial treatment of the Fourteenth Amendment's Due Process Clause has denied to the people the great protection that Amendment promises. And it effectively weakens the law of the land in each state. In most states, judges are elected for terms instead of being appointed for life, and it must require almost super-human effort for judges to be able to totally exclude any concern for the popular "acceptability" of their decisions. The certain knowledge that Supreme Court review would require state courts to give each individual the full protection of due process of state law would doubtless strengthen the resolve and clarify the thinking of state appellate judges. The Supreme Court has failed to carry out the mandate of due process of law in the Fourteenth Amendment and has substituted for it a different and far less valuable meaning.

Too often, appellate courts, state and federal alike, either incorrectly paraphrase or fail to mention serious legal questions raised, so that both the people involved in the lawsuit and their lawyers must hold the unspoken belief that the appellate court *could not* write a sound opinion honestly refuting the arguments made. This is not due process of law; it substitutes professional inadequacy or judicial inattention for government of laws. Due Process of Law in the Fourteenth Amendment is a promise never realized, just as the Privileges and Immunities Clause remains a mandate never obeyed.

---

18. See above, pp. 121-122.

19. In *Twining v. New Jersey,* discussed above, p. 130, in relation to its due process holding, Twining claimed his right against self-incrimination secured by the Bill of Rights, was protected against state violation by the Privileges and Immunities Clause of the Fourteenth Amendment. The Supreme Court said only that since the decision in *Maxwell v. Dow,* "the question is no longer open in this court." This apparently successfully blocked further and more careful consideration of the meaning of the clause.

Freedom of the Press:

With the adoption of the First Amendment, a position of Federal neutrality was taken toward the great freedoms that are so useful in protecting the people governed against abuses by government itself. In *Beauharnais v. Illinois,* Justice William O. Douglas wrote:

> "The First Amendment says that freedom of speech, freedom of press, and the free exercise of religion shall not be abridged. That is a negation of power on the part of each and every department on government. . . . Today a white man stands convicted for protesting in unseemly language against our decisions invalidating restrictive covenants. Tomorrow a negro will be hailed before a court for denouncing lynch law in heated terms. . . . Emotions sway speakers and audience alike. Intemperate speech is a distinctive characteristic of man. Hot heads blow off and release destructive energy in the process. They shout and rave, exaggerating weaknesses, magnifying error, viewing with alarm. So it has been from the beginning; and so it will be throughout time. The Framers of the Constitution knew human nature as well as we do. They too had lived in dangerous days; they too knew the suffocating influence of orthodoxy and standardized thought. They weighed the compulsions for restrained speech and thought against the abuses of liberty. They chose liberty."

If one would read, in inspiring rhetoric with accurate historical references, the reasons for protection of the great First Amendment freedoms one could find no better starting place than the most recent Supreme Court decisions on these subjects. One who reads such decisions can hardly escape the conclusion that these fundamental freedoms are well worth protecting; and that the best response to unpopular ideas—whether religious or moral, economic or political, serious or trivial —is to permit the ideas to be sounded so that they may either win over the majority or suffer repudiation by the majority, depending upon their intrinsic worth.

The cheapening of the Due Process Clause of the Fourteenth Amendment has had its most absurd results in connection with these cherished First Amendment freedoms. Though the First Amendment in the plainest possible language *does not command* that the people's enjoyment of these rights shall not be infringed, but only forbids *Congress* to pass *any law* infringing those rights, this restriction has been converted by the Supreme Court into a supposed identical restriction on the power of every state government, except that the federal government is given greater restraining power over the exercise of these freedoms than the state governments.

Every individual dislikes restraints upon his freedom and strives for as much freedom as possible. But given absolute freedom, I might enrich myself by killing you instead of working for you. And your gun might shoot further and your aim be truer than mine, so for our own self-protection, each of us must choose government and law to protect us from the terrible hazards of totally unrestrained and irresponsible freedom. And if we treasure freedom, we must insist upon the supremacy of constitutions and laws over the arbitrary caprice of individual rulers, be they executives, legislators or judges.

Speech, the press, religion, the right to assemble have all been used to infringe the liberty of those who disagree and to do them great harm. When settlers fled to America to secure freedom of religion, they promptly made their rules denying freedom of religion to those who wanted to worship differently or not at all. Speech and the press have been used to arouse people to needlessly infringe the freedom of others. *All freedoms* must have their limits or anarchy will result, the state constitutions are written to protect these essential freedoms, but also to allow for that minimum amount of control which must exist to protect the safety of the majority and of minorities alike.

The pretense that the power of the state government and the power of the federal government in regard to these freedoms are identical has inevitably and inexcusably led to a crippling of the states' powers to impose limits upon the irresponsibility of absolute freedom. It has also led to the enactment of federal laws infringing the freedom of the press, though the First Amendment says quite plainly that Congress shall pass no such law.

By its course of decisions, the Supreme Court has deprived the people of every state of the right to amend their constitutions and to pass such laws as are compatible with their traditions concerning these great freedoms. To this extent, the Court has nullified, in every state, the republican form of government, of which the Constitution declares: "The United States shall guarantee to every State in this Union a republican form of government, ..." The Court's decisions injurious to those freedoms have been rendered in the name of freedom.

Judges reach their benches through the exercise of political appointive power, and are not apt to be politically naive. One might anticipate that, in the substitution of the meaningless "fundamental principles of liberty and justice" for the constitutionally commanded due process of state law, judges would have a natural and deep appreciation for those particular freedoms so useful in the arts of democratic politics, the freedoms of speech and of the press. It is therefore not surprising that these would be among the first "fundamentals" to be placed in the empty receptacle of "Due Process of Law." Disregarding the varying contents of the law of the land in each state, the Supreme Court has formulated for every state its current ideas of what should be the content of each state's law of the land in regard to the press, speech, religion.

Freedom of the press stands in an entirely different category from *all* the other rights "protected" by the Federal Bill of Rights. The Americans had enjoyed and used the press as a valuable instrumentality to achieve their freedoms, but this was a right still in the process of being formulated, not an ancient freedom to be perpetuated, but as a new freedom to be created. In his work on *Constitutional Limitations,* Judge Cooley wrote in the 1870's history of freedom of the press:

> "At the common law, however, it will be found that liberty of the press was neither well protected nor well defined. The art of printing, in the hands of private persons, has, until within a comparatively recent period, been regarded rather as an instrument of mischief, which required the restraining hand of the government, than as a power for good, to be fostered and encouraged. Like a vicious beast it might be made useful if properly harnessed and restrained. The government assumed to itself the right to determine what might or might not be published; and censors were appointed without whose permission it was criminal to publish a book or paper upon any subject. . . .
>
> "The American Colonies followed the practice of the parent country. Even the laws were not at first published for general circulation, and it seemed to be thought desirable by the magistrates to keep the people in ignorance of the precise boundary between that which was lawful and that which was prohibited, as more likely to make them avoid all doubtful actions. The magistrates of Massachusetts, when compelled by public opinion to suffer the publication of general laws in 1649, permitted it under protest, as a hazardous experiment. For publishing the laws of one session in Virginia, in 1682, the printer was arrested and put under bonds until the king's pleasure could be known, and the king's pleasure was declared that no printing should be allowed in the Colony. . . ."

Cooley was writing primarily of the constitutional restraints upon state governments, but this excerpt accurately demonstrates the status of freedom of the press —a freedom sought, a freedom whose limitations were still in the process of formulation, a freedom still in the process of expansion. This freedom of the press consisted primarily of freedom from censorship.

James Madison was one of the authors of both the First Amendment and the free press provisions of the Constitution of Virginia. Under his leadership, the First Amendment was written to prohibit Congress from making *any* law "abridging the freedom . . . of the press . . ." This had coupled with it no provision reserving to Congress the power to punish abuses of that freedom. It pretended to restrict and destroy the powers of no governmental agency but the Congress. But the free press provisions Madison and his associates placed in the Constitution of Virginia was quite different:

> "That the freedom of the press is one of the great bulwarks of liberty, and can never be restrained but by despotic governments, and any citizen may speak, write, and publish his sentiments on all subjects, *being responsibile for the abuse of that liberty.*"

To abridge is to reduce, to abbreviate, it reduces the scope of any liberty to penalize those who exercise that liberty, and Congress is totally denied the power to abridge the freedom of the press to the slightest extent. In Virginia, the state was forbidden to restrain—by censorship, injunctions, the requirement of licensure, or other means—the exercise of anyone's freedom to print treasonous, obscene, libelous or blasphemous matter, or propaganda encouraging criminal behavior. But Virginia was free, by its pre-determined law, to declare any type of publication or speech an abuse of the freedom of the press, and provide civil or criminal liability as a means of imposing responsibility upon the speaker, the writer, or the publisher for his illegal acts in the abuse of these protected freedoms. Most states, in their constitutions, followed this same course to varying degrees. But no basis can be found in any provision of the Constitution of the United States for the Congress to claim power to impose responsibility upon people for the abuse of these First Amendment rights.

Yet such responsibility was imposed by an Act of Congress and the Act was enforced by the Supreme Court, despite the First Amendment, in a wartime case, *Schenck v. United States.* The Court's opinion was written by Justice Oliver Wendell Holmes, Jr., one of our greatest judges, but he made mistakes [20] as do all judges. He was a patriotic man, had fought in the Civil War, and in his patriotic decision of this case, he gave the nation a phrase he should never have written: "Clear and Present Danger." Unlawfully elevated to status as a part of the Constitution, it provides the means for enforcing laws made by Congress in an area in which the Constitution denies Congress any law-making power.

The case was decided during the war-time fervor of World War I, under a 1917 Espionage Act making it criminal to attempt to obstruct the "recruiting and enlistment service of the United States . . ." Schenck, a Socialist, had 15,000 leaflets printed: He asserted conscription was illegal involuntary servitude,[21] he urged his readers not to submit and criticised the war as benefiting "Wall Street's chosen few." Indicted and convicted for this use of his freedom of the press, his

---

20. A great student of the common law, Justice Holmes, when sitting as a state judge, once held that when two trains approach a rail intersection at the same time, it is the duty of each to stop and wait until the other has passed.
21. See the discussion of *Arver v. United States,* above, pp. 69-71.

conviction was upheld by the Supreme Court. The Court's opinion did not indicate that the propaganda inspired a single draftee to refuse to report, or even to file a lawsuit contesting the validity of the draft laws. The Court sought to justify this conviction:

> "The question in every case is whether the words used are used in such circumstances and are of such a nature as to create *a clear and present danger* that they will bring about substantive evils that Congress has the right to prevent."

The Constitution's absolute denial of power was thus converted into a denial of power unless Congress should feel the urgency of the situation demanded that it exercise the power flatly denied to it by the Constitution. In truth, such denials of power by the Constitution mean that the power cannot be lawfully exercised under *any* circumstances.[22]

Mr. Justice Holmes' opinion in the case made it clear his judgment was colored, even controlled, by patriotism:

> "When a nation is at war many things that might be said in time of peace are such a hinderance to its effort that their utterance *will not be endured* so long as men fight, and that no court could regard them as protected by any constitutional right.[23]

The Supreme Court's landmark case on freedom of the press, *Near v. Minnesota,* added to the befuddlement as to the meaning of due process of law by concentrating on the common law history of freedom of the press without making any inquiry as to what this might have to do with the law of the land in Minnesota.

Near and his associate Guilford were subjected to litigation in the Minnesota case of *State ex rel. Olsen v. Guilford,* arising from their publication of a newspaper filled with hatred for Jews. Typical: "It is Jew, Jew, Jew, as long as one cares to comb over the record."

Minnesota had a law authorizing injunctions against engaging in the business "of regularly and customarily producing, publishing or circulating, . . . a malicious, scandalous and defamatory newspaper, . . ." An injunction was issued prohibiting Near from engaging in such a business, and if Near should violate this injunction, he would be subject to punishment of a year's imprisonment without any right to

---

22. Consider the provision that the United States shall guarantee to each state a republican form of government. If a governor should become so popular that he could completely control government, effectively abolishing the legislature and acquiring power to dispense with elections and name his own successor, this would be an abolition of the republican form of government in that state. Congress would be required to restore to the state a republican form of government, probably by an Act scheduling an election under Federal control to choose delegates to write a new state constitution. Presented with more than a clear and present danger, but the accomplished fact of a major constitutional violation, Congress could not seek to remedy this by enacting a bill of attainder, ordering that the 1-state dictator be put to death, because the Constitution prohibits the passage of any such bills.

23. Is this not a confession of bias? Given the very best judges, occasions will arise in which their impartiality will be overshadowed by powerful emotions arising from compassion, patriotism, prejudices of their time and culture. The aim of every judge should be to exclude all such biased judicial attitudes, not to hold them up as examples to be followed.

trial by jury, this being the historical means of enforcing injunctions. On appeal, the Supreme Court reversed the injunction judgment. It quoted from the opinion of the Minnesota Supreme Court, including the sentence, "It is a matter of common knowledge that prosecutions under the criminal libel statutes do not result in *efficient repression or suppression* of the evils of scandal." This was contrary to the entire philosophy of freedom of the press guarantees, that there should never be *efficient repression or suppression* of the press, but only imposition of liability for misconduct in publishing, with a jury to stand between the citizen and the government in the government's attempt to impose the penalty.

The Minnesota Supreme Court had recognized that its constitution prohibited censorship or any requirement of governmental permission to publish anything, and said that "no agency can hush the *sincere and honest* voice of the press; . . ." Near gave every appearance of sincerely and honestly hating Jews and a host of local governmental officials [24] and competitors, but the Minnesota court failed to recognize that the injunction is among the most effective ways of destroying the freedom [25] to "publish their sentiments on *all* subjects." The Minnesota court tried to justify the injunction statute by pointing to a number of other statutes authorizing injunctions to combat liquor, prostitution, itinerant carnivals and noxious weeds, without, however, claiming that the state's constitution promised that the right to engage in prostitution or grow noxious weeds should forever remain inviolate.

The United States Supreme Court adequately demonstrated that the Minnesota injunction was a restraint on the right to publish,[26] but did this as a general comment on the common law of freedom of the press, without relating it to the law of Minnesota, so instead of giving Near the benefit of the law of the land in Minnesota, the Court in essence determined itself the scope of the law of the land on this subject in every state, which it had no power to do. With its excellent research facilities, the Supreme Court can obviously contribute greatly to the understanding of popularly-used state constitutional phrases, but the right to determine the scope of freedom of the press in Minnesota belonged to the people of Minnesota.

In the field of freedom of the press, as in few others, do we find demonstrations

---

24. Near was entitled to a reversal of the injunction destroying his freedom of the press in regard to future publications, because when Minnesota did this, it took this liberty from him without power to do so under Minnesota's law of the land, as found in its constitutional provision that all persons may "publish their sentiments on all subjects, being responsible for abuse of such right."

25. The injunction is a particularly pernicious means of restricting liberty, for when the injunction is violated, the punishment is historically, and still quite commonly, imposed by the judge who issued it; a person prohibited by an injunction from doing something is sometimes viewed as being prohibited from violating the spirit as well as the precise words of the injunction—he is prevented from evading it by only respecting the letter and disregarding the essence of the injunction. For this reason, an injunction against publication must cause a publisher to constantly hesitate as to what he might publish, even if he believes it to be true and even if he believes it to be something the public needs to know in furtherance of sound government.

26. The Court quoted from Madison and others as to the purpose of freedom of the press, to tolerate no advance restrictions, or previous restraints, on what could be printed. The Court quoted from Blackstone, who wrote of the freedom to publish, but added that "if he publishes what is improper, mischievous or illegal, he must take the consequence of his own temerity."

of the evil of the false assumption that Supreme Court decisions are a part of the supreme law of the land, instead of merely attempted interpretations of the supreme law. By disregarding the historical meaning of due process of law, that government must move in accordance with the law of the land when it deprives a person of his life, liberty, or property, the Supreme Court set out to discover a uniform law as to the limits of the press' freedom from governmental control, never pausing to notice the obvious: That there was no uniform law as to the freedom of the press in the various states. This was coupled with Mr. Justice Holmes' patriotic creation of the slogan "clear and present danger," which blocked further exercise of the judicial intellect [27] on the basis essential to respect for the imperative of judicial integrity, the actual meaning of words written into the constitutions and laws.

Two more recent cases on subjects of popular excitability will indicate the extent of destruction, solely by Supreme Court decisions presumed to be law, of the twin bodies of law protecting the freedom of the press and holding the press responsible for its abuses of this great freedom, protected not for the benefit of the press, but for the benefit of the people.

These two cases involve subjects that were of grave public concern when the decisions were rendered, Communism in *Dennis v. United States,* and black striving for equality in *New York Times v. Sullivan.*

Only three years after the end of World War II, the Government prosecuted a number of American Communist leaders, including Eugene Dennis, for conspiracy to teach or advocate the overthrow of the Government of the United States by force or violence.

At the height of the most grave and real concern over Communism's threat to the existence of the American government, in 1951, the United States Supreme Court rendered its decision in *United States v. Dennis.* The Communist leaders were prosecuted under a Federal law, the Smith Act. This law made it a crime to speak, to print, or to assemble in advocating the overthrow of any government in the United States by force or violence, though the First Amendment, in plain, simple, and unmistakable language, denies Congress and Congress alone the power to make laws "abridging the freedom of speech, or of the press; or the right of the people peaceably assemble, and to petition the government for a redress of grievances." Yet Communist leaders were convicted in a Federal District Court in New York, over their protests that the Smith Act violated the First Amendment, and the United States Supreme Court affirmed their convictions over the same protests.

The state of New York, where these events occurred, *had* strong laws against such speech and activities enacted within its constitutional authorization to impose responsibility for abuse of the freedom of speech.[28]

---

27. Before the *Schenck* case, Justice Holmes has written in *Hyde v. United States:* "It is one of the misfortunes of the law that ideas become encysted in phrases and thereafter for a long time cease to provoke further analysis." This was the fate of his phrase, "Clear and Present Danger," which was to continue to serve as an excuse for the exercise of power denied to Congress by the Constitution.

28. As to the practicality of using criminal prosecutions to combat revolutionary preaching, the powers of the Federal Government, assuming the First Amendment's non-existence, pale beside the powers the state constitutions give to the state governments. If individual revolutionaries should abuse the freedom of speech by their teachings in different states, each state could successively prosecute them for violations

But by the time of the 1948 Communist conspiracy prosecution, the Supreme Court had virtually destroyed the powers of the states, acting within the limitations of their own constitutions, to impose responsibility for abuses of the freedoms of speech and the press.

One of the numerous cases in which the Supreme Court had declared such state laws invalid was a 1931 decision, *Stromburg v. California,* declaring too vague for enforcement a state anti-Communist statute that made it a felony to display "a red flag, banner or badge or any flag, . . . as an aid to propaganda that is of a seditious character." The prosecution was of a member of the Young Communist League, operating a youth camp indoctrinating children in Communist precepts. The conviction was reversed under the Supreme Court's application of the "clear and present danger" slogan, in its concern for the maintenance of "the opportunity for free political discussion to the end that government may be responsive to the will of the people and that changes may be obtained by lawful means, an opportunity essential to the security of the Republic, . . ." [29]

So the Communist conspiracy case, *Dennis v. United States,* presented an attempt by Congress to abridge the freedoms of speech and the press for the protection of the existence of the Federal Government, after the states' legitimate powers to furnish far stronger protection to the Federal Government they support had been crippled needlessly by Supreme Court decisions without constitutional basis. By simply comparing the language of the Smith Act with the language of the First Amendment, it would be impossible to enforce the law under which these men were prosecuted except by giving the congressional enactment supremacy over the Constitution.[30]

The Supreme Court sustained the convictions. In writing its opinion on whether this law of Congress violated the First Amendment, the Court did not so much as quote the First Amendment in any part of its opinion. The Court noted the Communists' reliance upon a number of cases in which the Court had held that attempts by states to punish abuses of the freedoms of speech, the press, and assembly were unconstitutional. The Court attempted to demonstrate the inapplicability of these by saying that such were cases "where a state court had given a meaning to a state statute which was inconsistent with the Federal Constitution. . . . Where the statute as construed by the state court transgressed the *First Amendment,* we could not but invalidate the judgments of conviction." This bit of sophistry disregarded the fact that the Amendment does not claim to limit the powers of any government but the Federal Government, and if it should, by

---

of the criminal laws in each state. Where a single Federal prosecution could harass the leadership of a revolutionary movement, prosecutions by many state governments could crush that leadership.

29. All of this was of no concern to the Court unless the legislation should violate the free press provisions of the California Constitution and thereby violate the Due Process Clause of the Fourteenth Amendment.

30. The First Amendment's clear and plain declaration that "Congress shall make no law" abridging these freedoms can lead to but one conclusion when compared with the "law" Congress made, making it illegal "to knowingly or wilfully advocate, abet, advise, or teach," to "print, publish, edit, issue, circulate, sell, distribute, or publicly display any written or printed matter," or to either organize or even *be a member* of any "society, group, or assembly of persons who teach, advocate or encourage the overthrow or destruction of any government in the United States by force or violence." This law clearly abridged the freedoms of speech and the press.

some warping of words, be applicable to state governments as well, then the restraints it imposes upon the Federal Government could be no less than its restraints upon the state governments.

In mentioning the First Amendment objections of the convicted Communists, the Court said:

> "One of the bases for the contention that the means which Congress has employed are invalid takes the form of an attack on the face of the statute on the grounds that by its terms it prohibits academic discussion of the merits of Marxism-Leninism, that it stifles ideas and is contrary to all concepts of free speech and a free press. . . . The very language of the Smith Act negates the interpretation which petitioners would have us impose upon that Act. *It is directed at advocacy, not discussion.*"

The Supreme Court's simplistic rationalization disregarded the fact that the First Amendment itself is not directed at forbidding advocacy as distinguished from discussion: The First Amendment extends its protections against intrusion by the Federal Government to *all speech,* and speech may be in the form of entertainment, instruction, discussion, enticement, or advocacy, and its content may be wise, foolish, true or false.

Philosophical adherence to the concepts of freedom of speech and the press demands the right to speak loudly and print persuasively, so that people may be induced to take action. The First Amendment, by its very words, was designed to remove completely the powers of the *Federal Government* as an impediment to the right to advocate action, even revolutionary action.

The Supreme Court's *Dennis* opinion, disregarding the words of the Constitution, substituted instead the various past opinions of the Court and attempted unsuccessfully to find some rational and fundamental meaning in them. But perhaps the only rational conclusion that can be derived from the large number of contrary decisions, sometimes extending "protection" to the freedoms of speech and the press and sometimes withdrawing that "protection," is this: When the certainty of the clear language of the First Amendment is abandoned and when the certainty of the plain meaning of the Due Process Clause of the Fourteenth Amendment is abandoned, there remains no protection but the unguided philosophies of individual judges [31] destined forever to ebb and flow in strength with the appointment and departure of different judges; that when the language of the Constitution is abandoned, the supremacy of the Constitution is abandoned, and the people have lost the only dependable protection they have against the inevitable tendency of government to tyranny.

---

31. A dissent favoring constitutional freedoms in the *Dennis* case includes: "Communism on the world scene is no bogey-man; but Communists as a political faction or party in this country plainly is. Communism has been so thoroughly exposed in this country that it has been crippled as a political force. Free speech has destroyed it as an effective political party. . . . But the command of the First Amendment is so clear that we *should not allow Congress* to call a halt to free speech *except in the extreme case of peril* from the speech itself." This ostensible defense of constitutional supremacy carries with it two glaring defects—the arrogant claim of judicial supremacy over the legislative branch and judicial willingness to disregard the Constitution if the degree of peril shall impress the judiciary as adequately extreme. The proper position of public servants in both these government branches is an attitude of subservience to the supreme law; but most of the supreme law consists of Acts of Congress pursuant to the Constitution, and all of this the legislative body can repeal. But the executive and judiciary are sworn to obey the valid acts of the legislative department and are its inferiors.

The other case we will notice on a subject of popular political excitement is a 1964 decision, *New York Times v. Sullivan*. The decision grew out of the newspaper's publication not of false news, nor a false editorial, but a mere fund-raising advertisement seeking contributions to aid Dr. Martin Luther King in the defense of criminal charges against him. The decision was rendered nine months before Dr. King stood before the King of Sweden to receive the Nobel Peace Prize for his efforts in Alabama and other southern states. The advertisement, like many fund-raising advertisements, was filled with both exaggerations and falsifications of facts, but the newspaper had no hand in either writing it or determining its content, but accepted it for publication without censoring it.

The advertisement claimed that when black students sang "My Country, 'Tis of Thee" [32] on the steps of the State Capitol Building in Montgomery, Alabama, their leaders were expelled from school, truck-loads of police ringed the campus, and when all students protested by refusing to re-register, the dining-hall was padlocked in an effort to starve them into submission. Regarding the truthfulness of the advertisement, the Supreme Court said in part:

> "Although nine students were expelled by the State Board of Education, this was not for leading the demonstration at the Capitol, but for demanding service at a lunch counter in the Montgomery County Courthouse on another day. Not the entire student body, but most of it, had protested the expulsion, not by refusing to register, but by boycotting classes on a single day; virtually all the students did register for the ensuing semester. The campus dining hall was not padlocked on any occasion, and the only students who may have been barred from eating there were the few who had neither signed a preregistration application nor requested temporary meal tickets. Although the police were deployed near the campus in large numbers on three occasions, they did not at any time 'ring' the campus, and they were not called to the campus in connection with the demonstration on the State Capitol steps, as the third paragraph implied. . . ."

As revealed by the Supreme Court opinions, Mr. Sullivan was a Montgomery City Commissioner having charge of the police department, he thought the advertisement libelled him, so he sued. Another commissioner thought the advertisement libelled him, so he sued, too. The Governor of Alabama thought the advertisement libelled him, because he was an *ex-officio* member of the State Board of Education, so he demanded and received a retraction. But the idea of suing out-of-state publishers for distributing in Alabama such offensive matter —which must have been extremely offensive to the people of the state because of the unfairness of its exaggerations and falsifications—caught on so well that a total of eleven suits were filed in Alabama courts against the *New York Times* and five such suits against CBS for one or more of its telecasts. In all, the suits sought damages in the total amount of $7,300,000. Commissioner Sullivan and his fellow commissioner each sued for a half-million dollars, and in each case, the Montgomery jury obligingly returned verdicts against the newspaper for the full amount sought. The Supreme Court reversed the Alabama judgment, which had been upheld in the full amount by the Alabama Supreme Court, and sent the case back for a second trial in accordance with its opinion.

The Constitution of Alabama, quoted by neither the Alabama Supreme Court nor the United States Supreme Court, guaranteed "the right to speak, write, and publish his *sentiments* on all subjects, *Being responsible for the abuse of that liberty.*" Though the advertisement contained many sentiments, it also contained

---

32. Actually, *The Star Spangled Banner*.

totally false statements of fact, and damage suits for libel had long been the means of holding people responsible for the abuse of printing false statements about others. *If* the advertisement constituted a libel directed at Commissioner Sullivan under Alabama law, then there were elements present from which a jury could have concluded the newspaper was guilty of gross irresponsibility in the publication. It did not demand of the advertiser the dates of the events and did not even check its own files of its past news columns to see if the incidents had occurred and were correctly described in the advertisement. When asked by Commissioner Sullivan to retract, the newspaper directed its own representative in Alabama to report on the facts, and his report catalogued a list of falsehoods in the advertisement, yet the newspaper printed neither a retraction nor an apology. *If* the judgment was in accordance with the law of the land in Alabama, it should have been affirmed.

The two appellate court opinions—Alabama and Federal—do not give enough information to determine whether the newspaper received due process of Alabama law, but they furnish grounds to suspect a lack of due process. In its early stages, the law of libel was strictly for the protection of individuals, not large groups of people insulted by some false statement; in an early American case, when cowardice was charged to a group of Revolutionary War soldiers, it was the group as a group that was insulted, and its commander was held not to have been personally libelled.[33] But it has generally come to be held that a statement about a small group might be a libel or false statement about each member of the group, as where one man told another that his daughters were prostitutes; this charged that each of them was a prostitute. Commissioner Sullivan's theory was that false statements about the entire Montgomery Police Department were false statements about him personally.[34]

In its opinion, the Supreme Court of Alabama did not describe the entire advertisement, but excerpted two paragraphs, one stating things said to have happened in Montgomery and the other, four paragraphs later, speaking of things said to have happened to Dr. Martin Luther King, Jr. Both paragraphs contained falsehoods.

But the entire advertisement was in no sense directed at the Montgomery Police Department. It concerned the black battle for equal voting rights and equality in admission to private restaurants and the conduct of those opposed to the black movement, whether anonymous individuals, business owners or public officials.[35] It presented Dr. King as the leader and inspirer of black youth, who were following his peaceful resistance example. The first and most flagrant act of police conduct claimed by the advertisement to have happened was not said to have happened in Alabama, but in Orangeburg, South Carolina. After incorrectly describing the events in Montgomery, the advertisement critically mentioned eight other southern cities, it described Dr. King's leadership and then described opposition attacks against him.

---

33. This and other such cases are discussed in Cooley, *Constitutional Limitations,* p. 531, n. 1.

34. This is clearly more akin to an insult to a large group as a group, rather than to the individuals who comprise a small group; like a man's daughters or the people living in a particular house.

35. Collectively referred to in the advertisement as "Southern violators of the Constitution," the "Southern violators" or "they."

The entire paragraph that concentrated on Montgomery [36] was insulting to the entire city and not narrowly directed at its police department. The opinions indicate that the case was tried as if the city itself had been libelled.

In charging that the police had "ringed" the campus, there was no charge of impropriety, because the advertisement neither stated nor implied the absence of some riotous conduct or threat of student riotous conduct which would and *should* have brought police in numbers to the campus. False statements about campus events, such as locking the school dining hall, concerned matters under the decisional authority of state educational officials, rather than local police officials. No improper conduct was either stated or implied that could be said to be directed at the local police in the entire article upon careful examination of the article.

In imposing liability on the newspaper, the Alabama Court did not demonstrate this to be required by the law of the land in Alabama. Every reference made by that Court to "group" libel was a reference to a small group, and the Court mentioned no case establishing that Alabama had so far departed from the common law that it had become the law of the land in Alabama that the regulating official of such a large group as a city police department is libelled by slurs against the department, though he is empowered to control the conduct of the department.

Of course, the insult here was really directed against the entire section of the country in which Alabama is located and against the entire city of Montgomery. The jury was presumably drawn mostly from the city, a part of the insulted populace. In every state, when verdicts are so large that they indicate the jury was moved by passion or prejudice instead of by deliberation upon the evidence, this is a ground to set aside the verdict and direct a new trial.

Bearing on liability, the Alabama court held the statements were libelous *per se,* which means that damage from the libel is assumed, and the victim doesn't have to prove his reputation was actually damaged by the false statement. Libelous *per se* statements are charges that one has committed a serious crime, falsehoods derogatory to business or professional ability or reputation, and the category under which the Alabama Court placed this case, a statement which "tends to bring the individual into public contempt . . ." But this was simply declared by the Court, not demonstrated by it. If I say you have murdered ten men by cutting off their heads, it may be assured that I have made statements that will bring you into public contempt, but not if you happen to be the chief of a head-hunting tribe and the statement is made to members of your tribe—it then becomes a compliment.

Was there any rational basis to impartially hold that the published statements brought the Montgomery police into contempt before the people of the city? Among the general reading public there, including the jurors, would the reaction to the advertisement be public contempt for their police? Or would it be anger at the false insult of their city, their state, their region? The true answer is clear unless refuted by the trial record in the case.

Aside from probabilities based upon the general facts, there is an indication that the jury acted through bias and passion. In the full-page advertisement, the

---

36. "In Montgomery, Alabama, after students sang 'My Country, 'Tis of Thee' on the State Capitol steps, their leaders were expelled from school, and truck-loads of police armed with shot-guns and tear-gas ringed the Alabama State College Campus. When the entire student body protested to state authorities by refusing to re-register, their dining-hall was padlocked in an attempt to starve them into submission."

factual statements of events said to have happened and the impassioned plea for financial support for Dr. King and his followers was contained in three columns of small type across the center of the page. The entire ad was signed at the bottom by the organization soliciting the funds, the "Committee to Defend Martin Luther King and the Struggle for Freedom in the South." But under the three columns containing the false statements appeared a large-type appeal for funds, "Your Help Is Urgently Needed . . . Now!!" Beneath this fund appeal appeared the names of more than fifty prominent Americans who endorsed the appeal. No fair-minded jury would hold these people jointly authored the factual statements —this was done by the organization, and the prominent individuals simply publicly declared their support of the appeal for funds; surely, they were not guilty of libel. Beneath this was an endorsement by a number of Southern ministers, including four from Alabama, signing the statement "We in the south who are struggling daily for dignity and freedom warmly endorse this appeal." They did not claim authorship of the factual statement, but only claimed they supported the appeal for money.

They, too, were sued, and the proof showed that they knew nothing of the advertisement, had neither seen nor heard of its factual statements prior to its publication, but merely authorized the use of their names to endorse pleas for contributions. But the jury and the Courts also held these four men, each liable to the police commissioner for the same amount as the newspaper, a half-million dollars.

From the opinions alone, without access to the records of the trial and with but the briefest research into Alabama law, there are quite strong indications that the *New York Times'* right to due process of law was violated, that it might not have received the benefit of Alabama's law of the land. The verdict, coupled with other circumstances, indicated that the jury was prejudiced and impassioned, and the Alabama Court did not adequately demonstrate that the judgment was justified by Alabama law in this respect; the Alabama Court's opinion in fact did not demonstrate that Alabama law had moved so far from the common law as to hold that statements about a large organization were statement's made "of and concerning" the organization's director; and the Court's opinion failed to demonstrate that the statements actually subjected Commissioner Sullivan to public contempt rather than public sympathy.

Treating the case as an ordinary lawsuit in an ancient field of law, it appears that the United States Supreme Court, particularly after examination of the entire record of the trial, might properly have held that the *New York Times* was denied due process of Alabama law and should be adjudged not guilty or granted a new trial before an impartial jury unless the Supreme Court of Alabama should deliver a new opinion actually demonstrating from past decisions that the law of the land in Alabama had been fully followed. But instead, the Supreme Court treated the case as a vehicle to announce another new rule of Constitutional Law, not commanded by the words of the Constitution, and not inferrable from any constitutional provision.

The Supreme Court chose in this case to revise the law of libel in every state. The Court found a decision to its liking by the Supreme Court of Kansas, holding that there is no liability for newspaper criticism of public officials unless the publicity, even if untrue, is motivated by personal malice against that official. In essence, the Supreme Court decreed abolition of the law of libel in every state, despite the fact that the different states differ in their laws of libel, and despite the fact that the law of libel can and did furnish a very real protection to the right of the people to rely on press publications as the basis of the information on which they vote.

Newspapers have great political power through their ability to protect politicians by concealing corrupt practices from the public; when this power is increased by granting to newspapers immunity from liability for their false statements unless made with malice toward the person defamed, then the right of the electorate to be informed before they vote is further impaired and the republican form of government in each state further endangered.

In political matters, the press seldom acts from malice toward a candidate it opposes; instead it tends to support a candidate, and unfair and false criticism of the opposing candidate is the means of winning the election and gaining first access to released news. Given license to act irresponsibly, it can become part and parcel of corrupt government. It is primarily through the wronged individual's right to hold the press responsible for its misconduct that the press can achieve the position of critic of government and the value of a free press to the people can be preserved.

Nothing in the Fourteenth Amendment's command that Alabama not deprive the *New York Times* of its freedom or property without due process of the law of Alabama empowered the Supreme Court to re-write the laws of all the states as to liability for printing false statements about people in public office. The *New York Times* did not appear to receive the full protection of Alabama's law of the land, but Alabama should be free, if its people will tolerate it, to make laws to penalize the press for abuses of its freedom, and to define those abuses by laws applicable equally to every large and small newspaper sold in Alabama. If the *New York Times* should find the freedom of the press as protected by the laws of Alabama too restrictive for its publishing policies, it could find protection by foregoing the limited profits it gains by selling 394 copies of the issue in Alabama.

Freedom of the Press and Obscenity:

It is in regard to obscene publications that the Supreme Court has most actively exercised its supposed power to determine the extent of freedom in each state. It has even assumed the power to "define" obscenity, and thereby determine precisely what conduct the state and federal legislative authorities may make criminal, and has done this quite poorly, because its definitions are beyond comprehension. In *Ginsburg v. New York,* a dissenting justice wrote of the Court's new position in relation to things smutty:

"Today, this Court sits as the Nation's board of censors. With all respect, I do not know of any group in the country less qualified first, to know what obscenity is when they see it, and second, to have any considered judgment as to what the deleterious or beneficial impact of a particular publication may be on minds either young or old."

On the same day, April 22, 1968, another justice wrote in *Interstate Circuit, Inc. v. City of Dallas:*

". . . The subject of obscenity has produced a variety of views among the members of the Court unmatched in any other course of constitutional adjudication. Two members of the Court steadfastly maintain that the First and Fourteenth Amendments render society powerless to protect itself against the dissemination of even the filthiest materials. No other member of the Court, past or present, has ever stated his acceptance of that point of view. But there is among present members of the Court a sharp divergence as to the proper applications of the standards . . . for judging whether given material is constitutionally protected or unprotected. . . .

Anti-obscenity laws have been popularly combatted by using the same argument that has been used against anti-marijuana laws, the argument that there is no scientific proof that they actually protect society against psychological or physical harm. But it should ever be remembered that making laws is not a matter of science. Never have the marijuana laws been based upon scientific judgement that marijuana is harmful and that cigarettes and whiskey are harmless; all are harmful, but the people would not tolerate laws outlawing cigarettes and whiskey. The weakening of marijuana laws has resulted primarily from the fact that the public has become increasingly intolerant of those laws, also.

The making of legislated law is not a matter of scientific foundation nor even of wisdom. A law becomes a law *solely* because legislators have the power to enact law and they have exercised that *power* by declaring a provision to be law. If the law is unwise, as many are, there is no benign governor-general given lawful power to nullify it or to substitute a new law, but the answer to the unwisdom of a law is popular realization that the law is bad, realization induced by persuasion.

Roth v. United States and *Alberts v. California* were the starting point, a federal criminal case and a state criminal case decided in a single opinion. There is a scholarly organization, the American Law Institute, which concerns itself with suggesting improvements in state and federal law, and it had by this time done considerable work on a proposed "Model Penal Code," hoped to be enacted by state legislatures. In the *Roth* case, the leading opinion (the first one of several written by different justices) quoted a lengthy definition of obscenity from an *ALI* tentative draft.[37] The leading opinion itself gave its definition of obscenity as "material which deals with sex in a manner appealing to prurient interest." But the Court discussed the matter much further.

The opinion adopted a part of a proposed definition by a group which has concerned itself with improving law, but which has no law-making authority under any law. The Court noted that at the time of the adoption of the First Amendment, which in no way addressed itself to the powers of state governments, all states declared obscenity illegal and the opinion then stated that "implicit in the history of the First Amendment is the rejection of obscenity as *utterly without redeeming social importance.*"

This italicized characterization of obscenity was a 1957 sociological-oriented characterization of the reasons for rejecting obscenity, in fact inaccurate and in history without foundation. The fact is that obscenity was made criminal because it embarrassed too many people and blasphemy was made criminal because it offended or angered people.

Then the Court compared the jury charges—one in the federal prosecution [38]

---

37. "A thing is obscene if, considered as a whole, its predominant appeal is to prurient interest, *i.e.,* a shameful and morbid interest in nudity, sex, or excretion, and if it goes substantially beyond customary limits of candor in description or representation of such matters. . . ."

38. In holding that the First Amendment did not bar Congress from making laws against obscenity, the Court followed common-law theory as to the scope of freedom of the press instead of taking as its premise the wording of the First Amendment.

for using the mails to transport obscene matter and the other a state prosecution for disseminating obscene matter—with its thinking on the meaning of obscenity, and held both convictions affirmed. One dissenting opinion noted the danger in the Court's decision, and called attention to the fact that the Court was announcing its own definition adapted from a definition only tentatively proposed by the American Law Institute, whose writers announced that their definition differed from that followed in most states [39]—involving a "test" of appeal to lustful instincts—and who announced that their test was designed to fit changed conditions in which there was greater public interest in the distribution of erotica: That it proposed to change law.

Then came *Fanny Hill.* Massachusetts followed its duly-adopted laws to condemn and remove from the market (the modern equivalent of book-burning) a book famous as the world's first obscene novel. The name of the case was *A Book Named "John Cleland's Memoirs of a Woman of Pleasure" v. Massachusetts.* There were seven separate opinions in the case, and the leading one, entitled to first place in the printing of opinions because three justices concurred in it,[40] claimed to elevate to the standing of a constitutional test of obscenity and a part of the supreme law of the land the inaccurate phraseology of "utterly without redeeming social value." This phraseology was in a field of the common law, in which definitions of crimes, used to instruct juries, are to be considered by them along with the evidence in determining guilt or innocence. The Supreme Court not only seized the power to define, but departed from the common-law practice of making definitions both accurate and easy to understand.[41] This Supreme Court phraseology was without meaning as a definition—it would equally well and equally ill apply to all English crimes, including murder, burglary, rape, incest, and even that rather un-American crime of "tumultuous petitioning," the tumultuous assembly of more than twenty persons to approach and petition Parliament for the redress of grievances.

One dissenting justice left no doubt but that the book disgusted him,[42] and it is rather amazing that a book honored by the literary world as the first obscene book should be held in all the Supreme Court's exercise of its intellectual powers not to be obscene at all. The various opinions fairly well summarize the book, and include reference to a number of "expert" opinions completely adequate to persuade anyone already persuaded. These opinions at least establish that when those

---

39. The obscene was defined as that offensive to chastity, the word being incorporated in the language of other criminal prohibitions, such as obscene publication.

40. No other opinion voting to reverse the Massachusetts judgment was supported by as many as three justices.

41. Larceny was defined as "the trespassory taking and carrying away of the personal property of another, with intent to steal," and burglary as "breaking and entering into the dwelling-house of another in the night-time, with intent to commit a felony."

42. Justice Clark said: "I have 'stomached' past cases for almost 10 years without much outcry. Though I am not known to be a purist—or a shrinking violet—this book is too much even for me. . . . This is presented to the reader through an uninterrupted succession of descriptions by *Fanny,* either as an observer or participant, of sexual adventures so vile that one of the male expert witnesses in the case was hesitant to repeat *any one of them* in the courtroom. . . . If a book of art is one that asks for and receives a literary response [as characterized by one of the pro-Fanny Hill expert witnesses], *Memoirs* is no work of art. The sole response evoked by the book is sensual. Nor does the orderly presentation of *Memoirs* make a difference; it presents nothing but lascivious scenes organized solely to arouse prurient interest and produce sustained erotic tension."

of the erudite intelligentsia are taken with obscenity, their education and erudition enable them to formulate rhetoric to declare their tastes intellectually desirable.[43]

The inaccurate "utterly without redeeming social value" characterization of the reason (in the 1790's) for bans on obscenity was an unimportant descriptive "test" in the *Roth* decision, it was announced by the same justice, with the concurrence of only one other justice, to be the controlling test in his opinion in a second case we have not mentioned, *Jacobellis v. Ohio,* and this meaningless test now gained the concurrence of a total of three of the nine justices for its elevation as a part of the supreme law. The Massachusetts Supreme Court had interpreted the "social importance" "test" as meaning that the book does not have to sink to the level of being "unqualifiedly worthless." It was on this announced basis that the three concurring justices voted to reverse, intalicizing "utterly" in their insistence that unless the book were unqualifiedly worthless, it could not be said to be *utterly* without any redeeming social importance.

Perhaps the most intelligent thing said about this judicial "test" of the limits of state legislative powers was written in the final dissenting opinion in the case, in which it was asked, "And why shouldn't the fact that some people buy and read such material prove its 'social value'?" [44]

In these decisions, we see the entire purpose of the First Amendment—to totally deprive the Federal Government of any power over the freedoms of speech and the press—evaded by shifting *all* of the nation's powers to determine what should constitute abuses of these freedoms from the state governments to the Federal Government, and at that, not to the law-making branch of the Federal Government, but to its judicial branch, which *The Federalist* had referred to as "the weakest of the three departments of power." [45]

Other opinions rendered the same day emphasize the Supreme Court's assumption of power to be the final censor of what the people may read. *Ginsburg v. United States* was a federal prosecution for violating the Obscene Mail Statute, which declares obscene matter non-mailable.[46] In the case, the publication *EROS* was tested by yet another clause of the American Law Institute's recommended legislation, not yet either recommended or legislated, because four of the fifteen articles in the publication "substantially exceeded community [what community the Court did not say] standards of candor," so that although the Court could not quite say that this publication was as "utterly without" as others,[47] still it was

---

43. One of the concurring justices thought the Constitution prohibits both state and Federal governments from either restricting freedom of the press or penalizing abuses of that freedom, but most of his opinion was concerned with a demonstration of his view that *Fannie Hill* was, indeed, a valuable contribution to literature. He appended a copy of a sermon in favor of Fannie.

44. He concluded his dissenting opinion with a statement that "if a State insists on treating *Fannie Hill* as obscene and forbidding its sale, the First Amendment does not prevent it from doing so."

45. So weak, indeed, that "all possible care is requisite to enable it to defend itself against attacks" of the executive and the Congress. And so it would have remained, and still been able to powerfully perform its functions, had Congress not permitted it to exercise powers not given to it. Of this, we shall see more later.

46. It thereby prohibits distributions at public expense and to this extent is not a censorship law so much as a withdrawal of partial government support.

47. This rationale is absurd, because if one obscene article shocks a reader's sensibilities, the shock is no less real if the next article fails to shock. An obscene painting whose action truely shocks is not rendered pure by the flowers in the background.

advertised with evil intent: Ginsburg pandered to the desire for obscene matter to the extent of seeking mailing permits at Intercourse, Pennsylvania and at Blue Balls, Pennsylvania.[48]

His publication was "exploited entirely on the basis of its appeal to prurient interests . . ." The Court gave its assurance that this was not federal censorship: "A conviction for mailing obscene publications, but explained in part by the presence of this element does not *necessarily* suppress the materials in question, nor chill their proper distribution for a proper use." The Court did not say how this could possibly fail to partially suppress distribution, at least among those who would not be tempted to purchase except by such a pandering advertisement. Nor did the Court say what "proper" use we may make of obscene matter, nor has it hazarded any guess of reasons for buying obscene matter other than the pleasure derived from it.

In the day's third case, *Mishkin v. New York,* the Court affirmed the conviction of a New Yorker engaged in the large-scale manufacture and sale of pornography of an inferior intellectual quality. The Court said:

> "We adjust the prurient-appeal requirement to social realities by permitting the appeal of this type of material to be assessed in terms of the sexual interests of its intended and probable recipient group; and since our holding requires that the recipient group be defined with more specificity than in terms of sexually immature persons, it also avoids the inadequacy of the most-susceptible-person facet of the *Hicklin* test."

The *Hicklin* test refers to instructions that whether the matter were obscene must be judged with reference with its effect upon the most susceptible person into whose hands it might be expected to come. The instructions are from an English decision, *Regina v. Hicklin,* rendered in 1868, almost a hundred years after American Independence, and having no remote bearing on the state of American law at the time the First Amendment was adopted. The English judge's opinion was followed shortly afterward by the Massachusetts Supreme Court in one opinion, and was followed by several federal courts for a time.

This is sufficient [49] to indicate the extent to which the Supreme Court has gone in presuming that it has the power to define the limits to which a state can legislate in regard to the abuse of the freedom of the press by printing and distributing obscene matter; the extent to which the Court has confused the states' legislative powers with the legislative powers of the Federal Government; and the extent to which the Court's varying opinions as to what state law *should be* have successfully been permitted to replace both the Constitution of the United States and the various state constitutions in determining the limitations placed on the states' law-making powers in an area in which the Constitution of the United States places no limitations whatever on those powers.

In so doing, the Court has arrogated to itself the power reserved to the peo-

---

48. This, also, is absurd. Advertising may be rendered obscene by its content, but it cannot make the publication advertised either more or less obscene, except that, by making plain the offensive nature of the publication, it may prevent easily-shocked people from ordering it.

49. Another rather unremarkable case, *Ginsburg v. New York,* holding more stringent tests of obscenity can be devised for the protection of children is worth reading for entertainment, because one of the justices appended to his opinion a number of interesting articles on the history of censorship and the motivations of censors.

ple [50] to determine the content of their state constitutions, and has to this extent destroyed the republican form of government in every state.[51] The only power given to federal judges is that defined by the Constitution itself. It extends to cases arising under the Constitution, under laws made pursuant to the Constitution, and under treaties made under the authority of the United States. With due regard for their oaths of office and for the limited scope of their jurisdiction, Federal judges are not morally at liberty to pursue their own differing philosophies without regard to the commands of the Constitution. When they differ, they are obligated to give their differences a more responsible consideration than merely to proceed in opposite directions until a new appointee shall shift the weight of their numbers to one side or another.

Each member of the Supreme Court should be able to trace his reasoning back a step further in the chain of logic, except perhaps for such judges as may have neither logic nor law in their chain of reasoning. Most of the judicial differences of opinion on the Supreme Court are caused by the failure to attempt to reach any agreement as to the meaning of due process of law based upon some understanding more fundamental than yesterday's opinion.

Far greater fidelity to the Constitution could be maintained if the justices would more carefully probe the meaning of "privileges and immunities of citizens of the United States" as contended for by the man who wrote it, but that they should probe its meaning with greater competence than that of its writer, who assumed without analysis that the entire Bill of Rights was included within the phrase, when only parts of the Bill of Rights guarantee rights, and other parts, particularly the First and Tenth Amendments, do not guarantee rights, but either deny powers to Congress or reserve powers to the people or the states.

The Freedom of Religion:

Given the Supreme Court's claimed rejection of Mr. Justice Black's opinions on the Congressional intent in proposing the Fourteenth Amendment to the states for adoption as part of the Constitution, and the Court's claimed power to "expand" the Fourteenth Amendment's Due Process of Law Clause to prohibit state infringement of such rights as Supreme Court Justices might from time to time come to view as fundamental, it was inevitable that the First Amendment's freedom of religion provisions would eventually come to be fastened upon the various state governments.[52]

The First Amendment denies Congress any law-making power in two religious areas—prohibiting the free exercise of religion, and establishing a state religion or state church. In *Abington Township School District v. Schempp,* a dissenting justice wrote:

> "As a matter of history, the First Amendment was adopted solely as a limitation upon the newly created National Government. . . . I accept . . . the proposition that the Fourteenth Amendment has *somehow absorbed* the Establishment Clause, al-

---

50. By the words of the Tenth Amendment.

51. In no recent case involving obscenity has the Court taken any note of the provisions of the constitutions of the states whose decisions it was reviewing.

52. The First Amendment says: "Congress shall make no law respecting an establishment of religion, or prohibiting the free exercise thereof;" and the Fourteenth Amendment says that no state shall "deprive any person of life, liberty, or property without due process of law . . . ." Hence, the Supreme Court holds, states may not infringe these rights by any process of law.

though it is not without irony that a constitutional provision evidently designed to leave the States free to go their own way should now have become a restriction upon their autonomy.[53]

In the companion case of *Sherbert v. Verner,* he wrote further of the clause regarding "an establishment" of religion:

"I think that the Court's approach to the Establishment Clause has on occasion. . . . been not only insensitive, but positively wooden, and that the Court has accorded to the Establishment Clause a meaning which neither the words, the history, nor the intention of the authors of that specific constitutional provision even remotely supports."

Some of the Court's religious decisions have been viewed with great and sincere consternation by many people. The Court's "outlawing" of the practice of holding public prayer and reading the Bible in the classrooms of public schools have been viewed with a measure of accuracy as depriving school children of their freedom of religion, and during an era of embattlement against "Godless Communism," the Court's holding that no state can require its office-holders to take an oath attesting to their belief in God has caused strong fundamentalist protests. Others who do not concern themselves with religion to any great extent appear to regard the entire subject as a tempest in a teapot.

But religion is not a trivial matter. Religion attempts to answer questions whose answers are from their nature incapable of proof, but questions which, sooner or later, must haunt almost every man in his pensive moments or in all his waking hours. Who am I? How came I to be? Is there in the future some system of rewards and punishments that will balance the acts of my life, or do the rewards and punishments exist only here and now, understandable only by exploring the concatenation of cause and effect? How did it all begin? How will it all end?

Science concerns itself with some of the same questions, but from the viewpoint of the mechanics by which it was accomplished rather than from a questioning of whether the accomplishment was guided by some supreme intellect. And if the mass of scientists regard modern religion as a pointless development of primitive religions, which assigned divine guidance to those unpredictable forces of nature—the wind, rain, sun, changing seasons and quivering earth, even this view must accord to primitive religion the honor of being the first science, the first attempt to find rational explanations for the seemingly irrational.[54] And many scientifically oriented people eventually find themselves driven to the conclusion expressed by Einstein, that all we really know about the causes of the origins of the earth and its life may be summarized in the simple phrase, "and there was light."

Religious belief demands action. It is not a simple matter of meditation. Religion commands that the believer walk unharmed over hot coals to demonstrate the power of his gods to grant safety; that the believer bow low before the altar, and drink and eat sanctified food; that he repeat prayers in unison with his fellow believers; that he pray in privacy and never in the company of other people;

---

53. When he is incapable of envisioning *how* the First Amendment can limit the powers of a state government, a judge is obligated to hold that those powers are not affected by the First Amendment.

54. Was not the theory confirmed by experiment? Did not the growing season follow the winter's prayers for its return?

that he pray that God guide the surgeon's hands; that he pray for the healing of his sick child, saving the child from the surgeon's knives; that he marry and have as many children as possible, abstain from marrying, or marry as many wives as he can support; that he pray for success in his business or wars or that he denounce both wealth and war; that he give a portion of his property to the church or that he denounce all property ownership and live a communal life with all property owned by the religious commune; that he sacrifice life or deflower the virgin on the altar to appease the gods; that he facilitate his worship with marijuana or LSD; that he bring the good news of salvation to others by aggressively explaining to them how hopelessly wrong are their religious beliefs; that he share the treasure of his religion with none but those born into it.

Government, the sweeper of streets, fighter of wars, printer of money, keeper of vital statistics, can add nothing creative and little intelligent to such a personal and fundamental area as religious belief. The traditional American view has been that there should be total separation between the church and the state, but this is not an inherited view of the English common law. It is an improvement Americans sought to make upon the law which caused many of them to flee from civilized England to primitive America. The Supreme Court has done a magnificent job of marshalling the historical information demonstrating the beginnings of the American traditions of freedom of religion and separation of the church and the state. About the only thing it has failed to demonstrate is the existence of some sound basis for its claim of power to act as it has in regard to religion.

Much emphasis is properly laid upon words spoken by Thomas Jefferson and James Madison, but their words cannot properly be substituted for the Constitution. They led the battle for separation of church and state in a single state, Virginia, and then Madison was a leader in the formulation and writing of the First Amendment. These men furnished national leadership, but there were twelve other states, and some of them had official state religions. The strength and fervor of Jefferson's and Madison's leadership arose in part from the fact that Virginians suffered from restraints upon their freedom of religion: The Episcopal Church was the official state church, but it is said that the majority of the people were not Episcopalians, yet were compelled to pay taxes to support that church.

Lord Baltimore was a devout Catholic, and fled to what is now Maryland for religious reasons. He fled from Virginia,[55] where he was refused the right to settle because he would not take an oath of allegiance to the king, parts of the oath being contrary to his religious beliefs.

At that stage, Virginians treasured the right to worship God in the manner they saw fit and the right to exclude from among them people who wanted to worship differently; but Baltimore, victimized by this thinking, insisted upon the right of the individual to live where he wished and to worship as he wished. *Neither* insisted upon any right to damn the worship of God: Both were motivated by positive religious beliefs.

So it is not surprising that Maryland's constitution should strongly emphasize the freedom *to worship,* not the freedom *from worship.*[56] While accepting the added protection of the First Amendment's denial to *Congress* of the power to abridge the freedom of religion, the people of Maryland declared their unwilling-

---

55. As related by the Supreme Court in *Torcaso v. Watkins.*

56. Just as the Federal Government does not entrust with power those who reject the Constitution, officers being required to swear to support it without mental reservation and without purpose of evasion.

ness to be governed by any office-holders but those who proclaimed and swore to their belief in God.[57] Yet in *Torcaso v. Watkins,* the Supreme Court of the United States held that Maryland could not require its officer-holders to take an oath containing "a declaration of belief in the existence of God." The Supreme Court thereby denied to the people of Maryland a power the First Amendment denies only to Congress; true, Maryland had refused Mr. Torcaso the right to assume his high office of Notary Public unless he should swear he believed in God. To this extent, the State of Maryland abridged Torcaso's freedom *from* religion, but Maryland did this in full accordance with Maryland's law of the land, the law the people of Maryland adopted in establishing their republican form of government.

Before the First Amendment, Rhode Island's Roger Williams expressed his view of religious freedom:

"There goes many a ship to sea, with many hundred souls in one ship, whose weal and woe is common, and is a true picture of a commonwealth, or human combination in society. It hath fallen out sometimes that both Papists and Protestants, Jews and Turks, may be embarked in one ship; upon which supposal I affirm that all the liberty of conscience I ever pleaded for turns upon these two hinges: that none of the Papists, Protestants, Jews, or Turks be forced to come to the ship's prayers or worship if they practice any. I further add that I never denied that, notwithstanding this liberty, the commander of this ship ought to command the ship's course, yea, and also command that justice, peace, and sobriety be kept and practised, both among the seamen and all the passengers. If any of the seamen refuse to perform their service, or passengers to pay their freight; if any refuse to help, in person or purse, towards the common charges or defence; if any refuse to obey the common laws and orders of the ship, concerning their common peace and preservation; if any shall rise up against their commanders or officers, because all are equal in Christ, therefore no masters nor officers, no laws nor orders, no corrections nor punishments; I say I never denied but in such cases, whatever is pretended, the commander or commanders may judge, resist, compel, and punish such transgressors according to their deserts and merits."

The Supreme Court quoted the first part of Roger Williams' statement, relating to total freedom in matters of religion, in its opinion in *Abingdon Township School District v. Schempp,* but the Court omitted quoting the last part of his statement, concerning the position that freedom of religion does not give the individual the right to violate laws, even if he complains that his religion commands it.[58] Yet this thinking is seen in many state constitutions, which both pro-

---

57. Its provisions on religion include: "That as it is the duty of every man to worship God in such manner as he thinks most acceptable to Him, all persons are equally entitled to protection in their religious liberty; wherefore, no person [should be disqualified from being] a witness, or juror, on account of his religious belief; provided, *he believes in the existence of God, and that under His dispensation such person will be held morally accountable for his acts, and be rewarded or punished therefor either in this world or in the world to come."* The Maryland Constitution states that no religious test should be required for public office "other than a declaration of belief in the existence of God." Any such oath is required to be "such as those of the religious persuasion, profession, or demonination, of which he is a member, generally esteem the most effectual . . ."

58. It has repeatedly happened that an individual who murdered then claimed that he was divinely commanded to do so, and is thought insane for making the claim. If

tect the freedom of religion and declare the power of law to remedy abuses of that freedom, a power totally denied the Federal Government by the First Amendment. Typical is a provision in the Constitution of Connecticut:

> "The exercise and enjoyment of religious profession and worship, without discrimination, shall forever be free to all persons in this state; provided, that the right hereby declared and established, *shall not be construed as to excuse acts of licentiousness, or to justify practices inconsistent with the peace and safety of the state.*[59]

Although all state constitutions guarantee the freedom of religion, the people in different states, in exercising their self-governing powers, have adopted differing provisions regarding the extent of freedom of religion and other aspects of the church-state relation: Exemption of the church from taxation, state contributions of financial support to churches on a discriminate or indiscriminate basis, the citizen's right to claim his religious beliefs as justification for his violation of the criminal laws. In practical effect, all this has been swept aside by the Supreme Court, imposing on the people in each state the Federal Government's lack of governing authority on this subject.

In 1947, in *Illinois ex rel. McCollum v. Board of Education,* a case involving religion in public education, the Court said:

> "Separation in the field of education, then, was not imposed upon unwilling States by force of superior law. In this respect the Fourteenth Amendment merely reflected a principle then dominant in our national life."

Yet the supposed realization and acceptance of the proposition that the states, by accepting the Fourteenth Amendment, had knowingly imposed upon themselves the identical denial of law-making powers that the First Amendment imposed upon Congress, was not then exactly hoary with age. The Supreme Court had declared only eight years earlier, in *Cantwell v. Connecticut:*

> "The First Amendment declares that Congress shall make no law respecting an establishment of religion or prohibiting the free exercise thereof. The Fourteenth Amendments has rendered the legislatures of the states as incompetent as Congress to enact such laws."

Not the least endeavor was made by the Court in that case to demonstrate the accuracy of this declaration.

In 1868, only eight years after the Fourteenth Amendment became a part of the Constitution, and thirty years *before* the Supreme Court's *Maxwell v. Dow* holding that none of the rights protected by the Bill of Rights were privileges or immunities of American citizenship, President Grant led an unsuccessful attempt

---

such were recognized as a legal defense to acts uniformly deemed to be morally wrong, it would call upon the judiciary to pass upon the depth of the individual's beliefs, and would entice others to plan to minimize the risk of punishment by falsely claiming religious beliefs. It might even enable some to persuade themselves they should murder, as the alcoholic who took comfort in his religion, secure in the belief that if it had not been predestined that he should continue drinking, he would surely have stopped.

59. We see repeated examples of such commands to the judiciary, "shall not be construed," based upon history's lessons as to the unfortunate capacity of the judicial mind to utilize language protective of rights as a means of violating rights.

to amend the Constitution to limit state legislative powers regarding religion.[60] The proposal failed to pass the Senate and was therefore never submitted to the states for approval. Its proposal and rejection so soon after the Fourteenth Amendment was adopted are totally inconsistent with the Supreme Court's recent assumption that the states, by accepting the Fourteenth Amendment, knowingly imposed upon themselves the prohibitions the First Amendment imposes upon the Federal Government.

Yet the Supreme Court has now proclaimed, in its various decisions, that virtually the entire content of the never-adopted amendment is a part of the Supreme Law of the Land, and has further declared that the reading of the Bible in public school classrooms is prohibited by the Constitution, though this was expressly permitted by the amendment offered in 1868, which had so little success that it never even reached the legal stage of being proposed.

The battle for religious freedom that led to the First Amendment shortly followed the battle led by Jefferson and Madison in Virginia. The event which triggered the battle there was not a denial to anyone of the right to worship, but a continuation of the pre-Revolutionary War habit of taxing to support the church. A tax was proposed in the Virginia Legislature for the support of churches, and each citizen was to have the right to designate a particular church as the recipient of his tax money. Madison's famous "Memorial and Remonstrance" to the legislature was simply a citizen's petition urging defeat of the tax. The Remonstrance [61] is the most excellent American declaration in favor of the separation of church and state.

The Remonstrance gives objections to the tax that would probably have been quite small in amount. Among its objections:

"Because, it is proper to take alarm at the first experiment on our liberties. We hold this prudent jealousy to be the first duty of citizens, and one of [the] noblest characteristics of the late Revolution. The freemen of America did not wait till usurped power had strengthened itself by exercise, and entangled the question in precedents. They saw all the consequences in the principle, and they avoided the consequences by denying the principle.[62]

---

60. Congressman Blaine proposed, and the House of Representatives passed the suggested amendment: "No State shall make any law respecting an establishment of religion, or prohibiting the free exercise thereof; and no religious test shall ever be required as a qualification to any office or public trust under any State. No public property, and no public revenue of, nor any loan of credit by or under the authority of the United States, or any State, Territory, District, or municipal corporation shall be appropriated to, or made or used for, the support of any school, educational or other institution, under the control of any religious or anti-religious sect, organization, or denomination, or wherein the particular creed or tenets of any religious or anti-religious sect, organization, or denomination shall be taught. And no such particular creed or tenets shall be read or taught in any school or institution supported in whole or in part by such revenue or loan or credit; and no such appropriation or loan of credit shall be made to any religious or anti-religious sect, organization, or denomination, or to promote its interests or tenets. This article shall not be construed to prohibit the reading of the Bible in any school or institution, and it shall not have the effect to impair rights of property already vested. . . ." Quoted, *Illinois ex rel. McCollum v. Board of Education*.

61. A copy of the Remonstrance is appended to a dissenting opinion in *Everson v. Board of Education*.

62. For further quotation from the Remonstrance, see below, p. 192.

This is what has happened to the liberty of the people in each state to decide for themselves the scope of protection of religious freedom they want written into their constitutions, and the question has now become entangled in many precedents without any valid demonstration in principle of how the Supreme Court is empowered to determine the scope and attributes of religious freedom in each of the fifty states. Consider the principles, and the unentanglement loses all its complexity.

Here are some of the decisions destructive of the republican form of government and the concomitant right of the people to determine the limitations upon the powers of their own state governments:

1939: *Cantwell v. Connecticut.* The Cantwell's were "members of a group known as Jehovah's Witnesses," and were prosecuted for the unlicensed solicitation of contributions from persons other than members of the soliciting church "for any alleged religious, charitable or philanthropic cause," in violation of a state law; this law was designed to assure that the solicitors actually spoke for the organization having some means of looking after and accounting for funds. The Supreme Court held this to be a law "respecting an establishment of religion or prohibiting the free exercise thereof," which the Court held to be equally beyond the power of Connecticut as beyond the power of Congress.[63] The Court took no note of provisions of the Constitution of Connecticut: "The exercise and enjoyment of religious *profession* and *worship*, without discrimination, shall forever be free to all persons in this state, . . ." Fund soliciting is action taken on the basis of religious beliefs and is not itself either religious profession or worship. Connecticut infringed the Cantwells' freedom of religion, but in full accordance with Connecticut's law of the land, which permitted that infringement.

1946: *Everson v. Board of Education.* The New Jersey legislature authorized local school boards to reimburse students for the cost of transportation to public and parochial schools. Though the Supreme Court was sharply divided as to the disposition of the case, all its members agreed—without any tracing of the historical meaning of due process of law as a requirement that the law of the land be followed in depriving a citizen of his life, liberty, or property—that the Due Process Clause of the Fourteenth Amendment prohibits both states and federal governments from making any financial contributions to any church.

The New Jersey Constitution spoke plainly of taxation for religious purposes:

> ". . . nor shall any person be obliged to pay tithes, taxes, or other rates *for building or repairing any church or churches, place or places of worship, or for the maintenance of any minister or ministry,* contrary to what he believes to be right or has voluntarily engaged to perform."

The transportation of Catholic school children did not even remotely come within any of the specific purposes for which the people of New Jersey had prohibited their government to tax.

1947: *Illinois ex rel. McCollum v. Board of Education.* Vashti McCollum was a taxpayer and parent in Champaign County, Illinois. A 1905 religious movement for daily instruction to impress upon children the belief that religion was more than a one-day-a-week habit led in Champaign to the practice of giving religious instructions in public school classrooms. With parental permission, students could attend classes taught by different Catholic, Protestant and Jewish

---

63. Discussed above, p. 158.

teachers, all paid by religious groups and none paid from public funds. Students whose parents did not require them to attend these classes had to attend ordinary secular classes or study halls.

The Constitution of Illinois, of whose content the Supreme Court took no notice, said:

> "No person shall be required to attend or support any ministry or place of worship against his consent, nor shall any preference be given by law to any religious denomination or mode of worship."

This clearly was not violated, because no tax burden was added and because the McCollum child was not required to attend the classroom that was a temporary place of worship (actually, a place of instruction) without his consent. The Court adopted Thomas Jefferson's paraphraseology of the meaning of the First Amendment—"a wall of separation between church and state" [64]—itself as inaccurate as most paraphraseology, and held that Illinois could not permit religious teachers to teach religion in its classrooms to students whose parents wanted them to learn religion there.[65]

1962: *Engel v. Vitale.* The New York school authorities, given law-making authority by the State's Constitution over its public education system, designed an official prayer, presumably intended to please Some One and offend no one:

> "Almighty God, we acknowledge our dependence upon Thee, and we beg Thy blessings upon us, our parents, our teachers and our Country."

Ten parents sued, claiming this prayer was contrary to their religious beliefs, and the New York court ordered the State Board of Regents to make additional

---

64. New York's provision for permitting religious instruction was upheld by the Supreme Court in a 1951 decision, *Zorach v. Clauson.* New York expended no public funds and used no public facilities, but merely excused children so they could leave school to go to church for their religious instruction. Though there was no intelligent basis for urging that this violated anyone's freedom, or tended to establish any religion, there were dissents indicating that paraphraseology had been completely substituted for the First Amendment. One dissenter wrote, in part: "My evangelistic brethren confuse an objection to compulsion with an objection to religion. It is possible to hold a faith with enough confidence to believe that what should be rendered to God does not need to be decided and collected by Caesar. . . . The wall which the Court was professing to erect between Church and State has become even more warped and twisted than I expected. Today's judgment will be more interesting to students of psychology and of the judicial processes than to students of constitutional law."

65. A dissenting opinion in the *McCollum* case quotes an interesting report by Thomas Jefferson, as Rector of the University of Virginia, recommending that the state-owned land be used to build a School of Religion as part of the state-owned University of Virginia, to be staffed by teachers furnished by different denominations, so that the religious students could attend "scientific lectures" and so the secular students could attend "religious exercises with the profession of their particular sect," this report by Jefferson being approved by James Madison and the other members of the University's governing board. Perhaps this wall of complete separation was to be constructed between the people forming their churches and the massive Federal Government, and it was to be left to each state's people to design the relationship they wanted between their churches and their smaller local governments controllable by legislators elected from each town and county.

regulations to assure that religiously-objecting pupils would not have to be present while the prayer was being recited in unison by other pupils. Although this protected the objecting students' freedom of religion, the Supreme Court held the Board of Regents' prayer to be a step toward an establishment of religion, held to violate the First Amendment's command that Congress make no law on that subject.

The Court took no vote of New York's constitution,[66] which contained no prohibition against establishing an official state religion.

1963: *Abington School District v. Schempp.* Two cases were decided in the single opinion concerning the reading of the Bible in public schools, one involving the Schempp family, who attacked the practice in Pennsylvania, and the other the Murray family, attacking the same practice in Baltimore. The Supreme Court held the practice illegal in both states as tending toward the "establishment" of a religion. The Schempps were Unitarians, objected to the reading of the unexplained text of the Bible, many of whose passages, in literal reading, were contrary to their religion. They introduced testimony demonstrating the objections of different religious groups to different versions of the Bible, including the Catholic objection to the King James translation, the Protestant objection to the Douay, and the Jewish rejection of the entire New Testament as almost sacreligious. By compelling the Schempps to choose between the embarrassment of excluding their children from the school-room and the subjection of their children to teachings contrary to their religious beliefs, Pennsylvania may well have deprived them of their religious liberty without due process of the state's law, because the Constitution of Pennsylvania not only guaranteed religious freedom, but added the additional guarantee that "no preference shall ever be given by law to any religious establishment or modes of worship."

On the other hand, the Murrays objected to any Bible-reading in the public schools on the ground that they were atheists and objected to any state claim of recognition of the existence of a god. With provisions having been made to excuse the Murray child from the Bible-readings, Maryland gave the child all the protection afforded by its fundamental law, the right not "to be compelled to frequent . . . any place of worship." Otherwise, the people of Maryland had chosen to guarantee themselves the positive right to worship God in each person's chosen way rather than a general freedom of religion, with its implied right not to be embarrassed by the state in any manner in one's rejection of any belief in the existence of any deity.

The destruction of the people's self-governing powers in any state can only induce feelings of frustration and political impotence. In the more important matters of daily life, it was the design of the Constitution that the people should be governed by their local governments, over which they could exercise effective political control. The people can discern and understand the difference between the nullification of their laws by clear commands of the Constitution of the United States that judges are competent to explain in plain language, and the substitution of different bodies of laws not commanded by the Constitution. But when steps in the attempted logical demonstration that the Federal Constitution commands change are slurred over because they *cannot be logically explained,* this is an encroachment upon the people's self-governing powers.

As Madison said, ". . . it is proper to take alarm at the first experiment on our

---

66. "The free exercise and enjoyment of religious profession and worship, without discrimination or preference, shall forever be allowed in this state to all mankind . . ."

liberties." The experimentation with imposing upon the people in divergent states the total denial of power that the First Amendment imposes upon Congress alone has prevailed too long. That Congress can make no law at all "respecting" the subject of religion is the law given to us by the First Amendment; that the Courts, denied *any* law-making power, cannot exercise greater law-making powers than Congress is beyond refutation.

If the "First Amendment Liberties" may be defined and limited by the Federal judiciary, then there is no reason why all liberty may not be so defined and limited. The Fourteenth Amendment's Due Process Clause protects more than the liberties listed in the First Amendment—it protects *all liberty,* by forbidding each state to deprive any person of liberty, liberty to print or preach, work or steal, begat or kill, but by the law of the land. But the Fourteenth Amendment leaves the exact defining of liberty to the law of each state, where it has always resided, except to the extent that it denies each state the power to infringe the privileges and immunities of citizens of the United States. This is no less an essential of the American scheme of government than is the supremacy of the Constitution itself, because it is a part of the Constitution.

When Madison proposed the First Amendment in Congress, its language stated that "no religion shall be established by law, nor shall the equal rights of conscience be infringed." Madison stated his understanding [67] that this only restricted the powers of Congress. But mere opinion was not enough for Congress, which re-wrote the First Amendment before submitting it to the states to make it clear that *Congress* was denied power by the Amendment. That is all the amendment meant then, when some states had official state religions. It is all the First Amendment means now, when New Hampshire could have laws empowering its cities to employ teachers of piety if it wished, and when the people in every state could re-write their constitutional provisions to imitate those in the First Amendment.

The right to determine the scope of liberty and the lines between the exercise of freedom and the abuse of freedom is nothing less than the total power to govern. This power does not belong to the Federal judiciary. When judges destroy existing law under the conscious or subconscious emotional response to the supposed will of the people, or under the temptation to conform to the most modern thinking of a self-declared intelligentsia, they do more than destroy law: They infringe upon the supreme power of the people themselves to determine the metes and bounds of the powers they choose to yield to their governments.

The people of Maryland protected their freedom of religion in a manner different from that chosen by the people of Virginia; they protected it the way they wanted to protect it, and the design by the people in convention of these fundamental limitations upon power is an essential characteristic of the republican forms of government in America. In Maryland, the people wrote another provision, so essential to the supremacy of written constitutions that it as truly embodies the essence of the Constitution of the United States as it is a written part of the Constitution of Maryland:

"That the provisions of the Constitution of the United States, and of this State, apply, as well in time of war, as in time of peace; and any departure therefrom, or violation thereof, under the plea of necessity, or any other plea, is subversive of good Government, and tends to anarchy and despotism."

---

67. As reviewed in a dissenting opinion in *Murdock v. Pennsylvania.*

VIII.

THE FEDERAL METAMORPHOSIS

TODAY, WHEN ONE contemplates the authoritarian, irresistably powerful federal judiciary, it is with a wistful feeling that one is drawn again to Hamilton's almost haunting remarks in *The Federalist* about the weakness, the helplessness of the judicial branch of the Federal Government, its lack of control over the sword, the purse, or direction over the strength or wealth of society. Read again:

> "This simple view of the matter suggests several important consequences. It proves incontestably, that the judiciary is beyond comparison the weakest of the three departments of power; that it can never attack with success either of the other two; and that all possible care is requisite to enable it to defend itself against their attacks. . . . And it proves . . . liberty can have nothing to fear from the judiciary alone, *but would have every thing to fear from its union with either of the other departments; . . .*"

The central idea by which the Constitution attempted to protect the people from tyrannical government was to divide all the powers of the federal government into the law-making powers, given to Congress, the law-enforcing powers, given to the President, and the power to judge whether the citizen should be subjected to particular rules or to the penalties for their violation, given to the judiciary. Hamilton asserted that the people in their general liberty had everything to fear from the judiciary if it should become combined, *"notwithstanding a nominal and apparent separation . . ."* with either the executive or the Congress.

The reason for this real fear is quite clear—if the judiciary begins to "allow" Congress to pass laws the Constitution gives Congress no power to pass, then the Congress will soon realize that its powers are without limit; that it can depend upon a perverted and corrupt judiciary to sustain and enforce laws which, if the Constitution were supreme, would not even be considered laws at all; as the legislative branch begins to look more and more to judicial sanction to justify its exercise of usurped powers, then the legislature becomes increasingly crippled in spirit so that it can no longer correct a judiciary which is itself corrupted by power; until finally—such being the love for power, the judiciary itself will begin gradually to make laws, to carry those laws into execution, and to pass judgment on whether the individual has violated a "law" made only by judges who have no lawful law-making power at all.

At the same time, the executive may lead or be drawn into these abusive practices, and corrupt legislators may give him or his inferiors limited amounts of both legislative and executive powers, so that innocent legislators may be held blameless of the harsh effects of laws made and enforced by executive lawmakers, and may be tempted to prove that they are harmless and entitled to reelection by the simple expedient of doing absolutely nothing. Such abandonment of lawful government necessarily requires the complicity of a corrupt judiciary, to enforce as law that which is not law.

Such a course of disregard for the Constitution would inevitably result in

164

tyrannical tendencies, in the massive increase of Federal power, and in the corresponding weakening of the power of the people, in the exercise of their political strength, to affect the decisions of their own government.

No one would deny that there has been an almost total metamorphosis in the method of governing the people of the United States since the turn of the century. Where once state governments governed men in the most important aspects of daily life, the Federal Government is now looked to as the source of remedies for social ills. Today, an important political aim of state governments, and even city governments, is to obtain as large a share of "federal money" as possible, little if any of this federal tax money being for the general welfare of the entire nation. Now, state governments are so relatively powerless that they are no longer trusted to solve truly compelling social problems. The immediate thought when a problem arises is that Congress is challenged to provide the solution.

Simultaneously with the vast strengthening of the governing powers of the Federal Government at the expense of the more controllable local governments, there has occurred a transformation in the methods by which the Federal Government exercises its governing powers. The exercise of expanded governing powers by the Congress has been too burdensome for Congress to efficiently bear, so Congress has created a multitude of bureaus and commissions, with the power to both make rules, enforce rules, and make a determination of whether such rules have been followed or violated in particular cases. Examples of these agencies are the Interstate Commerce Commission, regulating the trucking industry, the Food and Drug Administration, governing the standards of many consumer products, the National Labor Relations Board, concerning itself with labor-management relations, the Federal Communications Commission, and so on almost *ad infinitum.*

The metamorphosis of the Federal Government into a new type of government, wholly irreconcilable with our written Constitution, could not have occurred but for violation by federal judges of the imperative of judicial integrity.

The judicial warping of the Constitution involves mainly two constitutional doctrines, the doctrine of separation of powers among the three different branches of government, and doctrines regarding something called "implied powers." By one the scope of the power of the government was magnified and by the other the method of the permissible exercise of power was distorted.

A striking illustration of techniques in the abandonment of constitutional government occurred at the beginning of the Prohibition Era. That era seems to be pictured primarily as a demonstration of the futility of mere government attempting to control common human morals by illegalizing an attractive sin and thereby, in a sense, compelling large numbers of people to violate the law because *they will not submit to its rules,* and leading thence to unpopularity of law and disrespect for law. The era may be imagined as having begun by a sudden drying-up of sources from which all types of alcoholic beverages had theretofore been easily and lawfully available. It didn't happen that way.

The Amendment was proposed by Congress in 1917, accepted by the necessary number of states in 1919, and by its terms it became illegal one year later, on January 16, 1920, to sell, manufacture or transport intoxicating liquor in the United States, or to import or export it. The amendment was adopted, after many decades of contention, as a moral measure, to give Congress the power it lacked, to combat the purely local conduct of drinking whiskey, a problem prevalent in many localities. With such powerful and growing moral condemnation of liquor, and the Federal Government having no direct power to combat it, one would imagine the people in each state who were moved by such moral motivations could act through their own governments to outlaw the manufacture, sale, and possession of whiskey.

This was not only possible, but by the time the Eighteenth Amendment became law, every state, *without exception,* had legislated to forbid the possession or manufacture of any alcoholic beverage even as weak as beer.[1] Except for local option pockets and the superstition that Federal law could somehow be less futile than state law as a means of compelling everyone to embrace the announced morals of the majority, the Eighteenth Amendment was totally pointless. The fact that this pointless amendment was adopted adequately attests to the strength the movement had attracted the time World War I began. To live during that time and be able to recognize that the popular moral movement was nothing but a moral movement before the Eighteenth Amendment became law, a moral viewpoint which in no way could give Congress the power to legislate on the subject, would require a detachment from the mob spirit not to be expected from any but judges steeled to maintain their detachment from popular excitement.

A politically-responsive Congress responded politically by enacting a prohibition law it had no power to enact before the Amendment became law, and the Supreme Court put its seal of approval upon the Congressional usurpation. The Act of Congress was the Volstead Act, and the decision failing to recognize it as a violation of the Constitution was *Ruppert v. Caffey.*

Jacob Ruppert was a brewer. At the beginning of World War I, for the stated purpose of preserving needed grains and other foodstuffs for the war-fighting needs of the nation, Congress outlawed the use of such grains for the manufacture of intoxicating beverages. This was likely within Congress' power as a measure thought necessary to assure success in waging war. But the preservation of food supplies could be aided only by forbidding the use of *grains* to manufacture beverages, not by prohibiting the sale of beverages already manufactured, and Congress made no attempt to forbid the sale of such beverages or the manufacture of non-intoxicating beverages. Ruppert manufactured great quantities of non-intoxicating beer containing less than 2.75% alcohol, established by the pleadings [2] in the case as non-intoxicating, and Ruppert was legally free to both manufacture and sell this beverage in local-option New York.

The war ended with the signing of the Armistice on November 11, 1918. The soldiers returned home and peace settled upon the face of the land, but the customary treaty had not been signed to govern future relations between the former enemies. America was at war with no nation on earth. Yet almost a year later, on October 28, 1919, Congress passed over the President's veto the Volstead Act, for the stated purpose of carrying out the nation's war effort. To protect food supplies and preserve grain, of which there was no shortage,[3] Congress now went further than several years earlier when it actually had a war to fight: It prohibited the manufacture and also the sale of intoxicating beverages, and it

---

1. As summarized in *Ruppert v. Caffey.*

2. Facts established by pleadings are unquestionably true for the purposes of the lawsuit. It is by pleadings that the Courts learn what facts are disputed and must be determined by it or by the jury.

3. The facts set out in this paragraph were given in the dissenting opinion, and the Court's opinion took no notice of them.

enacted that anything containing more than one-half of 1% alcohol by volume was intoxicating, a falsehood.[4]

Though there was no war to necessitate such an enactment and no grant of power to Congress to pass laws requiring everyone in America to comply with even the most popular moral standards, the Supreme Court held Congress had the power to pass such a law! Here is the heart of the decision:

> "*If* the war power of Congress to effectively prohibit the manufacture *and sale* of intoxicating liquors in order to promote the nation's efficiency in men, munitions, and supplies *is as full and complete* as the police power of the states to effectively enforce such prohibitions in order to promote the health, safety, and morals of the community, it is clear that this provision of the Volstead Act is valid. . . . The police power of a state over the liquor traffic is not limited to the power to prohibit the sale of intoxicating liquors, supported by a separate implied power to prohibit kindred nonintoxicating liquors so far as necessary to make the prohibition of intoxicants effective; it is a single broad power to make such laws, by way of prohibition, as may be required to effectively suppress the traffic in intoxicating liquors. Likewise the implied war power over intoxicating liquors extends to the enactment of laws which will not merely *prohibit* the sale of intoxicating liquors, but will effectually *prevent* their sale."

The case was decided on January 5, 1920, just eleven days before the Eighteenth Amendment became a law applicable by its own terms to absolutely forbid all sales, manufacturing and transportation of intoxicating liquors; it struggled to demonstrate that Congress had the power to prohibit intoxicants and near-intoxicants under its "war powers," when the Constitution was immediately to give Congress the express power to deal with the evils of immoral intoxicants, at least to the extent that the people would stand for it. As a practical decision legitimately affecting the governing of the people, the decision was and remains infinitely trivial.

Yet in consideration of the conduct of judges, the case assumes a greater importance. With the aid of the lapse of time and change in popular opinions, the new law on intoxicants is easily recognizable as an actual attempt by Congress to legislate upon morals, by a law whose every provision was aimed at stamping out the existence of immoral intoxicants, under the claim that it was exercising its war-making powers. Thus, considering the judicial opinion on its merits in comparison with the judicial obligation to uphold the Constitution above all other laws, the opinion's principal characteristic is that it is intellectually dishonest.

The key words in the Court's chain of logic were the Federal Government's "implied powers" and the states' "police powers," by then a rough synonym for the entire power of the state legislature to pass laws to govern the conduct of the people in the state. The Court's opinion assumed that there existed something within the Government of the United States known as implied power, when the entire purpose of having a written constitution was to state in precise language the exact limits—though admittedly extremely broad limits—of Congress' power to govern, to the end that there might be no power other than that given by the Constitution. There is only power granted by the Constitution and power usurped

---

4. Such legislative definitions are often false definitions, but are not attempts by the legislature to change the meaning of the words. "Definitions" are used to define the scope of the law. This one simply meant it was made unlawful to sell any beverage with more than 0.5% alcohol by volume.

in violation of the Constitution. Under a constitution which expressly grants a list of specific law-making powers to the Congress, expressly denies to it another list of law-making powers, and expressly reserves *all other governmental powers* to the people or to the states, there are no other possible alternatives.

The Court's second false assumption was that the Congress' "implied" "war powers" could be equated in scope to a state's "police powers." This is contrary to the most rudimentary knowledge of the organization of American governments. The Federal Constitution only gives the Congress the power to pass laws on specific subjects, and the state constitutions generally give the state legislature all the state's law-making powers, without specifying the subjects on which these powers may be exercised. The state's law-making powers are then restricted by express provisions denying the legislature the power to make certain types of laws, some of the power-destroying provisions being in the state constitution, some in the Federal.

Our constitutional systems demand of Congress, "Prove you can make this law," and permit the state legislatures to say, "Prove we can't make this law, or it is law." Any rationale based upon an assumption that the scope of Federal legislative power and that of state legislative power are identical must proceed either from ignorance or from some factor that blinds the writer to unchanging fundamentals.

So it must be that the Supreme Court's *Ruppert v. Caffey* is intellectually dishonest, when it assumes that Congress' war-making power may be the source of an implied law-making power, even though the war had ended, and even though there is no such thing as implied power under the Constitution, when the Court then assumes that the implied law-making power of the Congress is identical to the state legislature's law-making power, though the two are quite different, and when the Court combines these assumptions to conclude that Congress had the power to enact moralistic legislation. So clearly was this known and understood to be beyond Congress' power that *after World War I began,* Congress had proposed and the states had accepted the Eighteenth Amendment for the sole purpose of giving Congress the power to enact such moralistic legislation. Yet the Supreme Court held Congress already had the power, after all. This is intellectually dishonest, a breach of the "imperative of judicial integrity."

Yet the justice who wrote the opinion was an honest man. He was deservedly among the most highly esteemed of all the great men who have sat on the Court, his name still revered: Justice Louis D. Brandeis.

Intellectual dishonesty is different from the dishonesty of the child with chocolate-covered chin who insists to his mother that he did not cut and eat the new chocolate cake. Intellectual dishonesty is primarily the disregard of fundamental truth in favor of some doctrine or dogma, often abstract, which has gained popularity and is in vogue in the particular discipline—whether law, science, economics or religion. In almost all fields, men may dispute—whether from greater insight or greater ignorance—the basic precepts held by other men of learning in the field. But in Constitutional Law, there is no fundamental truth but the words of the Constitution itself. All other knowledge is secondary or derivative. Judges *may not* honorably dispute the fundamental truths contained in the words of the Constitution, because they have solemnly sworn to uphold those words. They may only dispute the secondary or derivative knowledge.

Justice Brandeis' opinion was faulty because he centered his attention upon the desired legislative aim of prohibition and utilized for his thinking the judicially-developed secondary concepts of implied power and police power.[5]

In arriving at his decision, Justice Brandeis was entirely true to the discipline of the common law, which itself has no place in constitutional law: The assumption that the source to search for the content of the law is past judicial decisions. And the two concepts he utilized had long been accepted as an integral and valid part of the law. "Implied power" as applied to the power of Congress, was a paraphrasing of an express power given Congress by the Constitution, and "police power," a phrase applied to the state legislatures, was a phrase appearing nowhere in the Federal Constitution or the constitutions of any one of the then forty-eight states, a phrase paraphrasing nothing.

But these phrases flowed from the pen of Chief Justice John Marshall, who still towers in reputation among all succeeding American appellate judges as the greatest judge produced by America. Beginning eighteen years after his appointment to the bench, Chief Justice Marshall wrote three magnificent essays on the scope of Federal legislative powers, in his opinions in *McCulloch v. Maryland,*[6] *Gibbons v. Ogden,*[7] and *Brown v. Maryland.*[8] The language in these opinions was in large part to supersede the language of the Constitution itself in the judicial decision-making process.

Necessity and Propriety:

Most of Congress' law-making power is found in a single clause, the Necessary and Proper Clause, for which the shorter "implied power" has been substituted. The Constitution gives Congress the power to do various things,[9] and it then empowers Congress

> "To make all laws which shall be necessary and proper for carrying into Execution the foregoing Powers, and all other Powers vested by this Constitution in the Government of the United States, or in any Department or Officer thereof."

Almost all of Congress' immense law-making powers are concentrated in this express grant of power in the Necessary and Proper Clause.

The language of the Necessary and Proper Clause was framed by the Constitutional Convention's Committee on Detail. The Committee wrote the precise words to carry out the decisions already made by the entire Convention as to the shape and scope of the new government. The entire Convention had resolved in general terms that the Congress ought to have power to legislate on matters of

---

5. Within the framework of the organization of federal power, the Court's critique of opposing arguments on comparison with the non-classification of state powers into a power to prohibit whiskey and beer and a separate implied power to prohibit the sale of similar beverages was completely invalid. If wartime necessity should compel the reduction or elimination of civilian grain consumption then, apart from other constitutional objections, the Federal Government might directly ban or reduce all civilian uses of grains, whether for alcoholic beverages, non-alcoholic beverages, or even bread.

6. Discussed below, pp. 171-177.

7. Discussed below, pp. 178-181.

8. Discussed below, pp. 178, 181-185.

9. See above; Chapter III.

general interest, matters on which the states could not effectively legislate separately, or on which harmony throughout the country was desired.[10]

But probably the greatest fear was that a national government would exercise general law-making powers, denying the people local control over what they were free to do and what they were required to do by law. So the Committee on Detail and the entire Convention chose not to use such general language as harmony of the states or general interests requiring uniformity. Politics and social relations are intrinsically so disharmonious that such language would have left a political Congress free to attempt to achieve harmony in all the affairs of life. Instead, it was determined to give Congress only a specific list of law-making powers, with the Necessary and Proper Clause to provide the rules for inferring from some powers the existence of other powers.

Many of the things Congress was empowered to do did not even involve law-making at all.[11] The specific powers listed in the Constitution to make laws to control the conduct of the people—as distinguished from the conduct of the Government—is an extremely short list. There are law-making powers that do not affect the general populace within the states,[12] but the specific law-making powers to be exercised as law-making powers over the general populace of the nation were only these: To regulate interstate and foreign commerce and commerce with the Indian tribes; to make uniform bankruptcy and naturalization laws; to regulate the value of money coined by Congress and by foreign governments; to grant patents and copyrights to inventors and authors; to provide for the punishment of counterfeiters of Securities and coins of the United States; and to provide the punishment for treason. *And that is all.*

The constitutional grant of law-making power to Congress was not a grant of power to make all laws on which either Congress or the people might believe there should be national uniformity [13] but only the power to make laws on specific subjects. It was anticipated that there might later appear other areas in which

---

10. "That the Legislature of the United States ought to possess the legislative Rights vested in Congress by the Confederation; and moreover to legislate in all Cases for the general Interests of the Union, and also in those Cases to which the States are separately incompetent, or in which the Harmony of the United States may be interrupted by the Exercise of Individual Legislation."

11. For example, the borrowing of money involved no more law-making when Congress was empowered to do it than when a board of directors of a private corporation is empowered by stockholders to borrow money. Coining money involves law-making no more than does the printing of premium stamps to be redeemed in the purchase of merchandise. Establishing post offices and post roads involves law-making no more than does the establishment of a railroad; both require hiring men to do the necessary construction and then maintaining such equipment and personnel to furnish service to members of the public who want to buy it.

12. These are the total power to govern within the District of Columbia and areas inside states which have come to be known as "Federal Enclaves," where no state law exists, the power to define and punish piracies and felonies on the high seas and offenses against the laws of nations, to make rules for the government of the army and navy, and to provide for disciplining the militia.

13. A constitutional provision for uniformity is found in authorization to states to enter into compacts, which become binding when approved by Congress. On a less formal basis, uniformity is also achieved, where the need for it is felt, by the simple expedient of copying laws previously enacted by the legislatures of other states, and by the intentional enactment of identical laws on different subjects by many or all states previously recommended for uniform enactment.

uniformity was desirable, and to accomplish this, a method for amending the Constitution was provided.

To provide for the resolution of disputes when Federal law required one result and state law required another, two devices were adopted. One was the supremacy clause, providing that laws made pursuant to the Constitution should be a part of the supreme law of the land, anything in the state constitution or law to the contrary notwithstanding. So if a conflict developed in the application of such conflicting laws, the state law was automatically voided. And on Federal enclaves, lands purchased within a state with the consent of the state legislature "for the Erection of Forts, Magazines, Arsenals, dock-Yards, and other needful Buildings," Congress was given exclusive legislative power, as it was over the District of Columbia. So in Federal post offices, court-houses, and other such government property acquired in that manner,[14] state law no longer exists. In effect, such installations are no longer parts of the state, and there can be no conflict because, while state law governs the outside street, only federal law applies within the building.[15]

But the great grant of law-making power was achieved by the Necessary and Proper Clause, because Congress is empowered to do many non-governing things, such as taking the census, whose achievement is facilitated by laws requiring cooperation. Men opposed to new laws proposed in Congress or enacted by it have at times objected on the argument that the new laws are not actually necessary to accomplish a purpose Congress was empowered to accomplish, because there were other, possibly better ways to accomplish it. To the argument that Congress could not pass a law unless the law were *absolutely necessary* to the exercise of the Congressional power, Chief Justice Marshall gave an impressive answer in *McCullough v. Maryland*. He noted that in writing and in common useage, "necessary" often means only that one thing is "convenient,[16] or useful, or essential to another." He continued:

"A thing may be necessary, very necessary, absolutely or indispensably necessary. To no mind would the same idea be conveyed, by these several phrases. This word, then, like others, is used in various senses; and, in its construction,

---

14. When the Federal Government purchases land without enactment of consent by the state legislature, the area continues to be governed by state law.

15. To minimize both variance in laws and the need to be bothered with governing such small areas, Congress periodically enacts an "assimilation law," adopting for all Federal Enclaves the law of the surrounding state, so that the only difference between the law of the state and of the Federal Enclaves within it consists of changes in state legislation made since the last enactment of an assimilation law.

16. Marshall did not use this word standing alone, with the implication that Government can do whatever it believes convenient. He used it in context, relating to the enactment of a law as being a convenient way of exercising a power. In referring to means of achieving objectives, convenience contrasts with inconvenience. No man with a bucket, considering the problem of transferring water from a full barrel into an empty barrel would view a cup as a convenient means of accomplishing the result, and if the full barrel were at a higher altitude, he would not consider a bucket convenient for this purpose except in the absence of a tube to serve as a siphon. Marshall did not use "convenient" as a means of destroying "necessary" in the Constitution, but as a means of explaining it. There is a world of difference between John Marshall read in context to gain understanding and Marshall excerpted for use as a text to expand governmental power.

the subject, in context, the intention of the person using them, are all to be taken into view.

"Let this be done in the case under consideration. The subject is the execution of those great powers on which the welfare of a nation essentially depends. It must have been the intention of those who gave these powers, to insure, as far as human prudence could insure, their beneficial execution. This could not be done by confining the choice of means to such narrow limits as not to leave it in the power of Congress to adopt any which might be appropriate, and which were conducive to the end. It would have been an unwise attempt to provide, by immutable rules, for exigencies which, if foreseen at all, must have been seen dimly, and which can be best provided for as they occur. To have declared that the best means shall not be used, but those alone without which the power given would be nugatory, would have been to deprive the legislature of the capacity to avail itself of experience, to exercise its reason, and to accomodate its legislation to circumstances. If we apply this principle of construction to any of the powers of the government, we shall find it so pernicious in its operation that we shall be compelled to discard it. . . ."

A simple case which demonstrates the relation of the Necessary and Proper Clause to the specific congressional law-making powers, and the operation of both under the Supremacy Clause is a 1913 decision, *McDermott v. Wisconsin.* It was concerned with the Federal Food, Drug and Cosmetics Act [17] and a Wisconsin law on the same subject. Many states had undertaken, in varying and conflicting ways as they desired, to regulate the business of permissible labelling on packaged and canned foods sold in retail sales within the state. For precisely the same purpose—the protection of consumers, Congress enacted its Food and Drug Act under its power to control or regulate commerce among the states. Congress made it illegal to ship any packaged foods in interstate commerce unless the foods were labelled in accordance with the Act. This would achieve a uniform standard except as to food both produced and sold locally *if the law could be enforced.*

The law might be enforced by inspection. Simply establish inspection points at every place where ships, trains or trucks carried goods across state lines, slit open shipping cartons, inspect the jars and cans to assure proper labelling, and thereby furnish employment to every politician in all parties and bring the nation's commerce to an immediate halt. Congress chose a more practical, cheaper, and less disruptive manner as being a reasonably necessary means of enforcement. Congress enacted that it should be illegal to remove the labels from any such containers until after sale in retail stores. Under this provision, all disruptive inspections could be avoided. An inspector could stroll through a few large stores and have a panoramic view of the labelling practices of manufacturers who shipped in interstate commerce.

This provision for enforcement of the ban against shipment across state lines was certainly reasonably necessary to carry out Congress' power to make the regulation as to how things should be labelled. Indeed, in light of the impracticality of other possible enforcement methods, this method, once suggested, would be considered by most to be absolutely necessary to enforce the prohibition on shipment.

McDermott was a Wisconsin grocer, and he ordered and received from Chi-

---

17. The "Pure Food and Drug Act."

cago a quantity of canned syrup labelled "Karo Corn Syrup," and sub-labelled "10 per cent Cane Syrup, ninety per cent Corn Syrup." He put the cans on his store shelves in Wisconsin, where the state law sternly required the cans to be labelled "Glucose flavored with Sugar-cane Syrup."

Of course, Wisconsin had the power to make laws as to how its grocers should label their goods. But the Federal labelling laws were within Congress' power to regulate shipments between states and within its necessary and proper enforcement powers to make sure the labels should remain on the cans so they could be casually inspected. Federal law required the particular label to remain on the can until its retail sale, and Wisconsin law required the label to be replaced with a different label having different wording. The two laws conflicted in their operation, so the Wisconsin law was void, because laws made by Congress pursuant to the Constitution are part of the Supreme Law of the Land, anything in state laws to the contrary notwithstanding. It has nothing to do with whether the subject of labelling syrup cans on the shelves of a Wisconsin store should more appropriately be governed by Congress or by the Wisconsin Legislature. Under the constitutional system, the solution to such a problem of conflicting laws requires no grave pondering, but only the application of a simple formula.

Chief Justice Marshall, a proponent of a strong federal government and a strong judiciary, contributed immeasurably to the attainment of both ends, with his great powers of reasoning and written rhetoric. His decision in *McCullough v. Maryland,* as we have noted, was one of his great essays on constitutional powers. It involved an unpopular institution, the Bank of the United States.

The Bank of the United States was a corporation incorporated by an Act of Congress, on the recommendation of Alexander Hamilton, Secretary of the Treasury. Many Revolutionary War debts of both the Continental Congress and the states remained unpaid, bonds having been issued by these various governments to raise the necessary money, in gold and silver coin, to finance the war. Hamilton proposed that all these war debts be paid by the Federal Government through the instrumentality of a nationally chartered bank by issuing its own bonds, at full value, in exchange for the greatly depreciated bonds of the states and the Continental Congress. The First Congress created the bank, with private stockholders, so that the bank served both as an instrumentality of the government and as a private profit-making venture.

McCullough was the manager of a branch office of the Bank of the United States in Maryland. There was then no official American paper currency [18] and banks issued their own notes which passed from hand to hand much as paper money does today. Maryland imposed a stamp tax on all such bank notes issued in the state by any bank other than one incorporated by the Maryland legislature. An individual could borrow money from the Bank of the United States in Maryland and would be given the spendable bank notes, which anyone could cash in at the bank for gold and silver coin minted by Congress' authority. These notes issued by the Bank of the United States did not have the Maryland tax paid on them, hence the state's suit against Manager McCullough to collect the tax.

Chief Justice Marshall expounded the Necessary and Proper Clause, demonstrating that the formation of a bank to re-finance and further delay payment of the Revolutionary War debts was a reasonably necessary means of accom-

---

18. No American currency was issued by the Federal Government until the time of the Civil War.

plishing payment of those debts.[19] But the fact that this may be a necessary and proper means of paying the debt does not prove that in empowering the bank to go further and engage in the ordinary banking business of making loans to individuals for their private use, Congress was paying the war debt or doing anything else reasonably necessary to carry out any of the other powers given to it by the Constitution. And it was this type of activity, apparently unnecessary to carry out any governmental power, that Maryland was attempting to tax.

Here was one of the two deficiencies in Marshall's great opinion: He demonstrated that Congress may utilize the formation of a corporation to carry out any of its powers, and he demonstrated that such a corporation would be immune, as is the Government itself, from all state taxes and regulations in carrying out the ends Congress was authorized to accomplish. But he never got around to demonstrating that making loans to private citizens by issuing bank-notes to them is necessary to carry out any of the powers of Congress. Maryland was not trying to tax any bank business of transporting the Government's treasures through the state from one part of the country to another, nor any other governmental function performed by the bank, but only its private, profit-making business of issuing its bank notes. The Supreme Court rendered the decision against Maryland *without ever attempting to answer the essential question* of whether Congress could authorize the bank, as as artificial legal being, to engage in these private, non-governmental, profit-making functions Maryland was attempting to tax.

The second deficiency in the opinion is that it occasionally refers to the necessary and proper law-making power as an implied power. Though he repeatedly referred to the requirement of some degree of necessity before Congress could exercise the "inferred power," he at one point bordered on stating that just because the proposed law concerned the same subject as some express grant of power, Congress could legislate on it without there being the slightest degree of necessity. Marshall wrote:

> "Take, for example, the power 'to establish post-offices and post-roads.' This power is executed by the single act of making the establishment. But from this has been inferred the power and duty of carrying the mail along the post-road, from one post-office to another. And, from this implied power, has again been inferred the right to punish those who steal letters from the post-office, or rob the mail."

If the establishment of post-offices consisted only in building post-office buildings and equipping them with the 1800 equivalent of postage scales, stamps, cancelling devices, and then chaining and sealing the doors with government seals to assure that no one would steal government property, then it is true that it would be totally unnecessary to accomplish such a construction project to go further and provide people to carry the mail, and make laws to jail those who might rob the mail carrier.

---

19. Thus Congress was *expressly* empowered to simultaneously create the banking corporation and authorize it to perform these governmental functions by the Necessary and Proper Clause. Congress could not, by separate enactments in the following years, empower this governmental entity to manufacture men's shirts for a profit, then offer bookkeeping services to the public for a profit, and then lend money to borrowers for a profit, for none of these could be necessary to any extent to the exercise for any powers created by the Constitution. They could not be made necessary by combining one or more of them with the original incorporation statute.

But the power to "establish post offices" could hardly be equated to "constructing post-office buildings." One cannot establish a newspaper by merely building a structure and installing type-setting and printing machines in it. It will never become an established newspaper until it is peopled with reporters, re-write men, editors, pressmen and others engaged in actually producing a daily or weekly newspaper reporting news-worthy events. And post-offices and post-roads cannot be established without peopling them with working personnel to make them operate as post-offices and post-roads, accepting, conveying and delivering mail.

If there be any doubt that these words refer to the establishment of real post-offices instead of to the conduct of construction projects, all doubts are dispelled by reference to the Constitutional Convention. The formal resolutions made it plain that the scope of governmental powers should include the preservation of all powers of the earlier Congress under the Articles of Confederation.[20] The brevity and purity of the Constitution's language tends to simplicity, but the simplification of language was not devised to reduce the existing governmental power, but to preserve it or, in some cases, to enlarge it. The post-office provisions of the Articles of Confederation gave the Congress "the sole and exclusive right and power of . . . establishing and regulating post-offices from one state to another, and of exacting such postage on the papers passing thro' the same as may be requisite to defray the expences of the said office . . ."

The word "establish" meant more than to merely organize by constructing buildings; it meant to put into operation that which was to endure, as Marshall put it, for the ages, and the word was used with the same connotations elsewhere in the Constitution.[21] Carrying the mail back and forth is part of establishing post-offices "from one state to another," in the quaint words of the Articles of Confederation, not implied as something subsidiary which might be done or omitted, but an essential ingredient of the permanent act of establishing the establishment. If the maintenance of the permanent system of post-offices should require, in order to assure that the mail should continuously and dependably flow through those post-offices, that some law be passed to effectively prevent mail robberies, then the demand of necessity and the historic justification of propriety expressly empowered Congress to pass a law prohibiting robbery of the mails. There was nothing "implied" about it. It was a power *expressly granted* by the Necessary and Proper Clause. Implications are inferred, of course, but different people can infer different results from the same premise. The Constitution did not leave to the unguided judgement of judges the general prerogative of inferring from one power over the people another different power simply on the basis of judicial opinions as to what powers the Government might find convenient to exercise. Instead, it set out the exact thinking process judges must follow in inferring the existence of powers, the tests of both necessity and propriety.

---

20. Above, n. 10.

21. When the Convention wrote "WE THE PEOPLE . . . do ordain and establish this CONSTITUTION . . ." this did not declare an intent to try an experiment in government, but to establish a permanent, operating establishment to perform its functions century after century. The declaration of the motive to "establish justice" the yearning expressed was for the permanent and continuing establishment to the greatest possible extent, of justice between individuals and between man and his government.

Chief Justice Marshall's brief reference to the constitutional provision for creation of post-offices came dangerously close to an unwarranted claim that Congress had some implied law-making power to make laws on any subject specifically mentioned in the Constitution, though other constitutional provisions contradict any such assumption.[22]

A single sentence from *McCullough v. Maryland* has most often been quoted as the basis for departure in the thinking of many subsequent judicial decisions on whether Congress has an "implied power" to make a desired law:

> "Let the end be legitimate, let it be within the scope of the Constitution, and all means which are appropriate, which are plainly adapted to that end, which are not prohibited, but consist with the letter and spirit of the Constitution, are constitutional."

Too often, the single word "appropriate" has been unthinkingly used to dispose of the question of whether a particular law passed by Congress was "necessary" to any degree. But for a law to be appropriate and consistent with the letter and the spirit of the Constitution, was used by Marshall in elaborating the meaning of "proper" in the clause giving Congress the power to make laws necessary and proper to carry out all other governmental powers.

For a law to be necessary to carry out some governmental power, Marshall's understanding was that the law must be plainly adapted to achieve an end the Constitution empowers Congress to achieve. It must appear that the law is in fact a means to achieve the end and that the end is within the grant of power to Congress. Where the only constitutional basis for a law enacted by Congress is the Necessary and Proper Clause, no court can be true to its obligations unless it seeks to discover the purpose or end sought by Congress to be achieved: If it is clear that the end is not within any of the areas in which Congress is given specific powers, or if the law is plainly unnecessary as a means of accomplishing

---

22. For example, it is in no way necessary to coin money, a manufacturing from precious metals, that government be able to punish counterfeiting coin, because this is a fraudulent crime punishable by the state in which it occurs. The Articles of Confederation had given Congress the power to regulate the value of coins issued by the Congress and by the states, and the Constitutional Convention's Committee on Detail, in bringing these powers forward, not only added the Necessary and Proper Clause but also added the authorization to punish counterfeiting the current coins of the Nation; this would have been unnecessary but for the recognition that the Necessary and Proper Clause did not empower Congress to punish counterfeiting. One delegate thought that the power to borrow money might include the power, as necessary, to issue paper money, but the Convention perceived this was untrue: The Committee on Detail had originally proposed giving Congress the power to issue paper, but this, in the form of the "Continentals" issued during the Revolution, had inevitably caused serious inflation, so the power to issue paper money was stricken from the draft of the Constitution. Elseworth suggested the language as altered, giving Congress power to punish "counterfeiting the securities and current coin . . ." Securities referred to government-issued bonds necessary to borrow money. Minutes earlier, in joining the chorus against the government ever being empowered to issue paper money, Elseworth had said: "By withholding the power from the new Government more friends of influence would be gained to it than by almost anything else. Paper money can in no case be necessary. Give the Government credit, and other resources will offer." See Madison's notes, *Documents Illustrative of the Formation of the Union,* pp. 475, 556-557, 560. The delegates to the Convention clearly knew that necessity meant necessity.

some end Congress is empowered to accomplish, then the law is beyond Congress' power to enact. Simple intellectual honesty requires the courts to so declare it. Otherwise, they are denying the Constitution their fidelity and giving it instead to a conflicting and inferior law.

The great shortcoming of Marshall's opinion in *McCullough v. Maryland* was that the chief justice did not even attempt a rational demonstration that something in the Constitution gave Congress the power to engage in the banking business for the private profit of investing citizens.[23] The evil of the decision was that it even spoke of implied power, because the power to carry out other powers is expressly granted, not implied. Could Justice Brandeis actually have concluded in the *Ruppert* case that it was "necessary" to *any slight extent* to outlaw the sale of beer in order to make war [24] when in fact and as a matter of common knowledge, Congress was not making war against anyone?

Chief Justice Marshall's strength was his ability to forcefully bring forth every conceivable argument to demonstrate the correctness of his decisions; he also knew his Constitution, and the difference between actual holdings of a court and mere *dicta* used to illustrate the correctness of the decision. This is more a criticism of the judges who have followed Marshall than of Marshall himself: The great jurist wrote so much, and so quotably, that his words came to be regarded almost as holy writ in the field of Constitutional Law, and largely replaced the thinking process among lesser intellects who followed him on the high court.

Marshall knew that the Necessary and Proper Clause was inserted in the Constitution to keep Congress from making claims to some generalized "implied

---

23. Alexander Hamilton's original argument in favor of establishment of a national bank was the source of most of Marshall's thinking in this opinion. Hamilton's was the argument of the advocate, and it persuaded President George Washington. But in its endeavor to prove the Federal power to authorize the bank to make loans by issuing its bank-notes, Hamilton's argument was sophistry. For example, he conceded that in creating corporations, the Congress could only create corporations to do what it was expressly empowered by the Constitution to do, but being unable to find anything in the Constitution authorizing the Government to lend money, he completely shifted his ground when he came to the new banking corporation's powers to lend money, saying that the individual citizens forming the corporation could lend money so nothing additional was given to them by the governmental grant of the power to lend money. But, according to Marshall's decision, this aspect of their profitable business was given immunity from taxation. It would require too much space to list and describe the sophistries in Advocate Hamilton's argument, but one of the more striking is the argument that the power to borrow money presupposes banks to lend it (is it not true that only banks can buy government bonds?), and *if there were no banks,* the Government would have to create one from which to borrow. With his concession that the Federal Government can create corporations to do only what it is expressly empowered to do by the Constitution, this reduces itself to the argument that if there were no source from which to borrow money, the Government could borrow from itself, by borrowing from the corporation which performs its functions. See Hamilton, "Official Opinion, as Secretary of the Treasury, on the Constitutionality of a United States Bank, 1791," Veeder, *Legal Masterpieces,* pp. 214, *et seq.*

24. The "war powers" are separately detailed in the Constitution as the powers to declare war, grant letters of marque and reprisal, raise and support armies, provide and maintain a navy, make rules to govern the army and navy, exercise detailed powers in regard to the militia, levy taxes for the common defense, and make laws necessary and proper to carry these powers into execution.

178   *Judicial Tyranny*

power." Its purpose was to state precisely what powers could be inferred from those powers expressly stated: The power to make laws both necessary and proper to carry out the other powers given to Congress and to the other branches of the Government. Though Marshall insisted in his decision on the Bank of the United States that the Necessary and Proper Clause was a grant of power to Congress (which it was), rather than a restraint on congressional power, he soon referred to it, in *Gibbons v. Ogden,* as "this limitation on the means which can be used" to carry out governmental powers. Marshall knew what the Necessary and Power Clause meant, but his unwarranted paraphraseology of this express grant of power as an "implied power" has led succeeding generations of judges to countenance that gradual encroachment upon the people's rights that the draftsmen of the Constitution sought to prevent by writing the Necessary and Proper Clause.

Interstate Commerce and Necessity:

The area of broadest encroachment upon the right of the people to be free from uniform law [25] not tailored to their local needs is under the Interstate Commerce Clause. This clause was designed to give Congress immense powers, and much of the modern understanding of this clause is based upon two Marshall opinions which followed shortly after *McCullough v. Maryland: Gibbons v. Ogden* and *Brown v. Maryland.*

The facts in the two cases are simple and the legal issues not very complex. The Constitution gives Congress the power to regulate commerce among the states, with foreign nations, and with Indian tribes. Congress had enacted a law under this clause to regulate the coasting trade, providing for the licensing of ships to engage in this trade. Under this law, the shipowner was given the license, or right, to engage in hauling passengers and freight between any ports in the nation, whether sea-ports or inland ports accessible from the sea. Mr. Gibbons owned two such ships, which plied their way between New York City and Elizabethton, New Jersey. Federal law, enacted under the Commerce Clause, gave him the right to do this. But the New York Legislature had passed a law giving a monopoly to Robert Fulton to sail steam vessels into, out of, and between all New York ports, and Fulton had sold to Mr. Ogden the right to navigate to and from New York City in trips between that city and Elizabethton, New Jersey. Federal law gave Mr. Gibbons the right to sail between those ports in violation of Ogden's state-granted monopoly. The Supremacy Clause of the Constitution provided the simple answer: New York law must yield to Federal law made pursuant to the Constitution, and Gibbons was free to exercise the navigational rights given him by Act of Congress, anything in the laws of New York to the contrary notwithstanding.

Brown v. Maryland presented a more subtle problem. Maryland imposed a license tax, or privilege tax of $50.00 each year, upon each importer who engaged in the business of wholesaling foreign goods in the original bales or packages in which they were imported. This law was attacked on two grounds. First, the Con-

---

25. And therefore freedom from any restrictive laws to the extent that the people might be able to persuade their legislators not to enact such laws; needless to say, the legislators are far more susceptible to popular influence when they are part-time legislators living in their own communities than when they become part of the distant governmental community, subject to the temptation to confuse persuasive lobbying with popular pressure.

stitution forbids any state to lay duties on imports and exports. This tax was not a duty on imports, because a duty is a tax on the thing imported.[26] This tax was imposed solely on the business of wholesaling imported goods, not on either the importation itself, the trans-shipment of imported goods, and the tax was in the fixed amount of $50.00 annually, whether the businessman should sell only $25.00 or a million dollars in imported goods. Chief Justice Marshall held the tax to be an unconstitutional duty on imports, but this was a false holding, because license taxes and duties on goods were as entirely different when the Constitution was written as they are today.

A more difficult question, and the one we are concerned with, was whether the Maryland tax violated the Commerce Clause, because the tax intefered with commerce with foreign nations, and the Constitution gave Congress the sole power to regulate commerce with foreign nations.[27] The Supreme Court held the Maryland tax unconstitutional on Commerce Clause grounds as well as on the ground that it was a duty imposed on imports.

In the first decision, *Gibbon v. Ogden,* Marshall responded to the question, What is commerce? The case involved the navigation of ships between ports in two different states, and the New York licensees under Robert Fulton's state monopoly claimed that commerce subject to federal control only included bartering, buying and selling, and transportation of goods, but did not include the navigation of ships. Marshall replied:

> "This would restrict a general term, applicable to many objects, to one of its significations. Commerce, undoubtedly, is traffic, but it is something more; it is intercourse. It describes the commercial intercourse between nations, and parts of nations, in all its branches, and is regulated by prescribing rules for carrying on that intercourse. The mind can scarcely conceive a system for regulating commerce between nations, which shall exclude all laws concerning navigation, which shall be silent on the admission of the vessels of the one nation into the ports of the other, and be confined to prescribing rules for the conduct of individuals, in the actual employment of buying and selling, or of barter."

The power to control commerce among the states clearly included the power to regulate shipping between states, whether the goods be transported by ship or by land vehicles. And though commerce was and is primarily selling and exchanging goods, selling the service of transporting people between states was an essential part of commerce, demonstrated, as Marshall related, by the fact that the Constituition forbade a particular type of maritime regulation—a requirement that ships clear any port on the way to another—to be imposed under the power to regulate commerce.[28]

---

26. The import duty is based upon the quantity of measurement of the items imported, by package, bottle, weight, value, or other measure, so that the greater the quantity imported, the higher the duty.

27. It was a historical fact that one of the prime causes leading to the adoption of the Constitution was the existence of varying state laws imposing conflicting interferences with and burdens upon interstate and foreign commerce, so that here was a state licensing law contrary to one of the basic purposes of the Constitution.

28. Any argument that the right to regulate commerce among the states must stop at the state line was untenable: The Articles of Confederation, in a similar provision, gave Congress the power to regulate the trade with Indians "not members of any State, *provided that the legislative right of any State within its own limits be not in-*

In *Gibbons v. Ogden,* Marshall wrote [29] of other aspects of the problem of conflicts between Federal and state powers in regulating the activities of the commercial world. What of the power to regulate the purely internal commerce of a state? A barber's sale of his services? Renting a truck to a man to transport his furniture from one house to another in a city entirely within a single state? The sale of a carriage or an automobile by an Albany, New York dealer to an Albany resident? Congress was authorized to regulate only three types of commerce, that with Indians, with foreign nations, and commerce among the states. Marshall wrote:

> "Comprehensive as the word 'among' is, it may very properly be restricted to that commerce which concerns more states than one. The phrase is not one which would probably have been selected to indicate the completely interior traffic of a state, because it is not an apt phrase for that purpose; and the enumeration of the particular classes of commerce to which the power was to be extended would not have been made had the intention been to extend the power to every description [of commerce]. The enumeration presupposes something not enumerated; and that something, if we regard the language or the subject of the sentence, must be the exclusively internal commerce of a state."

In a short statement of his conclusions on the lack of congressional power to regulate the internal commerce of a state, Marshall wrote:

> "It is not intended to say that these words comprehend that commerce which is completely internal, which is carried on between man and man in a state, or between different parts of the same state, and which does not extend to or *affect* other states."

Here was a mere hint that perhaps commerce totally within a single state, but which only *affects* other states in some manner, might be within the power of Congress to control. This was the germ of an idea that was to grow and grow. But it was a germ contrary to the very words of the Constitution. And Marshall's opinion, aside from his rhetoric, demonstrated deep understanding of the nature of the power of Congress in relation to commerce among the states—not the power to regulate all things affecting commerce, but this: "It is the power to regulate; that is, to prescribe the rule by which commerce [among the states] is to be governed."

Remember the case of the Wisconsin grocer who was required by the Federal Pure Food law to leave the original labels on his Karo syrup until the containers were sold, and not to replace those labels with labels required by Wisconsin law. It would have affected commerce between Chicago and Wisconsin not the slightest if McDermott had switched the labels on his syrup to conform to Wisconsin law. Congress was empowered to pass a law requiring McDermott to leave the original labels on the product because it was a law necessary and proper to achieve the enforcement of the basic federal law regulating commerce among the states, the

---

fringed or violated." The Constitution omits this provison, but instead makes federal laws supreme over conflicting state laws.

29. This writing had meaning for the distant future of today, some of it as wisdom utterly forgotten, and some as catch-phrases to be amplified into doctrines foreign to the Constitution and destructive of the Constitution as the law for the government of government.

act of making it illegal to ship goods in interstate commerce unless they were labelled as required by Congress.

The congressional power to enact laws beyond the strict regulation of commerce among the states is derived from the Necessary and Proper Clause and can be derived from no other source—certainly not from the fact that here are factors which "affect" commerce with other states.

Marshall discussed the nature of congressional power regarding commerce: "It is the power to regulate; that is, the power to *prescribe the rule by which commerce is to be governed.*"

By the plain language of the Constitution, the power given Congress in regard to commerce among the states is the power to make regulations governing the conduct of commerce, but it may make those regulations for any purpose it desires, with any motive that may move its members.[30] But no power is given Congress to encourage, protect or promote commerce: When the Constitution gives such power to Congress, it expressly says that Congress may *promote* the progress of arts and sciences by providing for patents and copyrights. No power is given Congress to *engage* in commerce: When the Constitution empowers Congress to itself perform good works, it expressly gives Congress the power to "coin money" and to "establish post offices."

The conduct of commerce is the business of private citizens who are subject to rules governing them. Congress is given no power to govern them in affairs outside of commerce among the states, nor to protect commerce, nor to combat influences which retard the development of commerce, nor is it given the power to do anything except to regulate commerce, to make rules governing it, and to make laws necessary and proper to carry out the power to regulate.

It was urged in *Gibbons v. Ogden* that just because Congress is given the power to regulate commerce among the states, no state can make laws governing or affecting interstate commerce. Marshall properly refused to attempt to answer this question because it was not involved in the case.

This question came before the Court in the case involving Maryland's fifty dollar annual license fee for engaging in the business of selling imported goods as a wholesaler, *Brown v. Maryland.* As we have seen, Marshall incorrectly held the license fee to be a duty on imports and that a Federal duty on goods imported for sale would give the importer the right, under Federal law, to sell the goods.[31] The Chief Justice wrote:

---

30. Such regulations may be made for any purpose, just as Congress might declare war for any purpose—to defend the nation, to distract the people from internal dissentions by endeavoring to unite them in a war elsewhere, or even to fight an aggressive war to conquer the world. When Congress enacts a law within one of its express powers, courts cannot properly question its motives, just as when Congress exercises a power it can claim only by virtue of the Necessary and Proper Clause, the courts cannot properly avoid questioning its motive, or the ends it seeks to attain.

31. Marshall's opinion that the license tax to engage in the business of selling amounted to a duty on imports was a patent absurdity. He noted that Congress had elected to tax, in the imposition of its duties, only things actually destined for America, exempting goods temporarily unloaded to be re-shipped to another country. From this he jumped to the conclusion that Congress was taxing things brought into the country for sale. Of course, things may be imported for purposes other than resale—Italian stone to build a mansion, French wine imported by a private citizen for his own consumption, manufactured parts to be incorporated in machinery for local sale. The duty is paid in order to lawfully bring the property into the country, and thereafter, ownership entitles the owner to do any lawful thing with it.

"The object of importation is sale; it constitutes the motive for paying the duties; and *if* the United States possess the power of conferring the right to sell, as the consideration for which the duty is paid, every principle of fair dealing requires that they should be understood to confer it.[32]

But taxes are imposed because Government has the power to take by force, and the tax payment is not a purchase for anything except in the case of license taxes. The right to sell derives from ownership, not from any supposed permission given by the United States Government. The motive for importing a pistol may be to murder someone, but payment of the duty is not a purchase of the right to commit murder.

The Court then turned to the real and substantial question in the case, whether the Maryland licensing law conflicted with the mere grant to Congress of the power to regulate commerce by making rules as to how commerce with other states and nations could be conducted. Marshall referred back to his correct conclusion in *Gibbons v. Ogden* that the power to regulate commerce does not stop at state lines, but may be exercised within every state to control commerce between states. He then returned to his incorrect conclusion that a duty on imports is a license to sell the imported goods.

He wrote:

"To what purpose should the power to allow importation be given, unaccompanied with the power to authorize a sale of the thing imported? Sale is the object of importation, and is an essential ingredient of that intercourse, of which importation constitutes a part."

He then held that the duty on imports authorized the importer to sell, this was a federal law, therefore:

"Any penalty inflicted on the importer for selling the article in his character as importer, must be in opposition to the Act of Congress which authorizes importation".

It was immaterial that Congress didn't even know it was enacting a licensing law.

The real question was whether Maryland could pass the law when Congress had the power to regulate interstate commerce but had enacted no law on the subject. The purpose of adopting the interstate and foreign commerce clause in the Constitution was to abolish conflicting state regulations which would tend to become retributive, as they had under the Articles of Confederation. A licensing law forbids every person in the state to engage in the business until he purchases the license, or privilege, from the government. The Maryland law prohibited everyone from selling imported goods. It did not directly regulate commerce with a foreign nation. To order and purchase wine from France to be delivered in Baltimore is to engage in commerce with a foreign nation. But when a Baltimore importer sells a case of wine to a Baltimore wine dealer, with what

---

32. Again and again, in irrational decisions, it can be seen that the Court does not assert the truth of its basic premise—the court says that *if* this premise is true, this conclusion follows, then the court acts as if it had proven the conclusion. This was done in *Ruppert v. Caffey,* beginning, "*If* the war power . . . is as full and complete as the police power of the states . . ."

nation is he engaging in commerce? France? England? Spain? None. He is engaging in internal commerce entirely within Maryland.

Could Maryland pass a law forbidding the importation of goods? It could not, because this would be regulating a subject which only Congress can regulate. Nor could Maryland regulate foreign commerce by making it illegal to import anything for sale without a license, for this would simply prohibit importation. Then could Maryland move one step away, and make it illegal for anyone to sell or use anything that had been imported? Clearly not, because this would be but an attempt to indirectly prohibit that which Maryland could not directly prohibit, commerce with a foreign nation. It would be the same in intent and effect as a prohibition against importation.

The defect in Maryland's legislation was not that it conflicted with some superior federal license to sell—there was no such federal license granted by the duty laws. The defect of Maryland's legislation was that it had no application except that it concentrated upon the importation of goods, a matter within the exclusive control of Congress. Importation and importation alone was made the test of whether the owner of goods should have the right to sell them without state permission.

If Maryland had instead required a license of all wholesale sellers without regard to the source of the goods sold, the law would not make importation the test of denying the owner of goods the right to sell them without license, but would apply to all wholesale sellers, whether selling foreign or domestic goods. A state cannot control the way in which a bus engaging in the interstate transportation of passengers is operated, if this is the only subject of the law, because this is within Congress' exclusive powers.

But a state can enact that all drivers must stop at red lights and may drive when the light changes to green, and this must be obeyed by the interstate bus driver, because the state is not regulating commerce among the states. It is regulating the internal matter of whose turn it is to drive through the intersection. But if a state should enact that all drivers of busses transporting passengers through the state should be forbidden to drive into cities during certain rush hours, the state would be attempting to regulate commerce among the states, and no other subject, though its purposes might be entirely local.

Chief Justice Marshall had spoken in *Gibbons v. Ogdon* of the remaining power of states to regulate their own internal affairs, "whether of trading or police." This was shortened in *Brown v. Maryland* to "Police Power."

In the *Gibbons* case, Marshall had spoken of the various types of state laws, police, health, trade, for the purpose of emphasizing that no matter what type of law was involved, no matter how clearly this was within the state's powers to control by its laws, if it should come into conflict with a valid law enacted by Congress, then under the express provisions of the Supremacy Clause, making laws enacted pursuant to the Constitution a part of the Supreme Law of the Land, the state law must yield to the Federal law.

From this humble start, "Police Power" grew immensely. It became a shorthand way of referring to the state's entire governing power, and the Supreme Court for many years thereafter reviewed cases to decide whether a particular type of law came within the state's police powers, when the real question was whether the state law in question violated the Federal Constitution or some law enacted by Congress pursuant to the Constitution. The scope and extent of state legislative power was never any business of the Supreme Court, unless the state should attempt to exercise powers vested exclusively in Congress, until the adoption of the Fourteenth Amendment with its direct restraints upon state powers.

So this was the legacy of Chief Justice John Marshall in regard to the understanding of the greatest powers given to Congress, the commerce power, war power, power to make laws necessary and proper to carry out the other powers: That there existed in state governments something known as *police power,* a phrase which never made any logical contribution to a decision of whether Congress had power to pass a law, but only served to brand a particular type of state law as beyond Congress' power and to invite state courts to unwittingly use the police power label to circumvent state constitutional prohibitions; that the federal commerce power included not only the power to regulate commerce, but possibly the power as well to regulate things affecting commerce; and that there might be something know as implied power, covering things "affecting" some subject on which Congress was given the power to legislate, though the only inferred power provided by the Constitution was that to enact laws necessary and proper to carry out powers particularly provided by the Constitution.

Future years were to see competent repudiation by the Supreme Court of these harmful doctrines hinted by Marshall, but Marshall's rhetoric was to remain, a strong enticement to future judges to substitute it for the thinking process, as indeed they have.

Brown v. Maryland was repudiated by the Supreme Court in *Thurlow v. Massachusetts* and a number of other state cases reported under the title of *License Cases.* Congress enacted laws authorizing the importation of spirituous liquors and Massachusetts, Rhode Island, and New Hampshire enacted license tax laws, requiring sellers of liquors and wines to first obtain licenses to engage in the business. It was argued that the federal import licenses gave the dealers the right to sell such spirituous beverages contrary to state law, which Marshall said to be the effect of the duty in the *Brown* case. The Supreme Court held the conduct of these businesses to be within Congress' taxing powers, but also held that they were local businesses, local commerce, not subject to Congress' power to govern by regulations or rules, because this was not commerce among the states or with foreign nations.

One justice in the *License Cases* wrote this prelude to his discussion of *Brown v. Maryland:* "In cases of alleged conflict between a law of the United States and the Constitution, or between the law of a State and the Constitution or a statute of the United States, this court must pronounce upon the validity of either law with reference to the Constitution; but *whether the decision of the court in such cases be itself binding or otherwise must depend upon its conformity with, or its warrant from, the Constitution. It cannot be correctly held, that a decision, merely because it be by the Supreme Court, is to override alike the Constitution and the laws both of the States and of the United States."*

In the *License Cases,* the local laws only required licensing of the local businesses of selling alcoholic beverages, which businesses operate entirely within the state even if their stocks include Scotch and Irish whiskeys and French and Italian wines. No matter how much these may merely affect commerce with those foreign nations, the conduct of those businesses is not commerce among the states or with foreign nations, and is not within Congress' power to regulate. The purchase of Scotch whiskey *from Scotland* is foreign commerce within Congress' power to regulate, but the sale of that whiskey by a Massachusetts seller to a buyer in Massachusetts is not foreign commerce.

Twenty years after the *License Cases,* the Supreme Court considered another branch of *Brown v. Maryland* in cases reported under the heading of *License Tax Cases, United States v. Vassar* and a number of other cases jointly decided. Taxes called license taxes were imposed by Congress on the businesses of selling liquor and dealing in lotteries. The particular businesses were illegal in the states where they were conducted, and the Congressional Act made it a federal criminal offense to engage in these businesses without paying the federal license tax. The Court correctly held that the tax was valid and that its payment did not confer on the taxpayer any right to carry on the businesses, but merely prevented the business activity from being a violation of *Federal law*. After noting that Congress could grant people the right or license to carry on businesses in interstate or foreign commerce, the Court said:

> "But very different considerations apply to the internal commerce of domestic trade of the States. Over this commerce and trade Congress has no power of regulation nor any direct control. This power belongs exclusively to the States. No interference by Congress with the business of citizens transacted within a State is warranted by the Constitution, except such as is strictly incidental to the exercise of powers clearly granted to the Legislature."

Thus, contrary to Chief Justice Marshall's holding that a Federal duty on imports gave the importer the unrestricted right to sell imported goods immune from all state laws, the Supreme Court now correctly held that a lawful Federal excise tax on the conduct of a business, even though required to be paid before the citizen could conduct the business, gave him no right to conduct such a business immune from state laws.

But what of the congressional desire to go beyond commerce between different states, and regulate internal affairs of a state? Can Congress do this, as Marshall implied, merely because such internal business may "affect" commerce with another state, or is Congress limited, as the Constitution says, in its commercial regulations, to making laws necessary and proper to carry out its regulations of commerce, as it did in the Food and Drug case we have discussed, *McDermott v. Wisconsin?*

The Supreme Court's strongest refutation of Marshall's hint that Congress might have authority to make laws on all matters affecting commerce came in an 1888 decision, *Kidd v. Pearson*. In that case, Iowa enacted a law making it illegal to manufacture or sell liquor in the state. Kidd set up a distillery and produced liquor which he sold to customers in other states, in interstate commerce. An Iowa court ordered the distillery closed, and it was claimed that this Iowa law attempted to control commerce in whiskey between Iowa and other states, which only Congress could control. The Supreme Court held that Iowa, not Congress, had the exclusive power to control and regulate the manufacture of whiskey within its borders, and could forbid all such manufacture, regardless of how much it "affected" commerce among the states or with foreign nations. The Court said:

> "No distinction is more popular to the common mind, or more clearly expressed in economic and political literature, than that between manufactures and commerce. Manufacture is transformation—the fashioning of raw materials into a change of form for use. The functions of commerce are different. The buying and selling and the transportation incidental thereto constitute commerce; and the regulation of commerce in the constitutional sense embraces the regulation at least of such transportation. . . . If it be held that the term includes the regulation of all such manu-

factures as are intended to be the subject of commercial transactions in the future, *it is impossible to deny that it would also include all productive industries that contemplate the same thing.* The result would be that Congress would be invested, to the exclusion of the States, with the power to regulate, not only manufacture, but also agriculture, horticulture, stock raising, domestic fisheries, mining—in short, every branch of human industry. . . .

"We find no provisions in any of the sections of the statute under consideration, the object and purpose of which are to exert the jurisdiction of the State over persons or property within the limits of *other states;* or to act upon intoxicating liquors *as exports;* or while they are in the process of exportation or importation. Its avowed object is to prevent, not the carrying of intoxicating liquors *out of* the State, but to prevent their manufacture, except for specified purposes, *within* the State. . . . Can it be said that a refusal of a State to allow articles to be manufacured within her borders (for export) any more directly or materially affects her external commerce than does her action in forbidding the retail within her borders of the same articles after they have left the hands of the importer? That the latter could be done was decided years ago; and we think there is no practical difference between the two cases.[33]

The possible existence of "implied power" hinted by Marshall, or the power to make laws "affecting" any subject Congress was empowered to regulate, came under careful consideration by the Supreme Court in a post-Civil War case, *Ex Parte Milligan.* Because of the excitement of war, the Supreme Court deferred deciding the case until the war had ended, to assure that the case would have their dispassionate concentration, an admirable attitude seldom seen since then.

During the Civil War, President Lincoln issued a proclamation:

". . . all persons discouraging volunteer enlistments, resisting military drafts, or guilty of any disloyal practice, affording aid and comfort to rebels against the authority of the United States, shall be subject to martial law and liable to trial and punishment by court-martial, or by the sentence of any court-martial or military commission."

Here was a false claim of some inherent power, as head of state or as commander-in-chief of the army, to impose dictatorial martial law upon private citizens. Congress then passed a law providing that all military commanders should report the names of all citizens of the loyal states who might be arrested, reporting the names to the federal courts, with the citizen to be freed if not indicted by a civilian grand jury within the time provided by this law.

Milligan was arrested by military officers, charged and tried by a court-martial, which sentenced him to death for plotting to capture a Federal arsenal, release prisoners from it, and join rebel forces in Kentucky. The Attorney-General

---

33. This clear meaning of the Commerce Clause was reaffirmed by the Supreme Court in 1922 in *Oliver Mining Co. v. Lord.* The Court held a Minnesota tax on mining not to be either a tax on exports or an attempt to regulate interstate commerce, though ore from the mines was loaded directly onto railroad cars and most of these were then hauled out of state. "Mining is not interstate commerce, but, like manufacturing is a local business, subject to local regulation and taxation. . . . Its character in this regard is intrinsic, is not affected by the intended use or disposal of the product, is not controlled by contractual engagements, and persists even though the business be conducted in close connection with interstate commerce."

sought to defend Lincoln's proclamation, and the military's obedience to it, on the ground that the office of military commander-in-chief, the President's constitutional office, necessarily included the power to combat such interference by direct use of his armed forces.[34]

This was simply a rational extension of John Marshall's incorrect assertion that the government can have some implied powers, even though it has a written constitution expressly listing all its powers; that it might have powers to regulate those things "affecting" the subjects within its jurisdiction, such as interstate commerce, war, bankruptcy. Here are parts of the Supreme Court's ruling, in Milligan's *habeas corpus* case,[35] as to whether the military commander's tribunal had the power to try and sentence Milligan:

> "No graver question was ever considered by this court, nor one which more nearly concerns the rights of the whole people; for it is the birthright of every American citizen when charged with crime, to be tried and punished according to law. . . . The decision of this question does not depend upon argument or judicial precedents, numerous and highly illustrative as they are. These precedents inform us of the extent of the struggle to preserve liberty and to relieve those in civil life from military trials. The founders of our government were familiar with the history of that struggle; and secured in a written Constitution every right which the people had wrested from power during a contest of ages. . . .
>
> "Time has proven the discernment of our ancestors; for even these privileges [trial by jury, etc.], expressed in such plain English words, that it would seem the ingenuity of man could not evade them, are now, after the lapse of more than seventy years, sought to be avoided. Those great and good men foresaw the troublous times would arise, when *rulers and people would become restive under restraint,* and seek by sharp and decisive measures to accomplish ends deemed just and proper; and that the principles of constitutional liberty would be in peril, unless established by irrepealable law. The history of the world had taught them that what was done in the past might be attempted in the future.
>
> "The Consitution of the United States is a law for rulers and people, equally in war and in peace, and covers with the shield of its protection all classes of men, at all times, and under all circumstances. No doctrine, involving more pernicious consequences, was ever invented by the wit of man than that any of its provisions can be suspended during any of the great exigencies of government. Such a doctrine leads directly to anarchy and despotism, but the theory of necessity on which it is based is false; for the government, within the Constitution, has all the powers granted to it which are necessary to preserve its existence, and has been happily proved by the result of the great effort to throw off its just authority."

---

34. The Attorney-General argued: "The Commander-in-Chief has full power to make an effectual use of his forces. He must, therefore, have power to arrest and punish one who arms men to join the enemy in the field against him; one who holds correspondence with that enemy; one who is an officer in an armed force organized to oppose him; one who is preparing to seize arsenels and release prisoners of war taken in battle and confined within his military lines."

35. Milligan was not engaging in war when he was arrested: "Milligan, not a resident of one of the rebellious States, or a prisoner of war, but a citizen of Indiana for twenty years past, and never in the military or naval service, is, while at his home, arrested by the military power of the United States, imprisoned and, on certain criminal charges preferred against him, tried, convicted and sentenced to be hanged by a military commission, organized under the direction of the military commander of the military district of Indiana. Had this tribunal the legal power and authority to try and punish this man?"

The Court, however, went on to speculate on a question not even remotely before it. The Court said that this martial law might be exercised in case of an actual invasion, when the Courts and governments were no longer operating in a given area of the country. But in that portion of its opinion, the Court was not writing on constitutional law. Certainly, this could and some day may happen. But when it does, that part of the country simply will no longer be constitutionally governed. It will instead be governed only by the gun in the hands of the military, uncontrolled by law. Constitutional government consists of a civil government, actually governing, and subjecting itself—or being compelled by its citizens to subject itself—to the supremacy of a constitution in all matters and at all times. Rule by brute force of guns in the hands of the military is uncontrollable by judges, cannot be restrained by them, and does not require their theoretical rationalizations for support.

Essential power, "necessary" power, is not inherent, does not inhere in the nature of the office, but is granted by the Constitution or created in a manner expressly provided by the Constitution. If there were any inherent power in the office of the presidency, then surely the nature of the office would empower the President to require written reports from his department heads, yet this is a separate power granted by the express words of the Constitution!

Before we examine the Twentieth Century's warping of the Constitution's provisions in order to achieve vast expansion of the Federal Government's powers over details of daily life, we need to return to a second premise mentioned early in this chapter: That massive expansion would be beyond Congress' power to effectively handle, and could be achieved only by the creation of a bureaucracy of boards and commissions.

The Separation of Powers:

It was the entire theory of the Constitution of the United States that it gives no power to government other than the powers expressly set out. And in particular, the Constitution does not give powers to the Government in general, but gives the powers to the separate departments of government. This was done to avoid the arbitrariness of the emperor or king, who could effectively govern as a master over a slave. That is, he could make those rules he desired to make, could interpret them the way he wanted to interpret them, remaking them as he went, and could decide according to his whim upon the application of his rules to individual situations in their enforcement. Essentially, this is a government by whim rather than by law.

A practical application of this doctrine of separation of powers between the different departments of government is seen in the *Milligan* decision, in which the Supreme Court declared void the death sentence imposed by a military tribunal under claim of martial law powers. The Court said:

> "Every trial involves the exercise of judicial power; and from what source did the Military Commission that tried him derive that authority? Certainly no part of the judicial power of the country was conferred on them; because the Constitution expressly vests 'in one Supreme Court and such inferior courts as the Congress may from time to time ordain and establish,' and it is not pretended that the commission was a court ordained and established by Congress. They cannot justify on the mandate of the President; because he is controlled by law, and has his appropriate sphere of duty, which is to execute, not to make, the laws; there is no 'unwritten criminal code to which resort can be had as a source of jurisdiction.' "

In writing the Constitution, its authors were influenced by the experience in Great Britain, which had evolved into a constitutional monarchy in which the powers of making laws, executing laws, and passing judgment had been separated into different corps of officials. The men who wrote the Constitution were also tremendously influenced by the writings of Montesquieu, which are liberally quoted throughout *The Federalist*. In such high regard was Montesquieu held that in one of the *Federalist* articles, Madison evidently felt constrained to defend the fact that the Federal Constitutional scheme envisoned some overlapping of powers. After writing of the British Government, Madison said:

> "From these facts, by which Montesquieu was guided, it may clearly be inferred that, in saying that 'There can be no liberty where the legislative and executive powers are united in the same person, or body of magistrates,' of 'if the power of judging be not separated from the legislative and executive powers,' he did not mean that these departments ought to have *no partial agency in or no control over, the acts of each other. . . .**

By the system of construing the Constitution which Chief Justice Marshall so often espoused and which reason verifies as valid, the express statements in the Constitution of these and a few other exceptions imply that *there cannot be* any other lawful exceptions to this separation of powers: That but for his action of approving or disapproving legislation, the President could not exercise *any* of the law-making powers of the Federal Government; that but for making those few appointments which they are permitted by Congress to make, the judiciary cannot lawfully exercise *any* of the legislative or *any* of the other executive powers of the Federal Government.

By saying that *the* legislative power of the United States was vested in Congress, *the* executive power in the President and *the* judicial power in the courts, the Constitution expressly stated that the particular types of powers could be exercised only by those particular departments of government. That conscious and studious support of the doctrine of separation of powers is essential to the maintenance of liberty is an obligation American judges have historically recognized in their decisions of cases, and its theoretical implications have not escaped their attention.[36]

---

36. This doctrine is written into all state constitutions as well as the Federal Constitution, and an application of it was seen in an old West Virginia case, *Shepherd v. Wheeling:*

"The enactment of an ordinance by a city council, or the enactment of a statute by a legislature, being in each case the exercise of legislative power, the repeal of such ordinance or statute must likewise be the exercise of legislative power. It does not require any precise definition of judicial power, or any nice discrimination as to its extent and limitations to determine that the act of repealing a statute is not the exercise of judicial power. . . .

"When, in the course of determining the rights of the parties to a particular suit or controversy, the court finds it necessary to ascertain whether or not a statute is unconstitutional, the court must necessarily pass upon that question; *but in doing so, it does not annul or repeal the statute it finds in conflict with the Constitution. It simply refuses to recognize it, and determines the rights of the parties just as if such statute had no existence. . . .* The opinion or reasons of the court may operate as a precedent for the determination of other similar cases, but it does not strike the statute from the statute-book; it does not repeal or 'supersede, revoke or

The Constitution recognizes that the judicial power of the United States will be shared by courts inferior to the Supreme Court, because it empowers Congress to create inferior courts. It recognizes some presidential powers will be exercised by inferiors, because it empowers the President to require a written opinion from "the principal Officer in each of the Executive Departments, upon any Subject relating to the Duties of their respective Offices." Even without the express recognition of the necessity for inferior executive departments, it is clear that necessity and propriety would empower Congress to make laws creating executive departments with department-heads and employees to help the President perform his duty of enforcing the laws, his duty to keep himself aware of the state of the union and to report to Congress on this subject from time to time. The existence of subsidiary officers in the executive and judicial departments are recognized as being entirely within one department or the other, and not inter-mixed between the two departments.

But in the entire Constitution, there is no word, no hint, not the slightest basis for any inference that any of the law-making power vested in Congress may be exercised by any other body. Congress establishes the rules and laws to govern the nation within the scope of its law-making powers, but by its nature, rule-making is something that could be done—and often has been done—by an individual in seclusion. But the Constitution provides for this rule-making or law-making power to be given to a larger body of representatives, it states exactly how they shall be chosen, and it states exactly how they shall exercise that power. The Constitution gives the legislative power of the United States to Congress and to Congress alone.

Legislative power consists of three things in its exercise: First, a rule to govern people in some of their conduct is proposed. Second, variations, conflicting interests, are considered, and the proposal is altered into a complete and final proposal of a rule which is to become law or which is not to become law. Finally, the decision is made, purely as a bare exercise of power, that this proposed law will or will not become law.

The exercise of law-making power consists no less in determining whether and when that rule will become applicable than in determining what the content of the rule will be.[37] If a law is imposed by the exercise of governmental power to govern the conduct of people subject to that power, law-making or legislative power has been exercised.

Congress might enact a law giving to some administrator the power to make rules determining whether certain products may be shipped in interstate commerce. The administrator promulgates and declares such a rule, announcing that a particular product which does not meet standards proclaimed by the administrator cannot be shipped from one state to another. The rule is respected, obeyed, and enforced. The day before the rule was made, that product could be freely shipped from one state to another. Upon proclamation of the administrator's rule, that product can no longer be shipped. Law-making power, legislative power, has been exercised.

The mode of exercising this law-making power was that a single officer of

---

annul' the statute. The parties to that suit are concluded by the judgment, and *no one else is bound.*"

37. Indeed, the middle step of suggesting variations and debating the merits of proposed legislation may be omitted, but this final step of declaring that this shall or shall not become law can never be omitted.

government issued an edict declaring that a previously non-existent rule should henceforth be a law governing the people. The Constitution says that the power to make laws shall be vested in Congress. It says this power shall be exercised by voting on the proposed law by one house of Congress, and then taking a vote on that *identical* proposal, without any change, by the other house of Congress, and if it passes both houses, sending it to the President for his approval; when the approval is obtained, or the identical measure is passed by the necessary majorities over the presidential veto, "it shall become a Law."

There is no question of "delegation" of legislative power. To concern one's attention with the possibility of "delegating" legislative power is to refuse to give one's attention to the Constitution in deciding constitutional issues. When law is formulated by a means other than that provided by the Constitution, then the Constitution has not been followed in making law. To recognize such regulations as law is to depart from the Constitution. It is, as Marshall maintained,[38] to blind oneself to the Constitution and see only law, to disregard in fact what has been established by reason, the supremacy of the Constitution. The enforcement of such an administrator-made law is an act which violates the Constitution and dishonors the oath of office.

In the operation of the government, the President is the chief executive, and his is the responsibility for executing the laws of the nation. He may make judgments, or his department heads or their inferiors may make judgements between conflicting laws, as judgments *must be made* in the enforcement of laws as to whether to take *any action*.[39] But regardless of what decisions the President and his inferiors may make as to the proper resolution of conflicting laws, regardless of what policies may be established as to which laws shall be more watchfully enforced and which treated with benign neglect, the entire body of law is nevertheless law. It is not changed and does not die from the rarity of its enforcement. But to hold that Congress can "delegate" its law-making power, to claim that this power can be passed on by Congress to some other favored person or group of persons, not elected by the people, is to uphold as law that which is not law.

Recognize that perhaps—in spite of the constitutional scheme which gives all the law-making power to Congress and prescribes the exact steps that must be followed to convert a written proposal into law—Congress may give some of its law-making powers to an agency, so expert in making its rules about a particular industry, is it not then simple to give this agency the power to enforce its rules and to determine whether its rules have been violated? But this is precisely the *principal evil that the Constitution sought to avoid.* So in the bare assumption that the congressional power to make law may be delegated to the slightest extent, there is very, very great danger.

How came such a foolish supposition that Congress' exclusive law-making powers might be handed over to others? How did anyone ever come to imagine that law might be originated and declared effective by some board or commission instead of by successive approvals of the same written proposal by the different houses of Congress? Where did such an idea originate?

---

38. In *Marbury v. Madison.*

39. They may make practical judgements because of budgetary limitations or from the experience that juries will not convict for any but the most aggravated violations of particular statutes. If there are not enough officials to do all the work, priorities may be established, and some laws may be enforced more aggressively than others simply because of the physical impossibility of any other alternative.

It began with Chief Justice John Marshall.
In *Wayman v. Southard,* the great chief justice wrote:

> "It will not be contended that Congress can delegate to the courts, or to any other tribunals, powers which are strictly or exclusively legislative. But Congress may certainly delegate to others, powers which the legislature may rightfully exercise itself. . . . The line has not been exactly drawn which separates those important subjects which *must* be entirely regulated by the legislature itself, from those of less interest, in which a general provision may be made, and power given to those who are to act under such general provisions to *fill up the details.*"

It was an unhappy day when the great chief justice uttered the words indicating—without giving the slightest reason for it—that Congress could "certainly" delegate some of the powers belonging to it: It was a sad day when this declaration was made and no James Madison noticed it and rose to declare, as in his Remonstrance,[40] upon the propriety of the people taking exception to the least experimentation with their liberty:

> "The preservation of a free government requires not merely, that the metes and bounds which separate each department of power may be invariably maintained; but more especially, that neither of them be suffered to overleap the greater Barrier which defends the rights of the people. *The Rulers who are guilty of such an encroachment, exceed the commission from which they derive their authority, and are Tyrants. The People who submit to it are goverened by laws made neither by themselves, nor by an authority derived from them, and are slaves.* The freemen of America did not wait till usurped power had strengthened itself by exercise, and entangled the questions in precedents. They saw all the consequences in the principle, and they avoided the consequences by denying the principle.

The Metamorphosis:

The suppositions hinted by Chief Justice Marshall for the most part lay dormant until the exciting days that came with the approach of the Twentieth Century, bringing with them the Populist Movement, the Labor Movement, the Prohibition Movement, bringing increased demands for increased regulatory activity on the part of the Federal Government.

After the Civil War, mere moral considerations began to enter into the Supreme Court's solutions of constitutional questions where they had no place. Two examples of this occurred shortly before the turn of the century when lotteries came under serious moral disapproval. These cases were *Douglas v. Kentucky* and *Stone v. Mississippi.*

The large-scale operation of lotteries in states where they were lawful, including Kentucky and Mississippi, necessarily involved contracts entered into not only with the customer-gamblers but also with the persons involved in the sale of the lottery tickets. Despite the existing contracts, Kentucky and Mississippi moved to make lotteries illegal, though the Constitution prohibits any state from making any law "impairing the Obligation of Contracts."

---

40. It is some indication of the former degree of congressional reliance upon law rather than hordes of administrators to govern the country that in 1879, after more than 100 years of national existence and after it had become a world power, Congress passed an act authorizing the employment of 35 agents to enforce the nation's revenue laws.

The city of Frankfort, Kentucky, sold a "scheme of lottery" under which the buyer was essentially to act as sales manager for Frankfort in the sale of lottery tickets. The city ordinances providing for the lottery scheme and the consequent contracts were made in strict accordance with state statutes. So this contract with Frankfort was not only lawful and enforceable, but was *encouraged by state law,* and Douglas was the owner of the contractual right to operate the lottery. By adopting a new constitution in 1891, Kentucky outlawed lotteries. The Supreme Court held that despite the unconditional denial of the power to every state to impair the obligation of contracts, Kentucky could nullify the existing contract and could prosecute and imprison Douglas for carrying out his contractual rights. The Court said:

"This Court had occasion many years ago to say that the common forms of gambling were comparatively innocuous when placed in contrast with the widespread pestilence of lotteries; that the former were confined to a few persons and places, while the latter infested the whole community, entered every dwelling, reached every class, preyed upon the hard earnings of the poor, and plundered the ignorant and simple. . . .

"Is a state forbidden by the supreme law of the land from protecting its people at all times from practices which it conceives to be attended by such ruinous results? Can the legislature of a state contract away its power to establish such regulations as are reasonably necessary from time to time to protect the public morals against the evils of lotteries?"

We see a clear indication that mere moral judgment and popular need are adequate to overcome an express prohibition of power contained in the Constitution of the United States and aimed at every state government. To answer the question it asked in the quotation above, the Supreme Court went back a few years to *Stone v. Mississippi,* in which the Court had said, "No legislature can bargain away the public health or the public morals." In support of this sweeping declaration that the Constitution's prohibition against impairing the obligation of contracts should not be safe from state violation when the state and the Supreme Court should consider current moral judgments adequate to outweigh the Constitution's supremacy, the Supreme Court cited no constitutional provision, past decisions, or any other real or imagined authority. The Court simply utilized sloganeering to permit an existing contractual obligation and an express constitutional command to be subordinated to the overriding supremacy of current and changing moral views, without regard to the position of every provision of the Constitution as a part of the supreme law of the land. Whether the moral judgments of a state government were wise or unwise was and is no concern of the Federal judiciary when it is called upon to judge the existence of state governmental power under the Constitution.

Congress then utilized its power to regulate commerce in aid of morality, by enacting a law making it illegal to transport any lottery tickets in interstate commerce. Champion was convicted of transporting a quantity of lottery tickets from Texas to California in violation of this law, and *Champion v. Ames* became a historic landmark in regard to congressional regulatory powers over interstate commerce. Champion claimed the *prohibition* of commerce is not a regulation of commerce, that Congress is empowered only to regulate commerce as it exists, not to destroy commerce by prohibiting it. But the Court held the prohibition itself to be a form of regulation, within the power of Congress. The Court followed the language of Marshall in *Gibbons v. Ogden* that the power to regulate inter-state commerce is plenary unless exercised in violation of some express provision of the Constitution, and that the voters' patience is its only limitation.

Champion v. Ames represented a step toward Twentieth Century regulations, apparently further than Congress had gone before. In this law, Congress pro-hibited shipment of a product between states for the purpose of affording pro-tection in a subject of local moral concern in many states, but Congress did this without regard to whether the lottery tickets were being shipped into states which condemned or permitted them.[41] With this decision came the realization that here could be a potent weapon for controlling all sorts of local problems. The case also presented an example of Congress using its power for an ulterior motive. A popular motive and purpose, but a purpose primarily local though prevalent in many localities.

The immateriality of the Congressional motivation was considered by the Supreme Court the year after *Champion v. Ames* in *McCray v. United States*. This decision involved a tax imposed by Congress on oleomargarine, which in its manufactured state, had the appearance of lard. Manufacturers customarily used a coloring agent to give it the appearance of butter, the same coloring agent used by dairies to make butter look like butter. Congress taxed uncolored mar-garine, and imposed a tax forty times as great upon colored margarine. The Court held that even assuming the congressional purpose to be the destruction of the margarine manufacturing business, Congress did this by imposing an excise tax upon a manufactured product and this was within the power of Congress to ac-complish. The Court well refuted the argument that it had some power to correct abuses by Congress,[42] holding that where Congress is actually exercising a power granted to it, its ulterior motivations cannot destroy its power.[43]

---

41. A frustrating 1889 decision, *Leisy v. Hardin*, followed Marshall's irrational (import duty = license to sell) thinking in *Brown v. Maryland*. The Court held that an Illinois law forbidding the sale of beer in the state could not be enforced to prevent the purchase in Illinois by Illinois people from an Illinois dealer of kegs of beer the dealer had previously purchased from Iowa. In practical effect, this nullified the power of every state to prohibit the sale of anything because a local dealer could always import goods for resale. Congress rapidly made it illegal to transport such objects in interstate commerce into a state in which their sale was prohibited by state law, and this law was upheld by the Supreme Court in *Re Rahrer*.

42. "It is, however, argued, if a lawful power may be exerted for an unlawful pur-pose, and thus, by abusing the power, it may be made to accomplish a result not in-tended by the Constitution, all limitations of power must disappear and the grave function lodged in the judiciary, to confine all the departments within the authority conferred by the Constitution, will be of no avail. This, when reduced to its last analy-sis, comes to this: that, because a particular department of the government may exert its lawful powers with the object or motive of reaching an end not justified, therefore it becomes the duty of the judiciary to restrain the exercise of a lawful power when-ever it seems to the judicial mind that such lawful power has been abused. But this reduces itself to the contention that, under our constitutional system, the abuse by one department of the government of its lawful powers is to be corrected by the abuse of its powers by another department.

"The proposition, if sustained, would destroy all distinction between the powers of the respective departments of the government, would put an end to what confidence and respect for each other which it was the purpose of the Constitution to uphold, and would thus be full of danger to the permanence of our institutions. . . ."

43. This principle was reaffirmed in 1936 in a better-known case, *Sonzinsky v. United States*, in which congressional taxing power was used to suppress commerce in machine guns, silencers, and other underworld weapons.

The turn of the century was a time of great change, of insistent efforts by laborers to organize into labor unions, of growing public distrust for large corporations, a distrust that had shortly before led to strong anti-trust legislation. The same year the Supreme Court decided Congress could use its taxing power to destroy the oleomargarine industry,[44] the Court held an Act of Congress unconstitutional because of the motivation of Congress.

The new law was the Railway Labor Act, providing for arbitration of labor disputes and providing a general railroad labor-management regulatory scheme recognizing labor unions as legitimate social organizations. This law made it a crime for any railroad or railroad agent to discriminate against an employee because of his membership in a union. In *Adair v. United States,* Adair was convicted of discharging an employee of a railroad company because of his membership in a labor union. The employee was a locomotive fireman. The railroad was engaged in interstate commerce by hauling goods and passengers for profit across state lines. The employee was also engaged in interstate commerce by helping to keep the train running to carry passengers and freight. The working together of the railroad and its employee in engaging in interstate commerce was a new aspect of commerce among the states which Congress sought to regulate by the Railway Labor Act.

The Supreme Court resorted to common law contrary theory, saying:

"The right of a person to sell his labor upon such terms as he deems proper is, in its essence, the same as the right of the purchaser of labor to prescribe the conditions upon which he will accept such labor from the persons offering to sell it. So the right of the employee to quit the service of the employer, for whatever reason, is the same as the right of the employer, for whatever reason, to dispense with the services of his employee. It was the legal right of the defendant, Adair,—however unwise such a course might have been,—to discharge Coppage because of his being a member of a labor organization, as it was the legal right of Coppage, if he saw fit to do so,—however unwise such a course on his part might have been,—to quit the services in which he was engaged, because the defendant employed some persons who were not members of a labor organization. In all such particulars the employer and employee have equality of right, and any legislation that distrubs that equality is an arbitrary interference with the liberty of contract which no government can legally justify in a free land."

This was a good statement of economic theory and of common law, and to establish its authenticity, the Supreme Court cited a large number of cases, every one of which was a common-law decision by a state common-law court.

In this case, the Supreme Court simply refused to recognize that Congress could regulate that aspect of interstate commerce which concerned the relationship between the railroad company and its employees, and their terms of employment, in actually operating a train transporting goods across interstate commerce. All its reasoning related to the unwise nature of the law,[45] which was none of its business.

---

44. It didn't work because the manufacturers sold the margarine and the dye in separate packages, and the people bought it.
45. "One who engages in the service of an interstate carrier will, it must be assumed, fully perform his duty, whether he be a member or not a member of a labor organization. His fitness for the position in which he labors and his diligence in the discharge of his duties cannot, in law or sound reason, depend in any degree upon his being or not being a member of a labor organization. It cannot be assumed that his

For a lengthy period, the popular pressures for wage-hour legislation, union recognition, and similar legislative aims aroused considerable judicial anger, which dictated the content of Supreme Court decisions on those subjects and which blinded the Court to the provisions of the Constitution itself. Congress had exclusive legislative powers in the District of Columbia, so that it could pass laws for that area on any subject,[46] but in 1922, the Court held in *Adkins v. Children's Hospital* that this congressional power could not be stretched to the point of maintaining wage and hour regulations to govern the District of Columbia. A Children's Hospital employee sued to enjoin enforcement of this legislation and in holding the law void, the Court quoted from an earlier opinion [47] condemning the audacity of the New York Legislature in presuming to limit the work day to 10 hours. Against a background of economic understanding, the reasonableness of the congressional enactment [48] was the sole standard utilized by the Supreme Court for passing upon the constitutionality of the law, and the question of reasonableness was not legitimately connected with any provision of the Constitution. The Court correctly prophesied that the power to forbid employees to pay less than a stated amount would eventually be used to forbid employees to receive more than a stated amount fixed by government.[49]

---

fitness is assured, or his diligence is increased, by such membership, or that he is less fit or less diligent because of his not being a member of such an organization. It is the employee as a man, and not as a member of a labor organization, who labors in the service of an interstate carrier."

46. Except areas excluded from its powers, such as the First Amendment freedoms.

47. "Statutes of the nature of that under review, limiting the hours in which grown and intelligent men may labor to earn their living, are mere meddlesome interferences with the rights of the individual . . . whose rights are interfered with, unless there be some fair ground, reasonable in and of itself, to say that there is material danger to the public health or the health of the employees if the hours of labor are not curtailed."

48. "The law takes account of the necessities of only one party to the contract [of employment]. It ignores the necessities of the employer by compelling him to pay not less than a certain sum, not only whether the employee is capable of earning it, but irrespective of the ability of his business to sustain the burden, generously leaving him, of course, the privilege of abandoning his business as an alternative to going on at a loss. Within the limits of the minimum sum, he is precluded, under penalty of fine and imprisonment, from adjusting compensation to the differing merits of his employees. It compels him to pay at least the sum fixed in any event, because the employee needs it, but requires no service of equivalent value from the employee. It therefore undertakes to solve but one half of the problem. The other half is the establishment of a corresponding standard of efficiency; and this forms no part of the policy of the legislation, although in practice the former half without the latter must lead to ultimate failure, in accordance with the inexorable law that no one can continue indefinitely to take out more than he puts in without ultimately exhausting the supply."

49. "Finally, it may be said that if, in the interest of the public welfare, the police power may be invoked to justify the fixing of a minimum wage, it may, when the public welfare is thought to require it, be invoked to justify a maximum wage. . . . If, for example, in the opinion of future law-makers, wages in the building trades shall become so high as to preclude people of ordinary means from building and owning homes, an authority which sustains the minimum wage will be invoked to support a maximum wage for building laborers and artisans, and the same argument which has been here urged to strip the employer of his constitutional liberty to contract in one direction will be utilized to strip the employee of his constitutional liberty to contract in the opposite direction. A wrong decision does not end with itself; it is a precedent,

The Court's opinion as to the wisdom of laws by which government establishes such variables as wages, hours, and profits appears to be unquestionably true as a matter of rational economic theory.[50] There are surely economic laws beyond the power of government to evade without subjecting its people to the consequences, laws to which all governments are helplessly subjected, just as there are natural laws above government and moral laws so deeply imbedded in popular conscience that government lacks the power to change them. But so far as constitutional law is concerned, when Congress acts within the scope of power expressly given to it by the Constitution, as in the power sought to be used in the *Adkins* case to govern the District of Columbia, or the power to regulate interstate commerce, then Congress has the power to make foolish laws as well as wise laws, the power to restrict as well as to protect the citizen's liberty. Whether laws are wise or foolish is never legitimately the concern of the federal judiciary. This is legislative business.

Perhaps the most famous early labor law decision was a 1917 case, *Hammer v. Dagenhart*, famous because of the dissenting opinion of Justice Holmes, since generally accepted as correct.[51] Congress tackled the problem of child labor, already the subject of legislation by many state governments. Congress made it illegal for any manufacturer to ship any goods in interstate commerce if these were produced in a plant in which any child under sixteen years of age had been permitted to work *more than eight hours in any day within thirty days* before the shipment. This law did not attempt to deny manufacturers the right to employ children, to have them work twelve hours a day, or at night. It simply prohibited shipment of their goods in interstate commerce for thirty days after use of such labor in excess of the standards enacted by Congress. The Supreme Court held this law unconstitutional.

The Court mentioned various past decisions in which strong moral or health needs had motivated Congress to close the channels of interstate commerce to particular products for consumer protection because the products themselves were objectionable,[52] but held that because Congress' ulterior motivation in this child labor legislation was solely to combat local problems, and Congress could not use its interstate commerce regulatory powers for that purpose.

Dissenting, Mr. Justice Holmes said:

> "The objection urged against the power is that the states have exclusive control over their methods of production, and that Congress cannot meddle in them; and taking the proposition in the sense of *direct meddling* I agree to it and suppose that no one denies. it. But if an act is within the powers specifically conferred on Congress, it seems to me that it is not made any less constitutional because of indirect effects that it may have, however obvious it may be that it will have those effects; and that we are not at liberty upon such grounds to hold it void."

---

and, with the swaying of sentiment, its bad influence may run from one extremity of the arc to the other."

50. See Ludwig von Mises, *Human Action.*

51. But as his own words show, Justice Holmes would never have countenanced the decisions since his dissent in *Hammer v. Dagenhart* came to be accepted.

52. This motivation (protecting the recipients rather than the producers of the products) is purely ulterior from a constitutional viewpoint, because it is local. When poisonous food shipped from another state causes death, it is a death that occurs locally, one of many deaths that occur locally every day and in every state.

Justice Holmes recognized that in matters merely affecting commerce with other states, like manufacturing, mining, the operation of retail stores, the purchasing habits and protection of consumers in their immediate transactions, Congress has no direct power whatever to make law on such matters, and its enactments in that area, unless authorized by the Necessary and Proper Clause, are legislative usurpations. But when Congress does have the power to act; as in levying taxes, regulating interstate commerce, or some of the other specific areas mentioned by the Constitution, its reasons or motivations, no matter how plain, no matter how local, are of no legitimate concern to the courts.[53]

The scope of recognized legislative power was greatly affected in Supreme Court decisions by animosity toward labor and wage-hour legislation, and the trend toward passing judgment upon the legislative aims, the supposed legitimacy of such aims, and the need for their achievement can be seen in judicial treatment of anti-trust legislation and in the legislative regulation of railroad rates in interstate commerce. All this paved the way for the complete destruction of the Necessary and Proper Clause and the complete disregard for both the constitutional limitations upon the scope of Congress' commerce powers and the fundamental doctrine of separation of legislative, executive, and judicial powers which was to occur in the administration of President Franklin D. Roosevelt.

In 1890, Congress passed an anti-trust law, making it illegal for persons to "monopolize or attempt to monopolize, or combine . . . with other persons to monopolize trade and commerce among the several states . . ." After enactment of the 1890 anti-trust law, the first case considered by the Supreme Court in which the government attempted to suppress a private monopoly was *United States v. E. C. Knight Co.* There were several corporate defendants, all engaged in refining and selling sugar. The American Sugar Refining Company entered into contracts to purchase the refineries, equipment, and plants of four other major sugar refining companies, thereby gaining control of almost all the sugar-refining business in the United States.[54]

The Court said:

"Commerce succeeds to manufacture, and is no part of it. The power to regulate commerce is the power to prescribe the rule by which commerce shall be governed,

---

53. Justice Holmes wrote: "The act does not meddle with anything belonging to the states. They may regulate their internal affairs and their domestic commerce as they like. But when they seek to send their products across the state line they are no longer within their rights. If there were no Constitution and no Congress, the power to cross the line would depend upon their neighbors. Under the Constitution such commerce belongs not to the states, but to Congress to regulate. It may carry out its views of public policy whatever indirect effect they may have upon the activities of the states. Instead of being encountered by a prohibitive tarriff at her boundaries, a state encounters the public policy of the United States which it is for Congress to express. If, as has been the case within the memory of men still living, a state should take a different view of the propriety of sustaining a lottery from that which generally prevails, I cannot believe that the fact would require a different decision from that reached in *Champion v. Ames.* Yet in that case it would be said with quite as much force as in this that Congress was attempting to intermeddle with the state's domestic affairs. The national welfare as understood by Congress may require a different attitude within its sphere from that of some self-seeking state. It seems to me entirely constitutional for Congress to enforce its understanding by all the means at its command."

54. But any citizen remained free to invest his wealth in building and operating a competing sugar refinery.

and is a power independent of the power to suppress monopoly. But it may operate in repression of monopoly whenever that comes within the rules by which commerce is governed or whenever the transaction is itself a monopoly of commerce."

The Court's holding was that Congress could not suppress monopolies by a direct declaration of their illegality when the monopoly was only in manufacturing, agriculture, or some other thing which might subsequently result in sales and shipments in interstate commerce. This was a correct holding.

The next case that was to enter into the development of governmental power theories in anti-trust law was not an anti-trust case, but a labor case, *In re Eugene Debs*. Debs was the principal leader of the American Railway Union, and his organization was attempting to unionize the employees of the Pullman Company. Their weapon was to use violence to assure that the trains would not run with Pullman cars coupled to them.

The Supreme Court said this in its *Debs* decision:

> "It is curious to note the fact that in a large proportion of the cases in respect to interstate commerce brought to this court the question presented was of the validity of state legislation in its bearings upon interstate commerce, and the uniform course of decisions has been to declare that it is not within the competency of a state to legislate in such a manner *as to obstruct interstate commerce*. If a state with its recognized powers of sovereignty is forbidden to obstruct interstate commerce, can it be doubted that any *mere voluntary association of individuals* within the limits of that state has a power which the state itself does not possess?"

This is one of the more confused statements in the Court's history. Language in prior opinions which refers to obstructions of interstate commerce by state law was itself not derived from the Constitution. The judicial process of declaring state laws nullified by the Constitution must always be based upon the Supremacy Clause of the Constitution, which provides that the Constitution and all laws made pursuant to it are the supreme law of the land, anything in any state constitution or laws to the contrary notwithstanding. It was *law as law* that was expressly invalidated by the Supremacy Clause. The clause had nothing to do with acts of individuals.

To say that the grant of power to Congress to regulate interstate commerce nullifies any state attempt to use that power by making a law regulating interstate commerce (whether burdensome or beneficial) is one thing. It is an entirely different thing to say that Congress has the power to make a particular law forbidding some practice in interstate commerce, and that the mere existence of the exclusive power to make law makes it illegal for a citizen to do such an act that Congress *could* prohibit, even though Congress has not prohibited such conduct. Such rationale is simply irrational. It was an attempt to justify an unauthorized injunction which the Court was determined to uphold.

If a thousand citizens decide they no longer like and will not buy a certain product, they then remove the economic motivation for the shipment of that product and in a sense obstruct commerce. This is none of the Federal Government's business, and cannot be made subject to any federal control either by the executive, legislative or judicial branches, except in disregard of the obligation to support the Constitution. Congress' power over commerce among the states is not a power to protect, encourage, promote or injure commerce, but to regulate it, which Congress may do for these purposes or for any ulterior purpose.

Despite its total irrationality, here it was: An assumption uttered by the Supreme Court that Congress had some power from some source to prevent individuals from "obstructing" commerce among the states and that this power could be utilized by the courts even when Congress had not exercised its supposed lawmaking power by condemning any particular type of "obstruction" of interstate commerce.

This judicial absurdity needlessly found its way into anti-trust law five years after the *Debs* decision in *Addyston Pipe & Steel Company v. United States.* The case involved an application of the anti-trust laws solely to interstate commerce, to a combination to control sales across state lines, so that there could be no doubt of the fact that the power of Congress was being used here to combat a monopoly in interstate commerce.[55]

Though Congress could enact such a law for whatever purpose it desired or for no purpose other than to gratify its yen to regulate things, the Supreme Court felt called upon in the *Addyston Pipe* case to rationalize as to an exciting and different basis for the federal legislation:

> "If certain kinds of private contracts do directly, as already stated, limit or restrain, and hence regulate, interstate commerce, why should not the power of Congress reach those contracts just the same as if the legislation of some state had enacted the provisions contained in them? The private contracts may in truth be as far-reaching in their effect upon interstate commerce as would the legislation of a single state of the same character. . . . Commerce is the important subject of consideration, and anything which directly obstructs and thus regulates that commerce which is carried on among the states, whether it is state legislation or private contracts between individuals or corporations, should be subject to the power of Congress in the regulation of that commerce."

The Supreme Court was soon to repeat its performance of expanding a law within Congress' legislative power to cover a subject totally beyond its powers. The case was *Houston, East & West Texas Railway Co. v. United States,* decided in 1913. The Interstate Commerce Act of 1901 made it unlawful for any railroad subject to the act to "make or give any undue or unreasonable preference or advantage to any particular . . . locality . . . in any respect whatsoever, . . . or to subject any particular . . . locality . . . to any undue or unreasonable prejudice or disadvantage in any respect whatever."

This language had application to rates and also, presumably, to a willingness to offer railroad services. Then Congress very carefully provided that "the provisions of this act shall not apply to the transportation of passengers or property, . . . *wholly within one state,* and not shipped to or from a foreign country from or to any state or territory . . ." In very simple language, this new law applied only to interstate commerce.

---

55. Under this arrangement, when municipalities desired pipe for water distribution systems, the pipe companies agreed that they would have a private bidding among themselves, and the high bidder, the one who would lose in public bidding, would unofficially be awarded the contract by the association of competitors. Then all the parties would bid to the public agency purchasing the pipe, with bidding rigged so that the high bidder at the private bidding would be the low bidder in the actual letting of the contract. More distant bidders could bid freely, but the freight rates were so high that it was assured that the eastern and far western bidders could not get the contracts.

Shreveport, Louisiana was located a few miles east of the Texas line, and the railroad company in this case hauled from Shreveport to Dallas, Houston, and many other points within the state of Texas. This was interstate commerce subject to federal regulation and, assuming the legality of the powers granted to the Interstate Commerce Commission, the Act permitted determination by that agency as to whether railroads were guilty of discrimination requiring a corrective order.

Texas regulations governed the railroad's operations in Texas, and those regulations favored Texas shipments made and delivered entirely within the state of Texas. Texas fixed its rates considerably lower than the rates [56] charged by the railroad on interstate shipments. So this was discrimination, but the discrimination was between interstate commerce, which Congress ordered regulated, and intrastate commerce, which Congress had no power to regulate and which Congress had solemnly declared should not be subjected to its law. The Interstate Commerce Commission held its hearings and established new rates for the interstate shipments, these rates being maximum rates to be applied to shipments on the railroad from Shreveport, Louisiana, westward to Houston and other named places in Texas. These new rates were even higher above the Texas rates than they had been before the new schedule was approved. The ICC then ordered that subject to the maximum rates it established for shipments from Shreveport westward into Texas, the railroad should charge no higher rates on those westward shipments than it charged on shipments eastward from Houston for an equal distance as the westward rates from Shreveport.

In effect, the Commission said that although its approved rates were higher than the official Texas-approved rates, that as far as it was concerned, the railroad could charge these higher rates it approved, so long as the rates it actually chose to charge for shipments from Shreveport toward Houston did not exceed the rates it charged for shipments from Houston toward Shreveport. The ICC thus ruled that the railroad could not charge more than the new maximum ICC rate or the maximum internal Texas rate, *whichever was lowest*.[57]

The railroad endeavored to present this as an effort by the Interstate Commerce Commission to control local rates. The falsity of this argument is that the case presented no question of supremacy of Federal over state law, because the ICC had made the Federal rates conform to the state rates.

A court which then existed to review Interstate Commerce Commission rulings, the Commerce Court, incorrectly viewed this ICC ruling as requiring the internal Texas rates to be lowered to conform to ICC-approved rates.

---

56. The rates charged under Texas regulations were somewhat lower than the highest rates permitted on the railroad's interstate shipments. For example, a shipment in interstate commerce from Shreveport, Louisiana, of 100 pounds westward to Lufkin, Texas, cost 69¢, while a shipment of 100 pounds from Houston, Texas, eastward to Lufkin, six miles further, cost 50¢, giving Houston Shippers a 19¢ edge over Shreveport shippers in selling their goods in the Lufkin market.

57. Thus, if the ICC-approved rate was 50¢, and the Texas-approved rate for internal shipments was only 40¢, the ICC order entirely forbade discrimination, and made the railroad free to comply with the ICC ruling in one of two ways—if the railroad could persuade Texas to increase its approval of rates to 50¢, it could charge that rate on all shipments in both directions, but if it could not persuade Texas to increase its approved rates, then the railroad was required by ICC to charge 40¢ on both interstate and intrastate shipments.

The Supreme Court, instead of denouncing the decision of the Commerce Court as attempting to accomplish that which Congress had no power to accomplish and had expressly commanded should not be attempted—the control of local rates—proceeded to attempt a justification of the Commerce Court's misstatement of law and misstatement of the effect of the ICC rate decision. The Court said:

> "Wherever the interstate and intrastate transactions of carriers are so related that the government of the one involves the control of the other, it is Congress, and not the state, that is entitled to prescribe the final and dominant rule, for otherwise Congress would be denied the exercise of its constitutional authority, and the state, and not the nation, would be supreme within the national field."

Here is the judicial assumption that the power of Congress to control one subject can be combined with a power, which Congress does not possess, to control another subject, simply because they are related and there is a congressional desire that both be uniformly controlled. The principal defect in this type of quasi-thinking is that it disregards the fact that the Constitution gives no implied power to Congress, but instead, expressly provides the only permissible test—consistent with the imperative of judicial integrity in construing the Constitution—to determine whether an inferred power to make law has been given to Congress, this being the test of the Necessary and Proper Clause. Of course there existed a relation between the internal Revenue rates and the internal Louisiana rates, but there existed nowhere any overriding power to regulate that relation.

In *Northern Securities Co. v. United States,* the Supreme Court used federal anti-trust statutes to prevent J. P. Morgan and his associates from consolidating competing railroads to build a larger railroad empire. When World War I came, the nation's system of railways appeared to be inadequate for the demands of war. They were inadequate, the Supreme Court said in *Railroad Commission of Wisconsin v. Chicago, Burlingame & Quincy Railroad Company,* because "the anti-trust law was thought to forbid [central control] under private management, and by the use of government credit . . ."

Private monopolies were thought evil because they might discriminate in the rates and services, but now that Congress had outlawed such discrimination by the Interstate Commerce Act, the principle justification for making anti-trust legislation applicable to interstate railroads disappeared.

Faced with the existence of the anti-trust laws as a burden upon commerce in the operation of the railroads, instead of repealing these laws, to permit business to meet the national challenge of World War I for the government, Congress decided that the logical solution was for the government to take over the operation of the railroads because the government did not have to pay any attention to the anti-trust laws. So this was done by an Act of Congress. After Federal seizure of the private property of the railroad companies, and after a period of their operation by the government, the expense of the ordinary operation of these confiscated properties had grown so great (due "to the rapid rise in the prices of material and labor in 1918 and 1919,") that the owners of the railroads wouldn't take them back unless some provision be made to enable them to survive and recover from government management.

So Congress enacted the Transportation Act of 1920, which set up a revolving fund of $300,000,000 to lend money to the railroads until they could recover from the fiasco and reestablish the railroads as operating businesses. A new theory in federal railroad rate-fixing was adopted to help the railroads recover. Theretofore, the Interstate Commerce Act had merely forbidden discrimination. Now, the Transportation Act amended the Interstate Commerce Act and directed that the railroad rates be so fixed that a railroad would make an annual profit of 5.5% of the value of the railroad properties.

Attempting to justify this congressional usurpation, Chief Justice Hughes wrote in *Railroad Commission of Wisconsin v. Chicago, Burlingame & Quincy Railroad Company:*

> "It is objected here, at it was in the *Shreveport* case, that orders of the Commission which raise the intrastate rates to the level of the interstate structure violate the specific provision of the original Interstate Commerce Act, repeated in the amending acts, that the Commission is not to regulate traffic wholly within a state. To this, the same answer must be made as was made in the *Shreveport* case. . . . that such orders as to intrastate traffic *are merely incidental to the regulation of interstate commerce, and necessary to its efficiency.*

These foolish statements are based on the assumption that Congress has some power to guarantee the rate of income or profit of those engaged in commerce. Congress' power is to *regulate* interstate commerce, not to aid it, hinder it, protect it, or to do anything other than to regulate it, which Congress may do for any purpose.

In this series of cases, we see the unnoticed legitimation of false constitutional doctrines: That even when Congress is exercising its powers in areas in which it has the exclusive legislative power, as in the regulation of interstate commerce or governing the District of Columbia, its enactments may be judicially measured against the common law, economic theory, or moral theories, to determine whether the laws are within the proper scope of "police power" as viewed by the judiciary. That Congress may combine things it is empowered to regulate and things it has no power to regulate and may regulate both. That Congress, in enacting laws for ulterior motives, may enact laws necessary to the success of its ulterior motives, though totally unnecessary to the exercise of its constitutionally-granted powers.

Some have assumed that prior to the depression which brought Franklin D. Roosevelt to office, the Nation was governed in accordance with the Constitution, and that the depression and the Roosevelt administration brought about judicial abandonment of sound constitutional principles, the bending and warping of those principles to make possible Roosevelt's program for combatting the Great Depression; that after the president sought unsuccessfully to "pack" the Supreme Court, the advanced ages of those on the Court brought to the president the opportunity—earlier denied by public opinion—to pack the Court with judges who would be subservient to the president's political aims. Not true.

The abandonment of constitutional precepts began long before Roosevelt became president. It began and slowly developed over a course of many years, with occasional decisions which pretended that the absolute rules contained in the Constitution were not absolute rules after all, but were rules which could be made to yield to a reasonable degree to make possible that which people felt simply must be achieved, or to protect the people from unwise experimentation by a Congress which lacked the judicial insight to recognize the true nature of things. All that happened during the long Roosevelt administration was that past infidelities to the Constitution were carried further toward their logical extreme. When constitutional absolutes are abandoned, there remain no guidelines but the whims of those who temporarily exercise the legislative, executive, and judicial governing power. Pretend that mere interpretations of the meaning of the Constitution by the Supreme Court of the United States or by any other body are themselves supreme, and are a total answer to questionings about constitutionality—concede this power to any court, and we concede that the Constitution is no longer the supreme law of the land. Take this essential step and sooner or later, the total destruction of constitutional government becomes inevitable.

The abandonment of the aim of government by law, a necessary correlative to the assumption that judicial opinions and paraphraseology can ever establish the meaning of a written constitution, eventuates in tyrannical and lawless government, and this is unavoidably so. The transformation of constitutional government into a more authoritarian government tending toward dictatorship can never occur except by disregard of fundamental law as to what subjects the Federal Government is authorized to govern and except by abandonment of the Constitution's central theme of separation of powers.[58]

Strengthening the Foundations for Authoritarian Government:

The absolute necessity of destroying the principle of separation of powers before a truly authoritarian government can be established—benign and benevolent in its origin—is required because dictatorial control of the minute details of daily moral, social, economic and political life cannot be achieved when all the law-making powers are permanently kept in the hands of Congress. Before true tyrannical government can be achieved, there must be room for more arbitrariness than is possible under a government whose law-makers must proceed slowly until they discover the public will and must answer to the voters for *all the law* enforceable by the power of the Federal Government: A legislative body whose lawmakers cannot hide behind some supposed rule-making power vested in executive departments, judges, and "administrative agencies" answerable to no one. An authoritarian government cannot exist in a nation whose government strictly adheres to the doctrine of separation of powers.

The abandonment of the doctrine of separation of powers came in 1911 in a decision which, assumed to be a part of the supreme law of the land, was to be used further in the 1930's as a demonstration that laws could be enacted by the nation's armies of anonymous administrators. In *United States v. Grimaud,* the official exercising the nation's law-making power was the Secretary of Agriculture. He made a criminal law. The government had embarked upon a program, under congressional enactment, to conserve the forests of the nation, by permitting the president to declare whatever areas he might select to be national forest reservations.[59]

---

58. This assumes that the people would retain the good sense to reject attempts to openly change the Constitution to the extent necessary to institute a lawful dictatorship. Of course, if the Constitution should be amended to give the president law-making power, and empowering him to issue edicts to carry out his ulterior motivations as well as to exercise his lawful powers, this, though foolish, would be an entirely lawful creation of dictatorship here.

59. This power to protect "national" resources was not among the powers granted to Congress by the Constitution, hence there is no lawful authority for *any* action on this subject by Congress or any other Federal agency. Forests grow within states, and any desire to protect them could have been accomplished by state legislation.

The government had no power to exercise general law-making authority over these lands, because the Constitution gives Congress exclusive legislative authority over such land only when it has been purchased, with the consent of the state legislature, *for the purpose* of constructing forts and other needful buildings. Bare land or forested land, purchased by the government for the purpose of preserving it as bare or wild land, is governed by state law, at least according to the Constitution. But such lands became government property and the government as a property-owner has its rights, as does any other property-owner. This includes the right to say what will be done with the property, the right to exclude trespassers, the right to give or deny people permission to use its land. There is no law-making involved in any of these functions of a property-owner. This is simply the land-owner's control of its property.

Congress, in placing these lands under the control of the Secretary of Agriculture, authorized him to make "regulations" to govern the public's use of those public forest lands. And Congress enacted "guidelines" to be followed by the Secretary of Agriculture in making his regulations, intended to "improve and protect the forests and to secure favorable conditions of water flows." Congress also enacted, in regard to regulations made by the Secretary of Agriculture, that "any violation of the provisions of this act *or such rules and regulations* shall be . . ." a criminal offense.

It pleased the officer in charge of the Sierra Forrest Reserve in California to promulgate a regulation declaring that all persons must obtain permits before grazing more than six head of stock on the forest lands. This became a regulation by executive edict, and under the Act of Congress, it thereby became, by virtue of the exercise of will by a member of the *Executive Branch* of the Government, a criminal offense to graze more than six sheep within the reservation without permission. Grimaud grazed sheep on the land without permission, and he was indicted for committing a felony against the United States.

The Supreme Court held this delegation of law-making power lawful, and held the violation of a mere rule made by an executive official to be a criminal offense. The moment before the regulation was promulgated, it was not a criminal offense to graze sheep on the reservation without permission. Both the decision as to what conduct should become a criminal offense and the decision as to whether and at what moment this conduct should become a criminal offense, were made by an executive official. The executive thus made law. The Constitution contains no hint that Congress can authorize any body or official other than itself to make law. When it pretends to do so, it endeavors to authorize a procedure for making law different from that set out in the Constitution: The successive approvals of the identical proposed law by the two separate houses of Congress, followed by approval of the enactment not by some park manager or other inferior officer in the executive branch of government, but by the President of the United States, acting personally.

However, the Supreme Court said of the problems arising on these federal reservations acquired for purposes other than the construction of forts and other buildings.

"In the nature of things it was impracticable for Congress to provide general regulations for these various and varied details of management. Each reservation had its peculiar and special features; and in authorizing the Secretary of Agriculture to meet these local conditions, Congress was merely conferring administrative functions upon an agent, and not delegating to him legislative power. The authority actually given was much less than what has been granted to municipalities by virtue of which they make by-laws, ordinances and regulations for the government of towns and cities. Such ordinancies do not declare general rules with reference to rights of persons and property, nor do they create nor regulate obligations or liabilities, nor declare what shall be crimes, nor fix penalties therefor.[60]

By the flat declaration in the Supreme Court's opinion, permitting such delegation simply because it was impractical for Congress to make laws on such myriads of details, the Supreme Court substituted practicality for the Constitutional declaration that the legislative power is vested in Congress as the test of constitutionality. Certainly it is impractical for Congress to make minute and differing rules for every Federal forest reservation and park. Therefore, the practical solution is not to have such laws making it a criminal offense to violate any rule made by some administrator.[61]

The Federal Government has a right to protect its property, and much must be done by the Federal Government as a property owner which involves absolutely no making of law.

Congress can empower forest rangers, park superintendents, and others to make all sorts of decisions and rules, rules which derive not from Congress' power to govern the citizens of the nation, but from the government's standing as an owner of property. By the same token, if a citizen owns a building, he has the power, or right, to decide who may be given permission to enter the building and who may be denied that permision. Such rules, in and of themselves, have nothing to do with law-making.

Congress, as part of its authority over publicly-owned property, legally owned by the United States, can pass a law making it a criminal offense for anyone lacking permission to trespass upon the government property.[62] This would be a criminal offense created by Congress. A state government can do the same thing, making it a criminal offense within the state for anyone to trespass upon a landowner's land without the owner's permission, and whether a crime is committed would depend upon the fact of whether the owner gave his permission to the person to come upon his land. But the private landowner in giving or refusing his permission would not be making or changing law. The law would constantly state that whoever trespasses upon the private property of another, without the owner's permission, is guilty of a crime.

---

60. This comparison by the Supreme Court of this "delegation" with the powers given to city governments by state legislatures was inane: State practices, whether lawful or unlawful, cannot invalidate any provision of the Constitution of the United States. And of course, state constitutions empower the legislatures to create city governments and to provide for the organization of their powers, including their exercise of legislative powers. No provision for empowering bureaucrats to legislate appears in the Constitution of the United States.

61. This does not mean that "administrative regulations" are evil, so long as the distinction between regulations and laws is remembered. Indeed, no government could operate without bureaucrats and regulations.

62. Such a law would apply equally to sheep-grazers, hikers, and Sunday-school classes unless Congress should itself enact permission for such particular groups to use government lands. The Constitution expressly empowers the government to protect governmental property by a provision of the seldom-read Article IV, but this does not empower Congress to give legislative power to the president for this or any other purpose.

So Congress could have enacted a law making it a crime for anyone to trespass upon the Government's lands, even though the fact of trespass would be contingent upon whether the citizen had permission from the appropriate official to come upon those lands in accordance with the property owner's "regulations." Congress did not do this, but instead claimed to pass some of its law-making power to the Secretary of Agriculture.

When law-making occurs outside the legislative branch of the Federal Government, and by a procedure different from the procedure commanded by the Constitution, it is governmental lawlessness.

Grimaud v. United States was a valuable foundation stone in structuring the new scheme of government, which was to be developed from and after the 1930's; but the development did not originate in the 1930's and it actually *could not have originated then* but for past infidelity to the Constitution found in occasional Supreme Court opinions reaching back to the words of Chief Justice John Marshall.[63]

When the pressure of the Great Depression brought forth that new law, however, it also brought forth rather surprised and almost unbelieving cries of protest from the Supreme Court itself that the Constitution was being violated. These final cries urging the supremacy of the Constitution in the 1930's were cries of futility—the futility of attempting to fit together the supremacy of the Constitution and past Supreme Court decisions that had failed to uphold that supremacy.

Economic depression and the election of Roosevelt brought with them a statutory scheme to impose economic dictatorship upon all details of the nation's business life. The battle was joined in a case that won as its sobriquet "The Sick Chicken Case," *A. L. A. Schechter Poultry Corp. v. United States.* The case derived its name from a charge of commission of a crime against the United States —selling an "unfit chicken" to a retailer in New York City for resale to some purchaser in New York City. The Court's opinion does not reveal whether the unfitness of the chicken sold by this New York company was due to sickness, being underweight, or other cause. The Schechter Corporation was indicted for a number of other serious offenses against the United States, including the heinous criminal act of permitting customers to choose the chickens they wanted to purchase.[64]

All these offenses—there were eighteen counts charging different crimes— occurred within the City of New York, and all involved sales by a New York

---

63. These principles of infidelity to the Constitution, legitimized in rare decisions over a period of many decades, were taken as authoritative enunciations of the content of the supreme law of the land in the 1930's, were carried toward their logical extremes, and no one could think of any reason why these principles could not be carried a little bit further. In truth, the violations of the Constitution first occurred in the original enunciations of such principles, and once constitutional principles were abandoned, there was no basis in human reason for refusing "permission" to carry the new principles somewhat further, except by renunciation of the original unwarranted decisions.

64. That men of good will could make such dictatorial insistences and could successfully prosecute without arousing public revolt tends to demonstrate that the general public, whose attention is directed to diverse individual cares, lacks the capacity to detect such dangerous changes in governmental practices and to realize the danger in them.

company to New York City customers for use within New York City. The only connection any of this had with interstate commerce was that the chickens being sold had originally been purchased from other states and brought to New York City. The case concerned, then, the processing and sale of chickens wholly within one state after an interstate commerce transaction had taken place.

The scheme of economic dictatorship sought to be imposed by the National Industrial Recovery Act was designed to correct the prevailing unemployment and disorganization of industry which was the depression.[65] Congress did not enact specific laws imposing duties, in understandable language, upon citizens whose activities might bring them within the scope of such a law and of Congress' legislative powers. Instead, it provided for the creation of "codes of fair competition," which were supposed to be written to carry out all the various and possibly conflicting congressional "policies" designed to end the depression as painlessly as possible.

The National Industrial Recovery Act claimed to empower the President to approve codes of fair competition suggested by industrial associations, and if such industrial associations should fail to materialize, or should fail to create an acceptable set of self-governing rules, the President was empowered to make up his own set of rules to govern any business that failed to exercise the law-making powers given to it and to the President.

All this was for the purpose of encouraging a resumption of commercial activity among the different states, by regulating not only commerce among the states, but also by regulating internal businesses within each state. The poultry-marketing industry in New York City and surrounding counties adopted one of those things known as the "Live Poultry Code," which undertook to impose minimum wages, maximum working hour limitations, and to guarantee employee rights to join labor unions in every business within the area engaged in marketing poultry. The "Code" also forbade the sale of "coops" or "half-coops" of chickens except by requiring the purchasers to accept the group of chickens selected by the seller.

The Supreme Court held the entire scheme to be a violation of the Constitution. The Government attempted to justify it on the ground that the economic depression was a national crisis, which Congress *must have the power to remedy*,[66] but

---

65. In the broadest language, Congress declared that there were some national "policies": "It is hereby declared to be the policy of Congress to remove obstructions to the free flow of interstate and foreign commerce which tend to diminish the amount thereof; and to provide for the general welfare by promoting the organization of industry for the purpose of cooperative action among trade groups, to induce and maintain united action of labor and management under adequate governmental sanctions and supervision, to eliminate unfair competitive practices, to promote the fullest possible utilization of present productive capacity of industries, to avoid undue restriction of production (except as may be temporarily required), to increase the consumption of industrial and agricultural products by increasing purchasing power, to reduce and relieve unemployment, to improve standards of labor, and otherwise to rehabilitate industry and to conserve natural resources."—None of which was any of Congress' business.

66. The Court explained: "Extraordinary conditions may call for extraordinary remedies. But the argument necessarily stops short of an attempt to justify action which lies outside the sphere of constitutional authority. The Constitution established a national government with powers deemed to be adequate, as they have proved to be both in war and peace, but these powers of the national government are limited by

this foolish argument had long since been refuted in the Civil War crisis case, *Ex Parte Milligan*.[67] Concerning the delegation of law-making power to the President and the industrial associations permitted to write the "codes," the Court made detailed comment upon the *breadth* of law-making powers to frame these codes of civil and criminal law.[68] This necessarily implied that the "delegation" would have been lawful if more narrowly drawn. All the Court need have said was that the Constitution empowers only Congress to make law, provides a procedure to be followed by Congress in making law, and that the constitutional method of making law can be changed only by amending the constitution itself, which is beyond Congress' power to accomplish; and that when Congress attempts to substitute for the constitutional means a different system of making law, by providing that upon presidential edict, whether alone or following a private citizens' committee's suggestions, a particular code of law should become law, then Congress has exceeded its powers under the Constitution.

Turning next to the subject to interstate commerce, and the government's claim that the Interstate Commerce Clause of the Constitution gave Congress the power to regulate the chicken business in New York City,[69] the Court said of this supposed power to regulate a state's internal chicken-marketing business:

> "The undisputed facts thus afford no warrant for the argument that the poultry handled by defendants at their slaughterhouse was in a *'current'* or *'flow'* of interstate commerce and was thus subject to congressional regulation. . . . Decisions which deal with the stream of interstate commerce—where goods come to rest within a State temporarily and are later to go forward in interstate commerce—and with the regulations of transactions involved in that practical continuity of movement, are not applicable here. . . ."

The Supreme Court then continued with an attempt to distinguish between things which directly affect interstate commerce and things which only indirectly affect commerce among the states, a dichotomy it had applied in the *Shreveport Rate Case* and other cases assuming that Congress could regulate things which directly affect interstate commerce.

The artificial distinction of a supposed difference between things directly

---

the constitutional grants. Those who act under these grants are not at liberty to transcend the imposed limits because they believe that more or different power is necessary. Such assistance of extra-constitutional authority was anticipated and precluded by the explicit terms of the Tenth Amendment, 'The powers not delegated to the United States by the Constitution, nor prohibited by it to the States, are reserved to the States respectively, or to the people.' "

67. See above, pp. 186-188.

68. "As already noted, the President in approving a code may impose his own conditions, adding to or taking from what is proposed; as 'in his discretion' he thinks necessary 'to effectuate the policy' declared by the act. . . . [Administrative agencies'] recommendations or findings in no way limit the authority which §3 undertakes to vest in the President with no conditions than those there specified. And this authority relates to a host of different trades and industries, thus extending the President's discretion to all the varieties of laws which he may deem to be beneficial in dealing with the vast array of commercial and industrial activities throughout the country."

69. Though the regulation was not imposed by Congress, but by the President pursuant to sweeping powers pretended to be "delegated" to him by Congress.

affecting and things only indirectly affecting interstate commerce—a difference only in degree and a difference often difficult to discern—is a distinction not based upon the Constitution. In the *Schechter Poultry Case,* the Court should have abandoned past decisions, should have read and recognized the supremacy of the Constitution as it was written instead of pretending that there is any constitutional difference between things which directly and things which only indirectly affect commerce among the states.[70]

The same year in which the Supreme Court decided the *Schechter Poultry Case,* 1936, also brought decision upon the validity of another Act of Congress, one which placed the nation's coal industry under economic dictatorship, thereby immensely burdening the commerce among the states, enacted upon the theory that Congress was somehow removing "burdens" from interstate commerce.

The law was the Bituminous Coal Conservation Act of 1935 (designed, of course, to increase the mining and thereby reduce the conservation of coal), and the Supreme Court's decision declaring the law unconstitutional was *Carter v. Carter Coal Co.* Where the 1933 National Industrial Recovery Act merely invited industries to draw up their own industrial codes covering wages, hours, collective bargaining, and unfair methods of competition, under the coercive threat that the President might inflict upon them codes of his own devising, the 1935 Act to regulate the coal-mining industry left far less initiative to the coal-mining companies,[71] even providing that a minority of coal-mine operators should be bound by labor-management contracts entered into by the majority of the operators.

In this case, the government sought once again, as the executive department so often does when it becomes excited about some new type of law it has succeeded in persuading Congress to enact, to justify this sweeping attempt to regulate something other than interstate commerce—the productive activity that precedes sales across state lines—upon a theory that the government has some general governing power to meet emergencies in a particular way that it feels such emergencies should be met, regardless of whether the things sought to be required are within the scope of the stated legislative powers of the Federal Government.

Once again, the Supreme Court refuted the claim of the existence of general

---

70. The Court did note that the Tenth Amendment recognizes that the Constitution gives the Federal government only those powers that were delegated to it, and the delegation includes the power to regulate interstate and foreign commerce, with no delegation of the power to protect or encourage commerce, to regulate things merely affecting commerce, or to indirectly regulate any activity which it might *indirectly* affect by the use of its delegated powers. As to such non-delegated powers, the Amendment reserves the power over these to the states or to the people. If the Constitution governed, the people in any state would be free to adopt the old English rule of law, that all men are free to engage in any of the common callings of life.

71. This law divided the nation's coal-mining areas into 23 coal districts, each governed by a district board empowered to establish minimum prices. It provided a formula for fixing prices based upon "approved" costs, which included "district board assessments" for board "operating expenses," a tax imposed by the board. The Act also required collective bargaining between mining companies and unions representing their employees, and provided that when wages should be fixed by such contracts with the producers of two-thirds of the nation's coal output, all coal mines under the Act should be required to pay these minimum wages negotiated by other companies in other parts of the country.

governing powers outside the powers granted by the Constitution. After describing the broad language of the preamble [72] to the Bituminous Coal Conservation Act, which recited the various general aims Congress hoped to accomplish, the Court said of this supposed general law-making power Congress was attempting to usurp:

> "The proposition, often advanced and as often discredited, that the power of the federal government inherently extends to purposes affecting the nation as a whole with which the states severally cannot deal or cannot adequately deal, and the related notion that Congress entirely apart from those powers delegated by the Constitution, may enact laws to promote the general welfare, have never been accepted, but always definitely rejected by the Court. Mr. Justice Story, as early as 1816, laid down the cardinal rule, *which has every since been followed* [73]—that the general government 'can claim no powers which are not granted to it by the Constitution, and the powers actually granted must be such as are expressly given, or given by necessary implication.'. . . The convention . . . made no grant of authority to Congress to legislate substantively for the general welfare, . . . and no such authority exists, save as the general welfare may be promoted by the exercise of the powers which are granted. . . ."

The Court commented upon the importance of the continuing viability of state governments, of leaving them under the necessity of solving their own local problems, and of recognizing that Congress has no power at all to legislate in such cases, saying that the abandonment of these local powers and responsibilities would reduce them to "geographical subdivisions of the national domain." [74]

---

72. The preamble declared Congress' motive for enacting the law, and the Court said it was important ". . . because it makes clear, except for the pure assumption that the conditions described 'directly' affect interstate commerce, that the powers which Congress undertook to exercise are not specific but are of the most general character —namely, to protect the general public interest and the health and comfort of the people, to conserve privately-owned coal, maintain just relations between producers and employees and others, and promote the general welfare, by controlling the nationwide production and distribution of coal. These, it may be conceded, are objects of great worth; but are they ends, the attainment of which has been committed by the Constitution to the federal government? This is a vital question; for nothing is more certain than that beneficent aims, however great or well-directed, can never serve in lieu of constitutional power."

73. These words are inaccurate, as we have seen; and they may well have granted the seal of judicial approval to prior deviations from the Constitution.

74. "The determination of the Framers Convention and the ratifying conventions to preserve complete and unimpaired state self-government in all matters not committed to the general government is one of the plainest facts which emerges from the history of their deliberations. And adherence to that determination is incumbent equally upon the federal government and the states. State powers can neither be appropriated on the one hand or abdicated on the other. . . . Every journey to a forbidden end begins with the first step; and the danger of such a step by the federal government in the direction of taking over the powers of the states is that the end of the journey may find the states so despoiled of their powers, or—what may amount to the same thing—so relieved of the responsibilities which preservation of the powers necessarily enjoins, as to reduce them to little more than geographical subdivisions of the national domain. It is safe to say that if, when the Constitution was under consideration, it had been thought that any such danger lurked behind its plain words, it would never have been ratified."

And the Court might have added that during the Framers' Convention, the idea of making the states subdivisions of the National Government was specifically suggested and immediately and strongly rejected by the convention.[75]

These two 1936 decisions, *Schechter Poultry Corporation v. United States* and *Carter v. Carter Coal Co.,* were the Supreme Court's last great outcries in favor of the supremacy of the Constitution as an instrument for the government of the Federal Government, and even they were infected with decades of assumptions that the meaning of the Constitution could be traced to the great essays by Chief Justice Marshall instead of to the Constitution itself; that there was some purpose and distinction between things which directly affected interstate commerce and things that only indirectly affected it; and that such hazy distinctions had something to do with the scope of congressional power of regulation. Thus, all the defects of past infidelity to the Constitution, which could have been corrected in the *Schechter* and *Carter* cases by powerful affirmations that the Constitution means precisely what its own simple language claims it to mean, were defects in past rationalizations which the Court failed to renounce. They were to become the seeds for the subsequent establishment of a giant bureaucracy responsive to no one.

Structuring the Metamorphosized Government:

The years immediately following, 1937, 1938, 1940, saw the successful expansion of federal power beyond the limits permitted by the supreme law. These years also saw an exercise of legislative power in a manner totally different from that prescribed by the Constitution, and yet an exercise of legislative power whose validity has never been directly passed upon by the United States Supreme Court. Perhaps the reason the Court has not passed upon the scheme in any case was that it was the Supreme Court itself which exercised this portion of the law-making powers of Congress.

For it was during this period that the procedural rules earlier adopted by Congress were superceded by the Federal Rules of Civil Procedure and the Federal Rules of Criminal Procedure, which were written by various committees and promulgated by the Supreme Court itself. The Constitution says that law shall be made by successive enactments by the houses of Congress, followed by presidential approval. Congress enacted that this particular brand of law, the rules to govern the conduct of the business of the federal courts in the trial of civil and criminal cases, could be made by promulgation by the Supreme Court, and that such rules should then become law unless voided by Congress at its next session; despite the precise steps provided by the Constitution for making laws, Congress created a different law-making procedure for this type of law.

Judicial proclamation followed by congressional non-disapproval were thus substituted for congressional enactment followed by presidential approval. These procedural rules, numbers of them claiming to replace statutes enacted by Congress, were promulgated, have been altered by successive promulgations, and are accepted as law. Hamilton said that we have everything to fear from the combination of the judiciary with either of the other branches of government, notwith-

---

75. Hamilton proposed a plan under which the legislative branch could legislate on all subjects, the President would have absolute veto power over new laws, as would the governor of each state, each state governor to be appointed by the President, and the President, all senators and judges appointed for life. *Documents Illustrative of the Formation of the Union,* pp. 979-980.

standing an apparent separation, and his wisdom exceeded that of judges who would not withstand the temptation to engage in formal legislating.

The Supreme Court decisions of 1937, 1938, and 1940 which favored the New Deal legislative programs were decisions totally unforeseeable by those who wrote and publicly debated the adoption of the Constitution, who were schooled in the study of government and experienced in its tyranny, and who endeavored to guard against the very type of authoritarian government that was upheld in these Supreme Court decisions.

After the *Schechter Poultry* and *Carter Coal* decisions had upset President Roosevelt's plans [76] the president's disenchantment with the Supreme Court reached the point in February, 1937, of impelling him to make his "court-packing" suggestion. He suggested that Congress authorize him to appoint a new justice to the United States Supreme Court for each justice then sitting who was over seventy years old. This was an unpopular suggestion, but later that same year, the Supreme Court's opinions began to de-emphasize the Constitution.

In 1937, the Court passed upon the constitutionality of the National Labor Relations Act in *National Labor Relations Board v. Jones & Laughlin Steel Corporation.* The purpose of the Labor Act was to fully regulate the relations between employers and employees represented by labor unions to the full scope of its constitutional power to do so. Of course, the Constitution gave Congress no power whatever to regulate such relationships. So the principal power utilized by Congress to achieve its announced ulterior motive of regulating labor-management relations was its power to regulate commerce among the states. Congress did this by establishing the National Labor Relations Board and empowering the Board "to prevent any person from engaging in any unfair labor practice *affecting commerce.*"

Congress then defined commerce for the purposes of this law in terms of trade among the several states, *i.e.,* it terms of the scope of the congressional power granted by the Constitution, and it defined "affecting commerce" as anything "in commerce, or burdening or obstructing commerce or the free flow of commerce or having led to or tending to lead to a labor dispute burdening or obstructing commerce or the free flow of commerce." The scope Congress claimed for its law was not only the power to regulate commerce, but also to regulate labor-management relations of all businesses which affected commerce among the states whenever (that is, *if* and *when* it should happen that) an unfair labor practice be committed which *might* cause a labor dispute that *might* burden or obstruct the free flow of commerce among the states.

The Supreme Court, in Chief Justice Hughes' opinion, admitted that the manufacturing of steel was not a part of commerce among the states, but only activity intimately affecting commerce, the Court describing the situation of Jones & Laughlin as an example of "the close and intimate relation which a manufacturing industry may have to interstate commerce . . ." To say this is to say that such industrial activity is not a part of the commerce among the states which Congress is empowered to regulate.

The National Labor Relations Act made it illegal for employers to commit certain unfair labor practices, including discrimination against employees for membership in a labor union, and it provided for the National Labor Relations Board

---

76. As written into the National Industrial Recovery Act and the Bituminous Coal Conservation Act.

to hold hearings and made determinations as to whether such unfair labor practices had been committed; then the procedure was for the orders made by the Board to be enforced by courts.

Jones & Laughlin's Alquippa, Pennsylvania plant alone [77] employed approximately ten thousand men, and the unfair labor practice charge against the steel company in this case charged it with having discharged several employees because of their union membership. The company was found guilty and the Board directed it to reinstate and pay back pay to the employees. Though manufacturing is not commerce at all, and though the men who were discharged were employed in the manufacturing aspect of the business rather than those aspects involved in sales and transportation of products across the state lines, the Supreme Court sustained the National Labor Relations Act as constitutional and held the Labor Board's decision to be enforceable in the manufacturing portion of Jones & Laughlin's business.

In holding the Act constitutional, the Supreme Court did not have to resort to the language of the Constitution, because it had before it a few past examples, some of which we have noticed, of its own assumptions that the power to regulate the conduct of commerce between states included the power to remedy things which might obstruct or burden commerce with other states and the power to promote commerce among the states, even by means other than the regulation of that interstate commerce.

Jones & Laughlin was engaged in Pennsylvania in reducing its own iron ore to pig iron, manufacturing its pig iron into various iron products and steel, and then into various steel shapes, wires, etc., so that its products "are to a large extent manufactured without reference to pre-existing orders and contracts and are entirely different from the raw materials which enter at the other end."

The Supreme Court said:

> "Although activities may be intrastate in character when separately considered, if they have such a close and substantial relation to interstate commerce that their control is essential or appropriate to protect that commerce from burdens and obstructions Congress cannot be denied the power to exercise that control."

The Court's holding was that Congress may combine commerce, which it is given the power to regulate, with some other thing which it is not given the power to regulate and may regulate both in combination.[78] This is contrary to the Constitution, a conclusion which cannot be inferred except by abandonment of the words of the Constitution.[79]

---

77. The National Labor Relations Board described the company's operations as being likened to the heart of a highly integrated body, the Board saying of its two Pennsylvania plants: "They draw in the raw materials from Michigan, Minnesota, West Virginia, Pennsylvania in part through arteries . . . controlled by [Jones & Laughlin]; they transform the materials and then pump them out to all parts of the nation through the vast mechanism which [Jones & Laughlin] has elaborated."

78. As was inevitable, this irrationality has been administratively carried to great extremes: Today, even colleges and universities are held subject to the laws regulating things affecting interstate commerce because they buy books, supplies, and food from out-of-state sources.

79. The Constitution says that Congress may regulate commerce among the states and may make all laws necessary and proper to exercise that power of regulation, and

The National Labor Relations Act not only violated, and continues to violate, the Constitution by usurping the power to regulate things that only affect interstate commerce, but it also violated, and continues to violate, the Constitution by granting a measure of the nation's judicial powers to a political board, the National Labor Relations Board. The Courts are commanded to enforce the orders of the Board if those orders are supported by "substantial evidence," a standard of review customarily applied by appellate courts to the decisions of trial courts and juries.

The next year, 1938, the Supreme Court again sustained NLRB orders in a case involving a manufacturer much smaller than Jones & Laughlin, *National Labor Relations Board v. Fainblatt*.[80]

The Court again claimed for Congress the power to regulate things merely related to its actual constitutional powers. A dissenter wrote:

"Manifestly if such attenuated reasoning—possibility massed upon possibility—suffices, Congress may regulate wages, hours, output, prices, etc., whenever any product of employed labor is intended to pass beyond state lines—possibly if consumed next door. Producers of potatoes in Maine, peanuts in Virginia, cotton in Georgia, minerals in Colorado, wheat in Dokota, oranges in California, and thousands of small local enterprises become subject to national direction through a Board.

"Of course, no such result was intended by those who framed the Constitution. If the possibility of this had been declared the Constitution could not have been adopted. So construed, the power to regulate interstate commerce brings within the ambit of federal control most if not all the activities of the nation; subjects states to the will of Congress; and permits disruption of our federated system."

In 1938 began the abandonment of congressional law-making power to private groups of competitors on the successful false pretense that this was other than law-making in a manner different from that provided by the Constitution. *United States v. Rock Royal Co-Operative*, sustained a complex milk-marketing law governing the area which produced milk for sale in New York City. The complex executive-made law was submitted to a referendum in which a dairymen's league was permitted, by the terms of the enactment, to cast the votes of its entire membership, and the code devised by private competing businessmen, promulgated by the Secretary of Agriculture, and then voted on by private businessmen, became "law" by virtue of their vote. This "code" was held by the

---

that powers not granted to Congress are reserved to the states or the people. The Supreme Court said in the *Jones & Laughlin* case, as in earlier decisions which did not go so far in their facts, that Congress has the power to prescribe the rules by which interstate commerce is conducted, and rules by which all things affecting interstate commerce may be conducted, and the additional power to destroy any and all practices that might obstruct interstate commerce. This is simply an untruthful interpretation of the Constitution. A strike which interferes with a manufacturing operation that precedes interstate commerce bears the same relation to such commerce as does a farmer's decision that he will not plant crops that would otherwise be shipped in interstate commerce.

80. The manufacturer in this case did not even own the raw materials or the products, but was a mere contract manufacturer. It received pre-cut materials from the Lee Sportswear Company, sewed these materials into completed garments, and shipped the garments to Lee in New York from Fainblatt's New Jersey plant. The Court held Congress had the power to regulate the employer-employee relationship in this small manufacturing plant.

Supreme Court to be valid law.[81] The dissenting justices in the *Rock Royal Co-Operative Case,* apparently realizing that the tide of the times was running against constitutional government, wrote only a brief paragraph about the passing of the law-making power and the law-making procedures from the hands of Congress and the procedures set out in the Constitution into the hands of private organizations according to new procedures designed by Congress:

> "If perchance Congress posses power to manage the milk business within the various states, authority so to do cannot be committed to another. A cursory examination of the statute shows clearly enough the design to allow a secretary to prescribe according to his own errant will and then to execute. This is not government by law but by caprice. Whimseys may displace deliberate action by chosen representatives and become rules of conduct. To us the outcome seems wholly incompatible with the system under which we are supposed to live."

Yet Congress knew how to pass laws that could accomplish sweeping results without exceeding the congressional law-making powers. In *Mulford v. Smith,* concerning a tobacco marketing quota law, the Supreme Court said:

> "The statute does not purport to control production. It sets no limits upon the acreage which may be planted or produced and it imposes no penalty for the planting and production of tobacco in excess of the marketing quota. It purports to be solely a regulation of interstate commerce, which it reaches and effects at the throat, —the marketing warehouse."

With these decisions, and others which accompanied them, and with the nation then going into its greatest war, the continued proliferation of administrative agencies both determining what law will be, enforcing law, and deciding whether law has been violated in individual cases, has shown no sign of abatement.

Thus, by such a never-ending evolutionary process, there is now a federal agency for almost everything, most of it none of the business of the United States Government. Some federal agency busies itself with endeavoring to extend its regulatory power to its widest possible extreme, reaching into almost every aspect of everyday life within every state in the union. There are even laws requiring the agencies to talk to each other on particular subjects. The agencies make rules which must be sought out to determine what a citizen is free to do and what he is forbidden to do, and these rules are contained in a monstrous work of many

---

81. If the New York Legislature should authorize all the prostitutes of New York City to agree to and vote upon a "code" for the conduct of prostitution, surely every thinking person in the city would realize that this code was not law proclaimed by a body empowered to exercise legislative authority given to it and exercising that authority by the procedures ordained to render its proclamations law. The subject involved in the Supreme Court's decision was on a higher plane, the importance to the public more pressing, but the question as to the existence of power was precisely the same as if the New York Legislature should endeavor to empower the city's prostitutes to make law. All that is needed to recognize this is intelligent analysis, and not even a very high degree of intelligence. For judges to fail to detect such clear and obvious distinctions, when the essence of their duty is the discernment of the nature of things, is impossible unless they tightly close their eyes against the Constitution and act upon the unthinking and fundamentally dishonest assumption that whatever government wishes to do, government must be able to do.

volumes, called the Code of Federal Regulations. No detail is too minute for the rule-markers' attention. For example, one regulation promulgated in the late 1960's, very carefully defines some of its terms, including definitions to help farmers judge the quality of their carrots, defining rough carrots as those which are not smooth and smooth carrots as those which are not rough.

Perhaps the height of congressional disregard for the Constitution of the United States came with the enactment of something called the Economic Stabilization Act of 1970. The real law-making part of this act is contained in a single paragraph:

> "The President is authorized to issue such orders and regulations as he may deem appropriate to stabilize prices, rents, wages, and salaries at levels not less than those prevailing on May 25, 1970. Such orders and regulations may provide for the making of such adjustments as may be necessary to prevent gross inequities."

It finally pleased the President to issue his edict on August 15, 1971, and total economic dictatorship came to the United States, a state of absolute governmental lawlessness, subject only to the duty of every judge in the nation before whom any part of it might come to recognize usurpation as usurpation. Something at last was being done about inflation! [82] The people cheered and the commentators pontificated for a brief span. No court held this to be unconstitutional. It successfully met the tests of yesterday's wartime judicial examples of infidelity to the Constitution.

When the Founders' Convention came together for the last time, Benjamin Franklin's comments were read to these wise men. Among his words:

> ". . . I think a general Government necessary for us, and there is no form of government but what may be a blessing to the people if well administered, and [I] believe further that this is likely to be well administered for a course of years, and can only end in Despotism, as other forms have done before it, when the people shall have become so corrupted as to need despotic government, being incapable of any other."

---

82. Of course, the controls did not work, as they have never worked when they have been tried, because they cause shortages which increase prices, and men do not sell their property for less than its value. Such measures simply attack the results of inflation rather than its cause—the course of governmental misconduct in printing money not immediately redeemable in full with gold or silver coin held in the treasury in adequate amounts to redeem all outstanding paper currency. See White, *Fiat Money Inflation in France.*

Part IV

"IN LAW AND IN EQUITY"

IX.

"IN LAW AND IN EQUITY"

WHEN CYRENIUS RULED as Governor of Cyria, there went out a DECREE from Caesar Augustus, that all the world should be taxed.

On October 29, 1969, the United States Supreme Court directed [1] a trial court ". . . to issue its DECREE and order, effective immediately, declaring that each of the school districts here involved may no longer operate a dual school system based upon race or color, and directing that they begin immediately to operate as unitary school systems within which no person is to be effectively excluded from any school because of race or color . . ."

The decree of government, whether a decree of a federal court or a decree of Caesar, is a command issued by government to people, absolutely requiring their obedience, a command backed by a threat of death, imprisonment, or other punishment.

In times such as these, when literally millions of people are deeply disturbed by the extent of control exercised by federal courts over local affairs, no one writing on the subject of the fidelity of the federal judiciary to the Constitution of the United States can evade the responsibility of giving major attention to this present problem. Many believe federal judges haxe exercised powers that do not belong to them, and have made of the Supreme Court not a proper judicial body but a "haven for reform movements," as Mr. Justice Harlan phrased it.[2] There is an uneasy sense that things are not being done properly.

Such response is not unknown in history. Holdsworth,[3] the leading historian of English law, tells of one period in English history when local officials became balky in the face of requirements of the central government of the nation. Writing of such county officials, Holdsworth said:

> "It is obvious that persons set to govern under such a system as this will be educated by their experiences. They will acquire some ideas of their own, if not as to the policy which they would like to see adopted, at least to the faults of the policy which they are asked to assist in carrying out. Having some practical knowledge of government in the concrete, it will be difficult to convert them by specious arguments to a belief in a policy of which they are suspicious. *They may not be able to confute the arguments,* but they will have an instinctive fear of measures which seem to threaten the foundation of their political creed.[4]

During the era of which Holdsworth wrote, the king dissolved Parliament, as was his royal prerogative, but only Parliament could levy taxes, so the king

---

1. In *Alexander v. Holmes County Board of Education.*
2. See above, Ch. II, n. 4.
3. References in this chapter to Holdsworth's treatise, *A History of English Law,* will be by the author's name with volume and page numbers.
4. VI Holdsworth 60.

ran short of money. Gifts were solicited for the king among his loyal subjects, but if such gift-giving should become customary, then Parliament might never be reconvened, and the rights of the people gained over several centuries might be lost through the lack of that essential eternal vigilence for only a single generation.

The justices of the peace in one of England's counties met to consider the plea for a gift to the king, and their response has a simple eloquence. They stated that they had but one fear about making the gift to their king: "The exceeding prejudice that may come to posterity by such a precedent." They said that they were grevously concerned that the king's great needs, the great needs of the government itself, should be supplied, and "that nothing but the fear of the *just blame of after ages* could have abated our forward disposition to perform a service itself so requisite." [5]

We, too, owe a debt to our posterity, one that may be more pressing than the need to take swift action upon unproven threats of injury to the ecological balance in particular areas. The preservation and transmission to our posterity of liberty itself is an obligation all Americans must bear, whether we recognize it or not.

There have long been uneasy feelings, and open objections, that the federal judiciary has exceeded its powers. Let us look at those powers. The Constitution vests all the judicial power [6] of the United States in the Supreme Court and in such inferior courts as may be established by Congress. There are some aspects of federal judicial power that we need not here consider.[7] When the Supreme Court and the inferior federal courts act upon petitions brought by local citizens against governmental officials claiming that official misconduct—such as the exclusion of a child from a school because of his race—violates the Constitution, the federal courts act under one particular provision of the judicial article of the Constitution. It says, "The judicial Power . . . shall extend to *all Cases in Law and in Equity,* arising under this Constitution, the Laws of the United States, and Treaties made, or which shall be made, under their authority . . ."

This is the judicial power claimed to be exercised by the federal judicial system in the mass of litigation in which federal judges give detailed instructions to local officials as to how they shall perform their official functions, whether those functions be the assignment of pupils to schools, decisions as to building new schools, the discipline of pupils, the discipline or punishment of prisoners in a state penitentiary, and a large number of other subjects. In law and in equity.

What do these words mean—cases in equity? Here, again, as in the meaning of "due process of law" when our Constitution was written, it is not so much a matter of opinion as it is a matter of reading old books. The word "equity" has a connotation of fairness, of rightness, of justice. Long ago, when the Lord Chancellor administered the law of equity in the English Chancery Courts, with his principal "sub-judge," the Master of the Rolls, the lawyers who practiced in

---

5. VI Holdsworth 62.

6. Judicial power is uniquely distinct from executive and legislative powers; it is the power to act in particular disputes between particular citizens, requiring of them certain conduct enforceable by the arms of government.

7. This includes admiralty cases, suits against foreign ambassadors, and suits brought against state governments by other states or by foreign nations. The Supreme Court often applies international law for decision of such cases between governments.

the chancery courts liked to refer to the Lord Chancellor as the "keeper of the king's conscience." [8]

The Supreme Court is wont to speak of its "equity powers," but the Constitution says nothing of equity powers; it speaks of the federal courts deciding cases in equity, particular types of cases. In exercising these injunction-issuing powers, issuing decrees requiring local governing officials to do particular acts in particular ways, the federal judiciary has utilized a device called the "class action" in which an individual or a small group of individuals claim they speak for a massed body of people; hence the federal judiciary acts to resolve disputes between a local government and thousands of citizens governed by that government: the resulting decree, commanding that government officials shall make decisions in the manner commanded by the courts, is claimed to be an exercise of "equity powers." None of this was even remotely within the scope of "cases in equity" when that phrase was written into our Constitution.

One cannot oversimplify the meanings of cases in law and cases in equity by simply saying that the powers of the chancery courts included the power to issue injunctions decreeing that the law shall be obeyed in particular cases. This, depending upon the content of the law, can reach dictatorial proportions.

When we speak of cases in law and in equity, we speak of particular brands of law administered by particular courts. The common law was administered by the Court of Kings Bench and courts inferior to it. The equity law was administered by the Court of Chancery. At the time of American Independence, these were the judicial systems which administered law in England, the law courts and the courts of equity, two institutions whose brands of law had very strong and particular earmarks. The resolution of disputes in the entire English nation was in the hands of the law courts and the equity courts. [9]

But it was not always so. It was not so when Captain John Smith in 1606 "set sayle from Blackwall . . . in search of Virginia," [10] nor when the Council of Pilgrims received their charter in 1621, nor when the governing scope of this chartered group was expanded in 1628, to cover everything "which lies and extends between a great river there, commonly called Monomac, *alias* Merrimac, and a certain other river, there called Charles River, being in the bottom of a certain bay, there commonly called Massachusetts, *alias* Mattachusetts, *alias* Massatusetts Bay."

In those days, there existed in England *three types of law* administered by three separate courts, administering law over the people throughout the realm of the King of England. Those were the days of a great English judge named Lord

---

8. One of England's leading legal commentators of the past, Lord Seldon, wrote of this idea: "Equity is a roguish thing; for law we have a measure, know what to trust to; equity is according to the conscience of him that is Chancellor, and as that is larger or narrower, so is equity. 'Tis all one for the measure of the chancellor's foot. What an uncertain measure would this be! One chancellor has a long foot, another a short foot, a third an indifferent foot. It is the same thing with the chancellor's conscience."

9. There were or had been other specialized courts such as the admiralty courts and the courts administering the "law merchant" over mercantile transactions, instead of the government of individuals throughout the land.

10. Captain John Smith, *Generall Historie of Virginia, New-England, and the Summer Ifles.*

Coke.[11] Of the third court, which in addition to the courts of law and the courts of equity exercised judicial power over the whole of England, Lord Coke wrote: "It is the most honorable court (our Parliament excepted) that is in the Christian world. . . . This court, the right institution of ancient orders being there observed, doth keep all England quiet." And Bacon said of it that it was "one of the sagest and noblest institutions of this kingdom." A lawyer who practiced in the court described it as being a court open to everyone "from king to beggar." [12] This court, administering the third type of English law, was called the Court of Star Chamber.

Equity and the Lawless Judiciary:

The federal courts are vested by the Constitution with jurisdiction to determine cases in law and cases in equity. In 1641, the powers of the Court of Star Chamber had become so tyrannical that the court was abolished by the English Parliament. The powers of the Court of Star Chamber are not vested in any federal court. Yet they bear some similarity to the powers of the court of equity and the powers of the court of law. To determine the scope of judicial powers granted to the federal courts when the Constitution empowered them to decide cases in law and in equity, one must examine the brand of power withheld from the federal courts and abolished in England 135 years before American Independence, the powers exercised by the Court of Star Chamber: A court which began as a most praiseworthy institution of justice and ended as the most infamous institution of judicial tyranny that has ever existed in the English-speaking world. And in considering the Court of Star Chamber, we shall learn of the powers that are *not* granted to the federal judiciary by the Constitution.

It may be difficult to understand the difference among these three types of judicial power exercised in England and to understand the characteristics of the two types of judicial power that were transplanted in America without knowing something of the manner in which they grew. The history of the growth of these judicial systems is intertwined with the history of the relation between the King of England and his subjects. During and for centuries before the establishment of the American colonies, the king had been referred to by men of law as the fountainhead of justice. This was no mere colorful figure of speech. It was an actual and factual summary of the relation between the king and his subjects. Throughout early English history, there were courts which administered justice to the people, but the king was always considered present as the fountainhead of justice, who could and did do justice among his subjects, just as King Solomon had done many centuries earlier. The king exercised control over the judges and he personally went about the country holding court and dispensing justice between his subjects. He had all the powers needed to dispense justice. He could

---

11. More than a century before Blackstone, Lord Coke wrote so learnedly of English law that at the time of American Independence, Blackstone was more readily available to American lawyers, but Coke was still the real authority. His language was even then outdated, but the statute books in many American states today contain statutes phrased in obscure language that are direct quotations from the writings of Lord Coke.

12. I Holdsworth 506-508.

take from one and give to another if justice demand it, and he could order one put to death if the offense demanded it.[13]

The common law courts, the Court of the King's Bench, the justices in the various counties of England, determined disputes under the common law, while the king sat with his council to advise him in the exercise of his royal prerogatives, which included making war, the suspension of law, the pardoning of criminals, and in general governing the land under the common law and under the laws made by Parliament.

The king's council was composed of those he chose, those who gravitated to him and were accepted by him, those who had influence with him. And one of the officers who was always a member of the king's council was the Lord Chancellor. His was something of a clerical role in the beginning. He kept the enrolled acts of Parliament in his custody, and he maintained the office that issued the writs in the name of the king, among them the writs of election ordering new parliamentary elections. Other writs were the authorizations which empowered the judges of the nation to hear and decide particular lawsuits.

Every citizen was entitled to sue another citizen by obtaining a writ to arrest and bring the other citizen into court and authorizing the common-law judges to hear and decide the case. But the law often proved inadequate to do justice. Wrongs would be committed, yet there would be no particular writ [14] authorizing a lawsuit to compel the wrong-doing citizen to make good his wrongful act. Where the law offered no remedy and the wrong was clear, the king's subjects sought and obtained justice from the king himself. There slowly began to develop a practice on the part of the Lord Chancellor of exercising a part of the power of the king to do justice among the people.

The king in his council had from ancient times issued injunctions forbidding citizens from doing particular acts to other citizens, and this power gradually devolved upon the chancellor in particular types of cases, though still retained by the king and used by him whenever he chose. The chancellor during early times was normally a clergyman, because the position required one learned in books and the clergy were the most ready source of people competent to perform the chancellor's duties.[15] In many cases where the remedy at law was not adequate, the chancellor, by issuing the king's injunction, could remedy wrongs. The king in his council continued to do justice, to hear and determine disputes, but many subjects in which the remedy at law was inadequate fell into patterns customarily handled by the chancellor until the point was reached that a chancery court was in full operation, its procedures copied after the ecclesiastical courts.

---

13. One of the earlier English writings, called *The Mirror of Justice,* supposed to copy writings from the reign of Alfred the Great, the Saxon king who ruled from 871 A.D., tells of the king's treatment of judges who failed to follow law in their decisions: "He hanged Athelsan because he judged Herbert to death for an offense not mortal. . . . He hanged Therberne, because he judged Oscot to death for a fault whereof he was acquitted before. He hanged Oscitell, because he judged Catlin to death by record of the coroner, without trial of the truth."

14. There were different kinds of writs for different types of cases, such as the writ of ejectment to recover possession of real property, the writs of *detinue* and *replevin* for recovery of personal property, the writ of *assumpsit* which fathered the law of contracts, and a number of variations of writs of trespass.

15. With the passage of the Statute Mortmain, outlawing church ownership of property, the clerical chancellors started enforcing uses, which they developed into the law of trusts. See above, p. 16.

Throughout, the primary function of the chancery court was to do justice between the king's subjects. If a man sold one tract of land twice, then the law might enforce either sale, because this enforcement would come about by reason of one purchaser filing a suit, or obtaining a writ from the chancery clerk, to institute a suit against the seller of the property in the Court of King's Bench, the law court. The other buyer would not be involved in that suit, and ownership of the land might be determined by the law court adversely to his interests.[16] The chancery court customarily brought into one suit everybody who had any possible interest in the property dispute, unhampered by the requirement of a separate writ to commence a separate suit between separate individuals.

But the king in council continued to sit and to administer justice. The king's council *was the Court of Star Chamber.* Those who were members of the king's council, including the Lord Chancellor and the Lord Chief Justice of the law courts,[17] were members of the Court of Star Chamber. In the natural work-dividing process, by which tedious work had to be done in the solution of judicial disputes, the natural tendency to divide work led to the Court of Star Chamber gradually evolving into the highest court in England. It operated as a court with regular procedures, while the king's council remained the highest political organ of the state in which the king worked through his council in governing the country, in making war, in carrying out the prerogatives which inhered in kingship.[18]

Blackstone quoted from an earlier writer that the Star Chamber had become

"both a court of law to determine civil rights and a court of revenue to enrich the treasury: The Council Table by proclamations enjoining the people that which was not enjoined by the laws, and prohibiting that which was not prohibited, and the star-chamber, which consisted of the same persons in different rooms, censuring the bench the breach and disobedience of those proclamations by very great fines, imprisonments, and corporal severities; so that any disrespect to any acts of state, or to persons of statesmen, was in no time more penal and the foundations of right never more in danger to be destroyed."

The Court of Chancery sat to do justice between citizens in civil cases, mainly involving groups of people or trusts or the righting of fraudulent transactions, and the Court of Star Chamber, though it tried civil cases, mainly sat in the exercise of the king's prerogatives in cases affecting interests of state. Thus the Court of Star Chamber gradually became more of a criminal court in which it was possible to dispense with such non-essentials as the right against self-incrimination, trial by jury, and other inconveniences that could bar the imposition of the royal will. The chancery court and its injunctions were used to do justice among the people, as were the common-law courts, and the Court of Star Chamber was more an instrument of state.

The Chancery Court was not utilized to supervise the acts of government officials. The injunctions issued by the Chancery Courts, or courts of equity,

16. This problem was complicated by the fact that suits were commenced by physically arresting the defendant and bringing him into court, and it was theorized that once he was in the court's custody, no new suit could be brought because this would require that he be taken out of the court's custody by arresting him on the second suit, which could not be done.

17. This was the position held by Lord Coke.

18. Tradition says the Court of Star Chamber was so called because it met in a chamber decorated with stars.

were not used to control and regulate the conduct of public officials in public office. The Court of Star Chamber exercised this power. A similar power was exercised by the law courts. The Court of King's Bench, however, did not regulate the manner in which officials chose to perform their duties. Instead, they issued writs to compel government officials to do things in which the officials had no discretion, no choice as to whether to do or how to do particular official acts. Where the law *absolutely required* an official to do something or *absolutely prohibited* him from doing some act, then the Court of King's Bench could issue writs on applications by injured persons, requiring or prohibiting exactly what the law itself required or prohibited.

One of these writs was called the writ of *prohibition,* issued by the law courts to government officials to prohibit them from doing something that the law absolutely forbade them to do.[19] Another was the writ of *mandamus,* which ordered government officials to do things that they refused to do, though the law positively required them to do such acts, and gave them not the slightest choice, or discretion, as to how to perform the duty.[20]

So between the law courts and the chancery courts, the law courts heard ordinary cases and on occasion commanded or prohibited governmental officials as the law itself commanded or prohibited, but neither the law courts nor the equity courts had the power to supervise government officials in the manner in which they exercised their discretion. A sheriff could choose jurors, and the courts could not lay down guidelines or give instructions to him as to what jurors to choose unless the law prescribed the exact methods that must be followed by the sheriff.

But the central government of England, the king and those who carried out his policies as well as the laws enacted by Parliament, did have control over the manner in which lower governmental officials performed their duties, and this control was exercised by the King in Council and by the Court of Star Chamber. This political control was no part of the jurisdiction of either the courts of law or the courts of equity. A political injunction was no part of the powers of the court of equity, which were vested in the federal judicial system when it was empowered to decide cases in equity.

The distinction between the brands of law administered by the chancery court, the law courts, and the Court of Star Chamber is far greater than a difference in names. The injunction against the private citizen and the *mandamus* against a public official are totally different from each other. The private citizen by injunction, at the suit of another citizen, may be instructed exactly what to do and as to the manner in which he shall do it, in order to remedy the wrongful acts he has done in the past in violation of law. But the orders of the law courts, in form of the writs of *prohibition* and *mandamus,* in no way interfered with the manner in which officials exercised their discretion, for if the law courts had done this, then the courts themselves would have been taking over the functions

---

19. The writ was often used by the Court of King's Bench against other courts which attempted to adjudge lawsuits beyond their jurisdiction to decide. The writ was widely used against the ecclesiastical courts to prevent them from claiming jurisdiction over ordinary law cases.

20. If a judge refused to hold court, a writ of *mandamus* could be issued by a higher court, commanding him to hold court, or to decide a case he had long since heard and had no excuse for not deciding, but the writ could not command the judge as to how he should decide a case.

of these governmental offices. This was done instead by the chief executive, the king, acting with and through his council and through the Court of Star Chamber, bodies that were in close contact with him and responsive to his wishes. The Court of Star Chamber was a political institution exercising political control and carrying out political objectives.

The chancery courts and the law courts were essentially subservient to law, and subservience to law was a point of pride with them. But the Court of Star Chamber was subservient to none but the king. It utilized torture to carry out its powers, but this torture occurred in a cruel age, was utilized to bring order to a riotous society, and was supported by popular approval. It was, Holdsworth says, an attribute of the age in which the torture occurred rather than merely of the court which used it,[21] though by law the use of torture was throughout said to be illegal.[22]

The principal attribute of the Court of Star Chamber, the attribute which eventually brought it into disfavor, was that it was a lawless court. Where the courts of law and of equity sat to do justice under law, the Court of Star Chamber sat to achieve desired purposes, no matter what the law required. If law would not bring about the result it desired, then it made new law that would bring about that result, so that it governed by whim. The Court of Star Chamber disregarded law, disregarded precedent which was the keystone of the common law, and punished that which it felt needed to be punished, regardless of whether the law prohibited it. It exercised regal powers in issuing injunctions, it exercised the powers of the law courts in deciding ordinary cases, and it tried persons for criminal "offenses" not carrying the death penalty, even if those offenses were not made illegal by law. It was a dictatorial body, first engaged in restoring order to society and then in political persecution.[23] The manner in which the Court of Star Chamber moved to accomplish its wonders is instructive.

The first thing a new government does is to achieve protection for itself as a government and respect for its institutions and officers. Whether these are essential or not, they appear to be necessary for a government to effectively govern, and they in fact are the most jealously-guarded interests of government: The protection of government itself, including the protection of its judicial processes, by laws such as those requiring obedience to court orders.[24]

The Court of Star Chamber used these particular laws that existed for the protection of the judicial system and it expanded these laws to govern the people

---

21. I Holdsworth 506; V Holdsworth 196.

22. V Holdsworth 186-188.

23. Once such power is vested it cannot be controlled. When it is recognized that any court can sit above the law instead of being controlled by law, then it will sit above the law to accomplish political as well as judicial purposes.

24. Chief Justice Marshall wrote in *McCullough v. Maryland* (above, pp. 171-177) that the Federal Government had from the very first enacted criminal statutes on the various general subjects on which it was empowered to legislate, regardless of whether those laws were "necessary and proper." But this statement was inaccurate. The First Congress enacted criminal statutes in areas in which it was expressly given total and exclusive legislative authority, such as the District of Columbia, laws creating crimes on the high seas, and the like. Its only other criminal enactments were statutes for the protection of the judicial processes, enacted as being necessary and historically proper for carrying out judicial powers created by the Constitution. There were perjury statutes, laws making it illegal to steal records of the federal courts, and laws making it criminal to interfere in particular ways with judgments of the federal courts.

in matters having nothing to do with the protection of the courts. It used its power to try people and inflict criminal penalties upon them to punish criminal offenses that were punishable by the ordinary criminal laws, and to thereby deprive such citizens of the right not to be prosecuted except upon an indictment, of the right to trial by jury, and of the right not to be compelled to give testimony against themselves.

One example of this is the crime of contempt of court. This had "always" been a criminal offense in England. This means that it was an offense punishable by grand jury indictment followed by trial by jury. No judge in early England had any authority to imprison people as punishment for contempt of court. The courts had authority to cause a citizen to be apprehended and brought before them for contempt of court, and once there, a bargained fine and apology might serve as a substitute for criminal prosecution,[25] but if a court really thought a citizen should be imprisoned for contempt of court, or if the citizen refused to bargain for a fine, punishment could be imposed only after indictment and trial by jury, and then, of course, only if the jury found the citizen guilty.[26]

The Court of Star Chamber, however, being all-powerful, held itself able to punish the crime of contempt of court committed in any court in the realm. Judges began on occasion to refer contempts to the Star Chamber, and the Court of Star Chamber brought before it citizens and tried them without indictments, without juries, and exercised its own judgment as to guilt or innocence and as to the term of imprisonment to be imposed. This was the origin of the idea that judges alone have some power to punish people for contempt of court, for refusing to obey injunctions, showing disrespect to the judge, and other such acts.[27]

The protection of the courts and their authority from contemptuous refusals of obedience easily spread by a combination of Star Chamber habits and an act of Parliament into protection extended to judges and other magistrates from all criticism. The Star Chamber said: "Let all men take heede how they complayne in wordes against any magistrate, *for they are gods.*" [28]

Early in the recorded portion of English judicial history, a writ was authorized under which one citizen could sue another one for falsely bringing about his

---

25. III Holdsworth 391.

26. III Holdsworth 392-393. In one early case, while a judge of the Court of King's Bench was presiding, a prisoner awaiting trial for some offense threw a brick at and narrowly missed the judge. This was not a matter for the judge to exercise some supposed power to punish the citizen for the crime of contempt of court. Justice did move rapidly. An indictment was immediately drawn, the grand jury indicted, there was a short jury trial not requiring much evidence on either side, followed by a guilty verdict and the imposition of the death penalty. But it was done in accordance with law as it then existed, not by the whim of an individual judge. III Holdsworth 393.

27. After the Court of Star Chamber was abolished, one English judge wrote a decision saying that the ordinary law courts had the power to punish people for contempt, to determine what the penalty would be, and to then pass sentence. But the judge who wrote this opinion did not even deliver it. That undelivered opinion, departing from past law, and adopting the lawless rule of the Court of Star Chamber (which dispensed with jury trial in all cases) became the foundation of all subsequent English and American law declaring judges alone empowered to determine whether a person was guilty of contempt of court and to impose a sentence upon him. III Holdsworth 393. This is one of our living heritages from the Court of Star Chamber.

28. V Holdsworth 209.

indictment. One of the expansions or courses of decisions in disregard of law made by the Star Chamber lay in the origin of the law of libel. To achieve a desired result of a minimization of public scandal, rather than to decide cases under law, the Star Chamber began punishing people for making false statements against officials, magistrates, clergymen, and this course of punishing the utterance of false statement was to become a part of the law administered by the Court of King's Bench after the Star Chamber was abolished.[29] With the appearance and growth of printing, the king in council exercised control over all such publications, granting or denying permission to print, and the Star Chamber exercised censorship control over publications as a part of the king's prerogative. This became the law of libel.[30]

In the early 1300's, Parliament passed a statute to protect people from being abused by conspiracies to misuse the judicial processes by obtaining false indictments against innocent citizens. The principal part of this statute read:

"Conspirators be they that do confeder or bind themselves by oath . . . that every of them shall aid or support the enterprise of each other falsely and maliciously to indict or cause to be indicted, or falsely to acquit people, or falsely to move or maintain pleas . . .[31]

This conspiracy law was actually law made to remedy injuries suffered by individuals by a perversion of the legal processes of the courts.

The Star Chamber took this idea of conspiracy, disregarded the main part that involved abuse of the individual through misuse of the judicial processes, and made it an instrumentality for imprisoning citizens for making agreements or acting together for disapproved purposes. In the Star Chamber, the essence of the thing punished by imprisonment became the act of freely discussing disapproved subjects or plans. The very liberty of citizens was itself diminished by the lawlessness of the Star Chamber in creating and developing its conspiracy doctrines. Though no crime be committed, the Star Chamber punished mere agreements or conspiracies to commit crimes, and even conspiracies to commit civil wrongs which might be the basis of civil lawsuits but were not criminal offenses at all.[32] They punished this self-created crime under a definition they created, though they had none of Parliament's law-making powers, and they imprisoned people in disregard of the fundamental rights supposed to be guaranteed by law, such as jury trial.

The Court of Star Chamber stood above the law. It did whatever it felt the needs of society and the state demanded. Being empowered, in the exercise of the king's prerogative powers, to accomplish desired results and to treat matters that were considered to be of sufficient importance to the state, the Star Chamber ruled, "exhorbitant offenses are not subject to the ordinary course of law." [33] The Court acknowledged no subservience to law nor even to the precedents of its own past decisions, saying, "We can make an order according to the nature and necessity of the thing itself." [34]

A contemporanous writer, Hudson, in his *Treatise on the Star Chamber*, de-

---

29. V Holdsworth 208-209.
30. VIII Holdsworth 238-239.
31. III Holdsworth 403.
32. III Holdsworth 405-406; V Holdsworth 203-205.
33. IV Holdsworth 87.
34. IV Holdsworth 87.

scribed the Court of Star Chamber as "the curious eye of the state and the King's Council, prying into the inconveniences and mischiefs which abound in the commonwealth." He said that it punished errors that "might prove dangerous and infectious diseases," and that it required the performance of such things as it thought needful "thought no positive law nor continued custom of the common law giveth warrant to it." [35]

The Star Chamber went further, commanding sheriffs to disobey writs of *habeas corpus* issued by the law courts inquiring into the legality of the imprisonment of citizens, and it gave sheriffs express instructions as to what responses they should make to the Court of King's Bench, the response being that the prisoner was being held in prison on the express personal command of the king or queen.[36] It thus controlled the discretionary functions of such officials. It even imprisoned jurors for returning not guilty verdicts in criminal trials in the Court of King's Bench. In short, the Court of Star Chamber was the instrument of tyranny utilized by the King in Council; it operated in the manner of a court, except that its procedures were totally contrary to those required by the law of the land.[37]

The Chancery Court's powers and processes were different from those of the law courts, but the Chancery Court did not exist for the purpose of imposing the government's will on the people, or for the purpose of controlling the officers of government in the way they carried out the obligations of their offices and in the way they chose to perform their discretionary governmental functions. Because when a court exercises this power, then the court itself is performing those governmental functions. All of this type of lawless jurisdiction was the jurisdiction of the Court of Star Chamber: The issuance of royal injunctions to enforce the king's prerogatives or will, the utilization of criminal procedures to punish acts which were not crimes under the law of the land, and the utilization of both civil, criminal and injunctive processes to control officials of government in the manner in which they carried out their functions. The Star Chamber jurisdiction was the type of jurisdiction that was abolished in England by Act of Parliament in 1641.

When Parliament abolished the Court of Star Chamber in 1641, it also outlawed the powers of the King in Council as a judicial body throughout England. But before Parliament destroyed these powers, which have nothing to do with the powers of courts deciding cases in equity, King Charles I was beheaded and England lived for a time without a royal monarch. With the restoration of the monarchy and with the abolition of the Court of Star Chamber and the powers of King in Council to exercise royal prerogatives in the manner of the Star Chamber, this power of prerogative government, or lawless government, of government above the law and not accountable to law, was hoped to be abolished in England.

However, the King's prerogative did not die and was not abolished by the terms of the Star Chamber Statute except within the home land. Some matters continued to be matters of the King's royal prerogative. His right to govern as he saw fit rather than as law commanded. One of the branches of the King's prerogative powers that continued to live after the Court of Star Chamber was destroyed was the King's prerogative powers over the colonies chartered by him,

---

35. I Holdsworth 504.
36. I Holdsworth 512; VI Holdsworth 35.
37. I Holdsworth 393, 512; IV Holdsworth 83-84, 87, 273-274; V Holdsworth 184.

wherever they might be.[38] This included the prerogative powers over the American colonies. They were still subject to such powers which in England were destroyed with the destruction of the Court of Star Chamber.

This remnant of the power of King in Council, the power to rule by prerogative, became so objectionable in America that the Continental Congress was finally moved to declare that the American states are "absolved from all allegiance to the British Crown, and that all political connection between them and the state of Great Britain, is and ought to be totally dissolved . . ." Thus did Star Chamber powers end in America on July 4, 1776. They have never since lawfully existed here.

This same type of tyrannical power which insisted that it was above the law, that it could control the discretion of government officials in disregard of the procedures established by law, and could instruct them as to how they should perform their obligations of office, that it could essentially govern as a matter of prerogative, this same brand of government that cost Charles I his head in England led at last to the American Declaration of Independence.

The prerogative powers of the King and the Court of Star Chamber, so recently destroyed in the long and costly Revolutionary War, were not reestablished thirteen years later when our Constitution was written. The prerogative powers of the Court of Star Chamber do not exist within the federal government, were not created by that portion of the Constitution that gives federal courts the power to determine cases in equity. The lawless court is an institution which cannot legally exist under the Constitution of the United States.

Ours was designed to be a government of laws, and the laws were designed to be made by a Congress elected by and responsive to the people, not by hordes of administrators answerable to no one, whose orders are enforced by courts under the claim that they are exercising the powers of courts of equity.[39] The decision of cases in equity did not include the use of injunctive powers to enforce governmental policies against the people nor to govern the people by governing their local officials. The jurisdiction to decide cases in equity refers to ordinary cases, not to the use of injunctive powers to compel people to obey the will of government.[40]

Judicial Power and Political Affairs:

Some early decisions of the Supreme Court considered the question of federal judicial power from an entirely different approach, *i.e.,* the approach of What is Judicial Power?

---

38. With the restoration of the monarchy and the Bill of Rights in 1688, virtually all these powers were actually taken over by the Parliament.

39. Early in our national history, the Supreme Court wrote of its equity jurisdiction in *Fontain v. Ravenel:* "The courts of the United States cannot exercise any equity powers, except those conferred by Acts of Congress, and those judicial powers which the high court of chancery in England, acting *under its judicial capacity* as a court of equity, possessed and exercised, at the time of the formulation of the Constitution of the United States. Powers not judicial, exercised by the chancellor, merely as the representative of the sovereign, and by virtue of the king's prerogative as *parens patriae* are not possessed by the [Federal] Circuit Courts." This was in accord with the rationale that had been utilized by Chief Justice Marshall in *The Trustees of the Philadelphia Baptist Association v. Hart's Executors.*

40. As to the views of Madison and the Constitutional Convention, see below, p. 243.

It is clear that some things cannot be resolved by judicial power, which is primarily exercised in disputes between individuals or in criminal prosecutions of individuals. If one state should arm its National Guard troops and send them to attack another state, no judicial order could be effective under such circumstances, though state officials would be directly violating a provision of the Constitution. The enforcement of the constitutional prohibition against a state making war would have to be undertaken by the Congress and the President, the two separate and superior branches of the three branches of government.

The Supreme Court has recognized that this type of dispute is simply not a dispute of a judicial nature. The importance of decisions which discuss the question of whether a dispute is a political or a judicial dispute arises under other provisions of the judicial article of the Constitution; these discussions have nothing to do with that part of the Constitution that gives Federal Courts jurisdiction of all cases in law and in equity arising under the Constitution and laws of the Nation.

Other provisions, for example, give the Supreme Court itself jurisdiction to act as a trial court in suits in which one state sues another or in which a foreign nation sues a state. It is particularly in this type of case, in which the authority is given to the federal courts, but primarily to the Supreme Court, in addition to the jurisdiction to decide cases in law and in equity, that the distinction between judicial controversies and political controversies is important.

A leading early example of an attempt to invoke this type of jurisdiction is an 1831 decision by Chief Justice Marshall, *The Cherokee Nation v. Georgia*. From the beginning of American settlement, Indians had been a formidable obstruction at times to the establishment of civilized colonies, and the colonies, the representatives of the British Crown, and later the states and the Congress of the Confederacy under the Articles of Confederation, had dealt with Indians by making "treaties" with them, though they were not nations in the sense that European nations were members of the family of nations.

By these treaties, the area occupied by the Indians as their hunting grounds had been successively reduced, and a part of the State of Georgia was occupied by Cherokee Indians under a series of treaties entered into between the Congress of the Confederation and the Cherokees and subsequently between President George Washington and the Cherokee Nation. The last such treaty recognized the Indian rights to occupy this area within Georgia as their hunting grounds.

Georgia decided to take over these hunting grounds. Its legislature passed laws extending county lines into the hunting grounds, declaring it illegal for Indian courts to exercise jurisdiction, and generally having the effect of banishing the Indians from their own hunting grounds, from their homeland. Considering the treaties to be a part of the supreme law of the land, Georgia's actions violated the supreme law and were unconstitutional. The Constitution gives the Supreme Court jurisdiction as a trial court to entertain and decide suits by foreign nations against individual American states, so the Cherokees sued the State of Georgia in the Supreme Court, seeking an injunction against Georgia's endeavors to exercise its sovereignty over the Indians and their hunting grounds.

Chief Justice Marshall expressed sympathy for the Cherokees, but carefully and at considerable length considered the question of whether the Indian Tribes, as they are referred to by the Constitution itself, were a "foreign nation" so as to enable them to sue Georgia in the Supreme Court. He held the Cherokee Nation was not a foreign nation and that the Supreme Court had no jurisdiction, or power, to consider the case, *even if the Constitution was then being violated by Georgia.* The chief justice wrote:

> "That part of the bill which respects the land occupied by the Indians and prays the aid of the Court to protect their possession, may be more doubtful. The mere question of right might perhaps be decided by this court in a proper case with proper parties. But the court is asked to do more than decide on the title. The bill requires us to *control the Legislature of Georgia, and to restrain the exertion of its physical force.* The propriety of such an interposition by this court may well be questioned. It savors too much of the exercise of political power to be within the proper province of the judicial department. . . .'"

"If it be true that the Cherokee Nation have rights, this is not the tribunal in which those rights are to be asserted. If it be true that wrongs have been inflicted, and that still greater are to be apprehended, this is not the tribunal which can redress the past or prevent the future."

It is clear that Chief Justice Marshall did not dodge decision of the case merely because it was a hot political issue. He never feared taking positions in cases in which there was a great deal of political interest. His opinion made it clear, though he spoke of the lawsuit as one which attempted to get the court to make a determination of a political issue, that the court's actual decision was based upon the fact that it had no jurisdiction of the case, no power to decide the case, because the suit was not brought by a foreign nation against a state, but was brought by an Indian Tribe against a state, and of such suits, the Constitution had given the court no jurisdiction. Further, history demonstrates that Chief Justice Marshall did not in the slightest shrink even from this huge question of the legality of the conduct of the State of Georgia, political though the question was.

The following year, an ordinary lawsuit, of the type clearly within the judicial powers of courts of law, came before the Supreme Court, Chief Justice Marshall decided the case, and with no show of reluctance declared the acts of the State of Georgia to be illegal, so doing as a step in deciding the lawsuit. The case was *Worcester v. Georgia,* an appeal from a conviction for a criminal offense after trial in a Georgia court. The Legislature that took over the Indian hunting grounds declared all Indian laws nullified, declared the Indian courts lacking in any power to render judgments and stated that citizens of Georgia could obtain licenses to settle the Indian lands by swearing their allegiance to the State of Georgia. The legislature also made it a criminal offense for any white man to live within the Cherokee territory without having obtained such a license.

Worcester was a missionary whose home was in Vermont, and he had been sent to Georgia by his church with the authorization of the President of the United States as permitted by the treaty between the United States and the Cherokee Nation. He was therefore residing within the huntgrounds of the Cherokees. So the direct question of the validity or invalidity of Georgia law was involved in this ordinary criminal appeal, an ordinary criminal conviction of Worcester for living within the reservation without having obtained a license from the State of Georga to live there. Marshall held the Georgia legislation to be contrary to the treaty made with the Cherokee Nation, and therefore to be a void law, because treaties made under the authority of the United States are part of the Supreme Law of the Land. The Supreme Court reversed Worcester's conviction and sentence of four years' imprisonment.

President Andrew Jackson, hearing of the decision said: "John Marshall has made his decision. Now let him enforce it." But there was no legitimate question of enforcement. The Supreme Court was exercising its ordinary appellate jurisdiction in an ordinary criminal case, it reversed the judgment of a Georgia court as it was empowered by law to do, and Worcester was set free.[41]

Perhaps the greatest impetus to the idea that the powers of the ordinary chancery courts to issue injunctions in lawsuits between private citizens could be utilized to control the acts of government officials occurred in an emergency in the life of the Bank of the United States, at one of those low ebbs in the Bank's popularity. The case was *Osborn v. Bank of the United States.* It happened in Ohio. Ohio tried to destroy the bank as far as its Ohio operations were concerned. It passed a law, which must have been aimed at that bank, making it illegal for any bank other than one licensed by the state to engage in the *private banking business* in Ohio. It imposed a tax on all such unauthorized banks in the amount of $50,000 on each office of the bank which accepted deposits or which discounted or made loans on private notes. This covered the Bank of the United States in its private, non-governmental profit-making functions.

The bank had two offices in Ohio so that the "tax" on it totalled $100,000 per year. The duty of collection was imposed upon the state auditor, Mr. Osborn. The Ohio law stated that if the tax should not be paid by a fixed date, the auditor should issue a warrant for the seizure of the amount of the tax, which should be seized from the bank's banking rooms, its vaults, or wherever it might be found in the bank. Auditor Osborn made it known that he was going to enforce the law.

Under Chief Justice Marshall's ruling in *McCullough v. Maryland,*[42] it was held that the bank had been constitutionally created and was exempt from state law. If that decision be credited, therefore, the Act of Congress creating the bank and somehow empowering it to engage in private banking business for profit was a part of the supreme law of the land, not subject to the state's taxing powers. If a state officer should proceed to seize bank assets, he would be exceeding his powers as limited by the Constitution, invalidating conflicting state laws. This would come strictly within the old common law writ of prohibition, under which state law courts could prohibit officials from doing acts prohibited by the law itself.

Instead of seeking such a writ, the Bank of the United States sought and obtained an injunction from a federal equity court, but by the time the injunction was served, the bank's $100,000 was resting securely in a bound trunk in Auditor Osborn's office. The injunction for its return would have been the same in substance as a writ of *mandamus,* commanding what the law commanded, assuming the bank was lawfully chartered to engage in private business. However, Chief Justice Marshall treated the entire matter as an ordinary equity case, in which an injunction was being issued against one private party on behalf of another private party instead of being issued against a governmental official. He noted that if the

41. In reaching the decision, the Supreme Court held the entire course of conduct by the Georgia Legislature illegal, but this decision of illegality was not the judgment of the Court. The judgment was that Missionary Worcester had been unlawfully convicted and that the conviction was reversed. As to the political issues arising from Georgia's actions, these were none of the Supreme Court's business, as the Court correctly held the year before in *The Cherokee Nation v. Georgia.* The political issues were solved by the political departments of the Government in favor of Georgia and against the Cherokee Nation.
42. Discussed above, pp. 171-177.

state law were void, as he held it to be, then it gave no authority for the state auditor to hold the money. This, of course, is *always* true in *mandamus* cases and does not justify an injunction. By assuming that the ordinary powers of a court of equity, long used to do justice between individuals, could be brought to bear on government officials, Chief Justice Marshall laid the groundwork for judicial determination and regulation of the mode of conduct of government affairs which in England had been abolished with the abolition of the Court of Star Chamber, and which was not a part of the powers of the courts of equity.

The results have been far-reaching. So far-reaching, that Marshall doubtless would never have taken part in the expansion of the supposed equity powers of the federal courts that has occurred in the Twentieth Century.[43] In the Twentieth Century, and particularly since 1950, the idea that the powers of a court of equity [44] include the power to issue injunctions to regulate the way public officials perform their duties, has come into its own. It came into its own largely through the device of a new type of suit designed by the federal courts, and supposedly the same thing as a type of case tried by the courts of equity when our Constitution was written.

But the motivation for the creation of this new type of lawsuit came in part from the Supreme Court's course of decisions in which it held that some types of controversies were "political" and could not be considered by the courts. These considerations are quite appropriate in deciding whether judicial power is being appealed to in cases in which states are being sued by other states or by a foreign government in the Supreme Court, where the Court sits as a kind of international law tribunal. But such considerations have no legitimate bearing in ordinary suits in law and in equity.

Chief Justice Marshall well realized the difference between the two types of cases, and demonstrated it in his decisions on Georgia's take-over of the Cherokee lands. His statement that the question of the legality of Georgia's actions was more of a political than a judicial controversy was a statement made by him

---

43. Marshall's understanding of the nature of judicial power was stated by him in *Osborn v. Bank of the United States:* "Judicial power, as contradistinguished from the power of the laws, has no existence. Courts are the mere instruments of the law, and can will nothing. When they are said to exercise a discretion, it is a mere legal discretion, a discretion to be exercised in discerning the course prescribed by law; and, when that is discerned, it is the duty of the court to follow it. Judicial power is never exercised for the purpose of giving effect to the will of the judge; always for the purpose of giving effect to the will of the legislature; or, in other words, to the will of the law." In modern times, Congress loves to leave matters to the "discretion" of judges, but as used today, "discretion" is a euphemism for whim. An example is the modern criminal statute, which empowers judges to impose sentences for "no more than" 5, 10, or 25 years. The idiosyncracies of different judges are prime factors in determining the length of sentences. Equal justice under law is impossible when penalties are determined by the whims of individual officers rather than the law of the land. See *Yick Wo v. Hopkins,* discussed below, p. 270.

44. We note a change of emphasis from the power to decide cases in equity to the powers used by the courts of equity to enforce their decisions. This is comparable to confusing the differences to hear criminal cases and civil cases with the differences in remedies which may be utilized in the different types of cases to remedy the defendant's violation of law, imprisonment of the defendant or giving judgement against him for monetary damages.

almost as an afterthought, though it was quite appropriate.[45] This statement received great and unwarranted amplification in the 1840's in an opinion written by Chief Justice Taney.

The case was *Luther v. Borden*. It grew out of a totally political controversy, but the case itself was an ordinary lawsuit of which the Federal courts had jurisdiction. Chief Justice Taney mistakenly placed his opinion on the basis that the court had no jurisdiction of the dispute because it was a political matter. The dispute arose from a series of happenings known as "Dorr's Rebellion." Could anything be more political?

Dorr set up a new government in Rhode Island alongside the existing government, and this was the rebellion. The rebellion grew out of the fact that Rhode Island did not have a state constitution. It was the only state in the nation without a constitution. The government had continued to govern under its charter when the Revolution occurred; nobody managed to stir up enough interest among the people of Rhode Island to bring about the adoption of a constitution, so the government of the state continued under the charter, or under tradition, for almost seventy years. Population shifts and changing population patterns resulted in malapportionment in the state legislative body so large that citizens in parts of the state could not effectively make their voices heard.

Repeatedly, unsuccessful attempts had been made in the legislature to call a constitutional convention, but the legislators, representing the people who had elected them, were satisfied with their control of the entire state.[46] Dissatisfied citizens finally began to hold meetings, and these voluntary citizens' meetings resulted in an agreement among the citizens to hold a constitutional convention even without the legislature's authorization. They held their convention, wrote a constitution, and inserted in it provisions allowing all adult males who were citizens of the state to vote on the proposed constitution.

Rhode Islanders, or those who wished to do so, came, voted, and the outcome favored the new constitution, and there followed an election of a new legislature and a new governor, Governor Dorr. Seeing that the people were serious, the state legislature had in the meantime begun motions to call its official constitutional convention and procedures were well under way to write another constitution, this time an official one. However, "Governor" Dorr, having been duly elected under the unofficial new constitution by the popular vote of the people who voted, advised the Governor to inform the legislature that he and the people's new body of legislators constituted the lawful government of Rhode Island. The Governor (the official governor, that is) communicated the message to the Legislature (the one sitting in the legislative chamber, that is) and that Legislature disagreed. It insisted it was the legislature.

Governor Dorr proceeded to endeavor to seize the state's arsenal in order effectively to put his new popularly-chosen government in command of the affairs of the state, but he failed in his military attempt. The legislature sitting in the legislative halls moved rapidly, the new government never got off the ground, and there was no interruption in the governing of Rhode Island by the existing government.

---

45. The actual decision, as we have seen, was that the Court had no authority to decide the case because the Cherokee Nation was not a foreign nation so as to entitle it to the services of the Supreme Court as a trial court.

46. This situation recurred to some extent in wider areas in states throughout the nation in the Twentieth Century. See below, Chapter X.

Shortly afterward, the new official Rhode Island constitution went into effect. Dorr was tried and convicted for his rebellion and was sentenced to prison. Luther was one of Dorr's supporters in the new government, and a warrant for Luther's arrest was isued by the old government during the rebellion. Officers came to Luther's home and arrested him. Luther sued Borden for breaking down his door and breaking into his house to make the arrest.[47] The suit was for trespass to real property. It was a plain common-law type of suit, it being one of the very oldest types of lawsuits anciently entertained by the common-law courts, anciently started by means of the writ of trespass *quare clausum fregit*.[48] There was nothing exceptional about the case except that it happened in the middle of a great political dispute but aside from this, it was about as ordinary a lawsuit as a lawsuit can be.

Did Borden break into Luther's house? Certainly. Was he a trespasser, or did he have lawful authority to break into Luther's house? Luther claimed he did not have authority, and Luther's claim was based upon the argument that the government of Rhode Island was not the government of Rhode Island but that instead, Dorr's government was the government of Rhode Island. The fact of the matter was that the existing government of Rhode Island had never ceased for a moment to govern the state, and that Dorr's government had never for a moment attained actual power as a government. The Rhode Island laws were administered without interruption throughout Dorr's short "rebellion."

But instead of treating this as the ordinary lawsuit it was, having simple legal questions, the Supreme Court covered the same ground only to conclude that this type of lawsuit, trespass to real property under stressed conditions of political upheaval, was not within the powers of the federal judicial system to decide. A lawsuit over one man breaking into another man's house in a state in which there existed one and only one governing government was supposedly not the type of case a court of law could decide.

Mr. Luther wanted the Supreme Court to determine that the Dorr government was the lawful government of Rhode Island instead of the established government, but the Court pointed out the practical impossibility of a court determining under such circumstances whether Mr. Dorr had won the "election." [49] In the heat of the conflict, the President had called out state militia to be available to go to the aid of the *established government* of Rhode Island in the event the legislature or governor of the state should call for help.[50] Speaking of the presidential action—and the President himself must make the high political decision

47. Mr. Luther succeeded in moving to Massachusetts after the "Rebellion," and as a resident of Massachusetts, he sued Bordon, the officer in charge of the arrest party executing the Rhode Island warrant in Rhode Island. He could sue in the federal court because the Constitution permits a citizen of one state to sue a citizen of another state in a federal court rather than a state court if he desires.
48. This phrase is usually abbreviated Trespass q.c.f. by law students, and seldom used by anyone other than law students.
49. "The written returns of the moderators and clerks of mere voluntary meetings, verified by affidavit, certainly would not be admissible [in evidence]; nor their opinions or judgments as to the freehold qualifications [land ownership] of the persons who voted. These require actual knowledge of the witness of the fact of which he testifies in a court of justice. How, then, could the majority of freeholders have been determined within a *judicial proceeding?*"
50. This is the only circumstance in which the Constitution authorizes the President to quell disorder within a state unless the state is invaded.

as to which is the lawful government of a state under such circumstances, the Supreme Court ruled:

> "After the President has acted and called out the militia, is a circuit court of the United States authorized to inquire whether his decision was right? Could the court, while the parties were actually contending in arms for the possession of the government, call witnesses before it and inquire which party represented the majority of the people? If it could, then it would become the duty of the court (provided it came to the conclusion that the President had decided incorrectly) to discharge those who were arrested or detained by the troops in the service of the United States government, which the President was endeavoring to maintain. *If the judicial power extends so far, the guarantee contained in the Constitution of the United States is a guarantee of anarchy, and not of order.* Yet if this right does not reside in the courts when the conflict is raging, if the judicial power is at that time bound to follow the decision of the political, it must be equally bound when the contest is over. It cannot, when peace is restored, punish as offenses and crimes the acts which it before recognized, and was bound to recognize, as lawful.[51]

In this line of thinking, Chief Justice Taney completely misinterpreted the nature of judicial power. His assertion was based upon the false assumption that when the Supreme Court decides a point of law as a step in deciding a lawsuit, all governmental officials are obligated to dedicate themselves to carrying out that view of the law. But such legal decisions are nothing more than steppingstones to the decision of the lawsuit for one side or the other, a decision binding only upon the parties to the lawsuit.

The Court was also grossly incorrect in its assumption that it could not pass upon the legality of the President's acts if necessary to the decision of the lawsuit. The Court did not have before it any application for a writ of prohibition to restrain the President of the United States from calling out any militia. If it had had such a lawsuit, to prevent the President from exercising discretion, any order obviously would have been beyond the power of any court simply because the president *had discretion* which a court could not seize.

The solution of the litigation in *Luther v. Borden* was in no way complex. Courts function as agencies of existing civil governments, and with the one unalterable fact that the original government of Rhode Island never ceased to govern, there was really nothing much to argue about in *Luther v. Borden*. In asking the federal court to declare Dorr's government to have been elected the lawful government of Rhode Island in the course of deciding his trespass lawsuit against Mr. Borden for breaking into his house, Luther was asking the court to decide an issue having nothing to do with the decision of the lawsuit. It was a fact that the Rhode Island government was the governing government, regardless of its popularity, and that Borden went under authority of a warrant of that government to break into Luther's home and arrest him. There was therefore no trespass, however much abstract theory and his own popularity may have justified "Governor" Dorr's actions.

The Courts and Classes of Citizens:

We bring our interest to bear upon a land-mark decision of 1922, which height-

---

51. Chief Justice Marshall could have asked the same questions, and used the same negative answers, to refuse to reverse the conviction of the missionary in *Worcester v. Georgia,* above, p. 233.

ened the frustration over the possible existence of unconstitutional laws and the inability of citizens to bring before the courts their complaints about such laws. These were two cases, *Massachusetts v. Mellon* and *Frothingham v. Mellon,* decided in a single opinion.[52]

Congress passed a law in the interest of motherhood and safe childbirth. The purpose of the law was to reduce infant mortality through programs to be administered by the various states. The states were invited by Congress to institute such programs, an appropriation of money was made to be divided among the states according to formula; this law created a bureau to administer the program and to oversee the disbursement of money to aid the obedient performance by the state governments, and empowered this bureau to disapprove disbursements in any state which might fail to perform as it had agreed in accordance with the regulations to be promulgated.

The Constitution empowers Congress to levy taxes to pay the debts of the United States and to provide for the nation's common defense and general welfare, but there is no provision empowering it to tax to provide for the private welfare of individual citizens, though their welfare may need improving throughout all the states in the country.

So Massachusetts sued Secretary of the Treasury Mellon to enjoin him from making any disbursements under the Maternity Act. The injunction sought was similar to the relief offered by the common law legal writ of prohibition, but Massachusetts was not a taxpayer, and although it presented most weighty arguments,[53] Massachusetts was nevertheless attempting to use judicial offices to control the entire course of action by the government in this matter. Massachusetts itself, apart from its citizens, was not injured by the unlawful expenditures by the Federal Government. The Supreme Court held Massachusetts had no interest in the matter, and could not maintain the suit.

But Mrs. Frothingham had also sued. She claimed she was suing as a taxpayer who resided in Massachusetts, and that her taxes were being increased for the benefit of individuals in many states rather than for the general welfare of the entire nation. Her assertion of unconstitutionality was quite clearly correct. It was correct because such activity as feeding hungry citizens is for the personal welfare of the hungry citizens as distinguished from the general welfare of the combined states. Spending money to improve the personal welfare of millions of citizens was not within the non-lawmaking objects Congress was authorized to achieve by spending money, such as establishing post offices, maintaining armies and navies, paying the debts of the federal government, and the like—and if this could be done for individual citizens on the basis of their hunger as they might be

---

52. Massachusetts filed its original suit against the Secretary of the Treasury in the Supreme Court, which is constitutionally given trial court jurisdiction over suits filed by states; Mrs. Mellon sued in the trial court in the District of Columbia, whose decision was eventually appealed to the Supreme Court, so the Court disposed of the two cases simultaneously in a single opinion.

53. The arguments were based upon both taxation theory and the fact that this scheme of taking a large amount of tax money from Massachusetts and spreading it to individual citizens throughout the nation was contrary to the fundamental taxing scheme of the Constitution, just as today's "revenue sharing" schemes, under which the proceeds of federal taxation are distributed to state governments, is falsely pretended to be in support of the Constitution's scheme of federalism, which it arrogantly violates.

scattered at random throughout the states, then it could just as easily be done for individuals who hungered and found their needs recognized because they knew congressmen. Charity to private citizens, achieved by using money extorted by means of the tax laws, is not within any of the purposes the Constitution authorizes Congress to accomplish.[54]

But constitutionality of a particular use of tax money was not decided by the Supreme Court in *Frothingham v. Mellon.* The Court decided that the federal judicial power to hear cases in law and in equity did not permit the federal courts to issue an injunction against the Secretary of the Treasury to prohibit him from spending tax money.

Mrs. Frothingham claimed that she had a right to sue as an ordinary taxpayer, whose tax bill was increased by the appropriation for the aid of some mothers. The Supreme Court said of the position of the individual taxpayer:

"His interest in the moneys of the Treasury—partly realized from taxation and partly from other sources—is shared with millions of others; it is comparatively minute and indeterminable; and the effect upon future taxation of any payment out of the funds so remote, fluxuating, and uncertain that no basis is afforded for an appeal to the preventive powers of a court of equity."

This was an attempt by a citizen to use the powers of a court of equity, or more properly, the prohibition-issuing powers of a law court, to do what courts could not do when the Constitution was adopted—to prohibit government itself from carrying out a pretended law purely because it was unconstitutional.

What would Mrs. Frothingham have done if, instead of endeavoring to speak for every taxpayer in the nation, she had only tried to file a lawsuit to protect only her own selfish interests? Mrs. Frothingham's interest was in the amount of tax she had to pay. Taxpayers have always had access to the courts of *law* to obtain a determination of whether they really owe the tax. Do I own the property taxed? Have I done an act which subjects me to the tax under a particular taxing law? Or does the law itself mean something different from what the tax collector claims it means, so that I don't owe the tax? Or is the tax law unconstitutional, so that I do not owe the tax? [55] A taxpayer normally follows some procedure established by the laws enacted by Congress, such as paying the tax under protest and then filing a suit against the tax collector, to recover taxes wrongfully extorted from him.[56]

---

54. Chief Justice Marshall expressed this in *Gibbons v. Ogden:* "Congress is not empowered to tax for those purposes which are within the exclusive province of the states." However, this is inaccurate, because when Congress makes a law that is necessary and proper to carry out federal powers granted by the Constitution, this law overrides state law though the subject may normally be within the exclusive province of the states, as in *McDermott v. Wisconsin,* above. p. 172. Marshall should have stated that Congress is not empowered to tax except for those purposes it is empowered to achieve by the Constitution.

55. We saw earlier how Daniel Hylton used judicial processes to settle his argument with the Government over whether he owed a tax on his many carriages, *Hylton v. United States,* above, pp. 79-80.

56. So if Congress should impose a tax upon every automobile in the country at $50.00 per year, an individual might contest his liability for the tax on many grounds. He might claim he no longer owned the automobile on the date the tax became due; or his vehicle was not an automobile of the type Congress intended to tax, because it was not manufactured commercially but was a home-made dune-buggy with a

Mrs. Frothingham could have protested her tax payment in this manner. She could have claimed that the maternity charity law increased her tax burden by some exact refundable amount in a year's time. It may have been twenty cents, perhaps even one dollar. She may have insisted that she was entitled to a reduction of her income tax by that twenty cents or one dollar for the year in which her money was illegally appropriated to be given to other citizens. But this was a general appropriation, coming from general federal funds, and the Collector of Internal Revenue may have insisted that there were billions of dollars that the government had received under citizens' wills as bequests which had gone into the treasury and had never been ear-marked in congressional appropriations for particular purposes— that, as far as either the Collector or Frothingham was concerned, the Government might be giving away its charitable funds, not its tax money. The Collector may have disallowed her claim for her twenty cent tax refund on this ground, on the ground that the maternity money was coming from accumulations from past taxes rather than from the current year's tax receipts, or he may have argued that she was entitled to no more than a eleven cent tax refund. Or the Internal Revenue Service might have decided that the entire twenty cents was simply not worth arguing about, and it may have agreed with Mrs. Frothingham and reduced her taxes by twenty cents.

This was her only interest in the dispute. Her claim allowed, she would not have been able to appeal her winning decision to the usual judicial tax-dispute settling machinery. She had no right to control the United States Government, but only the right to obtain settlement of her dispute with the government over the amount of her taxes, either in the procedure of the Internal Revenue Service or in the judicial procedure for reviewing the Service's decisions in individual cases.[57]

Mrs. Frothingham's position, except for twenty cents or some other small but unknown sum, was precisely the same as every citizen of the United States, including wealthy tax-paying children too young to vote, people prevented from voting for various legal or illegal reasons, people saved from taxation by their poverty. Actually, she sought to speak for all the people of the United States, to use the powers of the courts to give directions to the executive branch of the government that that branch should recognize the supremacy of the Constitution. This was beyond the powers of the courts of law or equity, though the Constitution was clearly violated.

The Government of the United States was designed as a republican form of government, and that form of government provides a method by which citizens may control the actions of government. That method is by participation in elections and the threat of future participation in a certain direction if officials do not change their behavior. The individual citizen has no right to boss his government. To the contrary, it is the theory of the republican form of government, as distinguished from the democratic, or mob-rule, form of government, that the

---

lawnmower engine; or that it was a direct tax that could not be imposed without apportioning it among the states according to population. But his purpose would be to save the $50.00, and the real issue decided would be: Does this man owe the Government $50.00?

57. The powers of the court of equity did not extend to the control of the acts of government. Nor did this power extend to the deliverance of abstract pronouncements as to the content of the law. The power existed to settle disputes between people in which the law was such that the legal remedies were inadequate to protect legal rights.

citizens do not govern, but that they select individuals to govern them. They are not self-governed, but are governed by officials of their choice. The mere fact that the Constitution is violated does not itself give any court the power to do anything about it. Except where individuals are injured by the law, the remedy lies with the people, and one individual cannot presume to speak for all the people of the nation; not even the President can do this.

In deciding the Frothingham portion of the cases of *Massachusetts v. Mellon* and *Frothingham v. Mellon,* the Supreme Court correctly said:

> "We have no power *per se* to review and annul acts of Congress on the ground that they are unconstitutional. That question may be considered only when the justification for some direct injury suffered or threatened, presenting a justiciable issue, is made to rest upon such an act. Then the power exercised is that of ascertaining and declaring the law applicable to the controversy."

The Supreme Court insisted that the judicial powers of the United States were restricted to cases in law and in equity and did not include higher powers—powers which, though the Court did not take note of it, were exercised by the Court of Star Chamber and the King in Council. But does this judicial restraint not permit violation of the Constitution? Of course it does. But for this there is no proper remedy but eternal vigilance and political agitation.

But wait! *What if Mrs. Frothingham had exercised her political rights?* What if she had engaged in protest? Marched with a sign and made speeches? Built up an organization of a million taxpayers? Surely, they could sue to forbid the Secretary of the Treasury from paying out this maternity benefit money. Couldn't they?

But greater numbers really make no difference. The million people would still be trying to use the judicial branch to control the executive branch of government. They would be appealing to the power of King in Council and Court of Star Chamber. If they should prevail, using this legally non-existent judicial power, where did they obtain the right to speak for the other hundreds of millions of citizens *who chose not to join their organization* and *not* to be concerned about the expenditure of federal money for unauthorized purposes. We should not dismiss lightly the idea that if a few citizens seek to use Star Chamber powers to impose their will upon the government of the entire nation, *they are a threat* to the existence of the republican form of government. They are a threat to the sanctity of popular government in which the political strength of the entire population is the only force that can compel the powerful government and its officers to perform their duties as required by law, as the populace did so beautifully under Dorr's leadership in Rhode Island, forcing their legislators to convene a lawful constitutional convention. The only permanent guaranty to the continued existence of constitutional government is today, as it has always been, the eternal vigilance of the citizens against tyranny within their own government. Vigilance both eternal and informed.

Federal courts are prone to speak of their "equity powers" or their "remedial equity powers." The Constitution says nothing about giving the federal judiciary "equity powers." Instead, it gives them jurisdiction of cases in equity, and there is a world of difference between the two. "Equity powers" may easily be stretched into the unqualified power to issue injunctions, governmental writs commanding instant and strict obedience under threat of imprisonment. But by merely giving the federal judiciary power to decide "cases . . . in equity" such a threat of tyrannical government was avoided, because of the vast body of equity jurisprudence that greatly limited the awesome powers of the chancellors to compel obedience.

Even this safe wording in the Constitution caused concern in the great mind of James Madison. In his notes of the convention that wrote our Constitution, he recorded an objection he made one day:

> "Mr. MADISON doubted whether it was not going too far to extend the jurisdiction of the Court generally to cases arising under the Constitution & whether it ought not to be limited to cases of a Judiciary Nature. The right of expounding the Constitution in cases not of this nature ought not to be given to that Department."

Madison's objection was overruled not because the other delegates felt it was proper to give the judiciary such broad powers, but because it was "generally supposed that the jurisdiction given was constructively limited to cases of a Judiciary nature." [58]

And the powers of the federal judiciary were in fact constitutionally limited by merely giving them power to entertain cases in equity, which did not include the Star Chamber power to govern the people by directing their governmental officials in the way they should perform their official duties, nor the power to issue injunctive decrees against some of the people to command them to obey government "policies." The constitutional manner of compelling the people to obey governmental orders is not the injunctive enforcement of "cease and desist orders" issued by a political administrator, but by the enactment of criminal laws and their enforcement by criminal prosecutions, preserving to the citizen subjected to government's power all of the many rights secured to those charged with criminal offenses, including the right to trial before a jury which might possibly consider such government "policies" to trivial to warrant the imposition of imprisonment.

Protecting the Absent Multitudes:

Despite the fact that the coercive powers of a chancery court over governmental officials to regulate the way they perform their duties, as a means of governing the people by governing their officials, was not a part of equity jurisprudence at the time the Constitution was written and the limits of federal judicial powers established, this misuse of the injunction was instituted by means of a device called the class action. By this device, the courts pretend that they have before them large numbers of people seeking "judicial relief" because they have before them a small group of people claiming to represent a "class" of many people needing protection from the judiciary.

This is supposed to be a further development of a class action that existed under the common law at the time of the Constitutional Convention. Actually, at that time, there was no such thing as a type of lawsuit known as a class action, an action in which large numbers of people with a common or like interest (such as a million taxpayers) could join together and compel a governmental official to come before a judge for judicial determination of whether his official acts were

---

58. Madison's Notes on the Federal Convention, *Documents Illustrative of the Formation of the Union,* p. 625. Madison also noted comments by John Dickenson, famous for his pre-Revolutionary War leadership provided in open letters written to the British people: "Mr. DICKENSON was strongly impressed with the remark of Mr. Mercer as to the power of the Judges to set aside the law. He thought no such power ought to exist. He was at the same time at a loss what expedient to substitute. The Justiciary of Arragon he observed became by degrees, the lawgiver." *Ibid.,* p. 549.

being done as required by law, so that he might be minutely instructed as to how he shall perform his discretionary duties in the future.[59] The questions of whether officials had acted lawfully formerly came up in lawsuits between individuals brought to settle their real individual disputes, or in suits brought by government against individuals, such as criminal prosecutions or land condemnations. Under modern "class action" theories, the courts falsely pretend that thousands or hundreds of thousands of people have come into court, through their "representatives," asking that some government official be compelled to do something.

To understand more fully what has happened, we will look at the old English "class action," which was not then known as a class action. In fact, it was not known as anything. It had no name. It was not a type of lawsuit. It was simply called what it was—an exception to a procedural rule. The conversion of this procedural exception into a startlingly different and new type of lawsuit is similar to the Star Chamber's conversion of the civil lawsuit for conspiring or confederating to cause the innocent to be wrongfully indicted into the crime of conspiring to commit either a crime or a civil wrong, regardless of whether any crime or civil wrong were afterwards actually committed.

There is one other attribute of judicial power we must first mention. It is a fundamental attribute of judicial power which holds true in every society and under every system of law. It is one of the characteristic things that distinguishes judicial power from legislative power. Legislatures enact upon the entire mass of citizens. Citizens do not appear before the legislature unless it chooses to hear them. They may ask to be heard, but the request may be either granted or denied. The legislature makes law because it is given power to make law, and it has pleased the legislature to use that power by declaring that a proposed rule is now law binding upon all the people.

Judicial power, on the other hand, does not act upon the mass of people. Instead, it settles a dispute between definite and identified people. It does not act like the biblical king who found himself fascinated by a woman, ordered her husband impressed into the army and placed in a dangerous position, so that after his sudden death, the king was able to take the lovely widow for his own. This was the exercise of regal power by decree, by command, similar to the exercise of legislative power.

Instead, judicial power is exercised by ruling between competing arguers, after giving both sides the equal opportunity to present evidence and arguments.[60] But

---

59. Such questions as the legality of monetary appropriations are not immune from the power of the judiciary to pass upon, if raised in proper judicial proceedings. The customary method of adjudicating such questions is that the officer directed by legislation to spend money is legally advised that the expenditure is constitutionally forbidden, so he refuses to issue a government check. Then the citizen entitled to the check seeks *mandamus* to compel the official to issue his check, as in *Kendall v. United States ex rel. Stokes*. But when the entire legal brotherhood becomes entranced with the idea that mere judicial opinions can replace the Constitution as the supreme law, and the judiciary falls into the habit of seldom recognizing the unconstitutionality of congressional usurpations which increase judicial and governmental powers, it seems never to occur to government lawyers to follow the proper course of advising their superiors to disobey unconstitutional congressional enactments.

60. Commenting upon the fact that no person is bound by a judicial decision unless he has been cited to appear and given the opportunity to be heard on the issues, the Supreme Court said in *Galpin v. Page:* "Judgment without such citation and opportunity wants all the attributes of a *judicial determination;* it is judicial usurpation and oppression, and never can be upheld where justice is justly administered."

to hear, the court must have the contenders before it. And the entire process is in no way voluntary, bcause if the people could voluntarily settle their dispute, they might just as well choose a third individual to mediate it for them without expense, and agree that they would do in accordance with his decision.

In a suit before a judge maintained by governmental power, the person who is being sued is brought before the court by force. This was once done by physically arresting him and bringing him bodily into the presence of the judge; but for about a century, it has been done by issuing a writ, most often called a writ of summons, served upon an individual physically within the state's jurisdiction, commanding him to appear in court and present his defense to the suit against him.

The court's power to pass judgment in the case, if the defendant does not appear and contest it, depends upon there actually having been an order sent out from the court and received by the defendant, served upon him in the place and manner provided by law, commanding him to appear. Otherwise, the court is merely exercising regal power. If I complain that you have run over and killed my child, I cannot go before a judge, tell him the sad story, and receive an order that you pay me a large sum of money. All I can receive is an order that you appear and answer my charges, a writ of summons. In the exercise of judicial power, the order to pay may be made later, or not at all.

But sometimes, a defendant is not present. He may be in another country or another state, so that he cannot be served with the summons. He may simply be hiding out to avoid being served with the writ commanding his appearance. But if he has property within the court's jurisdiction, the court may be authorized by law to seize and hold the defendant's property. This may bring the defendant in to personally submit to the court's jurisdiction. But if he does not then come in to defend the lawsuit, then the lawsuit is tried without him to the extent of the value of his property seized.

This may give the plaintiff less than he is entitled to receive. It cannot give him more than the value of the seized property, because the court has before it only the property, not the defendant. There must be something before the court to give it a real dispute—people who have been commanded to appear and have chosen not to do so, or their property which has been seized to stand in their place to the extent of its value. Without one of these, the court is merely issuing orders to people who have not been brought within its power by being required to appear and defend: It is exercising regal power, not judicial power.

We have seen that one of the attributes of the chancery court was that it did justice where the procedures of the law courts were inadequate. There were remedies in the law courts, types of lawsuits that could be filed, but they simply would not result in the achievement of justice. Often the reason was that the dispute was so complex, that there were so many different people whose interests were involved, that all of them simply could not be brought before a jury in a dispute narrowed down to distinct issues that could be presented to the jury in an orderly manner.

So here was the claim, and the true claim, of the Court of Equity: Where the types of lawsuits that can be filed in the law courts are wholly inadequate to achieve justice, bring your disputes to this court and bring all the disputants before it, and justice will be done to the extent possible. And to assure that entire justice would be done, that the complete mess would be straightened out and no ends left dangling to be the subjects of additional lawsuits going on forever, as

Dickens liked to picture it, the courts of equity required that *every individual* who had any interest in the complex dispute be brought before the Court.

The origin of the so-called "class action" which was not called a class action at the time of our Constitution, was simply this: The chancey courts said that although we have inflexible rules requiring that all parties having any interest in the dispute must be brought before the court, this time, we will dispense with that rule. This time, for very narrow reasons, we will let you maintain your suit in the court of equity even though you have not brought before the court everyone who has an interest in the dispute. We will do this because it is commanded by justice, though we would usually dismiss a suit in which all interested parties are not brought before the court. This was kept from being an exercise of regal power as to the absent defendants because the court of equity had in its control the property owned by the many people who owned interests in it, just as the law courts substitute a defendant's property for the defendant himself when the court seizes control of the property by means of a writ known as the writ of attachment.

The "class action" as it existed when the Constitution was written was not a type of lawsuit at all, but simply an exception to a fundamental procedural rule of the chancery courts. It did not authorize the chancery courts to control government officials and to regulate government conduct and activities. Even as a mere exception to a rule, the "class action" law was still in the process of development, still not completely certain, and still very seldom used, when our government came into being.

Of the English cases most commonly cited as proof that there existed in England a type of lawsuit known as the class action, *none of them* called themselves "class actions," *none of them* involved any pretense that the powers of a court of equity included the power to regulate the conduct of government, but *all of them* related to the ownership of property and to the rights and liabilities that went with property ownership.

In none of the English cases, nor in any other cases cited by them, was the reasoning related to any question except whether the chancery court would go ahead and try the case even though there were many people who were not before the court but who had ownership interests in the property involved.

Typical of the English "class action" cases was the first one truly of this type, *Chancery v. May,* decided in 1722. In that case, eighteen people contributed money and joined into a partnership of eighteen shares to engage in a business. They had to have an organization because there were so many of them, so they elected a manager and a treasurer. As the years passed, the eighteen shares were divided and sold, much as shares of corporate stock are today, so that by 1720, there were eight hundred members of this partnership. At that time, the treasurer and manager were voted out of office and new ones elected. The new manager discovered that the old management team had embezzled over fifty thousand pounds. This sum belonged to the eight hundred owners, among them both the new officers and the old officers. Chancey, of the new management team, sued May, the old treasurer, and others formerly involved in management, for this huge embezzlement, although Chancey owned only a 1/800th share of the stolen money. However, he sued for it to be replaced into the partnership treasury, not to go into his own pocket. He stated in his pleading that he was suing on behalf of all the eight hundred owners except for the few who were being sued for their thievery.

The former officers claimed Chancey could not sue for the entire amount, but only for his limited interest, and that instead, in order to fully settle the property rights involved, all the eight hundred share-owners would have to be brought into the suit, each to receive his own share. All owners must be before the court so that equity could do complete justice to everyone under the usual rule that all parties having an interest in the controversy must be brought before the court of equity. As a practical matter, however, a suit by the one representative, elected by and representing all the owners, and expressly entitled to have possession of the money of all eight hundred owners in his possession, could successfully get the money back into the partnership till where it belonged, and where each of the 800 partners would receive his share by the usual and customary profit-dividing process followed by the group. As the Chancellor put it in *Chancey v. May,* there would be "no coming to justice, if all were to be made parties."

This was the final major English "class action" type of suit in equity commonly cited that was decided before the American Revolution. It was a suit between common owners of property and the Chancery Court was performing its function of doing justice between disputing individuals in a situation in which the law courts could not adequately do justice because it would require eight hundred different lawsuits. There could be no doubt as to the identity of the eight hundred people involved—they were the *known owners* of the partnership property. They were not joined together for the purpose of filing a lawsuit, but the lawsuit happened because of the fact that they were joined together by their ownership interests. And because justice was better served by permitting the chosen representatives of all the common owners of the stolen fund to handle the suit for them, with the recovered fund to go into the existing common treasury, the Court permitted these few plantiffs to represent both themselves and their fellow owners of the same fund.

This is what most [61] of the rest of the English "class action" cases were about.[62]

---

61. The two most often-cited pre-Revolutionary War "class action" cases, *Brown v. Vermuden* (1676) and *The City of London v. Richmond* (1701) were not actually class action situations. *Vermuden* involved a remnant of feudal law, in which the land in an area owed obligations to a lord or a church. A vicar had sued the land, naming a number of prominent land-owners to defend, with the resulting chancery judgment establishing that the land owed the vicar a portion of its lead-ore production, but leaving for a future hearing the question of the price the vicar was entitled to receive for each measure of ore. Years later, a succeeding vicar sought to enforce this old judgment against Brown's land; Brown was not a party to the old suit and his land had not been owned by one of the owners sued in the old case. Contrary to modern "class action" theory, Brown was held not bound by the old judgment but was allowed to file a Bill of Review, which permits complete re-litigation of the case. The *Richmond* case involved a speculative trust designed to make profits out of an engineering water-supply line built to furnish water for London. Richmond was trustee receiving title for hundreds of investors, and Richmond promised to pay London a flat sum each year for all the left-over water after the prisons and tankard-bearers were supplied. The trust beneficiaries purchased shares in the venture, just as corporate stockholders do today, but they didn't promise to pay London anything, though they would be entitled to share the profits. But the venture failed because the pipe only carried 6 tons of water an hour instead of 20 tons as the engineers had predicted. It did not even make enough money in water sales to pay London its annual fee, much less to return a profit to investors. When London sued Richmond for the annual fee, he defended on the claim that all the trust beneficiaries had to be individually sued. But Trustee Richmond alone was liable, and the 900 trust beneficiaries assumed no liability. This was no class action situation in which one individual was allowed to stand in for many.

Suits were either brought on behalf of the common treasury, or else the treasury was effectively seized by subjecting its custodians to the court's injunctive powers, just as law cases were commenced in the defendant's absence by seizing the defendant's property—that is, judicial power was exercised rather than regal power.

The English method of use of the "class action" that nobody called a class action at the time of our Constitution—an exception to the general rule requiring all the common owners of property to be brought before the court in a suit in equity involving the disposition or division of that property—is the method by which the "class action" exception has been used in the federal judicial system for the greater portion of our history. A necessary device in a private lawsuit between individuals where there are a large number of individuals sharing ownership in the same property.

Before the Twentieth Century, it was never thought that individual citizens, even though each possesses a right—a political right—to be governed in accordance with the Constitution, could band together with a large number of other individual citizens, and utilize the nation's judicial power to compel executives and legislative officers to exercise their authority in the manner directed by the Constitution. Never before this century was it thought that this little bit of old English procedural law applied in the courts of equity in property cases could be used as a means for allowing the courts to exercise executive and legislative powers by themselves making executive and legislative decisions and giving instructions as to how executive and legislative powers should be used.

Early American cases were repetitions of the English cases in which persons controlling the treasury of societies of individuals were brought before the courts, the court thereby obtained control of the treasury property, and was able to control its disposition without having all the owners before the court. *Smith v. Swormstedt* is probably the best-known early decision of the Supreme Court. Suit was filed by the complainants for themselves and on behalf "of the travelling and worn-out preachers in connection with the Society of the Method Episcopal Church South . . . against the defendants to recover share of a fund called the Book Concern . . . claimed to be of the value of some $200,000."

At the time of the Civil War, the Methodist Church split, and the southern branch went its separate way. The Book Concern, which subsequently became the Methodist Publishing House, had then long been in operation to make profits

---

62. All the other English "class action" cases involved the effective seizure of a jointly-owned fund of money by litigating whether an injunction should be issued against individuals holding the fund. In addition to *Chancey v. May* (1722), discussed above in the text, were *Good v. Blewitt* (1807), *Pearce v. Piper* (1808), *Cockburn v. Thompson* (1809), and *Meux v. Maltby* (1818). The *Blewitt* case was a suit by a ship captain against the owners to obtain his and the crew's percentage shares of prize money from a privateer operation, with the money held by the court itself for future division among the sailors who might appear and prove their claims. All the other cases involved the common treasury of a business-type venture. Typical is the *Cockburn* case, in which many persons contributed money to a joint treasury to be used in forming a corporation known as the Philanthropic Annuity Association, and when they were unable to qualify for incorporation, some of the contributors sought an injunction compelling the treasurer to make a *pro rata* refund to all contributors. It was an exercise of judicial power because the court had the fund within its physical jurisdiction and could dispose of it. Yet Lord Eldon, a most learned and competent Lord Chancellor, evinced considerable strain over whether the court of equity could do this without all the owners being before the court.

to care for worn-out preachers in their retirement. Those in the northern branch did not seek to hinder their southern brethren's departure, but did seek to keep all the money. The southerners claimed they were entitled to their share of the wealth as members of the same original organization. It would have been pointless to require all southern Methodist preachers to join in suing the northern preachers for division of the common treasury; those representing the organization of the southern preachers were allowed to sue the northern preachers who controlled the sum of wealth and property known as the Book Concern, so that the Court had that wealth under its control and could divide it between the contending owners in the exercise of ordinary judicial power.

"Class actions" continued into the 1920's to be simply a convenient means of allowing a suit to be maintained on behalf of thousands of people to protect their identical but separate ownership interests in a single large fund of money, where separate suits might unjustly increase the shares of some and thereby diminish the shares of others: Cases in which the funds of the entire group were owned by individuals comprising the group and no co-owner owned an identifiable separate stack of coins.

This is similar to our relation with the Government of the United States, but the relation between each of us and the Government is not one of ownership of property. It is the relation of citizen to his government. If the Government misbehaves in its general conduct, as distinct from its relation to a single individual, our only legitimate remedy is and must always remain the joint political remedy. But the Twentieth Century saw the birth and growth of the idea that people might sue to protect some general interest distinct and different from common ownership of particular property or wealth.

Usurpation for the Protection of Classes:

The year 1950 saw the combining of spurious class action thinking with the idea that courts of equity might regulate governmental officials in a conflict regarding a subject more exciting than the joint ownership of a treasury—Communism. The case was *Joint Anti-Fascist Refugee Committee v. McGrath.* McGrath was Attorney-General of the United States. Concerned over possible Communist infiltration into the Federal Government,[63] Congress amended the Hatch Act, governing political activities by federal employees, to empower the President to weed out civil service employees whose loyalty to the United States was suspect. A part of the program involved the determination of whether different organizations that government employees might join came within the categories of totalitarian, fascist, communist, or subversive organizations. These determinations were to be made by the Attorney General, who was to maintain a list of such organizations, generally viewed as a list of Communist or Communist-front organizations.[64]

The Attorney-General made official determination that the Joint Anti-Fascist Refugee Committee was such an organization, and the Committee sued the

---

63. For factual description, See *Dennis v. United States,* above, pp. 142-144.

64. The Attorney-General was required by statute to publish the names of such suspect organizations in the *Federal Register,* a publication in which federal regulations must be published to become effective. He published the name of the Joint Anti-Fascist Refugee Committee, with the result that any federal employee who was a member was required, in order to retain his employment, to demonstrate that he was a loyal American citizen in a Loyalty Review Board hearing.

Attorney-General for an injunction requiring the removal of its name from the subversive list. The Committee complained that the list damaged its fund-raising capacities, and the procedure for listing the Committee was itself high-handed, because the Committee was given no advance notice and no right to defend itself before the Attorney-General, no right to present evidence to him. This complaint was quite true. The Executive Order, the means by which the President had given instructions to his inferior, the Attorney-General, in the discharge of the presidential duty to take care that the laws be enforced, directed the Attorney-General to place organizations on the list only after an "appropriate determination" had been made by him that such organizations came within one of the condemned categories.

The Committee was refused the injunction it sought by both the trial court and the Court of Appeals,[65] but the Supreme Court reversed these decisions, and sent the case back for trial. The Court said:

> "An 'appropriate' governmental 'determination' must be the result of the process of reasoning. It cannot be by arbitrary fiat contrary to the known facts. This is inherent in the meaning of 'determination.' It is implicit in a government of laws and not of men. Where an act of an official plainly falls outside the scope of his authority, he does not make that act legal by doing it and then invoking the doctrine of administrative construction to cover it."

The Supreme Court held that the mode of proceeding before the Attorney-General, on hearsay reports from FBI agents or on whatever basis the Attorney-General used for his listing, was lacking in due process of law. But the Constitution does not command that the Government shall always follow due process of law; it commands only that a person's life, liberty, or property not be taken without due process of law. Government employment is itself neither life, nor liberty, nor property; all employment is terminable at the will of either the employer or the employee, with or without reason, unless it is protected by private contract or by some special law, such as the civil service laws. By the Hatch Act Amendment, the civil service laws were effectively changed, and such employment became terminable by reason of suspicion, just as it was formerly terminable by reason of political motivation.[66] So there was no constitutional violation

---

65. The Court of Appeals, whose opinion was titled *Joint Anti-Fascist Refugee Committee v. Clark,* pointed out that the Attorney-General was only doing for the President that which the President could have done personally without being subjected to injunctions telling him how to perform his duties. The Court then said: ". . . [only] the members, not the Committee, can seek redress for alleged impairment of the members' constitutional rights of freedom of speech and assembly. Those rights are personal to the individual members. . . . Contrary to the contentions of the Committee, nothing in the Hatch Act or the loyalty program deprives the Committee or its members of any property rights. Freedom of speech and assembly is denied to no one. Freedom of thought and belief is not impaired. Anyone is free to join the Committee and give it his support and encouragement. Everyone has a constitutional right to do these things, but no one has a constitutional right to be a government employee."

66. Excellent judicial rules, absolutely essential to the fair administration of justice, can be utterly stupid when applied to other situations of everyday life. The presumption of innocence until one has been proven guilty beyond a reasonable doubt is essential when the state is endeavoring to imprison a citizen and deprive him of his liberty for many years to come. In everyday life, the fact that a man is merely highly suspected of committing repeated rapes or embezzlements is adequate to persuade any

in this case, and the Constitution carefully withheld any grant of over-riding authority to the courts to supervise the other departments of government which by design stand separate from and superior to the courts except in the decision of individual lawsuits.

The Supreme Court based its decision upon the language of the presidential order to the Attorney-General in which the President instructed that such listings of subversive organizations should be made upon the basis of an "appropriate determination" of facts. What is appropriate when the purpose of the inquiry is to remove disloyal citizens from public employment and when one of the essentials of such inquiry is that the scope of knowledge the government has gained be kept highly secret? The type of inquiry required under these circumstances, not involving the taking of life, liberty or property, might call forth different opinions, but to government faced with infiltration of the type feared in the 1950's, then the revelation to the enemy of the full scope of information and its sources might appear to the President to be foolish.[67] If the President, instructing his Attorney-General to make an "appropriate determination," should be dissatisfied with the manner in which the Attorney-General carried out his instructions, he could instantly, effectively, and completely control the way the Attorney-General carried out his instructions.

In presuming to regulate the manner in which the Attorney-General carried out the President's instructions, the Supreme Court exercised power belonging only to the President, executive power, in violation of the constitutional provision giving that power only to the President, and in exercising supervisory authority over the manner in which executive officials performed their discretionary duties, the Court exercised Star Chamber jurisdiction, not given by the Constitution to any federal court.

The combination of the spurious "equity powers" and spurious class action rationalizations came into full flower in a 1968 case, *Flast v. Cohen.* Flast was one of a number of citizens, a member of a "class" composed of taxpayers, presumably pretending to have authority from some source to represent all the taxpayers in the country. Congress had passed an act, donating public money to improve the elementary and secondary education programs administered by the various states, particularly as such programs benefitted low-income families and underpriviledged children, a subject which is not and never has been any of the business of the United States Government.

Flast and her fellow-plaintiffs sued as federal income-tax payers to obtain an injunction under the powers of federal courts to decide cases in equity. Flast

---

prudent individual not to entrust him with his daughter for a date or his money for safe-keeping. All prudent men act upon probabilities and mere suspicions in important matters, at the same time agreeing that a very high degree of certainty should be demanded when government moves in judicial proceedings to take one's life, liberty or property.

67. In one of the several opinions in this case, a member of the Court wrote: "In this day when prejudice, hate and fear are constantly invoked to justify irresponsible smears and persecution of persons even faintly suspected of entertaining unpopular views, it may be futile to suggest that the cause of internal security would be fostered, not hurt, by painful adherence to our constitutional guarantees of individual liberty." This political and moral observation expresses wisdom above that of the witch-hunting zeal of frightened public officials. But it was more suited for public or political utterance than for judicial writing in a case not within the judicial power of the United States.

granted her (and supposedly my, your and all other taxpayers') approval of the use of federal tax funds to aid the underprivileged in educational institutions not operated by religious bodies, so that this part of the program was safe, condoned and verified as good by all those taxpayers Flast somehow got the authority to represent. However, Flast objected strenuously to the use of tax funds so as to aid, directly or indirectly, in the operation of schools by any religious organization, claiming that this would be "a law respecting an establishment of religion" in violation of the First Amendment. The Supreme Court's opinion does not reveal that she claimed that the use of this "Federal money" to finance teaching ordinary academic subjects in church-operated schools increased her tax bill in any appreciable amount, or that she had sought a refund of her overpayment of taxes in that amount. She merely desired, with the aid of the courts, to supervise expenditures by executive officers of the United States.

The suit could not be maintained under the rationale of *Frothingham v. Massachusetts*,[68] so the question was presented as to whether that case was correctly decided. The Supreme Court began its discussion of the powers of federal courts under Article III, the Judicial Article of the Constitution. The Court said: "In terms relevant to the question for decision in this case, the judicial power of federal courts is Constitutionally restricted to 'cases' and 'controversies.' " But the word "cases" does not appear all by itself; it appears as a part of the phrase "cases in law and in equity."

The Court then discussed at length the question of whether the limited capacity of a citizen as a taxpayer actually constitutionally *prevented* the courts from entertaining suits by taxpayers to regulate the Government, or whether this was simply an example of judicial restraint, with the courts actually having the regulatory power but having restrained themselves from using it out of respect for the other departments of government. The Court then proceeded to announce its ruling, without any rational demonstration of its source or validity, that as long as a citizen is a taxpayer, he can maintain a suit to prohibit government officials from taking action if the government action would violate some express prohibition of the Constitution, like the prohibition against establishing a religion as contained in the First Amendment. As a source of this particular ruling of law, the Court cited nothing. Among all the rights and prohibitions contained in the Constitution, there is no constitutional provision that the benefit of any of these protections shall inure more fully to taxpaying citizens than to non-taxpaying citizens. The Court could just as well have said that *Massachusetts v. Mellon* involved protection afforded pregnant mothers of unborn children, while *Flast v. Cohen* involved protections for children already born. This would have been just as valid a distinction, and like the distinction between taxpaying and non-taxpaying plaintiffs, would have made not the slightest difference. Nor is any difference found in the distinction between congressional acts violating express prohibitions of the Constitution and those acts not authorized by the Constitution. For those acts not authorized are expressly removed from the powers of Congress by the Tenth Amendment to the Constitution. The perception of this requires no deep and abstract reasoning ability. All it requires is legislative, executive, and judicial willingness to read and obey.

The Supreme Court stated that it did not overrule *Frothingham v. Mellon*. But one member of the Court contended that the *Frothingham* decision should be overruled, saying:

---

68. Summarized above, pp. 239-242.

"The judiciary is an indespensible part of the operation of our federal system. With the growing complexities of government it is often the only place where effective relief can be obtained. *If the judiciary were to become a super-legislative group sitting in judgment on the affairs of the people, the situation would be intolerable.* But where wrongs to individuals are done by violation of specific guarantees,[69] it is an abdication for courts to close their doors.

"I would not be niggardly therefore in giving private attorneys-generals [70] standing to sue. I would certainly not wait for Congress to give its blessing to our deciding cases clearly within our Article III jurisdiction. To wait for a sign from Congress is to allow important constitutional questions to go undecided and personal liberty unprotected."

The learned justice did not give any suggestion as to where the courts supposedly obtained power to combat the evil of allowing "important constitutional questions to go undecided." As to "wrongs to individuals" done by "violation of specific guarantees," the writer gave no hint as to how *any* individual might be wronged, or his liberty restrained, by using funds from the Federal treasury to buy an arithmetic book for a Catholic or Jewish child, or for many such children. The opinion must surely have had some logical coherence to its writer, but that coherence, if it exists, is deeply concealed.

The only infringement of personal rights was simply the slight taxation of the citizen for purposes not authorized by the Constitution. The Constitution does not grant Congress the power to do works of charity.[71] Insofar as tax money is extorted from the individual taxpayer by force of law, that individual's rights are infringed when the money is taken from him for the illegal purpose of giving it to others, but he has legal recourse by the ordinary course of law to protect this infinitesimal sum of his property from government seizure, at least if the taxing law earmarkes the money for its intended illegal use. *Flast v. Cohen* did not involve the existence or infringement of any constitutional rights or individual rights or liberties. It involved only an insistence by Citizen Flast, and those of limited number who joined her, that obedience to the commands of the Constitution should be enforced to the extent, *but only to the extent,* they wanted enforcement.[72]

---

69. This is an inaccurate reference, because the First Amendment contains no specific guarantees. It only contains prohibitions against the use of power by the Federal Government, judicially altered into a greater prohibition against state governments and a lesser prohibition against the Federal Government. See above, pp. 137-149.

70. Legislative action has sometimes authorized what may accurately be called "private attorney-general" law enforcement in particular cases. These are known as *qui tam* actions, in which any citizen is authorized to sue to enforce a statutory penalty against anyone engaging in the reprehensible conduct condemned by the statute; these laws sometimes give all the penalty money to the citizen who sues, and sometimes divide it between him and the government. There was no legal *qui tam* authorization enacted in this case.

71. Even if one assumes it to be an act of charity to "give" money seized by legal processes from its owners, as distinguished from the sacrifice of one's own money voluntarily brought about by charitable motivations.

72. A far sounder, more responsible, and more judicial attitude was shown by Mr. Justice Harlan, who rejected the supposition that the federal courts could regulate the manner of performance of the executive functions of government at the request of individual citizens. He wrote: "The taxpayer cannot ask the return of any portion of his previous tax payments, cannot prevent the collection of an existing tax debt, and

When judges claim power to tell government officials how to discharge their duties, in minute detail, then judges are exercising the powers of those governmental officials. Whether a federal court is acting as Secretary of Health, Education and Welfare, as a local school board or as a prison warden governing prisoners, the formulation of instructions as to how government officials shall perform their duties, in the absence of the invasion of an individual citizen's legal rights, is a power exercised by the judiciary only by usurpation. It is a violation of the Constitution. Such violations carry with them the seeds of immense harm to the body politic and diminish the existence of the republican form of government. They can only eventuate in judicial tyranny.

---

cannot demand adjudication of the propriety of any particular level of taxation. His tax payments are received for the general purposes of the United States, and are, upon proper receipt, lost in the general revenues. . . . The interests he represents, and the rights he espouses, are, as they are in all public actions, those held in common by all citizens. To describe those rights and interests as personal, and to intimate that they are in some unspecified fashion to be differentiated from those of the general public, reduces constitutional standing to a word game played by secret rules. . . . I do not doubt but there must be 'some effectual power in the government to restrain or correct the infractions' of the Constitution's several commands, but neither can I suppose that such power resides only in the federal courts. We must as judges recall that, as Mr. Justice Holmes wisely observed, the other branches of the Government 'are ultimate guardians of the liberties and welfare of the people in quite as great a degree as the courts.' . . . The powers of the federal judiciary will be adequate for the great burdens placed upon them only if they are employed prudently, with recognition of the strengths as well as hazards that go with our kind of representative government."

X

THE REPUBLICAN GUARANTEE

FROM THEIR OWN past experience and historical knowledge that democracies become tyrannical because of their immediate over-reaction to supposed evils, from their dread of the return to monarchy, and from their fear that a continent of small states would lead to neighborhood wars and invite foreign aggression, the men who wrote the Constitution settled upon the republican form of government. They settled upon the federated republic as the most perfect form of government, with a federal government presiding over numerous small state governments, but with each state government having total governing power and responsibility within the spheres in which its power existed.

The republican form of government differs from mob rule, which is democracy. Democracy, the unpredictable government by the whims of an entire mass of people, is probably inherently more tyrannical than any other form of government. But in the republican form of government, the people do not govern; they *are governed* by a government. The people do not own the money in the public treasury; the government owns it. The essence of the republican form of government is that although we do not govern ourselves but are governed by a government, it is a government whose office-holders, exercising *their* judgment or discretion as to how we shall be governed, are elected by us and are answerable to us in the public elections. If they exercise their judgment in a manner unacceptable to us, then we, not individually but by the massed weight of our numbers, may refuse to return them to office. But always, it is their judgment, not ours, that governs us.

In the hope of forever protecting the people in each state from tyrannical government in their daily lives, it was provided in the Constitution that the "United States shall guarantee to each State a republican form of government." Such command, coupled with the law-making power given Congress by the Necessary and Proper Clause, required and empowered Congress to perpetuate republican government in each state, and not to permit such governments to deteriorate into either democracies or dictatorships.

This command, though addressed to the entire government of the United States, has been viewed as a command to Congress rather than the judiciary, because Congress has the power to appoint registration officials, schedule an election, and ordain a new state convention to permit the people to write a new state constitution. The judiciary lacks the capacity to attempt such a venture. It has no control over either the purse-strings to finance it or the sword to protect it from the existing powers of a non-republican state government.

The people choose their rulers in the republican form of government. But to be republican in form, government does not have to imitate the structure of the Federal Government, which was itself based upon the structure of the British Government. Many variations might be suggested. A state could provide for a small council of wise men elected by the people of the entire state, to be empowered to affirm or veto detailed laws suggested by the executive; the council might be empowered to nominate a small number of persons from among the city mayors in the state, with the people to choose from among the nominees. Such a government would be republican in form.

But when a state government imitates the federal government in form and organization, as all of them do to varying extent, problems arise. There are questions as to who shall be permitted to vote and when legislators are selected from different geographic areas, problems arise from shifts in population. Different areas electing one legislator each may start with populations about equal, but the shifting population results in a small number of people being able to elect one legislator, while in another area, a much larger number of people are also permitted to elect only one legislator.

This situation occurred during the first half of the Twentieth Century, doubtless greatly amplified by the vast improvements industry made in manufacturing techniques, transportation, communications and farm mechanization. Yet though Congress was required to guarantee to each state a government republican in form, no provision of the Constitution made any specifications nor empowered Congress to make any specifications as to the size or population of legislative districts electing delegates to the state legislatures. As urban pressures for a greater voice in government rapidly increased, the Federal Constitution was searched for some basis which could be used to compel state governmental reformation to more nearly accord with the thinking of urban majorities. The only provision of the Constitution that might be stretched to render aid in this situation was the Equal Protection Clause of the Fourteenth Amendment. It was on the basis of this clause that the Supreme Court finally ruled that the courts could remedy the worsening situation.

The Equal Protection Clause. With that label, one can envision all sorts of equality that may be required by the federal judiciary. But in reading and pondering its actual language, without any preconceived desire to reach a particular result, one finds in the Equal Protection Clause one of the most puzzling concepts for practical application in the entire Constitution. And it is one of the greatest concepts for the protection of human rights to be found in the Constitution. As such, it has been misused in much the same manner as the Due Process Clause of the Fourteenth Amendment.[1] Before venturing into what has been called the quagmire of legislative apportionment, we should carefully consider the meaning of this clause that has afforded deliverance from the quagmire.

Equal Protection of the Laws:

This clause brings to mind the same ideas as that conveyed by the Declaration of Independence in its statement that all men are created equal. But it has some of the same draw-backs as Jefferson's declaration, because all men are not created equal except in the sense that each is born naked and shocked at the traumatic ejection from the warm, safe nest. Some are born with the brains of an Einstein or a Newton, but most are not; some with the voice of a Carouso, but most can hardly sing; some with great beauty, but most without enough beauty to attract much attention, many quite plain, and some even ugly; some are born with strong and vigorous bodies, others with incurable defects that condemn them to a brief span of a few painful years.

Human equality, on any scale on which one may desire to measure it, exists only in daydreams and wishful thinking. Thomas Jefferson knew that men are created unequal. The Equal Protection Clause of the Fourteenth Amendment was not written in the light of an unthinking reading of Jefferson's declaration

1. See above, Chapter VII.

that all men are created equal.[2] It was written in the light of the idea Jefferson expressed—that before the law, the artificial but powerful majesty of the law, as before God, each citizen as an individual must be equal to each other citizen as an individual, regardless of their different talents and stations in life.[3]

Let us consider a few possibilities about the meaning of equal protection of the laws, reminding ourselves that this is a new part of the Supreme Law of the Land: "No *State* shall . . . deny to any person within its jurisdiction the equal protection of the laws." It may be that measures we would like to achieve we can no longer achieve, no matter how wise their achievement appears to be. For equality before the law of the state is now commanded.

I am free to come and go as I wish, and my freedom is protected by law. I may sue whoever interferes with this freedom in an illegal manner, and if I am kidnapped, officers of the law will come to my aid to the fullest possible extent. But another man is totally denied his freedom, the law itself commanding that he cannot move. He is denied the freedom I enjoy because he is a prisoner in the state penitentiary. The law guarantees my freedom to the widest possible extent and the law of the same state totally destroys my fellow citizen's freedom. Is this a denial of equal protection of the laws? Is it forbidden by the Constitution? Or will we disregard the Constitution and be governed instead by our sense of practicality, by an assertion that government *must be able* to imprison criminals?

My neighbor and I can walk into a building that is open to the public, but he, by virtue of status granted him by law, is given access to many parts of the building that I am denied the right to enter. Many people work in the building, and they eagerly cater to his slightest wish because of the status given him by law, while my wishes are of no consequence there. The protection, the privileges he enjoys there because of his legal status greatly exceed that given me. The reason is that the place is a hospital and he is a licensed medical doctor. The license was granted to him by the state government. Is this a denial of equal protection of the laws?

I am free to come and go as I wish all day long, almost without limit except as I may intrude upon the rights of others. Four members of my family are denied this freedom; they are in the custody of state authorities, charged by law with the obligation to obey those state authorities, and totally deprived of their individual freedom. They are school children. The state forces them to attend school every day and it doesn't require me to attend school at all. Is this a denial of equal protection of the laws—with one set of laws applying to me and another set applying to my children?

We feel that the Equal Protection Clause cannot be applied to outlaw such necessary laws as these. And if all of them are not necessary,[4] does the mere desirability of law make law permissible if it actually denies equal protection of the laws to different citizens? Most laws which treat different people differently exist because they were desired and because there was some logical reason

2. Not expressed as an isolated abstraction, the Declaration expresses the idea of equality in the endowment with inalienable rights, including the rights to life, liberty and the pursuit of happiness.

3. Even this concept of equality before the law is contrary to the practical ends men desire to use state law to achieve. Men do not desire equality; they want superiority, if not in ability, then in the recognition and share of the wealth they receive.

4. Many people believe no one should be imprisoned for any act, many believe that public schools are a mistake, that it is unfair to require one man to pay for the education of another's children.

for treating people differently. Some reason always exists or can be contrived.

But if we concede that laws which do not actually afford equal protection to different people may be legitimated simply because there is a legitimate reason to treat different people differently, we are assigning to the Equal Protection Clause the same test of reasonableness that the Courts have substituted for the meaning of the Due Process Clause. The Fourteenth Amendment does not say that no state shall deny equal protection of its laws to people unless the state has a good reason for doing so. There is no qualification in the Equal Protection Clause. It completely and totally takes from state government the power to deny equal protection of its laws to any person within its jurisdiction.

The Equal Protection Clause may fairly be read with common sense, and with the assumption that those who wrote it had common sense. It means what it says in the light of American tradition, that every person should stand equal before the law. One man is in prison while I am free. But the same law applies to both of us, equally and impartially, and the only reason he is imprisoned while I am free is that he chose to commit a crime and I chose not to do so. My doctor friend and I once stood equal before the law, each of us uneducated, each of us denied the right to perform surgical operations by laws prohibiting mayhem and the unauthorized practice of medicine. He chose to go to medical school, to do the things required by state law that any citizen must do to achieve the right to practice medicine. I was free to follow that course, but I decided not to do so. We were treated equally. And even my child and I are treated equally, because each of us faces a requirement that he attend school a minimum number of years beginning at the age of six. It simply happens that I have fulfilled that requirement and he has not. But it applies equally to each of us.

Some of these obvious examples, can be viewed in an unquestioning manner as having as their basis the assumption that when there is some reasonable and explainable reason for a law, then the state can treat people differently, sending the criminal to prison and leaving the upright man free. This unthinking assumption would say that particular laws may be made applicable only to particular classes of people, like children, women, criminals, doctors, lawyers, farmers. But this is not the valid distinction between the obvious examples we have noted. The Equal Protection Clause requires that each person be given equal protection of the laws, and when penalties fall on some and favors come to others by virtue of law, it must not be because the people are given different degrees of protection of the laws.

The different treatment accorded by law must be so accorded because all are treated the same instead of being treated differently: All rewarded or penalized according to *their own acts done after the law was formulated.* Equal Protection of the Laws can be given extremely valuable meaning—its natural meaning— without qualifying it by any test of reasonableness. When one so qualifies it, he says that the state does not have to accord equal protection of the laws to all people, but can deny such equal protection whenever the state has any reason acceptable to judges. This destroys the entire purpose of the Equal Protection Clause and is directly contrary to its express language.[5]

---

5. When two children lived side by side, one black and one white, and one child was permitted to go to a nearby school while the other was denied that right, the two children were denied equal protection of the laws. It makes no difference whether the denial was reasonable or unreasonable, based upon unfair discriminatory motives or upon rational or rationalized theories. The Fourteenth Amendment's Equal Protection Clause prohibits a denial of equal protection of the laws *for any reason or upon any theory.*

But what of natural differences? Men are men and women are women. When a law provides that a woman may be employed no more than six hours a day while a man may be employed eight hours a day, they are denied equal protection of the laws. There were reasons thought adaquate for this difference in the protections furnished by law to different individuals because of their individual attributes. But the Equal Protection Clause was designed to destroy the powers of state laws to treat different people differently. Government finds it very difficult to accept the fact that the Equal Protection Clause by its plain language, without the modifying interpretations that directly conflict with its words, totally denies state government the power to grant special privileges to any person or groups of persons, except by general laws which offer that privilege to every person who may do the things specified for achievement of the privilege.

If a state's laws permit anyone to operate a taxicab, all receive equal protection of the law. Great qualifications may be added, such as requirements that people have license tags on their taxicabs, that they have drivers' licenses, that they have insurance coverage in large amounts, that they have physical examinations to assure that they may safely drive without injury to the public, and many other such regulations. As long as the requirements, however slight or however burdensome, apply equally to everyone who wants to drive a taxicab, all receive equal protection of the laws.

But add to this one additional requirement: Taxicab drivers shall not exceed a certain number, because if there are more than that number, there will be more than the public needs. Then when that number is filled, those citizens—twenty or one hundred or however many—are granted the privilege of driving taxicabs by complying with the laws, and all other citizens are denied the right to obtain the privilege of driving taxicabs though willing and able to comply with those same laws. This is a denial of equal protection of the laws. No matter how excellent a reason a state may have for giving superior privileges to some people and denying them to others, the Constitution forbids each state to deny equal protection of its laws to any person within its borders.

And so to the right to vote. The weight of that vote. The distribution of voters. How many candidates a voter can vote for and how many voters a candidate can appeal to. In *Baker v. Carr,* persons from Memphis, Nashville, Knoxville and Chattanooga, Tennessee, claimed that they were being denied equal protection of the laws because they were not allowed to vote for a number of candidates according to the comparative populations of their cities and of the small counties of the state. But if Equal Protection of the Laws applies to voting rights, were the city people being denied equal protection, or were the small county people being denied equal protection? Extensive information furnished in the Supreme Court's opinion revealed that people in the county in which Memphis is located were allowed to elect eight representatives to the State Legislature. As a comparison between the treatment of individual citizens rather than a consideration of problems involved in the organization of a republican form of government, which was given less protection, the rural man allowed to cast one vote for one legislator, or the urban man allowed to cast eight separate votes for eight legislators?

This is a more accurate inquiry: Can it be said that the Equal Protection Clause has any application whatever to voting rights? The right to vote has never existed without the imposition of qualifications which had to be met before the individual could aquire the right to vote. There are good reasons for this, but the Equal Protection Clause in its language is qualified by no grant of permission of states to deny equal protection of its laws to some people even if the state has a good reason for doing this.

Here, again, we find an aspect of practicality not before considered. The Equal Protection Clause is not designed for the protection of citizens; it is designed for the protection of people, all people. The wise, the fool, the sane, the insane, the adult, the child, the American, the foreigner, are each entitled to equal protection of the laws. The Russian attending college in New York City is a person. Can the state of New York deny him the right to vote in its elections, eventuating in a denial to him of the right to vote in American presidential elections? There is no doubt but that the people who wrote and voted for the adoption of the Fourteenth Amendment knew that the protection of its Equal Protection Clause was to be extended to foreigners as well as to Americans, to every human being who should come within the jurisdiction and power of a state government. This was declared repeatedly on the floors of both the Senate and the House of Representatives during the debates which led to the adoption of the Fourteenth Amendment, and some legislators were quite unhappy about this aspect of its application.

In the debates, great dissatisfaction was expressed over the thought that the proposed amendment would extend to Indians rights identical to those enjoyed by the people generally, and California was unhappy at the threat that such rights would be extended to Chinese aliens living within its borders. However, it was fully understood and acknowledged by Congress that the benefits of the Equal Protection Clause, like the Due Process Clause, would inure to the benefit of foreigners, travellers, and persons from other states, just as it would inure to the benefit of citizens of the state.

But it was not their understanding that a state, in permitting the people in one of its counties to vote, must extend that right to vote for a member of the state legislature to a vacationer temporarily camping in the county, equally as it might extend that right to a citizen and taxpayer with a vital interest in the selection of a state legislator. It was not the understanding of the Congress that the Equal Protection Clause addressed itself to the right to vote. Because Congress understood this, and accepted this, Congress went further and proposed the Fifteenth Amendment to prohibit states from denying any person the right to vote on account of his race. This was done because the Equal Protection Clause—by then fully adopted as part of the Constitution—had nothing to do with voting rights.

The distinction in the Equal Protection Clause, which is a valid one, and which was understood by those who wrote and debated it, is the distinction between treating all people equally on the one hand, and on the other hand, giving all people the equal protection of the laws. Protection of the laws is extended by the governing authority over the people governed, that is, over all persons, citizens or non-citizens, who might at that moment be physically within the state and subject to the government's powers.

But constitutions speak primarily of another subject, and that is the organization of government itself. While one man may serve as governor, all men may not serve as governor at the same time. The existence of public office implies that some person will be installed in such office and will wield the powers of the office and that *all other persons* will be excluded from that office and the exercise of its powers. The concept of equal protection of the laws refers to the existence of governing powers over the people, and not to the internal organization of the government itself. Not everyone can be a legislator. Being a legislator is not a part of the business of being furnished protection by state law, but is instead participation in the operation of state government.

Under the Equal Protection Clause, if the clause be given its natural meaning, anyone can engage in any type of work for the purpose of earning a livelihood and the state laws cannot limit types of work to particular persons and exclude all other persons from following that line of work. But in the operation of its government, each of its legislative seats must be filled by one person and all other persons must be excluded from that seat.

In considering the republican form of government, no one has ever contended that every person within a geographical area should be permitted to vote—to participate in the governmental function of selecting individuals to perform the functions assigned to various governmental offices. At the time of the formation of the Constitution and when the Fourteenth Amendment was written, voting was regarded as an act of participation in government. This was an essential part of the operation of a republican form of government. At both times, it was specified by law who should fill this particular office, the office of acting as an *elector* for certain other offices.

When the Constitution was written, it was specified that the *electors* voting for Congressmen should, in each state, have the same qualifications as the *electors* for members of the lower or most numerous house of the state legislature, and this is still provided by the Constitution. At that time, the persons who were to choose the United States Senators were *electors* defined by the Constitution, and *these electors* were the members of the state legislature rather than the people. The *electors* who elected the president were also officers of government performing a function of government, the function of electing the President of the United States. These, also, were identified by the Constitution as *electors,* who were directed to be chosen in such manner as the state legislature might direct. In each state the legislature had the full power to provide the method of choosing *electors* to perform the governmental function of electing the President of the United States. One state's legislature might provide that the entire legislature should choose the presidential *electors;* another might provide that the *electors* would be popularly elected by the people; and another might provide for the selection of these *electors* by a convention.

Different persons serve as electors for different offices. In a given state, a governor may serve as the elector or appointing authority who selects many of the officers who exercise particular governmental powers. Some officials may be chosen by the members of the legislature, acting as electors for those offices. Some may be chosen by city councils, county courts, or other bodies, and the choice of people who will appoint or elect officers of government is a part of the functioning of government itself. The Equal Protection Clause refers to the exercise of the *power of government by the state over the people within its jurisdiction*. It has nothing to do with the organization or operation of government itself and the selection of persons to perform the various functions of government.

The Equal Protection Clause, in its literal and natural meaning, has no bearing upon the right of individuals to vote,[6] upon the question of how many legislators

---

6. The Equal Protection Clause did not, when it was written, have anything to do with the right to vote, because when one exercises the right to vote, he is performing a function of government for the benefit of himself and his fellow-citizens, though selfish motivations will sometimes govern the way he performs this governmental function. But personal motivations also have their effect in the performance of the functions of office in many higher offices of government, from the city halls to the presidential office.

or congressmen shall represent a particular area, or upon any other aspect of the process for electing public officials. This is why Congress proposed and the states accepted the Fifteenth Amendment, concerning the rights of Negro to vote,[7] the Seventeenth Amendment, changing the electors who choose United States Senators from the members of the state legislature to the electors for the largest house of the state legislature, the Nineteenth Amendment, concerning women's rights to vote, and the Twenty-First Amendment, providing that the right to vote for federal officials should not be denied or abridged by any reason of the failure of any person to pay a poll tax or any other tax.

The Constitution expressly speaks of the effect of amendments. It provides the machinery for adopting amendments and it states that when any amendment shall have been adopted, it "shall be valid *to all intents and purposes, as a part of this Constitution, . . .*" The Constitution commands that each amendment shall be considered not merely as a change in the Constitution as it previously stood, but as a *part of* the Constitution to the same extent as if it had originally been written into the Constitution. This is a command to be observed by Congress in proposing amendmens and to be observed by the courts in construing those amendments.

In the light of this constitutional command, how does the Equal Protection of the Laws provision stand? The Constitution commands in Article I that the electors for Congressmen, and in the Seventeenth Amendment that the electors for Senators, shall be the same as the electors for the members of the lower house of the state legislature. This recognizes and condones the state practice of giving some the right and denying others the right to be electors for the lower house of the legislature; it directly contradicts any supposition that the Equal Protection Clause requires the state to permit every person to be an elector for the lower house of its legislature. There is nothing in the Constitution that *entitles any person* to be an elector for the lower house of the state legislature; but there are provisions that forbid the state from denying persons the right to vote in *any* election—lower house of the legislature, governor, city council, or any other office, for particular reasons, the voter's *sex* or *race*. But black people and women may still be denied the right to vote for the lower house of the legislature, and therefore for senators and congressmen, for reasons of their failure to meet voting qualifications *unrelated* to sex or race. These distinctions in the Constitution would be pointless—indeed, meaningless—if the same Constitution mandatorily required the state to extend equal rights to serve as electors to all persons in all elections.

The Fourteenth Amendment itself, addresses itself to a state denial to persons of the right to vote. It says that if any state shall deny any of its adult male inhabitants the right to vote, then the populaion of the state, for the purpose of congressional apportionment—deciding how many congressmen the entire state is entitled to elect—shall be reduced by the number of adult males the state has denied the right to vote. This would not only be unnecessary but inane if the Equal Protection Clause appearing in the same amendment commanded that the state allow all citizens, and indeed all persons, to exercise the right to vote and thereby to participate in the government of the state.

7. None of these amendments *entitles* the protected group to vote. Instead, they merely deny the state the power to refuse to permit the person to vote *by reason of race, sex, etc.* It is not denial of the right to vote that is now constitutionally prohibited, but the denial for specific reasons.

In reading cold documents, we cannot divorce ourselves from reality and forget the circumstances under which those documents were written.[8] What if everybody in Congress was certain that by writing the Equal Protection Clause, which applies to foreigners as well as Americans, there was being secured to the freed Negro citizens the right to vote in all elections? We would have to take this fact into account to truthfully explore the meaning of the Equal Protection Clause, despite what all common sense now tells us it means.

The institution of slavery was one of the leading causes of the Civil War, and there was great moral protest against its continuation. Slavery was a condition in which a human being was owned by another, to be bought and sold, willed or inherited. It had nothing to do with voting rights, but rather with the state of the slave, which was the same as the state of livestock except that he was human, had human intelligence, and his person was given superior protection, at least under the laws of some southern states, to the extent that he had access to the courts for effective judicial protection.[9] But primarily, he was by law an owned chattel. Yet though wanting him to be free, many who sympathized with the slave's plight did not desire his company. Nor did they consider him entitled to equality or capable of engaging in government.[10] Many wanted him to be free, but to be free down there, in the South.

---

8. For example, in accurately reading an old English writing regarding the rights of a hussy, we could not close our eyes to the lexicography of the era and correctly understand the writing; we would have to be aware of the fact that "hussy" then meant housewife.

9. An example is an old Tennessee decision protecting the personal rights of slaves, *Bob v. The State.*

10. There were some in Congress who from the beginning accepted the idea of the total equality of black and white people in political matters. However, few of the northern states then permitted blacks to vote. In 1851, the people of Indiana overwhelmingly adopted a constitutional amendment, which stated in part "No Negro or mulatto shall come into or settle in the State after the adoption of this Constitution." This provision was quoted by Indiana's Congressman Niblack on the floor of the House of Representatives on June 18, 1866, as quoted in *The Congressional Globe,* the Supreme Court's usual source of reference to congressional debates at that time. He spoke in defense of the Indiana constitutional provisions, citing a case in which the state of Connecticut had criminally prosecuted a woman for operating a school for free Negro citizens. He also quoted from a speech by Abraham Lincoln in his first election campaign:

"Now, Gentlemen, I don't want to read at any greater length, but this is the true complexion of all I have ever said in regard to the institution of slavery and the black race. This is the whole of it, and anything that argues me into this idea of perfect social and political equality with the Negro is but a specious and fantastic arrangement of words, by which a man can prove a horse chestnut to be a chestnut horse. . . . I have no purpose to introduce political and social equality between the white and black races. There is a physical difference between the two which, in my judgement, will probably forbid their ever living together upon the footing of perfect equality, and inasmuch as it becomes a necessity that there must be a difference, I, as well as Judge Douglass, am in favor of the race to which I belong having the superior position."

In December, 1865, an election was held among the white voters in Washington, D. C., on whether the right to vote should be extended to free black people in the city. The results were reported in Congress on January 8, 1866: This was the third largest voter participation in the city's history, with 6,556 persons voting, of whom only 35

There was never any serious pretense in Congress that the proposed Equal Protection Clause of the Fourteenth Amendment would secure to the freedmen the right to vote.[11] Further exploration of the situation at that time makes this quite clear. During the course of the Civil War, the southern states in fact were not being governed by the government of the United States and regardless of anything the Constitution might say, they were governed by separate and different governments enforcing different laws.[12] Throughout that conflict, the United States Government maintained that the southern states were still, by law, a part of the United States and must be brought back into the nation and subjected to its government and laws. Throughout the Civil War, the South insisted that it was no longer a part of the United States. Federal victory was achieved, and then practical problems arose. Here was a vast area in which millions of slaves had been given their freedom, an area filled with and run by people who had rebelled against the authority of the United States.

Then a strange thing happened. The South began to maintain that it was a part of the United States, as if the Civil War had never occurred. The North, the Government of the United States, which throughout the war had maintained that the South could not dissever itself from the Nation, now began to maintain that the South was no longer a part of the United States, but was a conquered territory. Each section, freely changing positions, followed the theoretical line which supported the practical ends to be achieved.

There was a very real problem with which Congress had to contend. The South was filled with rebels. Most of its population had forsworn allegiance to the United States. They had tried their best to dissolve the Union and to become a separate country. Their return as a part of the nation presented a threat to the government itself and to the continued freedom of the slaves.

The Constitution provides for the apportionment of members of the House of Representatives according to the population of each state, counting all free people and three-fifths of the non-free people. But suddenly, with the adoption of the Thirteenth Amendment freeing the slaves,[13] there ceased to be any non-free people. So suddenly all the black population, unable to vote, would be counted as fully as white persns to determine how many Congressmen these states could select. Not only this, but the increased southern representation in Congress would be reflected in the number of electoral votes the southern states would be able to cast for president.[14] So with re-admission to the Union, the rebels would

people voted to extend voting rights to the free Negro people. At that time, there was no strong outpouring of public or congressional sentiment in favor of extending voting rights to free black people.

11. Debates and soul-searching were to lead to a more humane view. It was not until three years after the Fourteenth Amendment was approved by Congress for submission to the states that the Congressional sense of obligation brought Congress to the point of proposing the Fifteenth Amendment to outlaw denial of the right to vote because of race.

12. The fact of actual separation is amplified by Harvard historian George M. Fredrickson's account of the intellectuals' response to the crisis, *The Inner Civil War*.

13. Lincoln's Emancipation Proclamation was made only in his capacity as Commander-in-Chief of the army, to be effective upon the Army's capture of the rebel lands; it required an actual change of law, as provided by the Thirteenth Amendment, to terminate the property ownership in slaves.

14. This is because each state's electoral votes for president is the total of its senators and congressmen; and the equality of senatorial representation gave southern states an advantage disproportionate to their populations.

be permitted greater strength than ever in the Federal Government, though they could not be expected to change their constitutions and laws to permit the freedmen to vote.

This picture was quite clear as repeatedly referred to on the floors of Congress. The rebels lost the Civil War and their southern nation, but if recognized as a part of the nation, they would gain control of the entire nation, with their increased representation and their Democratic allies in the North, and slavery might again be instituted so strongly that it could never be eradicated. The threat was real and practical. It must be prevented!

Congress determined to exclude the southern states from returning to participate in the Federal Government until Congress should be satisfied that the government was in no danger of being seized by the rebels by legal and constitutional means, simply by the exercise of voting rights.

The thinking proceeded along the line of excluding the South from participation in government, to the extent necessary to allow the Republican Party to retain control. There were proposals to exclude from representation in the House of Representatives any state that refused to permit people to vote on the ground of race; but this wouldn't work, because almost all states, northern and southern, followed this course. It was proposed to exclude from the population count an entire race if that race should be excluded by any state from participation in the right to vote. But this would also reduce the number of Congressmen for some of the loyal states that had substantial numbers of black citizens. The least harmful provision was one which would subtract from the total population of any state the number of adult men who were denied the right to vote. If both New York and South Carolina should deny all black men and insane men the right to vote, the number of men in these categories would be subtracted from each state's population, but this would be far more harmful to South Carolina than to New York. This was the provision that was finally written into the Fourteenth Amendment. It did not pretend to deny the states the power to make the right to vote dependent upon race. It merely reduced the number of congressmen that could be elected by that state. This would have been a pointless provision if the Equal Protection Clause guaranteed all black men the right to vote or if it had any other connection with voting rights.

This was one problem. Another grave problem was the southern leaders. One could hardly visualize these major leaders returning to sit in Congress, there to undo the war's achievements, yet they were popular and could be expected to run for office and to win elections. To combat this possibility, Congress passed a law in 1865 to disqualify the rebels from holding federal office by requiring them to swear their non-participation in the rebellion.[15] Some states enacted similar laws, a Missouri statute requiring such an oath not only as a condition for holding public office, but also as a condition to practicing law, being an officer of a private corporation, or engaging in religious ministry.[16] The Missouri statute

---

15. This law required each office-holder, including lawyers authorized to practice in the Federal courts, to take an oath: "I have never voluntarily borne arms against the United States since I have been a citizen thereof; that I have voluntarily given no aid, countenance, counsel, or encouragement to persons engaged in armed hostility thereto; that I have never sought nor accepted, nor attempted to exercise, the functions of any office whatever, under any authority or pretended authority in hostility to the United States, that I have not yielded a voluntary support to any pretended government, authority, power or constitution within the United States hostile or inimical thereto."

16. This oath required the person to affirm not only his non-participation in the rebellion, but also that he had never even been guilty of not being "truly and loyally

even required one to swear of a lack of pro-rebel sympathy during the war years.

These laws created or increased penalties for acts or sympathies that were less criminal or not criminal at all when committed, and were suspect as being *ex post facto* laws or bills of attainder, forbidden by the Constitution. Also, the president had pardoned most participants, yet here was an additional penalty sought to be imposed—disqualification from practicing law in federal courts, and the presidential pardoning power which was constitutionally granted, absolute in its terms, and beyond the power of Congress to qualify. Yet this congressional disqualification law pretended to bar from office and federal law practice many leaders in the rebellion, contrary to the pardoning power. The invalidity of these state and federal laws was quite obvious.

After considerable debating of the proposed Fourteenth Amendment, it was committed for private study by the powerful "Committee of Fifteen," a joint congressional committee that included both Congressman Bingham, author of the Equal Protection Clause, and Congressman Thad Stevens, caustic-tongued leader of the House who had genuine affection for both the Negro race and the Republican party. Only days after the proposed amendment was committed to this powerful committee, the Supreme Court, sitting in the same building, heard oral arguments on March 14, 1866, on a case in which a pardoned Arkansas legislator was claiming his right to practice before the Court, *Ex Parte Garland,* and heard arguments from March 15 to March 20 on a similar case appealed by a Missouri minister claiming his right to preach without swearing to his past lack of rebel sympathies, *Cummings v. Missouri.* It would be unrealistic to suppose that these arguments, and the written briefs filed before them, did not come to the attention to the committee and the houses of the Congress, though the Court's opinion overruling these laws was not rendered until after the Fourteenth Amendment had been proposed to the states.

The Amendment as proposed by the Committee of Fifteen would have forbidden all who aided the rebel cause from voting for federal officers until 1870, and, as was Stevens' hope, would leave only those supporting Union policies as active voters, so that Republican control would be assured until the security of the southern area was satisfactorily assured. The temporary qualification of this proposal was not accepted by the Senate,[17] which proposed the language as it now stands in the Fourteenth Amendment, disqualifying from federal office anyone who had previously taken an oath to support the Constitution as an officer of state or federal government, and subsequently engaged in rebellion or given aid or comfort to the enemy. But the language of the Amendment allows Congress [18] to remove this disqualification, so this provision of the amendment, to the extent that the penalty of forfeiture of the right to hold public office was

on the side of the United States against all enemies thereof, foreign and domestic . . ." This even spoke of the citizen's mental attitude during the years of rebellion. The requirement that people swear to no past involvement, increased the penalties for such involvement and in some cases effectually made criminal conduct that was not criminal when it was done.

17. This provision stated that until July, 1870, ". . . all persons who voluntarily adhered to the insurrection, giving it aid and comfort, shall be excluded from the right to vote for Representatives in Congress and for electors for President and Vice-President of the United States."

18. "But Congress may, by a vote of two-thirds of each house, remove such disability."

concerned, effectively nullified the presidential pardoning power, *previously exercised,* and transferred this much of the pardoning power from the president to the Congress.

Thad Stevens, realizing that rebels who had not previously taken oaths to support the Constitution would not be barred from election to Congress by this provision, criticised it on the floor of the House on June 13, 1866:

> "This I cannot look upon as an improvement. It opens the entire elective franchise to *such as the States might choose to admit.* In my judgement it endangers the Government of the country, both State and National; and may give the next Congress and President to the reconstructed rebels. With their enlarged basis of representation, *and the exclusion of the loyal men of color from the ballot box,* I see no hope of safety unless in the prescription of proper enabling acts,[19] which shall do justice to the freedmen and enjoin enfranchisement as a condition-precedent."

Though the Equal Protection Clause was then in its final form as to be proposed to the States, Stevens' comments acknowledging that each state could still determine voting qualifications [20] and that the black citizens were certain not to be granted voting rights, exclude any possibility that Stevens thought the Equal Protection Clause had anything to do with the performance of the governmental function of serving as electors for public office. He knew that the Equal Protection Clause had nothing to do with voting rights; so did everybody else in the Congress. That is why Congress did not attempt to pass laws under the new amendment to seek to enfranchise the freedmen, but instead, four yaers later, proposed the Fifteenth Amendment forbidding denial of the right to vote in any election "on account of race, color, or previous condition of servitude."

A third major problem existed in the South after the Civil War. The Negro slaves were freed, but they were helpless. They owned nothing, and though they had skills and knowledge, many lacked knowledge of how to look after themselves in a free society, how to care for money, how to be free. Some of the southern states moved rapidly to bring the freedmen as nearly as possible back into a state of slavery. They limited personal freedom—a thing entirely different from the ownership of slaves and from involuntary servitude—by passing laws that prohibited them from coming into towns without passes, denied them the right to own property even if able to purchase it and to find an owner willing to sell to them, and otherwise denied them the equal protection of the laws of those states. The plight of the freedmen as being legally incapable of owning property,[21] and as being persons treated differently because of their race, was one of the principal reasons for the proposal of the Equal Protection Clause of the Fourteenth Amendment.

The Equal Protection Clause did not bloom all at once into its final form. Its first version was presented to the Senate by Senator Fessenden on February 13, 1866:

---

19. Acts prescribing conditions, such as the adoption of particular state constitutional provisions, for re-admission of the southern states into the Union.

20. By establishing qualifications to vote for delegates to the most numerous house of the state legislature.

21. A few of the southern states virtually re-instituted slavery. Prohibiting the freedmen from owning or leasing property, those states had vagrancy laws making it a criminal offense to wander about the country without visible means of support. This

"The Congress shall have power to make all laws which shall be necessary and proper to secure to the citizens of each State all privileges and immunities of citizens in the several states; and to all persons in the several states *equal protection in the rights of life, liberty, and property.*"

Voting rights were viewed as political rights as distinguished from personal and property rights, the rights of life, liberty, and property defined and governed by the entire body of law in each state.

This version, which promised equal protection of the rights of life, liberty, and property in the different states, was recognized by the Senate as being an impossible provision, because state laws protecting these individual rights from invasion by other people differed in their provisions from state to state; this would have transferred almost the entire law-making powers of the nation from the state legislatures to the Congress, to secure uniformity where diversity was essential.

On January 19, 1866, Senator Trumbull broached the central theme of the clause not yet written. One of the leaders in the adoption of the Fourteenth Amendment, Senator Trumbull quoted to the Senate from the President's State of the Union Message:

"Good faith requires the security of the freedmen in their liberty and their property, their right to labor, and their right to claim the just return of their labor.

"Monopolies, perpetuities, and class legislation are contrary to the genius of free government, and ought not to be allowed. Here there is no room for favored classes or monopolies; the principle of our Government is that of equal laws and freedom of industry. Wherever monopoly attains a foothold, it is sure to be a source of danger, discord and trouble. We shall but fulfill our duties as legislators by according 'equal and exact justice to all men,' special privileges to none."

The subject of the grant of special privileges or monopolies—superior protection to some people and inferior protection to others—was the subject of the Supreme Court's first consideration of the Equal Protection Clause. This came in a group of cases reported under the single title, *The Slaughter-House Cases,* decided in 1873. It was in this very first case that the idea was introduced, that the Equal Protection Clause did not guarantee equality before the law to all men.

New Orleans had a problem with slaughter-houses, scattered where their owners had located them throughout the city, offending the sensibilities of the people. On the principle that property must be used so as not to injure the neighboring property or people, the Supreme Court quoted one of the country's most respected authorities on (state) equity law, Chancellor Kent: "Unwholesome trades, slaughter-houses, . . . may all . . .be interdicted by the law. . . ."

But the sensibilities of New Orleans and its people were not protected by the expedient of merely making it illegal to operate slaughter-houses within the city. Instead, a law was gotten through the Louisiana Legislature.

---

was an ancient type of law. But they provided a new penalty, that anyone found guilty of vagrancy should be sentenced to involuntary servitude and, in effect, should be sold into slavery for a period of 3 months, 6 months or a year. This was not prohibited by the Thirteenth Amendment, which outlawed slavery and involuntary servitude *except as punishment of a crime,* and vagrancy was a crime. Nothing in the Fourteenth Amendment or any subsequent amendment outlaws this practice, unless the judge's individual philosophy of justice be substituted for the actual provision of the Constitution as the supreme law of the land.

This law did not merely prohibit everyone from keeping and slaughtering cattle in New Orleans, and require everyone to do so at points removed a given distance from the city—this would have been equal protection of the laws, a disqualification which applied equally to all but which permitted all to engage in the business on equal terms. Instead, the law closed the business to all people save seventeen favored persons formed into a single corporation. This was a denial of equal protection of the laws, it was a law that favored some people over other people instead of treating all equally.

This law was attacked by the butchers on the ground that it violated the Equal Protection Clause, but the Supreme Court upheld the violation.

The Court asserted that the statute was "aptly phrased" for the purpose of removing the slaughter-houses from the city, which indeed it was. Then the Court stated: "And it must be conceded that the means adopted by the Act for this purpose are appropriate, are stringent and effectual." But still, it gave great protection to the chosen seventeen, and denied all protection to all others who wanted to do this type of business.

To attempt answering this objection, the Supreme Court said that the Legislature could have granted the exclusive privilege of owning slaughter-houses to the City of New Orleans, a municipal corporation, and that it could therefore give this exclusive right to some private corporation. The effect on the butchers, the Court reasoned, would be precisely the same whether the exclusive privilege of slaughtering cattle were given to the city government or a private company—in either case, the private citizens would be forbidden to continuing operating their small slaughter-houses in the city.

In this rationalization, the Supreme Court missed the entire meaning of the Equal Protection Clause. If Louisiana had outlawed the operation of this business by all New Orleans people and given the right solely to the government of New Orleans, all people would have been equally protected by this law, all equally denied the right to engage in the business. In selecting some private citizens to be incorporated and given the exclusive right to operate the business, the Louisiana Legislature followed an entirely different course. It gave some people a superior protection and denied this protection to all other people. This was a denial of equal protection of the laws to two competing groups of people.

While *The Slaughter-House Cases* represent a negative refusal to give any rational meaning to the Equal Protection Clause, a more positive forecast of its future "meaning" was brought about by California's treatment of its alien Chinese population. These people, as argued during the debates over the adoption of the Fourteenth Amendment, simply would not assimilate into the western ways, but came to California from their Chinese homeland, worked during their working years, and then returned with their savings to China, if not during their lives, then in their caskets after death.

San Francisco adopted laws aimed at the industrious Chinese laundrymen. The first such set of laws to come before the Supreme Court required laundrymen to have health certificates, drainage inspections, and certificates of inspection of all their heating appliances for heating irons, and these laws also prohibited the conduct of wash houses and laundry businesses from ten o'clock at night to six o'clock in the morning.

The first person prosecuted and sent to jail for violation of the city ordinance was non-Chinese, at least in name, Francis Barbier. The Supreme Court said in *Barbier v. Connolly:*

There is no *invidious discrimination against anyone* within the prescribed limits of such regulation. There is none in the regulation under consideration. . . . It is not legislation discriminating against anyone; all are subject to the same restrictions and are entitled to the same privileges under similar conditions."

This accurately states the meaning of the Equal Protection Clause.

Laundryman Barbier complained that the ordinance denied him equal protection of the laws because it prohibited him from following his trade during the night hours while it permitted people engaged in other businesses to follow their trades at night. But in fact, the law simply provided that everyone, no matter who, should be subject to these particular regulations in the conduct of the business of operating a laundry. It applied just as much to the carpenter, if he should decide to operate a laundry, as it did to this individual who was already operating a laundry.

But the Supreme Court gratuitously remarked that this ordinance which applied equally to all did not *invidiously discriminate* against anyone. In fact, the San Francisco regulations reviewed in this case did not discriminate at all, invidiously or non-invidiously. But this phrase "invidious discrimination" was to become a catch-phrase used in announcing whether particular state laws are viewed as violating the Equal Protection Clause, a phrase given meaning in the mind of the individual judge, and otherwise devoid of meaning; certainly, it is without meaning as related to the idea expressed in the Equal Protection Clause.

The first Chinaman famous for his subjection to San Francisco's laundry was Yick Wo, whose name is a landmark in constitutional law. *Yick Wo v. Hopkins* presented a more extensive set of laundry laws.[22] By this ordinance, it was made illegal for anyone to carry on a laundry business in a wooden building within the city limits "without having first obtained the consent of the board of supervisors, . . ." Most of the houses in San Francisco were wood, of the more than 300 laundries, only 10 were built of materials other than wood, and two-thirds of all of them were operated by Chinese, present in the United States under a treaty with the Emperor of China.

Though Yick Wo's laundry had passed inspection by the San Francisco Fire Department, the Board of Supervisors refused to renew his license. At the same time, it refused to renew licenses of any Chinese launderer, while renewing the licenses of all but one of the Americans in this business. The case involved both the Due Process Clause and the Equal Protection Clause of the Fourteenth Amendment, both having been violated by San Francisco.

The ordinance itself violates the Due Process Clause because it did not provide for the grant or revocation of the licenses on the basis of law, but this could be done purely on whim, and due process of law requires that rights of property and liberty be terminable only by the law of the land. The Supreme Court said:

". . . if an applicant for such consent, being in every way a competent and qualified person, and having complied with every reasonable condition demanded by any public interest, should, failing to obtain the requisite consent of the supervisors to the prosecution of his business, apply for redress by the judicial process of *mandamus* to require the supervisors to consider and act upon his case, it would be a sufficient answer for them to say that the law had conferred upon them au-

---

22. This ordinance, passed *four years before* the ordinance involved in the *Barbier* case, did not result in the arrest of Yick Wo until after the Supreme Court's decision of the *Barbier* case.

thority to withhold their assent, without reason and without responsibility. The power given to them is not confided to their discretion in the legal sense of that term, but is granted to their mere will. It is purely arbitrary, and acknowledges neither guidance nor restraint."

The Supreme Court's decision sustained Yick Wo's *habeas corpus* petition by freeing him from jail, but the decision was quite jumbled in that it did not say when it was talking about due process of law and when it was talking about equal protection of the laws, and it often spoke in terms of "police powers." [23]

At the conclusion of its opinion, however, the Court firmly identified the denial of licenses to all Chinese, while granting licenses to Americans, as a denial of equal protection of the laws.[24] So from the negative beginning in *The Slaughter-House Cases,* the Court arrived at the correct meaning of the Equal Protection Clause, though it wrote confusingly in its *Yick Wo* decision, and though it planted the seeds for future denials of equal protection of the laws in its unfortunate use of the phrase "invidious discrimination."

From these beginnings, the Supreme Court continued, reluctantly deciding Equal Protection cases, apparently unwilling to face the fact that the Equal Protection Clause requires state governments to assure that all individuals will stand equal before its laws, regardless of how great an interest the state may believe it has in treating different individuals differently. The Court also failed to recognize that *this is all the Equal Protection Clause means.*

Without centering its attention upon the Equal Protection Clause itself, and drawing its inferences from the language of that part of the Supreme Law of the Land, the Supreme Court retained ideas that a state's interest might be adequate to entitle the state to treat different people differently, that a state might discriminate unevenly between individuals, and thereby deny them equal protection of the laws, if the discrimination were not "invidious" in the opinions of the judges. Through these cases, the Supreme Court gradually developed a new and meaningless meaning which it substituted for the Equal Protection Clause. Some of these cases are:

1931—*Smith v. Cahoon,* building upon a 1925 decision, *Frost v. Railroad Commission of California.* These cases involve a new and popular legislative movement, to regulate the business of hauling passengers and freight by motor vehicles. This was a subject of which the "public interest" supposedly required administrative regulation because of the possibility of unfair prices and of a refusal to render service to some shippers.

---

23. Unless one recognizes the great distinction between the application of laws to govern people and the power to select people to engage in the operation of government, either as voters or office-holders, the Equal Protection Clause, reading it in the full strength of its unqualified language, would have entitled these citizens of China to vote in San Francisco, if they should meet all voting qualifications generally applied.

24. "And while this consent of the supervisors is withheld from [Yick Wo] and from two hundred others who have also petitioned, all of whom happen to be Chinese subjects, eighty others, not Chinese subjects, are permitted to carry on the same business under similar conditions. The fact of this discrimination is admitted. No reason for it is shown, and the conclusion cannot be resisted, that no reason exists except hostility to the race and nationality to which the petitioners belong, and which in the eye of the law is not justified. The discrimination is therefore illegal, and the public administration which enforces it is a denial of equal protection of the laws and a violation of the Fourteenth Amendment of the Constitution."

With the appearance of the trucking industry, trucking firms began to appear and offer their services to all who desired to ship freight, and other trucking companies had contracts to haul freight for particular customers. Mr. Smith had such a contract in Florida which was to lead him to become a part of the famous decision of *Smith v. Cahoon.* Smith's contract was to haul groceries for the A & P Tea Company's chain of retail stores. Florida enacted a law applying to common carriers—carriers that had regularly published rates, routes, and time schedules for making periodic trips to haul freight. A key provision of this type of public service commission regulation is that the business man obtain something called a "certificate of public convenience and necessity" before he can engage in business as a common carrier. To show that the *public's* convenience required a truck line to operate, it must be shown that the public needs this service. The Florida statute provided that when a trucker wanted to "operate in a territory . . . already served by a certificate holder," the trucker could be granted this certificate: "Only when the existing certificate holder or holders serving such territory fail to provide service and facilities to the satisfaction of said commission."

So once a company obtained a certificate of convenience and necessity, it in theory was free from competition and held a monopoly granted by the state until such time as some competitor should prove by the testimony of customers that they could not get adequate service from the existing motor freight lines.[25] In state action granting these monopolies or partial monopolies, some people were afforded the right to engage in the business and others were denied that right, simply because state officials felt that there were already enough people enjoying that right. This was an obvious denial of equal protection of the laws.

In *Smith v. Cahoon,* the Supreme Court seized upon the fact that the Florida law exempted from its control contract carriers hauling exclusively "agricultural, horticultural, dairy or other farm products and fresh and salt fish and oysters and shrimp from the point of production to the assembling or shipping point . . ." The Court viewed this as being a denial of equal protection of the laws.

The Court said:

> "But in establishing such a regulation, there does not appear to be the slightest justification for making a distinction between those who carry for hire farm products, or milk or butter, or fish or oysters, and those who carry for hire bread or sugar, or tea or coffee, or groceries in general, or other useful commodities.[26]

25. Needless to say, without this type of regulation, anybody who wanted to could buy a truck, purchase the license tags, permits, and whatever insurance coverage the law might acquire, and could then offer his services to the public for whatever price he chose to ask. If the price were low enough and he succeeded in obtaining business and adequately serving his customers, the public would be served and he would earn profits. If his price were too high, he would go broke. So there is a natural regulation in the absence of state regulation and planning, just as there is when someone opens a grocery store and either makes money or loses money, so that the public is either served or the businessman learns that the public does not desire to be served by him, at least at the prices he asks.

26. In these common carrier cases, there was a theory that common carriers "dedicate" their property to public use, thereby enabling the state to regulate their rates and grant or deny them the right to use this great public privilege. In *Frost v. Railroad Commission of California,* California had required both common carriers and contract

This questioning concerned a matter that was none of the Supreme Court's business. The state legislature was free to require special licenses or stringent requirements of all who hauled fish and oysters, and it would be extending equal protection of its laws to all citizens if it let every citizen and every person temporarily in the state haul fish and oysters on precisely the same terms. The fact that one who carried grapes did not have to comply with a law regulating oyster-hauling would make no difference, because if the grape-hauler should decide to haul oysters then he, too, would have to comply with that law, and if the oyster-hauler should decide to haul grapes, he would be free from the requirements of that law in the grape-hauling portions of his business. The Equal Protection Clause commands that equal protection of the laws be granted to all *persons,* not to all *acts done by persons.*

Concerning the state's decision as to what businesses it wanted its new legislation to regulate, the Supreme Court said: "But the constitutional guarantee of equal protection of the laws is interposed against discriminations that are entirely arbitrary." This effectively destroys the power of the state to legislate unless the judiciary is competent to understand and does agree with the state's legislative policies.[27] Such rationalizations are not within either the words or the purpose of the Equal Protection Clause. However, *Smith v. Cahoon* did present a classic example of the denial of equal protection of the laws—in permitting limited numbers to engage in a business into which entry was denied to all others, an example that went totally unrecognized by the Supreme Court, as the Court continued its process of changing the Equal Protection Clause from the plain meaning declared by its language to a totally different meaning.

1939—Minnesota ex rel. Pearson v. Probate Court of Ramsey County: This was a writ of prohibition case, not an equity case, in which a citizen sued in the name of the State of Minnesota in the state courts, to prohibit a local probate court from conducting a certain type of proceeding, on the ground that under the Equal Protection Clause, the Court could not lawfully conduct the case. The case went to the heart of the Equal Protection Clause. Pearson was charged with *being a psychopathic personality,* one having "such conditions of emotional instability, or impulsiveness of behavior or lack of customary standards of judgement, or failure to appreciate the consequences of his acts, or a combination of any such conditions, as to render such person irresponsible for his conduct with re-

---

carriers to obtain a certificate of convenience and necessity before engaging in business; the Supreme Court held this unconstitutional, as a taking of the contract carrier's property, requiring it to "dedicate" its facilities to public use, the Court also expressing the opinion that the law's primary purpose was to "protect the . . . common carriers . . . by controlling competitive conditions." Faced with this decision, the Florida court endeavored to get around it in *Smith v. Cahoon* by saying that the statute applicable to both common carriers and contract carriers did not apply to contract carriers in those provisions "properly applicable" only to common carriers. The Supreme Court accepted this premise and held that, because no businessman could tell what applied to contract carriers and what applied only to common carriers, the whole law was void for uncertainty. Having decided the case, the Court nevertheless continued writing, for some reason, its comments on the Equal Protection Clause.

27. All legislative power is essentially arbitrary, because laws become laws only by virtue of majority vote. Most regulatory laws probably cause more harm than good if carefully analyzed. See Spencer, *The Man Versus the State.* But an essential of the doctrine of separation of powers is the power to judge whether proposed laws are harmful or beneficial is a power given to the legislative branch, not to the judicial.

spect to sexual matters and thereby dangerous to other persons." As construed by the Supreme Court of Minnesota, this law spoke of a person's conduct which demonstrated him to be a sexual psychopath.

The penalty was sterilization. It was to be imposed under probate court procedure, without trial by jury. On the basis of medical testimony, a judge was to determine whether the individual was a psychopathic personality, so as to require him to be subjected to a vasectomy without his consent. The Supreme Court held the state had the power to do this. Among the Court's comments:

> "Equally unavailing is the contention that the statute denies appellant the equal protection of the laws. The argument proceeds on the view that the statute has selected a group which is a part of a larger class. *The question, however, is whether the legislature could constitutionally make a class of the group it did select.* That is, whether there is any rational basis for such selection. We see no reason for doubt upon this point. Whether the legislature could have gone farther is not the question. The class it did select is identified by the state court in terms which clearly show that the persons within that class constitute a dangerous element in the community which the legislature in its discretion could put under appropriate control. As we have often said, the legislature is free to recognize degrees of harm, and it may confine its restrictions to those classes of cases where the need is deemed to be clearest. . . ."

However, reflection indicates that legislative creation of "classes" of individuals with the enactment of special laws to apply to those classes, reasonable or unreasonable, is a denial of equal protection of the laws between a person in the selected class and a person outside that class, if the legislation refers to classes of people instead of particular types of conduct; if the law actually refers only to conduct and the law is equally applicable to all, then the matter is of no legitimate concern to the federal judiciary.[28]

This is not to say that the Supreme Court ruled correctly in holding that Minnesota could lawfully procede with its probate-trial proceeding to sterilize Pearson. As thoroughly demonstrated by the Supreme Court in its post-Civil War decision of *Cummings v. Missouri*,[29] in which the State of Missouri imposed a penalty of deprivation of the right to be a minister upon one who held southern sympathies during the Civil War, the imposition of loss of a liberty is, to the person so deprived, a penalty, so as to make the legislative act imposing it for post conduct a bill of pains and penalties. By the same token, the imposition of compulsory sterilization was the creation of a penalty,[30] which was the creation of a

---

28. In Germany, Adolf Hitler created a legal class consisting of Jews, and decreed their death. His "rational" aim was to populate the country with what he believed would be a superior race. He restricted the operation of his decree to the groups deemed most dangerous to the achievement of governmental ends. Such rationale as used by the Court to justify unequal treatment of persons is but a refusal to honor the Equal Protection Clause.

29. Discussed above, p. 266.

30. In 1939, the Supreme Court still had not come to the realization—as it has not at the time of this writing—that the privileges and immunities of citizens of the United States, as protected by the Fourteenth Amendment, include the right to trial by jury upon indictment by a grand jury before the imposition of criminal penalties. Sterilization, castration, and decapitation are all penalties imposed upon people when the state imposes them by force, and in any view dedicated to the supremacy of the Constitution and to the principle of government by laws, state imposition of severe penalties cannot

criminal offense. Although the *Pearson* case did not involve a denial of equal protection of the laws, as the Minnesota courts had construed it, the Supreme Court on its own should have recognized the illegality of imposing criminal penalties without indictment by grand jury and without trial by jury.[31]

1941—*Skinner v. Oklahoma:* Skinner was convicted of stealing chickens in 1926, armed robbery in 1929, and another armed robbery in 1934. Oklahoma passed a new law, while Skinner was in prison, proclaiming to be an "habitual criminal" any person convicted of more than two felonies reflecting moral terpitude (roughly, dishonesty) with the exception of a few named crimes, such as violation of the whiskey prohibition laws, tax laws, political offenses, and embezzlement. If a person should be found guilty of being an habitual criminal under this new statue, after a trial before a jury, he should be subjected to sterilization. If one assumes that the Privileges and Immunities Clause of the Fourteenth Amendment had its most obvious meaning, as a guarantee to each citizen of the United States of all privileges and immunities of Federal citizenship, against violation of these privileges by state governments, so as to secure to each the protection of the Federal Bill of Rights,[32] then Mr. Skinner would have been immune from punishment by sterilization.

As applied in this case, the Oklahoma law clearly offended the double jeopardy and *ex post facto* prohibitions, but the Supreme Court desired to write about the Equal Protection Clause.

For the feature of the Act which condemned it, the Court seized upon the Act's exclusion of the crime of embezzlement from those crimes for which mandatory sterilization could be ordered upon conviction for the third offense. The Court compared embezzlement with larceny.

This legislative distinction made by Oklahoma had nothing to do with the Equal Protection Clause. Oklahoma's law applied in identical terms to all individuals, no matter who the individual might be: If he three times committed larceny, he was subject to compulsory sterilization. The subjection to the penalty in the case of the crime of larceny, and the immunity from that penalty in the case of the crime of embezzlement, applied equally to all individuals who might commit either crime.

The Supreme Court sought to justify its "equal protection" ruling in *Skinner v. Oklahoma* in this manner:

"A clerk who appropriates over $20.00 from his employer's till . . . and a stranger who steals the same amount are both guilty of felonies. If the latter repeats

---

be rendered anything other than the imposition of criminal penalties. Its nature cannot be changed by state (or federal) declaration that the penalty is not considered a penalty but a treatment, it is imposed for benign purposes, and the individual should cooperatively forego trial by jury and present himself for sterilization as a good citizen should, because it will benefit the general public.

31. There is a great practical difficulty in recognizing that a government proceeding that imposes penalties is in fact a criminal prosecution when the government chooses to call it by a different name. That difficulty is that the Federal Government has so many penalties it imposes by procedures that deny the citizen the right to jury trial and other criminal protections, that the recognition that these procedures are criminal would interfere with the enforcement of administrative regulations by imposition of "civil" penalties, because jurors on occasion might refuse to impose the penalty because of the triviality of the offense.

32. Discussed above, pp. 134, *et seq.*

his act and is convicted three times, he may be sterilized. But the clerk is not subject to the pains and penalties of the Act no matter how large his embezzlements nor how frequent his convictions. . . . Marriage and procreation are fundamental to the very existence and survival of the race. The power to sterilize, if exercised, may have subtle, far-reaching and devastating effects. In evil or reckless hands it can cause races or types which are inimical to the dominant group to wither and disappear. There is no redemption for the individual whom the law touches. Any experiment which the State conducts is to his irreparable injury. He is forever deprived of a basic liberty."

Of course, all of this could just as truly be said about the penalties of life imprisonment and electrocution, each of which terminates procreative activity, and it smacks more of empathy for the one penalized in a particular way than a detached rendition of professional judgment on the basis of written law. The supposed guaranty of "just and equal laws" upon which the Court relied is a guaranty that does not appear in the Constitution and will never appear there unless the people shall take leave of their senses, because it would effectively empower the courts to engage in the legislative process, by judging the justice of every law according to their own non-legislative judgment, immune from the power of the people to recall by rejection in the next election.

We thus see the gradual change in the meaning assigned to the Equal Protection Clause from its natural meaning to a different meaning devised by judges. It began with the simple proposition that all persons, citizens and aliens, women and men, black and white, should stand equal before the law of the state as the law governed those persons; that when a legislature should decide to impose regulation upon some particular type of human conduct, the legislature might deny to all persons engaged in a business the right to operate it at night, but this was not a denial of equal protection of the laws. The law applied impartially to every person as he should bring his activities within the class of activity regulated by the legislation.

But the Supreme Court changed this clause in its application to the assumption that legislators could create different classes of people and could grant one level of protection of the laws to one class of people and a lower level of protection of the laws to another class, and that this was perfectly lawful if a single condition be met: That the legislative reasons and justification for discriminating against every individual in the unfavored class was such as to strike judges as not constituting invidious discrimination. This is the very result that the language of the Equal Protection Clause prohibits! In the process, the Court never once noticed —save in comments acknowledging that when the Fourteenth Amendment was adopted, virtually everyone in Congress classified rights as being either civil rights or political rights—that being subjected to the protection of governing laws was a thing entirely different from being authorized to participate in the conduct of government itself.

The Republican Guarantee:

Experience teachers that the people generally are not vitally concerned with government. Each citizen is concerned with his own affairs, earning his living, enjoying his recreation, protecting and raising his family, and in times of sound and responsible government, is content to leave the problems of government to elected officials, though exercising his right to criticize government. While some are perpetually excited about all governmental affairs, the responsible people who do the world's work give most of their attention to their own affairs instead of to government: The doctor concentrates his attention on medicine, the builder on building, the trader on commerce. Some room is left for interest in what government is doing, and when government misbehaves, it attracts the close attention of great numbers of people who would otherwise be doing constructive things. And when government begins to grow tyrannical, there is temporarily no more constructive human activity than to bring government back into its proper and restricted role.

The republican form of government permits citizens to spend their time in constructive pursuits instead of concerning themselves with political intrigue and wasting their time on governmental problems which they are, for the most part, equipped to solve neither by education, study, experience, nor inclination. The republican form of government gives the citizen one safeguard which no other government permits him. Large numbers of citizens, representing the entire population, are permitted to vote against the politicians they distrust the most by voting for the ones they distrust the least. The people do not govern themselves, but they have the absolute power to refuse to return to office any official they dislike, and they are not required to have the slightest reason for refusing to renew his term of office, either rational or irrational.

It is in the right to vote that the republican form of government has its greatest strength and weakness. The weakness arises from the lack of any satisfactory method of answering the constantly recurring questions: Who shall vote? How many representatives shall the different areas be allowed to select? These questions constantly recur because the world constantly changes.

In order to achieve government at a level sufficiently high so that the people's representatives can make responsible decisions when the decision popularly demanded would be wholly irresponsible, there must be some restriction to assure that those voting will have the detachment to cast their votes with at least some sense of responsibility. To achieve responsible government, the electorate must have enough sense to recognize that quite often, the most responsible act a legislature can perform is the act of refusing to act.

Some claim to believe everyone should be allowed to vote, but such an approach would be suicidal. If we study our experience, instead of being guided by wishful thinking, by the pretense that human nature is different from what it is, we must conclude that the mass opinion of the total populace of any nation is at a rather low level. This simply means that we do not have the time for a careful study of the issues. We use our minds to control our actions, but no one makes a thorough analytical study to determine his course of action in all the affairs of life.[33]

The knowledgeable voter knows enough about government, causes and effects, the nature of people, and the world's past to make intelligent decisions as to how he should vote, with his decision influenced by an almost instinctive judgment as to whether a candidate can be trusted with the power he seeks. He realizes that the achievement of power over other people's affairs is the aim of every politician.

In political affairs, as the right to vote is constantly expanded, we find that

---

33. Television fare is usually on a rather low intellectual level, but it is on that level because that is the level which succeeds in persuading buyers to purchase products. If they could be better persuaded by a higher level of program and commercial content, then the higher levels would appear. Mass decisions are made with the minimal use of human intelligence. Many of our decisions are of poor quality because we are ignorant of facts which, if we knew them, would lead us to different decisions.

those who concern themselves with political prognosis and with the chances of various candidates, speak more and more of a candidate's charisma, which has no bearing upon his qualifications to hold high office except in the Pied Piper aspects of the office. Large masses of people become excited so easily and when excited, demand instant action, and cheer whoever convincingly promises power or glory or an easier life, or whatever else may be the passing moment's desire. Adolf Hitler was a very popular leader in Germany, winning the adulation of excitable youth and awakening the patriotic fervor of many older citizens, and the German people did not rise to prevent his torture and murder of millions of Jews. The city political bosses in America have been popular leaders in their own cities, and it was their popularity which retained them in office or power despite the harsh and arbitrary way they often treated their opponents.

It was strong popular demand that brought about the foolish Prohibition Amendment to the Constitution which, as we have seen,[34] was totally pointless. Present excitement over population grown and ecology may or may not be warranted. Whether warranted or not, the strength of the excitement depends purely upon the popular appeal of the movement, and the state of popular knowledge is necessarily always far behind the state of available knowledge.[35] In times of excitement, excited people—whether a lynch mob or an entire overwrought population—do not want things to be carefully studied and wisely considered. They want action! Yet serious matters involving activities which greatly benefit mankind need to be studied and handled intelligently instead of taking precipitous and harmful action under compulsion of the demands of a nation-wide mob, We, the People.

Government acts with such irristible force, destroying life and property, damaging useful private businesses, and interfering with the freedom of citizens, that responsible government action almost always requires considerable restraint and matured judgment. Mob action is never mature and never restrained. For this reason, sound government in the interests of all the citizens demands that politicians be responsible people who can expect that most of the voters will have the good sense to recognize responsible decisions as being responsible, to refuse to penalize politicians for being competent officers of government. This requires a responsible electorate, an electorate with mature judgement.

---

34. See above, p. 166.
35. A great deal has been written about the plight of the world from an ecological viewpoint. The need for immediate action has often been urged so strongly that harsh measures have been taken in places against businesses that perform useful services and may well have been doing comparatively little permanent damage. The basis for some of the concern has proved questionable. Much information was disseminated about the danger of mercury poisoning to aquatic life, and was proven by tests showing the amount of mercury present in fish; finally, someone made such a test upon a fish which had been preserved in a museum, having been caught many years before heavy mercury pollution started, and it was found to have the same level of mercury as today's fish. Dangerous concentrations of DDT in the world's soils was proclaimed and proven by world-wide soil tests run by many different people. Finally, a scientist ran such a soil test upon a sample that had been taken from the earth and kept shielded from air since before DDT was invented. Although difficult tests showed there was no DDT in the old soil, the common testing procedure revealed the same high quantity of DDT in this soil never exposed to DDT. Without knowledge as to which test was run by each experimenter throughout the world, it was impossible to say that there were *any accurate statistics* on DDT concentration in soils.

The politician receives some natural protection in his desire to make responsible decisions in the forgetfulness of the public.[36] The politician reacts to this natural protection afforded him in the manner that few voters have failed to notice: As election time approaches, politicians become far more responsive to public desires, even if those desires are irresponsible.

From these considerations, it is clear that people thinking about political theory and about a method of devising a government, might quite rationally design a method which would spread the right to vote among as large body of responsible voters as possible and which would, at the same time, endeavor to exclude the irresponsible from voting. Without any experiment ever being conducted, or being needed, reason indicates that if the voting age were lowered to six years, with every child over six being permitted to vote, there would inevitably be politicians promising programs of free candy with school lunches, more extensive recesses, and other benefits that might be thought adequate to delight the imaginations and win the support of children at different age levels.

Reflecting upon the inescapable facts of human nature, one designing a government would not overlook the fact that many adults are totally irresponsible. Many adults have never grown up to mental adulthood. Many men beget children and abandon them. Many adults cannot fulfill the obligation to go to work on time, day after day. Many cannot manage their financial affairs by living within their means and are driven, often repeatedly, to the bankruptcy courts to rid themselves of their debts instead of honestly paying their creditors. Many adults simply have never developed the ability to be responsible.

One designing a republican form of government, if he desired to perpetuate sound and stable government, might reasonably reach the conclusion that for those people who are responsible and productive, one of the major pleasures of life is their work, their production, building houses, laying pipes, manufacturing machines, flying airplanes, or engaging in any of the vast number of useful and complex human enterprises that are essential to the continuation of a civilized society for the benefit of all—a society in which people can work and use their earned money to purchase reasonably dependable products of their choice. Designing a republican form of government, the designer might well conclude that the government is best which governs least, which gives protection where protection is needed—because there will always be dishonest men and thieves at every level in society—but which leaves to the productive citizen the greatest possible freedom to plan his own life and to live it as he wants to live it, without senseless governmental interference: One designing a republican form of government might well conclude that the right to vote should be restricted to those productive elements in society and denied to the parasitic elements.[37]

---

36. The politician knows that, almost without exception, whatever he does in the early part of his term will be forgotten by the public at large at election-time but that anything he does toward the end of his term that angers too many people will be remembered at election time.

37. The strong inclination of more productive and creative people to run their own affairs might be expected to render them resistant to the lure of governmental promises, most of which are more harmful than beneficial in their promise of great benefits at little cost. For example, minimum wage laws always destroy the ability of some to earn their own livings performing useful services, because their services are simply not worth as much as the minimum wage. And the lure of such laws as the Social Security Act borders on the fraudulent. The amount of retirement benefits drawn by most workers

One designing a republican form of government might well conclude that those who take no joy in their work and have no end for their existence, being essentially parasitic in their outlook, should not be allowed to vote; that such a citizen's vote might reasonably be assumed to be for sale. If too many irresponsible and immature citizens were given the vote, one considering a republican form of government might conclude that the government could well deteriorate into a government by bribery, in which the politician, for self-protection, would be compelled to bribe the parasitic voters with public moneys taken from the productive voters, by promising to the parasites more and more money and a greater and greater share of the earnings taken by force of law from the mature and responsible members of society. Such a government, one might conclude, would carry in it a possibility of its own self-destruction through massive stupidity, dishonesty, and greed.[38]

These reflections are not presented as truths that must be recognized. But they are presented with the assertion that they were views held by the men who founded our country from an immense wealth of experience and study, views which no intelligent man concerned with problems of government can disregard. They are views that may be forced upon one by the application of studious and systematic reflection upon the weighty problems of self-government. They are therefore views that no serious thinker can disregard in favor of the current mob psychology of *any era*—views no serious thinker or writer can reject without consideration and discussion and still claim to be intellectually honest.

These views had their weight and effect with the men who founded our government. In most states at that time, no one was permitted to vote unless he was a property-owner. The use of property in those days did not have to await the installation of electric wires and pipe lines, and property ownership should have been relatively easy for the frugal to come by. The continuing ownership of property was an indication that the owner had a measure of maturity and self-control, and had assumed the responsibilities of adulthood that many never assume. A modern equivalent might be ownership of property or the earning of an annual income above a relatively low level almost universally attainable by those with enough understanding to be able to vote responsibly. The irre-

---

after the age of 65 is small compared to their contributions. If instead of having his "contributions" taken from him by law, the worker had deposited $500 a year at 4% in an annual compounding account, and at the end of a 40-year work life (25-65) had started withdrawing $3,000 a year, with the remaining moneys still drawing interest at 4%, and he died at the end of 10 years' retirement, there would remain $23,180 of his own money for his widow or heirs; if he worked 45 years instead, and survived ten years, the amount remaining for his family would be $36,181. With the enlargement of Social Security benefits to include medical expenses, all such money goes immediately to doctors and hospitals, necessarily greatly increasing medical charges made to persons not within this program, and the added expense of these benefits not covered by contributions is that the program becomes more insolvent every year.

38. A tragic picture of an actual occurrence of this trend, bearing an uncomfortable similarity to present American conditions, can be found in accounts of the beginning of the decline of the Roman Empire. One of the more readable and readily available of such accounts is the beautifully researched and written life of Cicero by Taylor Caldwell, *A Pillar of Iron*. A theoretical description of this trend, and possibly its inevitability, is the subject of Charles Fontenay's *Epistle to the Babylonians*. As to the economic mechanism, see "Observations on the Causes of Decline of Ancient Civilizations" in Ludwig von Mises' *Human Action*.

sponsible, drunken husband who works only half the time might well not be able to meet that income level. But does such an irresponsible man actually have the quality of judgment and reliability that voters should have in order to give their politicians an adequate sense of security to enable them to make rational, mature decisions in governing the people? Property ownership, then almost universally a voter qualification, cannot honestly be said to be irrational.

Another common voting qualification was that the voter must be an adult, twenty-one years of age. This was an arbitrary dividing line between childhood and adulthood which favored extending the right to vote to some childish persons, because at least today, the mature outlook is not commonly achieved until nearer the age of twenty-five or thirty. It takes some experience in addition to age to really become an adult and this includes experiencing the harsh facts of adult responsibility.

Another common qualification was that the voter must be male. Women for the most part did not even control their own property, which was held in the husband's name. Woman had her influence but it was the tradition that she should defer to and be protected by her husband. As late as the time of the Congressional debates over the Civil War amendments, it was argued that woman could rely upon the voting of her husband or father to protect her interests, and that if the women were given the right to vote, this would simply double the votes of the husbands without changing the result. With changing times, state legislatures began to concede to women the right to vote as changing social conditions and industrialization lured more women out of the home and into the commercial and industrial world.

It may be said with absolute accuracy that when the Constitution was written, no responsible leader believed that everyone should have the right to vote. None do today. Voting has never been a right extended to all citizens, but the right to vote has always been denied to a large portion of the citizens, if only the children. The right to vote is customarily exercised only by a minority, even in landslide elections.

Giving the right to vote to some representatives (adults not convicted of serious crimes, etc.) of all the people, there remains the constantly recurring question of how many representatives each person shall be allowed to vote for, the problem of apportionment of representatives among the voters. When our government was formed, it was considered that every group of citizens in each geographical location should have the right to elect a representative to the legislative body. Throughout our history, as will be seen, a general compromise has been followed in most American states, which gives the voting edge, at least in one house of the state legislature, to the minority living in rural areas.

It has been considered that the urban people do not really understand rural problems, and vice-versa, though the contributions of each group are essential to the well-being of the other. The most natural compromise which recognizes that each must be given the right to some voice in government is the compromise traditionally reached in America: Giving the representational edge to the urban populace in one legislative house and to the rural in the other.

Under this arrangement, politics becomes a matter of compromise in practical governing, instead of the tyranny of people in a represented area riding roughshod over the interests of people in an unrepresented area. In order to legislate, the two houses must compromise, must recognize their conflicting interests when these are of sufficient intensity.

No one can contest the fact that this is the system which many thoughtful and intelligent people have concluded to be the best possible compromise of the representational problem, and that it is therefore a rational solution. This was the compromise reached in establishing the government of the United States. Each state was given representation in the House of Representatives roughly according to population, but in the Senate, each state was given two Senators, no matter how large or small its area or population, and the Constitution provides that the principle of equal representation of the states in the Senate shall *never be changed* by amendment.[39] Under this device, all the people in America have a voice in the government by their votes or by the votes of the qualified voters among them, and anyone may attain the right to vote by achieving the voting qualifications, whatever they may be in the different states.[40]

When the Constitution was written, distrust of the general populace existed as did distrust of government.[41] The most important single office was by design the office of president, and the President was to be elected by specially-chosen electors from each state, with the state legislature to provide the method of choosing the electors. The Legislature itself could elect this small group of men to vote for President, it could require a convention, or it could authorize the people to elect the presidential electors. Apparently, it was their hope that the wisest and most respected men in the state would be chosen to exercise their own individual judgment and make their best choice of the person to be President. The President was to be chosen on the basis of ability rather than popularity, and his selection was removed from the direct power of the people.

Senators were to be elected by the state legislature, not by the people, so that the Senators would be protected from popular pressures and would be a stabiliz-

---

39. The Constitution is not amendable in this respect. Only by abandoning the entire Constitution and the adoption of a new constitution written at another convention could this protective device is discarded.

40. At the time of the 1970 census, more than half of the people in the United States lived in nine of the fifty states. Were it not for the principle of equal representation in the Senate, the selfish interests of the people in those nine states, or perhaps the ten or eleven largest states, would likely result in a coalition whereby that portion of the people would govern all the remaining people in the nation. The foresight of the men who wrote the Constitution prevented this. Though the majority of the people live in nine states, they have only 18 senators, while the minority living in the other 41 states have 82 members in the Senate. But in the House of Representatives, the ten or eleven most populous states have more representatives than the other 39 or 40 states. Under this arrangement, each group of states must listen to the others and by compromise, laws are enacted that are acceptable in most parts of the country.

41. Comments by some members of the Constitutional Convention included: Alexander Hamilton—"We are now forming a republican government. Real liberty is neither found in despotism or the extremes of democracy, but in moderate governments." Elbridge Gerry—"The evils we experience flow from the excess of democracy. The people do not want virtue, but are the dupes of pretended patriots." James Madison— "Democratic communities may be unsteady, and be led to action by the impulse of the moment.—Like individuals, they may be sensible of their own weakness, and may desire the counsels and checks of friends to guard them against the turbulency and weakness of unruly passions. . . . The man who is possessed of wealth, who lolls on his sofa, or rolls in his carriage, cannot judge the wants or feelings of the day laborer. . . . Land-holders ought to have a share in the government, to support these invaluable interests, and to balance and check the other. They ought to be so constituted as to protect the minority of the opulent against the majority . . ." *Documents Illustrative of the Formation of the Union,* pp. 125, 810-812.

ing influence upon the House of Representatives. But who was to vote for members of the House of Representatives? This was from early in the Constitutional Convention conceived to be the representative body of the great body of the people, chosen by the people. But as to qualifications to vote for members of Congress, it was provided—and is still provided by the Constitution—that the voters in congressional elections in each state should be the same as those voting for the largest house of the state legislature. Except for the automatic qualification of electors for Congressmen as being the same as the qualification for electors for state legislators, the Federal Government had absolutely no control over any state's decision as to the voting qualifications of those permitted to vote for any officer of the Federal Government.

The Federal Government has shown fidelity to the constitutional command that the Congressmen should be apportioned among the states every ten years according to population. Since around the turn of the century, the apportionment of congressional representation among the states has occurred automatically under machinery provided by Congress for administrative solution of the mathematical problem of how many congressmen should be elected by the people of each state. State legislatures, however, often failed to reapportion themselves, so that as more people moved from the farms into the cities, the rural areas tended to retain their large numbers of representatives while the urban areas failed to gain additional state legislative representatives to reflect and represent their increased populations.

Gradually, with repeated failures by many state legislatures to reapportion themselves, decade after decade, many legislatures tended by the early 1960's to become rurally dominated, so that to a substantial measure, it appeared that the city people found themselves without adequate representation to solve problems unique to the urban areas. Laws needed or desired by city people were not passed because city people lacked sufficient numerical representation to compel compromise in the state legislatures, which exercised general governing power over them.

But since the nation's beginnings, it has constantly been the judgment of people designing state and local governments that people within each county unit should have some representation in the state legislature, limited though the population might be in many counties. Nor has this decision to allow comparatively small rural bodies of people to have an effective voice in their state government been brought about entirely by time lapses and the failure of state legislatures to reapportion themselves. In more than one state, the people themselves, possibly respecting the conservative and less pressurized thinking of the farmers and small community inhabitants, have consciously and intentionally chosen to leave control of one of the state legislative houses in the hands of the rural interests. That is to say, the urban majority has *intentionally given veto power* over proposed laws to the rural minority by giving them control of one legislative house.

Such have been the practical considerations of American politicians and leaders in designing American governments after they have studied the best way to achieve sound, responsible, fair, and lasting government that will best serve the needs of all the people.

Always, the power and responsibility of performing the fundamental task of dividing the states into legislative districts has resided in the legislature chosen by the people, or in some states, the power has resided in the people themselves, exercised in referenda following constitutional conventions. Never before the 1960's have the courts claimed for themselves this fundamental legislative power.

The Regal Prerogative:

By the 1960's, representation had become lop-sided in many states. Still, could it be said that this was not the republican form of government guaranteed by the Constitution? All the people who really weilded the power of government, the governors and legislators, were elected by the qualifed voters among the people. Of course, the matter of qualification to vote had to some extent been altered by amendments to the Constitution.[42] But the problem of remaking government to protect the rights of masses of voters, to apportion the legislature, to reform government itself, has always been viewed in America as a matter left to the people in each state, who could act through their representatives in their own state government or, in appropriate cases, through the power of Congress, to bring about change. Congress could always act to guarantee to the people in any state a republican form of government, though in fact, Congress has never acted for this purpose except at the time of initial admission of states into the Union. Perhaps the American state that came nearest to a government so designed that it could be rationally argued it was not a republican form of government was the state of Georgia.

Georgia's peculiar method of compromising between the desire for political power on the part of the many rural counties and the few urban counties, most notably the county in which Atlanta is located, was its county unit system. In the state House of Representatives, the state Senate, and even in state-wide races for governor and other offices, this county unit system was followed. Each of the least populous counties was given an evaluation weight of 1, each of a smaller group of more populous counties was given a weight of 2, and each of the most populous counties was allowed three unit votes. In electing a governor, representatives or senators, the votes of the people in the three smallest counties equalled in effect the votes of the hundreds of thousands of people in the county where Atlanta is located. Atlantans were ruled from the farmlands, and they lacked the slightest veto power—muscle to demand compromise from representatives of the rural interests. But even in Georgia there was a shading from its larger counties through intermediate counties, and down to the large block of sparsely-populated counties, so that on many issues, counties of medium population could be expected to vote with the large counties and some compromise achieved in legislative issues.

If Congress had acted upon its own power under the constitutional requirement that the United States guarantee to Georgia a republican form of government, this would have presented a very deep question of whether Georgia's government had actually become so lop-sided in representational qualities that it could truly be said to have ceased to be a republican form of government so as to authorized Congress to take action as required by the Constitution.[43]

---

42. First, an amendment for the benefit of the newly-freed black citizens, declaring that no citizen should be denied the right to vote on account of race, followed by amendments barring states from denying the right to vote because of sex, failure to pay poll tax, and finally, in federal elections, denying the right to vote on account of age to persons over 18 years old.

43. It is doubtful if Congress would have utilized barren assumptions of opposition voting between urban and rural representatives. With legislative votes customarily re-

We have examined the powers of the courts of equity as they existed when the Constitution was adopted, and have seen that the remaking of an entire government simply was not within the powers of a court of equity; that this was not the type of dispute-settlement powers granted to the federal judicial system when it was created and given the power to decide cases in equity.

In 1949, almost thirty years ago, in the case of *South v. Peters,* Georgia citizens endeavored to use the equity powers of the Federal courts to achieve revision of Georgia's system of government in its county unit device of electing state government officials. The Supreme Court held in the case that the federal equity powers could not be used to accomplish this result. The heart of the Supreme Court's very brief opinion in the case appears in a single sentence:

> "Federal Courts consistently refuse to exercise their equity powers in cases posing political issues arising from a state's geographical distribution of electoral strength among its political subdivisions."

Here we see no declaration that an endeavor to remake a government is not a case in equity but instead the implication that the "equity powers" exist and could be used for this purpose, but we do not deign to grant to the people of Georgia the benefit of the exercise of our power in their behalf. We have seen that this implication is contrary—totally contrary—to the nature of equity jurisprudence, which extended to disputes between private citizens but did not empower such courts to take over the discretionary functions of state officials and tell them how to perform those functions.[44]

The people of Georgia could not sue the government of Georgia itself in the United States Supreme Court, which had original trial-court jurisdiction over lawsuits against states, because the Eleventh Amendment to the Constitution expressly destroyed all existing federal jurisdiction to entertain suits brought by individuals against a state—and the Judicial Article of the Constitution had *never given* the federal courts jurisdiction of any suits brought against any state *by its own citizens.*

Yet by failing to explore the historic and very limited nature of the powers of a court of equity, and by failing to declare that the federal judicial system totally lacked the power to give any aid to the people of Georgia, the Supreme Court in *South v. Peters* actually held out to Georgians hope for the future by stating that the federal courts refuse to use their equity powers in such political disputes. There was hope for Georgians: The Court's mind might be changed in the future.[45]

---

corded, Congress would likely require statistical analyses of actual votes on urban/rural issues, along with testimony concerning compromises between the opposed groups of interests in the two legislative houses.

44. We have seen that this is totally contrary to the nature of equity jurisprudence, which concerned itself with disputes involving individual citizens and groups of citizens, not with the discretionary functions of governmental officials.

45. A decade after *South v. Peters,* on June 8, 1959, a unanimous Supreme Court decided *Lassiter v. Northampton County Board of Elections,* upholding the power of North Carolina to require successful completion of a literacy test to qualify to vote. A black woman refused to even take the test, and the Supreme Court said: "The ability to read and write . . . has some relation to standards designed to promote intelligent use of the ballot. Literacy and intelligence are neutral on race, creed, color and sex, as reports around the world show. . . . [Where] newspapers, periodicals, books

During the fifteen years that followed the decision of *South v. Peters,* there were two amendments to the Constitution. Neither of them [46] in any way affected the voting rights of Georgia citizens and neither of them affected the scope of the judicial powers of the United States to control voting rights in state or federal elections. Neither of them enlarged the equitable powers of the federal courts, or empowered those courts to protect political rights according to the political theories held by the judges of those courts. There were no material changes in the Constitution during the fifteen years that followed the Court's decision of *South v. Peters.* Yet fifteen years after that decision, the United States Supreme Court came to the aid of the people of Georgia. Nothing changed but the voting count among the justices of the Court.

The case was *Wesberry v. Sanders.* This was the first case in which the Supreme Court endeavored to demonstrate that there was a controlling body of federal law to determine apportionment questions. The Court had shortly before this strengthened its intimation in *South v. Peters* that the federal courts might have the power to do something about the apportionment situation should they choose to grant the people the benefit of the exercise of that mighty power.[47] But no attempt had been made to explain the source of some federal law that might actually govern and solve the problems of apportionment of a state's area into voting districts for any election. And *Wesberry v. Sanders* was concerned with congressional apportionment for a Federal election, not apportionment for state elections of state officials.

In *Wesberry v. Sanders,* the meaning of the Constitution was warped almost beyond belief. The purpose was a popular one but so were the purposes of the Court of Star Chamber when it moved to ruthlessly restore order to a disordered society.[48] The Supreme Court's holding in the case was that in each state, the state must be divided into congressional districts of population as nearly equal as possible. No language in the Constitution can honestly be interpreted as issuing any such command. The Constitution does not even command that the states themselves have strict representational equality according to population, because it guarantees to even the smallest state one member in Congress.

In seizing control of the complexion of the Congress of the United States, the Supreme Court exercised an immense power, which exercise of power the Congress supinely accepted, though Congress itself has the power expressly given to

---

and other printed matter canvass and debate campaign issues a State might conclude that only those who are literate should exercise the franchise." Thus, although the Court emphasized the "reasonableness" of the test in view of the "state interest," the Court also held that the regulation of voting rights is within the exclusive power of the State. So, however, is the right to operate laundries in wooden buildings, marry and procreate and virtually all other aspects of daily life. All the Court need have said was that the matter was within the exclusive regulatory power of state government, absent refusal to permit voting on account of race. The Equal Protection Clause properly had nothing to do with voting rights, just as the Court's customary "Equal Protection" rationale had nothing to do with the meaning of the Equal Protection Clause.

46. These amendments limited the presidential office to two terms and granted the people of the District of Columbia the right to vote in presidential elections.

47. See below, *Baker v. Carr,* pp. 291, *et seq.*

48. There is very grave danger in admitting that it is *ever* legitimate for any government official to exercise power when the law does not give him that power, even if the objectives he attains by using the power are objectives we yearn to achieve.

it by the Constitution to do exactly what the Supreme Court did, and though the Constitution did not give that power to the Supreme Court.

In his dissent, Mr. Justice Harlan explained why,[49] if respected and followed by other states, the Supreme Court's enunciation of a new constitutional provision would result in changing the congressional districts electing all but thirty-seven of the four hundred thirty-five members of the House of Representatives. This large assumption of power by the Supreme Court over the House of Representatives would have been thought impossible throughout most of America's history; it should have been supported, if a correct decision, by reasoning so strong as to irresistably demonstrate that the result was commanded by the plain words of the Constitution. The decision did not even approach such a demonstration. To the contrary, it was a decision which sought to justify the result it imposed by false rationalization instantly transparent to any student of the Constitution. And by such false rationalization, the Supreme Court arrogantly seized for the judiciary powers given to Congress.

Here is the reasoning utilized by the Supreme Court to endeavor to support its announced decision that the Constitution requires (and has always required) each congressional district in a state to be as nearly as practicable equal in population. The Court stated that the population of Georgia's congressional districts widely varied, from the largest district of over 823,000 people to the smallest district of slightly over 272,000 people, each district electing one Congressman. The Court said of this apportionment law first enacted in 1911 and never changed since then: "The apportionment statute thus contracts the value of some votes and expands that of others." This statement is false. In the largest as in the smallest district, each voter was allowed to cast one vote and only one vote, which went into the totalling process to elect one congressman and only one congressman. The value of each voter's vote in each of the districts was subject to being "cancelled out" by one vote cast by one voter for the opposing candidate. Each voter's vote had precisely the same effect in each district; the value of neither individual vote was contracted and the value of neither was expanded.

The Court sad: "We hold that, construed in its historical context, the command of Art. I, § 2, that Representatives be chosen 'by the People of the several States' means that as nearly as is practicable, one man's vote in a congressional election is to be worth as much as another's." To buttress its conclusion as to the rule to be imposed upon every state legislature, requiring them to reapportion the state for the purpose of Congressional elections, the Court quoted from James Madison in No. 57 of *The Federalist:*

> " 'Who are to be the electors of the Federal Representatives? Not the rich more than the poor; not the learned more than the ignorant; not the haughty heirs of distinguished names more than the humble sons of obscure and unpropitious fortune. The electors are to be the great body of the people of the United States. . . .'

---

49. "I had not expected to witness the day when the Supreme Court of the United States would render a decision which cast grave doubt upon the constitutionality of the composition of the House of Representatives. It is not an exaggeration to say that such is the effect of today's decision. The Court's holding that the Constitution requires States to select representatives either by elections at large or by elections in districts composed 'as nearly as practicable' of equal population places in jeopardy the seats of almost all the members of the present House of Representatives."

"Readers surely could have fairly taken this to mean, 'one person, one vote.' . . ."

Actually, readers of Madison could have taken this to mean no such thing, because they would not have stopped reading where the Supreme Court stopped quoting. Readers would have gone on to read the very next sentence, after his statement that the voters should be the great body of the people, with its implication that everyone should be able to vote:

"They [the great body of the people] are to be the *same who exercise the right* in every state of electing the corresponding branch of the legislature of the State."

Madison was speaking of the entitlement of individuals to vote, not of the relative size of voting districts, and the complete text negates any assumption that the portion quoted by the Supreme Court implied that every member of "the great body of the people" was to be entitled to vote.

But the Supreme Court virtually ignored the fact that those who wrote the Constitution refused to write into it any command that congressional districts be apportioned by population. They adopted a very different device for determining the areas from which Congressmen should be elected.

The states were perfectly free to require that all congressmen be elected by the qualified voters of the entire state, and they were free to divide the state into congressional districts. The Constitution expressly stated that the legislatures should be empowered to determine the time of holding congressional elections, the places (or districts) in which to hold the elections, and all such details except the qualifications of voters, which were determinable by the qualifications for voting for representatives in the larger house of the state legislature.

But it was recognized that a state might give disproportionate strength to the people in a particular area by so establishing the places, or districts, for holding elections that most congressmen would be elected by a minority of the voters. To protect against this, the Constitution gives Congress—not the judiciary—the power to make overriding regulations as to the times and places of electing members of Congress in each state. It is because Congress has exercised this power that the congressional elections are held the same day throughout the nation. The Constitution contains no rules as to how Congress should exercise this power. It is free to require that the people of the entire state vote on all congressional seats, to divide the state into districts, to disregard county lines or be governed by them. This was the protective device created by the Constitution itself in unmistakable language, to protect the people against state legislative abuse of the power to divide the state into congressional districts. And when Congress passes uniform laws on this subject, all states are clearly denied any power to further legislate, because this was the purpose of giving Congress overriding control.

Justice Harland beautifully demonstrated the falsity of the Court's rationalization in support of its new claim of power belonging to Congress. When the Constitution was written, there existed wide disparities in the population of state legislative districts in a number of states, and most notably in South Carolina, and Madison was called upon to defend the fact that the Federal Congress was given *any power* to override state legislatures in dividing the states into congressional districts. As quoted by Justice Harlan, Madison said:

"Besides, the inequality of the Representation in the Legislatures of particular States, would produce a like inequality in their representation in the Natl. Legislature, as it was presumable that the Counties have the power in the former case [control of the state legislature] would secure it to themselves in the latter [election of congressmen]. *What danger could there be in giving a controlling power to the Natl. Legislature?**

Georgia had not been reapportioned for congressional elections since 1931, and population shifts had obviously occurred since then in Georgia as in other states; and numbers of states had not re-drawn their congressional district lines since 1900, 1910, or 1920. One gains the impression from reading the various Supreme Court opinions on congressional apportionment that here was a national scandal, a national disgrace, in which numerous state legislatures had violated the solemn obligation to reapportion, imposed by a sense of fairness according to a population-based standard which in fact was not written into the Constitution in any place.

This was likely also the general popular opinion. But the strange thing, unnoticed by the Supreme Court in *Wesberry v. Sanders,* is that the state legislatures were not violating law, *but were obeying law.* As reviewed in prior Supreme Court decisions (holding the courts not empowered to act in such cases), the standing congressional enactment had *forbidden the state legislatures to change the congressional district lines unless the total number of congressmen allowed a state should be increased or decreased.*

As to what should guide the state legislatures in such redistricting as Congress permitted them to perform, Mr. Justice Harlan reviewed the history of Congress' districting laws. As reviewed by him, with quotations from past congressional acts and past Supreme Court decisions, Congress had for many decades expressly required that the state legislatures apportion the state in to districts of equal population for Congressional elections. In 1929, Congress intentionally dropped this requirement that districts be equal in population and intentionally left to each state the discretion as to how to perform this political function when it was to be performed.

This intentional rejection by Congress of the old requirement that each congressional district should have equal population was rejected repeatedly by Congress on a number of occasions thereafter. Bills were introduced, attempting to impose on the states a requirement that they reapportion into approximately equally-populated legislative districts, and each such bill was rejected by Congress. The only power created by the Constitution to revise, alter, or veto state legislative political judgments as to the size and shape of congressional districts had been resoundingly exercised in a manner contrary to the political theories now espoused by the Supreme Court. By seizing and exercising this congressional power in *Wesberry v. Sanders,* the Supreme Court can hardly be said to have done less than wilfully violate the Constitution. It must be considered wilful, because the fact of the usurpation was brought to the Court's attention in the unquestionable facts related in Mr. Justice Harlan's dissent, of which the Court is charged with knowledge.

Power to Re-Make State Governments:

How came the Supreme Court to assume that it might exercise powers to control the performance of discretionary governmental functions by non-judicial officers? This was a type of power historically exercised by the Court of Star Chamber and the King in Council, not by the courts of equity in deciding cases in equity. Even before deciding *Wesberry v. Sanders,* the Supreme Court claimed to have demonstrated that the powers of the courts of equity included the power to regulate the manner of performance by state officials of these discretionary functions. They are necessarily discretionary functions, because mathematical lines can be drawn in millions of different arrangements within any state. Fine political judgement as well as infantile arithmetic enters into the performance of these functions, and renders them discretionary.

This regal power to control the discretionary decisions of non-judicial officers, which had never been anything but regal power, or executive power when exercised by the executive head of government controlling the decisions of his subordinates in the executive branch, was granted by the Supreme Court to the federal trial judges, themselves often politically selected from one of two opposing political factions or parties. Into the hands of these judges, many lacking any prior lengthy judicial experience to demonstrate their capacity for the proper performance of the judicial functions, was suddenly thrust the powers of governors-general, the delegated powers of King in Council, to reform and reshape state governments.

As common sense might have predicted, the results were high-handed, and indeed, the Court spoke in the tones of royal prerogative, of the royal grant of permission, and it moved with the appearance of conscious enjoyment of this immense ruling power that had now been discovered, after so long lying dormant. After lying domant, in fact, since July 4, 1776.

The following cases reflect this regal language from these latter days of the United States Supreme Court:

1964—*Reynolds v. Sims:* Suit was brought by all the city people in Alabama (we know all these hundreds of thousands of people sued, because a few people sued, claiming they represented "all similarly situated Alabama voters") against some election officials to accomplish judicial reapportionment of the Alabama legislative districts, and the Alabama Legislature met to propose to the people of the state certain constitutional amendments, hopefully adequate to come up to the current judicial standards supposedly required by the Constitution of the United States. The Supreme Court said of some of the Alabama happenings, "With the crazy-quilt existing apportionment *virtually* conceded to be invalid, the Alabama Legislature *offered two proposed plans for consideration by the District Court, . . .*" Assuming the quotation accurately summarized the events, no legislature ever has any business *submitting* any of its legislation for approval by a mere judge.[50] One of the complaints in the Declaration of Independence concerned the king's withholding his approval of legislation. The executive power to grant or withhold approval of legislation is not lawfully lodged in any judge in the federal judicial system. Whenever it is exercised by judges, it is exercised by usurpation, for it is not a judicial power.

1964—*Roman v. Sincock:* "After attempting to deliniate some guidelines for the Delaware Legislature to follow in reapportioning, the court below, with an eye toward the impending 1964 elections, *gave the General Assembly until Oc-*

---

50. Throughout America, the sole remnant of the regal legislative-approving power, where it exists, is vested in the executive, either president, governor or mayor. Proposals in the Constitutional Convention to vest such powers in the judiciary were carefully considered and firmly rejected. See *Documents Illustrative of the Formation of the Union,* pp. 548, 756, 849, 852. It is the legislative function to enact, not to submit enactments to judges, and it is the judicial duty to disregard unconstitutional enactments, but the judiciary has no proper involvement in the enacting process.

tober 1, 1963, *to adopt a constitutionally valid plan.*" Legislatures stand in the place of the people of a state and exercise the law-making power delegated to them by the peole. No judge ever has any prerogative to "give" any legislature a deadline for taking *any* action on *any* subject.

1966—*Burns v. Richardson:*

The State remains free to adopt other plans for apportionment, and the present interim plan will remain in effect for no longer time than is necessary to adopt a permanent plan. . . . For present purposes, HB 987 may be treated together with the existing House apportionment as a new, overall *proposal for interim apportionment.* . . . We direct the District Court to enter an order appropriate to adopt the plan as the court's own for legislative apportionment applicable . . . until . . . another interim plan for reapportionment of the Hawaii legislature *suggested* by the legislature is approved by the court.

Legislative enactments are neither proposals nor suggestions, and the presumptous language used by the Supreme Court toward the Legislature of Hawaii is characteristic of the type of action taken by the federal judiciary.[51]

In 1962, the United States Supreme Court discovered that courts of equity had the power to re-make state governments. Before the exercise of a power that has never been claimed or used in the entire history of the federal judiciary, some theory must be contrived to endeavor to demonstrate the existence of the power. The theory was contrived as the means of solving state legislative reapportionment problems in *Baker v. Carr,* a case from Nashville, Tennessee.

The Supreme Court's opinion in *Baker v. Carr* is a true masterpiece of deceptive reasoning. It must be considered outstanding for its intellectual gymnastics. Mr. Justice Frankfurter, dissenting from the decision,[52] wrote of its unwisdom as a policy decision:

"We are soothingly told at the bar of this Court that we need not worry about the kind of remedy a court could effectively fashion once the abstract constitu-

---

51. The regal language accompanying the federal judiciary's regal conduct suggests that regal language follows the exercise of regal powers, and perhaps the use of such language encourages its users to enlarge their regal conduct when they find themselves not reprimanded.

52. Justice Frankfurter wrote of the disregard of past decisions: "The Court today reverses a uniform course of decisions established by a dozen cases, including one by which the very claim now sustained was unanimously rejected only five years ago. The impressive body of rulings thus cast aside reflected the equally uniform course of our political history regarding the relationship between population and legislative representation—a wholly different matter from the denial of the franchise to individuals because of race, color, religion or sex . . . Disregard of inherent limits of the effective exercise of the Court's 'judicial power' not only presages the futility of judicial intervention in the essentially political conflict of forces by which the relation between population and representation has time out of mind been and now is determined. It may well impair this Court's position as the ultimate organ of 'the supreme Law of the Land' in that vast range of legal problems, often strongly entangled in popular feelings, on which this Court must pronounce. The Court's authority—possessed of neither the purse nor the sword—ultimately rests upon sustained public confidence in its moral sanction. Such feeling must be nourished by the Court's complete detachment, in fact and in appearance, from political entanglements and by abstention from injecting itself into the clash of political forces in political settlements."

tional right to have courts pass on a state-wide system of electoral districting is recognized as a matter of judicial rhetoric, because legislatures would heed the Court's admonition. This is not only a euphoric hope. It implies a sorry confession of judicial impotence in place of a frank acknowledgement that there is not under our Constitution a judicial remedy for every political mischief, for every undesirable exercise of legislative power. The Framers carefully and with deliberate forethought *refused to so enthrone the judiciary.* In this situation, as in others of like nature, appeal for relief does not belong here. Appeal must be to an informed, civically militant electorate. In a democratic society like ours, relief must come through an aroused public conscience that sears the conscience of the people's representatives. In any event, there is nothing judicially more unseemly nor more self-defeating than for this Court to make *in terrorem* pronouncements, to indulge in merely empty rhetoric, sounding a word of promise to the ear, sure to be disappointing to the hope."

Mr. Justice Frankfurter's prediction of judicial inability to accomplish the result of reformation of the shape of state governments evidenced his misjudgment of the ends to which the federal judiciary was capable of being swept in its excitement, and of the depths to which the people's sense of political viability had sunk, as state governments bowed before the will of judges.

As a case perfect for the Supreme Court to announce its new assumption of power, Tennessee's was an excellent choice. The state constitution imposed a mandatory duty upon its legislature to reapportion itself every ten years, but the legislature had not done this for sixty years. Clearly, the legislature had disobeyed the commands of the state constitution. But even given this indisputable conclusion, there remained immense problems in assuming the federal judiciary might supervise the performance of these functions.

First, no provision in the Federal Constitution requires that state officials obey the commands of their state's constitution.

Second, the Tennessee Constitution did not require assignment of legislators strictly by population; it provided that each county should be permitted to elect at least one representative to the state legislature, just as the Federal Constitution provides that each state, even the smallest, may elect one Congressman to the Federal House of Representatives.

Third, the jurisdiction to decide cases in equity did not extend to control the manner in which governmental officials made their discretionary decisions, an insurmountable problem. It could not be explained away, but could only be disregarded in the pretense that courts of equity had general governing powers instead of simply powers to resolve complex disputes between individual citizens and groups of citizens.

Therefore, the problems involved in maintaining a suit in a federal trial court to compel reapportionment of state legislative districts are insoluble, if one concentrates his attention upon the Constitution itself in carrying out the sworn obligation to support and defend it. Reformation of election districts in the federal courts had been attempted many times before *Baker v. Carr,* and never had the federal courts found themselves permitted by law to exercise any such power. By commanding a republican form of government for each state, the Constitution vests in the people's representatives in each state the power to reform and reorganize the political structure of state government. By assuming to exercise this power, the federal courts would actively and effectively destroy this most fundamental aspect of the republican form of government.[53]

---

53. Long ago, Mr. Justice Douglas commented in his dissenting opinion in *Snowden*

In *Baker v. Carr,* for the first time in American history, the Supreme Court decided—or sort of decided—that federal trial judges have this power to remake the legislative representational scheme of the state government. It remained for Mr. Justice Harlan, in his dissent, to pinpoint a fundamental error in the Court's rationalization:

"Once one cuts through the thicket of discussion devoted to 'jurisdiction,' 'standing,' 'justiciability,' and 'political questions,' there emerges a straight-forward issue which, in my view, is determinative of this case. Does the complaint disclose the violation of a federal constitutional right, in other words, a claim over which a United States District Court would have jurisdiction [under federal statutes]? . . . The majority opinion does not actually discuss this basic question . . ."

This was the primary defect of the Supreme Court's opinion in *Baker v. Carr,* aside from its specious reasoning. The Court never answered the questions involved in the lawsuit, whether the Constitution commands apportionment of State legislatures according to population and if so, whether the federal judicial system has the authority to compel obedience to that command. Instead, by a review of cases under which this power had *never been exercised,* the Supreme Court claimed to have demonstrated that the power *actually exists.*

In the lawsuit, Mr. Baker sued Secretary of State Carr and other officials having duties in the state electoral process, claiming that the 1901 legislative apportionment act had become invalid because of changes in population patterns. He and the other citizens joining with him from all the major cities in the state asked that the election officials be enjoined from conducting any further elections under the old apportionment scheme alleged to be unconstitutional.

One of the most misleading citations used by the Supreme Court to attempt to support its specious reasoning in *Baker v. Carr* was its citation to *Wood v. Broome* and a similar case, *Mahan v. Hume.* In each of these cases, citizens of a state had sought to use federal judicial power to bring about reapportionment of state legislative districts. Of *Wood v. Broome,* the Supreme Court said that a federal district court had "permanently enjoined officers of the State of Mississippi from conducting an election of Representatives under a Mississippi redistricting act, we reviewed the Federal questions on the merits and reversed the district court." Of *Mahan v. Hume,* the Supreme Court said: "A similar decree of a District Court, . . . concerning a Kentucky redistricting act was reviewed and the decree reversed." The implication was that the Federal courts had already been deciding reapportionment-type cases on the merits and that this supports a conclusion that such courts have power in equity cases to compel reapportionment.

Actually, in the *Wood* case, a federal trial court had held illegal a Mississippi apportionment of the state into congressional districts for election of Congressmen; it did this on its theory as to the meaning of the Constitution and the Acts of Congress prescribing the methods of congressional apportionment. The Supreme Court, weighing the merits of the case, found that the trial court had ruled incorrectly in its decision that federal law required apportionment to be based upon population. Considering there was no valid lawsuit at all in the case, the Supreme

---

v. Hughes: "I agree that the equal protection clause of the Fourteenth Amendment should not be distorted to make the federal courts the supervisor of state elections. That would place the federal judiciary in a position 'to supervise and review the political administration of a state government by its own officials and through its own courts' . . .—matters on which each state has the final say."

Court did not even go into the question of whether the federal courts could afford a remedy if the Constitution were violated. To the contrary, the Supreme Court said in *Wood v. Broome:*

> "it is unnecessary to consider the questions raised as to the right of the complainant to relief in equity upon the allegations of the bill of complaint, or as to the justiciability of the controversy. . . . Upon these questions the Court expresses no opinion."

So contrary to the implication sought to be conveyed by the Court's opinion in *Baker v. Carr, Wood v. Broome* was not a decision that federal courts of equity are empowered to do anything about malapportionment, even if it should violate both the Constitution and Acts of Congress, because the Supreme Court itself said in *Wood v. Broome* that it *was not passing judgment on that question.* A holding that citizens *cannot* use federal courts to achieve a desired result claimed to be commanded by the Constitution cannot logically be warped into proof that the federal courts *do have the power* to afford the remedy they have always refused to afford.

The earlier case of *Colgrove v. Green,* in which the Supreme Court held that federal judicial power could not accomplish congressional reapportionment according to population, was discussed by the Court in *Baker v. Carr.* The court said that this decision had been urged upon it as authority that the Federal courts lacked jurisdiction over the subject-matter of congressional apportionment. The Court said: "Appellees misconceive the holding of that case. *The holding was precisely contrary to their reading of it.*"

The holding was not precisely contrary. It was the express holding of *Colgrove v. Green* that the federal courts of equity could not accomplish reapportionment of congressional districts.

The Supreme Court said in *Colgrove v. Green:* "We are of the opinion that the petitioners ask this Court what is beyond *its competence* to grant." In speaking of the relief sought, an injunction to compel reapportionment, as being beyond the competence of the Court, the Court was speaking in terms of the limits of its power. The Court sought to demonstrate the wisdom of this denial of power to the judiciary. But it used as an example the fact that the Constitution expressly requires Congress to apportion the congressional seats among the several states [54] on the basis of population, and that Congress had sometimes failed to perform this duty. As to the scope of federal judicial power, the Court said in *Colgrove v. Green:*

> "It never occurred to anyone that this Court *could* issue mandamus to compel Congress to perform its mandatory duty to apportion. 'What might not be done directly by mandamus, could not be *attained indirectly by injunction.*' Chaffee, *Congressional Reapportionment* (1929), 42 Harvard L. Rev. 1015, 1019."

This was not an affirmation of "subject-matter jurisdiction," as claimed by the Supreme Court in *Baker v. Carr.* It was a declaration that the federal judiciary lacked the power, or jurisdiction, over suits brought to compel even congressional reapportionment.

Seeking to establish that there was "subject-matter jurisdiction" and therefore that a federal court of equity had power to take this enormous action that Ten-

---

54. As contrasted with apportionment within a state.

nesseans asked it to take in *Baker v. Carr,* the Supreme Court then proceeded to cite a number of *"Per Curiam"* opinions (unsigned opinions "by the court") rendered in a number of cited cases. The Supreme Court had decided each of these cases by *refusing to use* federal judicial powers to perform the function of legislative apportionment. Of these dismissals, the Supreme Court said in *Baker v. Carr:* "None was dismissed for want of jurisdiction of the subject-matter."

Considering the subject-matter to be the power of the federal judiciary to remedy state legislative malapportionment, this statement by the Supreme Court was false. A number of the cases were expressly dismissed upon the ground that there was no substantial question of federal law involved in them, *i.e.,* that this subject was not within the scope of federal constitutional rights and federal judicial powers. For example, in one of the cases cited by the Court, *Tedesco v. Board of Supervisors of Elections for the Parrish of Orleans,* the Supreme Court's entire statement was: "The motion to dismiss is granted and the appeal is dismissed for want of *a substantial federal question."* [55]

After reviewing some political cases,[56] the Supreme Court announced that it found no reason why it should not exercise jurisdiction over the performance of a Tennessee legislative function. The Court said:

"The question here is the consistence of state action with the Federal Constitution. We have no question decided, or to be decided, by a political branch of government co-equal with this Court. Nor do we risk embarrassment of our government abroad, or grave disturbance at home *if we take issue with Tennessee* as to the constitutionality of her action here challenged.[57]

It is clearly true that the case involved neither international repercussions nor the risk of grave internal political disruptions. But it is equally clear that this quotation evidences an entirely irrational theory: The theory that it can be assumed from the non-existence of some of the reasons which occasionally restrain courts from exercising power proves that the power legitimately exists. In truth, lawful federal judicial power is derived only from the Constitution—never from the assumption that the people will not question the lawfulness of judicial pronouncements, hence no grave disturbance can result, so the power is legitimate. This rationalization justifies all usurped power of every *coup d'etat.* It is a rationalization foreign to the theory of constitutional government.

As bearing upon its equity powers, the Court mentioned two cases "which held that federal equity power *could not be exercised* to enjoin a state proceeding to remove a public officer." The Court's characterization of this limitation upon

---

55. The same statement was made in *Remmey v. Smith,* and a number of these cases cited in *Baker v. Carr* simply dismissed the appeal without stating any reason, quite often simply by referring to the *Colgrove* decision.

56. Including Chief Justice Taney's mistaken decision of *Luther v. Borden,* the Dorr Rebellion case involving a trespass to real property in Rhode Island, in which the chief justice visualized the disruptive effects that could result from judicial endeavors to actually control the conduct of the President. This, as we saw, was a case decided on a point in no way properly involved in the decision of the simple lawsuit.

57. The fact of the non-existence of one or more particular reasons to defeat judicial decision could never establish the positive existence of the power to· "take issue with Tennessee" by regulating and reorganizing its government, in the face of the fact that the Constitution carefully withholds from the judicial branch of the federal government any power to even hear suits against a state by citizens of that state, of another state, or of a foreign government.

federal equity powers was explained away by the Court with one sentence upon which it amplified at length:

> "But these decisions explicitly reflect only a traditional limit upon equity juris-prudence, and not upon *federal courts' power to inquire into matters of state governmental organization.*"

This was another of the Court's misunderstandings. The only power given to the federal courts in this regard is the power of the courts of equity in deciding cases in equity, which power is so tyrannical in its nature, including the power to deprive people of their liberty by ordering them to do specific acts, that equity jurisdiction consists of nothing but this power *with its traditional limits.* Remove the traditional limits, and you have not equity powers, but the powers of the Court of Star Chamber and of the King in Council, which are not vested in any court in the Federal judicial system.[58]

It was the mighty will of government, through the Supreme Court, that all the state legislatures should be apportioned in accordance with the latest and most liberal political theories on population-based legislative apportionment. The Supreme Court, by satisfying itself that various objections which had been successfully raised to bar the exercise of this power by federal courts in many different cases had no application to this particular case, irrationally claimed to conclude that the Court had the power to do what it had always ruled could not be done or was not required by federal law.

So the Supreme Court sent the case back to the trial court to consider the only questions involved in the case. But the Court's opinion gave a rather strong indication that the Court expected the trial courts of the United States to take over and somehow assure that the laws of each state would be changed to arrive at legislative apportionment on some population-related basis. The Court made no attempt, and did not even claim to have attempted, to demonstrate that state legislative malapportionment violates some provision of the Constitution.

Claimed Theoretical Basis for Compelling Reapportionment:

Where legislative election districts are unevenly populated, commonly every voter is allowed to vote to elect one legislator or one congressman, the only difference being that some congressmen and legislators have much larger constituencies than do others. However, it is quite clear that if the right of individuals even to cast a ballot is not subject to the absolute equality commanded by the Equal Protection Clause of the Fourteenth Amendment, that clause certainly has no relation to the adoption of particular voter ratios based upon abstract refinements of theories as to the republican form of government.

Less than three years before its decision in *Baker v. Carr,* the Supreme Court held that North Carolina's literacy voter qualification law did not violate the Equal Protection Clause, and that North Carolina could refuse to permit a black woman to vote because of her inability to read.[59] It was contended in *Baker v.*

---

58. The fact that equity powers did not extend to the use of those powers to usurp the functions of other officers of government, though quite inferior in rank, was not a mere discretionary withholding of action. It was the difference between the scope of equity powers, existing to do justice between citizens, and of the tyrannical Star Chambers, existing to enforce the will of government upon the people.

59. Discussed above, n. 45.

Carr that the Equal Protection Clause somehow requires state legislative districts to be equal in population. The general tone of the Supreme Court's opinion conveyed the message that the federal district courts were expected to create some rationale to demonstrate a connection between the Equal Protection Clause and the size of state legislative districts.

But how could the Equal Protection Clause, concerned with the rights of individuals, have anything to do with political theories as to the republican form of government and how such a government could best be organized? This question, unanswered in *Baker v. Carr,* was to remain without any Supreme Court endeavor to answer it for two more years, until 1964, when the Supreme Court delivered its Equal Protection rationalization in *Reynolds v. Sims.*

Reynolds v. Sims was more than a case: It was one of a family of cases, all *en utero,* awaiting simultaneous birth on June 15, 1964, when the opinions were handed down in a number of cases involving the apportionment of state legislative districts. *Reynolds v. Sims* undertook the reapportionment of the Alabama legislature, *W. M. C. A. v. Lomenzo* altered New York government, *Maryland Committee for Fair Representation v. Tawes* revamped Maryland government, *Roman v. Sincock* disapproved the legislative apportionment among Delaware's three counties, *Davis v. Mann* provided a new safeguard omitted by Madison and others of the Founding Fathers in writing Virginia's constitution, and *Lucas v. Forty-Fourth General Assembly of the State of Colorado* administered lessons to the people of Colorado as to the meaning and sanctity of the republican form of government.

All the opinions being released the same day, the Alabama case was necessarily chosen intentionally as the case in which to "prove" that when the Constitution says that no state shall "deny to *any person within its jurisdiction* the equal protection of the laws," this means that each legislator has to represent a district containing approximately the same number of people as those represented by each of the other legislators.

Alabama's arithmetic was horrible. The state legislative districts had not been reapportioned for sixty years, the Supreme Court related in *Reynolds v. Sims,* so that "Jefferson County, with over 600,000 people, was given only one senator, as was Lowndes County, with a 1960 population of only 15,417, and Wilcox County, with only 18,739 people." Worse than this, "only 25.1% of the State's total population resided in districts represented by a majority of the members of the Senate, and only 25.7% lived in counties which could elect a majority of the members of the House of Representatives. Population-variance ratios of up to about 41-to-1 existed in the Senate, and up to 16-to-1 in the House." [60]

So a brief mathematical examination of the Alabama discrepancies gave a shocking picture. Does it not seem that if a small minority of the people are given control of the state government and their representatives empowered to rule all the people that this is a destruction of the republican form of government which the Constitution requires the United States to guarantee? In the business of re-making state governments, perhaps Congress could have passed a special

---

60. Some of the other states would have been poor choices to use to attempt to demonstrate that the personal guarantee of each *individual's* equality in subjection to state law required that each legislator be chosen from a district equal in population to districts choosing every other legislator. Alabama was the best choice because the arithmetical comparisons between the sizes of different legislative districts was most impressive.

law to carry out its duty and power to guarantee to Alabamians this republican form of government: Such a law might have required that a population-based constitutional convention be held by the people of Alabama, but the Congress had not seen fit to take any such action. If it had, it might possibly have noted some elements other than bare majority figures in deciding whether it was called upon to exercise this power.

If Congress had waited until 1970 to consider this question, the 1970 census might give it pause to wonder whether the cities subjected to such discrimination were actually entitled to rule the state. A majority of the state's population in 1970 was 1,722,082 people. Only four cities in the state had populations exceeding 100,000 and of these, all had populations less than 200,000 except Birmingham, which had slightly over 300,000 people. These four cities had a combined population of slightly over 762,000 people, less than one-fourth the state's 1970 population. In considering the rural-urban imbalance of Alabama's legislature, if Congress in 1970 should take into account the populations of the twenty largest cities in the state, it would have descended in city sizes to the town of Enterprise, Alabama, with its population of 15,591 people, and the total population of these twenty cities still would not constitute one-half the state's population.

Going further, Congress would have found that to conglomerate enough Alabama cities to arrive at a majority of the state's population in 1970, it would have to consider every Alabama town having a population in excess of 5,000 people except the towns of Piedmont (5,063), Pleasant Grove (5,090), and Fultondale (5,163). Under this mathematical theorizing, Fultondale should be expected to vote with the country people, while the representatives of the 5,251 people of Roanoke, Alabama, would vote with the urban majority of which they were a part.[61]

Moving to Alabama's county populations, one finds a number of small counties in which the bare majority of the county's population lives in the county seat, within its city limits, and there is ground for suspicion that if several counties be combined into a voting district, the city voters, if they vote for a better-known city candidate, might well leave the rural people without any voice in state government.

No intelligent judgment can be passed upon the question of whether lop-sided representation by percentage figures actually destroys the republican form of government, because all the representatives attained their seats by being elected by some of the people, and all the qualified voters in the state were permitted to participate in the selection of one or more representatives.

But of this is concerned with the republican form of government, the method of organizing state government and its representation so that the people living in each area will have some voice in government, and so it will be assured that the people living in no area will, as a practical matter, be totally unrepresented. A

---

61. Actually, Fultondale might be supposed more urban than rural in outlook because it is one of the cities located in the same county where Birmingham is located. County populations are the only valid basis for comparison, because many people live outside the larger or smaller cities; Birmingham has only 48% of the county's population. Alabama statistics would seem to indicate that the rural people should have a substantial voice in state government, with 41.8% of its people living in 80% of the state's counties which have no cities with a population over 20,000 people, and with over 450,000 of its people living in counties that do not have a single town with as many as 5,000 people.

traditional American system of organizing state governmental powers has been to have local law-enforcement and taxing officials elected by the people in each county, with alterations in county government made by the state legislature, which necessitates the people in each county having some voice in the legislature so their needs can effectively be made known. Theories as to the organization of the republican form of government have no apparent relation to the right of each person within a state to equal protection of the laws of the state as they govern such people.

In *Reynolds v. Sims*—at last!—came the Supreme Court's attempt to demonstrate some connection between the Equal Protection Clause and the aim of massive legislative reapportionment in the various states. Put aside republican form of government, political theory and proceed upon the real subject of the existence of judicial power to act and of a command compelling the judiciary to act—the protection of an individual's specific constitutional rights.

The Supreme Court began its attempted demonstration of the connection in Part II of its opinion in *Reynolds v. Sims* with this sentence: "Undeniably the Constitution of the United States protects the right of all qualified citizens to vote, in state as well as in federal elections."

The Constitution of the United States only protects the right of each qualified citizen to vote in *Federal elections, for Congressman, Senator, and presidential electors,* by its provisions that the persons entitled to vote shall be the same as those entitled to vote for representatives to the most numerous house of the state legislature. But aside from these particular elections, the Constitution is silent in regard to the right to vote, except that it denies states the power to refuse to permit people to vote for particular reasons, such as race, sex, and non-payment of poll tax. The qualified voter can enforce his political right to vote by going into a state court, without making the slightest appeal to the Constitution of the United States.[62] The Constitution has absolutely nothing to do with the practical enforcement of the right of a state's citizen to vote in one of its elections.

To support its false premise, the Court began with the citations to two cases, *Ex Parte Yarbrough* and *United States v. Mosley*. The *Yarbrough* case involved the simple question of denial of the right to vote to Negro citizens because of their race; the Fifteenth Amendment expressly states that people cannot be denied the right to vote for this reason. This cannot be expanded by any rational thinking into a claim that the Constitution protects the right of every qualified voter to vote. The Constitution does not even claim to protect the right of racial minorities to vote; it simply makes it illegal for states to deny them the right to vote because of their race.

After citing more cases based upon express constitutional provisions concerning the denial of the right to vote for particular reasons, the Court concluded, "And history has seen a continuing expansion of the scope of the right to suffrage in this country." This is true, but the expansion of voting rights has been achieved by changes in state laws and by state and federal constitutional amendments. It cannot be interpreted as the establishment of a trend empowering courts to make such changes as they wish.

---

62. Such political rights are not property rights, nor "liberty"—involving freedom from restraints, nor life, as are protected by the Fourteenth Amendment. These political rights are enforced in state courts by *mandamus* or similar judicial remedies, just as state court actions afford relief when property rights are violated and liberties infringed.

After recitation of this historical background which established nothing, the Court proceeded, as its second step, to discuss its holding in *Baker v. Carr,* the Tennessee legislative reapportionment case. In summarizing *Baker v. Carr,* the Court said in *Reynolds v. Sims:* "We intimated *no view* as to the proper constitutional standards for evaluating the validity of a state legislative apportionment scheme." So admittedly still without any endeavor to explain was the question of how there can possibly be a denial of equal protection of the laws to any individual within a state by virtue of the comparative sizes of the state's legislative districts, even assuming that the Equal Protection Clause were concerned with the right to participate in the structural organization of government rather than being concerned with subjection to government's laws.

The Court then briefly discussed a Georgia case which came between *Baker v. Carr* and *Reynolds v. Sims.* This was *Gray v. Sanders,* which declared Georgia's county unit system to be unconstitutional in federal elections. This was a pernicious system in which votes were actually weighted and the votes of the people in Atlanta who voted for a particular candidate were discounted by a very substantial percentage, while the votes of individual voters who voted in very small counties were effectively increased by very large factors. In effect, the votes in the entire state of Georgia were not being accurately counted but were being distorted by artificial factors by which, as a concurring justice stated, the different votes of individual voters in the same constitutency were not being given the same weight. This proper decision was not based upon the Equal Protection Clause, [63] but contributed to subsequent "Equal Protection" decisions by coming the phrase "one person—one vote," an accurate slogan for that case, but inaccurate for all legislative apportionment cases that followed.[64]

The Court's discussion of *Gray v. Sanders* in no way touched upon the Equal Protection Clause, nor attempted any explanation relating the Equal Protection Clause to state legislative apportionment. In speaking of the two Georgia cases, the *Gray* case involving systematically inaccurate vote-counting in state-wide Federal elections and the *Wesberry* case on the supposition that election of the Federal House of Representatives "by the people" required each congressional district in a state to be equal in population to each other congressional district,[65] the Supreme Court in *Reynolds v. Sims* recognized that those two cases "are of course not dispositive of or directly controlling on our decision in these cases involving state legislative apportionment controversies."

63. Not disputed by the majority, the concurring opinion in *Gray v. Sanders* stated specifically that the decision was not based upon the Equal Protection Clause of the Fourteenth Amendment, and that the Fifteenth Amendment's prohibitions against the denial or impairment of voting rights on the ground of race was not adequate to require the decision rendered by the Court. The Court had emphasized in *Gray v. Sanders* the discriminatory effect the vote-counting system had upon Negro voting rights, with the large concentration of black population in Atlanta being established by census statistics. The case involved merely a prohibition-type injunction as to the manner of counting votes, and not the pretended use of the powers of courts of equity to remake state government.

64. *Gray v. Sanders* was not a legislative apportionment case. Essentially, it presented an attempted legalized form of massive vote-stealing in federal elections.

65. Like all statutes, the Constitution must be read in all its parts, and not by isolating particular phrases. The election "by the people" phrase appears in Article I, §2 of the Constitution, in the same sentence which states that the qualification to vote shall be determined by state laws, and the entire subject of how elections shall be conducted is controlled by Art. I, §4.

The Court concluded its pointless discussion of the *Gray* and *Wesberry* cases by saying:

> "Nevertheless, *Wesberry* clearly established that the fundamental principle of representative government in this country is one of equal representation for equal numbers of people, without regard to race, sex, economic status, or place of residence within a State."

The reference to a "principle of representative government," concerned the guarantee of a republican form of government, not the Equal Protection Clause, and was therefore as inappropriate to an attempted discussion of the Equal Protection Clause as it was inaccurate. The *Wesberry* case *did not establish* the things the Court credited it with establishing. The necessary disregard of race and sex were established by specific amendments to the Constitution, not by the *Wesberry* case. The illegalizing of "economic status" as a means of determining voter qualifications was done to a slight extent by the Twenty-Fourth Amendment, barring poll tax requirements for the privilege of voting in Federal elections only. As far as the Constitution is concerned, states are still free to impose some type of property ownership or other economic test upon the right to vote.

Finally, the Court proceeded with its endeavor to demonstrate that the Equal Protection Clause was violated by the malapportionment of the Alabama legislature. The Court stated the question as being whether the apportionment scheme "constitutes an invidious discrimination" so as to violate the Equal Protection Clause. We have seen [66] that the "invidious discrimination" "test" necessarily claims that a state may deny equal protection of the laws to some persons within its jurisdiction, contrary to the verbatim language of the Fourteenth Amendment, if the denial does not impress judges as being invidiously discriminatory, *i.e.*, if the judges view the denial as reasonable in view of state interests which the judges' philosophies lead them to view as sufficiently important. This does not achieve for the Constitution the position of supremacy it commands and the judicial oath of office requires.

The Court then proceeded with an attempted mathematical demonstration reminiscent of that attempted by the Supreme Court many years earlier in the old *Daniel Hylton Carriage Case*.[67] First, the Court said that a constitutional claim had been asserted by a claim "that certain otherwise qualified voters had been entirely prohibited from voting for members of their state legislature." [68] The Court then said that "it is inconceivable" that a state could permit citizens voting for legislators to have their votes multiplied by 2 in some parts of the state, 5 in other parts of the state, and 10 in other areas. But the Court cited no provision of the Constitution to demonstrate that even this system would be a violation

---

66. See above, pp. 268, *et seq.*

67. *Hylton v. United States,* discussed above, pp. 79, *et seq.*

68. Any type of constitutional claim can be *asserted,* and the fact that it has been asserted has no tendency to prove anything. Indeed, this precise claim was asserted some years after the decision of *Reynolds v. Sims,* when Congress sought to give the right to vote to 18-year-olds in both state and federal elections, and these voters, thereby becoming "otherwise qualified"—if Congress actually had this legislative power— to vote in all federal elections, were still held by the Supreme Court in *Oregon v. Mitchell* not to be qualified to vote in state elections, because the state not only *had* power to deny them the right to vote, but Congress could not even give them the right.

of the Constitution.[69] But assuming that it might be, the Court went on to say that "the effect of state legislative districting schemes which give the same number of representatives to unequal number of constituents is identical." But it is by no means identical. There is all the difference in the world between weighting the votes of two different voters in a single constituency and making legislative districts unequal in population.

If we live in adjoining districts, and my district, on a population basis, should be able to elect five legislators, while yours, on the same basis should be able to elect only one, but actually each of our legislative districts is assigned only one legislator, then your vote and my vote will have precisely the same weight in an election. Your vote and my vote will each be counted as one vote, no matter how many other people shall have voted. After our candidates are elected, each of us will have the same weight with our candidates, assuming no personal factors. Each of us can influence the candidate who thinks we voted for him last time or hopes we will vote for him next time. You cannot influence my candidate and I cannot influence yours, because we are from different districts. Each of us can influence one and only one legislator. We have been given precisely identical and equal *voting rights*.

The difference is not in your personal right and my personal right. The difference is that the representative of the massed body of people, of which I am a part, cannot overcome the vote of the representative of the massed body of people of which you are a part. The injury is not to the individual, but to the massive group *as a group*. It is in no sense a matter of individual rights. It is a matter of what type of apportionment may be necessary to achieve the republican form of government. Despite gross malapportionment, if the people governed are politically viable, government can be quite representative, and can be compelled to hear and heed the mighty voice of the people, as those who governed Rhode Island learned at the time of Dorr's Rebellion.[70]

From this endeavor to prove by arthmetic that which cannot be proven by arithmetic, the Supreme Court proceeded with its attempt to prove that the Equal Protection Clause is violated by unequally-populated legislative districts. The Court spoke of political rights and the historical and present importance of state legislative bodies. The Court then spoke of representative or republican government, saying:

> "But representative government is in essence self-government through the medium of elected representatives of the people, and each and every citizen *has an inalienable right to full and effective participation in the political processes of his State's legislative bodies.*"

This supposed inalienable right of each and every citizen does not exist, has never existed, is utterly unintelligent, and surely will never exist in the United States or anywhere else on earth. With many citizens being denied the right to vote,[71] with states still being constitutionally free to require literacy tests, prop-

---

69. Yet Congress could clearly view such an inaccurate vote-counting system as destructive of the republican form of government within a state, and could convene a new constitutional convention from the state's people.

70. *Luther v. Borden,* discussed above, pp. 236, *et seq.*

71. Citizens who are children, citizens who have been convicted of serious crimes, citizens who have been adjudged insane, are customarily denied the right to vote.

erty ownership qualifications, and any other voter qualification not expressly forbidden by the Constitution, the assertion that each citizen enjoys an equal right
of participation in the political processes is inane. Such an extensive grant of voting rights would be so injurious to the whole of society and to the future, so lacking in intelligent basis, as to be irrational.

Then moving to the Equal Protection Clause, after asserting the essentially republican form of government assumption that "a majority of the people of a
State could elect a majority of that State's legislators . . . ," the Court said:

> . . "And the concept of Equal Protection has been traditionally viewed as requiring
> the uniform treatment of persons standing in the same relation to the Govern-
> mental action questioned or challenged."

This is certainly not the accurate view of the meaning of the clause, and it has
not been the traditional view except in those cases where it was pretended that
the Equal Protection Clause was not violated when all individuals in the favored
class were treated differently from those outside the favored class.[72]

The Court virtually conceded that it was concerned with theories of the structure of the republican form of government rather than individual rights. The
Court said: "Our constitutional system amply provides for the protection of
minorities by means other than giving them majority control of state legislatures."
This is true in the case of some minorities, namely racial and religious minorities,
but rural minorities have no constitutional clauses designed to protect them.

The Court concluded:

> "The Equal Protection Clause demands no less than substantially equal state
> legislative representation for all citizens, of all places as well as of all races."

In summary, the Court reached its conclusion that the Equal Protection Clause
imposes this requirement upon the people of every state by beginning with an assertion that this requirement had not yet been found to exist in any prior decision,
proceeding with a discussion almost entirely concerned with theories of the structure of government instead of human rights, and looking upon its theories and
finding them to be good, the Court ordained that in order to achieve conformity
with this favored political theory as to the structure of state government, each
citizen should be vested with an individual right designed to support the favored
political theory. The Supreme Court did not so much as quote the Equal Protection Clause in any part of its fifty-one-page opinion in *Reynolds Sims*. As we
have seen, each major pronouncement in its chain of reasoning was untrue.

The Court then announced its additional conclusion that there is no analogy
between a state and its counties and the federal system, in which the state govern-

---

72. The clause was correctly applied in *Traux v. Raich*, when Arizona tried to legally
disqualify most aliens from working and being employed in the state, and the Supreme
Court held this to be a denial of equal protection of the laws, because it favored citizens
of Arizona over non-citizens; yet those two different groups of people were not persons
standing in the same relation to the Government of Arizona. One group consisted of
citizens with political rights and the other group consisted of aliens without political
participatory rights. The entire purpose of the Equal Protection Clause is to require that
government treat each person equally in the process of governing, without regard to
whether government desires to brand some as standing in a preferred relation to the
state.

ments have a limited sovereignty, counties being but political subdivisions of the state for administrative purposes; hence the Court concluded that population equality for voting districts was required for both houses of a state legislature, regardless of what the people of the state may have provided in their state constitution. But the Court found inadequate the fact that in denying the people in a county a voice in the state legislature, it was destroying the power of individual citizens to bring pressure upon their state government, and was not merely denying such a voice to county governing officials. It was denying to the people in this or that small county the right to send a representative to the legislature, when the county might greatly need to make changes in its governmental structure, as is done so often in so many states. This representational power often serves to protect the people from courthouse cliques, as well as bringing to sparsely populated counties money for state highway improvements and other public works needed for continued economic improvement.

As to such arguments, the Court said:

> "Arguments for allowing such deviations in order to insure effective representation for sparsely settled areas and to prevent legislative districts from becoming so large that the availability of access of citizens to their representatives is impaired are today, for the most part, unconvincing.[73]

A mere statement that we are not convinced neither replies nor gives any reason for the rejection of arguments. The most impressive rationale given by the Court was of the sloganeering type, "Again, people, not land or trees or pastures, vote." In coining such slogans the Court evidenced not the slightest concern for the fact that it was effectively disfranchising the people who owned the land, trees and pastures, as the Court, pretending to be concerned with individual rights, wrote of such political theorizing as legislative *"bicameralism, modernly considered . . ."*

The Transformation of Representational Rights:

Enough of theory. Let us see how the transformation of state governments was accomplished by temporarily destroying the republican form of government in each state: Not by ordaining the convening of a new state constitutional convention to allow the people themselves to do as they might wish, but by temporarily destroying this fundamental aspect of representative government, which the Court claimed it was attempting to protect. And in taking these gigantic steps, the Court was oblivious of the fact that such broad powers had never inhered in the jurisdiction of the courts of equity, but had been powers used by regal government and partially exercised in America by the royal agents, the governors-general.

Judicial re-making of state government necessitates the assumption of immense powers over the government. These powers must be assumed and exercised on behalf of at least some of the citizens of the state, despite the fact that no federal court had *ever* had lawful authority to entertain a suit against a state itself by some of its citizens. Nothing more sweeping could possibly be done to the state government of Alabama by making it a formal party than was done in this

---

73. This statement evidences a philosophy concerned primarily with the power and structure of government, no matter how injurious to the rights of individuals may be the implimentation of such plans.

case of *Reynolds v. Sims,* and the same holds true for New York,[74] Colorado,[75] Hawaii,[76] and the other states whose representational schemes the federal judiciary saw fit to revise.

After the Supreme Court had indicated in the Tennessee case, *Baker v. Carr,* that the Equal Protection Clause might have some relation to the subject of state legislative apportionment, *Reynolds v. Sims* was hastily filed in a federal court having jurisdictional over *part of Alabama.* Those who sued claimed to represent all taxpayers and voters of their home counties, and all other Alabama voters "similarly situated," though there was no pretense that the voters, under some republican device of government, had selected these intermeddlers for the purpose of litigating for their behalf. The so-called "class action" procedure was pretended to authorize individual citizens to represent large classes of people in filing such suits, though the entire classes did not share ownership of any property, association, or corporation.[77] By this device, sometimes known as a "legal fiction"—something pretended to be true though known to be false—everybody in the "underrepresented" parts of Alabama could be considered a part of the class, though no one claimed to know whether the majority of each of these constituent groups thought such reapportionment to be desirable or undesirable, wise or foolish. Thus, the will of the people of these state-republics is immaterial in this type of "litigation."

In April, 1962,[78] the District Court in Alabama took notice of the population and representational status of the state's counties and announced to the handful of citizens and the various election officials who were the plaintiffs and defendants in the case, the Court's "present thinking": If the legislature should fail to act in time for the November election—and the legislators had not been sued and brought into court, nor was the legislature in session—then the Court would have to do this legislative job itself on a temporary basis by consolidating a number of election districts and awarding the "released seats" to large counties suffering "the most egregious discrimination," so that, by loosing the rural stranglehold, the legislature itself would be able to reapportion itself and award proper representation rights to the people.[79]

The fundamental legislative apportionment scheme, including a provision that every county should have at least one member in the House of Representatives—to be nullified by the District Court's announced plan to consolidate legislative districts—was set out in detail in the state's constitution and was binding upon the legislature unless void because of its conflict with some provision of the Constitution of the United States. At the time the District Court announced its intent to exercise this power should the unconvened legislature fail to do so, the Supreme Court had not then even *attempted to demonstrate* that the Constitution has any

74. Discussed below, pp. 307-309.

75. Discussed below, pp. 309-311.

76. Discussed below, pp. 312-313.

77. Supposedly made law by the procedure of promulgation by the Supreme Court followed by non-veto by Congress, as distinguished from the constitutional procedure of enactment by the two houses of Congress followed by presidential approval. Discussed above, pp. 243, *et seq.*

78. Closely following the Supreme Court's decision of *Baker v. Carr* on March 26, 1962.

79. These events in the District Court were summarized in the Supreme Court's subsequent opinion reviewing the District Court's actions in *Reynolds v. Sims.*

provisions relating to state legislative apportionment. If the Alabama constitutional provisions should be void because of some still undetected conflict with the Federal Constitution, this would presumably require the people of Alabama to again exercise their constitution-writing authority by means of a convention.

Faced with the imminent seizure by a Federal judge of the prerogative of the people of Alabama to write and amend their own constitution, and therefore faced with the eminent and temporary destruction by the federal judiciary of this fundamental aspect of the republican form of government traditionally followed in America, the governor of the state acted by convening an extra-ordinary session of the legislature; it made a proposal to the people of Alabama to amend the state constitution and also enacted a provisionsal apportionment law, to be used in the event the existing constitution of Alabama should be held to violate the Constitution of the United States.

In the land where the Virginia House of Burgeses had insisted that it is unbecoming to free men to surrender the rights of the people they represented, even upon demand by lawful authority, legislators of Alabama bowed down before a federal judge's mere threat that he might seize the power of the people's "original and supreme will" [80] by ordaining some brand of law to be substituted for parts of Alabama's constitution, hopefully for a temporary period.

After the legislature enacted a new apportionment law that flagrantly violated the state constitution and a proposed constitutional amendment that could not even be submitted to the people until after the November election, the District Court found to its liking a part of one "plan" and part of the other "plan" so the Court combined the two into a plan of its own. It decreed that the November elections should be held under its own plan.

On the appeal of *Reynolds v. Sims,* the Supreme Court held that the legislative apportionment scheme provided by the people of the state in their aged constitution, as well as the legislature's new enactment and its proposed constitutional amendment, each violated the Constitution. However, it also held that the combined "plan" imposed upon the people by the District Court also failed adequately to conform to the "one person—one vote" slogan. As to the District Court's conduct in issuing an order held by the Supreme Court to violate the Constitution, being a part of the District Court's conduct of the case, the Supreme Court said: "We feel that the District Court in this case acted in a most proper and commendable manner." *Proper? Commendable?* How could it *ever* be proper or commendable for a judge sworn to uphold the Constitution to violate it? Upon this, the Supreme Court did not comment.

As to the District Court's temporary seizure of the power of the people of Alabama, the Supreme Court said in *Reynolds v. Sims:*

"Additionally, the court below acted *with proper judicial restraint* after the Alabama Legislature had failed to act effectively in remedying the constitutional deficiencies in the State's legislative apportionment scheme, in ordering its own temporary reapportionment plan into effect, at a time sufficiently early to permit the holding of elections pursuant to that plan without great difficulty, and in prescribing a plan admittedly provisional in purpose so as not to usurp the primary responsibility for reapportionment which rests with the legislature.[81]

---

80. In *Marbury v. Madison.*
81. Not a responsibility, this primary *right* belonged to the people themselves in approving or disapproving amendments to their constitution.

The New York apportionment case was *W. M. C. A., Inc. v. Lomenzo.* Another class action case, the suit was brought by a corporation [82] and *one citizen* from each of the state's most populous counties suing to obtain increased representation in the legislature. They asserted they needed to have the legislature "freed from the fetters imposed" by the state's constitution so as to "insure to the urban voters of New York State the rights guaranteed them by the Constitution of the United States." But in fact, the state's urban voters had comfortable majority control of *both houses* of their legislature. As the Supreme Court stated, the ten largest of the state's sixty-two counties had seventy-three and one-half percent of the population and controlled over sixty-two percent of the votes in each house. It was almost time for the regular reapportionment, which the Supreme Court recognized would be accomplished by the state itself, and people in the ten largest counties would still elect over sixty-one percent of the delegates to each house—there was no rural stranglehold as there might be in Alabama.

Where the people of Alabama were not entitled to *originate* constitutional reapportionment amendments, New York's constitution mandatorily required that every twenty years, the ballots list a single question for majority determination, "Shall a Constitutional Convention be held?" If the two-decade gap should cause unfair disparities in apportionment to appear, New Yorkers had a convenient method for calling a convention to remedy this and all other evils in the fundamental scheme of their own government. In recent times, the voters of the entire state, including the immense voting population of New York City, had voted on whether they desired reapportionment; each time, the majority had opposed legislative reapportionment. In short, New York's government was set up with a legislative apportionment scheme desired by the majority of the voters,[83] though offensive to the will of the suing minority composed of six citizens and one corporation.

Upon the petition of this minority of infinitesimal size, the Federal District Court held that the existing apportionment scheme, with the requirement that every county except the very smallest have at least one representative in the lower legislative house, did not violate the Constitution of the United States. The District Court held it to be rational, based upon historically accepted concepts. This meant that generations of people concerned with political matters had felt the representational scheme, with the people of each county separately represented, to be wise and politically needful, though this clearly rendered impossible the compliance with any non-existent "one person—one vote" slogan when irrationally applied to the size of legislative districts.

The United States Supreme Court disagreed. Though the people had repeatedly voted that this was the way they wanted their legislative apportionment to remain and though the majority's representatives controlling both houses had the power to submit constitutional amendments or enact legislation making changes, the Supreme Court was quite concerned over one aspect of the arrangement confirmed by the people themselves: Apportionment so arranged as to give the people in each county a voice in their government resulted in mathematical ratios of "about 21-to-1" in the House and "about 3.9-to-1" in the Senate. These were

---

82. Which was not even a member of the "class," and therefore not entitled to represent the "class" under the literal words of the Supreme Court-promulgated rules.

83. In 1957, only five years before this decision, the Governor of New York was said by the Supreme Court to have held a 1957 vote on whether to have a constitutional convention as being a vote on the issue of apportionment, but "a majority of the State's voters chose not to have a constitutional convention convened."

ratios between the number of voters electing a single representative in the most populous and the least populous legislative districts.

The Court made a number of these little mathematical comparisons as to the plight of the urban majority which elected the majority of the members of the legislature. But their majority control was not as great as equal mathematical ratios would produce, and the Court said: "No adequate political remedy to obtain relief against alleged legislative malapportionment appears to exist in New York." This was because there was no constitutional procedure by which the majority of the people could themselves *initiate* proposals for constitutional changes in the representational apportioning; the initiation would have to come from a majority of the legislators elected by this helpless majority of the people. However, the Court added a footnote comment, citing another case decided that same day, stating that this lack of power in the people was not "constitutionally significant." The expressed will of the state's people as to how their state government shall be organized is not constitutionally significant. The people are not free to prefer any rule over that of "one person—one vote."

A dissenter in the New York case pointed out the error in the Supreme Court's assumptions on which it claimed the power to compel state legislative reapportionment, even aside from the objections that the Court did not have the state government before it as a party and that there was no statute giving federal judicial power to entertain suits against states by individuals. The dissenter remarked upon the Court's declaration that it is a fundamental principle that there must be equal representation for equal numbers of people:

> "With all respect, I think that this is not correct, *simply as a matter of fact*. It has been *unanswerably demonstrated* before now that this 'was not the colonial system, it was not the system chosen for the national government by the Constitution, it was not the system exclusively or even predominantly practiced by the States at the time of adoption of the Fourteenth Amendment, and it is not predominently practiced by the States today.' "

Further, the dissenter wrote:

> "To put the matter plainly, there is nothing in all the history of this Court's decisions which supports this constitutional rule. The Court's draconian pronouncement,[84] which makes unconstitutional the legislatures of most of the fifty states, finds no support in the words of the Constitution, in any prior decision of this Court, or in the 175-year political history of our Federal Union. With all respect, I am convinced these decisions mark a long step backward into that unhappy era when a majority of the members of this Court were thought by many to have convinced themselves and each other that the demands of the Constitution were to be measured not by what it says, but by their own notions of wise political theory."

This excellent dissent received the same treatment as did the highly scholarly dissent by Mr. Justice Harlan in *Reynolds v. Sims:* It was totally disregarded by the Court, and it may be assumed that if these dissents were not unanswerable,

---

84. The ancient Athenian Draco framed the city-state's first written code of laws; it imposed the death penalty for the most trivial offense, so as to bring prevalent civil disorder to an end, lending Draco's name to laws that are harsh and unyielding. It is noteworthy that the prevalence of civil disorder later gave rise to another system of draconian laws administered by the Court of Star Chamber in England.

the Court would have answered them, as demanded by the imperative of judicial integrity. In intellectual decision-making, the wilful disregard of unanswerable arguments is simple dishonesty.

Since the time of Socrates, thinkers have known that accurate conclusions can never be reached by a rational demonstration which fails to perceive a refutation of its own argument. The classical name of the Supreme Court's inexcusable logical fallacy in these cases is *ignoratio elenchi,* which may bear the literal translation, "ignorance of the refutation." Here was no ignorance of the refutation. In these cases, the refutation was wilfully ignored.

So on June 15, 1964, for some rural people in New York no less than for others in Alabama, a meaningful right to participate in the republican form of government commanded for each state by the Constitution was destroyed by the United States Supreme Court, claiming to protect individual rights. In these and other cases simultaneously decided, the Court emphasized the utter helplessness, comparative helplessness, or slight helplessness of the people themselves to bring about amendments to their state constitutions to cause reapportionment. In each of the cases, the Court appended an identical footnote:

> "For a discussion of the lack of federal constitutional significance of the presence or absence of an available political remedy, see *Lucas v. Forty-fourth General Assembly of Colorado . . .*"

The footnote appended to the other cases and referring to the Colorado case was inaccurate, because the Colorado decision was in no way concerned with the ready availability to a remedy the people could use to directly amend their constitution to reapportion their legislature.[85] This is true because in Colorado the people *had this power* and had actually exercised it to express their collective will. Their will was plainly and clearly that they wanted no part of the Federal judiciary's newly-created constitutional right. The Supreme Court's response, in meaning though not in words, to the Colorado people's rejection of the blessings of its modern political theories imposed upon the nation was: The people be damned! Their government will be organized *the way we want it organized.*

The people of Colorado were not helpless. They had the power to initiate and bring about any state constitutional amendment they desired.

In this manner, some of the people of Colorado wrote two separate proposed amendments to their state constitution and these were submitted to the state's voters on a "one person—one vote" basis in 1962. One of the proposals, with a new scheme of legislative appointment was approved by the people of Colorado as organizing their state government the way they wanted it organized. The new amendment gave the rural people a majority of the representatives in one legislative house and the urban people a majority in the other house. The people of Colorado accepted this proposal by a vote of two-to-one. Not only this, but a majority of the people in *every county of the state,* both the heavily and sparsely populated counties, voted for this apportionment system. By voluntarily conceding to the rural minority control over one legislative house, the urban majority retained the power to remove this control by simple constitutional amendment,

---

85. These factors were of real importance in the Virginia, Delaware and Maryland cases, *Davis v. Mann, Roman v. Sinock, and Maryland Committee for Fair Representation v. Tawes.*

which the urban population could achieve whenever they desired it without awaiting any legislative action or judicial intermeddling.[86]

Yet the Supreme Court held the people of Colorado were not free to adopt
the form of government they desired, admittedly republican in form. The Court
held the people had to design both their legislative houses on the basis of its "one
person—one vote" philosophy. Pretending that the powers of a court of equity
included the power to remake the very form of government itself, the Supreme
Court said:

> "While a court sitting as a court of equity might be justified in temporarily re-
> fraining from the issuance of injunctive relief in an apportionment case in order to
> allow for resort to the available political remedy, such as initiative and referen-
> dum, individual constitutional rights cannot be deprived, or denied judicial effectu-
> ation, because of the existence of a non judicial remedy through which relief
> against the alleged malapportionment, which the individual voters seek, might be
> achieved."

This arrogant sophistry pretended it was dealing with the wisdom of delaying
judicial relief because political relief was practically in sight. The Court was
actually dealing with a popular rejection of its political philosophy, and its
answer was to damn the will of the majority. Is this actually concern with majority rights, minority rights, or with the increase of the judiciary's powers? [87]

If America were ruled by a king and he had treated the people of Colorado
the way the Supreme Court treated them on June 15, 1964, it would be popularly
viewed as a fit of royal pique at the audacity of some subjects who ventured to
reject the supposed benefits of regal wisdom. Tyrannical rule is no less tyrannical
when imposed by a judicial body than when it proceeds from the whim of a
single recognized tyrant.

Consider this comparison: Acting on the same day and hour, in opinions
issued simultaneously, a federal judge of Alabama was praised for temporarily
installing a plan without the consent of a single voter except for those few who
sued, though the "plan" adopted by the authority of his own unguided judg-

---

86. A dissenting justice said: "Thus, the majority [of the people of Colorado] has
consciously chosen to protect the minority's interests, and under the liberal initiative
provisions of the Colorado Constitution, it retains the power to reverse its decision to
do so. Therefore, there can be no question of frustration of the basic principle of majority rule." The dissenter also quoted from the trial judge:

> "The contention that the voters have discriminated against themselves appalls
> rather than convinces. Difficult as it may at times to understand mass behavior
> of human beings, a proper recognition of the judicial function precludes a court
> from holding that the free choice of voters between two conflicting theories of ap-
> portionment is irrational or the result arbitrary."

87. This misleading writing overlooks the fact that when one of perhaps 100,000
voters wishes to achieve for the entire group the right to elect two legislators instead of
one, he is not asserting an individual right, but is claiming to speak for 99,999 other
people to achieve a collective right for all of them—not the subject of the Equal Protection Clause. And when the entire 100,000 have directly spoken and resoundingly
rejected the view sought by the individual voter, the contention that the achievement
of this view through coercive judicial power is a use of equity powers to protect individual rights is devoid of any trace of rationality.

ment resulted in the majority of the members of the two legislative houses being elected by voters in areas having 27.6% and 43% of the state's population.[88] Yet the people of Colorado more nearly approached the "one person—one vote" "ideal" proclaimed by no provision of the Constitution, their constitutional amendment producing election of the controlling majority of the two legislative houses from areas having 33.2% and 45.1% of the state's population. The popular will of the people was condemned and the arbitrary whim of the judge praised. Concern for majority will? Group rights? Individual rights? Or the enhancement of powers claimed by the judiciary?

This high-handed attitude of the federal judiciary is demonstrated by subsequent decisions on the subject of state legislative apportionment, as the federal courts seized and exercised the powers of the people of California,[89] New York,[90] Florida,[91] and Hawaii.

---

88. Far more exciting statistical comparisons than this can be made. The legislative majorities were not elected by 27.6% and 43% of the people, but only by the voters among the people in areas whose populations totalled these percentages of the state's population. But for the actual voters, these percentages may be reduced by the percentage of the state's entire population that voted, and then one has a total of the voters selecting a majority of the legislators. But all the voters did not select the legislators; some voted for other candidates, and always, victorious candidates are selected *only* by the voters who vote for them. A candidate who receives only 50.01% of the votes in his race wins. Making these infantile computations, it can be seen that a majority of the members of the two houses of the Alabama legislature might possibly have been selected by only 4.15% and 6.46% of the people.

89. California's experience is reported in *Jordan v. Silver.* California had a system like that of Arizona, in which the people themselves could originate and adopt constitutional amendments without legislative action. The state's constitution formerly required all legislative districts to be equal in population, but the *people proposed and adopted* a constitutional amendment abolishing the equal population requirement. Repeatedly, they had been asked and had refused to restore the requirement of equally populated districts. These repeated affirmations by the people—the source of all sovereign power under all American political theory—were abruptly swept aside by the powerful federal judiciary. In the Supreme Court, the few voters who prevailed over the will of the people filed a motion, asking that the district court decision in his favor be affirmed without oral argument. The Supreme Court said: "The motion to affirm is granted and the judgment is affirmed." The proper mode of exercising judicial power is to hear, consider, and then decide.

90. New York's situation again came before the Supreme Court in *W. M. C. A., Inc. v. Lomenzo* in October, 1965. The New York Legislature had enacted four apportionment laws, called Plans A, B, C, and D. The New York courts held all of them unconstitutional, and a federal trial court ordered an election to be held under "Plan A." Both cases were appealed, and the United States Supreme Court affirmed both of them, the state decision holding Plan A to violate the state constitution and the federal decision ordering elections conducted under Plan A, anyway. Thus important provisions of the state's constitution, regarded as the heart of the republican form of government required to be perpetuated by the federal judiciary under the republican guarantee provision of the Constitution, were utterly nullified by the federal judiciary.

91. Florida's difficulties in endeavoring to please the federal judiciary are reported in *Swann v. Adams.* In the first case, the trial court decided to withhold action to see if the legislature to be elected in 1966 should enact acceptable law on this subject in 1967; the Supreme Court ruled: "We reverse and remand to the District Court so that a valid reapportionment plan will be made effective for the 1966 elections." This order mandated that the trial court itself should perform Florida legislative functions unless

The 1966 Hawaii case was one in which a federal trial judge probably exhibited the greatest degree of audacity ever exhibited by a federal trial judge, and for it, he was not impeached. But at least the Hawaiian District Judge showed a loyalty to law not otherwise shown in the federal judicial system. He accepted the proposition that it was the business of the people and their legislature to provide legislative apportionment, and that they rather than the courts must actually perform this function. The District Court recognized that the Hawaii Constitution stood in the way of appointment according to the political theories espoused by the United States Supreme Court. So the Hawaiian Court, as described by the Supreme Court on appeal of the case in *Burns v. Richardson,* "directed the legislature to submit to the electorate at an immediate special election the question, 'Shall there be a convention to propose a revision of or amendments to the Constitution?' " The Hawaii Legislature was enjoined by the District Court, pretending to exercise the powers of a court of equity, from *enacting any legislation* until it should propose this constitutional amendment provision to the people of Hawaii. So at least that court openly seized control of the state government of Hawaii instead of merely holding distant threats over the legislative heads and pretending that coerced legislation was free government.

The District Court, in one of its orders quoted by the Supreme Court, used language befitting the type of power it was exercising, regal power:

> "We believe that the Senate should be redistricted into single senatorial districts, although we may approve two-member districts if and only if the legislature can affirmatively show substantional reasons therefor. There may very well be valid reasons for one or two two-member districts in the neighboring islands but we perceive no justification whatever for other than single member districts on the Island of Oahu, particularly the heavily populated areas thereof."

The Supreme Court ceremoniously reversed the District Court's injunctions telling the legislature exactly what to do and how to do it, but the legislature had already obediently provided for a 1966 vote on whether a constitutional convention should be convened. As to this, the Supreme Court said:

> "We note that the electorate will vote at the 1966 election on the question of whether a constitutional convention should be convened. We see no reason, however, why the newly elected legislature should either be compelled to propose amendments or precluded from proposing them. The legislature will doubtless find reason enough to act in the fact that the District Court will retain jurisdiction over

---

the legislature should be recalled into session and should satisfactorily reapportion the legislative districts. The new apportionment law resulted in ratios between the voters electing a single representative in the most populous and the least populous voting districts of 1.3-to-1 and 1.41-to-1; even under the Supreme Court's concern for majority rule, these comparisons between extremes are meaningless unless they are prevalent. Swann and those who joined him in the suit proposed some local adjustments here and there, but the trial court upheld the legislated apportionment scheme. The Supreme Court said: "We reverse for the failure of the State to present or the District Court to articulate acceptable reasons for the variations among the populations of the various legislative districts with respect to both the senate and house of representatives." It requires no articulation and little perception to understand that one plan is law elected by representatives chosen by the people of the entire state of Florida, while the other is merely a proposal of individual citizens not shown by the opinion to have been elected by anyone.

the cause to take any action that may be appropriate pending the adoption of a permanent reapportionment which complies with the constitutional standards. . . ."

So while earlier cases had failed to reprimand trial judges for their misconduct, in this case, for the first time, the tactic of holding the threat of power seizure over the heads of state governmental officials was sanctified as the *preferred* method of bringing about submission to the Supreme Court's political philosophy. In the long course of its pretense that this result was commanded by the Equal Protection Clause of the Fourteenth Amendment, the Supreme Court never once took note that contemporary Congresses, in approving re-admission of southern states into the Union, had also approved state constitutions with provisions for every county to have at least one representative in the state legislature, every such state constitution being contrary to the "one person—one vote" absurdity. But they knew what the Equal Protection Clause meant; they simply could not foresee the distorted meanings the Supreme Court was to assign to it in the future.

In imposing its political philosophy upon the nation, the Supreme Court thus coerced the states into abandoning the Great Compromise solution which was the foundation of the federal government. The Court declared this solution inappropriate to the states and their counties, because the Federal Great Compromise was between representation in the House of Representatives, elected by the people, and in the Senate, elected by the state governments. This was an artificial and inaccurate comparison, because from the first in the Constitutional Convention, the delegates had agreed that there should be one large legislative house drawing its support directly from the people and a smaller house, which became the Senate, restraining the lower house.

The conflict settled by the Great Compromise was totally unrelated to the fact that one house was drawn from the people and the restraining house from the state governments. The conflict was on the issue of whether the national legislative power would be controlled by population, with the populous states actually ruling the rural states, or by geography, with the larger rural states ruling the greater populations in the wealthier states. By repeated references to committees, attempts were made to find solutions to this conflict between the large and small states, and repeatedly, the committees had reported an inability to find any fair solution other than the Great Compromise.

This wise federal compromise, with the added benefit of giving state governments a voice in the national government, was made to protect the people where they lived, not their shops, buildings, trees or pastures. The Great Compromise was, and will always remain, the only compromise adequate to protect people living in both sparsely and densely populated areas, that is, it is the only rational means of arranging representation to give the people in all areas a voice in government. Human nature is such that if the people in one area control a government governing other areas, the laws made by that government will rapidly begin to change to protect those who control it to the prejudice of those who have no control over government. The "one person—one vote" arrangement is irrational. It would not be adopted by free men in America, respecting each other's rights, but could only be imposed by tyrannical decrees.

The treatment accorded the problem of Missouri's congressional apportionment demonstrates the absurd extremes to which the Supreme Court has gone. The case was *Kirkpatrick v. Preisler,* decided in 1969, only a year away from the 1970 census. Missouri had devised a congressional apportionment that very closely reflected the figures produced by the last census taken, 1960. Indeed, by dividing the entire state population by the number of congressmen and arriving at the judicially perfect representational scheme. Missouri had provided districts that varied from the "ideal" by no more than 3.13%. This was the largest variation, the smallest departure from absolute perfection being 0.19%. Here is how the Supreme Court characterized these slight differences: "Finally, it is simply inconceivable that population disparities of the magnitude found in the Missouri plan were unavoidable." It is actually inconceivable that responsible men could infer that such trivial disparities are of a magnitude deserving notice.[92]

The Supreme Court affirmed the decision of a federal District Court that made changes in the plan adopted by law in order to achieve more perfect alignment with the outmoded 1960 census. Between 1960, whose census figures were the the measure of the judicially-revised congressional apportionment in Missouri, and 1970, the population of the entire state increased by 8.276%. This is considerably more than the trivial 3.13% maximum variation from the 1960 census figures that was declared to violate the provision of the Constitution that states that the House of Representatives shall be elected "by the people," omitting the following words which expressly restrict the voting qualifications to those of the people who are qualified to vote for members of the most numerous house of the state legislature.

Mr. Justice Harlan wrote of this decision:

"Marching to the non-existent 'command of Art. I, § 2' of the Constitution, the Court now transforms a political slogan into a constitutional absolute. Strait indeed is the path of the righteous legislator. Slide rule in hand, he must avoid all thought of county lines, local traditions, politics, history, and economics, so as to achieve the magic formula: one man, one vote."

Having found itself vested in the mid-1960's with authority to remake election laws, the Supreme Court proceeded during that decade to extend the burdens of its political theories to governmental units smaller than state governments.

Avery v. Midland County, in 1968, concerned the structure of American county courts, known as the Commissioners Court in Midland County, Texas.

As the county government evolved into one dealing primarily with rural problems, it had likewise evolved in Texas, as elsewhere, into a government elected primarily by the rural people.[93]

---

92. The Supreme Court sternly said: "We recognize that a congressional districting plan will usually be in effect for at least 10 years and five congressional elections. Situations may arise where substantial population shifts over such a period can be anticipated. Where these shifts can be predicted with a high degree of accuracy, States that are re-districting may properly consider them. *By this we mean to open no avenue for subterfuge.* Findings as to population trends must be thoroughly documented and applied throughout the State in a systematic, not an *ad hoc,* manner."

93. If this rural governing body should enrich itself by taxes imposed upon city property, this might not be totally unjust because at least the road improvement funds would benefit the city people whenever they left the city and the jury funds would likewise benefit the city people. If the county governing body should become too heavy-handed in the use of its slight powers, an urban majority could easily elect a representative to the state legislature, and he could utilize the state's legislative powers to remake local government in the county—at least when government was organized in accordance with the will of the people rather than the will of the judiciary.

Midland County was said by the Supreme Court to have a population (estimated) of 70,000 people. This included the estimated populations of the City of Midland, 67,906, and of three rural districts of 852, 414 and 828 people.[94] If, instead of following the rational scheme of apportionment Texans followed in allowing the rural people control in electing this rural governmental agency, they had instead adopted the irrational "one man—one vote" slogan of equally populated electoral districts, then to give only a *single* commissioner to all rural voters, the people of the City of Midland would have to be permitted to elect thirty-two members to the commissioners court, which would have deprived the rural people of any meaningful representational rights in this rural governing body. Or, if the commissioners court were maintained at a manageable size of 10 members, then 4,906 people would have to be carved from the City of Midland and joined with 2,094 rural people to provide one of the ten members of the court. On at least some occasions, this two-to-one urban majority of the "rural" electoral district would elect an urban representative, so that the ten-member county court would leave rural residents without any representation. The irrationality of any such arrangement in a government concerned with rural affairs was so obvious that Texans took the rational approach: The rural people were given the formal legal right, by districting, to elect the majority of the commissioners court.

The Supreme Court held that its equally-populated district rule must apply to every government, even the most local, in which officers are elected by the people by geographic districts, the Court saying: "It is now beyond question that a State's political subdivisions must comply with the Fourteenth Amendment." [95] The Court made this comparison:

> "If voters residing in oversized districts are denied their constitutional right to participate in the election of state legislators [which had not occurred in *any* of the reapportionment cases], precisely the same kind of deprivation occurs when members of a city council, school board, or county governing board are elected from districts of substantially unequal population."

It also spoke of the states "characteristically" providing for "representative government," in such local governments, all of which renders particularly inane the Court's decision that rural people, the ones "governed" by the rural governmental unit, must be disfranchised for all practical purposes in the organization of their rural governments.[96]

---

94. This beautiful job of estimating population as a basis for judicial government-remaking is self-branded as fake: The county population is rounded off to an even number, and one rural district of 828 people is estimated to have exactly twice as many people as another rural district of 414 people. Comparing these artificial 1968 estimates with the 1970 census, the actual county population was 91.57% of the "estimate," the City of Midland had a population of only 87.56% of the prior estimate, but the county's rural population rose to 285.7% of the estimate. It thus appears that the rural people of Midland County were arithmetically disparaged as well as factually denied any voice in their local rural government by this act of federal judicial tyranny.

95. This is absolutely true, but does not justify the "1 man—1 vote" slogan, because the Court never has demonstrated and *never will demonstrate* that the Equal Protection Clause requires adherence to the slogan—it is impossible to rationally demonstrate the truth of false assumptions.

96. In these cases, as in so many other areas of recent judicial adventures, the un-

Another case vied with *Avery v. Midland County* for the leading position on the scale of absurdity. *Harper v. Virginia State Board of Elections* was decided two years after the adoption of the Twenty-Fourth Amendment, which provides in part:

> "The right of citizens of the United States to vote in any primary or general election for President or Vice-President, for electors for President or Vice-President, or for Senator or Representatives in Congress, shall not be denied or abridged by the United States or any State by reason of *failure to pay any poll tax or other tax.*"

Internal examination of the Constitution thus reveals that only by amending it could state poll taxes be outlawed even as to "federal" elections, except that a state itself could abolish the qualification at any time. Yet only two years after this amendment became part of the Constitution, the Supreme Court decided that, after all, *the Court itself had had this power to determine voter qualifications since 1868.*

Of course, the Court proceeded upon its "invidious discrimination" rationalization in declaring a $1.50 poll tax outlawed in state elections. The Court said: "Wealth, like race, creed, or color, is not germane to one's ability to participate intelligently in the electoral process." Why not? Even assuming that a mere $1.50 can, without dishonesty, be characterized as "wealth," is there any rational reason why a person should be permitted to vote when local law requires him to pay the tax, if he is so lacking in ability that he has been unable to raise $1.50 or so lacking in foresight that he has not been sufficiently interested in public affairs to pay it before some qualifying deadline? And with reference to "one's ability" to vote intelligently, such laws have never related to the ability of the individual to vote intelligently, but to a determination of mass qualifications with the expectation that restriction of the right to vote to those qualified by adulthood, property ownership, and tax payment, there is a greater likelihood of adequate voter understanding to lead to the selection of responsible leaders.

In this state poll tax case, the Supreme Court held poll tax qualifications illegal in state elections. The voting qualification rule was a backward one, but possibly a wise one, and the constitutional amendment just adopted for "federal" elections confirmed the premise that prior to the amendment, the Constitution in no way prohibited poll tax qualifications. By its decision, the Supreme Court seized legislative powers recognized by the provisions of the Constitution as being vested in the separate states, and acknowledged *by every federal constitutional amendment concerning voting rights as still being within the law-making powers of each state,* controlled either by laws made by its legislature or constitutional provisions made by its people.

The Supreme Court misconstrued the plain meaning of the Equal Protection Clause and then, for the "enforcement" of the clause, exercised the rule-making powers expressly given to Congress by the Fourteenth Amendment. So Congress finally decided to exercise some of this law-making power itself, accepting the perverted rationalization [97] that if "discrimination" were "invidious," it could be

---

varying underlying rationale explaining all of them is not a dedication to the protection of rights of individuals, but instead, dedication to the aim of enhancing the powers of the federal judiciary.

97. In the Federal Convention, the delegates were firmly resolved that Congress should not be given the power to determine the voting qualifications of those who would

corrected. Congress enacted a statute declaring that eighteen-year-old citizens should not be denied the right to vote on account of age in any election, state, federal or local. It had several times used the same language in proposing amendments to the state legislatures, but if the Supreme Court could do it without constitutional amendment, then why couldn't the legislative authority do the same?

The Supreme Court, by a warped reading of the Constitution, upheld this enactment as applying to the elections of congressmen, senators and presidential electors. Of course, Congress had no such power. The Constitution itself says who shall be permitted to vote for these offices—the electors for the lower house of the state legislature. Today, any state could have a law limiting the right to vote for state legislators to individuals of any age, race or sex owning not less than 5 acres of land, his own home, or $2,500 in a savings account, and the Constitution of the United States would thereby restrict the right to vote for Congressmen and Senators in that state to those having the stated ownership qualifications. If Congress sought to vary these requirements, its enactment would be in direct violation of the Constitution's provisions. This cannot rationally be questioned.

In *Oregon v. Mitchell,* the Supreme Court went further and concluded that the power to determine the "manner" of holding elections included the power to determine voter qualifications. Hence, the Court ruled, Congress could determine voter qualifications for congressmen, senators and presidential electors, but not for state officials. But of course, the Supreme Court itself exercised this power as to state elections in its poll tax decision, *Harper v. Virginia State Board of Elections.*

Does this mean that in the exercise of usurped legislative powers, the legislative powers of the judiciary exceed those of the legislative body? Of course it does. Usurped power is by definition power whose existence is not founded upon law, power seized in disregard of law, and therefore power without limitation other than those imposed by the judiciary at the point where governmental power actually controls the conduct of people. When the judiciary itself becomes perverted from loyalty to law in any nation and gives its loyalty instead to its own political or philosophical ideas as the source of law, then tyranny is not an eventuality to be feared: It is a present actuality.

The Supreme Court's rationale and conduct in deciding *Oregon v. Mitchell* cannot be defended.[98] As quoted in Mr. Justice Harlan's dissenting opinion, Madison warned that if Congress could regulate voting rights and the qualifica-

---

choose congressmen. See *Documents Illustrative of the Formation of the Union,* pp. 873-876.

98. The Supreme Court would more soundly, and more in accord with the imperative of judicial integrity it claims to follow, always ask itself how the Constitution might be worded if it were intended to reach the end the Court now desires it to reach. It is unquestionable that if the Constitution actually gave Congress the power to determine voting qualifications, not only would the 15th, 17th, 19th, 24th and 26th Amendments have been totally unnecessary, but the provision upon which the Supreme Court relied in *Oregon v. Mitchell* would have been written to say: "The times, places, and manner of holding elections and the qualifications of electors for Senators and Representatives, shall be prescribed by state law, but the Congress may . . ." If the Framers of the Constitution had intended to give Congress the power it usurped by lowering the voting age to 18, then the Constitution would have been written to grant this power to Congress.

tion of electors to vote for federal office-holders, then the Congress could "by degrees subvert the Constitution." That great judge also quoted Madison's opinion as to the "safest" persons to whom to restrict the voting rights: "The freeholders of the Country"—those meeting a real property ownership quali- fication.

The ever-increasing power of central government and the continual diminution of the powers of local government—subject to the restraining influence of an angry populace that surrounds it—will inevitably result not only in judicial tyranny over the ordinary details of every-day life, but in a tyrannical national government. It is highly unlikely that this trend will be reversed. It is too delight- ful to both voters and local government to receive bribes from an immense federal treasury filled with fake, devalued currency.

The delights of irresponsibility outweigh the burden of a debt we owe to furture generations whom we will have left on earth and whom we will subject to the government we have provided. Never can a wealthy heir be more profligate in the waste of his inherited wealth than has been Twentieth Century America in the irresponsible destruction of its priceless political heritage.

And at a time not so far distant as it has been, when the last trace of human liberty shall have been swallowed up in the regimentation of citizens who have never known true liberty from pointless governmental restraints, always imposed under the fraudulent pretense that human rights are being more fully protected, a fitting epitaph for the best-designed government that ever existed on the face of the earth may be found in those wise words of Alexander Hamilton:

> ". . . liberty can have nothing to fear from the judiciary alone, but would have everything to fear from its union with either of the other departments . . . , *not- withstanding a nominal and apparent separation . . ."*

XI.

EQUAL PROTECTION IN PUBLIC EDUCATION

IT HAS BEEN our invariable theme that there is no intelligent basis for criticism of any judge in the decision of constitutional law cases except that the judge has breached the imperative of judicial integrity by failing to decide cases as commanded by the Constitution; that this may be caused by his stupidity in failing to understand the Constitution, his laziness in failing to do the work necessary to learn the meaning of the terms found in it, or his intellectual dishonesty in failing or refusing to obey the Constitution's commands; that it is never permissible to substitute mere judicial interpretations for the Constitution itself as the supreme law of the land; that every judge in the nation is obligated to be subservient to the Constitution and to disregard Supreme Court interpretations which are contrary to the meaning of the Constitution; and that when any judge substitutes mere interpretations for the Constitution, he violates his solemn oath of office to support the Constitution as the leading component of the supreme law of the land.

In no area of Constitutional Law are the correctness of these premises more evident than in the subject of race relations; and in no area has the federal judicial system come closer to a state of absolute judicial tyranny than in righting racial wrongs.

In deciding *Plessy v. Ferguson*,[1] the Supreme Court did an immense wrong to the Negro people of America. The Supreme Court espoused the quasi-logic of those who desired to perpetuate racial segregation. Holding state-required racial segragation not to be a violation of the Equal Protection Clause, the Court thought in terms of a conglomerated body of black people and a conglomerated body of white people, ignoring the fact that the Clause has nothing to say of masses or classes of people. It speaks only of the individual, the single, solitary person being subjected to the power of state government. It destroys the state's power to deny to that person the equal protection of its laws. When Louisiana gave each white person the right to ride in "white" railroad cars, but denied that right to each black person, then Louisiana was denying to each black person the equal protection of its laws. What could be more clear?

In the fifty-eight intervening years between *Plessy v. Ferguson* and *Brown v. Board of Education of Topeka*, holding racial segregation by law in the public schools to be a violation of the Equal Protection Clause, the judges of the United States, intelligent men truly dedicated to justice, blinded themselves to the Constitution. They unquestioningly accepted —unquestioningly believed they *had to accept*—these Supreme Court rationalizations as a substitute for the Constitution, as if the opinions of this small group of public officials had become a part of the Supreme Law of the Land.

By this misconduct in public office which was the decision of *Plessy v. Ferguson* the Supreme Court led the nation to cause immense damage to countless millions of Americans. Decade after decade, they were illegally denied equal protection of the laws by virtually all the states.

---

1. Discussed above, pp. 59, *et seq.*

By the laws of some states, it was made illegal for restaurants and other businesses to permit both black and white people to be served in the same rooms, to use the same restrooms or drinking fountains, to use the same public swimming pools, to intermarry, and to attend the same public schools. Black people were required to occupy only the rear seats in busses of privately-owned city transportation systems.

By its lawless decision, the Supreme Court led the nation in a lengthy era of racial discrimination. By their unthinking acceptance of the premise that judges are obligated to defer to the opinions of the Supreme Court as to the meaning of constitutional provisions, the judges of the nation aided and abetted the leadership afforded by the Supreme Court in fastening habits and attitudes of racial discrimination upon generations of black and white citizens. As a part of the supreme law of the land, the Equal Protection Clause of the Fourteenth Amendment was destroyed.

Finally, after a series of decisions in which individual black students sought and attained the right of entry into white state universities, the Supreme Court ruled in *Brown v. Board of Education of Topeka* that racial segregation in the public schools achieved by state law violates the Equal Protection Clause. If a state could not require racial segragation in the operation of its public schools, how could it do so by any of its other laws? Both the question and the answer were immediately obvious to all thinking people. That which Eric Hoffer called the ordeal of change [2] came upon the nation, and the ordeal was to be a traumatic one.

Many members of both the major races had come to an unspoken acceptance of the idea of the racial inferiority of the Negro. How could the black man tolerate the condition imposed upon him by law and by custom except by subconsciously accepting, and trying to live up to, this idea of group inferiority? All men love justice, and how could the white man tolerate and engage in the unjust treatment of the Negro, the paternalistic manner in which he was used, except by accepting the proposition of inherent mental inferiority of the black? Gunnar Myrdal, in his sociological study, *An American Dilemma,* one of the non-legal works cited by the Supreme Court in *Brown v. Board of Education,* asserted that the Negro people in fact were inferior, but presented the now accepted explanation that such inferiority was the result of discrimination rather than its justification.

As was anticipated, those white people with ingrained attitudes of unquestionable white superiority found it very difficult to accept the idea that state government must treat black people and white people exactly the same way. These attitudes were naturally deepend in those areas having larger percentages of black population. To thousand of these people, the idea that their white children or *any white children* must associate with black children in the public schools was intolerable. To many, freedom was perverted and they were being subjected to tyrannical government no less foreign in nature than if it had come from the hands of a conquerer, though actually, freedom was only being granted to those to whom it had been denied.

Alabama found its university officials subjected to a judicial decree requiring the university to admit a young black lady to its student body. There was powerful popular revulsion to this admission, and the governor of the state carried out his promises to the people by standing at the gates of the university to bar the student's admission. There was an almost ceremonial confrontation between the

---

2. Hoffer, *The Ordeal of Change.*

governor of the state and a representative of the attorney-general of the United States. The ceremony ended when the governor yielded to the threat of superior force.

But what had the appearance of a ceremonial encounter in Alabama had no ceremonial aspects in the State of Arkansas. There, the confrontation was deadly serious. The people of Arkansas and the people of Little Rock were angry. The participants were angry, the governmental officials were angry, and in their anger, they did not act with the good grace and the respect for law that governmental officials should show. The facts were described by the United States Supreme Court in 1958 in *Cooper v. Aaron*, just four years after the Court had declared in *Brown v. Board of Education* that racial segregation by law in the public schools violates the Equal Protection Clause.

The case presents two examples of inexcusable audacity. The first is the audacity of Arkansas public officials in their conduct in public office; the second is the Supreme Court's audacity in the opinion it wrote. The case hardly deserved the Supreme Court's attention at all, because it was an extremely simple case, properly decided by the lower court.

The Supreme Court reviewed the facts. Its original *Brown* decision was actually two decisions. The Court decided the first half of the case in 1954, declaring state-imposed racial segregation illegal, and waited a year to render its decision as to what should be done about it. Three days after the first half of the decision, which soon came to be known as *Brown I*, the Little Rock School Board announced it intended to abide by the Court's decision as soon as the Court should determine the proper course of action to be followed. The Board then began developing a plan to end compulsory racial segregation, by first admitting Negro children to the top three grades of Little Rock's Central High School. Negro citizens were disappointed in the limited scope of the "plan," and sued the school board in this case which became *Cooper v. Aaron*.

However, the federal District Court in Arkansas approved the plan limited to the top three grades, and the approval became the final judgment of that trial court. The validity of that final judgment was not before the Supreme Court for review in *Cooper v. Aaron*. Following the judgment, plans were made to admit nine Negro children to Central High School in Little Rock.

In the meantime, the government and people of Arkansas had declared themselves strongly opposed to abandoning state-imposed racial segregation in the public schools. The state's constitution was amended to expressly command the Arkansas Legislature to oppose "in every Constitutional manner the Un-constitutional desegration decisions . . . of the United States Supreme Court." [3] Though Arkansas enunciated such formal policy, the Little Rock School Board continued with its plans to admit the nine Negro children to Central High School. It arranged for the support of the city administration and the police department, and apparently had the support of the responsible citizenry of Little Rock in performing it unpopular obligation. But the School Board reckoned without the Governor of Arkansas.

On the day before the school was to open for the new school year, Governor Faubus issued a declaration that Central High School was "off limits" to "colored

---

3. If state officials actually believe that the Supreme Court has itself violated the Constitution and by so doing possibly usurped power in any of its decisions, it is quite proper for the state to dedicate itself to righting acts of judicial lawlessness particularly if, as did Arkansas, the state commands its officials to combat such acts only in "every constitutional manner."

students," and he dispatched the Arkansas National Guard to the school to assure that no black child would gain access to its hallowed halls. This leadership sparked tempers that were close to the surface and the governor found himself supported by mob enthusiasm. He was subjected to a writ of prohibition-type injunction, restraining him from using force to interfere with obedience to the desegregation judgment. These proceedings against the Governor of Arkansas were affirmed on appeal,[4] had become a final judgment, and were not before the Supreme Court for decision in the case of *Copper v. Aaron*. After the governor's obstruction was removed by the separate lawsuit against him individually, the black children were escorted into the school by local and state police officers, but an angered mob had gathered. They were of such a temper that the police removed the nine children from the school mid-morning of the first day of school.

Then President Eisenhower sent regular army troops into Little Rock and "admission of the Negro students to the school was thereby effected." These children remained in the school under the protection of federal troops and then of the federalized national guard for the remainder of the school year.

But the presence of the troops, the governmental leadership which had been furnished by the governor in opposition to the admission of the Negro children, and the extreme public hostility—claimed by the School Board to have been engendered and in fact clearly led by the state's governor and legislature—made education in the school virtually impossible. So the School Board petitioned the District Court in February, 1958, to do something about the situation. The Board reported to the Court the intolerable aspects of the educational situation, violence directed against the Negro students, hostility against the school administration, and extreme tension in the class-rooms. The Board asked the Court for permission to withdraw the Negro children from the school and to defer re-admitting any Negro students for a period of two and a half years.[5]

The District Court agreed with the Board that relief for the intolerable state of school morale and discipline was essential, and approved withdrawal of the Negro children. The students appealed, and the Court of Appeals reversed the trial court, holding that the court could not defer admission of the children and could not exclude them from the school. This was the issue that went before the Supreme Court for review, almost on the eve of the commencement of the new school year in the Fall of 1958, and the Supreme Court also held that the continued admission of the Negro students could not be deferred.

This was quite a simple issue, which might almost be called a non-issue. The School Board had been violating the Constitution by keeping the nine black children (and others) out of the white school on account of their race; under an order entered more than a year earlier by the District Court, the School Board was proceeding to discontinue its violation of the Constitution and, so far as the nine children were concerned, to conform its conduct to this limited extent to the requirements of the Constitution. Appellate proceedings had then taken place, the appellate court had affirmed the judgment of the trial court, and therefore, *whether right or wrong,* this had been fully and finally determined by judicial procedure: These children had a right to attend Central High School, and the School Board had a duty to admit them, imposed by the final judgment. This was a simple matter of a final judgment to be enforced, and one of the parties to the

---

4. In *Faubus v. United States.*

5. This was a petition to totally destroy the constitutional rights of those black children, because all were in the top three grades and would be graduated after another two and a half years.

suit in which the judgment was given, the School Board, wanted to temporarily nullify the judgment and, as far as the nine children were concerned, to permanently nullify the judgment already finally determined to be binding upon the Board.

The Board cited reasons: Unrest, objections by those who were not parties to the lawsuit to any black children being permitted to attend white schools— reasons that can never be recognized as valid reasons to set aside a final judgment. The School Board did not even appear to make any claim that the earlier judgment was wrong, but seemed to admit that the Constitution prohibits a denial of equal admission on the ground of race. The School Board simply found it inconvenient to comply with the final judgment conceded to be required by the Constitution.

It is a simple truth which cannot be refuted by reasoned argument that if the Constitution is the supreme law of the land as it declares itself to be, and if the Constitution requires such a result in the operation of a state's public schools, then no reason, no law, no excuse can prevail over the supremacy of the Constitution, no matter how unpopular may be the result commanded by it. This is essential to a government of laws as distinguished from government by the whims of individual rulers. So this was a simple lawsuit, actually one long since decided, in which the School Board was trying to set aside a final judgment when there were no grounds for nullifying the judgment.[6]

What we may call the sanctity of the judgment, of the direction originally given that these children be admitted to the school, was not related to the question of the Supreme Court's original anti-segregation decision of *Brown v. Board of Education,* but arose entirely from the fact that the decision had become final, determining the scope and measure of the rights and duties existing between the school board and the black children who sued.[7] But the Supreme Court completely misunderstood or mis-identified the issue, and the very simple issue, involved in *Cooper v. Aaron.*

Cooper v. Aaron did bring before the Supreme Court a record having the potentiality of upsetting the Court's serenity, a record relating the conduct of the Governor, the Legislature, and the people of Arkansas in impugning the integrity of the Court in its anti-segregation decisions,[8] but insults to the Court and reaction to these insults could not properly affect the Court's decision.

Amazingly, however, the Supreme Court commenced its opinion in *Cooper v. Aaron* with this statement it said was raised by the case:

---

6. Final judgments can be declared void on very narrow and specific grounds, such as that the judgment was obtained by fraud or that the court lacked jurisdiction.

7. The awesomeness of judicial power is not that it settles truth, which can never be established by the power of government, but is either true or untrue in itself. The awesomeness of judicial power is that once it settles a dispute, determining the rights and duties of individuals in a particular situation, then its judgment, right or wrong, wise or foolish, in enforceable by all the power and arms of government. The triviality of judicial power is that it settles no constitutional meanings except for the purpose of deciding an individual case, and its decision is in no sense binding upon any other human being except those who are parties to the lawsuit, and their agents, such as a superintendent and school principals employed by a school board.

8. This is among the hazards of judicial office, and no court should concern itself over the unpopularity of its decision. It is not a Court's function to defend its decisions or to comment gratuitously upon the conduct and opinions of those who disagree. Defense or praise of the quality of the work of all courts belongs to others, not to the courts themselves. Silence is the proper judicial response to criticism.

"[This case] necessarily involves a claim by the Governor and Legislature of a State that there is no duty on state officials to obey federal court orders resting on this Court's considered interpretation of the United States Constitution."

This simply misstated the issues in the lawsuit. The Governor was not a party to the appeal, but the parties were Cooper and other individuals, all School Board members, on one side, and on the other side, Aaron and others, all either Negro school children or their parents. The people asking to be relieved of the obligation to obey the desegregation order for two and a half years were not the Governor and Legislature, but the School Board, and they were asking it on their own, not in obedience to any command by the Governor or Legislature. They were in no way claiming that they were free from any duty to obey the District Court's final judgment. They admitted they were under a duty to obey but only asked the Court, pretty much as a matter of grace, to nullify or suspend the judgment for a period of time. And though they did not realize it, they were asking the Court, as a matter of grace, to suspend the Constitution.

The case did not necessarily or unnecessarily involve an claim by the Governor and Legislature of Arkansas that there was no duty upon state officials to obey the orders of state or federal courts. Indeed, the governor of the state had been made a party under special injunction proceedings against him, and had evidently *obeyed the injunction,* although he did unsuccessfully appeal the decision against him to the appropriate Federal Court of Appeals, as was his right. The judgment against Governor Faubus had become a final judgment, and was not in any manner before the Supreme Court for review. That his conduct inspired mob violence was one of the facts the Court could well notice, because it is pointless for a court to close out from its sight explanations of why events have occurred; but the Supreme Court did not have before it for review any claim by the Governor or legislators of Arkansas that they were under no duty to obey Federal Court orders directed to them.

The subject the Supreme Court wanted to discuss and soon got around to discussing was the supposed existence of some obligation on the part of government officials to agree with the Court's interpretations of the meaning of the Constitution. This is a totally different question from the question the Court stated at the outset to be necessarily involved in the lawsuit. Actually, neither of the questions was properly involved in the decision of the case.[9]

When it came to the question it wanted to discuss, the Court no longer stated it in terms of whether state officers are bound to obey Federal Court orders, which the Arkansas officials appeared to concede. This is the way the Supreme Court stated the question it wanted to discuss: "However, we should answer the premise of the actions of the Governor and Legislature that they are not bound to our holding in the *Brown* case."

Here, the Supreme Court considerably shifted its ground, and began weighing the actions of the Governor and Legislature, none of which were before the

---

9. The first question stated by the Court as to the duty to obey federal court orders was not involved. It is very clear that in a civil government having courts authorized to issue orders, anyone to whom a court issues an order is obligated to obey. But *orders* are issued to people involved in the lawsuit or to additional people brought into the lawsuit, not to the world at large. The Supreme Court's statement of the supposed question as to whether there is any "duty on State officials to *obey* Federal Court orders . . ." was in no way involved in the case.

Court and none of which were subject in any way to its adjudicative power.[10] The Court began its discussion with an allusion of Chief Justice Marshall's great decision of *Marbury v. Madison*, sustaining and demonstrating the duty of a court to rule upon the constitutionality of a statute when the court is asked to enforce or take action under the statute. As to the supposed obligation of other governmental officials to defer to Supreme Court opinions on the meaning of the Constitution, the Court excerpted a single sentence from Marshall's decision: "It is emphatically the province and duty of the judicial department to say what the law is."

It had been argued in *Marbury v. Madison* that it was not within the province of a court to even pass upon constitutionality of statutes, but that the Constitution was a set of commands to the Congress, that Congress passes upon constitutionality when it enacts a law, and that a court must only carry out the law to the letter and never question its constitutional validity. In refuting this contention, Chief Justice Marshall pointed out that it is the province of judges in deciding cases to look to the Constitution as well as to the statutes, and to rule upon constitutionality and then either enforce the statute or, believing it to be a nullity, to refuse to enforce it. There was not the slightest implication in *Marbury v. Madison*, from beginning to end, that the Supreme Court was in any way licensed to make an authoritive and final determination of the meaning of any provision of the Constitution. The burden of the opinion was only to demonstrate that the court could not close its eyes to the Constitution, but could and must rule upon constitutionality in the process of deciding lawsuits.

The Constitution requires that many state and federal officers swear to support the Constitution. Those who wrote the Constitution relied upon this obligation of honor, in hopes that the people would compel their executive, legislative, and judicial officers to honor their oaths of office. This requires each officer to use his mind to discover the meaning of the Constitution, with individual disputes as to rights and duties in various circumstances being finally determined—*as between the individuals involved*—by the judiciary in deciding lawsuits. The power to make a final and authoritative determination of the meaning of the Constitution or any of its provisions is a power which *does not exist*.[11]

Part of Marshall's determination in *Marbury v. Madison* was based upon the sanctity of the oath, he asserting that it would not only be immoral, but criminal,

---

10. It was not within the scope of the Supreme Court's authority or its functions to pass judgment upon those actions, though the actions themselves were unlawful and inexcusable.

11. A state judge in an early Tennessee case, *Bank of the State v. Cooper*, made these valid observations: "I acknowledge the force of authority of adjudication upon analogous cases. It oftentimes presents a forcible and conclusive argument. But it is a sufficient answer to the argument upon this point, to say that the cases and decisions referred to, though analogous, were not made in this precise case; and I can never follow precedent, in the line of analogy, when it leads to an infraction of the constitution. Hence the necessity of a frequent recurrence to first principles. *If we follow precedent, and move on according to the analogy of cases, we shall be led from step to step until the constitution itself will be lost amidst the subtleties of the law.* When precedent is established in the construction of statute or common law, I concede the propriety of following it, unless flatly absurd or unjust. *But every judge and other public officer, when called on to do an official act, must judge of the constitution for himself; for no precedent, however grave, and no adjudication, however respectable, can warrant a violation of that sacred instrument.*"

to require a judge to take an oath to support the Constitution and yet require him to close his eyes to the Constitution and see only the statute. He concluded his opinion in the case with the expression of this thought: ". . . and that courts, *as well as other departments,* are bound by that instrument." Here was no declaration that the courts alone are empowered to construe the Constitution, but a declaration that every officer who swears to uphold it must decide upon the meaning of the Constitution and then yield to its supremacy.

But in the brief quotation which the Supreme Court saw fit to excerpt and re-print in *Cooper v. Aaron,* the Court emphasized the single sentence in which Chief Justice Marshall, replying to the position that the judicial department was not allowed to compare statutes with the Constitution in deciding lawsuits, had asserted the judiciary could and must perform this function.

From this simple declaration, whose meaning is quite clear when it is read in context, the Supreme Court in *Cooper v. Aaron* drew this additional conclusion: "This decision declared the basic principle that the federal judiciary is supreme in the exposition of the law of the Constitution, . . ." The decision makes no such declaration and carries in it no such implication. Marshall was expounding upon the bare *duty,* not only of the Supreme Court but of every state and federal judge in the land, to determine the question of constitutionality of a statute in deciding a lawsuit involving the statute, and was in no way attempting to declare that the judicial department has any supreme authority from any source to establish truth beyond possibility of dispute, truth with which all men must agree.

The Supreme Court's statement in *Cooper v. Aaron* that *Marbury v. Madison* declared as a basic principle that "the federal judiciary is supreme" in determining the meaning of the Constitution is a falsehood, misstating the holding of a respected decision, and doing it by reprinting a single sentence out of context. Then, after falsely declaring that it had been established that federal judges are the supreme expositors of the meaning of the Constitution, the Supreme Court continued with the claim, ". . . and that principle has ever since been respected by this Court and the Country as a permanent and indispensible feature of our constitutional system." This is another false statement (though it may accurately summarize the opinions of laymen) which was never either respected or enunciated by the Supreme Court of the United States, insofar as diligent search has been able to reveal, until September 12, 1958, when the Court announced it in *Cooper v. Aaron.*

The Court then concluded this portion of its comments:

> "It follows that the interpretation of the Fourteenth Amendment enunciated by this Court in the *Brown Case is the supreme law of the land,* and Art. 6 of the Constitution makes it of binding effect upon States 'any Thing in the Constitution or Laws of any State to the Contrary notwithstanding.' "

For the first time in American history, the United States Supreme Court declared that its mere interpretations were the supreme law of the land above all other law.

Recognition of the Supreme Court as the supreme enunciator of the meaning of the Constitution is not, as maintained by the Court, indispensible to the preservation of our constitutional system; it is, instead, indispensible to the destruction of our constitutional system.

The Supreme Court took no notice of the earlier Supreme Court decision in

Thurlow v. Massachusetts,[12] holding that Supreme Court interpretations, when they incorrectly expound the Constitution, are not authoritative and are not law. Not only are they never a part of the supreme law, they are not even law at all; the components of the supreme law are set out in the Constitution and the Supreme Court cannot add as a part of the supreme law its own interpretations which are sometimes contrary to the Constitution. *Thurlow v. Massachusetts* contained a complete refutation of the tyrannical absurdities pronounced in *Cooper v. Aaron.* The Constitution is the supreme law. Judicial interpretations are never more than interpretations.

The Supreme Court's action in *Cooper v. Aaron*—posing a hypothetical question not involved in the decision of the case, giving to it a self-aggrandizing answer effectively increasing its own power and having no other result, and thus usurping regal prerogatives to itself—was a monstrous act of misconduct in public office. It deserved, and should have received, an official reprimand from the Congress.[13]

The real outcome in *Cooper v. Aaron* was correct. The *District Court's* judgment was final, and therefore inviolable, and entitled the nine black children to remain enrolled as students in their school. Not because it was based upon accepted Supreme Court theory. But simply because it was a *final* judgment. It could not be nullified because it secured equal protection of the laws of Arkansas to the children who sued.

But the fact that it is a denial of equal protection of the laws to deny some people the right to attend a particular school while their neighbors are permitted to attend it, and to make this denial solely because of race, is not to say that the Supreme Court has acted properly and decided correctly in its handling of cases arising from state maintenance of racially-segregated schools.

We have already seen [14] that the Supreme Court greatly warped the meaning of the Equal Protection Clause by bringing into it such invidious and immaterial considerations as how important it might be to a state to carry out a particular policy. It was quite important to Arkansas to classify children according to race and to deny all black children admission to white schools, so important that riots and civil strife resulted when compliance with the Constitution was required to a very limited extent. But such local considerations are totally unrelated to the correct meaning of the Equal Protection Clause.

In *Brown v. Board of Education,* the old case of *Plessy v. Ferguson* came again before the Supreme Court, which accepted jurisdiction and agreed to decide the constitutionality of laws requiring racial segregation of public schools. Thus in 1954, the Supreme Court finally had the opportunity to demonstrate the error, not only of *Plessy v. Ferguson,* but of the entire history of the Court's misinterpretation—truly, the Court's virtual destruction—of the Equal Protection Clause of the Fourteenth Amendment. But unfortunately, the Supreme Court disregarded the Equal Protection Clause in *Brown v. Board of Education* as fully as it had disregarded the clause in most of its prior decisions claimed to have been

---

12. Discussed above, pp. 184, *et seq.*

13. Whenever deserved, such a reprimand would help restore to the Federal Government the system of checks and balances envisioned by the Constitution, and now mostly dormant. When in truth not deserved, such a reprimand would be harmless: Any competent judge could refute it, because it is so much easier to demonstrate truth by reason than it is to mislead by specious rationalizations. Truth is surrounded by ready-made arguments.

14. See above, pp. 269, *et seq.*

decided under it. In a very real sense, the Supreme Court upheld *Plessy v. Ferguson* and its "separate but equal" doctrine in its decision of *Brown v. Board of Education.*

The case was argued before the Supreme Court not once, but three times. After the first argument, the Court ordered a second argument on particular questions, mostly on what had occurred in Congress in the process of proposing the Fourteenth Amendment to the states for adoption, and after it decided that state laws requiring racial segregation in public schools are unconstitutional, the Court ordered a third argument as to what should be done about it.

The Court summarized the racial segregation school laws in Kansas and other states from which cases were appealed,[15] and then said of the existing "separate but equal" doctrine: "Under that doctrine, equality of treatment is accorded when the races are provided substantially equal facilities, even though these facilities be separate." The Court then reviewed some of the university cases, in which equal physical facilities were maintained, but the intangibles that make a great professional school were missing in the school which only black students were permitted to attend. These cases had obviously upheld the "separate but equal" doctrine by demonstrating that the doctrine was violated by substantial inequality in educational benefits.

After speaking of the intangibles affecting graudate university education, the Court said:

> "Such considerations apply with added force to children in grade and high schools. To separate them from others of similar age and qualifications solely because of their race generates a feeling of inferiority as to their status in the community that may affect their hearts and minds in a way unlikely ever to be undone. The effect of this separation on their educational opportunities was well stated by a finding in the Kansas case by a court which nevertheless felt compelled to rule against the Negro plaintiffs . . ."

Regarding the effects of legally-required racial segregation, the court in Kansas had said:

> . . . [IT] is greater when it has the sanction of the law; for the policy of separating is usually interpreted [16] as denoting the inferiority of the negro group. A sense of inferiority affects the motivation of a child to learn. Segregation with the sanction of law, therefore, has a tendency to [retard] the educational and mental development of Negro children and to deprive them of some of the benefits they would receive in a racial[ly] integrated school system."

With very sound basis, the Supreme Court could have said more along this line, *e.g.,* in regard to the theory of self-fulfilling prophecy. Such sound psychological theory was relied upon by the Supreme Court to hold that racial segregation gives the Negro child an inferior education. On this basis, still failing to

---

15. In Kansas, the law authorized cities to maintain racially-segregated schools, and Topeka had followed this authorization by providing segregated schools in the elementary grades, but with the higher grades operated without segregation. Others cases decided with the *Brown* case involved schools in states whose laws required separate schools for black and white students, Kansas, South Carolina, Virginia and Delaware.

16. Such euphemistic treatment was pointless. All compulsory segregation laws are for the purpose of protecting one group from painful contact with another, commonly on the basis of general beliefs as to the inferiority of the excluded group.

demonstrate the obvious irrationalities of the "separate but equal" doctrine, the Supreme Court held it to be a denial of equal protection of the laws when children were segregated by law in public schools. The Court did not say precisely what aspect of *Plessy v. Ferguson* it was rejecting.

The holding was thus based not upon the constitutional illegality of compulsory racial segregation as such, but upon the perceived harm it did to a particular group of people, the black school children. How much simpler it would have been to directly reject *Plessy v. Ferguson* as a false interpretation of the Constitution! To hold that when each qualified white person is entitled by law to attend a school and each qualified black person is denied this right by law, this is a denial of equal protection of the laws. Constitutional denials of powers to state governments are in no way related to the question of whether harm is done by the exercise of this forbidden power.[17] The Court's entire discussion of harm to black children from compulsory racial segregation had no relation to the proper constitutional rationale for the decision of the case.

By giving the Equal Protection Clause its correct and obvious meaning, and by demonstrating the fallacies that render the "separate but equal" doctrine of *Plessy v. Ferguson* an invalid rationalization, the Supreme Court could and should have provided a sound basis for its decision—a basis founded upon the Constitution instead of the Court's own past errors. This could have deprived those intent upon perpetrating compulsory racial segregation of any reasoned basis for criticizing the *Brown* decision. Instead, by preceeding from empathy rather than law, the Supreme Court invited criticism of the false basis of its decision.

Even more clearly the Court invited accurate criticism by a separate decision it rendered the same day, *Bolling v. Sharpe*. This case involved compulsory racial segregation in the public schools of the District of Columbia, and as the Supreme Court recognized in its opinion, there is no Equal Protection Clause restraining the powers of the Federal Government. It is in no way constitutionally obligated to treat citizens equally, but is perfectly free to pass laws, within the scope of its law-making powers, which favor black people, white people, or people who are friends or relatives of former members of Congress or former presidents.

But the Supreme Court decided that the Government of the United States was also constitutionally obligated to treat Negro and white children alike. The Court held this to be required by the Due Process of Law Clause of the Fifth Amendment, which in fact, has absolutely nothing to do with either the quality, wisdom, fairness or justice of law. It is but an enunciation of the principle that when Government moves to deprive the citizen of his life, liberty or property, it must do this in accordance with the law of the land and all applicable provisions of that law.[18] If Congress should determine that the schools of the District of Columbia must be racially segregated, or even that all Negro or white children should be denied free education at public expense, this would be an end to the question as far as the actual provisions of the Constitution of the United States are concerned.

---

17. For example: Congress cannot deny defendants charged with felonies the right to trial by jury. If Congress should do this, the denial could not be legitimated by demonstrating that it did not harm the complaining defendant because, though the court found him guilty, he was so hopelessly proven guilty that a jury would have found him guilty also. It is always pointless to discuss whether people are harmed by the exercise of a governmental power when the Constitution does not permit the power to be exercised at all. The psychological harm to school children caused by racial segregation has no bearing upon the constitutionality of compulsory segregation.

18. Discussed above, pp. 126, *et seq.*

The heart, the real basis, of the Supreme Court's decision that compulsory racial segregation in the District of Columbia's public schools was supposedly unconstitutional, is to be found in a single sentence almost at the end of the opinion in *Bolling v. Sharpe:* "In view of our descision that the Constitution prohibits the states from maintaining racially segregated public schools, *it would be unthinkable* that the same Constitution would impose a lesser duty on the Federal Government." [19] Whatever may be thought of *Brown v. Board of Education, Bolling v. Sharpe* was a political decision, not reached by judicial thinking: A lawless edict by the Supreme Court to the United States Government.

It is unfortunate that *Brown v. Board of Education* embraced and reaffirmed *Plessy v. Ferguson,* while holding separate treatment unequal in public school operations on the basis of psychological, sociological, and philosophical reasons with which some might honestly disagree. This course gave opponents arguments having the appearance of validity: By agreeing with the Supreme Court's reaffirmation of *Plessy v. Ferguson,* they could urge that the opinion arose from the individual philosophies of the justices rather than from the supreme law of the land, and was therefore government by whim rather than government by law.

Thus, *Brown v. Board of Education,* this opinion later to be known as *Brown I,* not only invited criticism by the manner of its decision, but also invited argument as to whether the Constitution could be lawfully disregarded, and whether the Supreme Court could perform trial-court functions withheld from it by the Constitution. This furnished the basis for further legitimate criticism. [20]

In 1955 came *Brown II.* The Court spoke of the practical flexibility of a court of equity in shaping its remedies, [21] and said: "At stake is the personal interest of the plaintiffs in admission to public schools *as soon as practicable* on a non-discriminatory basis." This was incorrect. At stake was *the absolute right* of each of those children who sued to be *immediately* admitted to the nearby white school to whose admission he sought and from which he had been barred by state law in violation of the Equal Protection Clause.

The Court spoke of transition. It spoke of the public interest in eliminating obstacles in a systematic way. The Court stated that the Federal trial courts in the cases must require the defendant school boards to "make a prompt and reasonable start toward full compliance with our May 17, 1954, ruling." Then the Court indicated that the school boards might need additional time before they could actually admit these Negro children. Regarding the prospective difficulties, the Court said:

> ". . . the courts may consider problems related to administration, arising from the physical condition of the school plant, the school transportation system, personnel, revision of school districts and attendance areas into compact units to achieve a

---

19. This statement is almost a confession that the Court was being guided by its own sense of fairness instead of by a provision of the Constitution.

20. As we have noticed, political changes in laws are accepted more gracefully if drastic changes are put into effect by slow and gradual stages, so that people may become accustomed to them a step at a time. This type of sound political and legislative practice has no legitimate place in the proper exercise of judicial power in constitutional cases. The Supreme Court should have intuitively held fast to this principle without ever asking for argument on these absurd questions.

21. Such flexibility is involved when a court of equity specifically orders a trespasser to rebuild your garden wall he has destroyed, as contrasted with the inflexibility of the court of law, which merely awards damages to you for the trespasser's destruction of your wall.

system of determining admission to the public schools on a non-racial basis, and revision of local laws and regulations which may be necessary in solving the fore-going problems."

The presence of such problems could not lawfully excuse violation of the Constitution for the briefest moment, and the solution of those problems was not within the jurisdiction of any federal court to oversee. Any problems which might ensue, any reorganization that might become wise as a result, were strictly the problems of the local officials. Their obligation was not to suit public convenience to the Constitution but to obey the Constitution no matter how inconvenient or disruptive it might be to local government.

Ruling in *Brown II* that the Constitution must yield to convenience—for which is supreme when the commands of convenience are heeded and the commands of the Constitution are suppressed?—the Supreme Court abandoned the principle of government of laws in favor of temporary expediency. The Court treated the landmark case as a political act rather than a judicial decision.

Leaving the Supreme Court's abandonment of law and reason in its decisions of *Brown v. Board of Education,* let us briefly consider the meaning of the Equal Protection Clause as applied to public education.

The Clause commands that no state shall deny equal protection of its laws to any person within its jurisdiction. We have seen that this command is not violated by the fact that one man is imprisoned and another remains free when the imprisonment of the first man was caused by the fact that he violated the law prohibiting murder; equal protection of the laws has been afforded, because the law directs that every person who commits murder shall be imprisoned, after trial and conviction. Both the imprisoned man and the free man have been equally subjected to this law.

When we leave the realm of law-making and consider government as a provider of benefits to some citizens at the expense of all tax-payers, perhaps the situation will become more complex. There is a school located in a city in the center of a state, and there are hundreds of other schools located at other points throughout the state, scattered among the populace. We concentrate upon this one school and the laws admitting students to its benefits. Does the Equal Protection Clause command that every child in the state shall have an equal right to attend this particular school, perhaps better in facilities and faculty than any other? Of course it does. This is the specific command of the Equal Protection Clause.

But when the state makes this gift of public service to school children at everyone's expense, it may impose conditions so long as those conditions afford equal protection of the laws—so long as there is no discrimination between individuals who meet the conditions imposed by law. If the state determines that there will be a ten dollar admission fee for each week's attendance at the school, then equal protection of the laws has been afforded if the state indiscriminately imposes that ten dollar fee and indiscriminately admits every child who shall come bearing ten dollars.

The most common stated requirement for admission is a residence requirement. To every school child in the state, whether he lives one block or three hundred miles from the school, state law says that you will be admitted to attend this school as a student if you meet the condition of establishing your home within a given distance from the school; and if you do not establish your home within that distance, you will be denied admission. This is necessarily a valid admission requirement, valid because it is applied equally to all. The Equal Protection

Clause commands that all *individuals* be treated the same but does not deny the state the power to treat different *acts* differently.[22]

So schools had been established by state governments to serve the people living near them, except that before the *Brown* decisions, many states, in slowly dwindling numbers, had added an unlawful condition, a condition that depended not upon human conduct, such as moving into an area, but upon individual differences, racial differences. It was quite common that two schools would be built, a Negro school and a white school. In a sparsely-populated area, these might be the only schools. The white school would likely be located near a concentration of white people and the Negro school near a concentration of black people. The maintenance of school districts in and of itself in no way violated the Constitution. The Constitution is completely silent as to the organization of local governmental service districts.

But the Constitution was violated and equal protection of the laws denied black children by refusing to admit them to the white school in the middle of overlapping school districts on the sole ground of their race, that is, on individual differences rather than on the basis of differences in conduct; and the Constitution was violated in the same manner as to white children.

Many children, without regard to race, were quite lawfully denied admission to near-by high schools, not because of natural differences between the individuals admitted and those excluded, but because the excluded children had not performed the necessary preliminary acts—indiscriminately required of all individuals—of successfully completing elementary and junior high schools.

These distinctions are simple, obvious, and indisputable if one concentrates his attention upon the plain meeting of the Equal Protection Clause instead of concentrating upon the decision the thinker's philosophy leads him to deem most wise.

Essential to a proper reading and understanding of the Equal Protection Clause is the disregard of the misleading rationalizations of *Plessy v. Ferguson* and the ramifications of "vital state interests," "invidious discrimination," and other such inane concepts that have no rational relation to the Equal Protection Clause, they having been used primarily to deny citizens equal protection of the laws.

The Supreme Court's decision that racial segregation by law is illegal led to many administrative problems whose solution was no legitimate concern of the federal judiciary. School boards were faced with a situation in which they had children to be admitted to schools and schools of limited capacity to receive the children. The historical and most rational solution was for the school to serve a limited area surrounding it. In many places, school boards drew lines surrounding a formerly white school and lines surrounding a formerly black school. Every student in the state, black, white, Indian, Chinese or gypsies,[23] was free to attend the formerly black school by moving into the limits of the area it served, and every child in the state, regardless of the identity of his group heritage, was free to attend the formerly white school by moving into its area. This was full and complete compliance with the Equal Protection Clause of the Fourteenth Amendment.

If a school board should draw lines surrounding the existing schools along roads, highways or natural boundaries separating the area, and if it should see

---

22. This is discussed in greater detail above, pp. 257, *et seq.*

23. The groups mentioned in the congressional debates over the Equal Protection Clause.

that a single Negro family lived within the "white" area, and the Board should then add to the area served by the formerly black school an additional area comprised of the perimeter of the land owned by the single black family in the midst of the white community, this would be a denial to that black child of the right to go to the school within his district while the right was given to white children living next door, and it would be a denial of equal protection of the laws.

But what of the quality of schools? Some may be ancient, without gymnasiums, adequate libraries, or laboratory facilities for teaching sciences, while others may contain the most advanced facilities designed. Is this a denial of equal protection of the laws? Consider: Is it a denial of equal protection of the laws when a state, through one of its county governments, paves a road on which one hundred people live, while in another part of the state, there is a dirt road which is the source of unpleasant clouds of dust in dry weather and which becomes a muddy quagmire every time it rains? When a state paves one road, must it simultaneously pave every street, road, highway and alley in the state? Surely not. The state had paved the road and every person in the state is equally free to drive on that road.

The state's paving conduct is not a denial of equal protection of the laws because it does not involve, to *any* extent, *any* protection of the *laws*. It involves the use of public money to benefit the public generally and to specially benefit a few private citizens living nearby, but it does not involve any application of the laws governing the people. If public money is used to build an expensive school in one area and a shoddy school in another area, this is not an enactment or application of laws, but the disbursement of public moneys. Building schools, installing street lights, building swimming pools, and maintaining parks do not involve the protection of laws. This conclusion must be reached if one reads the Equal Protection Clause, instead of applying his own ideas as to how much attention government should pay to concepts of human equality. The Equal Protection Clause becomes involved when *law* is utilized to control access to such facilities.

But laws are involved in the operation of public schools, because laws require people to attend and forbid people to attend particular schools. Questions of equal protection of the laws can exist only when laws are utilized. If there is a dilapidated and unheated school in one place and the state's most modern school is only twenty miles distance, this alone does not indicate any denial of equal protection of the laws. If every child in the state is entitled and required to attend the old school upon his action of moving into its area and every child in the state is entitled and required to attend the new school upon moving into *its* area, then every child in the state, as an individual, is treated identically.

The mere fact that there is a school located here in which most or all the pupils are black and a school located there in which most or all are white is in itself meaningless. From these bare facts, no rational conclusion can be reached regarding the possibility of denial of equal protection of the laws. A swimming pool may be maintained by a state through one of its city governments; the pool may be located in an area of the city peopled exclusively by 20,000 Negro families. It may happen that day after day, none but black children can be seen enjoying it, though it is open to everyone who desires to use it. The fact that, as a matter of state and local law, the pool is open to all without regard to race, parentage, or national ancestry, and that fact alone, conclusively establishes that equal protection of the laws has been afforded.

That schools are involved instead of swimming pools does not render the ratio of black and white students attending a particular school the basis for any rational conclusion as to whether there has been a denial of equal protection of the laws.

There is a tendency to think that in the absence of racial segregation imposed by law, the two major races, both of whose members are required to attend the public schools, would settle into ratios in each school approximating the racial ratios in the general school population. This is irrational. It treats school children as if they were a mixture of freely circulating drops of water, subjected to the outside pressure of law forcing them at random through orifices into waiting student slots.

But the students are not freely circulating drops of water. They are human beings with wills of their own, guided and controlled by parents with their own individual wills. We cannot count the number of black children and white children in a school and from the totals arrive at any reasoned conclusion that deviation from population ratios is the result of exclusionary racial prejudice. It would be even more irrational to carry such "thinking" an additional step and conclude that the deviation from the general population racial ratio has been accomplished *by law*.

The problems of re-drawing school district lines in what were formerly overlapping white and black school districts, and of avoiding gerrymandering those lines so that in fact black children would not be excluded on the actual basis of their race, were found by some school boards to be almost insurmountable. They simply declared that all schools in the system were open to all students. Students were given the choice as to what school they wanted to attend and absolute and unerring fidelity to the Equal Protection Clause was thereby accomplished. In other areas, school district lines were drawn, but because of citizen objections,[24] additional rights were given on identical terms to all school children, regardless of race and regardless of the school district in which they lived: Each child was given the right, though assigned to attend the school in whose district he lived, to transfer upon request to a different school of his choice. Absolute equality before the law was thereby attained and in such equal treatment there was no denial of equal protection of the laws to any such child.

But where such plans that assured equality in admissions were adopted, there were still occasional situations in which equal protection of the laws was denied to black children, as where citizen conspiracies prevented them from exercising their legal rights [25] or where application of the rules led to an almost unthinking denial of admission because of race, possibly caused by the school board's failure to carefully analyze its own actions.[26] Such were isolated problems which the judiciary should—and did—have no difficulty analyzing and remedying.

---

24. This is not an "unreasonable" factor to be considered—if that had any rational bearing upon constitutionality—because it is our traditional claim that government exists to serve the citizens; citizens are not supposed to be government's serfs.

25. The clearest example of this type of violation of constitutional rights occurs which a lynch mob, fearing that a suspect rapist or murderer will not be given the death penalty, storms a jail and lynches the prisoner for the very purpose of imposing the death penalty upon him, of depriving him of his right not to be executed except upon judgment after a fair trial. Such gross misconduct has occurred in school cases, in which the school board opened the schools to all children of all races, and private citizens utilized brutal threats to cause black parents to withdraw their children. Such a course of events is described in *Brewer v. Hoxie School District No. 46*. Conduct like this is reportable, it can be factually proven by testimony, and black citizens subjected to this treatment are not without friends in any section of the country. Judicial powers are adequate to protect such citizens in these circumstances.

26. In *Raney v. The Board of Education of the Gould School District,* the school board announced that both the formerly black and the formerly white school would be

We have seen there was no branch of equity jurisprudence by which injunctive powers were used to govern the people through the subterfuge of controlling the conduct of those officials who had been chosen to govern the people. This type of government by judicial edict was an earmark and an evil of the infamous Court of Star Chamber. But it was in *Brown v. Board of Education* that the United States Supreme Court, without noticing what it was doing, invited the federal judiciary to assume this type of power not granted by the Constitution to any branch of the Federal Government.

In the *Brown* decisions, with the holding that state racial segregation laws are unconstitutional came the judicial obligation to order the immediate admission of those children to their schools. Instead, the Supreme Court concerned itself with the problem of how local school boards would rearrange their conduct of public business to admit the children. In the proper exercise of judicial power, this should have been entirely the plight of the school boards, selected to exercise their discretion, their judgement, their intelligence, to meet whatever problems might arise in the operation of schools are required by law. But instead of holding that the Constitution commands total obedience by governmental officials, as it always does, the Supreme Court held the boards obligated to devise methods to end segregation so that those children who had sued could be admitted to the schools. The federal trial courts were admonished to review such methods chosen by the local school boards.

So the stage was set for the local federal trial courts to oversee the conduct of school boards, to review their "plans," to approve, alter, or disapprove the plans, to determine how each school district would operate its affairs. The lower courts proceeded to exercise their new-granted Star Chamber jurisdiction. There are myriads of those lower-court cases in which plans were submitted, altered, and endless reams of testimony taken to the end that the federal trial courts could perform the functions of state government by giving or withholding approval of the discretionary governmental planning by government officials.

In these dreary rounds of plans, there are cases in which the courts permitted, sanctioned, and ordered gradual desegregation, disregarding the rights of individual people, the only rights protected by the Equal Protection Clause, and concerned themselves instead with the intricacies of the exercise of Star Chamber power to govern the people by controlling the decisions of their governing officials. There were situations in which "gradual" plans were approved, and these plans left many Negro children in the position of being excluded from schools by law because they were black instead of white; when an occasional black child asked the federal judiciary to admit him to the school he was qualified to attend, his petition was denied, because court approval had already been given to "plans" as supposedly doing all that could reasonably be required to bring school systems

---

open to all comers, and that if any child failed to register his selection by a given date, he would be deemed to have chosen the school he previously attended pursuant to the segregation system. But the number of black children who signed up for three of the grades in the "white" school exceeded the room capacity; allowing the white children to remain, the board accepted black children for those grades until the school-room capacities were reached, relegating the remaining black children to the "black" school. This was unconstitutional, because it gave priority to the white children who were originally assigned there on the basis of their race. A constitutional system would have been to accept both black *and* white children on a first come—first serve basis or by lot, and assign the remaining black *and* white children to the formerly black school, located nearby. There were no segregated residential areas in the community, in which the majority of the school children were black.

into conformity with the Constitution. The courts opined that because the system was being worked out to achieve conformity with the Constitution as rapidly as could reasonably be expected, the children's individual rights to equal protection of the laws were being accorded the full protection to which they were entitled. Of course, the Constitution has nothing to say about the organization and operation of school systems.

If one compares this national course of federal judicial conduct with the language of the Constitution, one can only conclude that the judges dishonored their obligations of office by commanding and sanctioning a continued course of systematic violation of the Constitution. But the federal judges did this in strict accord with the Supreme Court's illicit legal advice given in the *Brown* decisions.

Further judicial proceedings resulted from dissatisfaction with the fact that persons accorded equal protection of the laws did not choose to so exercise their rights as to bring about a commingling of children of different races in the same ratio in every school throughout the school system. Such proceedings and strong expressions of popular opinion occurred in the city of Charlotte, Mecklenburg County, North Carolina. These events came before the United States Supreme Court in *Swann v. Charlotte-Mecklenburg Board of Education,* decided April 20, 1971.

The holding of the Federal District Court in North Carolina required the denial to white children of the right to attend near-by schools on the sole ground that they were white, and required that they instead by sent across the city to schools that had been attended primarily by black children; and the District Court required a denial to black children, on the sole ground that they were black, of the right to continue attending the schools they had chosen to attend, and it required that instead they be sent into white neighborhoods to attend schools they had freely chosen not to attend.

The transportation of the children from one area to another was to be accomplished with school busses, which for many years had been used to transport school children to schools. Great public anguish followed this decision, and it centered around objections to "bussing." Transportation of children over longer distances did involve inconvenience, increased danger, increased monetary cost, and an unnecessary impediment to rapid parental action in the event of an emergency. But although the public clamor centered about the word "bussing," the use of busses was not the principal objection to the decision, either on the part of objecting citizens or from a legal and constitutional viewpoint.

From both viewpoints, the legal and the popular, the fundamental objection was that the Supreme Court was positively ordering the institution of a program of systematic racial discrimination. In principal, the situation would have been identical if it had involved only two schools and if these had been only a block apart. The principle offended is that the result decreed by the Supreme Court could not be achieved except by violation of the Constitution, by state action denying black children and white children admission to particular schools on the sole ground of their race.

The infamous *Plessy v. Ferguson,* which the Supreme Court incorrectly upheld and followed in *Brown v. Board of Education,* was now sponsored anew by the Supreme Court for the purpose of perpetuating the principal evil condemned by the Equal Protection Clause The Charlotte-Mecklenburg schools operated under a system which assigned every child to the school in the area in which he lived and gave to every child in the state an equal right to attend any of those schools by the simple procedure of moving into the area in which the school was located. Additionally, it gave to every child in Mecklenburg County, no matter which school zone he lived in, the right to go to any other school of his choice anywhere in the county.

But although absolute fidelity to the Equal Protection Clause was thus achieved and every child, black or white, was treated identically, the children and their parents did not elect in a manner satisfactory to the desires of those who wanted each school to be peopled with both Negro and white children in substantial numbers. The Constitution does not permit the law to be used to forbid racial association nor does it permit state law to be used to compel racial association. It mandatorily requires that state law grant *equal* protection to every person.

Racial segregation in schools cannot be achieved over the objection of children who do not want to be segregated except by violation of the Constitution and racial integration of the schools likewise cannot be achieved over the protests of objecting citizens except by violation of the Constitution. To rule otherwise would be to be guided by racial bias rather than reason.

Of course, the factual existence of segregation and integration constantly occur on public property, but when these are not commanded by the coercive power of state law, it is none of the business of the federal judiciary, nor even of the Congress. This happens when one sees that all the people on a public walk by the state-owned streets are, at a particular moment, are of a single race or are of different races; this happens not because of restraints imposed upon people by state laws, but because of the free decision of each individual in bringing himself to that place at that time. A condition which results from human freedom and individuality can never honestly and intelligently be confused with a condition caused by a governmental denial of freedom.

The District Court made it clear that the School Board must consider all possible alternatives, including transferring children without their consent on the basis of their race to achieve actual racial integration of student bodies in the different schools, a patent violation of the Constitution. The Court said:

> "There has been substantial de-segregation in many areas—mostly the rural areas —of this large and complicated school system. A majority of the black students, however, still attend segregated schools and seldom, if ever, see a white fellow-student. Many all-black and all-white schools still remain. The neighborhood school concept and freedom of choice as administered are not furthering desegregation."

The Board itself took a strong position before the District Court. It expressly stated that it did not admit that it had any duty to promote desegregation, which it obviously did not have, the Board refused to admit that it owed any duty to select school sites in such a manner as would promote desegregation, and it asserted "that the Constitution is satisfied when they locate schools where children are and provide 'freedom of transfer' for those who want to change schools." But the District Court disagreed, saying:

> "Freedom of transfer increases rather than decreases segregation. The school superintendent testified that there would be, net, more than 1,200 additional white students going to predominently black schools if freedom of transfer were abolished."

Freedom encourages the lack of subservience to the will of government, therefore freedom is an evil.

By this time, plans had been developed and announced in compliance with the District Court's exercise of its Star Chamber powers to regulate the manner in which governmental officials exercise their official discretion, as a means of indirectly ruling the people, and these plans called for the racially-discriminatory transfer of many Negro children because they were black, supposedly to cure the fact that other Negro children in the past had suffered discriminatory treatment because they were black by being assigned to schools they didn't want to attend and by being denied the right to attend the schools they wanted to attend.

In addition to the 21,000 "silk stocking" white people who earlier had signed angry protests, 19,000 Negro people signed protests against the destruction of *their* freedom.[27] In describing these popular protests against the destruction of part of their freedom, the District Court even commented upon people who had written anonymous letters to it:

> ". . . Comment from people who have not studied the evidence tends to ignore the law—the reason this question is before a *court,* for decision—and to concentrate upon public acceptance or what will make people happy. A correspondent who signs 'Puzzled' inquiries:

> " 'If the whites don't want it and the blacks don't want it, why do we have to have it?'

> "The answer is, the Constitution of the United States."

But the answer was not the Constitution of the United States. The correct answer to Puzzled's question was a false rationalization based upon slogans rather than reason, having the same quality as that immortlized in the fictional writing of George Orwell, in which it was insisted in the regimented and dictatorial society of *1984* that war is peace, love is hate, freedom is slavery. Let us achieve freedom by destroying freedom.

In the apportionment cases the courts viewed a collective "right" of masses of people and illogically inferred from this joint political right a non-existent individual right accorded to an individual citizen. In the school cases, they took an individual right of each separate school child, totally disregarded the fact that those rights had been fully secured by state law, and instead envisioned the nonexistent right of a massive group of black children to be intermingled with a massive group of white children, even though substantial numbers of individuals in each group did not want and actively opposed this end.

The District Court in Charlotte said: "Segregation of children in public schools, whether they be black or white, and *regardless of whether they do or don't want to stay apart,* is unlawful." This is not a respect for individual constitutional rights. It does not even concern itself with individual rights. It concerns itself solely with the achievement of regimented submission to the judicial will to test or attain conformity with educational or sociological theories.

The School Board's performance of its ever-retreating endeavors to produce a plan satisfactory to the District Court never produced one fully pleasing in the Court's sight, so the Court announced it would appoint its own consultant.[28] The Court then appointed as its "independent" consultant a Dr. Finger, who had

---

27. It is interesting that the Court did not utilize the statistical comparisons so often used by federal courts. Such comparison made here would reveal that a far greater percentage of black parents protested than the percentage of white parents.

28. The Court ordered: "The Defendants are directed to cooperate fully with the consultant. This cooperation will include but not be limited to providing space at the headquarters of the board of education in which he may work; paying all his fees and expenses; providing stenographic assistance and the help of business machines, drafts-

already been hired to testify against the school board and who had already testified against the school board.

Not surprisingly, Dr. Finger produced a plan that was pleasing in the Court's sight, and the Court approved it. The Court directed the School Board to deny children admission to particular schools on account of their race, and to bus them, bussing children who live in predominantly Negro school zones to schools located in predominantly white areas, and bussing white children who lived near *those schools* to schools in the neighborhoods from whence the Negro children had been bussed.

After review by the Court of Appeals for that circuit, the case came before the United States Supreme Court. But in that Court the appeal was hopeless, unless the Court could be persuaded to read the Constitution instead of its own contrived opinions. This is true because in 1968, the Supreme Court had decided *Greene v. School Board of New Kent County.* In that case, the Court had condemned the practice of allowing each child his freedom as to where he would attend school unless those free choices happened to agree with the dream of promoting development of a society in which all racial groups are intermingled at random.

The school board involved in the *Greene* case had argued that the Constitution *did not permit* assignments on the basis of race, so as to bring about the end of schools whose populations were predominantly of one or the other race, as something that could be achieved only by a denial of equal protection of the laws. The Supreme Court said of this correct argument: "The Board attempts to cast the issue in its broadest form by arguing that its 'freedom-of-choice' plan may be faulted only by reading the Fourteenth Amendment as universally requiring 'compulsory integration' [29] a reading it insists the wording of the Amendment will not support. *But the argument ignores the thrust of Brown II."* [30] Thus the Supreme Court insisted upon turning its back upon the wording of the Constitution as it again re-affirmed its false claim of the supremacy of its own mere interpretations över the Constitution, over all other laws, and over the people themselves.

The *Greene* case had involved only one white school and one Negro school. In the decision, the Supreme Court complained that in three years, "not a single white child has chosen to attend Watkins School, . . . although 115 Negro chil-

---

men and computers if requested, along with telephone and other communication services. . . . The defendants will provide this consultant with full professional, technical and other assistants which he may need in familarizing himself with the school system and the various problems to be solved in desegregating the schools."

29. This inaccurate attempted restatement of the School Board's argument does not even make sense. The School Board did not argue that the Fourteenth Amendment universally *requires* "compulsory integration." The Board argued, and argued correctly, that the Amendment universally *prohibits* compulsory integration just as it universally *prohibits* compulsory racial segregation.

30. The Court gave no hint as to what part of the "thrust" of *Brown II* inspired this comment, but this decision was directly contrary to *Brown II,* in which the Supreme Court *said* it was declaring *"the fundamental principle that racial discrimination in public education is unconstitutional. . . ."* The Charlotte-Mecklenburg Board's position and the position of the board in the *Greene* case were in full accord with the rationale of the *Brown* decisions, which the Supreme Court abandoned in these two cases. As the Supreme Court only referred to the *Brown* decisions in reply to the school boards' contentions, and as those decisions supported the school boards, the Court actually failed to attempt to give any answer to these valid contentions.

dren enrolled in New Kent School in 1967 (up from 35 in 1965 and 111 in 1966), eighty-five percent of the Negro children in the systems still attend all-negro Watkins School." The Court's principal complaint was that white children did not choose to seek to attend the all-Negro school. In reference to this manner in which free people made their own choices the way they wanted to make them instead of deferring to the purposes the Supreme Court desired to accomplish—a purpose whose accomplishment is beyond the lawful power of either the Supreme Court or any state government—the Supreme Court concluded in its *Greene* decision: "In other words, the school system remains a dual system."

But "dual system" in the context of the commands of the Equal Protection Clause is meaningless unless it refers to a system maintained by state laws which prohibit school children admission on the ground of race.

In the *Greene* case, the Supreme Court falsely stated: "We do not hold that 'freedom-of-choice' can have no place in such a plan." But that is precisely what the Supreme Court did hold, that the trial courts of the United States must enter decrees prohibiting freedom of choice unless experience should demonstrate that the people will so exercise their freedom, by "evaluation in practice" in the manner desired by the Supreme Court to increase integration ratios, even after segregation commanded by law has been totally destroyed.[31]

Particularly in the light of the *Greene* decision,[32] the appeal of the Charlotte-Mecklenburg Board of Education was hopeless unless the Court could be persuaded to examine the Constitution, which Marshall had held to be the duty imposed by the judicial oath of office.

In the *Charlotte-Mecklenburg* case, the Supreme Court misleadingly stated:

> "Our objective in dealing with the issues presented by these cases is to see that school authorities exclude no pupil of a racial minority from any school, directly or indirectly, on account of race; . . ."

But in its decision, the Court totally disregarded the only real constitutional issues unavoidably involved in the case: Whether the District Court had violated the Constitution by ordering a state governmental unit to engage in racial discrimination and whether the school board could honestly be charged with excluding any child from any school on account of race when the Board had opened *every* school to *every* child of *every* race.

So in this rationalization in the *Charlotte-Mecklenburg* case, the Supreme Court abandoned reason and substituted for it a specious and misleading word game. The Court sought to defend its decision in the case by saying, "But all things are not equal in a system that has been deliberately constructed and maintained to enforce racial segregation." The intellectual dishonesty of this statement is in its implication that the school system is being maintained to enforce racial segregation, when the simple honest assessment of the fact that each student was given full freedom to attend the school of his choice demonstrates

---

31. Freedom of choice qualified by any requirement that the freedom be exercised in the manner desired by the master is not freedom. It is slavery. Religious theoreticians seem to agree that divine authority gives each person the freedom to sin, the freedom to make his own decisions on whether he will kill, steal, commit adultery, or whether he will refrain from doing these things. If they are correct, then God knows what freedom really is. America's modern government has forgotten, or else the corrupting effect of power is such that those in power no longer care.

32. It was to the leadership of that decision that the District Court in Charlotte, North Carolina, had responded by closing its eyes to the Constitution.

conclusively that the use of law to segregate people according to their race has been discontinued and no longer exists. This is demonstrated even without paying any attention to the practical result of the termination of legally-compelled racial segregation: That increasingly larger numbers of black students were exercising this right by attending schools with white children.

From its entire opinion in *Swann v. Charlotte-Mecklenburg Board of Education,* it can only be concluded that the Supreme Court wilfully and intentionally refused to consider and discuss the language of the Constitution and the argument as to the clear conflict between that language and its own plans to be imposed upon the school systems of the nation's communities.

This is made even more clear from a companion case decided the same day, *McDaniel v. Barresi.* In that decision, the Supreme Court did recite the contentions made, including the contention that a school board's plan to achieve more extensive racial integration by denying children admission to particular schools and assigning them to other schools on the basis of race violates the Equal Protection Clause of the Fourteenth Amendment.

McDaniel v. Barresi came before the Court on appeal from the Supreme Court of Georgia. That Court, the Supreme Court stated, had upheld the Equal Protection contentions, "concluding first that the plan violated the Equal Protection Clause 'by treating students differently because of their race.' " Then the Court stated its rejection of the Georgia court's conclusion, but the only reason it gave for this rejection was to briefly summarize its holdings in the *Greene* case and in the just-decided *Charlotte-Mecklenburg* case, including a quotation of its assertion that: "In this remedial process, steps will almost invariably require that students be assigned 'differently because of their race.' " In neither the *Greene* nor the *Charlotte-Mecklenburg* case, however, did the Supreme Court actually attempt to answer the contentions that the Fourteenth Amendment bars courts from ordering or upholding action by units of state governments engaging in racial discrimination in the administration of rules or laws.

But in the opinion being reviewed, *Barresi v. Browne,* the Supreme Court of Georgia had expounded the meaning of the Equal Protection Clause very briefly. That Court said:

> "Thus, the United States Supreme Court has condemned the practice of denying Negro children admission to public school facilities available to white children similarly situated as a denial of equal protection of the laws. The complaint here is that white *and* Negro children are denied admission to public school facilities available to other white *and* Negro children similarly situated. In all logic, it must be condemned also. . . .
>
> "Nor can it be argued that 'effective inclusion' because of race is different from 'effective exclusion' because of race. Within the proscription of the Fourteenth Amendment, we see no difference. One is just as discriminatory as the other. The Clarke County Board of Education has attempted to achieve a pre-determined racial balance in its elementary schools by treating students differently because of their race. This neither squares with the Fourteenth Amendment nor its interpretation by the United States Supreme Court holding that 'racial discrimination' is unconstitutional."

The Supreme Court of Georgia, in daily exercising the scholarship needed in the decision of ordinary common-law equity cases, also noted a limitation upon judicial power once honored by the United States Supreme Court but long since forgotten: That for a school board to file a "plan" of how it proposed to run its district in the future and to ask a court (here, a Georgia state trial court) to "approve" the "plan" was but to ask the court to give legal advice, not an exercise of judicial power in the decision of an actual case, but the delivery of a fictional opinion on a hypothetical state of facts.

Assuming that the United States Supreme Court properly did its duty of actually reading the full opinions of all lower courts whose decisions it was reviewing, then the issue concerning the obvious meaning of the Equal Protection Clause prohibiting the use of state law to compel racial integration by engaging in racially discriminatory exclusions of thousands of black and white children from their schools, was clearly brought to the Court's attention. Yet the Court in the *Barresi* case, as it did in the *Greene* and *Charlotte-Mecklenburg* cases, blinded itself to the Constitution of the United States.[33]

Chief Justice Marshall wrote in *Marbury v. Madison:*

> "Why does a judge swear to discharge his duties agreeably to the Constitution of the United States, if that Constitution forms no rule for his government—if it is closed upon him, and cannot be inspected by him? If such be the real state of things, this is worse than solemn mockery. *To prescribe, or to take this oath, becomes equally a crime."*

But the misconduct of the members of the Supreme Court in their decisions in the *Greene, Charlotte-Mecklenburg* and *Barresi* cases far exceeded the dishonor envisioned and described by Chief Justice Marshall in *Marbury v. Madison.* Marshall faced lawyers who were arguing that the Court was obligated to close its eyes to the Constitution despite the oath of office. Driven by the compulsion of the duty to answer these arguments, he considered this argument that only Congress can judge the meaning of the Constitution, and that its laws, enacted in the manner prescribed by the Constitution, must be accepted and enforced by the judiciary. Marshall measured these pressing arguments against the judicial oath of office and against the entire Constitution, and proved by reason that a judge is *compelled* by subservience to law to view the Constitution and to recognize its supremacy over all other types of law.

But the modern Court faced no comparable argument that it was compelled to close its eyes to the Constitution: Instead, it faced pleas from lawyers that its members should open their eyes to the Constitution and should grant the Constitution its supremacy. Marshall, faced with demands that law required him to shut out the Constitution, obeyed the command of honor and supported the Constitution. Today's Supreme Court justices moved of their own wills to shut the Constitution, its words, and its supremacy out of their decisions.

In this course of decisions on racial segregation by law in the public schools maintained by state governments, in its factual claim of power to suspend the

---

33. That the Supreme Court's decision in *Swann v. Charlotte-Mecklenburg Board of Education* was reached by intellectual dishonesty is undeniable. A sadder thing about it is that the Court's violation of the Constitution was so obvious that it was noticed and correctly identified by the man in the street, the man unlearned in law, the man who may well never have even read the Constitution. The saddest thing about this clear judicial violation of the Constitution is that it is difficult to imagine any judicial frame of mind that could save this course of judicial conduct from the legitimate charge of wilful violation of the oath of office, by unanimous conspiracy among the Court's members, not one of whom raised his voice to analyze the conduct of the court and to point to the simple and obvious truth that its members, under color of their official positions, were violating the individual constitutional rights of thousands of North Carolina citizens.

Constitution, in its concern with administration of local government entities instead of the rights of individuals, the Supreme Court has acted in such a manner as to merit the criticism that its justices have been guilty of misconduct in public office. Nothing in the *Charlotte-Mecklenburg* rationalization is based upon the visualization of any child being presently denied admission to a school because of his race. It is all directed instead at the unsuccessful attempt to justify a present denial of admissions to schools on the ground of race in order that racial association in place of racial segregation may be compelled by force of arms—by law.

This course of decisions would have been changed not the slightest if the Court had been guided solely by a spirit of retribution against the white majority's rejection of the Court's ideas and the black minority's rejection of its sometimes unwelcome helping hand—which chose the destruction of individual freedom as the means of rendering its assistance, and with such spirit of retribution being strengthened by a conscious or sub-conscious desire to increase the power of the judiciary over the people at all costs.

It must be true that the corrupting influence of an excessive amount or usurped power may be a blinding influence adequate to distort judicial reasoning and to impel judges to an unreasoned acceptance of a proposition that reason could never demonstrate to John Marshall—that it is ever honorable for judges to disregard the Constitution and be guided only by inferior or secondary law.

This course of misconduct in judicial office has resulted in frustration of the people's belief and desire that they be lawfully governed. It has led to an immense and ungovernable increase of the power of the federal judiciary over the people.

To rule the people by ruling the officers they have chosen to govern them is to diminish and weaken the republican form of government and is to exercise a non-judicial power. This type of rule which controls the manner and content of decisions by those chosen locally to govern is an earmark of tyrannical government—government by one who stands above the law, ruling by arbitrary whim, and refusing to acknowledge that his acts and his decisions must always be governed by some superior and controlling law.

This type of governing power, when exercised by a judicial body, is judicial tyranny and judicial dictatorship. There are no bounds to it save such as may be imposed by the anger of an outraged citizenry who remain politically viable. Judicial tyranny is not an evil to be dreaded in the distant future. It is an evil that has come upon us, brought about by infidelity to the imperative of judicial integrity.

The judges of the nation, blinded by their near-deification of the Supreme Court, and intellectually crippled by the habit of assuming that Supreme Court opinions accurately expound the law and must be followed—though in fact they are neither supreme law nor even law, but only interpretations of law— have, presumably innocently, aided and abetted the Supreme Court's usurpations. They have even failed to be sufficiently astute to recognize as an exercise of regal power the Supreme Court's claim of the power to suspend the Constitution.

Long ago, Thomas Jefferson predicted:

"The germ of dissolution of our government is in the constitution of the federal judiciary, an irresponsible body . . . working like gravity by day and by night, gaining a little today and a little tomorrow and advancing its noiseless step like a thief over the field of jurisdiction until all shall be usurped from the states and the government of all shall be consolidated into one."

Part V

THE FINAL JUDGMENT

THE FINAL JUDGMENT

XII.

THERE IS NO popular objective so important as to justify disregard of the lawful limitations placed upon the powers of governmental officials. Nor is any official so high as to be justly immune from criticism of his conduct. When courts abandon the Constitution and utilize their powers to achieve desired objectives, this conduct cannot be tolerated and freedom preserved.

There was a time in the history of England when the king had powerful arguments to support his need to exercise extraordinary powers for a limited period, and of this request for urgently-needed powers, Lord Seldon said: "At this little gap, every man's liberty may in time go out." [1] It is in the preservation of the lawful forms of government and limitations of its powers that the rights of the individual are secured. There is no other—nor has there been any other—successful device to protect the individual against the power of government. The Supreme Court, in ever-increasing degrees, has dishonored its obligation to yield to the supremacy of the Constitution.

In the past two decades, the Court has warped beyond recognition and in disregard of their historically established meanings, the criminal procedures ordained by the Constitution; it has utilized claims of expanding personal rights to in fact expand its own powers by methods that have little benefited the personal rights of citizens. It has failed to live up to its obligation to weigh the Acts of Congress against the Constitution and to fearlessly refuse to recognize as law illegal congressional enactments. It has combined, as Hamilton warned, with the legislative and executive branches of the federal government, to declare lawful, on the most specious reasoning, exercises of power which are clearly beyond the powers given to those branches and beyond the powers given to the Government of the United States.

The Supreme Court, in cooperation with the other branches of the federal government, has reduced the interstate commerce clause of the Constitution to an absurdity, and has recognized as law immense usurpations by the Congress in regulating local affairs which are of no legitimate concern to the United States Government. It has destroyed the Due Process Clauses of the Constitution in their meaning established by simple scholastic research, and has substituted for them an artificial meaning that guarantees to the citizen nothing but the protection of such ideas of justice as the individual judges currently sitting on the Supreme Court may find adequately fundamental in their varying philosophies to deserve protection.

As was inevitable from the judicial embrace of this absurdity, the right to trial by jury—to the protection of a body of independent citizens standing between the individual and the power of government—has already begun to disappear: This achieved by the false pretense that the right to trail by jury now means something different from what it meant when those words were written into the Constitution.

The Court has warped the meaning of the Equal Protection Clause into a mean-

---

1. VI Holdsworth 38.

ing totally different from that expressed by the language of the clause and totally different from that intended by the men who wrote its language.

The Court has adamantly refused to recognize the Privilege and Immunities Clause of the Fourteenth Amendment as having its natural meaning and the meaning repeatedly proclaimed for it in the halls of Congress when the clause was written and was being debated—the guarantee to every citizen, against infringement by his own state government, of any and all of the rights guaranteed by the Bill of Rights to the Constitution of the United States.

And all this has been achieved with hardly a backward glance, without evidencing the slightest suspicion but that the Court itself is endowed with all wisdom, pretending there is no need to read and ponder the opinions and reasoning of men who sat on the bench of the Supreme Court between the last days of John Marshall and the closing years of the Nineteenth Century.

This has been achieved largely by the creation of paraphraseology, usually rhetorically attractive, by substituting there different words for the usually more precise and descriptive words written into the Constitution, and then by closing the judicial eyes to the Constitution itself and seeing instead the surviving remnants of yesterday's rhetoric or the pleasing creations of today's rhetoric. Police Power. Without Redeeming Social Importance. Clear and Present Danger. Justiciability. Affecting Commerce. War Power. Unitary School System. Scheme of Ordered Liberty. Invidious Discrimination. Separate but Equal. One Man, One Vote. The Remedial Powers of Equity. People, not Trees. *Ad infinitim, ad infinitim.*

" 'When *I* use a word,' Humpty Dumpty said, in a rather scornful tone, 'it means just what I choose it to mean—neither more nor less.'

" 'The question is,' said Alice, 'whether you *can* make words mean so many different things.'

'The question is,' said Humpty Dumpty, 'which is to be master—that's all.' [2]

And in Supreme Court decisions, too often it is not a question of the true meaning of words, but a question of who has the power. The power of government may declare that a tax imposed directly upon a man's total accumulated wealth is not a direct tax, but true meanings may not be changed. It is beyond the power of any government to destroy truth or to create truth from falsehood. Government can only compel obedience and seek to justify its conduct.

Judges have occasionally shown brief flashes of recognition of the deceptiveness of vague phraseology. In a case that was quite non-controversial, *Tiller v. Atlantic Coast Railroad Co.*, Justice Felix Frankfurter, mentioning the "uncritical use of words [which] bedevils the law," said of the evoluntionary growth:

"A phrase begins life as a literary expression; its felicity leads to its lazy repetition; and repetition soon establishes it as a legal formula, undiscriminatingly used to express different and sometimes contradictory ideas."

The felicitious paraphraseology becomes but a tool to "change" the meaning of fundamental law, and to abandon that law in favor of other "fundamental" precepts of justice more pleasing to the current philosophies of individual judges. In fidelity to the Constitution, why create the rhetoric? Why speak of "redeeming social importance" when it only raises other questions—How important?—Im-

2. Carroll, *Through the Looking Glass,* Ch. 6.

portant in whose judgment? Redeeming to what level of society, the level of the man who values the pornography enough to pay his hard-earned money for it?—Redeeming in the judgment of the jurors who valued the pornography so little that they voted the seller guilty?—Redeeming in the judgment of judges far removed from the pressures of ordinary life, but powerfully drawn to the latest literate productions of philosophical and sociological writers?

How much simpler it would be to forget the rhetoric and read the Constitution, the best-drawn and most wisely-conceived document of state ever written. And if the people do not like power to be limited and channeled as required by the Constitution, the people can make their wills known and their voices heard, and their representatives can change the Constitution.

But in the process of change, if we listen, the debate may educate our minds, improve our manner of thinking, and convince us that the devices adopted in the Constitution rest upon a deep understanding of unchanging human nature, and an uncompromising love of liberty. If we thoughtfully search our own minds, we may even conclude that there is no aim of government more praiseworthy than to expand to the greatest possible extent the freedom of every individual; that governmental power can never be expanded except by further limiting the freedom of one or more individuals; that of all civil rights which any individual possesses, the most fundamental is the right to be free of lawlessness in government, the right to be free of governmental interference except to the extent and in the manner provided by law; and that no matter how tasty the goodies may be, it is never a legitimate aim of government to play god—that by "giving" to an individual that taken by force of arms from its owners, government robs the favored individual of the right to be the master of his own fate, the right to nurture and improve his own individuality, the right to be free, to be a man.

Throughout the land, the child can sense the impotence of the parent, can sense not only the parental outrage and the lack of power to *demand* change, even in his own home town, but the lack of ability even to conceive of any constructive action which might increase the possibility of improvement. Throughout the land, one can perceive the unrest of the citizen who feels that he is victimized by taxation without representation for his views, while government is unable or unwilling to furnish him the protection he needs, yet demands and takes an unfair portion of the earnings of his labor, to the injury of his family and to the benefit of unseen parasites who make little or no contribution to their society, their posterity, or to themselves.

Considering the immense increase of federal power and the ever-growing interference by the federal judiciary, one can perceive a real and growing suspicion that much of the blame for the unhappy state in which the people now find themselves may be laid at the clay feet of the federal judiciary, the robed priesthood of the American civilization. The student must concur in the belief that much of the evil of this day would not have occurred but for the federal judiciary's infidelity to the imperative of judicial integrity.

A review of the work of the Supreme Court commands an attempt to answer a simple question earlier asked: So what? Does it really make any difference?

We must surely accept as true the assertions of those who claim that the Constitution of the United States is not sacred, that the people are not obligated to submit to rule by the dead hand of the past, that we owe no duty of ancestor-worship, and that the people are free to demand change in their Constitution whenever they desire it. But it is the *people* who have the right to demand change in their fundamental law, and the right to demand change is quite different from some supposed duty to suffer change imposed upon them by lawless usurpers of power.

It is true we owe no duty of ancestor-worship. But may we with equal assurance assert that we owe no duty to our distant posterity, brought here through our procreation? Sound morality and good conscience will not admit this. Sound morality does not demand that we preserve past governmental forms and limitations. But it does demand that we study those forms, as they were originally conceived with great genius, before depriving our posterity of the benefit of our design of government.

When we become dissatisfied with the scope and organization of our government, the discharge of our moral duty to the future requires that we do something more than and different from simply demanding a change in our Constitution: It demands that we or our representatives first determine whether we are dissatisfied with our Constitution or with the fact that it has been disregarded, with the fact that by gradual changes a form of government has been adopted that is totally and irreconcilably incompatible with the design of government established by the Constitution.

It should never be thought necessary to amend the Constitution—and further pollute it—for the purpose of returning our government *part of the way* in the direction of a law-abiding and constitutional government. Whenever government fails to respect law, the people should have the sense to detect it and the ability to make government hear their demand: That government cease its lawless misconduct, and again respect the lawful organization of and limitations upon its powers.

We owe no obligation of worship to our ancestry, from whose conduct we benefit or suffer. But we owe a very real obligation to the future. An obligation not to pollute our land, waters and air. An obligation not to destroy our forests and our irreplaceable natural wealth. An obligation not to poison our tillable land. But we also owe to the future an obligation not to allow tyrannical government to replace a responsive and responsible republican form of government; an obligation to preserve our political viability and the genius of our true from of government planned by an unmatched little assembly of men; an obligation to preserve freedom.

In the long run, it may happen that much environmental pollution can be remedied by allowing it to rest free from abuse for a time. But once established, tyrannical government cannot be combatted by a policy of benign neglect. Once established, its tyrannical nature can be destroyed only at the cost of human blood, and then after the suffering has become so intolerable as to inspire resistance.

But this time we may have already passed the point where resistance to a well-entrenched tyrannical government can have any hope of success. We may have reached a point in the scientific development of man where the complex state of communication facilities,weaponry, and dependence upon centralized and controllable sources of essential supplies would render even a population of many millions of people powerless to resist a truly tyrannical government with well-established organization and procedures.

We, today, partly because of our inventiveness, may well owe to our posterity a far greater obligation than have any of history's past generations. We may have already permitted ourselves to be lured far too close to the brink of a regimented, authoritarian Orwellian society where war is peace, love is hate, freedom is slavery. Too many faint traces are rapidly becoming more visible.

Perhaps the time has come for Americans to re-think the wisdom of those who, comparatively recently, decided to abandon the protection of a United States Senate better insulated from the necessity of rapidly responding to temporary and insubstantial changes in public opinion, and who substituted for it a Senate obligated by the instinct of self-preservation to respond quickly to voter pressure. We might pause to wonder what would be the degree of corruption in our Federal Government if it had a Senate free from direct voter pressure, and subjected to only that pressure strained through a slightly protective legislature, which recognizes *some* mature responsibility to a greater degree than do individual voters. We might wonder if the ratification of judicial appointments would have been more responsible had the United States Senate been better insulated from the brief whirlwinds of raging public opinion.

Perhaps the time has come for Americans to re-think the proposition that everyone who wants to should be permitted to vote on the comparative charismatic qualities of leaders, and the proposition that the function of voting is more of a personal privilege to be exercised that a solemn responsibility to be discharged. Present trends will inevitably enhance the further development of government by bribery, in which public money will increasingly be used to influence votes, with the consequent lessening of the degree of independent republican responsibility exercised by our representatives. If government thus gains the power of self-perpetuation, the freedom of those whose independence is not for sale will be in grave danger. Those individualists probably supply a leavening influence essential to the freedom of all.

And the time has definitely come for Americans to reconsider the question of whether the continued existence of government by bureaucracy rather than government of laws is not a mistake that could be abandoned without injury to anyone other than the bureaucrats who infest it.

But what of the judiciary which has "permitted" this governmental sickness to develop, the remote, supreme judiciary so powerful that it cannot even hear the voice of Congress? This is the proper response when the congressional voice contravenes the Constitution, but sometimes the voice of Congress is more true to the Constitution than the voice of the judiciary. When the judiciary sails off on a foolish tack, substitutes its philosophy for the Constitution, what possible practical remedy is there for this evil?

Some have urged the use of a remedy written into the Constitution as one of the "checks and balances" designed to protect the people from the government— the power of impeachment. Only one Supreme Court justice has been impeached, and though he richly deserved impeachment, the Senate acquitted him. There has developed a tradition that judges are not to be impeached, except possibly for financial indescretions. But for infidelity to the Constitution?—Never! The institution of the remedy of impeachment would be exceedingly difficult, when the judiciary shields from the public eye congressional infidelity to the Constitution. And the habitual use of impeachment might carry with it a real threat of rendering the Supreme Court subservient to Congress. But if faced with a judiciary which haughtily persists in acting dishonestly, impeachment should be utilized to remove dishonorable judges from office, if necessary by making it a criminal offense for a judge to wilfully violate his oath of office.

Some have urged more care in the selection of judges, but this could be achieved only by continuous public insistance that only qualified people be appointed, and the public never *continuously* insists upon anything. Also, the public may naturally be apt, as lay people, to confuse a dignified judicial appearance with the existence of judicial ability and temperament. Institutionalized selection procedures have proven themselves perfectly adapted to the unerring selection of whomever the political appointing authority desires to appoint. Some improvement might be achieved if the Senate should advise the President that it would not consent to the appointment of any Supreme Court justices except those appointed directly from among the body of state judges, until a majority on the Court should be former state judges. It is likely that among the nation's trial judges, the most competent will be found scattered here and there on state rather than federal courts. On state courts, their competence can be observed and judged through the years, as they improve their knowledge of our common-law heritage and as they perform their duties in an ordinary judicial atmosphere, instead of the Federal atmosphere of the exercise of supposed judicial power to attain political objectives and to control the use of political power.

It has also been suggested that federal judges should be subject to re-appointment or to periodic re-confirmation by the Senate, but this carries with it a very grave threat of damage to the Supreme Court's independence.

For despite its failures, the Supreme Court remains a most valuable institution whose independence should be protected. How else could the Supreme Court have withstood strong public criticism other than by its independent spirit? Its fault has not been in an excess of independence, but in intellectual poverty, the substantial emptiness of its decisions, its failure to be studious and introspective, its failure to adequately inspect past interpretations before rejecting them in preference to "interpretations" not based upon the Constitution, its failure to keep constant watch upon itself to assure that it will not become what it has become: The instrumentality of the destruction of the Constitution instead of the guardian of the Constitution's supremacy.

The principal fault in the Supreme Court is the thing that should be treated and remedied, and this cannot be attained by the pointless abuse of the Court. Nor can it be attained by robbing the federal judiciary of its independence by taking from judges the life tenure that promotes fearless independence. Of course there should be eliminated the temporary fault of foolish "interpretations" which have characterized the past seventy-five years but whose abandonment would result from honest and competent scholarship. But the principal fault of the Supreme Court is the fault that pervades the entire judicial brotherhood: An idea. And the soundest cure is not to assault the Court, but for the people to insist that the poisonous idea be eliminated and its foolishness declared and demonstrated by the Court itself for all the world to see.

And that idea is the idea that Supreme Court interpretations are law. Not just the idea that they are Supreme Law, but the idea that they are even law at all.

One with the opportunity can observe state *and federal judges* almost bitterly criticising the Supreme Court, and stating precise and correct reasons why Supreme Court decisions on particular points are false interpretations of the Constitution and of the law. These are good men, intelligent men, men dedicated to the proper performance of their duty. Yet when they mount the bench and are called upon to rule on the precise question on which they have criticised the Supreme Court, they loyally follow not their own beliefs but the interpretations by the Supreme Court. Their error is the error caused by the unquestioning acceptance of a totally invalid idea—that Supreme Court interpretations of law are themselves law which everybody is obligated to follow.

When an evil flows from a false idea, the most appropriate remedy is the destruction of that idea. The most appropriate remedy for the body of the citizenry to follow when they find the conduct of the judiciary unacceptable is to insist that judges live up to their oaths of office: That each judge is obligated to re-

learn the teachings of the common law, that the function of the judge is to studiously seek to discover the law, and to then give to *the law* his unquestioning
obedience. Communication is a two-way street, and the Supreme Court could
learn much from the nation's judges, if those judges would free themselves from
the shackles of subservience to a false idea, developed into blinding dogma.

The true obligation of every judge is to live up to his oath of office: To let his
judgments always reflect the supremacy of the Constitution, always true to the
Constitution as his study of its clear words lead him to interpret it, remembering
that those words always have the same meaning they had when they were first
written into the Constitution.

No judge, carefully considering the words of his oath of office, by which he
has sworn allegiance to the Constitution, can conclude on the basis of reason that
he is either obligated or permitted to support and defend some other judge's ideas
as to the meaning of the Constitution, when the judge finds those ideas completely
opposed to the results of his own thoughtful study.

This is the proper position of the United States Supreme Court: In the exercise
of judicial power in the decision of a lawsuit, its supremacy is unquestionable.
There comes a time when disputes between people must be brought to an end,
when there remains no place to which another appeal can be taken, and that
final stopping-place of every dispute that can properly be resolved by the use of
federal judicial power is the Supreme Court of the United States. In the exercise
of this power, the Supreme Court is supreme. Its judgments command unquestioning obedience by the people bound by them, unless it can be persuaded to
change its mind. But this is the full scope of judicial power—the simple decision
of lawsuits, the rendition of decisions binding upon the people who sued or were
sued, and their representatives, but binding upon no one else on earth. Except for
those people so bound by the judgment, no one else—neither President, Senators,
Congressmen, Governors, judges or lawyers—is under the slightest obligation
either to accept as correct or to pretend the correctness of any exposition of the
meaning of the Constitution by the Supreme Court of the United States.

In regard to the Supreme Court's expositions of the meaning or supposed meaning of the Constitution, this is the proper position of the Supreme Court: It is the
teacher of the nation's lawyers and judges, giving them in its opinions the benefit
of its insight, the knowledge flowing from its research, and the opinions produced
in part by the arguments it has heard. And as in the teachings of any teacher, the
students are not only free, but obligated, to disregard the teachings they find to
be false.

It is true that this approach would in time render it virtually impossible for
the Supreme Court to achieve desired objectives. But the Supreme Court *never*
has any business having *any* objectives to achieve. Its only proper objective is a
self-achieving one, to decide every lawsuit correctly, in accordance with law, and
in subservience to the supremacy of the Constitution. This is the objective the
oath of office binds every judge to seek to achieve.

The best remedy for the Supreme Court's exercise of its new-found powers
discovered this century is for the Court itself to perceive and confess the error of
its possibly innocent misconduct. Innocent, because ideas can be extremely misleading unless one stops to question them. But in a sense not innocent, because
anyone who accepts judicial office holds himself out as being intelligent enough
to discern truth and sufficiently energetic and dedicated to search for it.

But the Court having shown no overt signs of repentence, the next best remedy
is the slow but safer remedy of the people themselves, under the informed leader-

ship of a more studious press, insisting upon judicial fidelity to the oath of office. A studious press, a strong supporter of liberty, can and should not only report the good and evil flowing from judicial decisions, but should do more. The press should study the opinions and report their content, both the achievements and the miscarriages of justice *under law*. A studious press would read dissenting opinions, compare them with the majority court opinions, and if the dissent contains a complete or partial refutation that the majority has disdained to notice or to endeavor to explain away, the press should scathingly criticise the Court's decision as intellectually dishonest.

Too often, the Supreme Court has rendered opinions—many of which we have discussed—which took no note of a dissent totally demolishing the Court's opinion. But a dissenter's opinion, like that of any critic, should be carefully examined, because the dissenter is not really performing a function in which he is discharging any duty of office. The majority is deciding the lawsuit, exercising the judicial power, and the dissenter is simply expressing the reasons for his inability to join in the performance of this duty, knowing that his words can have no effect beyond their inherent persuasiveness.

Too often, the Supreme Court has blinded itself to the Constitution, and has in the same opinion absurdly proclaimed that it was obeying the imperative of judicial integrity. It is by that merciless imperative that the Court's performance should be judged. Attempted obedience to the imperative of judicial integrity on al occasions and in every case should be the standard of conduct demanded by the people of all judges.

The Supreme Court's proper position is not a position of national moral leadership. The Supreme Court's function is to decide lawsuits, its duty to search for the correct meaning of the Constitution in *all* its past opinions as well as from other sources.

In those bound volumes of reports of the decisions of the United States Supreme Court is a unique history of a nation, each decision speaking with the freshness of today, though many are filled with outdated legal jargon that cannot be rapidly read. In those books one finds fiery dedication, opinions like explosive belches of anger, restrained wisdom, many convincing explanations of the meaning of the Constitution which are now forgotten, catch-phrases that have lain for a time to be seized upon later and amplified far beyond the permissible bounds of reason, and no small amount of plain intellectual rubbish. The ability to distinguish among these in the search for truth is one of the essential qualifications for the competent performance of the judicial function. Some men have this ability and some do not. Unfortunately, when the ability is missing, it cannot be added or created from the trappings of high judicial office.

The ecclesiastical king's final advice concerned the difficulties of assessing the validity of ideas conveyed by the printed word: "One further warning, my son: the use of books is endless, and much study is wearisome." [3]

---

3. Ecclesiastes XI:12; *The New English Bible.*

AFTERWORD

EXPERIENCE SINCE THE COMPLETION OF THIS BOOK proves the validity of its premises and conclusions. Changes in membership of the Supreme Court has brought differing personal philosophies, but no sign of increased adherence to the supremacy of law or of the Constitution, and no abandonment of the Court's illicit view of its own past utterances as the supreme law.

To prove this would require extended writing, but when a book is completed, the writing must stop. But to demonstrate the correctness of this premise, I must mention the concurring opinion of one of the newer members of the Supreme Court in *Runyon v. McCrary*, decided June, 1976. He briefly discussed an irrational decision, upheld in this case, in which the Supreme Court had imposed upon *the individual citizen* the same obligation of racial impartiality that the Fourteenth Amendment imposes only upon *state governments*. He stated his "firm" "conviction" that the case was "wrongly decided" but voted to require that it be followed on the basis of "my understanding of the mores of today . . ." Sworn to decide in accordance with law, he stated he was voting contrary to his firm convictions as to the requirements of law. If this is integrity in judicial office, then intellectual honesty has somehow acquired a strange meaning beyond comprehension.

I wish to express my deep appreciation to my friend, Philip M. Carden, for his encouragement as he read each chapter during the writing; to Dominic deLorenzo, for his valuable re-write suggestions; to Mrs. Shirley George for her editing work; to Sam Moore, for his confidence in the American reader's ability to read and understand, and to those who, now by wise words, now by horrible examples, taught me constitutional law: The justices, past and present, of the United States Supreme Court.

Nashville, Tennessee
January, 1977

THE CONSTITUTION
OF THE UNITED STATES

WE THE PEOPLE of the United States, in Order to form a more perfect Union, establish Justice, insure domestic Tranquility, provide for the common defence, promote the general Welfare, and secure the Blessings of Liberty to ourselves and our Posterity, do ordain and establish this CONSTITUTION for the United States of America.

ARTICLE I.

SECTION 1. All legislative Powers herein granted shall be vested in a Congress of the United States, which shall consist of a Senate and House of Representatives.

SECTION 2. The House of Representatives shall be composed of Members chosen every second Year by the People of the several States, and the Electors in each State shall have the Qualifications requisite for Electors of the most numerous Branch of the State Legislature.

No Person shall be a Representative who shall not have attained to the Age of twenty five Years, and been seven Years a Citizen of the United States, and who shall not, when elected, be an Inhabitant of that State in which he shall be chosen.

Representatives and direct Taxes shall be apportioned among the several States which may be included within this Union, according to their respective Numbers, which shall be determined by adding to the whole Number of free Persons, including those bound to Service for a Term of Years, and excluding Indians not taxed, three fifths of all other Persons. The actual Enumeration shall be made within three Years after the first Meeting of the Congress of the United States, and within every subsequent Term of ten Years, in such Manner as they shall by Law direct. The Number of Representatives shall not exceed one for every thirty Thousand, but each State shall have at Least one Representative; and until such enumeration shall be made, the State of New Hampshire shall be entitled to chuse three, Massachusetts eight, Rhode-Island and Providence Plantations one, Connecticut five, New-York six, New Jersey four, Pennsylvania eight, Delaware one, Maryland six, Virginia ten, North Carolina five, South Carolina five, and Georgia three.

When vacancies happen in the Representation from any State, the Executive Authority thereof shall issue Writs of Election to fill such Vacancies.

The House of Representatives shall chuse their Speaker and other Officers; and shall have the sole Power of Impeachment.

SECTION 3. The Senate of the United States shall be composed of two Senators from each State, chosen by the Legislature thereof, for six Years; and each Senator shall have one Vote.

Immediately after they shall be assembled in Consequence of the first Election, they shall be divided as equally as may be into three Classes. The Seats of the Senators of the first Class shall be vacated at the Expiration of the Second Year, of the second Class at the Expiration of the fourth Year, and of the third Class at the Expiration of the sixth Year, so that one third may be chosen every second Year; and if Vacancies happen by Resignation, or otherwise, during the Recess of the Legislature of any State, the Executive thereof may make temporary Appointments until the next Meeting of the Legislature, which shall then fill such Vacancies.

No Person shall be a Senator who shall not have attained to the Age of thirty Years, and been nine Years a Citizen of the United States, and who shall not, when elected, be an Inhabitant of that State for which he shall be chosen.

The Vice President of the United States shall be President of the Senate, but shall have no Vote, unless they be equally divided.

The Senate shall chuse their other Officers, and also a President pro tempore, in the Absence of the Vice President, or when he shall exercise the Office of President of the United States.

The Senate shall have the sole Power to try all Impeachments. When sitting for that Purpose, they shall be on Oath or Affirmation. When the President of the United States is tried, the Chief Justice shall preside: and no Person shall be convicted without the Concurrence of two thirds of the Members present.

Judgment in Cases of Impreachment shall not extend further than to removal from Office, and disqualification to hold and enjoy any Office of honor, Trust or Profit under the United States: but the Party convicted shall nevertheless be liable and subject to Indictment, Trial, Judgment and Punishment, according to Law.

SECTION 4. The Times, Places and Manner of holding Elections for Senators and Representatives, shall be prescribed in each State by the Legislature thereof; but the Congress may at any time by Law make or alter such Regulations, except as to the Places of chusing Senators.

The Congress shall assemble at least once in every Year, and such Meeting shall be on the first Monday in December, unless they shall by Law appoint a different Day.

SECTION 5. Each House shall be the Judge of the Elections, Returns and Qualifications of its own Members, and a Majority of each shall constitute a Quorum to do Business; but a smaller Number may adjourn from day to day, and may be authorized to compel the Attendance of absent Members, in such Manner, and under such Penalties as each House may provide.

Each House may determine the Rules of its Proceedings, punish its Members for disorderly Behaviour, and, with the Concurrence of two thirds, expel a Member.

Each House shall keep a Journal of its Proceedings, and from time to time publish the same, excepting such Parts as may in their Judgment require Secrecy; and the Yeas and Nays of the Members of either House on any question shall, at the desire of one fifth of those Present, be entered on the Journal.

Neither House, during the Session of Congress, shall, without the Consent of the other, adjourn for more than three days, nor to any other Place than that in which the two Houses shall be sitting.

SECTION 6. The Senators and Representatives shall receive a Compensation for their Services, to be ascertained by Law, and paid out of the Treasury of the United States. They shall in all Cases, except Treason, Felony and Breach of the Peace, be privileged from Arrest during their Attendance at the Session of their respective Houses, and in going to and returning from the same; and for any Speech or Debate in either House, they shall not be questioned in any other Place.

No Senator or Representative shall, during the Time for which he was elected, be appointed to any civil Office under the Authority of the United States, which shall have been created, or the Emoluments whereof shall have been encreased during such time; and no Person holding any Office under the United States, shall be a Member of either House during his Continuance in Office.

SECTION 7. All Bills for raising Revenue shall originate in the House of Representatives; but the Senate may propose or concur with Amendments as on other Bills.

Every Bill which shall have passed the House of Representatives and the Senate, shall, before it become a Law, be presented to the President of the United States; If he approve he shall sign it, but if not he shall return it, with his Objections to that House in which it shall have originated, who shall enter the Objections at large on their Journal, and proceed to reconsider it. If after such Reconsideration two thirds of that House shall agree to pass the Bill, it shall be sent, together with the Objections, to the other House, by which it shall likewise be reconsidered, and if approved by two thirds of that House, it shall become a Law. But in all such Cases the Votes of both Houses shall be determined by yeas and Nays, and the Names of the Persons voting for and against the Bill shall be entered on the Journal of each House respectively. If any Bill shall not be returned by the President within ten Days (Sundays excepted) after it shall have been presented to him, the Same shall be a Law, in like Manner as if he had signed it, unless the Congress by their Adjournment prevent its Return, in which Case it shall not be a Law.

Every Order, Resolution, or Vote to which the Concurrence of the Senate and House of Representatives may be necessary (except on a question of Adjournment) shall be presented to the President of the United States; and before the Same shall take Effect, shall be approved by him, or being disapproved by him, shall be repassed by two thirds of the Senate and House of Representatives, according to the Rules and Limitations prescribed in the Case of a Bill.

SECTION 8. The Congress shall have Power To lay and collect Taxes, Duties, Imposts and Excises, to pay the Debts and provide for the common Defence and general Welfare of the United States; but all Duties, Imposts and Excises shall be uniform throughout the United States:

To borrow Money on the credit of the United States;

To regulate Commerce with foreign Nations, and among the several States, and with the Indian Tribes;

To establish an uniform Rule of Naturalization, and uniform Laws on the subject of Bankruptcies throughout the United States;

To coin Money, regulate the Value thereof, and of foreign Coin, and fix the Standard of Weights and Measures;

To provide for the Punishment of counterfeiting the Securities and current Coin of the United States;

To establish Post Offices and post Roads;

To promote the Progress of Science and useful Arts, by securing for limited Times to Authors and Inventors the exclusive Right to their respective writings and Discoveries;

To constitute Tribunals inferior to the supreme Court;

To define and punish Piracies and Felonies committed on the high Seas, and Offences against the Law of Nations;

To declare War, grant Letters of Marque and Reprisal, and make Rules concerning Captures on Land and Water;

To raise and support Armies, but no Appropriation of Money to that Use shall be for a longer Term than two Years;

To provide and maintain a Navy;

To make Rules for the Government and Regulation of the land and naval Forces;

To provide for calling forth the Militia to execute the Laws of the Union, suppress Insurrections and repel Invasions;

To provide for organizing, arming, and disciplining, the Militia, and for governing such Part of them as may be employed in the Service of the United States, reserving to the States respectively, the Appointment of the Officers, and the Authority of training the Militia according to the discipline prescribed by Congress;

To exercise exclusive Legislation in all Cases whatsoever, over such District (not exceeding ten Miles square) as may, by Cession of particular States, and the Acceptance of Congress, become the Seat of the Government of the United States, and to exercise like Authority over all Places purchased by the Consent of the Legislature of the State in which the Same shall be, for the Erection of Forts, Magazines, Arsenals, dock-Yards, and other needful Buildings;—And

To make all Laws which shall be necessary and proper for carrying into Execution the foregoing Powers, and all other Powers vested by this Constitution in the Government of the United States, or in any Department or Officer thereof.

SECTION 9. The Migration or Importation of such Persons as any of the States now existing shall think proper to admit, shall not be prohibited by the Congress prior to the Year one thousand eight hundred and eight, but a Tax or duty may be imposed on such Importation, not exceeding ten dollars for each Person.

The Privilege of the Writ of Habeas Corpus shall not be suspended, unless when in Cases of Rebellion or Invasion the public Safety may require it.

No Bill of Attainder or ex post facto Law shall be passed.

No capitation, or other direct, Tax shall be laid, unless in Proportion to the Census of Enumeration herein before directed to be taken.

No Tax or Duty shall be laid on Articles exported from any State.

No Preference shall be given by any Regulation of Commerce or Revenue to the Ports of one State over those of another: nor shall Vessels bound to, or from, one State, be obliged to enter, clear, or pay Duties in another.

No Money shall be drawn from the Treasury, but in Consequence of Appropriations made by Law; and a regular Statement and Account of the Receipts and Expenditures of all public Money shall be published from time to time.

No Title of Nobility shall be granted by the United States: And no Person holding any Office of Profit or Trust under them, shall, without the Consent of the Congress, accept of any present, Emolument, Office, or Title, of any kind whatever, from any King, Prince, or foreign State.

SECTION 10. No State shall enter into any Treaty, Alliance, or Confederation; grant Letters of Marque and Reprisal; coin Money; emit Bills of Credit; make any Thing but gold and silver Coin a Tender in Payment of Debts; pass any Bill of Attainder, ex post facto Law, or Law impairing the Obligation of Contracts, or grant any Title of Nobility.

No State shall, without the Consent of the Congress, lay any Imposts or Duties on Imports or Exports, except what may be absolutely necessary for executing its inspection Laws: and the net Produce of all Duties and Imposts, laid by any State on Imports or Exports, shall be for the Use of the Treasury of the United States; and all such Laws shall be subject to the Revision and Control of the Congress.

No State shall, without the Consent of Congress, lay any Duty of Tonnage, keep Troops, or Ships of War in time of Peace, enter into any Agreement or Compact with another State, or with a foreign Power, or engage in War, unless actually invaded, or in such imminent Danger as will not admit of delay.

ARTICLE II.

SECTION 1. The executive Power shall be vested in a President of the United States of America. He shall hold his Office during the Term of four Years, and, together with the Vice President, chosen for the same Term, be elected, as follows

Each State shall appoint, in such Manner as the Legislature thereof may direct, a Number of Electors, equal to the whole Number of Senators and Representatives to which the State may be entitled in the Congress: but no Senator or Representative, or Person holding an Office of Trust or Profit under the United States, shall be appointed an Elector.

The Electors shall meet in their respective States, and vote by Ballot for two Persons, of whom one at least shall not be an Inhabitant of the same State with themselves. And they shall make a List of all the Persons voted for, and of the Number of Votes for each; which List they shall sign and certify, and transmit sealed to the Seat of the Government of the United States, directed to the President of the Senate. The President of the Senate shall, in the Presence of the Senate and House of Representatives, open all the Certificates, and the Votes shall then be counted. The Person having the greatest Number of Votes shall be the President, if such Number be a Majority of the whole Number of Electors appointed; and if there be more than one who have such a Majority, and have an equal Number of Votes, then the House of Representatives shall immediately chuse by Ballot one of them for President; and if no Person have a Majority, then from the five highest on the List the said House shall in like Manner chuse the President. But in chusing the President, the Votes shall be taken by States, the Representation from each State having one Vote; A quorum for this Purpose shall consist of a Member or Members from two thirds of the States, and a Majority of all the States shall be necessary to a Choice. In every Case, after the Choice of the President, the Person having the greatest Number of Votes of the Electors shall be the Vice President. But if there should remain two or more who have equal Votes, the Senate shall chuse from them by Ballot the Vice President.

The Congress may determine the Time of chusing the Electors, and the Day on which they shall give their Votes; which Day shall be the same throughout the United States.

No Person except a natural born Citizen, or a Citizen of the United States, at the time of the Adoption of this Constitution, shall be eligible to the Office of President; neither shall any Person be eligible to that Office who shall not have attained to the Age of thirty five years, and been fourteen Years a Resident within the United States.

In Case of the Removal of the President from Office, or of his Death, Resignation, or Inability to discharge the Powers and Duties of the said Office, the Same shall devolve on the Vice President, and the Congress may by Law provide for the Case of Removal, Death, Resignation or Inability, both of the President and Vice President, declaring what Officer shall then act as President, and such Officer shall act accordingly, until the Disability be removed, or a President shall be elected.

The President shall, at stated Times, receive for his Services, a Compensation, which shall neither be encreased nor diminished during the Period for which he shall have been elected, and he shall not receive within that Period any other Emolument from the United States, or any of them.

Before he enter on the Execution of his Office, he shall take the following Oath or Affirmation:—"I do solemnly swear (or affirm) that I will faithfully execute the Office of President of the United States, and will to the best of my Ability, preserve, protect and defend the Constitution of the United States."

SECTION 2. The President shall be Commander in Chief of the Army and Navy of the United States, and of the Militia of the several States, when called into the actual Service of the United States; he may require the Opinion, in writing, of the principal Officer in each of the executive Departments, upon any Subject relating to the Duties of their respective Offices, and he shall have Power to grant Reprieves and Pardons for Offenses against the United States, except in Cases of Impeachment.

He shall have Power, by and with the Advice and Consent of the Senate, to make Treaties, provided two thirds of the Senators present concur; and he shall nominate, and by and with the Advice and Consent of the Senate, shall appoint Ambassadors, other public Ministers and Consuls, Judges of the supreme Court, and all other Officers of the United States, whose Appointments are not herein otherwise provided for, and which shall be established by Law: but the Congress may by Law vest the Appointment of such inferior Officers, as they think proper, in the President alone, in the Courts of Law, or in the Heads of Departments.

The President shall have Power to fill up all Vacancies that may happen during the Recess of the Senate, by granting Commissions which shall expire at the End of their next Session.

SECTION 3. He shall from time to time give to the Congress Information of the State of the Union, and recommend to their Consideration such Measures as he shall judge necessary and expedient; he may, on extraordinary Occasions, convene both Houses, or either of them, and in Case of Disagreement between them, with Respect to the Time of Adjournment, he may adjourn them to such Time as he shall think proper; he shall receive Ambassadors and other public Ministers; he shall take Care that the Laws be faithfully executed, and shall Commission all the Officers of the United States.

SECTION 4. The President, Vice President and all civil Officers of the United States, shall be removed from Office on Impeachment for, and Convention of, Treason, Bribery, or other high Crimes and Misdemeanors.

ARTICLE III

SECTION 1. The judicial Power of the United States, shall be vested in one supreme Court, and in such inferior Courts as the Congress may from time to time ordain and establish. The Judges, both of the supreme and inferior Courts, shall hold their Offices during good Behaviour, and shall, at stated Times, receive for their Services, a Compensation, which shall not be diminished during their continuance in Office.

SECTION 2. The judicial Power shall extend to all Cases in Law and Equity, arising under this Constitution, the Laws of the United States, and Treaties made, or which shall be made, under their Authority;— to all Cases affecting Ambassadors, other public Ministers and Consuls;—to all Cases of admiralty and maritime Jurisdiction;— to Controversies to which the United States shall be a Party;—to Controversies between two or more States;—between a State and Citizens of another State;—between Citizens of different States,—between Citizens of the same State claiming Lands under Grants of different States, and between a State, or the Citizens thereof, and foreign States, Citizens or Subjects.

In all Cases affecting Ambassadors, other public Ministers and Consuls, and those in which a State shall be Party, the Supreme Court shall have original Jurisdiction. In all the other Cases before mentioned, the supreme Court shall have appellate Jurisdiction, both as to Law and Fact, with such Exceptions, and under such regulations as the Congress shall make.

The Trial of all Crimes, except in Cases of Impeachment, shall be by Jury; and such Trial shall be held in the State where the said Crimes shall have been committed; but when not committed within any State, the Trial shall be at such Place or Places as the Congress may by Law have directed.

SECTION 3. Treason against the United States, shall consist only in levying War against them, or in adhering to their Enemies, giving them Aid and Comfort. No person shall be convicted of Treason unless on the Testimony of two Witnesses to the same overt Act, or on Confession in open Court.

The Congress shall have Power to declare the Punishment of Treason, but no Attainder of Treason shall work Corruption of Blood, or Forfeiture except during the Life of the Person attainted.

ARTICLE IV.

SECTION 1. Full Faith and Credit shall be given in each State to the public Acts, Records, and judicial Proceedings of every other State. And the Congress may by general Laws prescribe the Manner in which such Acts, Records and Proceedings shall be proved, and the Effect thereof.

SECTION 2. The Citizens of each State shall be entitled to all Privileges and Immunities of Citizens in the several States.

A Person charged in any State with Treason, Felony, or other Crime, who shall flee from Justice, and be found in another State, shall on demand of the executive Authority of the State from which he fled, be delivered up, to be removed to the State having Jurisdiction of the Crime.

No Person held to Service or Labour in one State, under the Laws thereof, escaping into another, shall, in Consequence of any Law or Regulation therein, be discharged from such Service or Labour, but shall be delivered up on Claim of the Party to whom such Service or Labour may be due.

SECTION 3. New States may be admitted by the Congress into this Union; but no new State shall be formed or erected within the Jurisdiction of any other State; nor any State be formed by the Junction of two or more States, or Parts of States, without the Consent of the Legislatures of the States concerned as well as of the Congress.

The Congress shall have Power to dispose of and make all needful Rules and Regulations respecting the Territory or other Property belonging to the United States; and nothing in this Constitution shall be so construed as to Prejudice any Claims of the United States, or of any particular State.

SECTION 4. The United States shall guarantee to every State in this Union a Republican Form of Government, and shall protect each of them against Invasion; and on Application of the Legislature, or of the Executive (when the Legislature cannot be convened) against domestic Violence.

ARTICLE V.

The Congress, whenever two thirds of both Houses shall deem it necessary, shall propose Amendments to this Constitution, or, on the Application of the Legislatures of two thirds of the several States, shall call a Convention for proposing Amendments, which, in either Case, shall be valid to all Intents and Purposes, as Part of this Constitution, when ratified by the Legislatures of three fourths of the several States, or by Conventions in three fourths thereof, as the one or the other Mode of Ratification may be proposed by the Congress; Provided that no Amendment which may be made prior to the Year One thousand eight hundred and eight shall in any Manner affect the first and fourth Clauses in the Ninth Section of the first Article; and that no State, without its Consent, shall be deprived of it's equal Suffrage in the Senate.

ARTICLE VI.

All debts contracted and Engagements entered into, before the Adoption of this Constitution, shall be valid against the United States under this Constitution, as under the Confederation.

This Constitution, and the Laws of the United States which shall be made in Pursuance thereof; and all Treaties made, or which shall be made, under the Authority of the United States, shall be the supreme Law of the Land; and the Judges in every State shall be bound thereby, any Thing in the Constitution or Laws of any State to the Contrary notwithstanding.

The Senators and Representatives before mentioned, and the Members of the several State Legislatures, and all executive and judicial Officers, both of the United States and of the several States, shall be bound by Oath or Affirmation, to support this Constitution; but no religious Test shall ever be required as a Qualification to any Office or public Trust under the United States.

ARTICLE VII.

The Ratification of the Convention of nine States, shall be sufficient for the Establishment of this Constitution between the States so ratifying the Same.

AMENDMENTS

ARTICLE I

Congress shall make no law respecting an establishment of religion, or prohibiting the free exercise thereof; or abridging the freedom of speech, or of the press; or the right of the people peaceably to assemble, and to petition the Government for a redress of grievances.

ARTICLE II

A well regulated Militia, being necessary to the security of a free State, the right of the people to keep and bear Arms, shall not be infringed.

ARTICLE III

No Soldier shall, in time of peace be quartered in any house, without the consent of the Owner, nor in time of war, but in a manner to be prescribed by law.

ARTICLE IV

The right of the people to be secure in their persons, houses, papers, and effects, against unreasonable searches and seizures, shall not be violated, and no Warrants shall issue, but upon probably cause, supported by Oath or affirmation, and particularly describing the place to be searched, and the persons or things to be seized.

ARTICLE V

No person shall be held to answer for a capital, or otherwise infamous crime, unless on a presentment or indictment of a Grand Jury, except in cases arising in the land or naval forces, or in the Militia, when in actual service in time of War or public danger; nor shall any person be subject for the same offence to be twice put in jeopardy of life or limb; nor shall be compelled in any Criminal Case to be a witness against himself, nor be deprived of life, liberty, or property, without due process of law; nor shall private property be taken for public use, without just compensation.

ARTICLE VI

In all criminal prosecutions, the accused shall enjoy the right to a speedy and public trial, by an impartial jury of the State and district wherein the crime shall have been committed, which district shall have been previously ascertained by law, and to be informed of the nature and cause of the accusation; to be confronted with the witnesses against him; to have compulsory process for obtaining witnesses in his favor, and to have the Assistance of Counsel for his defence.

ARTICLE VII

In Suits at common law, where the value in controversy shall exceed twenty dollars, the right of trial by jury shall be preserved, and no fact tried by a jury, shall be otherwise re-examined in any Court of the United States, than according to the rules of the common law.

ARTICLE VIII

Excessive bail shall not be required, nor excessive fines imposed, nor cruel and unusual punishments inflicted.

ARTICLE IX

The enumeration in the Constitution, of certain rights, shall not be construed to deny or disparage others retained by the people.

ARTICLE X

The powers not delegated to the United States by the Constitution, nor prohibited by it to the States, are reserved to the States respectively, or to the people.

ARTICLE XI

The Judicial power of the United States shall not be construed to extend to any suit in law or equity, commenced or prosecuted against one of the United States by Citizens of another State, or by Citizens or Subjects of any Foreign State.

ARTICLE XII

The Electors shall meet in their respective states, and vote by ballot for President and Vice President, one of whom, at least, shall not be an inhabitant of the same state with themselves; they shall name in their ballots the person voted for as President, and in distinct ballots the person voted for as Vice-President, and they shall make distinct lists of all persons voted for as President, and of all persons voted for as Vice-President, and of the number of votes for each, which lists they shall sign and certify, and transmit sealed to the seat of the government of the United States, directed to the President of the Senate;—The President of the Senate shall, in presence of the Senate and House of Representatives, open all the certificates and the votes shall then be counted;—The person having the greatest number of votes for President, shall be the President, if such number be a majority of the whole number of Electors appointed; and if no person have such majority, then from the persons having the highest numbers not exceeding three on the list of those voted for as President, the House of Representatives shall choose immediately, by ballot, the President. But in choosing the President, the votes shall be taken by states, the representation from each state having one vote; a quorum for this purpose shall consist of a member or members from two-thirds of the states, and a majority of all the states shall be necessary to a choice. And if the House of Representatives shall not choose a President whenever the right of choice shall devolve upon them, before the fourth day of March next following, then the Vice-President shall act as President, as in the case of the death or other constitutional disability of the President. The person having the greatest number of votes as Vice-President, shall be the Vice-President, if such number be a majority of the whole number of Electors appointed, and if no person have a majority, then from the two highest numbers on the list, the Senate shall choose the Vice-President; a quorum for the purpose shall consist of two thirds of the whole number of Senators, and a majority of the whole number shall be necessary to a choice. But no person constitutionally ineligible to the office of President shall be eligible to that of Vice-President of the United States.

ARTICLE XIII

Section 1. Neither slavery nor involuntary servitude, except as a punishment for crime whereof the party shall have been duly convicted, shall exist within the United States, or any place subject to their jurisdiction.

Section 2. Congress shall have power to enforce this article by appropriate legislation.

ARTICLE XIV

Section 1. All persons born or naturalized in the United States, and subject to the jurisdiction thereof, are citizens of the United States and of the State wherein they reside. No State shall make or enforce any law which shall abridge the privileges or immunities of citizens of the United States; nor shall any State deprive any person of life, liberty, or property, without due process of law; nor deny to any person within its jurisdiction the equal protection of the laws.

Section 2. Representatives shall be apportioned among the several States according to their respective numbers, counting the whole number of persons in each State, excluding Indians not taxed. But when the right to vote at any election for the choice of electors for President and Vice President of the United States, Representatives in Congress, the Executive and Judicial officers of a State, or the members of the Legislature thereof, is denied to any of the male inhabitants of such State, being twenty-one years of age, and citizens of the United States, or in any way abridged, except for participation in rebellion, or other crime, the basis of representation therein shall be reduced in the proportion which the number of such male citizens shall bear to the whole number of male citizens twenty-one years of age in such State.

Section 3. No person shall be a Senator or Representative in Congress, or elector of President and Vice President, or hold any office, civil or military, under the United States, or under any State, who, having previously taken an oath, as a member of Congress, or as an officer of the United States, or as a member of any State legislature, or as an executive or judicial officer of any State, to support the Constitution of the United States, shall have engaged in insurrection or rebellion against the same, or given aid or comfort to the enemies thereof. But Congress may by a vote of two-thirds of each House, remove such disability.

Section 4. The validity of the public debt of the United States, authorized by law, including debts incurred for payment of pensions and bounties for services in suppressing insurrection or rebellion, shall not be questioned. But neither the United States nor any State shall assume or pay any debt or obligation incurred in aid of insurrection or rebellion against the United States, or any claim for the loss or emancipation of any slave; but all such debts, obligations and claims shall be held illegal and void.

Section 5. The Congress shall have power to enforce, by appropriate legislation, the provisions of this article.

ARTICLE XV

Section 1. The right of citizens of the United States to vote shall not be denied or abridged by the United States or by any State on account of race, color, or previous condition of servitude.

Section 2. The Congress shall have power to enforce this article by appropriate legislation.

ARTICLE XVI

The Congress shall have the power to lay and collect taxes on incomes, from whatever source derived, without apportionment among the several States, and without regard to any census or enumeration.

ARTICLE XVII

Section 1. The Senate of the United States shall be composed of two Senators from each State, elected by the people thereof, for six years; and each Senator shall have one vote. The electors in each State shall have the qualifications requisite for electors of the most numerous branch of the State Legislatures.

Section 2. When vacancies happen in the representation of any State in the Senate, the executive authority of such State shall issue writs of election to fill such vacancies; Provided, That the Legislature of any State may empower the executive thereof to make temporary appointment until the people fill the vacancies by election as the Legislature may direct.

Section 3. This amendment shall not be so construed as to affect the election or term of any Senator chosen before it becomes valid as part of the Constitution.

ARTICLE XVIII

Section 1. After one year from the ratification of this article, the manufacture, sale, or transportation of intoxicating liquors within, the importation thereof into, or the exportation thereof from the United States and all territory subject to the jurisdiction thereof, for beverage purposes, is hereby prohibited.

Section 2. The Congress and the several States shall have concurrent power to enforce this article by appropriate legislation.

Section 3. This article shall be inoperative unless it shall have been ratified as an amendment to the Constitution by the legislatures of the several States, as provided in the Constitution, within seven years from the date of the submission hereof to the States by the Congress.

ARTICLE XIX

Section 1. The rights of citizens of the United States to vote, shall not be denied or abridged by the United States or by any State on account of sex.

Section 2. Congress shall have power to enforce this article by appropriate legislation.

ARTICLE XX

Section 1. The terms of the President and Vice President shall end at noon on the twentieth day of January, and the terms of Senators and Representatives at noon on the third day of January, of the years in which such terms would have ended if this article had not been ratified; and the terms of their successors shall then begin.

Section 2. The Congress shall assemble at least once in every year, and such meeting shall begin at noon on the third day of January, unless they shall by law appoint a different day.

Section 3. If, at the time fixed for the beginning of the term of the President, the President elect shall have died, the Vice President elect shall become President. If a President shall not have been chosen before the time fixed for the beginning of his term, or if the President elect shall have failed to qualify, then the Vice President elect shall act as President until a President shall have qualified; and the Congress may by law provide for the case wherein neither a President elect nor a Vice President elect shall have qualified, declaring who shall then act as President, or the manner in which one who is to act shall be selected, and such person shall act accordingly until a President or Vice President shall have qualified.

Section 4. The Congress may by law provide for the case of the death of any of the persons from whom the House of Representatives may choose a President whenever the right of choice shall have devolved upon them, and for the case of the death of any of the persons from whom the Senate may choose a Vice President whenever the right of choice shall have devolved upon them.

Section 5. Sections 1 and 2 shall take effect on the fifteenth day of October following the ratification of this article.

Section 6. This article shall be inoperative unless it shall have been ratified as an amendment to the Constitution by the legislatures of three-fourths of the several States within seven years from the date of its submission.

ARTICLE XXI

Section 1. The eighteenth article of amendment of the Constitution of the United States is hereby repealed.

Section 2. The transportation or importation into any State, Territory, or possession of the United States for delivery or use therein of intoxicating liquors, in violation of the laws thereof, is hereby prohibited.

Section 3. This article shall be inoperative unless it shall have beeen ratified as an amendment to the Constitution by conventions in the several States, as provided in the Constitution, within seven years from the date of the submission hereof to the States by the Congress.

ARTICLE XXII

Section 1. Restriction on terms of President.—No person shall be elected to the office of the President more than twice, and no person who has held the office of President, or acted as President, for more than two years of a term to which some other person was elected President shall be elected to the office of the President more than once. But this Article shall not apply to any person holding the office of President when this Article was proposed by the Congress, and shall not prevent any person who may be holding the office of President, or acting as President, during the term within which this Article becomes operative from holding the office of President or acting as President during the remainder of such term.

Section 2. Ratification, time limit.—This article shall be inoperative unless it shall have been ratified as an amendment to the Constitution by the legislatures of three-fourths of the several States within seven years from the date of its submission to the States by the Congress.

ARTICLE XXIII

Section 1. Presidential and Vice Presidential electors for District of Columbia.—The District constituting the seat of Government of the United States shall appoint in such manner as the Congress may direct:

A number of electors of President and Vice President equal to the whole number of Senators and Representatives in Congress to which the District would be entitled if it were a State, but in no event more than the least populous State; they shall be in addition to those appointed by the States, but they shall be considered, for the purposes of the election of President and Vice President, to be electors appointed by a State; and they shall meet in the District and perform such duties as provided by the twelfth article of amendment.

Section 2. Enforcement of article.—The Congress shall have power to enforce this article by appropriate legislation.

ARTICLE XXIV

Section 1. Voting in federal elections—Tax payment not prerequisite.—The right of citizens of the United States to vote in any primary or other election for President or Vice President, for electors for President or Vice President, or for Senator or Representatives in Congress, shall not be denied or abridged by the United States or any State by reason of failure to pay any poll tax or other tax.

Section 2. Power to enforce.—The Congress shall have power to enforce this article by appropriate legislation.

ARTICLE XXV

Section 1. Filling vacancy in office of president.—In case of the removal of the President from office or of his death or resignation, the Vice President shall become President.

Section 2. Filling vacancy in office of vice president.—Whenever there is a vacancy in the office of the Vice President, the President shall nominate a Vice President who shall take office upon confirmation by a majority vote of both Houses of Congress.

Section 3. Declaration of disability by president—Acting president.—Whenever the President transmits to the President pro tempore of the Senate and the Speaker of the House of Representatives his written declaration that he is unable to discharge the powers and duties of his office, and until he transmits to them a written declaration to the contrary, such powers and duties shall be discharged by the Vice President as Acting President.

Section 4. Determination of disability of president.—Whenever the Vice President and a majority of either the principal officers of the executive departments or of such other body as Congress may by law provide, transmit to the President pro tempore of the Senate and the Speaker of the House of Representatives their written declaration that the President is unable to discarge the powers and duties of his office, the Vice President shall immediately assume the powers and duties of the office as Acting President.

Thereafter, when the President transmits to the President pro tempore of the Senate and the Speaker of the House of Representatives his written declaration that no inability exists, he shall resume the powers and duties of his office unless the Vice President and a majority of either the principal officers of the executive department or of such other body as Congress may by law provide, transmit within four days to the President pro tempore of the Senate and the Speaker of the House of Representatives their written declaration that the President is unable to discharge the powers and duties of his office. Thereupon Congress shall decide the issue, assembling within forty-eight hours for that purpose if not in session. If the Congress, within twenty-one days after receipt of the latter written declaration, or, if Congress is not in session, within twenty-one days after Congress is required to assemble, determines by two-thirds vote of both Houses that the President is unable to discharge the powers and duties of his office, the Vice President shall continue to discharge the same as Acting President; otherwise, the President shall resume the powers and duties of his office.

ARTICLE XXVI

Section 1. Right to vote not denied to citizens eighteen years or older.—The right of citizens of the United States, who are eighteen years of age or older, to vote shall not be denied or abridged by the United States or by any state on account of age.

Section 2. Power to enforce.—The Congress shall have power to enforce this article by appropriate legislation.

BIBLIOGRAPHY

Frederic Bastiat, *The Law,* Foundation for Economic Education, 1972

Catherine Drinker Bowen, *John Adams and the American Revolution,* Little, Brown & Co., 1949.

William Blackstone, *Commentaries on the Law of England,* Jones Ed., Bancroft-Whitney Co., 1916.

Edmund Burke, *Words of the Right Honorable Edmund Burke,* London, 1855-1864.

Lewis Carroll, *Through the Looking Glass.*

Taylor Caldwell, *A Pillar of Iron,* Doubleday & Co., 1965.

Thomas M. Cooley, *Treatise on the Constitutional Limitations which Rest Upon the Legislative Power of the States of the American Union,* 4th Ed., Little, Brown & Co.

Charles Darwin, *The Origin of Species,* Penguin Classics Ed., 1968.

Documents Illustrative of the Formation of the Union, Government Printing Office, 1927, Reprinted *sub nom.* Tansill, *The Making of the American Republic,* Arlington House.

Feodor Dostoevski, *Crime and Punishment.*

Jonathan Edwards, *The Debates of the Several State Conventions on the Adoption of the Federal Constitution,* J. P. Lippincott & Co., 1881.

Charles L. Fontenay, *Epistle to the Babylonians,* University of Tennessee Press, 1969.

George M. Frederickson, *The Inner Civil War,* Harper & Row, 1965.

Alexander Hamilton, John Jay and James Madison, *The Federalist,* Modern Library.

S. I. Hayakawa, *Modern Guide to Synonyms,* Funk & Wagnalls, 1968.

Bruno Leoni, *Freedom and the Law,* Nash Publishing Corp., Los Angeles, 1961.

Ludwig von Mises, *Human Action,* Third Revised Ed., Henry Regnery & Co., 1966.

Samuel Eliot Morison, *The Oxford History of the American People,* Oxford University Press, 1965.

Gunner Myrdal, *An American Dilemma,*

New English Bible, Oxford University Press and Cambridge University Press, 1970.

George Orwell, *1984,* Harcourt, Brace & Co., 1949.

Roscoe Pound, *The Development of Constitutional Guarantees of Liberty,* Yale University Press.

Adam Smith, *The Wealth of Nations,* Modern Library, 1937.

Herbert Spencer, *The Man Versus the State,* The Caxton Printers, Ltd., 1969.

Harlow Shapley, Editor, *Science Ponders Religion,* Appleton-Century-Crofts, Inc., 1960.

Henry David Thoreau, *Civil Disobedience.*

Carl Van Doren, *The Great Rehearsal,* The Viking Press, 1948.

Van Vechten Veeder, *Legal Masterpieces,* Keefe-Davidson Co., 1903.

Andrew Dickson White, *Fiat Money Inflation in France,* The Foundation for Economic Education, 1959.

Holdsworth, *A History of English Law,* 7th Ed., Metheun & Co., Ltd., London, 1923.

TABLE OF CASES †

---

† Any reader who desires to read any of the original opinions of the Supreme Court discussed in this book may read them in the Official Supreme Court Reports (U.S.), available in most city libraries, and easily located with this table of citations. Other citations, such as to state decisions, Federal trial court (F.Supp.) and Courts of Appeals (Fed. or F.2d) decisions, and English decisions, are seldom available in public libraries, but may be found in law school libraries, some of which are open to the public. Anyone interested in receiving copies of Supreme Court decisions may get them very slowly from the Government and very rapidly in *United States Law Week,* published by the Bureau of National Affairs, Washington, D. C. At less expense, pamphlet editions, replaced by bound volums from time to time at a cost comparable to that of a weekly news magazine, are the *Lawyers Edition,* co-published by The Lawyers Co-Operative Publishing Co., Rochester, N. Y., and Bancroft-Whitney Co., San Francisco, and the *Supreme Court Edition,* published by West Publishing Co., St. Paul, Minnesota.

Oliver Iron Mining Co. v. Lord, 262 U.S. 172

Olmstead v. United States, 277 U.S. 438

Oregon v. Mitchell, 400 U.S. 112

Osborn v. Bank of the United States, 9 Wheat. (U.S.) 738

Pacific Insurance Co. v. Soule, 74 U.S. 433

Palko v. Connecticut, 302 U.S. 319

Pearce v. Piper, 34 Eng. Repr. 1

Pennoyer v. McConnaughy, 140 U.S. 13

Plessy v. Ferguson, 163 U.S. 537

Pollock v. Farmers' Loan & Trust Co., 158 U.S. 601

Pope v. Williams, 193 U.S. 621

Rahrer, Re, 140 U.S. 545

Railroad Commission of Wisconsin v. Chicago, Burlington & Quincy R. Co., 257 U.S. 563

Raney v. Board of Education of the Gould School District, 391 U.S. 443

Regina v. Hicklin, LR 3 QB 360

Remmey v. Smith, 342 U.S. 916

Reynolds v. Sims, 377 U.S. 533

Rex v. Miller, 20 St. Trials 870

Rex v. Woodfall, 20 St. Trials 895

Roman v. Sincock, 377 U.S. 695

Roth v. United States, 354 U.S. 476

Ruppert v. Caffey, 251 U.S. 264

Schenck v. United States, 249 U.S. 264

Scholey v. Rew, 90 U.S. 331

Shelley v. Kraemer, 334 U.S. 1

Shepherd v. Wheeling, 30 W.Va. 479

Sherbert v. Verner, 374 U.S. 398

Skinner v. Oklahoma ex rel. Williamson, 316 U.S. 535

Slaughter-House Cases, 83 U.S. 36

Smiley v. Holm, 285 U.S. 355

Smith v. Cahoon, 283 U.S. 553

Smith v. Swormstedt, 16 How (U.S.) 288

Snowden v. Hughes, 321 U.S. 1

Snyder v. Massachusetts, 291 U.S. 97

Sonzinski v. United States, 300 U.S. 506

South v. Peters, 339 U.S. 276

Starr v. United States, 153 U.S. 614

St. Joseph Stockyards Co. v. United States, 298 U.S. 38

State ex rel. Olson v. Gulford, 179 Minn. 40

Stone v. Mississippi, 101 U.S. 814

Stovall v. Denno, 388 U.S. 293

Stromburg v. California, 282 U.S. 359

Supreme Council of the Royal Arcanum v. Green, 237 U.S. 531

Supreme Tribe of Ben-Hur v. Cauble, 255 U.S. 356

Swann v. Adams (1966), 383 U.S. 210

Swann v. Adams (1967), 385 U.S. 440

Swann v. Charlotte-Mecklenburg Board of Education, 402 U.S. 1

Swann v. Charlotte-Mecklenburg Board of Education, (1965) 243 F.Supp. 667, (Apr. 23, 1969) 300 F.Supp. 1358, (June 20, 1969) 300 F.Supp. 1381, (Aug. 15, 1969) 306 F.Supp. 1299, (Nov. 7 and Dec. 1, 1969) 306 F. Supp. 1299

Tedesco v. Board of Supervisors of Elections for the Parish of Orleans, 339 U.S. 940

Tehan v. United States ex rel. Shott, 382 U.S. 406

Thurlow v. Massachusetts, 5 How. (U.S.) 504

Tiller v. Atlantic Coast R. Co., 318 U.S. 38

Torcaso v. Watkins, 367 U.S. 488

Traux v. Raich, 239 U.S. 33

Trustees of the Philadelphia Baptist Ass'n. v. Hart's Executors, 4 Wheat (U.S.) 2

Twining v. New Jersey, 211 U.S. 78

United States v. Cruikshank, 92 U.S. 542

United States v. E. C. Knight Co., 156 U.S. 1

United States v. Grimaud, 220 U.S. 506

United States v. Mosley, 238 U.S. 383

United States v. Rock Royal Co-Operative, Inc., 307 U.S. 533

United States v. Schooner Peggy, 1 Cranch (U.S.) 103

United States v. Vassar, 5 Wall. (U.S.) 562

United States v. Wade, 388 U.S. 218

Washington v. W. C. Dawson & Co., 264 U.S. 219

Weeks v. United States, 232 U.S. 383

Welsh v. United States, 254 U.S. 637

Wesberry v. Sanders, 376 U.S. 1

West Coast Hotel Co. v. Parrish, 300 U.S. 379

Wilson v. Black Bird Creek Marsh Co., 2 Pet. (U.S.) 245

WMCA, Inc. v. Lomenzo (1964), 382 U.S. 4

WMCA, Inc. v. Lomenzo (1965), 377 U.S. 633

Wolf v. Colorado, 338 U.S. 25

Wood v. Broom, 287 U.S. 1

Worcester v. Georgia, 6 Pet. (U.S.) 515

Yarbrough, Ex Parte, 110 U.S. 651

Yick Wo v. Hopkins, 118 U.S. 356

Zorach v. Clauson, 343 U.S. 306